Broadband Coding, Modulation, and Transmission Engineering

Broadband Coding, Modulation, and Transmission Engineering

Second Edition

By
Bernhard E. Keiser

Keiser Engineering, Inc.
Vienna, Virginia

© 1994 Bernhard E. Keiser
ISBN 0-13-083387-8

Published by
CEEPress Books
Continuing Engineering Education Program
George Washington University
Washington, D.C. 20052

BROADBAND CODING, MODULATION, AND TRANSMISSION ENGINEERING

Second Edition

Printed in the United States of America
by Mercury Publishing Services
a Capital Cities/ABC Inc. Company

MERCURY

PUBLISHING

SERVICES

12230 WILKINS AVENUE • ROCKVILLE, MD 20852

Library of Congress Cataloging-in-Publiation Data
KEISER, BERNHARD
  Broadband coding, modulation, and transmission engineer-
ing/
Bernhard E. Keiser.

p.   cm.

  Includes bibliographies and index.
  ISBN 0-13-083387-8
  1. Broadband communication systems. I. Title.
TK5102.5.K39 1989
621.38—dc19   88-21558
                          CIP

*To my wife Evelyn, and our children
Sandra, Carol, Nancy, Linda, and Paul*

Contents

PREFACE   **xv**

1 INTRODUCTION TO BROADBAND
COMMUNICATION SYSTEMS   **1**

    1.1   Types of Broadband Systems   2

    1.2   Requirements for Broadband Systems   3

    1.3   Transmission Principles   3

    1.4   Nontechnical Factors Affecting the Utilization of
              Broadband Systems   5

              Problems   6

              References   6

2 DIGITAL TRANSMISSION   **7**

    2.1   Definition of Digital Transmission   7

    2.2   Performance Measures   11

              2.2.1 Performance Objectives, 11 / 2.2.2 Performance
              Allocations, 13 / 2.2.3 Error Parameters, 13 / 2.2.4 Error
              Allocation, 16 / 2.2.5 International Objectives, 16 /
              2.2.6 Bit Count Integrity, 17 / 2.2.7 Channel Evaluation, 17

2.3   Network Topology   19

2.4   Switching   20

*2.4.1 Circuit Switching, 20 / 2.4.2 Message Switching, 20 /
2.4.3 Packet Switching, 20 / 2.4.4 Statistical Multiplexing, 21*

2.5   Digital Transmission via Band-Limited Facilities   22

*2.5.1 Synchronous versus Asynchronous Transmission, 24 /
2.5.2 Nyquist Theorems, 25 / 2.5.3 The Shannon
Theorem, 30 / 2.5.4 Timing and Synchronization, 34 /
2.5.5 Baseband Transmission, 37*

2.6   Digital Modulation Techniques   53

*2.6.1 Amplitude Modulation, 54 / 2.6.2 Frequency
Modulation, 57 / 2.6.3 Phase Modulation, 60 /
2.6.4 Amplitude-Phase Keying (APK), 68 / 2.6.5 Broadband
Modems, 76 / 2.6.6 Comparison of Modulation Methods, 76*

2.7   Multiplexers   83

2.8   Systems for Digital Transmission   85

*2.8.1 Applications of the Transmission Format, 86 /
2.8.2 Functional Aspects of Digital Transmission Systems, 86 /
2.8.3 Digital Hierarchies, 92 / 2.8.4 Hybrid Transmission Systems, 94*

2.9   National Digital Network Example: DDS   95

*2.9.1 DDS Network Interfaces, 95 / 2.9.2 DDS Fault
Isolation and Diagnostics, 95 / 2.9.3 DDS Quality, 97 /
2.9.4 DDS Limitations, 97 / 2.9.5 DDS Network
Synchronization, 97 / 2.9.6 Interconnection of National Digital Networks, 98*

2.10   Broadband Services   98

2.11   Error Control   100

*2.11.1 Loop or Echo Checking, 100 / 2.11.2 Automatic
Repeat Query (ARQ), 100 / 2.11.3 Forward Error
Correction, 101 / 2.11.4 Trellis-Coded Modulation, 112*

2.12   Transmission Protocols   116

*2.12.1 Protocol Functions, 116 / 2.12.2 Protocol
Categories, 117 / 2.12.3 High-Speed Transmission via Satellite, 117*

2.13   Glossary of Terms   118

Problems, 123

References, 125

3 VIDEO ENCODING   **128**

3.1   Analog Video Standards   128

*3.1.1 Color Transmission, 130 / 3.1.2 Modulation for
Transmission, 134 / 3.1.3 International Standards, 135 /
3.1.4 Uses of the Vertical Interval, 136*

3.2 Techniques for Increasing Picture Quality   136

*3.2.1 Transmission Format Categories, 136 /
3.2.2 Improvement Techniques, 137 / 3.2.3 Systems Using
High-Definition Formats, 139*

3.3 Digital Video Coding   140

*3.3.1 Source and Receiver Statistics, 140 / 3.3.2 Video Signal
Characteristics, 141 / 3.3.3 Characteristics of the Human Visual
Systems, 142 / 3.3.4 Picture Coding Approaches, 143 / 3.3.5
Intraframe Coding, 144 / 3.3.6 Interframe Coding, 160 /
3.3.7 Hybrid Coding, 167*

3.4 Digital Processing Within Television Receivers   168

3.5 Video Bandwidth Reduction   168

*3.5.1 Teleconference Video Systems, 169 / 3.5.2 Full Motion
Video at 56 kb/s, 171*

3.6 Conformance of Video Coding to International
Standards   172

3.7 Future Uses of Video Coding   174

Problems   174

References   175

4 MICROWAVE RADIO SYSTEMS   **177**

4.1 Microwave Propagation   178

*4.1.1 Radiation from a Point Source, 178 / 4.1.2 Line-of-Sight
Propagation, 181 / 4.1.3 Ground Reflection, 183 /
4.1.4 Refraction, 184 / 4.1.5 Diffraction, 186 /
4.1.6 Tropospheric Scatter, 188 / 4.1.7 Fading, 191*

4.2 Microwave Antennas   191

*4.2.1 Introduction, 191 / 4.2.2 Antenna Gain, 192 /
4.2.3 Antenna Patterns, 192 / 4.2.4 Antenna Types, 194*

4.3 Modulation of an RF Carrier   196

*4.3.1 Amplitude Modulation (AM), 196 / 4.3.2 Angle
Modulation, 198*

4.4 System Impairments   205

*4.4.1 Background Noise and Co-Channel Interference, 205 /
4.4.2 Intermodulation, 209 / 4.4.3 Intersymbol
Interference, 212 / 4.4.4 Adjacent Channel Interference, 213*

4.5 Regulatory Limits   214

4.6 System Design   217

*4.6.1 Coordination, 217 / 4.6.2 System Layout, 218 /
4.6.3 Link Budget, 220 / 4.6.4 Repeaters, 223 /
4.6.5 System Design Tradeoffs, 228 / 4.6.6 Reliability and Availability, 232*

4.7   System Examples   233

    4.7.1   Common Carrier Systems, 233   /   4.7.2   Special Systems, 240

    Problems   241

    References   243

5 SATELLITE TRANSMISSION   245

5.1   Frequency Allocations   246

5.2   Satellite Propagation   246

    5.2.1   Orbits, 246   /   5.2.2   Time Delay, 249   /   5.2.3 Atmospheric Attenuation, 249   /   5.2.4   Rain Depolarization, 251

5.3   Space Segment   253

    5.3.1   Transponders, 253   /   5.3.2   Satellite Power Sources, 269   /   5.3.3   Satellite Antennas, 270

5.4   Ground Segment   275

    5.4.1   Earth Station Antennas, 279   /   5.4.2   Interface Subsystems, 290   /   5.4.3   Earth Station Amplifier Techniques, 293   /   5.4.4   Echo Suppression and Cancellation, 293

5.5   Satellite Control   294

5.6   Link Budgets   295

5.7   Transponder Utilization   301

    5.7.1   Frequency Division Multiple Access (FDMA), 303   / 5.7.2   Time Division Multiple Access (TDMA), 304   /   5.7.3 Code Division Multiple Access (CDMA), 307   /   5.7.4 Summary, 309

5.8   Operating Systems   309

5.9   Direct Broadcast Satellites (DBS)   311

5.10   Spectrum Utilization   312

    5.10.1   Polarization Diversity, 313   /   5.10.2   Spot Beams, 320   /   5.10.3   Bi-Directional Links, 320   / 5.10.4   Companded Single Sideband, 320

5.11   Future Satellite Applications   321

    5.11.1   Land Mobile Radio, 321   /   5.11.2   Aeronautical Communication, 323   /   5.11.3   Geostar Satellite Data Nework, 323   /   5.11.4   Personal Radio, 324

5.12   Future Trends in Satellite Communications Systems   325

    5.12.1   Large Space Platforms (LSP), 325   /   5.12.2   Trends, 326

5.13   Glossary of Terms   327

    Problems   330

    References   331

6 OPTICAL TRANSMISSION   335

6.1   Advantages of Optical Fibers for Communications   336

6.2   Basic Elements of an Optical Fiber
         Communications System   337

6.3   Optical Fiber Materials   338

         *6.3.1   Plastic Fibers, 338   /   6.3.2   Glass Fibers, 338   /
         6.3.3   Plastic-Clad Silica, 338*

6.4   Wave Propagation Through Fibers   338

         *6.4.1   Path Geometry, 338   /   6.4.2   Modes in Fibers, 342   /
         6.4.3   Attenuation Characteristics, 343   /   6.4.4   Angular
         Division Multiplexing, 344*

6.5   Fiber Types and Their Characteristics   345

         *6.5.1   Single Mode Step-Index Fibers, 346   /   6.5.2   Multimode
         Step-Index Fibers, 347   /   6.5.3   Graded-Index Fibers, 347*

6.6   Group Delay Distortion   348

         *6.6.1   Intermodal Dispersion, 348   /   6.6.2   Material
         Dispersion, 348   /   6.6.3   Waveguide Dispersion, 350*

6.7   Optical Sources   350

         *6.7.1   Light Emitting Diodes, 350   /   6.7.2   Laser Diodes, 351   /
         6.7.3   Comparison Between Light Emitting Diodes and
         Lasers, 353   /   6.7.4   Light Source Modulation, 353*

6.8   Photodetectors   356

         6.8.1   Detector Types, 356   /   6.8.2   Methods of Detection, 359

6.9   Optical Fiber Transmission Systems   360

         *6.9.1   System Components, 361   /   6.9.2   Link Budgets, 372   /
         6.9.3   Wavelength Division Multiplexing, 374   /   6.9.4   Optical
         Fiber Applications, 375   /   6.9.5   Photonic Switching, 378*

6.10   Coherent Optical Systems   380

         *6.10.1   Description, 380   /   6.10.2   Advantages, 381   /   6.10.3
         Amplifiers, 382   /   6.10.4   Modulation and Detection, 382   /
         6.10.5   Applications Areas, 386   /   6.10.6   Implementation
         Requirements, 387*

6.11   Optical Fiber System Standards   387

6.12   Atmospheric Optical and Infrared Transmission   389

6.13   Free-Space Optical Transmission   390

6.14   Glossary of Terms   391

         Problems   392

         References   393

7 BROADBAND CABLE SYSTEMS 396

7.1   Performance Standards and Quality   397

7.2   Spectrum Utilization on Cable Systems   398

7.3   Basic Components of a CATV System   399

*7.3.1   Headend, 400   /   7.3.2   Main Trunk, 401   /   7.3.3
Distribution System, 407   /   7.3.4   Studio for Local Origin, 407*

7.4   Text Display Systems   407

7.5   Techniques for Maximizing System Bandwidth   409

*7.5.1   Reduction of Amplifier Distortion, 412   /   7.5.2   Special
Channeling Plans, 418   /   7.5.3   Special Techniques, 418   /
7.5.4   Special Systems, 418*

7.6   Addressable Control   419

*7.6.1   System Operation and Features, 420   /   7.6.2
Security, 420   /   7.6.3   Interface Between Cable System and
Television Receiver, 422*

7.7   Two-Way Cable Systems   423

*7.7.1   Two-Way System Techniques, 424   /   7.7.2   Two-Way
System Design, 424   /   7.7.3   Two-Way System Operation, 425   /
7.7.4   Two-Way Cable System Applications, 427*

7.8   Local Area Networks (LANs)   428

*7.8.1   CATV System Characteristics and the Development of
LANs, 430   /   7.8.2   LAN Classification, 430   /   7.8.3
Communication Protocols and Interfaces, 432   /   7.8.4   Network
Utilization and Capacity Allocation, 435   /   7.8.5   LAN
Applications, 437*

7.9   Integrated Services Digital Network (ISDN)   440

       Problems   441

       References   442

8 TRANSMISSION SYSTEM ALTERNATIVES 444

8.1   Coaxial Carrier Cable Systems   444

*8.1.1   System Features, 446   /   8.1.2   Frequency
Allocation, 446   /   8.1.3   Cable Characteristics, 447   /   8.1.4
Repeater Design Objectives, 448   /   8.1.5   System Layout, 448   /
8.1.6   Reliability, 449   /   8.1.7   LD-4 Digital Cable
System, 449   /   8.1.8   Future of Coaxial Carrier, 451*

8.2   Millimeter Waveguide System   451

*8.2.1   System Characteristics, 451   /   8.2.2   Waveguide Structure
and Characteristics, 451   /   8.2.3   Link Budget, 453   /   8.2.4
Repeater Stations, 453   /   8.2.5   System Status, 455*

8.3   Comparison of Broadband Transmission
Technologies   456

References, 456

Appendix A   INTERNATIONAL SYSTEM OF UNITS (SI)   **457**

Appendix B   FREQUENCY BAND NOMENCLATURE   **459**

INDEX   **460**

Preface

This book provides an engineering description of the methods used to process and transmit broadband signals. As such, it includes both the analog and digital transmission of data and graphic information, as well as multiplexed voice transmission.

The technological developments of the past decade have brought to the system designer a seeming wealth of possibilities for communications transmission. The selection of the best method for a given application, however, may be rendered difficult because much of the information is scattered among several texts and many different published papers. This text brings together in one volume a treatment of all broadband communication system types at a level readily understandable by the practicing engineer. It allows a detailed understanding and evaluation of each system type, and provides the information needed to structure special-purpose transmission systems.

The material has been developed over a period of ten years, during which the author has been teaching a popular continuing engineering education course on Broadband Communication Systems several times per year. This course often is attended by recent engineering graduates who express the need for more information at the senior and graduate level on the engineering of transmission systems for high-speed data and video, as well as for multichannel voice. Thus, the book has been written not only for the practicing engineer, but also to supplement more theoretical texts used in telecommunications engineering courses. Accordingly, problems are included at the ends of most of the chapters. Chief engineers and engineering managers also will find portions of the text useful in understanding the basic ideas and structure of broadband communication system for overall end-to-end system planning purposes.

While the emphasis of the book is on broadband systems and technology, the principles are applicable generally to narrowband systems as well. Readers interested in speech coding techniques are referred to the book *Digital Telephony and Network Integration,* [Van Nostrand Reinhold Company, Inc.], coauthored with Eugene Strange. Such media as high-frequency radio are not included because of their limited bandwidth per channel.

The term wideband is used by some to designate systems up to 1.5 or 2.0 Mb/s, with higher transmission rates being designated broadband. Others use the term broadband for any system whose bandwidth is in excess of voice bandwidth. This text uses the name broadband to encompass all systems operating at rates beyond those of voice systems, without further delineation.

Vienna, Virginia   *Bernhard E. Keiser*

Broadband Coding, Modulation, and Transmission Engineering

1

Introduction to Broadband Communication Systems

What is a broadband communication system? In this text the term means any telecommunication system capable of conveying information bandwidths in excess of voice bandwidth, which often is taken to be 3 kHz. In terms of digital transmission, a precise definition cannot be given, but the term will be taken to include digital transmission at rates in excess of 9.6 kb/s, since the 9.6 kb/s rate can be handled readily by a voice-band modem. This definition is oriented toward end-to-end transmission in which the user's access to the telecommunication system is via a bandwidth greater than that of the conventional analog local loop.

Any bounds that are set, of course, are arbitrary. One must recognize, for example, that 3 kHz voice bandwidths, since the early 1960s, have been transmitted using 64 kb/s digital streams. Moreover, 3 kHz analog service now can convey modem data well in excess of 9.6 kb/s.

Broadband communication systems are owned and operated by common carriers (those which make their facilities* available to all who request them), and by private carriers (those which make their facilities available to one or more users only).

Applications of broadband communication systems, as will be seen throughout this text, include computer-to-computer communication, television transmission,

---

* The word *facility* denotes an end-to-end transmission capability.

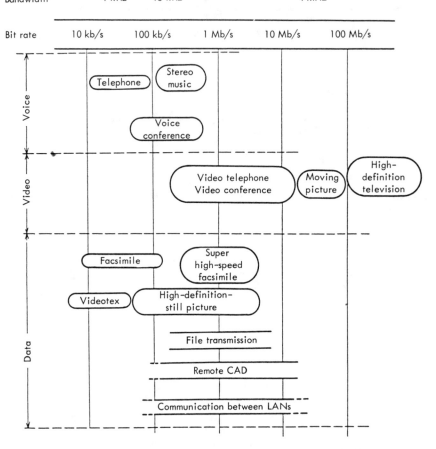

Figure 1.1 Bit rate and bandwidth requirements of various telecommunications applications. (From S. Harashima and H. Kimura, "High-speed and Broad-band Communication Systems in Japan," *IEEE Journal on Selected Areas in Communications,* July 1986. © 1986, IEEE. Reprinted by permission.)

video conference connections, telecommunications terminal equipment connections (multiplexers and concentrators), and various digital private branch exchange (DPBX) connections. Figure 1.1 [Ref. 1] shows the bandwidths and bit rates typically required for a number of telecommunications applications.

1.1 TYPES OF BROADBAND SYSTEMS

As a prelude to the discussion of the various types of broadband systems, this text first considers the preparation of information for transmission. Since an increasing amount of transmission is being handled on a digital basis, Chapter 2 is devoted to digital transmission, and includes a discussion of the types of switching being used, basic digital modulation techniques, coding, and error control. Also included are discussions of the digital hierarchy and digital transmission services. A discussion of analog modulation techniques can be found in Chap. 4. The conversion of broadband analog information, in the form of video, into digital forms is the subject of Chap. 3.

Beginning with Chap. 4, the text is devoted to telecommunications facilities. Both analog and digital transmission are discussed, but the emphasis is on digital because of its widespread prevalence and increasing importance. The primary facility types covered are microwave radio, satellite, and fiber optics. Subsequent chapters deal with coaxial carrier transmission, both for cable television and for common-carrier telephony. The text concludes with a chapter on millimeter waveguide transmission, and comments on future uses and trends in broadband communication systems.

Engineers being introduced to broadband communication systems technology may ask logically, "if a carrier simply provides a system as part of a service offering, why do I need a knowledge of the system's characteristics?" There are many positive answers to this question. (1) The transmission system is part of the end-to-end system, and thus its characteristics affect the capabilities and behavior of the end-to-end system. (2) The type of transmission system a user receives from a carrier depends upon what facilities are available between the points to be connected at the time when the connection is required. (3) Specialized transmission requirements may call for detailed technical discussions with the carrier. (4) Your requirements may necessitate the design of a special transmission system. (5) You may be involved in designing a new system for a foreign country.

1.2 REQUIREMENTS FOR BROADBAND SYSTEMS

An understanding of the speed and information requirements of a number of message types can be obtained from Table 1.1, adapted from [Ref. 2], which compares the transmission times of a number of message types sent at digital rates.

1.3 TRANSMISSION PRINCIPLES

Several basic parameters are common to every transmission system. These parameters are attenuation, phase shift, noise level, and saturation level. Their consequences in terms of transmission impairments are examined next.

The attenuation rate α is expressed in basic units of neper/meter (Np/m), where a neper denotes an attenuation to $1/e$ of the initial value. Thus 1 Np = 8.686 dB if values are expressed in voltage or current units. The dB, of course, is the most commonly used unit for attenuation.

The phase shift rate β is expressed in radian/meter. Thus the total phase shift for a line of length l is $\phi = \beta l$. For a sine wave of frequency f Hertz and wavelength λ meters, $\beta = 2\pi/\lambda$.

The group delay τ_g is defined as the time required for a given signal to progress

TABLE 1.1 DATA TRANSMISSION REQUIREMENTS

Message	Typical Number of Bits	Transmission Time, seconds		
		at 9.6 kb/s	at 64 kb/s	at 1.544 Mb/s
One second of digitized telephone speech, PCM	6.4×10^4	7	1	0.04
A page or a full CRT screen of text (uncompressed)	1 to 4×10^4	1 to 4	0.15 to 0.6	0.006 to 0.025
Facsimile image, black and white, two tone (compressed)	2 to 6×10^5	20 to 60	3 to 9	0.12 to 0.36
One second of video teleconference (moving image)	1.54×10^6	165	25	1
Full-page, three-color image, high quality (heavily compressed)	2 to 10×10^6	200 to 1000	30 to 150	1.2 to 6
20-cm floppy disk, single-sided, double density	5×10^6	500	75	3
One medium-sized disk unit (IBM 3310)	5×10^8	50 000 (14.5 hours)	7500	300

Source: From T. Mandey, "Assessing the New Services," *IEEE Spectrum*, Oct. 1979, © 1979, IEEE. Reprinted by permission.

through a line or other facility. If v denotes the speed of propagation on the line, then $f\lambda = v$. Since $v\tau_g = l$,

$$\tau_g = -d\phi/d\omega \qquad (1.1)$$

In the discussion that follows, the noise level N usually is thought of as being determined by thermal noise, but actually may be produced by any generalized disturbance within the channel, including cochannel interference. The saturation level is designated V_m.

Transmission impairments in a facility result because $\alpha \neq 0$, $\tau_g \neq$ constant, $N \neq 0$, and $V_m < \infty$. The result in a digital system is an error probability, p_{be}, often designated the error *rate* or, the bit error rate (ber). The p_{be} is a function of the carrier-to-noise ratio (C/N), as will be detailed in Chap. 2.

Analog system impairments in the case of video transmission include (1) picture distortion because $\tau_g \neq$ constant, $d\alpha/df \neq 0$, and $V_m < \infty$ and (2) "snow" because $N \neq 0$. Graphic system impairments include (1) distorted reproduction because $\tau_g \neq$ constant, $d\alpha/df \neq 0$, and $V_m < \infty$ and (2) gray background because $N \neq 0$. Digital video experiences various impairments depending on p_{be} and the coding technique used, as will be discussed in Chap. 3.

The categories of transmission impairments are displayed in Fig. 1.2. Note that the vertical direction is *level* whereas the horizontal direction is *bandwidth*. With respect to level, too high a signal results in saturation of the active components

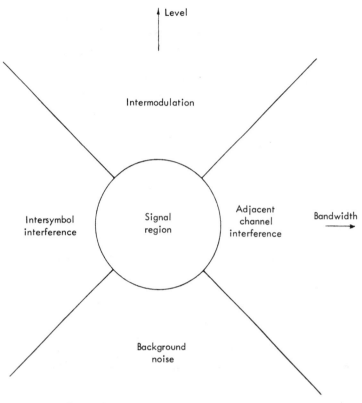

Figure 1.2 Categories of transmission impairments.

of a system and thus intermodulation. Too low a level results in impairment due to background noise, which actually may be considered in a general way to include not only receiver-generated noise, but any unwanted power in the channel, such as co-channel interference.

With respect to bandwidth, the use of too large a signal bandwidth results in adjacent channel interference, whereas too small a bandwidth causes an impairment known in digital transmission as intersymbol interference. Note that a form of intersymbol interference called *echo* can be caused by an unwanted transmission path or an impedance mismatch as well as by simple band limiting.

1.4 NONTECHNICAL FACTORS AFFECTING THE UTILIZATION OF BROADBAND SYSTEMS

Certain broadband transmission capabilities are feasible technically but are not in use because of government regulatory policies and franchise arrangements, economics of scale, and spectrum allocation agreements. For example, telecommunications across national boundaries often carries a requirement for an interface through a country's telecommunications authority, such as the postal service. Such requirements often are established to ensure that revenue sharing occurs on a prespecified basis. However, the given telecommunications authority may require the use of its own local subscriber lines, whose bandwidth capabilities may be limited to voice service only.

As another example, some countries prohibit customer data transmission because tariffs for such transmission have not been agreed upon.

On an international basis, the portions of the radio spectrum that can be used for telecommunications via satellite and microwave radio are limited because of needed allocations for radar and government applications.

Within the U.S. and Canada, long distance services are competitive, whereas within most other countries, long distance services are handled by the government, often the postal service. Local wireline service, however, is not competitive, being on a franchised basis in the U.S. and Canada, and being government owned and operated elsewhere. Within the U.S., however, competitive local nonwireline service exists in many forms, and often uses short-distance radio transmission. The name *by-pass* is used to describe such a service. By-pass is defined as the provision of telecommunications service other than via the public switched network. As such, even the franchised local carrier may engage in by-pass operation, which can assume a variety of forms. One category, private line arrangements, includes private line networks, private branch exchange (PBX) tie trunks*, foreign exchange (FX) lines†, and dedicated access facilities. These arrangements are often, but not always, limited to voice bandwidths. Another category, user-owned transmission facilities, includes private systems using microwave radio, satellite transmission, fiber optics, and two-way cable television facilities. By-pass by the common carrier may involve the provision of *dark fiber,* in which the franchised carrier simply provides the fiber connection and the user provides the electronics.

The digital termination service (DTS), described in Sec. 4.7.2.1, is an increasingly popular form of by-pass.

PROBLEMS

1.1 Derive Equation (1.1) from the information provided in Sec. 1.3.

REFERENCES

1. S. Harashima and H. Kimura, "High-speed and Broad-band Communication Systems in Japan," *IEEE Journal on Selected Areas in Communications,* SAC-4, no. 4 (July 1986), 565–72.

2. T. Mandey, "Assessing the New Services," *IEEE Spectrum,* 16, no. 10 (Oct. 1979), 42–50.

*A PBX tie trunk provides one or more voice channel connections between a PBX and the public telephone network or between two PBXs. Such trunks may be within a local service area, or may extend beyond it.

†An FX line allows a subscriber to have a number on an exchange that normally provides service to a different geographical area.

2

Digital Transmission

This chapter deals with the preparation of broadband signals for digital transmission. The emphasis is on digital techniques because analog techniques, including single sideband, are confined largely to voice bandwidth applications, and vestigial sideband is limited largely to broadcast television applications. As such, it is discussed in Chap. 3. Following the introductory discussions on network topology and switching is a theoretical development of digital transmission from the basic Nyquist and Shannon theorems to digital modulation and multiplexing. This is followed by a discussion of service offerings using these techniques. The chapter concludes with subjects of key interest to the subscriber to such services: error control and transmission protocols.

2.1 DEFINITION OF DIGITAL TRANSMISSION

Information bearing signals are said to be in digital form when they are limited to a discrete number of *levels*. The term level means not only amplitude, but also frequency and phase shift, and combinations of amplitudes, frequencies, and phase shifts. If only two levels are used, the signals are said to be *binary*. Three-level signals are called *ternary*, and four-level signals are called *quarternary*.

An analog signal is not limited to discrete levels, but may assume any level (within circuit limits). The analog detector must be designed to reproduce the analog level accurately, but has no way (other than the exceeding of amplitude limits) of distinguishing signal from noise or distortion within the pass band. The advantage of digital transmission is that noise of sufficiently low magnitude does not result in an erroneous detected level since the digital detector is designed with a set of thresholds. All received levels within prespecified thresholds are treated alike, the differences being attributed to noise and therefore ignored, Figure 2.1 illustrates these differences between analog and digital signals.

Because in digital transmission only a limited number of valid signal levels are sent, digital transmission has numerous advantages. First, waveform regeneration can be achieved, as will be discussed in Sec. 2.3. With waveform regeneration, there is no cumulative distortion or noise with distance. Accordingly, a digital system (using regeneration) can provide satisfactory operation with a lower carrier-to-noise

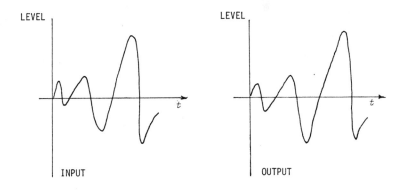

(a) Analog: all details must be reproduced accurately

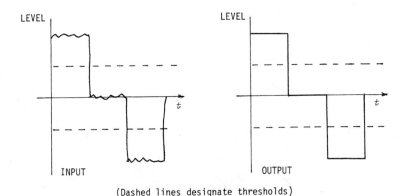

(Dashed lines designate thresholds)

(b) Digital: only discrete levels need be reproduced

Figure 2.1 Analog versus digital signals.

ratio than that required in analog transmission. In addition, all-digital transmission does not require conversion of the digital waveform to keyed sine waves (a function performed by modems, as discussed in Sec. 2.6), because the system is designed for digital signals. Moreover, digital transmission readily permits time-division multiplexing (TDM), which provides greater transmission economy than frequency-division multiplexing (FDM) because the time guard periods between TDM channels need occupy typically only one to two percent of the time domain, whereas filter guard bands between FDM channels typically occupy a higher percent of the frequency domain. In addition, FDM signals often cannot use the entirety of a filter pass band because of group delay alteration of the received waveform, with a consequent increase in bit error probability. Finally, digital transmission on a multichannel basis usually can be implemented more economically than analog transmission, i.e., greater large-scale economy results.

The digital processing of a signal for transmission may involve a number of steps whose names sound nearly alike. Thus, precise definitions of terms become important to an understanding of the individual steps.

1. *Source coding* is a process in which an analog input such as baseband video is converted to a binary stream, i.e., 1s and 0s. Chapter 3 discusses the source coding of video in detail. Some commonly used source coding techniques go by the names pulse code modulation (PCM), differential PCM (DPCM), delta coding, etc.

2. *Error coding* is applied to a digital stream for the purpose of detection and perhaps error correction. Section 2.11 discusses error coding and shows that such coding involves the addition of special error control bits to the information bit stream.

3. *Scrambling* refers to the alteration of a bit stream for a specific purpose, often the avoidance of a long run of zeros, so that clock information may be derived from the streams at the receiver. Scrambling also may be done to render the bit stream unintelligible to an unauthorized recipient. Scrambling is accomplished according to a preestablished set of rules which allows the receiver to reconstruct the originally transmitted bit stream.

4. *Channel* or *line coding* takes the digital stream, which may be in the form of a zero-volt level for a "0" (space) and a five-volt level for a "1" (mark), and converts the stream into the waveform to be used in the channel.

The foregoing steps all involve operations on the bit stream without translating it from its original location in the spectrum. Such operations thus are *baseband* techniques. To transmit the signal for an appreciable distance other than by certain coaxial cable systems, however, involves the use of a radio frequency or optical carrier, and thus the process of *modulation,* which involves changes of the carrier's amplitude or frequency or phase, or some combination of these parameters.

In some systems certain coding steps may be combined with digital modulation as a means of improving the bandwidth efficiency (b/s per Hz bandwidth) without a corresponding degradation in the error probability characteristics. Such combinations form the subject of Sec. 2.11.4, dealing with trellis-coded modulation.

Figure 2.2 illustrates the functions of a digital transmission system, as they have been described in the foregoing paragraphs, together with a multiplexer to combine channels together on a time or frequency division multiplexed basis and the modulator and up converter for transmission by a terrestrial or satellite radio system. Figure 2.2 shows only the sending end functions. The receiving end functions, of course, are their complements, i.e., decoders, descrambler, demultiplexer, demodulator, and downconverter.

Most digital transmission systems span distances great enough that signal distortion and noise occur because of the characteristics of the transmission medium, as noted in Chap. 1. Signal distortion caused by the transmission medium itself usually takes the form of amplitude versus frequency and phase versus frequency variations. Loss of signal level with distance, together with noise and distortion, makes the use of repeaters necessary. A repeater in a digital transmission system not only amplifies the signal along its path of travel, but may also reshape the pulses representing bits or symbols. (A *symbol* may be a single bit but often refers to a combination of two or more bits.) A repeater that reshapes the pulses is called a *regenerative* repeater. Figure 2.3 shows the functions performed in a regenerative repeater. The incoming signal first is amplified and *equalized*. The equalizer has an amplitude and phase characteristic versus frequency that is the inverse of that of the transmission path, thus yielding (ideally) an overall flat amplitude and linear phase characteristic versus frequency. Timing is derived from the received signal, often by a bandpass filtering process, and the signal is sampled at the appropriate times. Depending on the signal's number of digital levels, some limiting or other form of amplitude normalization may be done. The "regenerator" compares the actual signal level at each sampling instant with built-in thresholds. In Fig. 2.3, two thresholds are shown, resulting in normalized output values of $+1$, 0, and -1. Noise produces symbol or bit errors by causing the detected signal to be misinterpreted by the detector by falling on the wrong side of a threshold.

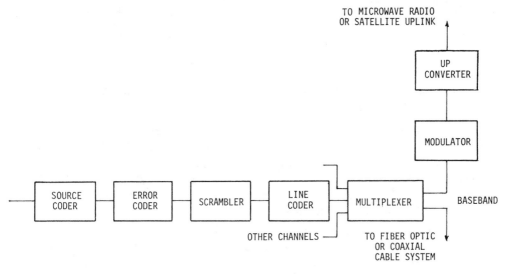

Figure 2.2 Functions performed in a digital transmission system.

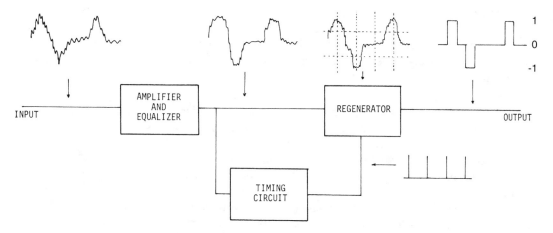

Figure 2.3 Regenerative repeater functions.

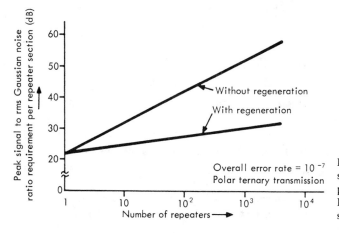

Overall error rate = 10^{-7}
Polar ternary transmission

Figure 2.4 Effect of regeneration on signal-to-noise ratio required per repeater section. (© 1970, Bell Telephone Laboratories, Inc. Reprinted by permission.)

Figure 2.4 [Ref. 7, Chap. 27] shows what peak signal to rms gaussian noise ratio (dB) is required per repeater section as a function of the number of repeaters to achieve an end-to-end bit error probability of 10^{-7} using polar ternary transmission. The ability of regenerative repeaters to work with significantly lower signal-to-noise ratios than are usable without regeneration is a primary advantage of digital transmission.

2.2 PERFORMANCE MEASURES

2.2.1 Performance Objectives

Performance is expressed in terms of availability and quality. Availability of a circuit refers to the percentage of time that the users can achieve their intended communication over the circuit. However, a circuit that might be usable for video might be unsatisfactory for data. Thus, the quality of a circuit is an important parameter also. When quality is inadequate, the circuit may be said to be unavailable. Quality parameters thus include such factors as bit error probability, bit count integrity, response delay, timing, slips, and jitter, as will be defined in subsequent portions of this chapter.

2.2.1.1 Definitions. *Failure* is any condition in which a circuit does not meet its performance specifications. Failure may occur either slowly or suddenly. The failure rate λ_r is the average rate of occurrence of failures during the lifetime of a circuit or a piece of equipment or a component.

The *mean time between failures* (MTBF) is the reciprocal of the failure rate, and thus is the total operating time divided by the number of failures during the period considered. The *mean time to repair* (MTTR) is the average time to perform fault isolation and replace or repair faulty circuits. If replacement is done, the term *mean time to replace* often is used instead. The MTTR plus time for travel and locating spares is the *mean time to service restoral* (MTSR).

Availability (A) is the portion of a total considered period during which a circuit functions satisfactorily, thus,

$$A = \frac{\text{MTBF}}{\text{MTBF} + \text{MTSR}} \tag{2.1}$$

Note that the foregoing definitions do not necessarily indicate hardware as the sole cause of circuit failure. In some cases, propagation anomalies, especially on microwave radio circuits, may be the cause.

Reliability, R(t), however, is usually a hardware-oriented term, and means the probability that equipment will serve without failure for a length of time t given by

$$R(t) = e^{-\lambda_r t} \tag{2.2}$$

The exponential characteristic is based on observations that component reliability decays exponentially with time, except for early failure ("infant mortality") and "end of life" failures. Accordingly,

$$\text{MTBF} = \int_o^\infty R(t)\, dt = \int_o^\infty e^{-\lambda_r t}\, dt \tag{2.3}$$

2.2.1.2 Effects of Impairments. As noted earlier, a circuit that might be usable for one purpose, e.g., video, might be unsatisfactory for another purpose, e.g., data. As will be seen in Chap. 3, digital video requires a bit error probability, p_{be}, of 10^{-3} to 10^{-4} depending on the coding technique used. Such factors as phase jitter, timing slips, and bit errors all degrade video performance as do such system-produced impairments as quantization noise and frame replenishment.

Data transmission is impaired by group delay distortion, timing slips, block error rate, and response delays, which limit throughput and efficiency. However, essentially error-free transmission can be achieved using the error control techniques described in Sec. 2.11.

2.2.2 Performance Allocations

A telecommunications circuit generally consists of a long haul segment or segments plus several short distance or local line segments. End-to-end performance degradation is the sum of the degradations along the various segments of the end-to-end circuit. Performance tends to vary with time because of circuit loading and, perhaps, propagation conditions; thus performance measures are expressed best on a statistical basis.

The first step in performance allocation is a statement of the end-to-end objectives, as described next.

2.2.2.1 Hypothetical Reference Circuit.

In telecommunication system design, use is made of a *hypothetical reference circuit* which represents the majority of practical circuit cases, thus reducing the designer's task to allocating performance for this one circuit [Ref. 1,] to its individual subsystems and equipment. The hypothetical reference circuit is constructed based upon circuit length, type of service, analog bandwidth, and/or digital bit rate, A/D and D/A converters and multiplexers/demultiplexers required. Figure 2.5 illustrates the factors that are used in structuring a hypothetical reference circuit. Figure 2.6 shows the factors among which its performance is allocated.

Each segment of a hypothetical reference circuit is representative of the transmission medium and the equipment to be used; accordingly, the segments are not necessarily worst cast designs. Figure 2.7 is an example of a hypothetical reference circuit. Reference circuits for telephony, especially analog, have been in use for many years. Reference circuits for wideband digital transmission are under development by both the Consultative Committee International for Telephony and Telegraphy (CCITT) and the Consultative Committee International for Radio (CCIR).

2.2.3 Error Parameters

A variety of ways of expressing a digital system's error performance have been developed. Some systems, such as coaxial cable and optical fiber, as well as satellite systems, exhibit random bit errors, typically one at a time. Other systems, especially those using fixed or mobile microwave radio, may exhibit bursts of errors. Full motion video transmission, i.e., ≥ 30 Mb/s, is more tolerant of both random errors and error bursts than is data transmission or motion-compensated video, e.g., 1.544 Mb/s, which may be seriously impaired in the presence of error bursts. Error correcting codes (see Sec. 2.11) are useful in a high-channel-error environment. The most commonly used error measures are the following:

1. Bit error probability, p_{be}. This is often called the "bit error rate" (ber) and is the average ratio of erroneous bits to the total number of bits sent.

2. Symbol error probability, p_{se}, is a measure used in systems which combine two or more bits into a "symbol" for transmission, as will be described in Sec. 2.6.

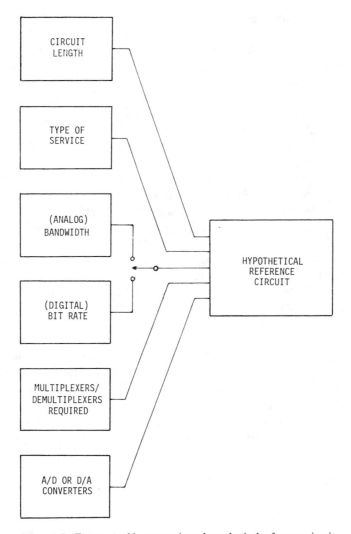

Figure 2.5 Factors used in structuring a hypothetical reference circuit.

The value of p_{se} is the average ratio of erroneous symbols to the total number of symbols sent. Its relation to p_{be} is discussed in Sec. 2.6.

3. Error-free seconds (EFS) is the probability that a one-second measurement interval is free of error.

Other measures include error-free blocks (the percent of data blocks that are error free), and the percent of time that the p_{be} does not exceed a given threshold error probability. The terms *errored second* (ES), *severely errored second,* and *failed second* will be defined later in this chapter in the discussion of T-carrier systems, Sec. 2.8, Systems for Digital Transmission.

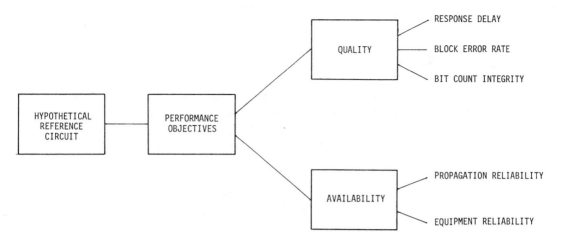

Figure 2.6 Factors among which hypothetical reference circuit performance is allocated.

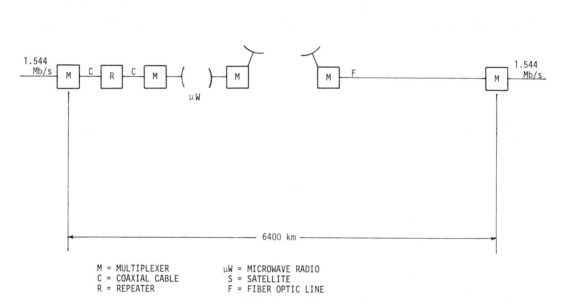

M = MULTIPLEXER   µW = MICROWAVE RADIO
C = COAXIAL CABLE   S = SATELLITE
R = REPEATER   F = FIBER OPTIC LINE

Figure 2.7 Example of a hypothetical reference circuit.

In the absence of error bursts, assuming a binomial error distribution (valid for statistically independent errors), the percentage of error-free seconds is

$$\%\,\mathrm{EFS} = 100(1 - p_{be})^R$$

where R = information rate, b/s. For example, to achieve $\geq 95\%$ EFS on a 1.544 Mb/s conference video circuit requires $p_{be} \leq 3.32 \times 10^{-8}$.

2.2.4 Error Allocation

The end-to-end error performance achieved on a given circuit is the result of the individual error performances of its links. If a circuit consists of identical sections, e.g., coaxial cable or optical fiber with uniformly spaced repeaters, errors may be allocated on a per km basis. More often, however, a circuit will be a tandem combination of various media with different repeater spacings and noise characteristics. Under such circumstances, if p_l = bit error probability per link and if the errors are statistically independent from one link to another, then [Ref. 2], for n identical links,

$$p_{be} = 0.5[1 - (1 - 2p_l)^n] \tag{2.4}$$

Often p_l is small enough that the probability of multiple errors on the same bit can be neglected. Then (2.4) can be approximated by the sum of the individual values of p_{be} per link, or

$$p_{be} \simeq np_l, \quad np_l \ll 1 \tag{2.5}$$

In the case of error-free seconds, if %(EFS)$_l$ is the percent error-free seconds per link, then for n identical links,

$$\%\text{EFS} \simeq 100 - n[100 - \%(\text{EFS})_l], \quad n[100 - \%(\text{EFS})_l] \ll 1 \tag{2.6}$$

For circuits whose links have differing error characteristics, equation (2.4) must be replaced by

$$p_{be} = 0.5\left[1 - \prod_{i=1}^{m}(1 - 2p_{l_i})^{n_i}\right] \simeq \sum_{i=1}^{m} n_i p_{l_i},$$
$$n_i p_{l_i} \ll 1 \text{ for all } i \tag{2.7}$$

where $p_l = p_{be}$ for link of type i and n_i = number of links of type i. The number of different link types is m.

Correspondingly, if %(EFS)$_{l_i}$ = percent error-free seconds for link of type i,

$$\%\text{EFS} \simeq 100 - \sum_{i=1}^{m} n_i[100 - \%(\text{EFS})_{l_i}],$$
$$n_i[100 - \%(\text{EFS})_{l_i}] \ll 1 \text{ for all } i \tag{2.8}$$

2.2.5 International Objectives

International standards are based on a 64 kb/s reference channel. CCITT Recommendation G.821 [Ref. 3] for a digital connection forming part of an Integrated Services Digital Network (ISDN) is based on a 27 500 km hypothetical reference for voice and data services. For voice services the p_{be} is to be $<10^{-6}$ for $>90\%$ of the available minutes. For data services, %EFS $> 92\%$. A connection is considered unavailable if $p_{be} > 10^{-3}$. A one month period is suggested as the measurement time for error rate.

The CCIR has issued recommendations, also based on a 64 kb/s reference channel, for digital radio systems [Ref. 4] and for satellite systems [Ref. 5]. For digital radio systems, the p_{be} shall not exceed 10^{-6} more than 0.4% of any month averaged over one minute intervals on a 2500 km hypothetical reference path. For satellite systems the p_{be} shall not exceed 10^{-6} more than 20% of any month averaged over ten-minute intervals.

The 64 kb/s channel is part of the basic ISDN service with a full duplex information-carrying capacity of 144 kb/s, corresponding to an aggregate transmission rate of 192 kb/s, including overhead for framing and housekeeping. The primary ISDN rates are 1.536 Mb/s (information) and 1.544 Mb/s (aggregate) based on North American standards and 1.984 Mb/s (information) and 2.048 Mb/s (aggregate) based on CEPT standards. Recommendations for error performance at these as well as the much higher rates suitable for full motion digital video, e.g., 90 Mb/s and 135 Mb/s, are under study by the CCITT.

2.2.6 Bit Count Integrity

Bit count integrity (BCI) is the preservation of the exact number of bits (or characters or frames) transmitted in a message or in a period of time. Thus given any two bits separated by m bits in a transmitted stream, the same two bits are separated by m bits in the received stream if BCI has been maintained. The loss of BCI corresponds to an outage that may result in the need for resynchronization.

If a digital signal is shifted by a given number of bits without a loss of alignment, the corresponding loss of BCI is called a *slip*. A *controlled slip* consists of the deletion or repetition of only a single bit, character, or frame. The user will lose data bits, but may not notice a controlled slip if digital video is being transmitted. Thus if the slippage is limited to complete frames, frame alignment will be preserved. CCITT objectives for the slip rate on international connections [Ref. 6], based on a 64 kb/s 25 000 km circuit, call for no more than 0.1% time lost on data transmission. The number of slips/hour for a fixed block length shall not exceed 6.0 for digital data (or 7.2 for voice-band data). For a variable block length, there shall be no more than 0.6 slips/hour.

Uncontrolled slips, as well as high p_{be} can cause multiplexing equipment to lose frame alignment. Such slips are much more likely to be noticed by the user than are controlled slips.

Just as p_{be} and EFS measures are allocated among the links of a circuit, so is BCI. From such link allocations one can establish performance requirements for the factors that produce loss of BCI, such as noise that prevents a timing recovery loop from producing bit synchronization, frame or pulse stuffing synchronization in multiplexers, and transients resulting from protection switching in redundant equipment.

2.2.7 Channel Evaluation

The ability of a channel to deliver an error-free or low p_{be} signal to the receiver is strongly related to the presence of amplitude and phase noise (jitter) on the signal. Display of the signal thus is important in evaluating the causes of channel performance degradation. Such a display can be produced by feeding the signal to the vertical axis of an oscilloscope. The symbol clock signal is fed to the external trigger of the oscilloscope. The horizontal time base is set equal to the symbol duration. This arrangement allows successive segments of the signal to be displayed superimposed on one another as a result of the persistence of the cathode ray tube. [Ref. 7] Figure 2.8 illustrates the types of displays that may result. In the absence of band limiting and noise, the display of the (a) portion of the figure is obtained. The result is called a fully open eye. Band limiting preventing the signal from reaching its full amplitude at the sampling instant produces the eye pattern of the (b) portion of the figure. As noted in Chap. 1, band limiting produces intersymbol interference (ISI). The effect of zero-crossing jitter also is illustrated in this drawing.

Since the amplitude does not reach its full value, there is an amount of eye "closure" as indicated. This closure can be related to the degradation due to ISI. Let δ = fractional closure. Then the peak degradation due to ISI is approximately $20 \log_{10} (1 - \delta)$. Thus for a 20% eye closure, the degradation is -1.94 dB. Note that symbol errors are produced if the amplitude is not over the threshold at the sampling instant. If the threshold is at 50% full amplitude, the band limiting thus has decreased the noise margin, but not produced symbol errors as such.

The eye diagram also displays zero crossing jitter. Such jitter may have an adverse effect on the performance of the symbol timing recovery circuits. The

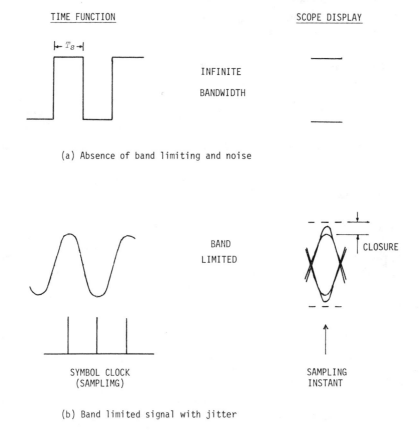

TIME FUNCTION

SCOPE DISPLAY

$\leftarrow T_s \rightarrow$

INFINITE

BANDWIDTH

(a) Absence of band limiting and noise

BAND

LIMITED

CLOSURE

SYMBOL CLOCK
(SAMPLIMG)

SAMPLING
INSTANT

(b) Band limited signal with jitter

Figure 2.8 Eye pattern displays.

consequence may be a degradation in the performance of cascaded regenerative repeaters.

2.3 NETWORK TOPOLOGY

Broadband communication systems may be built in a variety of network forms, depending on the application. A point-to-point configuration is illustrated in Fig. 2.9. The *data circuit terminating equipment* (DCE), sometimes called a *signal converter,* converts the ones and zeroes representation from the terminal's format (often binary) to that of the telecommunication system (often ternary, as will be seen in Sec. 2.5). If the transmission system is an analog one, the DCE is known as a modem. Alternatively, the DCE may be a multiplexer. The *data terminal equipment* (DTE) is a user device such as a front end processor or computer. The *end terminal* (ET) is the ultimate source or sink equipment, such as a video camera or video display. Often the DTE and ET are combined into a single piece of equipment, such as a work station.

A multipoint network is illustrated in Fig. 2.10. The multipoint configuration is useful in *broadcast* type applications in which a single source must transmit to

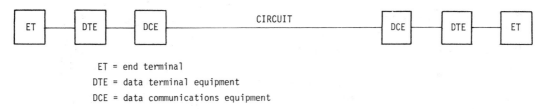

ET = end terminal
DTE = data terminal equipment
DCE = data communications equipment

Figure 2.9 Point-to-point network configuration.

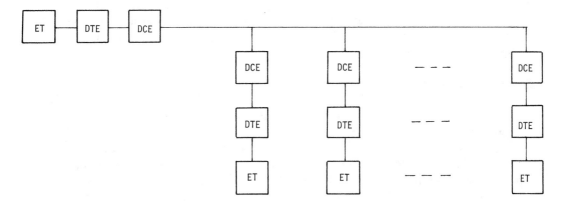

In a multipoint network, all terminals are connected to a common bus. All receive the same information. Some form of addressing is required if only one of the terminals is to respond to a given message.

Figure 2.10 Multipoint network configuration.

numerous terminals simultaneously. For transmission between specific ETs only, addresses must be used, and each individual terminal must be able to recognize its own address.

A discussion of, the ring, bus, and star network topologies, as used in local area networks, is included in Chap. 7.

2.4 SWITCHING

Switching of circuits is done when a given circuit is not needed all the time. Many broadband circuits are switched on a manual (circuit) basis, but the forms of automated switching presently used for low-speed data communications can be applied to wideband systems as well.

2.4.1 Circuit Switching

In *circuit switching,* the circuit is dedicated exclusively to the call or transaction for its duration. Circuit switching requires terminal compatibility in terms of information rate and framing.

2.4.2 Message Switching

In *message switching,* each switch in the network stores entire messages, forwarding each as soon as a circuit becomes available. Message switching can achieve a high degree of efficiency in that the peaks and valleys of demand on a circuit can be smoothed. This is done at the expense of delay in transmission. Terminal compatibility is not required in message switching since code, protocol and speed conversions can be done at the switches. However, such conversions require powerful processors at the switches, including many peripherals such as disk storage devices. The occasional large delays encountered in message switching render it unsuitable for interactive communication. Security and privacy may be poor if operational personnel at the switch can view the messages.

2.4.3 Packet Switching

In *packet switching,* each message is divided into short segments (packets), which then are stored and forwarded by the switches in the network. A packet may be 512 or 1024 bits long, i.e., the length of a line on a display screen. Each packet starts with a *header,* containing the address to which it is to be sent. Code, protocol and speed conversions are done at the switches. Blocking (circuit busy condition) is not noticeable to the user since packet switching entails a rapid exchange of short messages. Packet switching can produce high efficiencies in circuit utilization (see Chap. 7) while functioning with relatively short delays. Another advantage is that packet switching facilitates logical multiplexing, in which a large computer with a single high-speed access line can converse with many lower speed devices simultaneously. Packet switching allows for automatic traffic routing around failed portions of a network. The chief disadvantage of packet switching is its need for many small switches and processors.

The routing and control procedures in packet switching tend to be complex but effective. Three types of routing control have been defined. In *dynamic routing* the network nodes examine the address of each packet and select the outgoing line which will provide minimum delay to the destination. Thus a packet network using dynamic routing responds quickly to changes in network topology or traffic conditions, but the packets may arrive out of sequence. Accordingly, the packets all must be numbered so that they can be placed into the proper order for delivery to the recipient.

In routing using *virtual circuits,* all packets of the message follow the same route through the network, but other packets may be interspersed among them. Accordingly, the transmission delay may be greater than with dynamic routing.

Fixed path routing establishes successive connections known as *sessions* between any two end points. These connections always use the same path. Fixed path routing thus is vulnerable to node or link failures.

2.4.4 Statistical Multiplexing

In time-division multiplexing (TDM), time slots are assigned to users for the durations of their calls. The assignment of a fixed number of slots per unit time (fixed rate) is called synchronous TDM (STDM), and is discussed in Sec. 2.7. However, if the number of slots or the frame length is adjusted to the activity of the source (variable rate), the result is called asynchronous TDM (ATDM), or statistical multiplexing (STAT-MUX). Synchronous bit stream transmission and detection usually are used with both STDM and ATDM, and the framing formats usually are the same in both. The difference lies in the channelization within the frame, resulting from the variable frame lengths in ATDM.

The way in which STAT-MUX works compared with message switching and packet switching can be understood through the example shown in Fig. 2.11. [Ref. 14, Chap. 8]. In each case, message C arrives first at the sending end. Before C is complete B arrives. After C is complete, but while B still is in progress, A arrives. In message switching, B cannot start until C has finished. A must wait until B is finished. In packet switching, however, the first packet of C is sent. Then a packet of B is sent, followed by the second packet of C. After this comes another packet of B, followed by A, which happens to be only one packet long. All of the remaining packets then are B. In statistical multiplexing the frame sequence initially is defined as CBCB . . . , since B arrives right after C. Before the transmission of C has been completed, however, A arrives. Accordingly, the frame structure is redefined as CBACBA . . . . Upon completion of the C data, there is another redefinition to BABA . . . . When A has been completed, all time slots are devoted to complete B.

Packet switching thus transmits larger blocks of data than does STAT-MUX, and each packet contains a header. Each STAT-MUX time slot is shorter than a packet and contains only source data.

In conclusion, the message switch sends each message on a first-come first-served basis. Packet switching breaks up the messages to allow packets from various

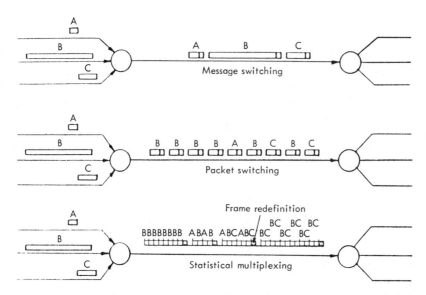

Figure 2.11 Comparison of message switching, packet switching, and statistical multiplexing. (From J. C. Bellamy, *Digital Telephony,* © 1982, Wiley. Reprinted by permission of John Wiley & Sons, Inc.)

sources to be interleaved. STAT-MUX breaks messages into even finer blocks (words) and adds periodic frame definition messages to allow the receivers to identify individual time slots and thus to switch the incoming data correctly. STAT-MUX provides an efficient means by which a line can be shared by multiple interactive terminals communicating with a host computer. A few active sources can each have a high channel data rate, or many active sources can each have a low channel data rate.

2.5 DIGITAL TRANSMISSION VIA BAND-LIMITED FACILITIES

Digital transmission involves rapid changes from one level to another. Such changes constitute pulses in the time domain. The corresponding frequency spectrum is given by the Fourier transform of the pulse. For a pulse of duration T_s centered at $t = 0$ and of magnitude A volts, the Fourier spectrum is

$$A(\omega) = \left(\frac{AT_s}{2\pi}\right) \left[\frac{\sin\left(\frac{\omega T_s}{2}\right)}{\left(\frac{\omega T_s}{2}\right)}\right] \tag{2.9}$$

This function extends to infinity in the frequency domain, so for actual transmission, the spectrum must be limited by filtering. Usually, transmission of the components up to $\omega_s = 2\pi/T_s$ provides a sufficiently good representation of the pulse that it can be detected correctly.

A view of the actual effect of a commonly used filter on pulse shape can be obtained by calculating the effect of a simple RC low pass filter on a step function. For a step function of A volts occurring at $t = 0$, the response of the low pass filter is $A[1 - \exp(-t/RC)]$ volts. Such a filter has a bandwidth to the -3 dB frequency of $1/2\pi RC$. Figure 2.12 illustrates these relationships.

This example illustrates the fact that band-limiting produces degradation of the pulse, resulting in a practical limit on the rapidity with which level changes can be transmitted by the system. In fact pulse spreading means that a given pulse may interfere with the next one to be transmitted, hence the name *intersymbol interference* (ISI).

Before proceeding further, the meaning of the term *bandwidth* needs clarification. The channels assumed by Nyquist and Shannon, as described below, consist of a flat response from a lower cutoff to an upper cutoff frequency, with zero response beyond the cutoff frequencies. The digital signals themselves have spectra extending to infinite frequency, and thus are limited only by circuit characteristics. The most commonly used bandwidth definitions in practice are the following:

The *noise bandwidth B* is the number of Hertz which, when multiplied by the temperature in K and by Boltzmann's constant, $k = 1.38 \times 10^{-23}$ J/K, yields the thermal noise power.

The *half-power bandwidth* is the range of frequencies above and below the frequency of maximum power within which the power level is at least 50% of that at

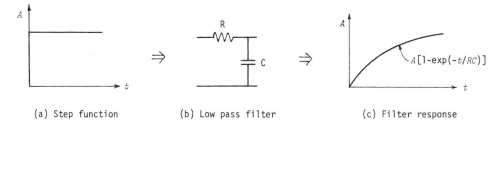

| (a) Step function | (b) Low pass filter | (c) Filter response |

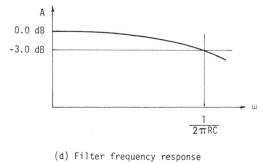

(d) Filter frequency response

Figure 2.12 Effect of RC low-pass filter on pulse rise time.

the frequency of maximum power. The half-power bandwidth is also called the -3 dB bandwidth. A single resonator band pass filter with a half-power bandwidth W_{-3dB} has a noise bandwidth $W = (\pi/2)W_{-3dB}$. For a two-pole filter with maximally flat group delay, $W \simeq 1.2\ W_{-3dB}$.

The *Carson's Rule bandwidth* is approximately the -20 dB bandwidth. It is often used in defining the band occupied by an (analog) frequency-modulated signal.

More generally, the *percentage power bandwidth B_p* is defined such that a specified percentage of the total power, $\%P_B$ is found within B_p, where

$$\%P_B = 100 \times \frac{\int_{-B_p}^{B_p} P(f)df}{\int_{-\infty}^{\infty} P(f)df} \qquad (2.10)$$

Note that the *percentage power bandwidth* refers to the amount of power within the band B_p, as distinguished from the relative power level at the edge of the band, as in the case of the -3 dB bandwidth, which thus is not the same as the 50% percentage power bandwidth.

The *null-to-null bandwidth* is the frequency span between the nulls defining the main lobe of a digitally modulated signal. This bandwidth definition is useful only for modulation techniques that have well-defined nulls. The *Nyquist bandwidth* of a nonreturn-to-zero pulse spectrum is its half-power bandwidth, and equals half its null-to-null bandwidth.

The *spectrum mask* is a curve of power spectral density (power in a specified bandwidth, e.g., 4 kHz or 1 MHz) as a function of frequency. The power spectral density outside the mask must be attenuated to specified levels. The spectrum mask is discussed further in Chap. 4, where specific masks are described.

2.5.1 Synchronous versus Asynchronous Transmission

Most broadband communication systems operate on a *synchronous* basis, which means that the bits are sent continuously in large blocks without the use of special start or stop pulses. The same operating speed is used by both the sending and receiving equipment. In fact, the receiver derives its timing from the received stream in commercial, as well as in many military systems. In addition, the receiver is designed or programmed to associate specific sequences of bits with frames or words, depending upon the application.

In *asynchronous* transmission the terminals transmit data characters independently, separated by start and stop pulses. The receiver identifies the beginning and end of each character by the receipt of these start and stop pulses. The stop pulse is longer than the start pulse or the data pulses. This not only distinguishes it from the other pulses but also provides compensation for differences in the transmit and receive clock frequencies.

2.5.2 Nyquist Theorems

The effect of band limiting on synchronous transmission has been described by the Nyquist theorems [Ref. 8], which specify the minimum channel bandwidth required to send a given symbol rate without intersymbol interference. Nyquist states that synchronous impulses at a rate of 2 *W* per second can be sent through a channel whose bandwidth is *W* Hertz, and that these impulses can be received without intersymbol interference. Note the use of *impulses* is specified. An impulse has infinite amplitude but zero duration; thus its energy is finite. Moreover, Nyquist's "channel whose bandwidth is *W* Hertz" has a flat response and linear phase within the pass band, but its response drops to zero at the edge of the pass band. The term "brick-wall channel" often is used to describe such a response. Figure 2.13 illustrates the characteristics of the brick wall channel. Its impulse response, $h(t)$, is the inverse Fourier transform of its transfer function, $H(f)$, where

$$H(f) = \begin{cases} T_s, & |f| \le \dfrac{1}{2T_s} \\[2mm] 0, & |f| > \dfrac{1}{2T_s} \end{cases}$$ (2.11)

$$h(t) = \int_{-\infty}^{\infty} H(f) \, exp \, (j2\pi f T_s) df$$ (2.12)

$$= \frac{\left[\sin(\pi t/T_s)\right]}{\pi t/T_s}$$ (2.12b)

The phase shift through $H(f)$ is zero for all frequencies.

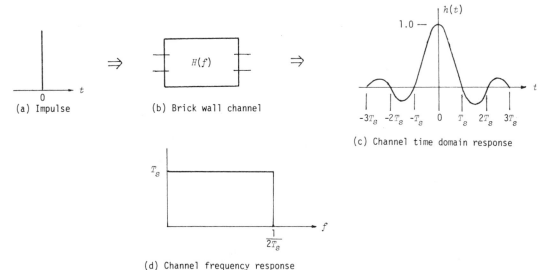

(a) Impulse

(b) Brick wall channel

(c) Channel time domain response

(d) Channel frequency response

Figure 2.13 Characteristics of brick-wall channel.

Note that Eq. (2.12b), plotted in Fig. 2.13(c), calls for an output before the input impulse occurs at $t = 0$! For this reason, plus the infinitely steep drop at $f = 1/2\,T_s$, the channel cannot be built. However, an understanding of the properties of this channel as well as its response is important in understanding the ramifications of the Nyquist theorems. In particular, at all multiples of T_s (except zero), $h(t) = 0$, i.e.,

$$h(nT_s) = \begin{cases} 1 \text{ for } n = 0 \\ 0 \text{ for } n \neq 0, \ n \text{ any integer} \end{cases} \tag{2.13}$$

Although the ideal channel is specified as one with zero phase shift, a linear phase shift within the pass band, $d\phi/df = 2\pi\tau$, simply corresponds to a time delay τ through the channel.

Note that the foregoing statements have placed no limit on the magnitude of the impulse energy. Thus the conditions for zero ISI apply equally well to multilevel inputs.

Thus far the discussion has dealt with impulses. The impulse has a flat spectrum for all frequencies whereas the rectangular pulse of duration T has the spectrum described in Eq. (2.9). For the rectangular pulse to produce an output of the type shown in Fig. 2.13 (no ISI), the brick wall channel transfer function must be modified by the inverse of the rectangular pulse spectrum, i.e., the inverse of Eq. (2.9), which is $[\pi f T_s]/\sin(\pi f T_s)$. Figure 2.14 shows the finite pulse input to the equalized brick wall channel, $H_e(f)$.

While we now have a real rectangular pulse, we still have an unrealizible channel. Moreover, the channel bandwidth W and the symbol duration T_s are

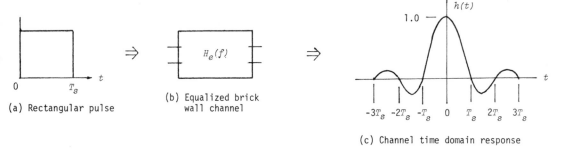

(a) Rectangular pulse

(b) Equalized brick wall channel

(c) Channel time domain response

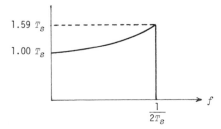

(d) Channel frequency response

Figure 2.14 Response of equalized brick-wall channel to rectangular pulse.

uniquely related; thus a small variation in W will result in a change in the times nT_s when the zeroes of $h(t)$, the channel output, occur. Alternatively, a small change in T_s will change the times when outputs occur. In either event, ISI will increase significantly.

The channel can be made realizable by allowing a smooth roll-off at the band edge in place of the brick wall characteristic. The smooth roll-off also eliminates the high degree of sensitivity of ISI to filter bandwidth and symbol rate. The frequency domain response to the impulse, Fig. 2.13(d), now becomes that of Fig. 2.15(a) [Ref.9] while the response to the rectangular pulse, Fig. 2.14(d), becomes that of Fig. 2.15(b) [Ref.9].

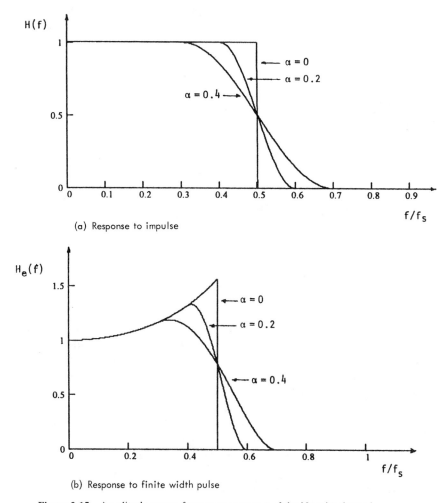

(a) Response to impulse

(b) Response to finite width pulse

Figure 2.15 Amplitude versus frequency response of the Nyquist channel.

The equations expressing the channel characteristics for impulse transmission are:

$$H(f) = \begin{cases} 1 \text{ for } 0 \leqslant f \leqslant \left(\frac{f_s}{2}\right)(1-\alpha) \\[2ex] \cos^2\left\{\left(\frac{1}{4\alpha f_s}\right)[2\pi f - \pi f_s(1-\alpha)]\right\} \\[1ex] \quad \text{for } \left(\frac{f_s}{2}\right)(1-\alpha) \leqslant f \leqslant \left(\frac{f_s}{2}\right)(1+\alpha) \\[2ex] 0 \text{ for } f > \left(\frac{f_s}{2}\right)(1+\alpha) \end{cases} \tag{2.14}$$

where α = channel roll-off factor, a measure of the excess bandwidth built into the channel

$\quad$ f_s = symbol rate

This characteristic, called the raised-cosine function, maintains the zero axis crossings of the impulse response, and thus provides transmission free of ISI. The phase response is linear with respect to frequency. For finite width pulse transmission, the equations are

$$H_e(f) = \begin{cases} \dfrac{(\pi f/f_s)}{\sin(\pi f/f_s)} \text{ for } 0 \leq f \geq \left(\dfrac{f_s}{2}(1-\alpha)\right) \\[3ex] \left[\dfrac{(\pi f/f_s)}{\sin(\pi f/f_s)}\right]\cos^2\left\{\dfrac{1}{4\alpha f_s}[2\pi f - \pi f_s(1-\alpha)]\right\} \\[1ex] \quad \text{for}\left(\dfrac{f_s}{2}\right)(1-\alpha) \leq f \geq \left(\dfrac{f_s}{2}\right)(1+\alpha) \\[3ex] 0 \text{ for } f > \left(\dfrac{f_s}{2}\right)(1+\alpha) \end{cases} \tag{2.15}$$

The maximum transmission rate is $2/(1+\alpha)$ baud/Hertz, where one baud is one symbol/second. Note that the term baud must not be confused with the term bit per second. Baud is the symbol rate whereas bit per second is the information rate. Note also that if the data stream modulates a carrier such that two sidebands are produced (doubling the occupied spectrum), the maximum double-sideband transmission rate is $1/(1+\alpha)$ baud/Hertz.

Example

A modem is designed to use phase-shift keying within a 3000 Hz bandwidth. If the channel response approximates a Nyquist channel with $\alpha = 0.15$, what maximum symbol rate can be accommodated by the channel?

Solution The maximum symbol rate will be $3000/1.15 = 2607$ baud.

One problem remains. An examination of the eye pattern shows that while the ISI has been brought to zero, the signal does not always cross zero at exact integer multiples of the symbol clock. This departure from the correct zero crossing points is called *data transition jitter*. Figure 2.16 [Ref. 10] shows the eye diagrams of digitally modulated signals using a technique called quaternary phase shift keying (QPSK) (see Sec. 2.6.3) for $\alpha = 0.2$ and $\alpha = 0.8$. The advantage of the larger value of α is clear. The jitter is caused by the fact that the effective center of each pulse varies from pulse to pulse based upon the surrounding data pattern. This jitter has an adverse effect on the symbol timing recovery circuit, tending to produce jitter in the recovered clock. For a multiplicity of repeaters, the clock jitter problem becomes serious. The solution to this problem [Ref. 8] is to reshape the original brick wall channel, Eq (2.11), to one which places zero level null points midway between

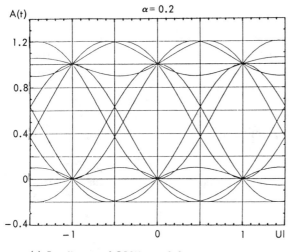

(a) Eye diagram of QPSK, $\alpha = 0.2$

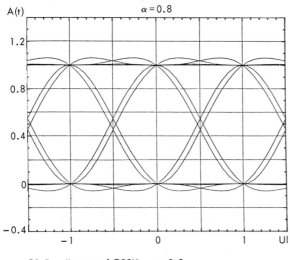

(b) Eye diagram of QPSK, $\alpha = 0.8$

Figure 2.16 Measured eye diagrams of raised-cosine channels. (From *Microwave System News and Communications Technology,* © 1986. Reprinted with permission.)

the existing nonzero level null points. Such simultaneous zero crossing conditions are achieved [Ref. 11] by the $\alpha = 1$ roll-off raised-cosine channel described by setting $\alpha = 1$ in Eq. (2.14), which yields

$$H(f) = 0.5 \left[1 + \cos\left(\frac{\pi f}{f_s}\right) \right] \qquad 0 < f < f_s \tag{2.16}$$

For rectangular pulses, rather than impulses, the equalizer must be added, resulting in

$$H_e(f) = 0.5 \left[\frac{(\pi f_s)}{\sin(\pi f_s)} \right] [1 + \cos(\pi f T_s)] \qquad 0 < f < \frac{1}{T_s} \tag{2.17}$$

While this characteristic removes the data transition jitter problem, it generally is not used because of the additional bandwidth required for $\alpha = 1$.

Thus far, the discussion of the Nyquist theorems has centered on the use of finite width pulses, and the need for an equalizer which effectively flattens the spectrum of these pulses as they pass through the Nyquist channel. For signals having shapes other than the rectangular pulse, a spectrum flattening equalizer still must be added for ISI-free transmission. The characteristics of this equalizer thus will be the inverse of the signal's spectral shape. An example of a nonpulse signal is the half sinusoidal wave shape used in minimum shift keying (MSK), which is described in Sec. 2.6.2.

In an actual transmission channel the Nyquist characteristics describe the desired end-to-end channel. The transmitted signal may be filtered using a frequency response that approximates the square root of the Nyquist channel, and the same square-root frequency response may be used to filter the received signal.

2.5.3 The Shannon Theorem

The discussion of Sec. 2.5.1 dealt with the bandwidth required to send a given symbol rate without intersymbol interference. If a given number of bits are associated with a symbol, the Nyquist expressions seem to imply a relationship between bandwidth and bit rate. However, there is another factor which must be included. That factor is channel noise, which is assumed to be additive white Gaussian noise (AWGN) with a probability density function $p(v)$, where

$$p(v) = \left(\frac{1}{\sigma \sqrt{2\pi}} \right) \exp\left[\frac{-(v - V_o)^2}{2\sigma^2} \right] \tag{2.18}$$

where V_o = mean or dc value, volts
σ = root-mean-square value, volts

For thermal noise, as typically encountered in communication systems $V_o = 0$ so

$$p(v) = \left(\frac{1}{\sigma \sqrt{2\pi}} \right) \exp\left[\frac{-v^2}{2\sigma^2} \right] \tag{2.19}$$

The noise is assumed to be AWGN for two reasons, (1) AWGN occurs commonly in communication systems; (2) AWGN effects can be analyzed more readily than can the effects of other noise types. (The effects of other noise types often can be shown experimentally to be comparable to the effects of AWGN of a given rms value for modest ratios of peak to rms value.)

Having defined the channel as one that is disturbed by AWGN, we look next at the meaning of the unit of information, the bit. Shannon [Ref. 12] defined the information associated with a source output or with a source state X_i as

$$I_{x_i} = \log_a p(X_i) \tag{2.20}$$

where $p(X_i)$ = probability of source state

where a, the base of the logarithm, determines the units in which information is measured. Since binary arithmetic is used extensively not only in transmission systems but also by digital computers, usually $a = 2$, in which case information is measured in *binary digits* or *bits*. While Eq. (2.20) describes the amount of information associated with source state X_i, usually the average information or *entropy* of a source is of most importance. The entropy of a discrete memoryless source, $H(x)$, is obtained by averaging over all source states. Given N such states,

$$H(x) = -\sum_{i=1}^{N} p(X_i) \log p(X_i) \tag{2.21}$$

Assume a source produces zeros with probability p_0 and ones with probability p_1. Then $p_0 + p_1 = 1$ and

$$H(p_0) = -p_0 \log_2 p_0 - p_1 \log_2 p_1 \tag{2.22}$$

This function is found to reach a maximum value of 1.0 if the zeros and ones are equally likely, i.e., if $p_0 = p_1$. Thus a discrete binary source produces one bit per binary symbol if both source states are equally likely.

In general, for any value of N,

$$p(X_i) = \frac{1}{N} \quad \text{for all } i \tag{2.23}$$

and the entropy is

$$H(x) = -\sum_{i=1}^{N} \left(\frac{1}{N}\right) \log_2 \left(\frac{1}{N}\right) = \log_2 N \tag{2.24}$$

The term *mutual information* [Ref. 11, Chap. 6] is a measure of the information that has passed through a channel. The maximum value of the mutual information is the channel capacity. Since the channel is fixed, maximization is with respect to the source (input) probabilities. For a *binary symmetric channel* (one for which errors in zeros and ones are equally likely), the channel capacity C_c is achieved when $p_1 = p_0 = 0.5$. The capacity is

$$C_c = 1 + p_e \log p_e + (1 - p_e) \log (1 - p_e) \tag{2.25}$$

where p_e = unconditional error probability

The unit of measure is bits per binary source symbol.

Example

Calculate the channel capacity for $p_e = 0.5$

Solution $C_c = 1 + 0.5(-1) + 0.5(-1) = 0$

The significance of this result is that for a 0.5 error probability the channel output is independent of the channel input, so the channel is transmitting no information! On the other hand, if $p_e = 0$ or 1, then the output is determined entirely by the input, so $C_c = 1$.

Example

A binary symmetric channel exhibits an error probability of 10^{-6}. What is its capacity in bits/binary source symbol?

Solution $C_c = 1 + 10^{-6}\log_2(10^{-6}) + (1 - 10^{-6})\log_2(1 - 10^{-6})$
$\quad\quad = 1 + 10^{-6}(-19.93) + (0.999999)(-1.44269 \times 10^{-6})$
$\quad\quad = 0.9999786$

Note that this is less than $1 - 10^{-6} = 0.9999990$.

For two or more channels in tandem, the error characteristics of each channel must be expressed in the form of a channel transition probability matrix, $[P(y|x)]$, where y denotes each channel output and x denotes each channel input.

$$[P(y|x)] = \begin{bmatrix} (1 - p_e) & p_e \\ p_e & (1 - p_e) \end{bmatrix}$$

The combined p_e then is applied to Eq. (2.25) to obtain C_c.

Example

A channel consists of three tandem transmission functions. The first and last are subscriber lines for which $p_e = 10^{-8}$. Between them is a long haul line for which $p_e = 10^{-6}$. What is the channel capacity in bits per binary source symbol?

Solution For the tandem combination.

$$[P(y|x)] = \begin{bmatrix} (1 - 10^{-8}) & 10^{-8} \\ 10^{-8} & (1 - 10^{-8}) \end{bmatrix}\begin{bmatrix} (1 - 10^{-6}) & 10^{-6} \\ 10^{-6} & (1 - 10^{-6}) \end{bmatrix}\begin{bmatrix} (1 - 10^{-8}) & 10^{-8} \\ 10^{-8} & (1 - 10^{-8}) \end{bmatrix}$$

$$= \begin{bmatrix} 0.99999898 & 0.00000102 \\ 0.00000102 & 0.99999898 \end{bmatrix}$$

Thus $p_e = 0.00000102$
$\quad\quad C_c = 0.99999782$ bits/binary source symbol.

Having defined channel capacity in bits per symbol and having determined the way in which capacity is affected by the error probability in the channel, the channel capacity in bits per second can be obtained next by simple multiplication.

$$C[\text{bits/second}] = C_c[\text{bits/symbol}] \times R[\text{symbols/second}]$$

The discussion thus far has been oriented toward binary symbols, i.e., one symbol designates one bit. In many communication systems, symbols may be ternary, quaternary, etc., as noted in Sec. 2.1. Thus the number of bits per symbol, C_c, may assume a value well in excess of one, although this value is degraded in the presence of channel errors, as seen in the foregoing example. With no noise in the channel, there would be no limit to channel capacity!

The truth of the last statement is echoed in a well known theorem known as the Shannon-Hartley Law, which states the limits on channel capacity C in terms of the signal-to-noise power ratio in the channel. This theorem states that the upper limit on error-free transmission is

$$C = W \log_2\left(1 + \left[\frac{P}{N_0 W}\right]\right) \quad \text{bits/second} \tag{2.26}$$

where P = received signal power
  N_0 = single-sided noise power spectral density

Note that the single-sided density is the total noise power N divided by the receiver noise bandwidth which, for the Nyquist channel, is the Nyquist bandwidth, $1/2T_s$, as illustrated in Fig. 2.13(d). Thus

$$N_0 = 2NT_s \tag{2.27}$$

Since σ denotes the rms noise level in volts, the normalized noise power (in a one ohm load) is σ^2, so an alternative expression to (2.27) is

$$N_0 = 2\sigma^2 T_s \tag{2.28}$$

Example

A channel has a 3400 Hz bandwidth to the -3 dB points and a 3600 Hz noise bandwidth; it provides a 35 dB ratio of received signal power P to noise power σ^2. What is the channel capacity C?

Solution   Since

$$\frac{P}{\sigma^2} = 35 \text{ dB} = 3162.3 \quad \text{and} \quad N_0 W = \sigma^2, \quad \frac{P}{N_0 W} = 3162.3$$

Thus, from (2.26)

$$C = 3600 \log_2(1 + 3162.3) = 41858 \text{ b/s}$$

Note that the characteristics of the example, a 3400 Hz bandwidth and a 35 dB signal to noise ratio, are what one might expect on a good analog subscriber line. Some state-of-the-art modems now allow 19200 b/s transmission on such a line and provide about a 10^{-5} bit error probability. Shannon says the rate *could* be 41858 b/s with a zero error probability! This tells us that even with the tremendous technological advances of the past decade, we still are far from the Shannon limit.

An alternative form of Eq. (2.26) is obtained [Ref. 11] by noting that for a channel running at full capacity $T_b = 1/C$. The energy per bit, E_b, then is

$$E_b = PT_b = \frac{P}{C} \tag{2.29}$$

from which

$$\left(\frac{E_b}{N_o}\right) = \frac{P}{N_e C} \tag{2.30}$$

Then

$$C = W \log_2\left(1 + \left[\frac{E_b}{N_o}\right]\left[\frac{C}{W}\right]\right) \tag{2.31}$$

This equation can be restructured to show the minimum value of E_b/N_o required for error-free transmission as a function of C/W. Thus

$$\left(\frac{E_b}{N_o}\right) = \frac{2^{C/W} - 1}{C/W} \tag{2.32}$$

Equation (2.31) shows that as E_b/N_o decreases, C/W decreases. However, as can be shown from Eq. (2–32), as $C/W \to 0$, $E_b/N_o \to \ell n\ 2$, or -1.59 dB. This is called the Shannon bound. Operation at $C < W$ is known as *power-limited* operation, whereas operation at $C > W$ is said to be *bandwidth-limited*. The significance of the Shannon bound will be discussed further in Sec. 2.11.

The discussion of Sec. 2.5.2 showed that the Nyquist theorem limit on symbol rate is $2/(1 + \alpha)$ baud/Hertz in a memoryless channel. The Shannon-Hartley Law, Sec. 2.5.3, states that $W \log_2(1 + [P/N_o W])$ is the maximum number of bits per second that can be sent error-free in a bandwidth W. The symbol rate (baud) and the information rate (b/s) are related by the number of levels M used in the system, where $M = 2^m$; thus M is a power of 2. The parameter m thus becomes a multiplier on the spectral efficiency of the transmission. Figure 2.17 shows the interrelations among the foregoing factors.

2.5.4 Timing and Synchronization

As noted in Sec. 2.5.1, in synchronous transmission, the receiver derives its timing from the received signal stream. Synchronization thus is the process whereby the receiver is made to sample the incoming bit stream so that each bit is properly identified (bit sync), and the bits constituting a particular channel are combined to provide the proper output (frame alignment).

The source clock may reside either in the terminal equipment (DCE or DTE), or in the telecommunications network itself. Section 2.9.6 discusses timing from the national network.

2.5.4.1 Derivation of Timing at the Receiver. Several levels of timing must be obtained at the receiver. Often the received signal will be a digitally modulated carrier. The modulation may involve phase shift keying so a reference carrier must be recovered to produce a baseband signal. Carrier recovery is discussed in Sec. 2.5.4.2. Following carrier recovery, symbol timing must be recovered. This is discussed in Sec. 2.5.4.3. Symbols are converted to bits which must then be identified as belonging to words, frames, or packets. Such identification is typified by the approach used in standard digital transmission formats and may involve the

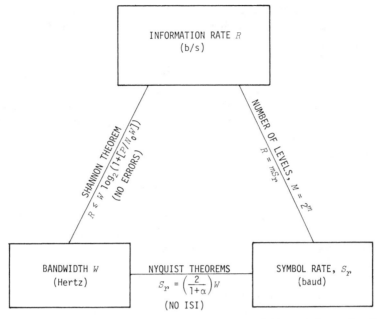

Figure 2.17 Relationships between information rate (b/s), symbol rate (baud), and bandwidth (Hz).

repetitive insertion of special bits or bit combinations into the data stream. The North American standard format uses such insertions and is described in Sec. 2.8.

2.5.4.2 Carrier Recovery. Demodulation of a phase-shift keyed or a suppressed carrier transmission requires that the receiver have available a carrier of correct frequency and phase. Recovery techniques include narrow bandpass filters and phase locked loops (PLLs). As the loop bandwidth is made smaller, the rms phase jitter decreases, but the receiver becomes less able to track transmitter carrier instabilities. In addition, an incorrectly tuned bandpass filter may lengthen the acquisition time for phase recovery. A bandpass filter used to recover an unmodulated carrier exhibits a phase jitter of $(WT_s)(N/2A^2)$ where N = noise power in the filter bandwidth and A = signal amplitude.

One carrier recovery circuit is shown in Fig. 2.18. The first bandpass filter eliminates noise except in the immediate vicinity of the carrier. Its width may be appreciably less than that of the modulated carrier since carrier recovery circuits operate outside the signal flow path through the receiver. The squarer produces components at dc and at twice the carrier frequency. The filter tuned to $2f_o$ retains

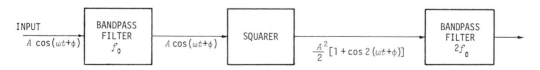

Figure 2.18 Squarer-bandpass filter carrier recovery.

the mean value of the output of the squarer and reduces its variance to an acceptable value. The output exhibits a phase jitter known as squaring loss. Its value is $(WT_s)\left[\dfrac{N}{2A^2} + \dfrac{N^2}{4A^4}\right]$.

One phase-tracking loop recovery system for suppressed carrier signals is known as the Costas loop [Ref. 13], and is shown in Fig. 2.19. Its performance is the same as that of the arrangement of Fig. 2.18 with the $2f_o$ bandpass filter replaced by a PLL. Without the loop filter, the Costas loop behaves the same as a single-resonator output bandpass filter.

For modulation types involving both in-phase (I) and quadrature (Q) carrier components, square-law recovery circuits cannot be used because the balanced statistical nature of the I and Q signal components causes the periodic term to disappear. Instead, fourth-power carrier recovery must be used. Accordingly, the output filter is tuned to $4f_o$. Otherwise, the configuration is the same as that of Fig. 2.17. In this recovery circuit the phase error depends on the data sequence, resulting in a jitter component known as *pattern jitter*. In addition, a *quadrupling loss* results from the use of the fourth-power recovery circuit.

2.5.4.3 Symbol Timing Recovery. The demodulated signal is a baseband waveform whose variations convey the symbol information that was transmitted. This baseband waveform must be sampled at the appropriate times to provide the symbol output of the receiver. The Nyquist bandwidth of the data stream is $1/2T_s$.

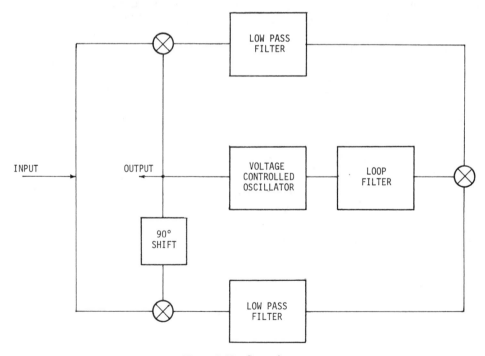

Figure 2.19 Costas loop.

Use of the squarer bandpass filter arrangement of Fig. 2.18 produces a sinusoidal component at $1/T_s$. The zero crossings of the filtered timing signal indicate the correct sampling times. Figure 2.20 is a block diagram showing the recovery of symbol timing.

The symmetrical bandpass filter produces a delay of the zero crossings of $T_s/4$ relative to the desired sampling times. However, if a PLL is used instead of the bandpass filter, the voltage-controlled oscillator of the PLL locks in quadrature with the input.

Timing jitter results from irregularities in the data stream, as well as from input noise. Increasing the number of symbols used in the estimation process decreases the timing jitter. However, techniques exist which actually improve timing recovery performance by either (1) doing timing recovery on known data sequences, such as the preamble of a data packet or (2) using the outputs of the data detectors. For either approach, timing jitter decreases as the signal-to-noise ratio increases up to about 15 dB, beyond which jitter generally is less than $0.1\ T_s$ for a channel roll-off factor $\alpha \geqslant 0.3$ and 25 symbols. Timing jitter also decreases as the filter roll-off factor α increases. For $\alpha \geqslant 0.3$, the jitter is less than $0.1\ T_s$ for a signal-to-noise ratio $\geqslant 15$ dB and 25 symbols, [Ref. 11, Chap. 7].

Carrier and symbol timing can be derived simultaneously, in some cases with superior results compared with separate derivation. For data-aided joint recovery of carrier phase and symbol timing for QPSK, using 25 symbols and $\alpha = 0.5$, a 15 dB signal-to-noise ratio provided a phase jitter less than 0.025 radians and a symbol timing jitter less than $0.15\ T_s$, [Ref. 11, chap. 7].

2.5.5 Baseband Transmission

In baseband transmission the data stream is represented by specific levels on a facility without frequency translation. Baseband transmission may be binary, in which each symbol represents one bit of information, or it may be multilevel, in which each symbol represents two or more bits of information. Multilevel transmission thus provides an increased spectral efficiency over binary transmission.

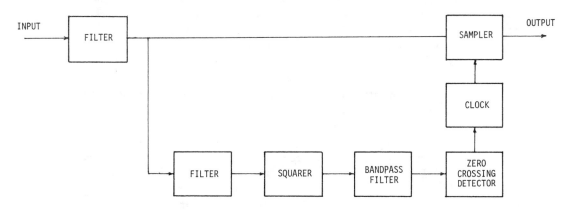

Figure 2.20   Symbol timing recovery circuit using squarer and bandpass filter.

In multilevel baseband transmission, a given symbol may be any one of $M = 2^m$ levels, and thus may convey m bits. Accordingly,

$$R = \left[\frac{2W}{(1 + \alpha)}\right] \log_2 M = \frac{2Wm}{(1 + \alpha)} \text{ b/s} \qquad (2.33)$$

2.5.5.1 Line Coders/Decoders. Bits or symbols can be represented in numerous ways on a transmission system. The line code describes the way in which the information is represented. The discussion at first is limited to binary transmission. First, some definitions are in order. In *antipodal* or *polar* coding, only two levels are sent; one is the opposite of the other. For a given received power, these two levels are as far apart as possible. In *unipolar* coding, one of the two levels is zero. This requires a decision threshold at half of the "on" amplitude. The "on" pulse may be called a *mark* while the "off" (zero) condition is called a *space*. Instead of the receiver's decision threshold being at the zero level, as is the case for polar coding, the decision threshold is placed at half the "on" amplitude. This requires a doubling of the transmit power and a corresponding 3 dB carrier-to-noise penalty compared with polar coding. In *bipolar* coding three levels are used, positive, zero, and negative. Two thresholds thus are required, and both positive- and negative-going noise can cause an erroneous threshold crossing. The result can be shown to be a 3.2 dB carrier-to-noise penalty relative to polar coding, [Ref. 14, Chap. 4].

Numerous digital signal encoding formats have been defined. Table 2.1 [Ref. 15] provides a definition of many of these formats, and Fig. 2.21 shows the corresponding waveforms. Which code is best for transmission purposes? The best code depends on a number of factors, such as spectrum efficiency, timing content, and error detection capability. Spectrum efficiency is very important in any telecommunications application. The nonreturn-to-zero (NRZ) codes exhibit nulls at n/T_s and a peak *density* at zero frequency. (A peak *density* does not necessarily imply the presence of a dc component.) The return-to-zero (RZ) code has its first null at $2/T_s$, along with a peak density at zero frequency. The diphase code, while having a zero density at zero frequency, exhibits a peak at $1/T_s$ and its first null at $2/T_s$. The most spectrally compact of the codes discussed is the bipolar return-to-zero code, which not only exhibits a null at zero frequency, but also at $1/T_s$. It reaches a peak at $1/2T_s$. While filtering is useful in controlling the bandwidth of all digital transmission techniques, starting with a relatively compact spectrum entails less signal modification due to filtering, and thus less degradation.

With respect to timing content, some of the line codes provide more data transition density, e.g., more level changes, than others, and thus improved performance of timing recovery circuits. This is important in allowing receivers to derive their clock from the received stream.

Certain of the line codes have a inherent redundancy as they are used. For example, the bipolar code actually is a three-level code even though it is used only on a binary basis. The number of bits per symbol that could be transmitted on it is $\log_2(3) = 1.6$. However, it is used only at one bit per symbol; hence its redundancy is 60%. Errors can be detected through the use of constraints in the allowed transitions among the different levels.

TABLE 2.1 DEFINITION OF DIGITAL SIGNAL ENCODING FORMATS

Nonreturn to Zero-Level (NRZ-L)
  1 = High level
  0 = Low level
Nonreturn to Zero-Mark (NRZ-M)
  1 = Transition at beginning of interval
  0 = No transition
Nonreturn to Zero-Space (NRZ-S)
  1 = No transition
  2 = Transition at beginning of interval
Return to Zero (RZ)
  1 = Pulse in first half of bit interval
  0 = No pulse
Biphase-Level (Manchester)
  1 = Transition from high to low in middle of interval
  0 = Transition from low to high in middle of interval
Biphase-Mark
  Always a transition at beginning of interval
  1 = Transition in middle of interval
  0 = No transition in middle of interval
Biphase-Space
  Always a transition at beginning of interval
  1 = No transition in middle of interval
  0 = Transition in middle of interval
Differential Manchester
  Always a transition in middle of interval
  1 = No transition at beginning of interval
  0 = Transition at beginning of interval
Delay Modulation (Miller)
  1 = Transition in middle of interval
  0 = No transition if followed by 1
     Transition at end of interval if followed by 0
Bipolar
  1 = Pulse in first half of bit interval, alternating polarity from pulse to pulse
  0 = No pulse

Source: From W. Stallings, "Digital Signaling Techniques," *IEEE Communications Magazine,* Dec. 1984, © 1984, IEEE. Reprinted by permission.

A commonly used line code is the bipolar return-to-zero (BRZ), illustrated in Fig. 2.22. It is also known as alternate mark inversion (AMI). Its 50% duty cycle during the ones interval was selected to simplify timing recovery in T1 line repeaters [Ref. 16]. Note not only the relatively compact spectrum but also the fact that each 1 produces a level (data) transition. With respect to error detection note that a single error produces a violation of the alternating one's polarity. Thus the elimination of any single one pulse, of either polarity, means that the next one will violate the polarity rule. Also, the appearance of a single one in place of a zero similarly will cause the alternating one's polarity rule to be violated. Accordingly, on-line performance monitoring can be done readily on lines using BRZ.

While BRZ provides a level change for each one, it provides none for a sequence of zeros. Level changes thus must be introduced artificially without alter-

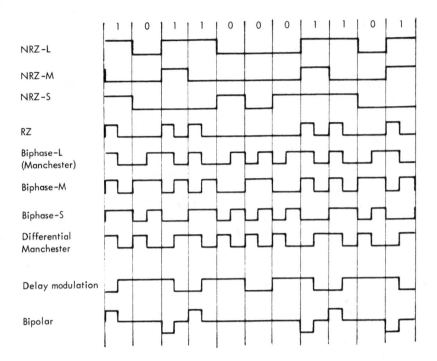

Figure 2.21 Digital signal-encoding formats. (From W. Stallings, "Digital Signaling Techniques," *IEEE Communications Magazine,* Dec. 1984, © 1984, IEEE. Reprinted by permission.)

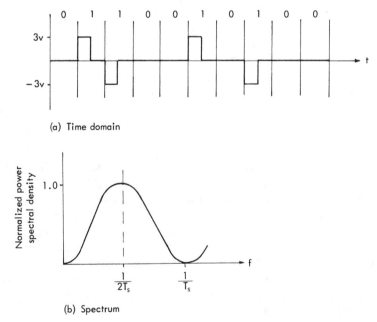

(a) Time domain

(b) Spectrum

Figure 2.22 Bipolar-return-to-zero line code.

ing the data stream. This is done by altering the waveform in a systematic, obvious manner at the transmitting end of the circuit and by removing the alterations at the receiving end, an unaltered bit stream is delivered to the user. Bipolar violations (BPVs) are introduced intentionally in this alteration process.

The need for such altered bit streams depends on the transmission rate, which governs the precision with which the receiver clock must operate; the signal format, whether polar, bipolar, or multilevel; and the pulse amplitude. These factors govern the number of consecutive zeros allowable.

For transmission at 1.544 Mb/s without restricting the data stream, the bipolar with eight-zero substitution (B8ZS) format has been devised, as illustrated in Fig. 2.23, [Ref. 17]. For transmission at the 6.312 Mb/s rate, the format used is bipolar with six-zero substitution (B6ZS) in which, for five or fewer zeros, the stream is bipolar, whereas for six zeros in a row, the output depends on the polarity of the one that preceded them. BPVs are produced as follows:

- If the one was a positive pulse, the output produced is $0 + - 0 - +$.
- If the one was a negative pulse, the output produced is $0 - + 0 + -$.

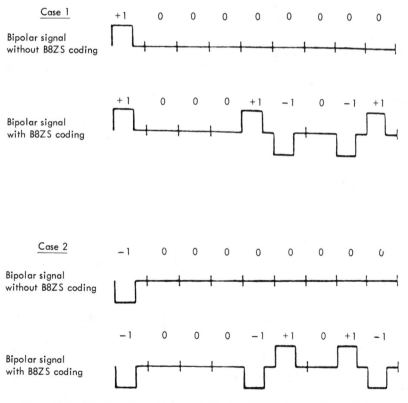

Figure 2.23 Bipolar with eight zero substitution (B8ZS) format. (From Technical Reference TR-TSY-000210, "Low Bit Rate Voice (LBRV) Terminals," Issue 1, 1986, © 1986, Bell Communications Research, Inc., Livingston, NJ.)

The receiver recognizes the pattern of BPVs and substitutes zeros instead. Figure 2.24 illustrates the B6ZS code.

For transmission at the 44.736 Mb/s rate, B3ZS is used, as illustrated in Fig. 2.24. Here each group of three consecutive zeros is replaced by B0V or 00V, where B is a one pulse that adheres to the bipolar rule, while V is a one pulse that violates the bipolar rule. The selection between B0V and 00V is made so that the number of B pulses between consecutive V pulses is odd.

The foregoing rates, 1.544 Mb/s, 6.312 Mb/s, and 44.736 Mb/s are standard rates used by transmission systems conforming to North American standards. Systems that conform to the European standards of 2.048 Mb/s, 8.448 Mb/s, and 34.368 Mb/s use high-density bipolar-3(HDB-3) coding that limits the allowable number of consecutive zeros to 3 by substituting the fourth zero with a BPV. For three or fewer zeros, the stream is bipolar. However, for every four zeros in a row, a 000V or B00V is substituted as shown in Fig. 2.24. The choice of 000V or B00V is made so the number of B pulses between consecutive V pulses is odd, and the polarities of the V pulses alternate. This arrangement prevents the occurrence of a dc component.

To improve the usage of transmission capacity, the 4B3T codes have been devised. In such codes, groups of four binary digits (16 possible code words) are converted into groups of three ternary digits (27 possible code words). The inherent 60% redundancy of BRZ noted previously is reduced to 20% because a given number of bits is transmitted by only three-fourths as many symbols, i.e., $(3/4) \times 1.6 = 1.2$. In using the 4B3T codes a *mode alternation* technique is used to minimize low frequency spectral energy. Each "mode" is an alternative ternary alphabet. The mode used is based on the past history of the signal. Since the decoder has the signal history, it can decode immediately. In a specific implementation of this concept, the MS43 code has three alphabets. Each group of three

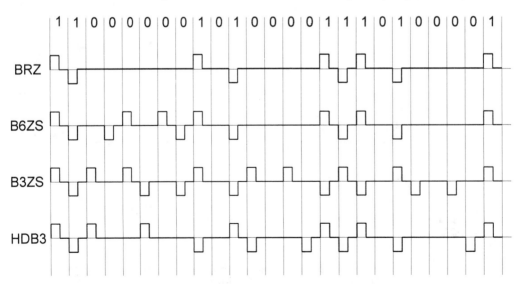

Figure 2.24 Use of bipolar violations in line coding.

ternary symbols is uniquely associated with one group of four binary digits. The decoder need not identify the alphabet used at the coder. The ternary word 000 is not used, so every word contains a positive or a negative 1, resulting in a high timing content.

Biphase-S coding, also known as coded mark inversion (CMI), provides a large number of level transitions and is used in the fourth level European systems, which operate at 139.264 Mb/s [Ref. 18].

Table 2.2 summarizes the repetition rates and codes used in the North American digital hierarchy [Ref. 19, Chap. 21].

The error performance characteristics of the line codes discussed above in an AWGN environment have been derived in numerous references [Ref. 1, Chap. 5; Ref. 14, Chap. 42]. The results, briefly, are as follows:

For polar NRZ, the bit error probability, p_{be}, is

$$p_{be} = \text{erfc} \sqrt{\frac{S}{N}} \tag{2.34}$$

where

$$\text{erfc}\,(z) = \left(\frac{1}{\sqrt{2\pi}}\right) \int_z^\infty e^{-x^2/2}\, \mathrm{d}x \tag{2.35}$$

and where S/N is the ratio of average signal level to noise power in the channel bandwidth.

For unipolar NRZ,

$$p_{be} = \text{erfc} \sqrt{\frac{S}{2N}} \tag{2.36}$$

For M level tranmission, (M equally likely independent symbols) the symbol error probability, p_{se}, is

$$p_{se} = 2\left(1 - \frac{1}{M}\right) \text{erfc} \sqrt{\frac{3S}{(M^2 - 1)N}} \tag{2.37}$$

in zero mean AWGN.

TABLE 2.2 REPETITION RATES AND CODES USED IN THE NORTH AMERICAN DIGITAL HIERARCHY

Signal	Rep. Rate, Mb/s	Tolerance, ppm	Format	Duty Cycle, %
Subrate	0.0024	–	Bipolar	50
	0.0048			
	0.0096			
	0.056			
DSO	0.064	+	Bipolar	100
DS1	1.544	±130	Bipolar	50
DS1C	3.152	±30	Bipolar	50
DS2	6.312	±30	B6ZS	50
DS3	44.736	±20	B3ZS	50
DS4	274.176	±10	Polar	100

+ Expressed in terms of slip rate.

Source: © 1977, American Telephone and Telegraph Company. Reprinted with permission.

Note that Eq. (2.37) expresses the probability of symbol error rather than bit error. If a symbol error occurs and the decoder randomly selects one of the other M-1 symbols then

$$p_{be} = \frac{(2^{m-1})}{(2^m - 1)} p_{se}$$
$$\simeq \frac{p_{se}}{2} \text{ for } m \text{ large}$$

(2.38)

However, in many cases, such as MPSK, as will be seen in Sec. 2.6, the selected symbol will be one of the adjacent ones. If gray coding has been done such that adjacent symbols differ by only one bit position, then a symbol error is likely to cause only a single bit error. In such a case, as S/N increases,

$$p_{be} \to \frac{p_{se}}{\log_2 M}$$

(2.39)

This relationship is valid for most values of p_{be} of interest in wideband communication systems, e.g., $p_{be} \le 10^{-3}$.

2.5.5.2 Scramblers/Descramblers.
The previous section has emphasized the importance of high timing content to allow the receiver to derive timing information from the received signal. However, characteristics of the source output affect the statistics of the data stream. Not only are long runs of zeros and ones undesirable, but periodic bit patterns of any type can result in spectral lines which may produce interference in other channels. The purpose of scrambling is the elimination of long runs of zeros and ones as well as the suppression of any spectral lines in the signal stream. Scramblers may add a pseudorandom sequence to the data stream or may perform a logic addition on delayed values of the stream, [Ref. 1, Chap. 5].

Some scramblers, such as those used in European systems, simply invert every other bit. Other techniques involve inverting the zeros and ones in streams where zeros usually predominate.

Combining the data stream with a pseudonoise stream provides a means whereby unwanted periodicities in a stream can be removed. Pseudonoise generators get their name from the fact that short segments, e.g., several seconds, of their output appear to be random numbers. However, the output actually is periodic, with the period being perhaps minutes or even hours long. If two pseudonoise generators are built alike, started in the same state, and clocked at the same rate, their outputs will be identical. Figure 2.25 is a block diagram of a pseudonoise generator. The individual flip-flop stages are started, each in a specific state, but not all zeros, and clocked simultaneously. Table 2.3 shows the output that is produced by the shift register of Fig. 2.25 by starting with the stages in states 1 0 1 0.

As can be seen from Table 2.3, even though the initial condition was alternate ones and zeros, the output appears to be random. In general, the maximum period τ of a pseudonoise generator is

$$\tau = \frac{(2^n - 1)}{f_0}$$

(2.40)

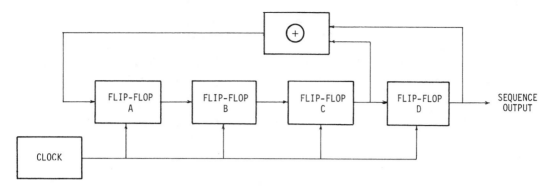

Figure 2.25 Pseudonoise generator using four-stage shift register.

TABLE 2.3 GENERATION OF PSEUDONOISE SEQUENCE
BY FOUR-STAGE SHIFT REGISTER

		Stage			
	Time	1	2	3	4
INITIAL CONDITION ⟶	1	1	0	1	0
	2	1	1	0	1
	3	1	1	1	0
	4	1	1	1	1
	5	0	1	1	1
	6	0	0	1	1
	7	0	0	0	1
	8	1	0	0	0
	9	0	1	0	0
	10	0	0	1	0
					↑
					Output

where n = number of shift register stages

f_0 = clock frequency

To illustrate the use of a pseudonoise generator, consider the following example:

Example

The input sequence 1 0 0 0 0 0 0 1 0 0 is to be transmitted. Both sending and receiving ends of the circuit have pseudonoise generators which are built alike, started at the same time in the same initial state, and clocked with the data stream. (The receiver derives its clock from the received stream.) Show that the receiver output is the same as the original input even though the transmitted stream is significantly different. The pseudonoise stream to be used is the one produced in Table 2.3.

Solution At the sending end, the pseudonoise stream is added bit by bit to the input stream to produce the transmitted stream. The received stream is assumed to be the same as the transmitted stream, i.e., no errors have occurred. (The purpose of the technique being demonstrated is to eliminate periodicities and long runs of the same bit in the transmitted stream; error detection and correction are separate issues to be treated later in this chapter.) At the receiver, an independently generated, but identical, pseudonoise stream is added to the received stream to produce the output, thus:

Input	1	0	0	0	0	0	0	1	0	0
Pseudonoise stream	0	1	0	1	1	1	1	0	0	0
Transmitted stream	1	1	0	1	1	1	1	1	0	0
Received stream	1	1	0	1	1	1	1	1	0	0
Pseudonoise stream	0	1	0	1	1	1	1	0	0	0
Output	1	0	0	0	0	0	0	1	0	0

As will be noted from Eq. (2.23), the maximum length of a sequence from a pseudonoise generator is $2^n - 1$. The actual length also depends on the initial states of the flip flops as well as the number and location of the feedback taps. For a suitable choice of initial sequence, half of the "runs" are of length one (really single bits, not runs!), one-fourth are the length two (two like bits in a row,), one-eighth of length three, etc. Thus, the number of runs of consecutive zeros or ones of length $n - 1$ is twice the number of runs of length n. In addition, the number of ones in a single cycle of the output sequence (a number of bits equal to the length of the shift register), is one greater than the number of zeros.

2.5.5.3 Correlative Level Encoding. The discussion of Nyquist's theorems in Sec. 2.5.2 noted that these theorems are based upon zero memory of past symbols. Stated another way, the symbols are generated independently of one another. There is no ISI among the symbols. Reaching the Nyquist limit would require channel filtering with $\alpha = 0$, i.e., the use of "brick wall" filters. However, the use of a preplanned amount of ISI allows transmission not only to, but even beyond, the Nyquist rate. The technique which allows this achievement is called *correlative level encoding*. Its purpose is to provide the transmission of a given bit rate in less bandwidth than would be required otherwise. Correlative level encoding introduces *correlation* among the levels transmitted, i.e., they no longer are independent of one another. This correlation can be produced either in the time domain (by combining adjacent symbols), or in the frequency domain (by overfiltering), but because the two domains can be related through the Fourier transform, the end results of the two approaches can be made equivalent. (However, not all overlapping pulses are produced by overfiltering an input, as will be seen in the description of $1 - D$ encoding in Sec. 2.5.5.3.1). Different multilevel formats are available, with various spectral properties.

In correlative coding, controlled interference is introduced between the symbols. Figure 2.26 shows binary symbols (two-level), in which each symbol is combined with the adjacent one to produce what is called *partial response coding*, another name for correlative level encoding. Figure 2.27 illustrates the time domain responses to individual pulses, and shows that the output only responds to half the amplitude of the input, hence the name *partial response*. The technique was de-

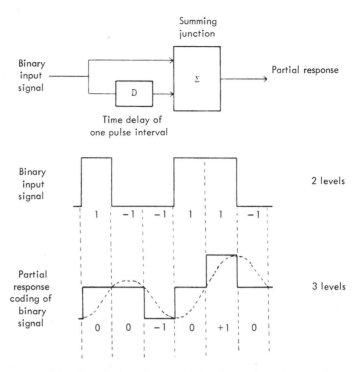

Figure 2.26 Introduction of controlled interference between symbols.

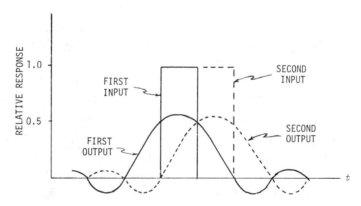

Figure 2.27 Output of partial response channel.

scribed first by A. Lender [Ref. 20], who called it *duobinary,* based upon its doubling the speed at which binary symbols can be transmitted otherwise by combining two adjacent pulses to form a multilevel signal.

The role of ISI can be seen in Fig. 2.28 [Ref. 14], where a two-level input results in a three-level output (a), and where a four-level input results in a seven-level output (b).

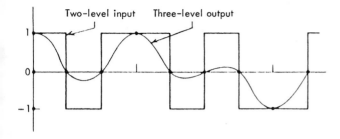

(a) Two-level input

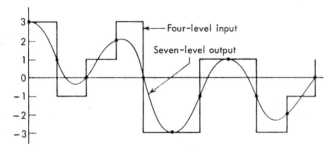

(b) Four-level input

Figure 2.28 Waveforms resulting from overfiltering to produce partial response signaling. (From J. C. Bellamy, *Digital Telephony,* © 1982, Wiley. Reprinted by permission of John Wiley & Sons, Inc.)

Because partial response signaling (PRS) is produced by correlating adjacent symbols, only certain transitions can occur in the waveform. Receipt of a level other than an allowed one in a given symbol interval means that an error has occurred. The following level constraints exist:

- A nonzero level may not be followed by the opposite polarity nonzero level at the next sampling instant.
- Nonzero levels of opposite polarity must be separated by an odd number of zero level samples.
- Nonzero levels of the same polarity must be separated by an even number of zero level samples.

A special technique called *precoding* allows the detector to establish the original sample value without comparison with the previous sample value. The result is the elimination of error propagation from one sampling time to the next. Figure 2.29 [Ref. 1, Chap. 5], illustrates the precoding concept. At the output a one appears either as +1 or as −1. Zeros appear as the zero level after applying mod-2 arithmetic, which converts the +2 level to zero.

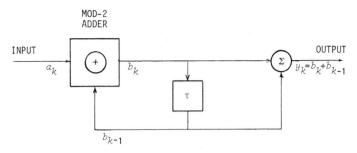

Figure 2.29 Precoding block diagram. (From D. R. Smith, *Digital Transmission Systems,* © 1985, Wadsworth, Inc. Reprinted by permission.)

2.5.5.3.1 *Partial Response Classes.* A variety of classes of partial response systems are possible. Figure 2.30 [Ref. 1, Chap. 5], shows a transversal filter which serves as the basis for the various PRS coding arrangements. Table 2.4 lists the classes as established by Kretzmer [Ref. 21]. The filter of Fig. 2.30 is generalized in the sense that various choices for the weighting coefficients h_n allow various PRS classes to be implemented. For example, Class 1, with which the name *duobinary* now is associated, involves adding the previous input to the present one. Often the delay operator D is used to denote a delay equal to one symbol interval, T_s. Thus,

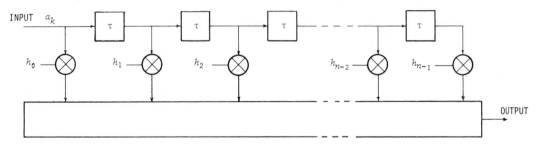

Figure 2.30 Generalized partial response filter. (From D. R. Smith, *Digital Transmission Systems,* © 1985, Wadsworth, Inc. Reprinted by permission.)

TABLE 2.4 PRS CLASSES

Class	Generating Function	Transfer Function	Received Levels
1	$y_k = a_k + a_{k-1}$	$2 \cos\left(\dfrac{\omega T}{2}\right)$	3
2	$y_k = a_k + 2a_{k-1} + a_{k-2}$	$4 \cos^2\left(\dfrac{\omega T}{2}\right)$	5
3	$y_k = 2a_k + a_{k-1} - a_{k-2}$	$2 + \cos \omega T - 2 \cos 2\omega T$	5
4	$y_k = a_k - a_{k-2}$	$2 \sin \omega T + j\,(\sin \omega T - \sin 2\omega T)$	3
5	$y_k = a_k - 2a_{k-2} + a_{k-4}$	$4 \sin^2 \omega T$	5

Class 1 may be called $1 + D$. Its spectrum has maximum density at zero frequency with nulls at $1/nT_s$, $n = 1, 2, 3, \ldots$. A special case not shown in Table 2-4 is $1 - D$, which uses a single cycle of a square wave across two signal intervals to encode each bit, as illustrated in Fig. 2.31(a). However, one bit only requires one symbol interval, as illustrated in Fig. 2.31(b), where the superposition of the "one" and "zero" symbols produces a positive, zero, or negative output level. The $1 - D$ spectrum is zero at zero frequency and has nulls at $1/nT_s$, $n = 1, 2, 3, \ldots$. The null at zero frequency results from the fact that neither of the two individual signals, Fig. 2.31(a), has a dc component. If the levels are replaced by 50% duty cycle pulses, and if differential encoding is used (zeros coded with same phases as previous symbol and ones with opposite phase), the result is BRZ. Thus, $1 - D$ coding is useful in shaping the transmitted spectrum.

A tandem combination of $1 + D$ and $1 - D$ produces $1 - D^2$ coding, which is Class 4 in Table 2.4. This coding is called *modified duobinary*. It can be produced by using a $1 - D$ encoder and a $1 + D$ channel response. Its spectrum is zero at zero frequency with nulls at $1/2nT_s$, $n = 1, 2, 3, \ldots$. Its waveform has three levels and error propagation can be eliminated by precoding.

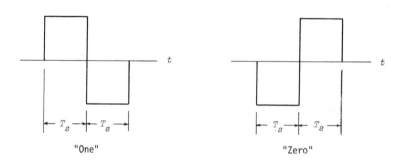

(a) Symbols one and zero

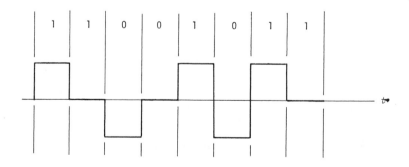

(b) Bit sequence using $1 - D$ encoding

Figure 2.31 Illustration of 1-D encoding.

Of the classes listed in Table 2.4, Class 1 (duobinary), and Class 4 (modified duobinary), are used most frequently because they are relatively simple, their spectra are relatively compact, and their performance is good, as will be described in Section 2.5.5.3.2. Class 4 systems are in use by the GTE TIC system, operating at 3.152 Mb/s [Ref. 22] and also by Western Electric in its data under voice 1A-RDS system with four-level inputs, as illustrated in Fig. 2.28(b). In general, an M level input to a duobinary system results in $2M - 1$ received levels. The precoder, Fig. 2.29, will have the mod-2 adder replaced by a mod-M adder.

For a given data rate, M-ary PRS requires fewer levels than does zero memory M-ary transmission. This is why the 1A-RDS system was built using $1 - D^2$ coding. With $2M - 1 = 7$ levels ($m = \log_2 M = \log_2 4 = 2$), the 1.544 Mb/s stream ($T_s = [1.544 \times 10^6]^{-1}$) occupies a spectrum whose first null is at $(1/m)(1/2T_s) = 384$ kHz. If the same spectrum conservation had been achieved with a zero memory system, $m = 4$ and $M = 2^4 = 16$ levels. The smaller number of levels means that a given channel noise level produces fewer errors, as can be seen from Eq. (3.37).

Another advantage of PRS lies in its application to digital subscriber loops [Ref. 23]. In conjunction with echo cancellation, modified duobinary coding has been found to reduce crosstalk by 2.85 dB compared with AMI, and a 2.1 dB reduction in jitter also has been achieved.

Longer correlation spans than D (duobinary), and D^2 (modified duobinary), can be used. A span of length D^n, $N \geq 3$, is called *polybinary*. These longer correlation spans result in more energy concentrated at lower frequencies, but require correspondingly longer memories.

The receiving configuration corresponding to the generating filter of Fig. 2.30 is shown in Fig. 2.32. The ISI is removed by selecting the weights, C_n, in accordance with the weights used in the generating function, as listed in Table 2.4.

2.5.5.3.2 Partial Response Performance. Partial response transmission results in $2M - 1$ levels at the receiver. In zero mean AWGN,

$$p_{se} = 2\left(1 - \frac{1}{M^2}\right) \text{erfc}\left[\frac{\pi}{4}\sqrt{\frac{3S}{(M^2 - 1)N}}\right] \tag{2.41}$$

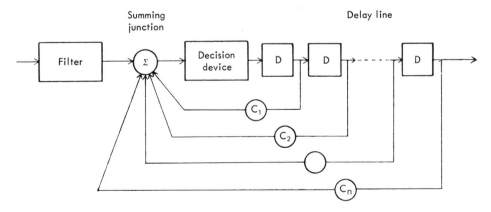

Figure 2.32 Decision feedback receiver.

with Eqs. (2.38) and (2.39) applying to the conversion to p_{be}. In a PRS system the distances between the signal levels are cut in half, causing a 6 dB reduction in error performance. About 2 dB of this is recovered because of the smaller bandwidth, and another 2 dB by virtue of there being less power on the channel.

Setting $M = 2$ in Eq. (2.41) results in the expression

$$p_{se} = p_{be} = \left(\frac{3}{2}\right) \text{erfc} \left[\frac{\pi}{4} \sqrt{\frac{S}{N}}\right] \qquad (2.42)$$

Comparison of Eq. (2.42) with Eq. (2.36) appears to indicate that duobinary performance is less than that of ordinary binary performance by about $\pi/4$, since the 3/2 factor is of much less significance than the argument of the erfc. The $\pi/4$ factor corresponds to -2.1 dB. However, Eq. (2.36) is based on the ideal Nyquist channel, whereas Eq. (2.42) is based on a practical channel. For an $\alpha > 0$ the comparison swings the other way, as was seen in the 1ARDS example of Sec. 2.5.5.3.1, where duobinary is found to require fewer levels than an M-ary zero memory system.

2.5.5.4 Equalization. Wideband transmission, whether for data or for video, requires that limits be placed on attenuation and group delay variations over the bandwidth of the channel. Many channels exhibit an attenuation decrease near the band edges, along with appreciable group delay variation. The result may be significant pulse dispersion and thus ISI, with consequent bit errors. While a fixed channel characteristic can be corrected with a preset equalizer, most channel characteristics are not precisely known, and may vary with time.

The linear transversal filter, shown in Fig. 2.33, is commonly used as the basis for the equalizer. In this figure, the cs and ds are coefficients describing the equalized signals, and correspond to amplifier gains. If these coefficients are variable, the device is called an *adaptive equalizer*. The taps are spaced τ units of time apart, where $\tau = T_s$. The equalizer output is sampled at the symbol rate and then fed to the detector or decision device. Suitable selection of the coefficients allows ISI to be cancelled. A decision-directed adaptive equalizer uses the receiver output to estimate the error voltages. The objective is to iteratively improve the tap gain settings. On poor channels, however, the adaptation process may be slow. A hybrid system attempts to reduce the settling time by starting with preset equalization and then switching to adaptive equalization once transmission is in progress.

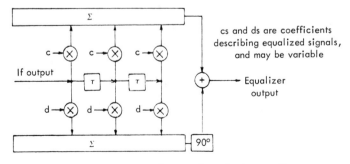

Figure 2.33 Transversal filter used as adaptive equalizer.

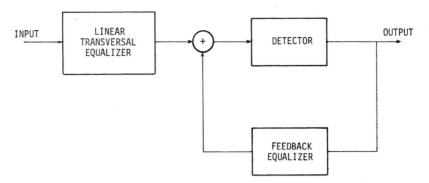

Figure 2.34 Decision feedback equalizer.

The *decision feedback equalizer* [Ref. 24] shown in Fig. 2.34, uses nonlinear filter techniques. After the linear transversal filter processes the signal, the result is fed back to a second transversal filter. The purpose of the feedback equalizer is to cancel ISI caused by previous symbols. The forward and feedback coefficients are adjusted continually to minimize the mean square error.

Several conditions tend to limit the performance attainable from equalizers [Ref. 1, Chap. 5]:

1. The channel may change faster than the equalizer response time. The solution is an increased step size for fast convergence initially, and then decreased step size for continuing operation.

2. The length of the equalizer (nT_s) may be inadequate for the ISI being encountered. The solution is a greater equalizer length.

3. Equalizer settings may drift during idle periods when actual data is replaced by repetitive patterns with insufficient data transitions. The solution to this problem is scrambling of the data stream.

2.6 DIGITAL MODULATION TECHNIQUES

The discussion of Sec. 2.5.5 dealt with baseband transmission, in which no frequency translation has occurred. There are numerous situations, however, in which frequency translation is desirable. One involves the use of frequency-division multiplexers, in which a multiplicity of baseband signals are combined to produce a group (12 voice channels), or supergroup (60 voice channels), or higher level combination. Another example is the case of modems used for transmission via a facility which does not handle the lowest frequencies well. An example is a telephone voice channel with its 200 Hz low frequency cutoff. Of major interest in wideband communications is the use of digital modulation in microwave radio and in satellite communication systems, as well as in coherent optical transmission systems.

A carrier, in general, is a sine wave, $A \cos (\omega_c t + \phi)$, whose amplitude A, frequency $f_c = \omega_c/2\pi$, and phase ϕ may be varied every T units of time. The carrier is said to be digitally modulated if A, f_c and ϕ are allowed to assume specific values or "levels" only. As before, the number of levels is designated M.

2.6.1 Amplitude Modulation

In digital amplitude modulation (AM), the carrier is allowed to assume specific levels. The simplest form of AM is on-off keying (OOK), which corresponds to direct multiplication of the carrier with a two-level (unipolar) line code. This digital modulation technique was used in 1847 by Samuel F. B. Morse to send the message "What hath God wrought!" from Baltimore to Washington on a pair of copper wires. The first electronic communication thus was digital! The term amplitude-shift keying (ASK) often is used to designate digital AM. Negative amplitudes or levels correspond to 180° phase shifts of the carrier relative to the positive levels.

For simple OOK,

$$A = \begin{cases} A_{max} \text{ for a 1 (mark)} \\ 0 \text{ for a 0 (space)} \end{cases} \tag{2.43}$$

An envelope detector is suitable for receiving since no information is conveyed by the phase of the carrier.

A two-level keying arrangement is used in noncoherent optical fiber systems because of the characteristics of laser diodes, as described in Chap. 6. In this case,

$$A = \begin{cases} A_{max} \text{ for a 1} \\ A_{min} \text{ for a 0} \end{cases} \quad A_{max} > A_{min} > 0 \tag{2.44}$$

Again, an envelope detector is used for reception. The most general form of ASK is double sideband (DSB), for which $A = (A_{max}/2)[1 + a(t)]$, where $a(t)$ is the modulating signal. The carrier, however, represented by the "1," conveys no information, so may be suppressed, yielding $A = (A_{max}/2)a(t)$, which describes the amplitude of a double-sideband suppressed carrier (DSB-SC) signal. Both sidebands, however, convey the same information, so one can be eliminated, yielding single-sideband (SSB). If the unwanted sideband is removed by a band-stop filter, the result may include only a vestige of the lower frequency components of the unwanted sideband. The result is known as vestigial sideband (VSB). The transmission of SSB or VSB may be done with or without a carrier. The carrier, while not conveying modulating information as such, may be very useful to the receiver as a reference. For this reason, analog television is transmitted over the air using VSB with the carrier present, as described in Chap. 3.

In the case of DSB-SC, if $a(t) = \pm 1$, the result has a constant amplitude but the carrier reverses phase. The result may be called phase reversal keying (PRK) or bi-phase shift keying (BPSK). As such, it is discussed in Sec. 2.6.3. However, it is mentioned here to pave the way for a later discussion of quadrature amplitude modulation (QAM) in Sec. 2.6.4 where the concept of "negative amplitudes" (actually carrier phase reversals) is important. Any technique that involves carrier phase changes requires a coherent demodulator so that these phase changes are recognized at the receiver. Figure 2.35 illustrates four-level ASK in which the

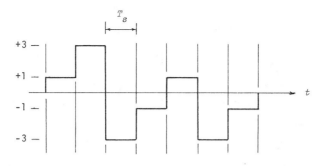

(a) Baseband form

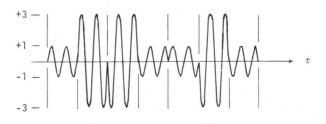

(b) Modulated form

Figure 2.35 Four-level ASK.

carrier frequency is twice the data clock frequency. Note the carrier phase reversals wherever the polarity of the baseband signal changes.

Coherent demodulation requires the receiver to have a local sine wave whose phase corresponds to that which was transmitted, with compensation for propagation delay.

Unless one sideband has been removed, the modulated spectrum is twice the width of the baseband spectrum. Figure 2.36 illustrates the spectrum of a single rectangular pulse, both at baseband, and surrounding a carrier frequency f_c. Note that the spectrum of the modulated signal is simply an upward translation of the baseband, with the lower sideband being a mirror image, about the carrier, of the upper sideband. The term *linear modulation* is sometimes used to designate such a translation. Thus the shaping as well as the bandwidth of the modulated signal are governed by the baseband signal $a(t)$.

In the case of coherent ASK demodulation, the spectrum shaping used (overall frequency response consisting of transmitter, channel, and receiver), should be *matched* to the received signal. This means that noise passed to the demodulator is

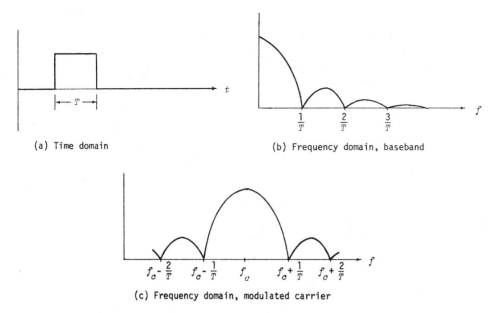

(a) Time domain

(b) Frequency domain, baseband

(c) Frequency domain, modulated carrier

Figure 2.36 Spectrum of pulse at baseband and as modulated onto a carrier using ASK.

minimized consistent with maximizing the distance between received levels, so that the symbol error probability is minimized. In the time domain, a matched filter is achieved by multiplying (correlating) the received signal with each of the receivable symbols or pulse shapes. The multiplier outputs are integrated across a symbol interval to find the overall average value during that interval. A separate integrator is used for each symbol. The integrator whose output is largest indicates the most likely transmitted symbol. In ASK the symbols differ only in amplitude and polarity, allowing a single matched filter to be used. Decoding then consists of comparing the output of the matched filter to each of the decision levels.

The output of a single correlator $h(t)$ and its integrator is expressed [Ref. 14. App. C] as

$$V = \int_0^T s(t)h(t)dt = \int_0^T |s(t)|^2 dt \qquad (2.45)$$

where $s(t)$ = signal being detected. V is a measure of the energy in the signal over the period T. In the frequency domain the matched filter response $H(f)$ is the complex conjugate of the channel pulse spectrum $S(f)$. Accordingly the matched filter output $Y(f)$ is

$$Y(f) = H(f)S(f) = S^*(f)S(f) \qquad (2.46)$$

Coherent decoding will be found, both in Sec. 2.6.6 as well as in later chapters of this book, to provide lower symbol error probabilities than noncoherent decoding. However, unless the modulation technique demands it, its added complexity makes it worthwhile only under conditions in which the received signal-to-noise ratio is near the threshold for acceptable performance.

2.6.2 Frequency Modulation

In digital frequency modulation (FM), the carrier is shifted to specific frequencies, one for each symbol. The term frequency shift keying (FSK) usually refers to binary digital FM, with the abbreviation MFSK designating the use of more than two frequencies. A major advantage of the forms of FSK (as well as PSK, Sec. 2.6.3), over ASK is the fact that their amplitudes are constant. A multiplicity of amplitude levels is a problem where amplifier saturation is encountered. Saturation will reduce, and may even eliminate, the distance between amplitude levels. The use of multilevel ASK thus requires amplifier linearity. A further advantage of FSK over ASK is the fact that the FSK demodulation threshold does not have to be adjusted continually if the received signal varies in strength, as may occur in certain types of radio transmission such as HF or microwave.

The general expression for an MFSK signal is $A \cos[\{\omega_s + 0.5a_M(t)\Delta\omega\}t]$, where $a_M(t)$ is a balanced M level baseband signal with equal numbers of positive and negative levels, and $\Delta\omega = 2\pi\Delta f$ is the difference frequency between the levels. Figure 2.37 illustrates a baseband signal and the corresponding frequency components for $M = 4$. The actual frequency spectrum of an FSK signal occupies a bandwidth of approximately $(M - 1)\Delta f$ for $\Delta f \gg \omega_s/2\pi$, the bandwidth of the baseband

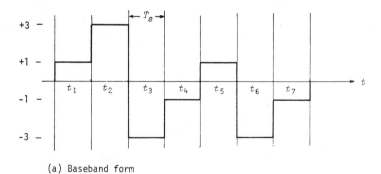

(a) Baseband form

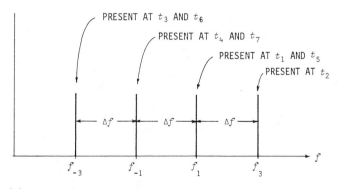

(b) Frequencies used to convey symbols

Figure 2.37 Four-level FSK.

modulation signal. The bandwidth is approximately $(M - 1)(1/T_s)$ for $\Delta f \ll \omega_s/2\pi$. The *frequency deviation* is defined as $(M - 1)\Delta f/2$. The *modulation index* is β, the ratio of the frequency deviation to the baseband width, $\omega_s/2\pi$, or

$$\beta = \frac{(M - 1)\Delta f \pi}{\omega_s} \qquad (2.47)$$

Coherent detection (demodulation and decoding) is achieved by comparing the outputs of two matched filters, as illustrated in Fig. 2.38(a), for $M = 2$. The box labeled STR performs symbol timing recovery, as described in Sec. 2.5.4.3, thus allowing the matched filter outputs to be sampled at the correct times.

The noncoherent detector, Fig. 2.38(b), simply performs envelope detection at each of the input frequencies and reaches its decision based on relative envelope magnitudes. Noncoherent FSK detection is used more often than coherent detection because coherent FSK is less than 1 dB better in terms of error performance in noise.

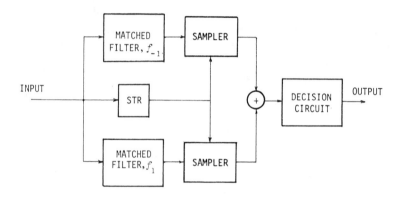

(a) Coherent detector

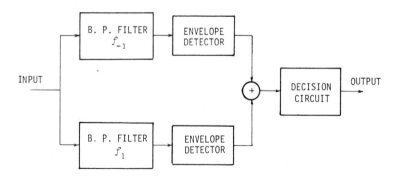

(b) Noncoherent detector

Figure 2.38   FSK detector concepts, $M = 2$.

In general, FSK is used most commonly in low rate asynchronous modems for data transmission over analog facilities. Where broadband data rates and low error probabilities are demanded, PSK (see Sec. 2.6.3) provides superior performance. However, a special form of FSK known as minimum shift keying (MSK) has some useful properties which make it worthy of discussion. MSK belongs to a class of FSK signals known as continuous phase FSK. Two frequencies, f_1 and f_{-1}, are spaced such that, during $T_s = T_b$, one symbol goes through 180° more phase shift than the other. This results in the maximum phase difference at the end of T_b with a minimum Δf. Phase continuity is maintained at signaling transitions. Figure 2.39 illustrates an MSK signal at a bit rate of $1/T_b$. Thus for a zero (f_{-1}) and a one (f_1), respectively, $\Delta\omega = \pi/T_b$, and the signals s are

$$s_0 = A \cos\left(\omega_c t - \left[\frac{\pi t}{2T_b}\right] + \phi_0\right) \tag{2.48a}$$

and

$$s_1 = A \cos\left(\omega_c t + \left[\frac{\pi t}{2T_b}\right] + \phi_0\right) \tag{2.48b}$$

where ϕ_0 is the phase at the beginning of the signal interval.

The primary advantage of MSK is the fact that its spectrum is very compact. From a maximum spectral density at the carrier frequency, the power drops to nulls at $\pm 0.75/T_b$. Moreover, the fraction of out-of-band power beyond these nulls is only 0.1%. This is achieved with a minimum frequency spacing of $1/2T_b$ Hz for $M = 2$, as indicated by Eq. (2.48). This means that during each symbol (bit) interval, the carrier phase changes by $\pm\pi/2$. Accordingly, a phase trellis, Fig. 2.40, can be used to describe the phase of an MSK signal as a function of time. Each of the paths corresponds to a combination of ones and zeros.

The power spectral density of an MSK signal is

$$S(\omega) = \frac{16A^2 T_b}{\pi^2}\left[\frac{\cos(\omega - \omega_c)T_b}{1 - \left(\frac{8}{\pi}\right)(\omega - \omega_c)^2 T_b^2}\right]^2 \tag{2.49}$$

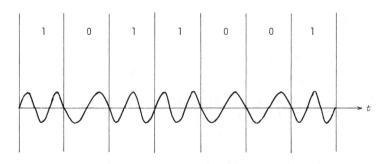

$$f_{-1} = 1/T_b \qquad f_1 = 1.5/T_b$$

Symbol rate = $1/T_b$

Figure 2.39   MSK waveform.

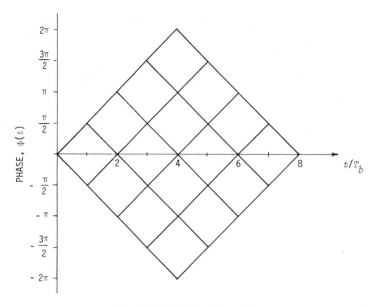

Figure 2.40 MSK phase trellis.

Note that at frequencies well beyond the carrier, ω_c, the spectrum falls off as ω^{-4}. Figure 2.41 shows the MSK spectrum as a function of $(f - f_c)T_b$, which is $(1/2\pi)$ $(\omega - \omega_c)T_b$.

Returning to MFSK, the optimum receiver is a bank of M matched filters. At each sampling time, $t = kT_s$, the receiver selects the largest filter output as the received symbol. For coherent MFSK detection an exact phase reference is required at the receiver. Noncoherent detection provides nearly the same performance (within 1 dB) and is much simpler. A bank of M filters is used, each centered on one of the M frequencies. An envelope detector is used at the output of each filter, and the largest detector output is taken to be the symbol sent.

2.6.3 Phase Modulation

In digital phase modulation (PM), the carrier phase assumes specific values, one for each symbol. The term phase shift keying (PSK) usually refers to binary digital PM, with the abbreviation MPSK designating more than two phases. As in the case of the FSK systems, the amplitude of a PSK signal remains constant under modulation.

The general expression for an MPSK signal is $A \cos(\omega_c t + \phi_n)$, $0 \leq t \leq T_s$ where $\phi_n = 2(n - 1)\pi/M$, $n = 1, 2, \ldots, M$. Figure 2.42 illustrates a baseband signal and the corresponding phases for $M = 4$. Note that the baseband signal is a symmetric M level NRZ baseband signal; in this case it has levels ± 1 and ± 3. In general, all allowed phases are equally probable; consequently, a "carrier" as such is not present since opposite phases cancel one another. However, the term "carrier recovery" is used to denote the production of a reference carrier for detection purposes, as was discussed in Sec. 2.5.4.2.

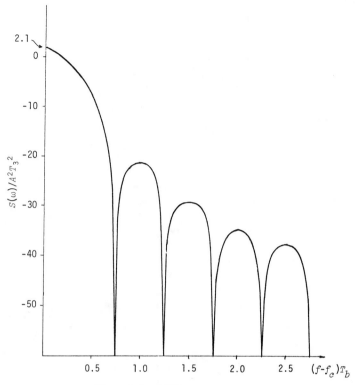

Figure 2.41 MSK spectrum.

As noted previously, digital detection involves identifying the value of a received level relative to a threshold, or boundary between different levels. In the case of amplitude or frequency shift keying a determination is made as to received amplitude level or frequency value. In the case of phase shift keying, decision thresholds, the dashed lines in Fig. 2.42(b), mark the boundaries between differing received levels. Noise constitutes a vector added to the tip of the signal vector. However, provided the resulting vector (signal plus noise) lies within $\pm \pi/M$ of the nominal phase value, the correct symbol will be detected.

The vector tip locations in Fig. 2.42(b) constitute signal states, and thus a polar plot of such points is called a *signal state space* diagram, or *constellation*. The distance between points divided by the maximum power level (a constant for phase modulation) is called the *Euclidean distance*. The Euclidean distance is a measure of the extent to which the system can tolerate noise. Thus for a given value of p_{be}, higher levels of modulation require larger values of carrier-to-noise ratio.

MPSK can be generated in any of several ways [Ref. 14, Chap. 6]. Multiple phases of the carrier frequency can be generated and the appropriate phase corresponding to each symbol can be selected; if desired, a switching arrangement can be used to select controlled delays corresponding to the desired phases. Alternatively, the MPSK signals can be produced as a linear combination of quadrature signals, or the desired waveforms can be synthesized using digital processing at relatively low

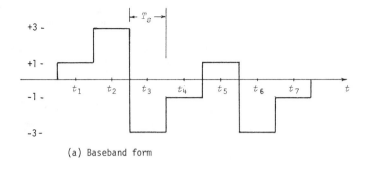

(a) Baseband form

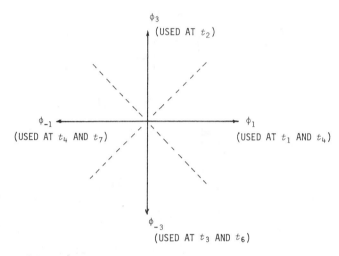

ϕ_3
(USED AT t_2)

ϕ_{-1}
(USED AT t_4 AND t_7)

ϕ_1
(USED AT t_1 AND t_4)

ϕ_{-3}
(USED AT t_3 AND t_6)

(b) Phases used to convey symbols

Figure 2.42 Four-level PSK.

carrier frequencies, as is done in voiceband modems. Figure 2.43 illustrates the steps used to produce an MPSK signal. The serial binary stream is converted to M multibit symbols, one of which at a time appears as a voltage on the appropriate output lead. As a result, two baseband signals, $a_I(t)$ and $a_Q(t)$ are produced at levels which correspond to a quadrature representation of the phases, i.e., 45° is represented as $(1 + j)/\sqrt{2}$, etc. The resulting amplitude modulated signals are summed to produce the desired constant level MPSK output.

Figure 2.44 illustrates the generalized spectrum of an MPSK signal, where M is the number of bits per symbol. The curve follows Eq. (2.50):

$$S(f) = T_s \left\{ \frac{\sin[(f - f_c)\pi T_s]}{(f - f_c)\pi T_s} \right\}^2$$

$$= mT_b \left\{ \frac{\sin[(f - f_c)\pi m T_b]}{(f - f_c)\pi m T_b} \right\}^2 \tag{2.50}$$

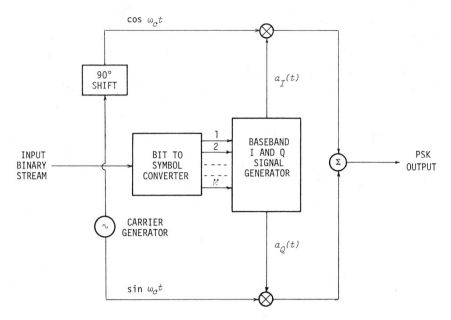

Figure 2.43 MPSK modulator.

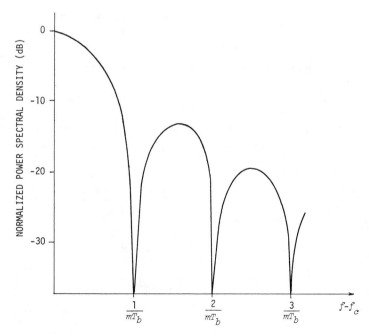

Figure 2.44 Generalized MPSK spectrum.

2.6.3.1 Phase Reference. The demodulation of amplitude or frequency shift keyed signals requires the establishment of amplitude and frequency thresholds at the receiver. Such thresholds can be established quite readily, on a basis independent of the received signal. However, the phase reference requires not only that the exact carrier frequency be established at the receiver, but also that the phase of that carrier be established properly since an incorrect (reversed) phase can result in a 100% bit error probability, p_{be}. The phase ambiguity produced by the carrier-recovery circuit thus must be resolved. One approach to such resolution is the use of a differential encoder and decoder, which operate based upon the principle illustrated in Fig. 2.45. This illustration is called differential quarternary phase shift keying (DQPSK). Its use is illustrated by the following table:

To send	Change phase by
11	$+45°$
01	$+135°$
00	$-135°$
10	$-45°$

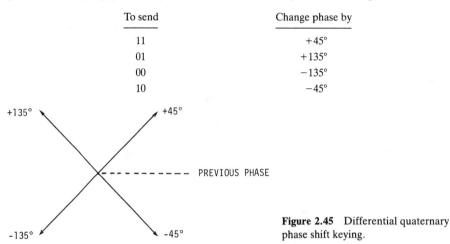

Figure 2.45 Differential quaternary phase shift keying.

The phase reference simply is the phase of the previously transmitted symbol. This technique can be applied to MPSK using any value of M. Consequently, the designation DPSK (differential phase shift keying) should not be used because it leaves the reader wondering how many phases M are being used.

Figure 2.46 illustrates a differential encoder. For BPSK, $T_s = T_b$. The corresponding decoder is illustrated in Fig. 2.47. Here an unmodulated carrier is

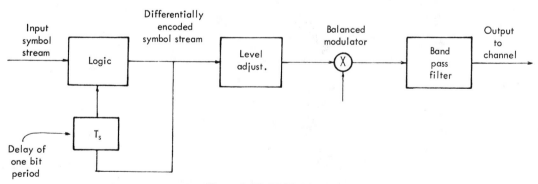

Figure 2.46 BPSK differential encoder.

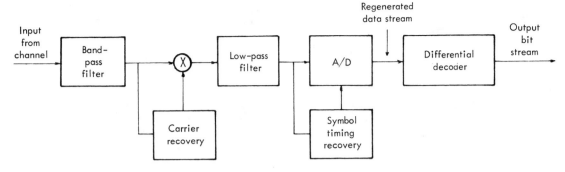

Figure 2.47 Coherent PSK demodulator with differential decoder.

"recovered" (produced by the demodulator) on a coherent basis, but symbol timing recovery is done on a differential basis. The differential decoder uses receive logic which is the inverse of the transmit logic. Generally MPSK systems require differential encoding because the detector cannot determine the phase of a recovered reference relative to the phase of the transmitted signal. For coherent PSK, as is used in some limited-power satellite applications, a unique word (special bit combination) must be transmitted at the start of a frame or at some other specified time to allow the detector to identify the received phases correctly. Coherent PSK, however, provides only about a 1 dB improvement over differential PSK, so its additional complexity cannot be justified in many applications.

A coherent demodulator is shown in Fig. 2.48. Instead of a coherent demodulator, a differential phase demodulator may be used as illustrated in Fig. 2.49. This approach performs differential decoding on the modulated signal.

An improvement in differential PSK has been devised [Ref. 25] in which the NRZ waveforms are smoothed to provide "controlled transitions," as illustrated in Fig. 2.50. Its power spectral density is more confined than that of either DQPSK or

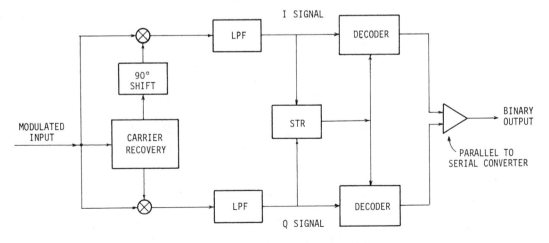

Figure 2.48 Coherent phase demodulator.

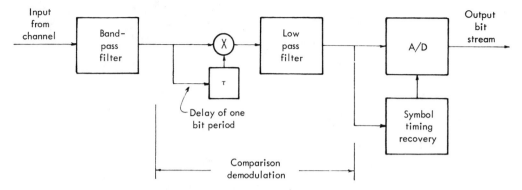

Figure 2.49 Differential phase demodulator.

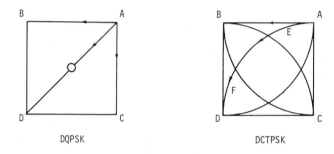

(a) Signal state space diagrams

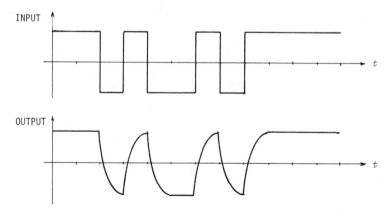

(b) I-channel waveforms of controlled transition processor

Figure 2.50 Differentially detected controlled-transition phase-shift keying. (From A. Yongaçoğlu and K. Feher, "An Efficient Modulation Technique for Differential Detection," *IEEE ICC '85*, © 1985, IEEE. Reprinted by permission.)

DMSK, even after hard limiting. Thus it has good power and bandwidth efficiency, while retaining the advantages of differential detection.

2.6.3.2 Phase Jitter. Phase *jitter* is the name given to phase noise in the receive clock of a digital system. Jitter is a short-term variation of the sampling instant, as distinguished from long-term variation, which is called *drift* or *wander*. Jitter causes transmission impairment in three ways [Ref. 1, Chap. 22]: (1) displacement of the sampling instant from its correct time increases the probability of missing the pulse to be detected, thereby reducing the noise margin and degrading the p_{be} performance; (2) excessive jitter results in STR circuit slips as a result of loss of phase lock or a cycle slip; (3) irregular spacing of the decoded samples of coded analog waveforms corresponds to distortion of the recovered analog signal.

Jitter and wander are caused by noise and interference which pass through the phase detector and filter and cause errors in the receiver clock (as it attempts to "hunt" the source clock) and thereby in the received stream. Wander results from temperature changes, which affect both conducted and propagated signals through changes in velocity of propagation as well as path length. Path length changes may result from having one terminal on board an aircraft or a repeater on board a satellite. A major cause of jitter is irregular timing information arising in regenerative repeaters and multiplexers because of data patterns in the stream from which the receive clock is derived, including the addition of stuff pulses. Irregular timing information also results from overhead bits added by multiplexers.

Jitter can be removed by the use of an elastic store (a variable length delay line), which provides bit rate averaging to reduce the jitter, thus absorbing the short-term instabilities in the receive clock. Accordingly, the transmit clock of a repeater or terminal using an elastic store will operate at a different instantaneous rate than the receive clock. Figure 2.51 is a block diagram illustrating the use of an elastic store to remove phase jitter. In operation, an increase in the input bit stream rate causes the instantaneous number of bits in the elastic store to increase. The increased storage level information, smoothed by a low-pass filter, causes an increase in the frequency of the voltage-controlled oscillator, which serves as the transmit clock. This increased frequency causes bits to be read out of the elastic store more rapidly and thus a suitable average bit level is maintained in the elastic store.

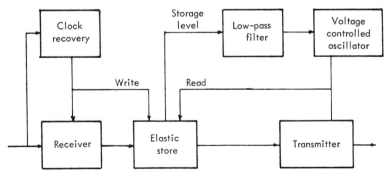

Figure 2.51 Use of elastic store to remove phase jitter.

2.6.4 Amplitude-Phase Keying (APK)

In MPSK, all signals are constrained to be of constant amplitude. The spacing of the signal state points thus is limited to $\phi_n = 2(n-1)\pi/M$. Removal of the constant amplitude constraint allows independent signals to modulate the real and imaginary axes. The result is a square, triangular or other array of signal state points, as illustrated in Fig. 2.52 for the case of four equally spaced levels on each axis. In general, this is an M-ary APK, or MAPK system. The result shown is known as 16-level quadrature amplitude modulation (16-QAM). Note that, in general, the signal states need not be in a square array (QAM). Thus QAM is a special form of APK. Figure 2.53, (courtesy Codex Corp.), is a photograph of a 64-state amplitude-phase keyed constellation showing the use of a triangular configuration, which allows the maximum Euclidean distance d_e between points. The increased Euclidean distance for 16-QAM compared with 16-PSK is illustrated in Fig. 2.54, which shows an improvement of $20 \log_{10} (0.471A/0.393A) = 1.59$ dB for 16-QAM over 16-PSK for a given peak power. This is the actual improvement obtained versus sinusoidal interference of random phase. Against additive white Gaussian noise (AWGN), the dB improvement is greater than 1.59 dB because of the amplitude probability distribution of AWGN. In general, the distance d_s between adjacent signal states is

$$d_s = A_{max} d_e = A_{max} \sqrt{2}(L-1) \qquad (2.51)$$

where L = number of levels on each axis

Figure 2.55 shows a QAM modulator and Fig. 2.56 shows a QAM demodulator. The splitter sends alternate bits from the input stream to the alternate converters. The low pass filters provide spectrum shaping, e.g., raised cosine filtering, with the overall shaping being split between the modulator and the demodulator. Since the spectrum is determined by the spectrum of the baseband signals applied, the spectrum shape is the same as that of MPSK of the same number of levels.

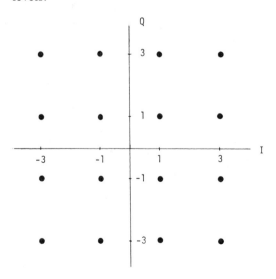

Figure 2.52 16-QAM constellation.

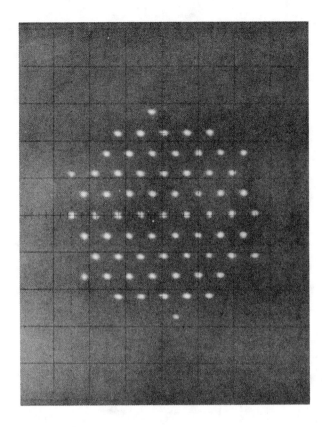

Figure 2.53 64-APK constellation. (Courtesy Codex Corp.)

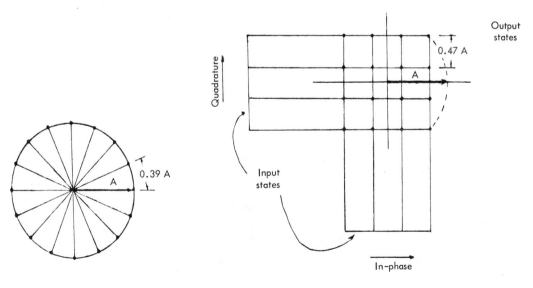

(a) Constellation for 16-PSK

(b) Constellation for 16-QAM and its deviation

Figure 2.54 Constellations for 16-PSK and 16-QAM.

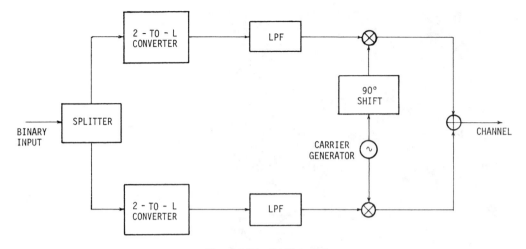

Figure 2.55 QAM modulator.

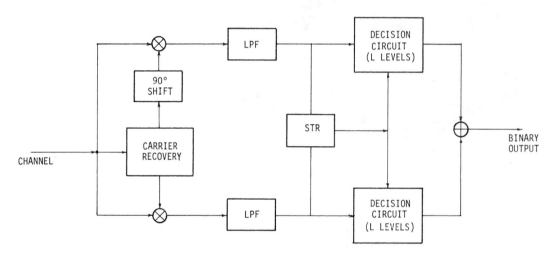

Figure 2.56 QAM demodulator.

While APK signals in general have better bit error probability performance than PSK signals because of greater Euclidean distance, the fluctuating amplitude of an APK signal means that it requires the use of linear amplification (at least a nonsaturated amplifier), to prevent the collapse of the outer signal state points into the inner ones.

QAM has found numerous applications in voiceband modems (modulator-demodulators) as illustrated in Tables 2.5 and 2.6. Such devices convert digital streams to the form of digitally modulated sine waves suitable for transmission within the 200–3200 Hz telephone band.

Quadrature signals can be used to represent MPSK signals using linear combinations of cos $\omega_c t$ and sin $\omega_c t$. In fact, such representation leads to one method of

TABLE 2.5 HALF-DUPLEX MODEM TYPES

Data rate	Symbol rate	n	Constellation	Type	Model	CCITT standard
2400 b/s	1200 Bd	2	QPSK	Fixed eq.	Bell 201 (1962)	V.26
4800 b/s	1600 Bd	3	8-PSK	Manual eq.	Milgo 4400/48 (1967)	V.27
9600 b/s	2400 Bd	4	16-QAM	Adaptive eq.	Codex 9600C (1971)	V.29
14.4 kb/s	2400 Bd	6	64-QAM	Rectangular	Paradyne MD14400 (1980)	V.24, V.28
14.4 kb/s	2400 Bd	6	128-QAM	8-State Trellis	Codex 2666 (1985)	V.33
19.2 kb/s	2743 Bd	7	64-State 8 Dimensional Trellis Coded Modulation		Codex 2680 (1985)	V.24, V.28

TABLE 2.6 FULL-DUPLEX MODEMS

Data rate	Model	CCITT standard	Notes
300 b/s	Bell 103/113		
1200 b/s	Bell 212A	V.22	
2400 b/s	Bell 2224	V.22 bis	error corr., 64-QAM
9600 b/s		V.32	error corr., dial-up lines

generating MPSK signals. This approach can be viewed as a direct result of the fact that, in MPSK, the amplitude is constrained to a fixed level whereas the phase assumes a discrete number of values.

A special form of QAM known as superposed QAM (SQAM) has several useful properties [Ref. 26]. SQAM has a more limited spectral occupancy than standard 4-QAM (QPSK) or MSK, and this limited occupancy is achieved even when the signals pass through a nonlinear amplifier. Many other modulation techniques suffer spectral spreading upon nonlinear amplification.

The SQAM signal is produced by using an impulse response that is a double symbol interval $(2T_s)$ raised-cosine pulse superposed on two weighted single interval (T_s) raised-cosine pulses. The signal thus is $(A/2)(1 + \cos\ [\pi t/T_s])$ $- (A[1-a]/2)(1 - \cos\ [2\pi t/T_s])$, where a is an amplitude parameter of the SQAM signal such that $0.5 < a < 1.5$, $-T_s < t < T_s$. Figure 2.57 illustrates the SQAM signal. Since the signal has twice the duration of the input symbol, the resulting SQAM signal is a function of two consecutive input symbols. The parameter a is selected to control the power spectrum and the envelope fluctuation of the signal.

The power spectral density of an SQAM signal is

$$S(f) = \left(\frac{A^2}{a^2}\right)\left[\frac{1}{1 - 4T_s^2 f_c^2} + \frac{a-1}{1 - T_s^2 f_c^2}\right]^2 \left(\frac{\sin\ 2\pi f_c T_s}{2\pi f_c T_s}\right)^2 \tag{2.52}$$

Figure 2.58 [Ref. 26] shows computed plots of the single-sided SQAM spectrum compared with QPSK (4-QAM) and MSK in a hard limited (nonlinear) channel. The advantages of SQAM in the presence of adjacent channel interference as well as in satellite systems (hard limiting in many cases), thus are apparent.

Sec. 2.6   Digital Modulation Techniques

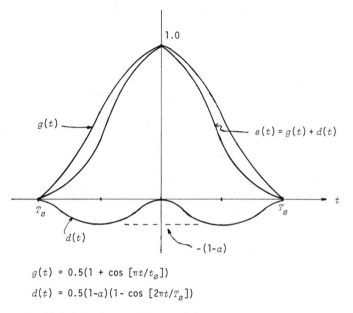

$$g(t) = 0.5(1 + \cos [\pi t/t_s])$$

$$d(t) = 0.5(1-a)(1- \cos [2\pi t/T_s])$$

Figure 2.57 SQAM signal, $A = 1$. (From J. S. Seo and K. Feher, "Performance of SQAM Systems in a Nonlinearly Amplified Multichannel Environment," *IEEE ICC '85,* © 1985, IEEE. Reprinted by permission.)

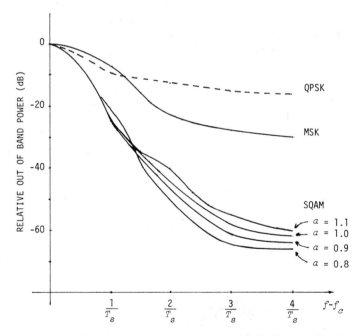

Figure 2.58 Out-of-band to total power ratio of SQAM, QPSK, and MSK signals via hard limited channel. (From J. S. Seo and K. Feher, "Performance of SQAM Systems in a Nonlinearly Amplified Multichannel Environment," *IEEE ICC '85,* © 1985, IEEE. Reprinted by permission.)

2.6.4.1 Offset Keying. A well-known technique for preventing spectral broadening in a nonlinear channel is the use of a constant amplitude signal. While such signals as QPSK are regarded as having constant amplitudes, bandpass filtering of a QPSK signal to limit its spectral occupancy causes the envelope to go to zero at each 180° phase reversal. Any subsequent nonlinear amplification reduces the envelope fluctuations and tends to restore the spectral sidebands to the values they had prior to filtering. For QPSK, bandpass filtering thus is useful only after nonlinear amplification. Further improvement can be achieved by limiting the phase changes at symbol transitions to ±90°, rather than the ±180° changes which may occur otherwise in QPSK. The ±90° limit can be achieved by offsetting the I and Q streams of a QAM signal by one bit period, T_b, i.e., by $0.5T_s$. This prevents the quadrature coefficients from changing state simultaneously. The result is called offset QPSK (OQPSK). A further advantage of offset keying is that it allows synchronization of reference recovery circuits to the incoming carrier at a 3 dB lower carrier-to-noise ratio than is possible with a corresponding aligned system.

Further reduction of out-of-band energy results by totally eliminating the phase transition between symbols, as is done in MSK, which can be viewed as a special case of OQPSK in which the NRZ level encoding (apply the waveform of Fig. 2.28(b) to Fig. 2.52), is replaced by half-sinusoid waveforms. The use of half-sinusoidal pulse shaping on both the I and Q channels of an offset QAM system results in the signals

$$A_i \cos \left(\frac{\pi t}{2T_b} \right) \cos \omega_c t \qquad (-T_b \leqslant t \leqslant T_b)$$

and

$$A_q \sin \left(\frac{\pi t}{2T_b} \right) \sin \omega_c t \qquad (0 \leqslant t \leqslant 2T_b)$$

where A_i and A_q are the amplitudes, e.g., ±1, on the I and Q channels, respectively, and $\cos (\pi t/2T_b)$ and $\sin (\pi t/2T_b)$ are the shaping factors on the two channels. The sums of these two signals then are:

$$A_i \cos \left(\omega_c t + \left[\frac{\pi t}{2T_b} \right] \right) \qquad A_i = A_q$$

and

$$A_q \cos \left(\omega_c t - \left[\frac{\pi t}{2T_b} \right] \right) \qquad A_i \neq A_q$$

These expressions are the same as those of Eq. (2.48), which describe the MSK waveform.

2.6.4.2 Quadrature Partial Response Signaling. Sec. 2.5.5.3 discussed correlative level encoding and showed its advantages in terms of spectrum efficiency. The application of partial response codes to the in-phase and quadrature channels of a QAM system is called quadrature partial response (QPR). Alternatively, a QAM modulator can be followed by a narrow bandpass filter that overfilters the quadrature signals. Figure 2.59 illustrates the resulting constellation. Points 1, 2, 3, and 4 are those of the original QAM signal. Points 5, 6, 7, 8, and 9 are produced as a result of using partial response coding or overfiltering (use of a filter with a bandwidth less than the Nyquist bandwidth). Correspondingly, four levels on each channel (I and Q) result in seven levels on each channel and thus 49-QPR. Note that over-filtering may be done either by low-pass filtering the original baseband, or by bandpass filtering the QAM signal. The filter characteristic usually is divided between the sending and receiving ends; thus the receiver not only completes the spectral shaping but also rejects out-of-band noise. The sending end filtering often is done after nonlinear amplification.

The filtering for QPR differs from the raised-cosine filtering done for non-correlative techniques in that a cosine shaped filter is used instead at both the sending and receiving ends resulting in a 2 dB loss in transmitted power. For equal peak powers (QAM and QPR), the overfiltering has the effect of increasing the information density by approximately 17%. While conventional QAM modulators are used at the sending end, the receiving end must be built to handle the additional levels which are present. Following demodulation, the detection done on each channel (I and Q) is the same as the PRS detection described in Sec. 2.5.5.3 [Ref. 27].

With partial response coding, 4-QAM becomes 9-QPR and can transmit 2 b/s per Hz, while 16-QAM becomes 49-QPR and can transmit 4 b/s per Hz. While 9-QPR appears to exhibit a net loss of 2 dB compared with 4-QAM, if one considers the fact that 2 b/s per Hz can be achieved on a practical channel ($\alpha = 1$) with either 9-QPR or 16-QAM, the comparison now favors 9-QPR by 1.9 dB for a given probability of bit error. Accordingly, as is discussed further in Chap. 4, QPR is a useful technique in digital radio systems.

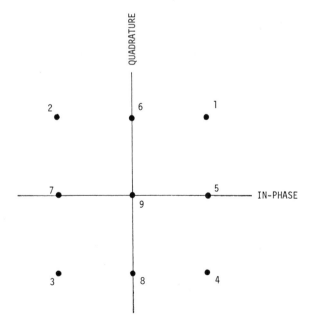

Figure 2.59 Signal state space diagram of 9-QPR signal.

Both Class I and Class IV QPRS systems degrade rapidly for symbol rates above the Nyquist rate. For example, with four input levels, eye closure occurs at 3% above the Nyquist rate; with eight input levels, eye closure occurs at only 1% above the Nyquist rate. Performance at 6 to 9% above the Nyquist rate [Ref. 28, 29] has been achieved by "chopping" the transmitted spectrum as shown in Fig. 2.60(a), where α is the percentage in excess of the Nyquist rate. In Fig. 2.60(b), a service channel has been added at the low frequency end of the spectrum as well. At $p_{be} = 10^{-9}$, for 225-QPRS at 6% above the Nyquist rate the required C/N is 35.3 dB. Without spectrum chopping, operation 3% above the Nyquist rate was not possible. At 3% above the Nyquist rate, spectrum chopping allowed a 10.6 dB C/N reduction for $p_{be} = 10^{-9}$.

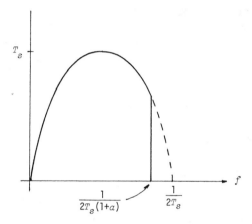

(a) Spectrum chopped to allow transmission to $2(1+\alpha)$ Bd/Hz

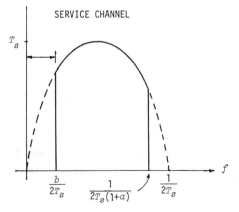

(b) Spectrum chopped to allow transmission to $2(1+\alpha)$ Bd/Hz plus service channel

Figure 2.60 Chopped spectra. (From K. T. Wu, I. Sasase, and K. Feher, "Improved Efficiency 15-Level Modified Duobinary PRS Above the Nyquist Rate," *IEEE ICC '85*, © 1985, IEEE. Reprinted by permission.)

2.6.5 Broadband Modems

Numerous modems have been built to convert high-speed digital streams to band-widths corresponding to an analog group (12 voice channels, 48 kHz bandwidth), an analog supergroup (60 voice channels, 240 kHz bandwidth), and other bandwidths.

Current standards for broadband modems often are based on digital stream rates which are multiples of the 8000/second sampling rate used for PCM voice. Table 2.7 [Ref. 30] lists the salient features of three CCITT recommendations for broadband modems. Some broadband modems interface directly with analog FM and SSB radio systems (see Chap. 4). The binary stream is encoded to M-ary, filtered, and applied to the baseband input of the transmitter. At the receiver, after demodulation, the M-ary signal is decoded to binary. The filtering may be raised cosine or partial response, and often is accomplished partly at the transmitter (to reduce interference to adjacent channels) and partly at the receiver (to reduce the noise bandwidth). The term *digital FM* has been used to describe the combination of a broadband modem and an analog FM radio system. The GTE seven-level modi-fied duobinary system providing 6.312 Mb/s in a 3.5 MHz bandwidth at 2 GHz is an example of such a system. Other examples include a 9-QPR system for transmitting twice the DS-3 rate (91 Mb/s) in a 40 MHz bandwidth in the 8 GHz band, as well as digital radios designed for U.S. Defense Department of applications.

2.6.6 Comparison of Modulation Methods

With the exception of special modulation techniques that combine modulation and coding, which are deferred until after the discussion of error coding, the basic digital modulation techniques now have been described. This description has shown that multilevel modulation techniques provide a transmission rate per unit bandwidth that is directly proportional to $\log_2 M$, where M is the number of levels. Complexity

TABLE 2.7 CCITT RECOMMENDATIONS ON GROUP MODEM CHARACTERISTICS

Characteristic	CCITT Rec. V.35	CCITT Rec. V.36	CCITT Rec. V.37
Data rates	48 kb/s	48, 56, 64, and 72 kb/s	96, 112, 128, 144, and 168 kb/s
Modulation type	AM, suppressed carrier	3-level partial response	7-level partial response
Equalization	N/A	N/A	Automatic adaptive
Scrambler	Self-synchronizing with length $2^{20} - 1$	Self-synchronizing with length $2^{20} - 1$	Self-synchronizing with length $2^{20} - 1$

Source: **Note:** The reproduction in this textbook of material taken from the publications of the International Telecommunications Union (ITU), Place des Nations, CH-1211 Geneva 20, Switzer-land, has been authorized by the ITU, from the Sales Sections of which the full text of the publica-tion, from which the material reproduced here has been taken, can be obtained. Choice of the excerpts reproduced has been made by the author and does not in any way affect the responsibility of the ITU.

and cost, of course, increase with the number of levels. Another factor is the requirement for linearity in transmission. Linearity is quite important in transmitting multiple amplitude levels, as encountered in the APK systems. The choice of coherent versus noncoherent detection has a significant impact upon receiver complexity and therefore cost. Ordinarily, the small, e.g., ≈ 1 dB, improvement achieved through the use of coherent detection limits its use to satellite receiving systems in which the relatively modest, e.g., 2–6 dB, link margins render coherent detection worthwhile.

For all of the digital modulation techniques, the bit error probability can be described as a function of the signal-to-noise ratio for a given number of levels. This description allows the system designer to determine the amount of power required on the channel. The various digital modulation techniques are compared next based upon their bit error probability performance. In performing such comparisons, a normalized form of signal-to-noise ratio is used. Generally, the noise is taken to be AWGN. The ratio is the energy per bit, E_b, to the noise power spectral density, N_o, which is the noise power in a 1-Hertz bandwidth. The ratio E_b/N_o is related to the ratio of the average signal power, S, to the noise power in the receiver bandwidth, N, by noting that $E_b = ST_b$, keeping in mind that the bit rate, $f_b = 1/T_b$ bits/second. Let the noise bandwidth of the receiver be designated B. Then,

$$\frac{E_b}{N_o} = \left[\frac{S}{N}\right]\left[\frac{B}{f_b}\right] \tag{2.53}$$

Thus, E_b/N_o is obtained by multiplying S/N by the bandwidth to bit rate ratio. In some cases, the energy per symbol, E_s, is of interest.

$$E_s = E_b \log_2 M \tag{2.54}$$

Note that all of the above ratios are dimensionless. In particular, the units for E_b are joules = watt seconds = watts/Hertz. Similarly, N_o is in watts/Hertz. Usually the ratios are expressed in decibels by taking $10 \log_{10}$ (ratio).

In the performance descriptions that follow, the noise is assumed to be AWGN, and zeros and ones are assumed to be equally likely.

To determine the performance of ASK, note that Eq. (2.36) for unipolar NRZ also is valid for OOK since all of the energy is used to transmit one of the binary states. Considering the values of both S and N of Eq. (2.36) in a one Hertz bandwidth, replace S by $E_s/2T_s$ and N by $N_o/2T_s$, yielding

$$p_{be} = \text{erfc}\sqrt{\frac{E_s}{2N_o}} \tag{2.55}$$

Instead of OOK (with states 0 and 1), the signal may convey states -1 and 1. In this case, $E_b = E_s/2$, and

$$p_{be} = \text{erfc}\sqrt{\frac{E_b}{N_o}} \tag{2.56}$$

This illustrates the 3 dB advantage of polar, e.g., balanced NRZ, over unipolar signaling.

For noncoherent OOK demodulation using a narrowband envelope detector with decisions at half maximum output amplitude [Ref. 31].

$$p_{be} = 0.5 \exp\left(\frac{-E_b}{2N_o}\right) \tag{2.57}$$

Since erfc $x \simeq e^{-x^2/2}/x\sqrt{2\pi}$, $x > 4$, Eq. (2.57) shows that there is less than 1 dB disadvantage in the use of noncoherent OOK detection compared with coherent OOK, Eq. (2.55).

For MFSK with coherent detection, [Ref. 32],

$$p_{se} \leqslant (M-1)\, \text{erfc} \sqrt{\frac{E_b \log_2 M}{N_o}} \tag{2.58}$$

This expression is an equality for $M = 2$. The upper bound is a good approximation for E_b/N_o values yielding $p_{se} \leqslant 10^{-3}$.

For noncoherent detection, [Ref. 1, Chap. 6].

$$p_{se} \leqslant \left[\frac{M-1}{2}\right] \exp\left(\frac{-E_s}{2N_o}\right) \tag{2.59}$$

Again, the expression is exact for $M = 2$, and is an increasingly good approximation as E_b/N_o increases beyond the value that yields $p_{se} = 10^{-3}$. Exact expressions for MFSK performance are given in Ref. 1, Chap. 6.

As M increases for a given E_b/N_o, these equations show that p_{be} decreases; correspondingly, for a given p_{be}, an increased M allows a reduced E_b/N_o. However, increasing M results in an increased occupied bandwidth, as can be appreciated from the discussion of Sec. 2.6.2. Such behavior results from the fact that the multiple frequencies constitute an *orthogonal* signal set, i.e., the symbols (frequencies) are uncorrelated over the symbol interval T_s.

In MPSK detection, the thresholds are expressed in terms of phase shift rather than in terms of detected amplitude or frequency. Figure 2.61 illustrates the concept of error distance for a QPSK signal. The signal vector S is of the proper phase but a noise vector N is added to it, producing a detected amplitude and phase at point d. In spite of the noise, symbol 00 will be detected correctly since point d is not outside the region $\pm \pi/4$. The *error distance* is the minimum amount by which noise can displace the received vector and produce a symbol error.

For coherent MPSK detection, [Ref. 14, App. C],

$$p_{be} = 2(\log_2 M)^{-1}\, \text{erfc}\, \sin\left(\frac{\pi}{M}\right) \sqrt{2 \log_2 M \left(\frac{E_b}{N_o}\right)} \tag{2.60}$$

Note that with respect to E_b/N_o, QPSK provides the same performance as BPSK. However, QPSK requires a 3 dB larger S/N than does BPSK. If the symbols are transmitted and received using the phase of the previous symbol as the reference (DMPSK), then

$$p_{se} \simeq 2\, \text{erfc} \sqrt{\left(\frac{2E_s}{N_o}\right)} \sin\left(\frac{\pi}{M\sqrt{2}}\right) \tag{2.61}$$

Equations (2.60) and 2.61) are plotted in Fig. 2.62.

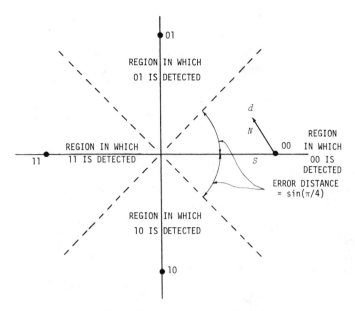

Figure 2.61 Error distance for a QPSK signal.

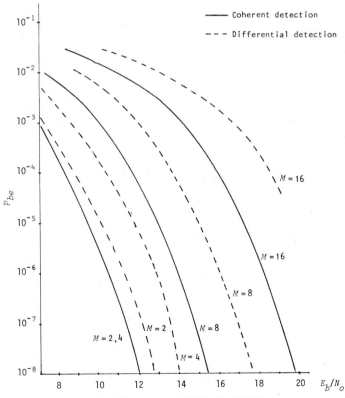

Figure 2.62 Bit error probabilities for MPSK.

A comparison of Eq. (2.60) with $M = 2$ for BPSK with Eq. (2.58) with $M = 2$ for FSK and Eq. (2.55) for ASK (OOK) shows that based on peak power BPSK is superior to FSK by about 3 dB and to ASK by about 6 dB. On an average power basis, BPSK is superior to both FSK and ASK by about 3 dB. This, combined with the spectral efficiency of MPSK systems, accounts for their extensive use in broadband communication systems. An increase in M causes a poorer p_{be} for a given E_b/N_o, as shown in Fig. 2.62, (MPSK signals constitute a nonorthogonal set) but results in improved spectral efficiency.

Example

A transmission system requires a bit error probability not to exceed 10^{-7}. The bit rate is to be 1.544 Mb/s. Determine the signal-to-noise ratio and bandwidth ($\alpha = 0.2$) required for 8-PSK. Repeat for 16-PSK.

Solution For 8-PSK, $p_{be} = 10^{-7}$ requires $E_b/N_o = 14.7$ dB. The symbol rate is $1.544 \times 10^6/\log_2 8 = 514\ 666$ Bd. The required -3 dB bandwidth is $514\ 666(1 + 0.2) = 617.6$ kHz. Taking the noise bandwidth B to be $\pi/2$ of this value, $B = 970$ kHz. Then $S/N = (E_b/N_o)(f_b/B) = (29.5)(1.544 \times 10^6/970 \times 10^3) = 46.96$, or 16.7 dB.

For 16-PSK, $p_{be} = 10^{-7}$ requires $E_b/N_o = 19.2$ dB. The symbol rate is $1.544 \times 10^6/\log_2 16 = 386\ 000$ Bd. The required -3 dB bandwidth is $386\ 000(1 + 0.2) = 463.2$ kHz. The noise bandwidth, $B = (\pi/2)(463.2) = 727.6$ kHz. Then $S/N = (E_b/N_o)(f_b/B) = (83.2)(1.544 \times 10^6/727.6 \times 10^3) = 176.5$, or 22.5 dB.

For M-ary QAM (MQAM), the error performance is given by Eq. (2.37), where M = number of levels on each axis. Substitute $(S/N) = (E_s/T_s)/(N_o/2T_s)$, which becomes

$$
\frac{S}{N} = \frac{\left(\dfrac{E_b \log_2 M}{T_s} \right)}{\dfrac{N_o}{T_s}} = 2 \log_2 M \left(\frac{E_b}{N_o} \right) \tag{2.62}
$$

Accordingly, [Ref. 1, Ch. 6], since the total number of levels now is $M = L^2$, with L levels on each axis

$$
p_{se} = 2\left(1 - \frac{1}{L}\right) \mathrm{erfc} \left[\sqrt{(\log_2 L) \left\{ \frac{6}{(L^2 - 1)} \right\} \left(\frac{E_b}{N_o} \right)} \right] \tag{2.63}
$$

Note that the number of levels L on each axis modifies the E_b/N_o ratio by $3/(L^2 - 1)$. Figure 2.63 is a plot of Eq. (2.63) with the conversion $p_{be} = p_{se}/\log_2 L$.

Figure 2.54 illustrates the reason for the superiority of high-level MQAM systems over high-level MPSK systems. For the MQAM systems, the signal state points are farther apart. In the example of Figure 2.54, the ratio 0.47/0.39, which is 1.59 dB, is the additional level of sinusoidal (CW) interference which 16-QAM can handle compared with 16-PSK. Against AWGN, the difference is even greater, as shown by a comparison of Fig. 2.62 and 2.63.

For M-ary QPR systems (MQPR), the error performance is based on Eq. (2.41), using Eq. (2.62) for S/N, and $M = L^2$. Then

$$
p_{se} = 2\left(1 - \frac{1}{L^2}\right) \mathrm{erfc} \left\{ \frac{\pi}{4} \sqrt{(\log_2 L) \left\{ \frac{6}{(L^2 - 1)} \right\} \left[\frac{E_b}{N_o} \right]} \right\} \tag{2.64}
$$

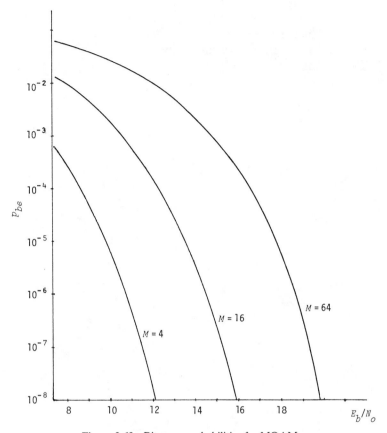

Figure 2.63 Bit error probabilities for MQAM.

since $E_s = \log_2 LE_b$. The $\pi/4$ factor in the argument of the erfc function corresponds to a 2.1 dB degradation with respect to E_b/N_o compared with MQAM. Thus, a bit error probability curve for 9-QPR would be displaced about 2.1 dB to the right of the 4-QAM curve; similarly, 49-QPR is 2.1 dB poorer than 16-QAM, and 225-QPR is 2.1 dB poorer than 64-QAM. As noted in Sec. 2.6.4.2, however, other factors often make MQPR systems preferable to MQAM systems.

Figure 2.64 compares the bandwidth efficiency (b/s per Hz) as a function of S/N to achieve $p_{be} = 10^{-8}$ for several MPSK, MAPK, and MQPR systems. For this comparison, $\alpha = 0.2$ was selected for the MPSK and MAPK system families, whereas an $\alpha = 0$ was assumed for the MQPR family. The Shannon limit, also shown, is for $p_{be} = 0$.

While AWGN is a predominant form of interference to cable and radio systems alike, other forms of interference and disturbance also must be anticipated. These include continuous wave (CW) sinusoidal interference from cochannel carriers, Rayleigh fading on certain radio paths, and delay distortion in transmission channels. Table 2.8 compares several of the techniques in terms of the value of E_b/N_o required to achieve the stated p_{be}, the values being typical of those tolerable in coded video, e.g., 10^{-2} to 10^{-4}, rather than in data transmission. The PSK systems shown are all based on coherent detection.

Figure 2.65 shows the effect of filter bandwidth on several of the systems in terms of S/N degradation [Ref. 33]. In this figure, B is the 3 dB double-sided bandwidth of a Gaussian-shaped filter characteristic, and T_s is the symbol duration.

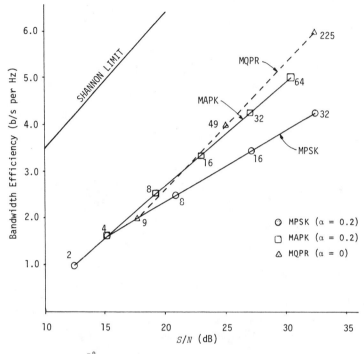

$p_{be} = 10^{-8}$ for MPSK, MAPK and MQPR
Numerals refer to the number of signaling states required.

Figure 2.64 Comparison of modulation methods.

TABLE 2.8 COMPARISON OF DIGITAL COMMUNICATION TECHNIQUES FOR DISTURBANCES OTHER THAN SIMPLE AWGN

Condition	p_{be}	BPSK	QPSK	8-PSK	MSK
CW interference at $S/I = 15$ dB	10^{-4}	9.2	9.8	15.8	
Rayleigh fading	10^{-2}	14.0	14.0	15.8	14.0
Quad delay distortion ($d/T = 1$)	10^{-4}	9.8	9.8		9.8
Lin. delay distortion ($d/T = 1$)	10^{-4}	9.6	15.8		15.8

Source: From J. D. Oetting, "A Comparison of Modulation Techniques for Digital Radio," *IEEE Trans. Communications,* Dec. 1979, © 1979, IEEE. Reprinted by permission.

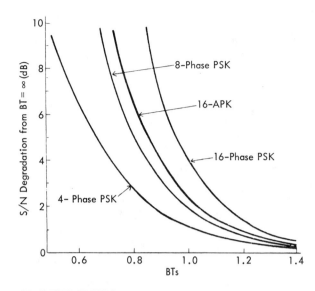

Figure 2.65 *S/N* degradation caused by Gaussian filter band limitation. (From H. Ishio et al., "A New Multilevel Modulation and Demodulation System for Carrier Digital Transmission," *IEEE ICC '76,* © 1976, IEEE. Reprinted with permission.)

2.7 MULTIPLEXERS

A multiplexer is a device that combines multiple signals into a single channel for transmission purposes. The combining may be done on the basis of giving each signal its own portion of the frequency spectrum, in which case the term frequency-division multiplexing (FDM) is used, or the signals may share time slots on the channel, in which case the process is called time-division multiplexing (TDM). Examples of broadband FDM systems include the Western Electric AR6-A microwave radio system discussed in Chap. 4, as well as cable television systems, which are channelized (North American standards) on the basis of each analog television channel having a 6 MHz bandwidth. The use of wavelength division multiplexing (WDM) in fiber optic transmission is another example of FDM.

The *FDM hierarchy* refers to the established grouping of voice channels as follows:

12 voice channels = 1 group (48 kHz bandwidth)

5 groups = 1 supergroup (240 kHz bandwidth)

10 supergroups = 1 mastergroup (2.52 MHz bandwidth)

6 mastergroups = 1 jumbogroup (16.984 MHz bandwidth)

The added bandwidth of the higher levels is used for special pilot and control signals needed in multiplexing and demultiplexing.

Many broadband systems are digital and function on a TDM basis. Unless otherwise stated, TDM operates by assigning specific time slots to specific channels. Sometimes this is called *synchronous* TDM, to distinguish it from asynchronous TDM, or statistical multiplexing, which was the subject of Sec. 2.4.4. The functions of coding and multiplexing may be performed together as is done in a channel bank in which the incoming analog waveform of each channel is sampled and the samples are interleaved and then coded (analog value is converted to a sequence of bits);

alternatively, coding may be done first and then interleaving. *Bit interleaving* refers to the assignment of a time slot that is one bit in length. The multiplexer acts like a commutator taking one bit from the first channel, one bit from the second, etc. In *word interleaving,* also known as *character interleaving* a specified number of bits, e.g., eight, from each channel is placed on the line at a given time. Accordingly, bits must be stored by the multiplexer while they are awaiting transfer to the line. Bit interleaving is used in the higher order TDM multiplexers.

Thus far, the bits from the individual sources are assumed to arrive at a uniform rate, or multiples of such a rate, from each source. If some of the rates differ slightly, the sources are called *plesiochronous* (nearly synchronous), and buffers are needed to provide a uniformly timed output. If the inputs are at rates that are not multiples of some common denominator, they are said to be *asynchronous* and a technique such as *pulse stuffing* (see Sec. 2.8.2) must be used to provide a synchronous output.

The *transmultiplexer* is used to interface between FDM and TDM lines. For example, translation can be done between two supergroups (480 kHz bandwidth) and five DS1 streams (7.72 Mb/s), with the conversion being based upon 8-bit quantization at an 8000/second sampling rate, which provides a standard pulse-code modulated (PCM) voice channel. Alternatively, two groups (96 kHz bandwidth) can be translated to one DS1 stream (1.544 Mb/s) or a supergroup (240 kHz bandwidth) can be translated to two European first level streams, totaling 4.096 Mb/s. The use of transmultiplexers instead of channel banks allows expensive signaling interfaces to be omitted.

Transmultiplexers are used in switching centers where conversions between TDM and FDM must be done because of the differing types of facilities being switched. Figure 2.66 is a block diagram illustrating the architecture of the Rockwell

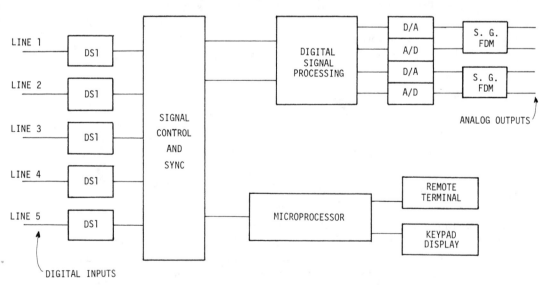

Figure 2.66 System architecture, Rockwell ADX-120 transmultiplexer. (Courtesy Collins Transmission System Division, Rockwell International.)

ADX-120 Transmultiplexer [Ref. 34], which translates between five DS1 lines (each carrying 24 voice channels), and two standard supergroups, each in the 312 to 552 kHz band (each carrying 60 voice channels). The ADX-120 accepts up to ±20 bits of incoming line jitter, maintaining bit count integrity as well as FDM performance. FDM jitter is 1° peak-to-peak maximum from 20 to 300 Hz.

2.8 SYSTEMS FOR DIGITAL TRANSMISSION

Digital transmission is accomplished using standard rates that constitute a "hierarchy" comparable to the FDM hierarchy discussed in Sec. 2.7. Just as the FDM format is based on the analog voice channel, so the digital format is based on the 64 kb/s PCM voice channel. In North American systems, 24 voice channels (a *digroup*) are multiplexed together, and a framing bit is added to each digroup, thus:

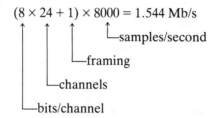

In European systems 30 voice channels are combined with two additional channels for frame alignment, alarms, and exchange signaling, thus:

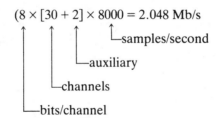

The 1.544 Mb/s rate is known as the DS1 rate. Systems which transmit at this rate are called T1 systems. The 2.048 Mb/s rate is called the CEPT-1 rate, the letters standing for the Conference of European Postal and Telecommunications administrations. As noted in Sec. 2.5.5.1, these first level systems use the BRZ line code.

First level systems utilize twisted-pair, coaxial cable, radio, and optical fiber as their transmission media. Higher level systems use all of these media but twisted pair. For operation on twisted pair and coaxial cable, a pulse shaping line driver is used to precompensate for anticipated line attenuation at the higher frequencies of the transmission band by shaping the pulse in advance [Ref. 35]. The result is that the pulses are relatively square as they arrive at their destination, such as a maintenance patch panel at a repeater or on the customer's premises. The amount of pulse predistortion is adjusted based upon the line length to be used. Adaptive equalizers also are used. Measurement of the received signal strength allows the cable length to be calculated, whereupon the circuit adapts automatically to the calculated length.

2.8.1 Applications of the Transmission Format

Use of the transmission format can be illustrated by looking at the types of traffic that can be included in a first level North American frame, as illustrated in Fig. 2.67 [Ref. 17]. In Fig. 2.67, the slots labeled "digital data" allow transmission at the 64 kb/s rate for each 8-bit slot. The slot labeled "μ-law PCM voiceband data" provides for the transmission of modem data at rates which depend upon modem capabilities, typically up to 9600 b/s half duplex on dial-up lines and up to 19 200 b/s half duplex on conditioned lines.

A "T1 Multiplexer" is a device that translates between one or more DS1 streams and a number of voice and/or data channels at a combined rate equalling 1.536 Mb/s, allowing for framing. Point-to-point as well as network applications are supported by these multiplexers.

2.8.2 Functional Aspects of Digital Transmission Systems

2.8.2.1 Framing. Framing is the determination of which groups of bits constitute characters and what groups of characters constitute messages. North American systems use *distributed* frame synchronization bits, as illustrated in Fig. 2.68 for a system operating at the DS1 rate. Every 193rd bit is a framing bit. To achieve framing or "sync," the detector looks at a sequence made up of every 193rd bit. There are 193 such possible sequences. The "sync search" mode hardware operates as follows: The bits (every 193rd), are shifted into a shift register in the receiver. The contents of this shift register are compared bit for bit with the contents of the sync character, which has been stored in another register. The process is repeated until a match occurs. When a match is found on two successive sync characters, a "character available" flag is raised at the beginning of each frame and often every 8 bits.

The sequences usually are examined one at a time, in which case the time to achieve framing is N^2 bit times, where N is the number of pulse positions in the

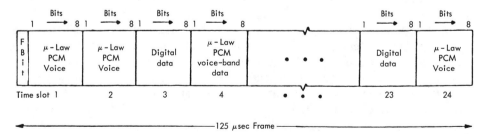

Figure 2.67 Full rate DS1 traffic mix. (From Technical Reference TR-TSY-000210, "Low Bit Rate Voice (LBRV) Terminals," Issue 1, September 1986, © 1986, Bell Communications Research, Inc., Livingston, NJ.)

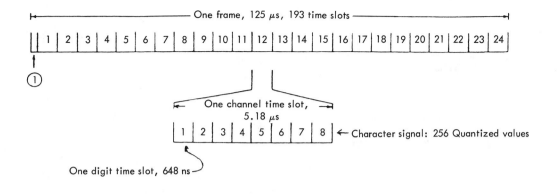

One frame, 125 μs, 193 time slots

One channel time slot, 5.18 μs

Character signal: 256 Quantized values

One digit time slot, 648 ns

① Odd frames: Frame alignment signal 1 0 1 0 1 0... repeated
Even frames: Common channel signaling (4000 bits/second)

Figure 2.68   Frame structure for T1 system using common-channel signaling.

frame. This results from the fact that, on the average, the receiving terminal dwells at a false framing position for two frame periods during a search, since the ones and zeros are statistically independent and equally likely. A search through all possible positions requires N such tests. Thus frame time = (average number of bit positions searched before framing bit is found) × (average number of bits to determine that an information position is not a framing position) = $(2N)(N/2) = N^2$. Thus for a T1 system, $N = 193$ and $N^2 = 37249$ or 24.125 ms. The maximum reframe time is twice this amount, or nearly 50 ms. If these times are too great, they can be reduced by the use of parallel searches.

If channel noise or equipment malfunctions or transients cause framing to be lost, the search must be reinitiated, just as is done when transmission begins.

Frame slips often result from timing inaccuracies. Specifications generally limit frame slips to a maximum of one in five hours. Frame slips result in error bursts and loss of synchronization on data circuits, as well as a variety of picture flaws in video and graphic transmission.

Framing errors can be useful in determining end-to-end circuit performance. However, digital switches as well as certain modems remove the received framing information and insert new framing. Accordingly, framing errors may be indicative only of circuit performance from the point of measurement to the point where the signal was reframed.

European systems use *bunched* framing bits contained in time slot zero (TS 0), as illustrated in Fig. 2.69. The bunched framing bits allow frame synchronization to be achieved more rapidly than do distributed bits examined on the sequential basis. However, error bursts may prevent framing from being obtained in a bunched arrangement. In addition, during the insertion of the bits in TS 0, the multiplexer must store the bit coming in from each of the channels; consequently, additional buffering is required at the multiplexer, and jitter occurs as the demultiplexer smooths the received data. Both the CEPT-1 and CEPT-2 (8.448 Mb/s) systems use

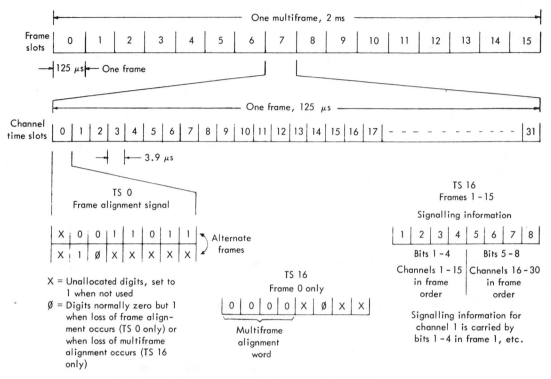

Figure 2.69 Frame and multiframe structure for CEPT-1 system.

bunched framing. The North American DS2 standard uses a combination of distributed and bunched framing bits.

Figure 2.70 shows an alternative DS1 format used commonly on North American systems. As shown there, as well as in Fig. 2.69, a *superframe* is a set of consecutive frames in which the position of each of the individual frames can be determined by reference to a superframe alignment signal. Frame alignment assures, for example, that Channel 1 from the transmitter is interpreted correctly as Channel 1 by the receiver. In the North American systems a superframe alignment signal (Fig. 2.70) identifies the signaling bits carried in the sixth and twelfth of each sequence of frames. The composite framing bit sequence can be seen to be 100011011100.

The *extended superframe* (ESF) format, also designated F_e, is an extension of the superframe structure from 12 to 24 frames, and includes a redefinition of the 8 kb/s framing bit stream at the DS1 level. ESF can provide continuous data link performance checks without interfering with ongoing traffic. Logic errors can be measured in real time. Protection against false framing is achieved by a 6-bit cyclic redundancy check (CRC-6), which can be used by both customers and carriers to monitor data link performance continuously. (A cyclic redundancy check is an error detection scheme in which the check character is generated by taking the remainder after dividing all the serialized bits in a block of data by a predetermined binary

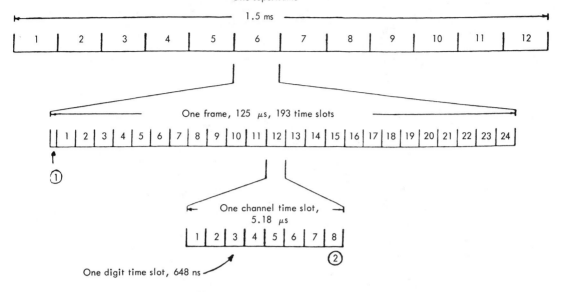

One superframe

1.5 ms

| 1 | 2 | 3 | 4 | 5 | 6 | 7 | 8 | 9 | 10 | 11 | 12 |

One frame, 125 μs, 193 time slots

| 1 | 2 | 3 | 4 | 5 | 6 | 7 | 8 | 9 | 10 | 11 | 12 | 13 | 14 | 15 | 16 | 17 | 18 | 19 | 20 | 21 | 22 | 23 | 24 |

①

One channel time slot, 5.18 μs

| 1 | 2 | 3 | 4 | 5 | 6 | 7 | 8 |

②

One digit time slot, 648 ns

① Bit 1 carries the superframe alignment signal (F) in even-numbered frames (0 0 1 1 1 0)
Bit 1 carries the frame alignment signal in odd-numbered frames (1 0 1 0 1 0)

② In frame 6, bit 8 is used to provide signaling channel A
In frame 12, bit 8 is used to provide signaling channel B

Figure 2.70 Frame and superframe structure for 24-channel (DS1) system using channel associated signaling.

number.) Table 2.9 describes the ESF framing bit (F-bit) assignments. The framing pattern sequence (FPS) performs the basic framing function. The facility data link (FDL) provides message bits at an overall 4 kb/s rate using X.25 level 2 protocol for such applications as protection switching, alarms, loopback testing, received line performance monitoring, supervisory signaling, network configuration information, and general maintenance information. The CRC bits, generated at the data source, are based on an nth degree polynomial which represents the data. The received CRC bits are compared with CRC bits computed at the receiver. If the received and computed sets match, the implication is that no errors occurred during transmission. A lack of match indicates one or more errors during the previous extended superframe. Since there are 64 possible combinations of the six bits, there is one chance in 64 that a burst of errors will cause a matching combination, giving the false indication that no errors occurred. Thus the CRC-6 detects 63/64, or 98.4% of the transmission block errors [Ref. 36].

While the CRC-6 is not intended to replace the customer's normal error control procedures, it can be used directly by the customer, unlike bipolar violations or the monitoring of a maintenance supervision channel (Channel 24), which usually are limited to the common carrier.

The ESF format is being implemented in designs of DS1 equipment which

TABLE 2.9 EXTENDED SUPERFRAME (ESF) F-BIT ASSIGNMENTS

Frame Number	Bit Number	F-Bit assignments			Robbed Bit Signaling
		FPS	FDL	CRC	
1	0		m		
2	193			CB$_1$	
3	386		m		
4	579	0			
5	772		m		
6	965			CB$_2$	A
7	1158		m		
8	1351	0			
9	1544		m		
10	1737			CB$_3$	
11	1930		m		
12	2123	1			B
13	2316		m		
14	2509			CB$_4$	
15	2702		m		
16	2895	0			
17	3088		m		
18	3281			CB$_5$	C
19	3474		m		
20	3667	1			
21	3860		m		
22	4053			CB$_6$	
23	4246		m		
24	4439	1			D

FPS = Frame Pattern Sequence (2 kb/s)
FDL = Facility Data Link Message Bits, m (4 kb/s)
CRC = Cyclic Redundancy Check (Check Bits CB$_1$ . . . CB$_6$) (2 kb/s)

frame on a pattern contained in the framing bit position of the DS1 signal, and can be used where both the transmitter and the receiver have the hardware and software capabilities to handle it. The D5 channel bank supports ESF.

2.8.2.2 Signaling. The reference to *robbed bit signaling* in Table 2.9 denotes the fact that in every sixth frame, bit number 8 (the least significant bit), is robbed from each channel and used for signaling purposes as needed. This arrangement thus differs from that of Fig. 2.68 where the signaling is confined to the framing bit stream.

Signaling in the CEPT-1 format (Fig. 2.69) allocates four digits, designated (a, b, c, d), to each channel. Time slot 16 is reserved for signaling in frames 1 through 15 of the multiframe. Since the channel time slot is 8 bits long, repeated at a rate of 8000/second, the total rate per channel time slot is 64 kb/s. Thus the rate per bit is 8 kb/s and, for 4 bits, 32 kb/s. Since each 4-bit signaling channel appears once per 16 frames, the effective information rate is 2 kb/s, quite adequate for signaling. Thus channel time slot 16 is extracted as a 64 kb/s stream which is subdivided to provide the 2 kb/s channels.

2.8.2.3 Pulse Stuffing. *Pulse stuffing* is the process of changing the rate of a digital signal in a controlled manner to align it with a different rate, usually without loss of information. It is also known as *bit stuffing,* and the CCITT refers to it as *justification.* Thus pulse stuffing is used to avoid the slips that would occur otherwise in interconnecting lines that are not synchronized. What is called *positive pulse stuffing* increases the rate of an incoming stream by the addition of stuff pulses as needed. Positive pulse stuffing is used in combining DS1 streams into DS2, DS2 into DS3, etc.

Pulse stuffing is a logical operation that is independent of the line code or modulation systems used. Each incoming channel is stuffed independently with bit interleaving usually being used. Thus each incoming channel is treated as a bit stream without regard to its framing structure.

To enable the receiver to identify the stuff bits, i.e., to distinguish them from the actual information bits, the frame contains stuffing specification bits designated C and special timing bits designated T, as illustrated in Fig. 2.71.

Desirable features of a pulse stuffing format are: (1) fixed length master frames, so that each channel is allowed to stuff or not stuff a bit in the master frame, (2) redundant stuffing specifications, providing redundant coding of the T bits for error protection, and (3) a distribution of the noninformation bits across the master frame to guard against burst errors. This makes the information flow as uniform as possible to aid in the clock recovery for the lower level signals, as well as to allow for a modest sized elastic store. For example, the DS2 format has three C bits for each T bit. All three Cs equal to zero means T is stuff but all three Cs equal to one means T is an information bit. The DS2 frame structure contains 1148 information bits, 12 framing (F) bits, 12 stuff control (C) bits, and 4 timing (T) bits. The result is a capability of 287 or 288 bits/channel.

An arrangement under consideration by the CCITT is called *positive-zero-negative stuffing.* It avoids the frequency offset required for positive pulse stuffing. A negative stuff is called a *spill,* but the spill bits actually are sent to the receiver via an overhead bit allocation. Because the stuffing circuitry is independent for each channel, synchronous channels can be mixed readily with asynchronous channels, a primary advantage of this technique.

2.8.2.4 Performance Definitions. Transmission using ESF involves the examination of every ESF for an error event. An error event occurs whenever an ESF contains either a CRC-6 error event or an out-of-frame condition or both [Ref. 37]. The CRC-6 signal is processed to determine *errored seconds, severely errored seconds,* and *failed seconds.* An errored second is a second containing one or more ESF error events. A severely errored second is a second with 320 or more ESF events. A failed signal state exists whenever 10 consecutive severely errored seconds

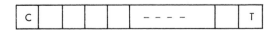

C = 0 means T is a stuff (null) bit
    T may be designed to be a 0 or a 1
C = 1 means T is information

Figure 2.71 Implementation of pulse stuffing.

occur. The failed state has ended when 10 consecutive seconds occur without a severely errored second. A failed second is counted for each second that a failed signal state exists.

2.8.3 Digital Hierarchies

The digital hierarchies consist of sets of standard transmission rates. Both the North American and the European hierarchies are CCITT standards. Table 2.10 summarizes these hierarchies and also lists the number of equivalent 64 kb/s voice channels that can be accommodated at each rate. Higher rates, often implemented on fiber optic systems, generally are multiples of the standard rates shown here, often the third level. In the North American system, multiplexers used to combine four DS1s into a DS2 are designated M12; those which combine 28 DS1s into a DS3 are called M13; and those which combine six DS3s into a DS4 are called M34.

The characteristics of digital multiplex equipment operating at various rates are listed in Table 2.11, [Ref. 1, Chap. 4]. These multiplexers use positive pulse stuffing with a 3-bit stuff control word and majority vote decoding. The multiplexing is done by cyclic bit interleaving in channel numbering order. The timing is derived from external as well as internal sources.

A new approach to the multiplexing of 28 DS1 signals to a DS3, and vice versa, is called *Syntran,* for synchronous transmission at the DS3 rate [Ref. 38]. Existing M13 multiplexers work on a partially synchronous partially asynchronous basis. Each DS1 may have independent timing, and pulse stuffing and bit interleaving are used for form the DS3 signal. As a result, the location of specific DS1s within the DS3 is not sequential. In Syntran, once the *F* bits have been located, all other bit locations are known. The format allows the direct multiplexing of bytes from 672 DS0s or 28 DS1s to form the DS3 signal, with no need for going to or from the DS2 level. All of the incoming bit streams must be traceable to a common clock or at least be very close to the same frequency, such as one part in 10^{11}. This is readily achievable because of the widespread availability of synchronization signals

TABLE 2.10 DIGITAL MULTIPLEX HIERARCHIES

Level	North American*	Japanese	European (CEPT)*
First	1.544 Mb/s (24 ch.)	1.544 Mb/s (24 ch.)	2.048 Mb/s (30 ch.)
Second	6.312 Mb/s (96 ch.)	6.312 Mb/s† (96 ch.)	8.448 Mb/s (120 ch.)
Third	44.736 Mb/s (672 ch.)	32.064 Mb/s (480 ch.)	34.368 Mb/s (480 ch.)
Fourth	274.176 Mb/s (4032 ch.)	97.728 Mb/s (1440 ch.)	139.268 Mb/s (1920 ch.)
Fifth		400.352 Mb/s (5760 ch.)	565.148 Mb/s (7680 ch.)

* CCITT Recommended Hierarchy
† Alternative: 7.876 Mb/s (120 ch.)

TABLE 2.11 CHARACTERISTICS OF DIGITAL MULTIPLEX EQUIPMENT

Characteristic	Aggregate bit rate (Mb/s)	Tolerance	Digital interface	Channel bit rate (Mb/s)	No. of channels	Channel code
Second Level						
CCITT Rec. G.743	6.312	±30	B6ZS	1.544	4	BRZ
CCITT Rec. G.742	8.448	±30	HDB3	2.048	4	HDB3
Third Level						
CCITT Rec. G.751	34.368	±20	HDB3	8.448	4	HDB3
CCITT Rec. G.752	32.064	±10	Scrambled BRZ	6.312	5	B6ZS
CCITT Rec. G.752	44.736	±20	B3ZS	6.312	7	B6ZS
Fourth Level						
CCITT Rec. G.751	139.264	±15	CMI	34.368	4	HDB3
North America	274.176	±10	—	44.736	6	B3ZS
Japan NTT	97.728	—	—	32.064	4	Scrambled BRZ

Source: From D. R. Smith, *Digital Transmission Systems,* © 1985, Wadsworth, Inc. Reprinted by permission.

traceable to standards such as the AT&T Basic System Reference Frequency (BSRF) or similar references of other common carriers.

Syntran allows the implementation of an *add-drop multiplexer* which allows the adding and dropping of DS1s without having to demultiplex the entire DS3 stream. Moreover, individual DS0 (64 kb/s) channels are identifiable in the DS3 stream; in addition, the locations of the DS1s within the DS3 can be rearranged by using a "Digital Cross-Connect System 3/1" which performs time division switching operations on the high speed signals themselves rather than having to demultiplex the DS3 into individual DS1s first.

The three modes of Syntran operation are (1) byte synchronous, which allows direct identification of DS0 channels from the DS3 framing information, but which requires multiplex equipment to frame on the DS1 signal when DS1s are multiplexed together to form DS3s; (2) bit synchronous, which allows DS1 identification from the DS3 frame, but requires a second level of framing before the DS0s can be identified; and (3) asynchronous, in which bit stuffing is used to multiplex DS1s to DS3. The third mode is comparable to the operation of the M13 multiplexer, and allows Syntran to interface with nonsynchronous networks.

The byte synchronous mode allows time-slot interchanges between DS3 streams. Syntran is not compatible with existing DS3 multiplex equipment, but is compatible with existing DS3 transmission equipment.

Because Syntran does not require the extensive overhead framing information needed by M13, a total of over 1.2 Mb/s within the DS3 signal becomes available for new features, such as possible common-channel signaling or a facility data link.

The Syntran format includes a 9-bit CRC (CRC-9), which allows the detection of 511/512, or 99.8% of all possible error bursts. The benefits of Syntran include flexible network architecture, reduced cabling and cross-connection congestion, minimization of the number of customer interfaces, and improved operation and maintenance capabilities as a result of the CRC-9 and the facility data link capability. The Syntran format can accommodate all of the currently defined ISDN services as well as broadband service up to the DS3 rate. Rapid provision of additional access lines to customers also can be achieved through the add-drop multiplex feature of Syntran.

2.8.4 Hybrid Transmission Systems

Along routes carrying insufficient digital or analog traffic to warrant separate systems, hybrid systems can be implemented for microwave or cable transmission. Such systems are especially prevalent along routes which have had analog service for a number of years, and along which there is a need to add digital service at minimum additional cost. A *data under voice* (DUV) system adds digital transmission in the portion of the baseband below existing analog channels, as illustrated in Fig. 2.72. For the DS1 stream this system (AT&T) uses a binary to four-level encoder (producing 772 kBd) which is followed by a Class 4 partial response filter that produces a seven-level signal having a spectral null at $1.544 \times 10^6/4 = 386 \times 10^3$

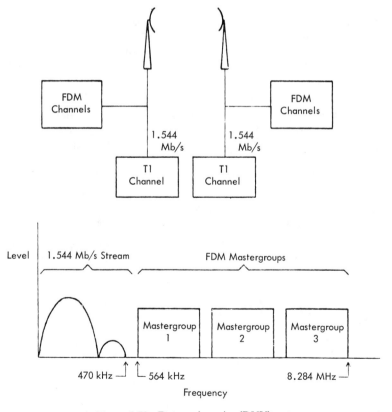

Figure 2.72 Data under voice (DUV) system.

Hz. Further filtering heavily attenuates all spectral sidelobes above 470 kHz; this filtering, together with bit stream scrambling, minimizes any interference to the FDM mastergroups, whose spectrum starts at 564 kHz. Other DUV systems have been implemented by Western Union and by CNCP Telecommunications.

An alternative approach, *data above voice* (DAV), also known as *data over voice* (DOV), implements a digital spectrum above the analog transmission. It allows full use of the lower part of the baseband by order wires (service channels) and by any lower frequency analog groupings. A third approach is *data above video* (DAVID). Rates up to 3.152 Mb/s have been implemented using the DAV and DAVID approaches by Spar Aerospace for CNCP Telecommunications, [Ref. 9. Chap. 8].

2.9 NATIONAL DIGITAL NETWORK EXAMPLE: DDS

Major countries throughout the world are implementing their own digital networks. Within the U.S., several competing long haul carriers have or are planning such networks. This section briefly summarizes the characteristics of one such network, the AT&T Digital Data System (DDS), as representative, in many ways, of other such networks throughout the world. The DDS is used to support Dataphone Digital Service, which is offered by the Bell operating companies on a point-to-point and multipoint basis at rates of 2.4, 4.8, 9.6, and 56 kb/s, as well as 1.344 and 1.544 Mb/s on a private line full duplex basis. Advantages to the user are a $p_{be} \simeq 10^{-7}$ on an end-to-end basis as well as extensive network diagnostics, test, and fault isolation procedures. The transmission facilities, known as the "digital data system" include unloaded twisted pairs with regenerative repeaters every kilometer between the customer and the serving switching center, T-carrier systems from the serving switching center to a higher level office known as a *hub*, and long-haul microwave or optical fiber or satellite transmission between hub offices.

2.9.1 DDS Network Interfaces

The user's signal often will be in the unipolar format, whereas the common carrier's signal is BRZ. The customer service unit (CSU) is for the user who furnishes separate timing recovery and signal conversion equipment. The CSU provides loop-around testing capability, regeneration of received line signals, and protection of the carrier network. The data service unit (DSU) is for the user who elects not to provide signal conversion devices, so the DSU includes both timing recovery and signal conversion. Because of the functional similarity between the CSU and DSU, some manufacturers simply provide a combined CSU/DSU.

2.9.2 DDS Fault Isolation and Diagnostics

A major DDS benefit to its users is the extensive amount of fault isolation and diagnostics built into the system. Figure 2.73 illustrates typical elements in a DDS transmission path, and shows the location of DDS test centers at the hub offices.

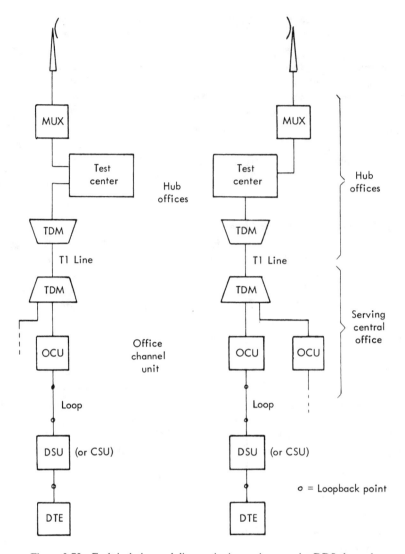

Figure 2.73 Fault isolation and diagnostics in a point-to-point DDS channel.

The hub office merges the DS1 data streams into higher level multiplexed states, e.g., DS2, DS3, etc., and connects incoming T1 lines to long haul trunks. The DDS test centers can perform direct monitoring on the subscriber's data stream, and can send out digital test patterns and activate loop-backs for rapid fault isolation. The benefit of these features is reduced down time. The OCU in Fig. 2.73 is an *office channel unit.* It is the counterpart of the user's DSU. It terminates the four-wire local loop, regenerates the bipolar signal, and prepares it for transmission through the TDM to the T1 line.

2.9.3 DDS Quality

The DDS design objective is an availability in excess of 0.9996, which is equivalent to an average annual down time of 210 minutes. Quality is 99.5% error free seconds (EFS), where the probability of an EFS is $p(EFS)$.

$$p(EFS) = (1 - p_{be})^R \tag{2.65}$$

where

R = data rate (b/s)

Quality is allocated to various segments of the overall network using a model in which a long haul network interconnects two local serving areas. In each local serving area there are two local T1 carrier lines in tandem with one baseband loop.

The error allocation is as follows:

- The two baseband loops account for 20% of the errors.
- The four local lines account for 30% of the errors.
- The long haul network accounts for 50% of the errors.

2.9.4 DDS Limitations

Along with the many advantages of DDS over analog transmission are several limitations of which users must be aware. DDS is available only in metropolitan areas. While analog extensions can be implemented to provide remote connections to DDS, such extensions result in modem charges, additional distance charges, and degraded error performance because of the additional tandem equipment.

DDS users have no dial back up without the use of analog modems, no alternate voice-data capability is available unless a voice digitizer is used, and no auxiliary slow speed control channels are included, as may be needed for customer-provided network diagnostics.

2.9.5 DDS Network Synchronization

For timing purposes the DDS network is configured as a master-slave tree, with the functioning data links distributing the synchronization signals. Timing then is recovered from the data stream. A master timing supply sets the frequency (BSRF) for the entire network. The reference for the AT&T network is located at Hillsboro, MO, with the frequency being fed into the nationwide network at St. Louis, MO. In addition, all major nodes in the network contain a nodal timing supply with a very long time constant. This supply is phase locked to the incoming timing signal. The nodal timing supply can run satisfactorily for several days if its inputs should fail, based upon its frequency memory capability and internal accuracy.

Secondary timing supplies operate in distant nodes of the tree and provide signals to all DDS equipment in each office where they are installed. All timing supplies are highly redundant for reliability. The unit of phase controlled at each node is the 125 μs interval that represents a multiplexing frame. The synchronization bit stream is the reference. Based on it, an elastic store in each data stream input maintains exact frame alignment from each source. Figure 2.74 illustrates the synchronization tree concept [Ref. 39].

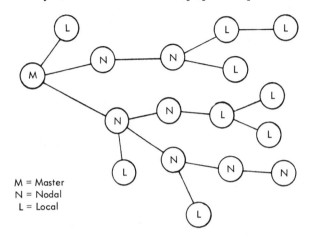

M = Master
N = Nodal
L = Local

Figure 2.74   DDS network synchronization tree. (Reprinted from *Bell System Technical Journal,* © 1975, with permission.)

2.9.6 Interconnection of National Digital Networks

The national digital networks of individual countries can be interfaced with one another on a plesiochronous basis. Such an interconnection uses buffers sized to accommodate the surplus or deficiency of bits that arises from the slight differences in bit rates between the reference rates of the two nations.

In operation, the interconnection protocol calls for repeating a block of eight DS0 bits if the buffer is nearly empty or deleting a block of bits if the buffer is full. The blocks are chosen as DS0 frames since deleting or repeating such frames (slipping) will not cause significant disturbance to the network. Slipping is allowed only once every 72 days per CCITT Recommendation G.811. This recommendation requires national networks and the TDMA frame rate to be held to $1 : 10^{11}$ over a 72 day period. One reference station derives frame timing from a very high stability clock that provides the timing reference for the network.

For operation via satellites, doppler buffers remove path length variations caused by satellite movement. Such buffers must accommodate up to 1.1 ms of peak-to-peak path length variation.

2.10 BROADBAND SERVICES

Numerous broadband services have been developed providing digital transmission directly to the subscriber. The Public Switched Digital Service (PSDS) is a generic name for a BOC switched offering at 56 kb/s [Ref. 40]. The AT&T service is based on a Circuit Switched Digital Capability (CSDC) at various local (Class 5) switching offices and is marketed as Accunet Switched 56. The Northern Telecom service is called Datapath. Both use *time compression multiplexing* (TCM) on the local loop.

In TCM the subscribers' digital signals are buffered at each end of the message channel, resulting in bursts which are timed to send data alternately through the local loop on a "ping pong" basis, i.e., transmission is in only one direction at a time, but the switching back and forth is done so rapidly that the user perceives the result as full duplex transmission. The CSDC data bursts are at 144 kb/s while the Datapath bursts are at 160 kb/s. PSDS is upgradable from 56 kb/s to 64 kb/s with the availability of 64 kb/s clear channel capability. Customer access lines are assigned 700-numbers. PSDS is viewed as one of the steps in the full-scale development of the Integrated Services Digital Network (ISDN) circuit switched services. Applications [Ref. 41] include bulk data transfer, network optimization by handling peak seasonal demands or traffic to destinations not warranting full period service, teleconferencing (both voice and video), computer-aided design from remote locations, high speed facsimile (one page in 6 seconds), connection of communicating word processors together, disaster recovery, and secure voice.

At the 1.544 Mb/s rate the High Capacity Terrestrial Digital Service (HCTDS) is offered by AT&T as Accunet T1.5 Service. This is private line full duplex *isochronous* (variations from synchronous rate are constrained within specified limits) service. The customer interface is at the DS1 rate through Network Channel Terminating Equipment (NCTE). Distances handled usually are less than 1200 km. A transfer arrangement allows customers to switch the long haul portion of a digital service between two locations in a local area. Central office multiplexing provides for the derivation of up to 24 voice grade connections in the central office. Through Customer Controlled Reconfiguration (CCR) users can access a Digital Access and Cross-Connect System (DACS) at the central office. The DACS is an all-digital automatic patch panel which connects incoming DS0 channels of a DS1 rate link to the various long haul services that can be accessed via Accunet T1.5. Automatic protection capability consists of switching to a spare circuit when the error rate of the working circuit exceeds a predetermined level. Accunet T1.5 service is compatible with AT&T Series 9000 satellite transmission service, which may be required where use must be made of an off-premises earth station because of on-site interference problems.

The High Speed Switched Digital Service (HSSDS) offered by AT&T as Accunet Reserved T1.5 Service provides 1.536 Mb/s or 3.072 Mb/s full duplex connectivity to customers on a reservation basis. Media used include satellite, cable, microwave radio, and optical fibers. Service also is available on a broadcast or multipoint basis, and international connections can be handled. Customers obtain service via a digital access line from their premises to an HSSDS switching center. Reservations are made in advance for specific connection times and places. Time is sold in 30-minute increments and reservations are made one hour to six months prior to call establishment. The switching centers are interconnected via digital radio as well as satellite. The interfaces with customer premises equipment are NCTE. Applications include video conferencing, bulk data transfer, high-speed facsimile, and high-speed data communications.

Skynet 1.5 service is provided via the Telstar satellite within the U.S. Pricing is usage sensitive. Accunet T45 service provides 44.736 Mb/s point-to-point transmission via the AT&T network of fiber optic routes within the U.S.

2.11 ERROR CONTROL

Users of telecommunication services may find that they have requirements for lower error rates than those provided by these services. In some cases, the user may provide its own transmission medium and, again, need to detect and correct errors to a greater extent than normally provided by the capabilities of that medium. *Error control* is a general term that encompasses both the detection of errors and the correction of at least some of these errors.

Before errors can be corrected, they first must be detected. The error detection techniques to be described are *loop* or *echo checking* and *automatic repeat query* (ARQ). These are followed by a discussion of coding for error control, and then the discussion of *forward error correction* (FEC). The section concludes with a special coding application called trellis-coded modulation, which is being used in several high-speed modems.

2.11.1 Loop or Echo Checking

In loop or echo checking, each character is echoed back to the originating console from the distant site. If the echoed message differs in any way from the message that was sent, an error has occurred, but there generally is a 50% chance that the error occurred on the return path. In any event, the errored portion of the message is repeated until it is echoed back correctly. Loop or echo checking is good in highly interactive applications. It is used mainly for terminal systems that do not contain the buffering capability needed for the more powerful schemes.

2.11.2 Automatic Repeat Query (ARQ)

In ARQ, redundant bits are sent to detect errors. If an error is sensed, retransmission is requested. The redundant bits generally are computed on a parity basis.

Example

A row of eight bits includes seven information bits and one redundant bit such that the modulo-2 sum of all of the bits is zero. If the information bits are 1001001, what is the parity bit?

Solution For the row to add to zero, the parity bit must be a one, because the sum $1 + 0 + 0 + 1 + 0 + 0 + 1 = 1$ already. The complete sequence then is 10010011.

If a single bit error occurs anywhere in the above sequence, the row will add to 1 rather than to 0, and the receiver will know that an error has occurred, and therefore request a repeat of the row or some other grouping of the bits found to be in error. The above example illustrates a single-error detecting code. More sophisticated error detection schemes exist and may be used with ARQ.

Stop and wait ARQ works on a half-duplex basis, and sends a positive acknowledgment (ACK) or a negative acknowledgment (NAK) after each block. The source waits for the ACK or the NAK before sending the next block (in response to ACK) or repeating the block (in response to NAK).

Continuous ARQ works on a full duplex basis, overlapping the data and control signaling times to reduce interblock overhead. When a NAK is received, either the source goes back N blocks or retransmits only the block in which the error has been detected.

Adaptive ARQ is used on high-frequency (HF) circuits whose characteristics may vary during the transmission of a message. The block length is shortened during noisy periods. Usually adaptive ARQ uses only two block lengths.

2.11.3 Forward Error Correction

Forward error correction, as the name implies, allows the receiver to determine, from the total set of received bits, which information bits are in error. This, of course, allows the erroneous bits to be corrected. Applications of forward error correction include DS1 transmission, defense applications, satellite communications, and deep-space programs. Also included are modems built to CCITT Standard V.32 for full duplex 9.6 kb/s data over dial up modems operating on voice bandwidth lines. This standard calls for trellis coding (see Sec. 2.11.4), rate 4/5, for a total 12 kb/s stream, and a 2400 Bd symbol rate achieved through the use of QAM.

Several definitions are needed in the discussion of error correction. The *Hamming weight* is the number of nonzero components in a code word. For example, if $c = (101101)$, then $W(c) = 4$. The *Hamming distance* is the number of positions in which two code words differ. Thus if $c_1 = (101101)$ and $c_2 = (111001)$, then $d(c_1, c_2) = 2$. In general, $d(c_1, c_2) = W(c_1 + c_2) = W(c_3)$, where c_3, for linear codes, is a code word. Thus, the distance between any two code words is the weight of the sum of the code words. As a corollary, the minimum distance d for a linear block code is the minimum weight of its nonzero code words.

The Hamming distance D of a code is the minimum Hamming distance of any two words of the code. The Hamming distance is of fundamental importance in establishing the error detection and correction capabilities of a code.

1. To *detect errors* requires a $D + 1$ code, since there is no way that D single bit errors can change a valid code word into another valid code word.
2. To *correct errors* requires a $2D + 1$ code because, even with changes, the original code word still is closer to the starting value than any other code word.

If a code has b information bits and n total bits, the code is referred to as an (n, b) code.

The use of redundant bits in providing error correction can be illustrated by the following example of a (7, 4) code [Ref. 42]. Given the four information bits I_1, I_2, I_3, and I_4. Let the parity bits be P_1, P_2, and P_3. Select each parity bit for an even number of 1s among itself and a selected subset of the Is. Let the encoding-decoding table be the following:

	I_1	I_2	I_3	I_4	P_1	P_2	P_3
P_1	X	X		X	X		
P_2	X		X	X		X	
P_3		X	X	X			X

Thus, select P_1 so that $I_1 + I_2 + I_4 + P_1 = 0$
select P_2 so that $I_1 + I_3 + I_4 + P_2 = 0$
select P_3 so that $I_1 + I_3 + I_4 + P_3 = 0$

Thus, if

$$I_1 = 1$$

$$I_2 = 0$$

$$I_3 = 0$$

$$I_4 = 1$$

Then,

$$P_1 = 0$$

$$P_2 = 0$$

$$P_3 = 1$$

and the code word is $1\,0\,0\,1\,0\,0\,1$.
Suppose the received word is $1\,0\,1\,1\,0\,0\,1$.

The first parity check passes.

The second parity check fails.

The third parity check fails.

In conclusion, one error has occurred. Only an error in I_3 will allow the first parity check to pass while the other two fail.

The term *coding gain* is used to describe the performance of coded signals in a noisy channel. Coding gain is defined as the difference in values of E_b/N_o required to achieve a given p_{be} with and without coding. The channel is assumed to be memoryless, i.e., successive symbols are independent of one another. In addition, the channel is assumed to have no bandwidth limitation, and to be disturbed only by additive white Gaussian noise. Under these circumstances, Shannon has shown that for $E_b/N_o > -1.6$ dB, (the Shannon bound) there exists a coding scheme which allows $p_{be} = 0$. Such an achievement would require a *soft decision* detector, which is described in Sec. 2.11.3.2. Moreover, for $E_b/N_o > 0.4$ dB, a *hard decision* (integrate and dump) detector can achieve $p_{be} = 0$. Thus, a soft decision detector can be said to have a 2 dB coding gain relative to a hard decision detector.

Coding gain is obtained at the expense of increased bandwidth because of the redundant bits that must be added for its achievement. It results in a decreased requirement for received signal power. Thus it is useful only where performance improvements are achievable by increasing signal power. Conversely, in the presence of intersymbol interference, as may be caused by multipath, a power increase does not decrease p_{be} and thus coding gain will not be useful.

2.11.3.1 Coding Types. In data transmission, the sending station groups the bits to be sent into blocks sometimes referred to as "structured sequences," [Ref. 43]. The structure may be either that of a block code or a convolutional code.

2.11.3.1.1 Block Codes. A *block code* is a code in which the redundant bits in a given block relate only to the information bits in the same block. A block code transforms a group of b information bits (or symbols) from a data source into a larger group of n bits (or symbols) by computing and inserting $n - b$ redundant bits (or symbols). An (n, b) block code for error control encodes a block of b information bits (or symbols) into a block of n code-word bits (or symbols). Each symbol is an M-bit byte. The *efficiency* or *rate* of the code is b/n. A high degree of protection is obtained for a large $n - b$, but the line efficiency then is low, long time delays are encountered, and the hardware is complex (large buffers are needed).

Most block codes for error detection and correction are parity check codes. The redundant bits usually are determined using modulo-2 arithmetic. Characters in a block can be checked using a combined horizontal and vertical parity scheme.

A special arrangement using parity bits that cover overlapping fields of message bits is known as a cyclic redundancy check (CRC). The CRC determines when received blocks have errors in them. Thus:

Let,

$$p_{be} = \text{probability of a bit being in error (channel bit error probability)}$$

$$(1 - p_{be}) = \text{probability of a bit not being in error}$$

$$n = \text{number of bits in block}$$

$$(1 - p_{be})^n = \text{probability of a block of } n \text{ consecutive bits not being in error}$$

$$1 - (1 - p_{be})^n = \text{probability of a block of } n \text{ bits being in error}$$

$$r = \text{length (bits) of CRC}$$

$$p_{re} = \text{probability of an undetected error in a block}$$

$$= \frac{1 - (1 - n_c)}{2^r}$$

$$B_t = \text{blocks per transmission}$$

$$B_{ret} = \text{average number of blocks that are likely to be received with undetected errors}$$

$$= B_t p_{re} = \frac{B_t[1 - (1 - p_{be})^n]}{2^r}$$

Example

For 10^9 blocks, each 1000 bits long, transmitted over a channel in which $p_{be} = 10^{-6}$ and for a 16 bit long CRC, what average number of blocks is likely to be received with undetected bit errors?

Solution

$$B_{ret} = \frac{B_t[1 - (1 - p_{be})^n]}{2^r}$$

$$= 10^9 \frac{[1 - (1 - 10^{-6})^{1000}]}{2^{16}}$$

$$= 15.25$$

A *cyclic code,* also called a *polynomial code* is a block code in which a data message of b bits is represented in terms of a $b - 1$ degree polynominal in the variable x. Thus if the data message is given by $a_{b-1}a_{b-2}\ldots a_1a_0$, the corresponding polynominal is

$$M(x) = a_{b-1}\, x^{b-1} + a_{b-2}\, x^{b-2} + \cdots + a_1\, x^1 + a_0$$

A key characteristic of the cyclic code is that any cyclic permutation or end-around shift of a code word results in another code word. The advantage of such codes is that simple feedback shift registers and modulo-2 adders can be used to perform the encoding and decoding operations. Thus encoding consists of operations on the message by feedback shift registers and modulo-2 adders.

Examples of cyclic codes include the Bose-Chaudhuri-Hocquenghem (BCH), the Golay, and the Reed-Solomon (RS) codes. The BCH codes have words of length $n = 2^m - 1$, $m = 3, 4, 5, \cdots$ and can correct any pattern of e or fewer errors using no more than me parity check digits. BCH codes are especially valuable in detecting and correcting randomly occurring multiple errors, i.e., errors which affect successive symbols independently. As an example, a $(15, 7)$ BCH code can provide a 1.0 dB coding gain. BCH coding $(127, 112)$ is being used on Intelsat V.

The Golay code is a $(23, 12)$ code in which one information symbol is repeated $2m + 1$ times. It corrects all combinations of m or fewer errors, but no patterns of $> m$ errors. Adding an overall parity check forms a $(24, 12)$ code with approximately a 2.2 dB coding gain.

In an RS code each symbol is represented as m bits. The block length is $2m - 1$ symbols $= m(2^m - 1)$ bits. The RS codes are well suited to correcting short bursts of errors. RS codes are used in the Joint Tactical Information Distribution System (JTIDS) in a $(31, 15)$ form and in the Air Force satellite system, AFSATCOM, in a $(7, 2)$ form.

2.11.3.1.2 Convolutional Codes. If the $n - b$ redundant symbols of a block also check information symbols in preceding blocks, the code is called *convolutional.* A block diagram of a convolutional encoder is shown in Fig. 2.75. Let b bits be shifted in at a time. The *constraint length K* of the code is the number of shifts over which a single information bit can influence the encoder output. Then bK is the element shift register length. In Fig. 2.75 there are n modulo-2 adders, each of which sums the states of several shift register stages. The state of the register is determined by the states of $b(K - 1)$ stages. These $b(K - 1)$ digits plus the next b digits uniquely define the n output digits. As an example, consider the convolutional coder for $K = 3$, $n = 2$, and $k = 1$, illustrated in Fig. 2.76. The code rate is $b/n = 1/2$, since $n = 2$ code symbols are generated for each $b = 1$ information bit. Because the constraint length $K = 3$, there are 3 bit shifts over which a single information bit can influence the coder output. The state of the coder is defined by the contents of the first $b(K - 1) = 2$ stages. (There are 4 possible states.) The encoder state plus the following input bit ($b = 1$) completely defines the $n = 2$ output symbols.

The convolutional coder of Fig. 2.76 can be described by the code tree of Fig. 2.77 [Ref. 44]. Each branch of the tree represents a single input bit with an input 0

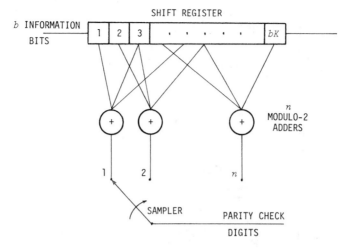

Figure 2.75 Convolutional encoder.

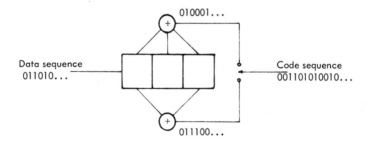

Figure 2.76 Convolutional encoder for $K = 3$, $n = 2$, $b = 1$. (From V. K. Bhargava, "Forward Error Correction Schemes for Digital Communications," *IEEE Communications Magazine,* Jan. 1983, IEEE. Reprinted by permission.)

corresponding to the upper branch and an input 1 corresponding to the lower branch. Accordingly, any input sequence of bits produces a particular path through the tree. As can be seen by inspection of the tree, the input sequence 0 1 1 0 1 0 produces the output sequence 00 11 01 01 00 10. Each node of the tree has been labeled with one of the following sets of bit pairs: {00, 01, 10, 11}, corresponding to the contents of the two left-most positions of the encoder register at that point in the tree. This number is called the state of the encoder.

The tree can be seen to contain redundant information that can be deleted by merging, at any given level, all nodes corresponding to the same encoder state. The redrawing of the tree with merging paths has been called a trellis by Forney [Ref. 45]. Figure 2.78 [Ref. 44] is a trellis for the coder of Fig. 2.76. Again, an input 0 corresponds to selection of the upper branch and an input 1 to the lower branch. Each possible input sequence corresponds to a particular path through the trellis. Thus, at each time unit, the trellis shows all possible transitions between states.

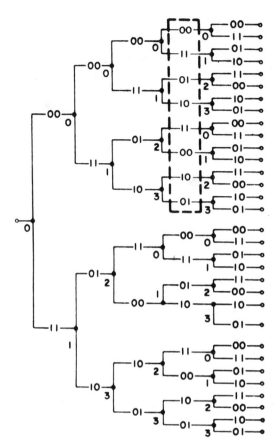

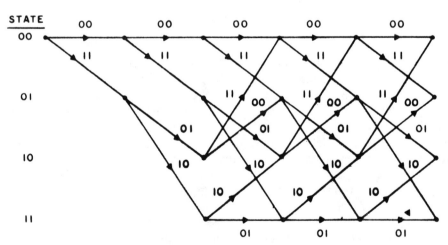

Figure 2.77 Tree for convolutional encoder of Fig. 2.76. (From V. K. Bhargava, "Forward Error Correction Schemes for Digital Communications," *IEEE Communications Magazine,* Jan. 1983, © 1983, IEEE. Reprinted by permission.)

Figure 2.78 Trellis for the convolutional encoder of Fig. 2.76. (From V. K. Bhargava, "Forward Error Correction Schemes for Digital Communications," *IEEE Communications Magazine,* Jan. 1983, © 1983, IEEE. Reprinted by permission.)

There are two possible paths leaving each state, corresponding to the two possible values that can be taken by the next input data bit.

2.11.3.2 Decoding Techniques.

The performance achievable using a given type of coding depends to a significant extent on the decoding technique used. An important concept in error detection is the *syndrome*. The syndrome is a special set of bits used to indicate whether or not a received sequence of bits contains errors. To obtain the syndrome the receiver first reencodes the received information bits to compute a parity sequence as was done in the encoder. The computed parity bits are compared with the bits actually received. The modulo-2 adder doing this comparison forms the syndrome. If no error has occurred, the directly received and the computed bits are identical, so the syndrome bits are zero. Nonzero syndrome bits indicate the presence of errors.

For error correction, the syndrome is processed further. As an example consider the (6, 3) code consisting of the following $2^3 = 8$ code words:

$$(000000), (001101), (010011), (011110),$$
$$(101011), (110101), (111000), (100110).$$

The minimum weight (of the nonzero code words) is 3, and therefore the minimum distance is 3. Therefore, this code is single error correcting because $2D + 1 = 3$, thus $D = 1$.

A second important concept in decoding is the use of hard or soft decisions. A digital demodulator usually quantizes the received voltage before processing it. The use of binary quantization results in a *hard decision,* i.e., the output is simply a 0 or a 1. With three-level or finer quantization, however a *soft decision* is said to be made. Soft decision demodulation thus determines whether the output voltage is above or below the decision threshold and computes a confidence number specifying how far the demodulator output is from the decision threshold. An example of 3-bit (8-level) quantization of a signal from a discrete memoryless channel is illustrated in Fig. 2.79, [Ref. 44]. In this figure $p(z|1)$ and $p(z|0)$ are conditional probability density functions of a matched filter output for a coherent PSK system. As can be seen, the soft decision demodulator determines a confidence value which specifies how far the output is from the decision threshold. Thus, the binary input results in an 8-ary output to the decoder, which follows the demodulator. This soft decision (8-ary) output, as noted in Sec. 2.11.3, generally results in about 2 dB improvement in coding gain over what can be achieved with only a hard decision.

2.11.3.2.1 Decoding of Block Codes.

Decoding techniques for block codes include table lookup decoding, algebraic techniques, and majority logic decoding. Many of the techniques are based on the use of hard decisions at the demodulator output, and the formation of a syndrome.

Table look-up decoding is based on the unique correspondence between the 2^{n-b} distinct syndromes and the correctable error patterns. For codes having only small redundancy, the error patterns can be stored in read-only memory (ROM) chips, with the address being the syndrome of the received word. The error pattern

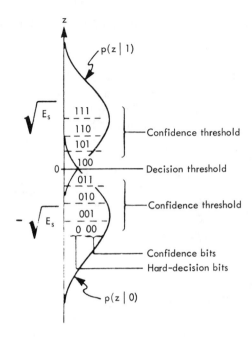

Figure 2.79 Three-bit (8-level) soft-decision quantization. (From V. K. Bhargava, "Forward Error Correction Schemes for Digital Communications," *IEEE Communications Magazine,* Jan. 1983, © 1983, IEEE. Reprinted by permission.)

then is added (modulo-2) to the received sequence in order to reconstruct the transmitted word.

Algebraic techniques include an iterative BCH decoding algorithm developed by Berlekamp [Ref. 46], which is useful for both block and convolutional codes in minimizing decoder complexity. The algorithm has been used by Massey, [Ref. 47], in the design of a minimum-length shift register. An "error-locator polynominal" is computed and its roots are obtained. The algorithm's complexity increases only as the square of the number of errors to be corrected. Decoders using the principle on a parallel basis have been operated at rates as high as 40 Mb/s.

To use soft decisions with this BCH decoding algorithm, another coding technique generally is *concatenated,* or placed in tandem with it.

An algebraic technique known as *permutation decoding* is based on the fact that if the weight of the syndrome for an (n, b) code capable of correcting E errors is at most E, then the information bits are correct. If the weight of the syndrome is greater than E, then at least one information bit is in error.

Some codes have a form of parity check equations that allows majority logic decoding. This is a simple form of *threshold decoding* (see Sec. 2.11.3.2.2) which is applicable to both block and convolutional codes. Since any syndrome bit is a linear combination of error bits, a syndrome bit represents a known sum of error bits. In addition, any linear combination of syndrome bits also is a known sum of error bits. Thus all 2^{n-b} possible combinations of syndrome bits are of the known sum of error bits available at the receiver. These codes are decoded on a bit-by-bit basis with several parity check equations being checked for every received bit. A majority of "votes" is used to determine whether each bit is a 0 or a 1.

2.11.3.2.2 Decoding of Convolutional Codes. The performance achievable from a code depends upon the decoding technique used. The decoding techniques are known as threshold, sequential, and maximum likelihood, with the Viterbi algorithm usually being used to implement the maximum likelihood approach.

In threshold decoding a majority count of parity check bits associated with an information bit is used to make decisions. Thus a syndrome is formed. The first 1 in the syndrome register indicates that an error has been detected. The syndrome bits immediately following indicate whether the error is among the parity bits or an actual information bit error. The syndrome pattern for double errors is the modulo-2 sum of the syndrome patterns for each of the individual errors. Hard decisions are used in threshold decoding, with 2 to 3 dB coding gain being attainable with relatively inexpensive decoders and a limited amount of redundancy.

In sequential decoding the decoder examines the received bit sequence to determine which of various allowed bit sequences were most likely to have been transmitted. The path with the largest likelihood is selected; the information bits corresponding to that path form the decoder output. Decoding depends on the Hamming distance between code words. The received bit sequence is compared with the code book consisting of all valid code words. The selected word is the one which has the minimum distance from the received sequence. Disadvantages of sequential decoding are that the storage requirements for the code book increase rapidly as the constraint length of the code increases. In addition, large numbers of decisions must be made rapidly to keep up with the incoming data.

In sequential decoding, variable length searches result from a fluctuating channel noise level. A buffer is needed if a firm decision has not been made before another data bit arrives. Any buffer overflow means a burst of errors at the output, with such error bursts being a major constituent of the error rate from sequential decoders. A scrambler after the encoder and a descrambler before the decoder can randomize the effects of channel error bursts. Such an approach is known as *interleaving* or *diffusing*. Sequential decoders usually make hard decisions because soft decisions cause significant increases in the required storage and computation. Coding gains on the order of 5 to 6 dB are provided. Because decoder complexity is not highly sensitive to code constraint length K, high K values, e.g., 40 or more, often are used to achieve very low values of p_{be}.

If all code words have an equal likelihood of being transmitted, the optimum decoding scheme to use is called *maximum likelihood* decoding [Ref. 43]. A brute force maximum-likelihood decoder calculates the likelihood of the received data on all of the paths through a code trellis. Since the number of paths for an N-bit information sequence is 2^N, the brute force method quickly becomes impractical as N increases. However, an algorithm due to Viterbi [Ref. 48] uses the structure of the code trellis to reduce the computational requirements. The Viterbi decoder calculates the likelihood of each of the two paths entering a given state and removes from further consideration all but the most likely path leading to that state. This is done for each of the $2^{b(K-1)}$ states at a given trellis depth. After each decoding operation, only one path remains leading to each state. The decoder then proceeds one level deeper into the trellis and repeats the process. In eliminating the less likely paths, the decoder does not reject any path which would have been selected by a brute-force maximum likelihood decoder.

The advantage of the Viterbi decoder is that the number of decoding operations for N bits is $N2^{b(K-1)}$, which is linear in N. This decoder is best for small values of K because storage requirements increase exponentially with K. Accordingly, many Viterbi coders are limited to $K \le 10$. Viterbi decoders work with both hard and soft decision demodulation. Soft-decision Viterbi using 8-level quantization provides more than 1.75 dB improvement in coding gain compared with hard-decision Viterbi.

Figure 2.80 [Ref. 43] compares $K = 7$ Viterbi with $K = 41$ sequential decoding of BPSK. Figure 2.81 [Ref. 49] shows the effect of increasing K for rate 1/2, 8-level quantization Viterbi. The solid curves were the results of computer simulation while the dashed curves are theoretical limits.

2.11.3.3 Burst Error Correction.   Error bursts, also known as *erasures,* may occur in any transmission system, but are found most commonly in systems involving radio propagation, especially those in which one terminal is in motion. Error bursts in such cases result from multipath propagation. Most error correction techniques are based upon errors occurring randomly, i.e., only one or a limited number in a given block or message. To achieve burst error correction, the redundancy must bridge the length of the burst, i.e., both the information and redundant bits of a block cannot be within the burst. Only if suitable redundant bits occur either before or after the burst can they be effective in achieving error correction. One approach is to interleave a delayed stream with an undelayed one. (The original stream is assumed to have been error coded.) Table 2.12 provides an example of the use of this approach. This simple example interleaves the original stream with itself delayed by four bit positions and thus can survive an erasure as

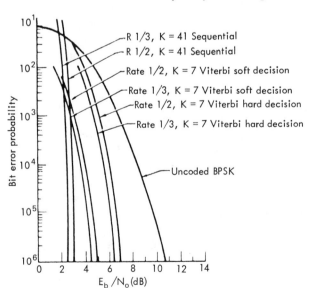

Figure 2.80   Performance comparison: Viterbi and sequential decoding. (From P. Sklar, "A Structured Overview of Digital Communications—A Tutorial Overview," *IEEE Communications Magazine,* Oct. 1983, © 1983, IEEE. Reprinted by permission.)

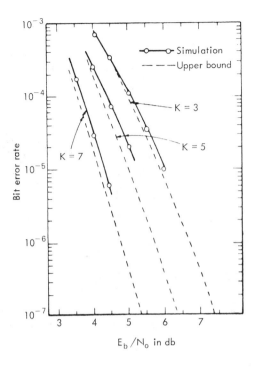

Figure 2.81 Effect of K on performance of rate ½, 8-level quantized Viterbi decoding. (From J. A. Heller and I. M. Jacobs, "Viterbi Decoding for Satellite and Space Communications," *IEEE Trans. Communications*, Oct. 1971, © 1971, IEEE. Reprinted by permission.)

TABLE 2.12 ILLUSTRATION OF INTERLEAVING FOR BURST ERROR CORRECTION

Original Stream							0	1	1	0	1	0	0	0	1	0	1	1	1	0		
Delayed Stream									0	1	1	0	1	0	0	0	1	0	1		
Combined Stream	0	0	1	1	0	1	0	0	0	1	1	0	0	0	1	0	1	1	1	0	0	1

long as four bit times in the original stream. This is done by switching alternate received bits into shift registers, and performing error checks on the resulting streams, delivering the valid one to the user if the alternative stream shows errors. Numerous interleaving methods are in commercial use, including compact audio disk recording. These disks also use forward error correction to reduce the noise that would result from scratches and other minor damage to the disks.

Other approaches to burst error correction arrange the code words as a matrix, sending one column at a time, or use special forms of threshold decoding. Special algorithms that can correct burst errors include the Gallager adaptive burst-finding scheme and diffuse threshold decoding, [Ref. 50].

2.11.3.4 Comparison of Coding Techniques.

Table 2.13 [Ref. 44] compares the coding techniques, indicating data rate ranges based upon digital integrated circuit technology. A comparison of block and convolutional coding is provided in Table 2.14. A summary of the types of coding and decoding most directly useful in various application areas is provided in Table 2.15.

TABLE 2.13 COMPARISON OF CODING TECHNIQUES

Technique	Gain at 10^{-5}	Gain at 10^{-8}	Data rate
Concatenated (Reed Solomon/Viterbi)	6.5–7.5	8.5–9.5	10 kb/s to 1 Mb/s
Sequential (soft)	6.0–7.0	8.0–9.0	10 kb/s to 1 Mb/s
Block (soft)	5.0–6.0	6.5–7.5	10 kb/s to 1 Mb/s
Concatenated (Reed Solomon/ Short Block)	4.5–5.5	6.5–7.5	>20 Mb/s
Viterbi (soft)	4.0–5.5	5.0–6.5	1 to 20 Mb/s
Sequential (hard)	4.0–5.0	6.0–7.0	1 to 20 Mb/s
Block (hard)	3.0–4.0	4.5–5.5	1 to 20 Mb/s
Block—Threshold	2.0–4.0	3.5–5.5	1 to 20 Mb/s
Convolutional—Threshold	1.5–3.0	2.5–4.0	>20 Mb/s

Reference: BPSK or QPSK on AWGN Channel

Source: From V. K. Bhargava, "Forward Error Correction Schemes for Digital Communications," *IEEE Communications Magazine,* Jan. 1983, © 1983. Reprinted by permission.

TABLE 2.14 COMPARISON OF BLOCK AND CONVOLUTIONAL CODING

	Block	Convolutional
Max. data rate supported	>100 Mb/s	Usually < 50 Mb/s
Typical code rates	7/8, 15/16	1/2, 3/4, 7/8
Typical delays	>2000 bit durations	30 to 100 bit durations
Length of error bursts corrected without interleaving	≤100 b/s	Usually < 20 bits

TABLE 2.15 SUMMARY OF CODING APPLICATION AREAS

- 10 kb/s to 20 Mb/s, AWGN, 10^{-5} ber—convolutional/Viterbi
- >20 Mb/s
  - —Reed-Solomon and short block (same gain as Viterbi, but with less complexity)
  - —Threshold
- 1 to 20 Mb/s, high gains
  - —Sequential (hard)
- 10 kb/s to 1 Mb/s
  - —Sequential (soft)
- System protocols requiring block transmission (e.g., TDMA)
  - —Block
- Small bit rate with high bandwidth efficiency
  - —Threshold (for satellite digital telephony)
- Mobile terminals (doppler offsets, multipath, fading)
  - —Reed-Solomon (soft)
  - —Threshold/interleaving
  - —Viterbi (soft)/interleaving

2.11.4 Trellis-Coded Modulation

In doing coding for error correction prior to modulation, the redundant bits and the message bits are handled simply as a bit stream, i.e., the redundant bits are not used to select the sequence of transmitted signal points. Accordingly, in terms of the information bit rate, coding results in a decrease in bandwidth efficiency. Trellis-coded modulation (TCM)* adds redundant code bits to the data stream within each symbol and thereby achieves coding gain without reducing the data rate or requiring additional bandwidth, [Ref. 51]. Accordingly, it is quite useful where bandwidth efficiency is important. Coding gains on the order of 3 to 6 dB are achievable. The name *trellis* is used because the schemes can be described by a trellis (state transition) diagram similar to the diagrams of binary convolutional codes.

Figure 2.82 shows the basis on which TCM is applied to a 14.4 kb/s modem. The result of adding the seventh bit is a 128-point constellation rather than the 64-QAM which would be used otherwise. Only certain sequences of the signal points are valid. The use of codes with large Hamming distances and careful selection of the mapping rules provides sequences with signal points far apart, i.e., large Euclidean distances. Maximum likelihood decoding then selects the valid sequence closest to the observed sequence using the Viterbi trellis search algorithm.

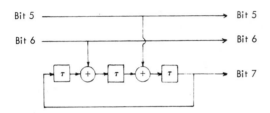

Figure 2.82 Application of trellis-coded modulation to 14.4 kb/s modem.

The CCITT has developed standards for modems using trellis-coded modulation. These standards are Recommendations V.32 for 9.6 kb/s modems and V.33 for 14.4 kb/s modems. (Recommendation V.32 also deals with modems not using trellis-coded modulation and operating at lower rates.)

A further advantage of TCM is that it can introduce a number of classes of points in the signal constellation. In what is called 8-state, 2-dimensional TCM, the classes of points are represented by the numbers in Fig. 2.83, [Ref. 52]. On the left is a 256 point TCM signal constellation. On the right, a small section of the constellation is extracted to illustrate the principle of signal point classes.

A total of eight bits is used to select one signal point. The three bits resulting from the convolutional encoder determine the class of the point (the number in Fig. 2.83). The remaining five bits determine the particular point within the selected class. Once one of the signal points is chosen, it is transmitted to the receiving modem.

Upon receiving the signal point, (point A in Fig. 2.84), the receiving modem starts the process of recognition (which signal point is it?). This process is best explained through example. Assume the position of the signal point was disturbed during transmission through the telephone line. The receiving modem initially "sees" the point closer to some other (incorrect) position, illustrated in Fig. 2.84. A modem based on the QAM technique would assign this point to the nearest (wrong) location in the constellation. Not so with TCM. The process of recognition with TCM consists of two steps—the coarse and the fine.

---

* The letters TCM also are used to denote time compression multiplexing in other contexts.

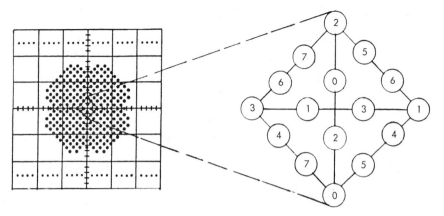

Figure 2.83 Classes of points in TCM constellation. (Courtesy Codex Corporation, 1986. Reprinted with permission.)

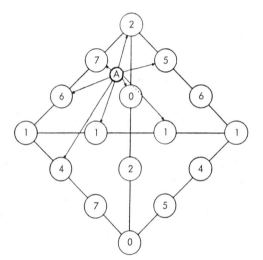

Figure 2.84 Received point A relative to expected signal states. (Courtesy Codex Corporation, 1986. Reprinted with permission.)

As illustrated in Fig. 2.84, [Ref. 52], eight distances to the nearest point in each of eight classes are measured. During the coarse step, the receiving TCM modem selects the closest signal point in each class as the most likely candidate to have been transmitted. Since there are eight classes, eight possible positions are identified. The distances between the received point and the eight possible positions are also measured and recorded.

At the second, or fine step, the recorded information is used to examine the dependencies introduced by the convolutional encoder. By taking into account past and subsequently received signals, the decoder will decide which of the eight signal points was most likely transmitted. The decoding algorithm examines several successively received signal points before making its decision.

In other words, the decoder is continuously looking backwards, comparing received data with newly presented information—only then is the final decision made on the signal point identification. The resulting performance gain can be quantified by examining signal-to-noise levels. Transmitting data with two times the number of signal points as TCM does, decreases performance by 3 dB using a conventional QAM receiver. However, the redundant encoding bit allows the TCM receiver to select point sequences or patterns, improving the performance by 6 dB. Hence, TCM provides a net performance gain of approximately 3 dB over conventional QAM techniques, depending upon line conditions. This gain is sufficient to cope with high levels of signal distortion and to provide reliable operation at rates above 9600 b/s.

Multidimensional TCM has been developed to provide good transmission at rates up to 19.2 kb/s on voice bandwidth lines. It concatenates four 2-dimensional signal constellations into one 8-dimensional constellation and then uses TCM encoding techniques to introduce dependencies only between 8-dimensional signal points, as shown in Fig. 2.85, [Ref. 52]. An example is 64-state, 8-dimensional TCM (64 × 8 TCM). Figure 2-85 illustrates four 2-dimensional 160 point signal constellations interconnected (concatenated) into one system.

Only one redundant bit is added per 8-dimensional signal point rather than one redundant bit added per each 2-dimensional signal point. Both the signal power and the number of points which need to be transmitted are saved because proportionally fewer redundant encoding bits are necessary. Although there are fewer encoding bits, these redundant bits are used in a more efficient manner through the more powerful 64-state trellis code compared with the 8-state, 2-dimensional TCM scheme.

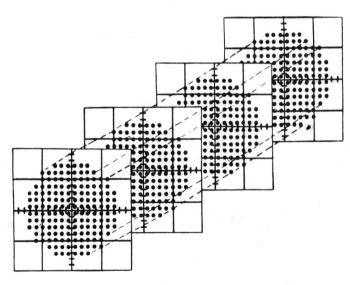

Figure 2.85 Eight-dimensional TCM. (Courtesy Codex Corporation, 1986. Reprinted with permission.)

Sec. 2.11   Error Control

By utilizing both 8-dimensional TCM and a higher symbol rate than the usual 2400 Bd, the noise immunity is improved and the number of points is reduced from 256 to 160, in each of the four concatenated 2-dimensional constellations.

As an example, the Codex 2680 modem at 19.2 kb/s collects data into 28-bit blocks instead of 7-bit blocks as in the Codex 2660 at 16.8 kb/s. A redundant bit is added to each block through a 64-state trellis encoder, and the resulting 29 bits are used to select an 8-dimensional signal point. Each 8-dimensional signal point comprises four successive 2-dimensional signal points selected from a 160 point 2-dimensional constellation. The sequence of 2-dimensional signal points are then transmitted at a symbol rate of 2743 Bd. The Codex 2680 modem provides $p_{be} = 10^{-3}$ on "better than 90% of D1 conditioned lines," [Ref. 53].

Although 8-dimensional TCM appears more complex than 2-dimensional, the concepts of signal point recognition in the receiver are essentially the same. This is also true for the backward looking mechanism. Therefore, the exploitation of signal point dependency is similar in both TCM schemes. A 64×8 TCM constellation provides an improvement of 5.4 dB compared with uncoded 128 signal point QAM at 16.8 kb/s.

2.12 TRANSMISSION PROTOCOLS

A protocol is a set of rules for operating a communication system. This section summarizes the functions of protocols, describes their categories, and outlines the application of a specific transmission protocol in high-speed transmission via satellite.

2.12.1 Protocol Functions

Protocol functions include framing, error control, sequence control, transparency, line control, timeout control, and starting control, as well as special cases, [Ref. 54].

Framing establishes which 8-bit groups constitute characters and what groups of characters constitute messages.

Error control provides for the detection of errors via longitudinal, vertical, or cyclic redundancy checks. Included are such functions as the acceptance of correct messages and requests for the retransmission of faulty messages.

Sequence control is achieved by the numbering of messages to eliminate duplicate messages, avoid lost messages, and properly identify messages that are retransmitted by the error control system.

Transparency denotes the ability to transmit information that contains bit patterns which resemble the control characters used to implement framing, error control and sequence control, without the receiving station identifying those bit patterns as control characters.

Line control is the determination of which station will transmit and which station(s) will receive, as applied to half-duplex or multipoint lines.

Timeout control establishes actions to be taken if message flow ceases entirely.

Starting control is used to start transmission in a communication system that has been idle.

Special cases involve establishing the transmitter output when no data is to be sent.

2.12.2 Protocol Categories

Protocol categories are delineated in terms of the message framing techniques used.

Character oriented protocols use special characters to indicate the beginning of a message (STX) and the end of a block of text (ETB). An example is the binary synchronous protocol (IBM BISYNC).

Byte count oriented protocols use a header which includes a beginning special character, a count indicating the number of characters in the data portion of the message, control information, the data itself, and block check characters. An example is the DEC digital data communications message protocol (DEC DDCMP).

Bit oriented (bit stuffing) protocols delineate which bits constitute messages by separating messages with a flag character, such as 01111110. Examples are the IBM synchronous data link control (IBM SDLC), the ANSI advanced data communications control procedure (ANSI ADCCP), THE ISO high-level data line control (ISO HDLC), and the CCITT X.25 packet transmission standard.

2.12.3 High-Speed Transmission via Satellite

As will be seen in Chap. 5, geosynchronous satellite circuits have a 0.6 second round trip delay time. If ARQ is used to achieve error control, overall message transmission may be slowed considerably. For example, a facsimile machine may send a line and then wait for an ACK or a NAK from the receiving end. Ways of solving this delay problem are the following:

1. Block by block. In this case, the block (or line) is sent. If the reply is an ACK, the next block is sent whereas, if the reply is a NAK the block is repeated. The problem with this approach is the delay encountered. To maintain transmission efficiency, large blocks are needed, and the channel should have a low probability of bit error.

2. Restart after error detection. This approach sends numbered blocks. If the reply is an ACK, the transmission continues. If the reply is a NAK, the sender repeats the block in error plus all following blocks. The problem with this approach is built-in inefficiency.

3. Continuous. In using this approach, numbered blocks are sent. If the reply is an ACK, the receiver forwards the block to the user. If the reply is a NAK, the receiver holds all blocks until the NAK'ed block is retransmitted within the stream and received correctly. This approach provides the best transmission efficiency, but at the expense of a larger buffer at the terminal than required for the other approaches.

Delay sensitive protocols such as the IBM 3270 BISYNC can be handled using a technique called *delay compensation through program emulation,* [Ref. 55]. Program emulation provides local acknowledgment and response to the FEP and control units. It can be done on a line-by-line basis using external "black boxes" or by emulation in networked statistical multiplexers, which allow multiple lines and good network efficiency. The X.25 and SNA/SDLC are well suited to large transmission delays because they can support multiple outstanding messages. They use an acknowledgment sequence number that starts at zero and increments to seven before cycling back to zero (modulo 128).

2.13 GLOSSARY OF TERMS

Asynchronous Transmission in which time intervals between transmitted characters may be of unequal length. Transmission is controlled by start and stop elements at the beginning and end of each character.

Availability Percentage of time that satisfactory data communication service is available. "Satisfactory" implies that terminal equipment and cables are in working order.

Baseband office An office in a DDS digital serving area that contains no DDS multiplexing equipment, but acts as a linkup point between the four-wire connection to a customer's station and an interoffice cable.

Bipolar NRZ Bipolar nonreturn to zero; the same as bipolar RZ, except that transitions between adjacent 1s do not stop at zero level.

Bipolar RZ Bipolar return to zero; a three-level code in which alternate 1s change in sign, e.g., 1011 becomes $+1, 0, -1, +1$, and transitions between adjacent 1s pause at the zero voltage level.

BPSK Bi-phase shift keying; keying in which the phase of the carrier assumes only two values, e.g., $0°$ and $180°$.

BPV Bipolar violation; a violation of the alternating $+1, -1$ pattern in a three-level code.

Byte A group of (usually) eight consecutive binary digits associated with a single user.

Byte stuffing A technique by which the bit rate of a digital stream is increased by repeating bytes and transmitting them at a faster rate. The information content of the stream is not increased.

CCITT Comité-Consultatif International Télégraphique et Téléphonique

Channel A medium (or means) of one-way transmission in either direction.

Circuit A means of communication between two points, consisting of associated send and receive channels. The two associated channels may be symmetrical, i.e., may offer the user the same capability in either direction of transmission, or they may be asymmetrical.

Control signals Signals used for synchronization, status, and remote testing.

CSU Channel service unit; a unit located on the customer's premises that terminates a DDS channel and is used with the customer's logic and timing recovery circuitry.

Data link The configuration of equipment enabling end terminals in two different stations to communicate directly. The data link includes the paired DTEs, signal converters, and interconnecting communications facilities.

Data mode A condition of the DSU with respect to the transmitter in which its data-set-ready and request-to-send circuits are on and it is presumably sending data.

DCE Data Communications Equipment; any equipment that connects to a DTE using an EIA RS-232 or CCITT V.24 standard interface.

DDS Dataphone Digital Service

DDS loop That portion of an individual customer's channel between the station and its associated office channel unit (OCU).

Downtime Time during which data communication is not available or is unsatisfactory (see Availability) because of malfunction. Time required for preventive maintenance is not included.

DSA Digital serving area; the combined geographical serving areas of a set of DDS serving offices, as specified in the appropriate tariff(s). The DDS office serving areas making up a DSA are not necessarily contiguous, and a DSA may overlap state and associated company boundaries; however, a typical DSA might encompass one urban area of a single associated company.

DSDS Dataphone Switched Digital Service

DSU Data Service Unit; a terminal located on the customer's premises for the purpose of accessing the DDS through a standard EIA or CCITT interface.

DTE Data Terminal Equipment; the configuration of equipment at the end points of a system segment contained between the signal converter interface defined by EIA Standard RS-232 and the information source or receiver utilized in a given application. It always includes at least one intermediate terminal and may include combinations of intermediate terminals and end terminals.

Duplex A communication mode in which transmission can occur in both directions simultaneously (also called "full duplex").

Duty cycle The percent of a single pulse period during which the voltage is nonzero.

DUV Data under voice; a system that provides for the transmission of one bipolar RZ signal at a 1.544 Mb/s rate (known as a DS-1 signal) over a microwave radio link.

Efficiency of data communications Percentage of one-second intervals in which data are delivered free of error.

EFS Error-Free Seconds

EIA Electronic Industries Association

End office A local office that passes on toward the hub only circuits that entered the office over local loops. The main function of an end office is to combine several individual customer channels by means of multiplexers, and to transmit the combined bit stream toward the serving test center.

End terminal An equipment consisting of the ultimate source or receiver, or both, in a digital data transmission system. It may include features designed to initiate or react to various end-to-end control procedures such as carriage return or line feed on a keyboard printer, but does not include features for the execution of control of communications procedures.

Forward channel A data transmission channel in which the direction of transmission coincides with that in which information is being transferred, i.e., from source to receiver.

Four-wire circuit A facility that provides two full-time, independent channels for transmission in opposite directions. It is historically associated with two wires for transmission and two wires for reception.

Front end processor A communications computer associated with a host computer. It may perform line control, message handling, code conversion, error control, and applications functions such as control and operation of special-purpose terminals.

Half duplex A facility that permits transmission in both directions, but only one direction at a time.

Hit Any disruption of service that persists for less than one second.

Homochronous Two signals are homochronous if their corresponding significant instants have a constant, but uncontrolled, phase relationship. Example of significant instant: bit period [homo = same].

Idle code A bipolar violation sequence transmitted to indicate that no data are being sent over the line.

Information channel The transmission media and intervening equipment involved in the transfer of information in a given direction between two terminals. An information channel includes the signal converters, as well as the reverse channel when provided.

Information path A discrete route by which information may be transferred between any two DTEs within a multipoint segment. (This term is not used in describing a point-to-point segment.)

Intermediate terminal A device functioning as a part of the data path within a DTE and including features for the execution or control of communications procedures. Its functions may also include code conversion, error control, multiplexing, or temporary buffering or storage of data. It may be a discrete item of equipment or an integral part of an end terminal.

Isochronous A signal is isochronous if the time interval separating any two significant instants is theoretically equal to the unit interval or to a multiple of the unit interval. In practice, variations in the time intervals are constrained within specified limits. Example of unit interval: bit period [iso = equal].

Local loop The cable pairs between an office and customer premises.

Long haul Transmission distances typically beyond 400 km utilizing microwave or coaxial cable facilities.

Long haul access multiplexing The multiplexing equipment in a hub office dedicated to combining circuits for efficient transmission to other local serving areas.

Looping A testing procedure that causes a received signal to be transmitted, i.e., returned to the source.

Multipoint A customer circuit with more than two end points. One end point is designated the control station.

Mux Multiplexer

Outage Any disruption of service that persists for more than one second.

PCM Pulse code modulation; the process in which analog signals are sampled, quantized and coded into a digital bit stream.

Plesiochronous Two signals are plesiochronous if their corresponding significant instants occur at nominally the same rate, any variation in rate being constrained within specified limits. Two signals having the same nominal digit rate, but not stemming from the same clock or homochronous clocks, are usually plesiochronous. There is no limit to the phase relationship between corresponding significant instants [plesio = near].

PLL Phase locked loop; a circuit containing a variable frequency oscillator whose phase is compared with a reference signal. By a suitable feedback mechanism, both signals are forced to agree in frequency and possibly in phase.

Point-to-point segment A class of system segment that permits communications between only two DTEs at a given time.

Protocols Sets of rules governing information flow in a communication system. Among the specifications included in protocols are:

• Procedures for establishing and altering relationships between devices in a system

- Formats for messages sent in a system
- Means for identifying devices
- Means for allocating permission to transmit among devices sharing a line
- Means for recovery from errors or failure
- Means to control the flow of data when a station is temporarily unable to process more.

QAM Quadrature amplitude modulation

QPSK Quaternary phase shift keying

Residual error rate The ratio of the number of bits, unit elements, characters, or blocks incorrectly received but undetected or uncorrected by the error control equipment, to the total number of bits, unit elements, characters, or blocks transmitted.

Reverse channel A data transmission channel used for supervisory and/or error control signals and associated with the forward channel, but having a direction of transmission opposite to that in which information is being transferred.

Short-haul Transmission distances typically less than 400 km.

Signal converter Equipment which changes the data signal into a form suitable for the transmission medium, or the reverse. An analog signal converter consists of a modulator and/or a demodulator.

Slip A defect in timing that causes a single bit or a sequence of bits to be omitted or read twice.

Station One of the physical input or output points of a communication system, including all intermediate terminals and the associated end terminals to which they are connected. Examples are stand-alone terminals, clustered CRT terminals and their control unit, and computer ports.

Synchronous Two signals are synchronous if their corresponding significant instances have a desired phase relationship [syn = together].

System segment A conceptual subset of a data transmission system containing the DTEs connected to a common channel. A system segment may be either point-to-point or multipoint.

TDM Time division multiplexing; the process of combining a number of digital signals into a single digital stream by an orderly assignment of time slots.

Terminal configuration The functional interconnection of an end terminal and one or more intermediate terminals within a DTE for a specified mode of operation at a given time.

Transfer delay A characteristic of system performance that expresses the time delay in processing information through a data transmission system.

PROBLEMS

2.1 A statistically representative set of ten data modems was found to exhibit the following failure characteristics:

1 failed once every 6 months, on the average
2 failed once every 7 months, on the average
2 failed once every 8 months, on the average
2 failed once every 9 months, on the average
2 failed once every 10 months, on the average
1 failed once every 11 months, on the average

Calculate the MTBF for this set of modems.

2.2 A data transmission facility has a 1.544 Mb/s rate and $p_{be} = 10^{-7}$. What is the percentage of error-free seconds?

2.3 A system consisting of seven links in tandem has a bit error probability of 10^{-6} per link. What is the end-to-end bit error probability?

2.4 Numerous bandwidth definitions have been devised, such as the -20 dB bandwidth, the half-power bandwidth, the noise bandwidth, etc. Explain why these bandwidths cannot be converted from one to another by simple formulas. What additional information is needed to convert from one bandwidth to another, i.e., a system's bandwidth is described using one definition; what is its bandwidth using another definition?

2.5 Figure 2.17 shows relationships between the Shannon and Nyquist theorems and the number of levels of a signal. However, one cannot, from the information in the figure, find one of the three relationships only by knowing the other two. Why not?

2.6 Proponents of correlative level encoding claim that it is capable of operating at symbol rates beyond the Nyquist limit. Are these claims valid? Why? Is the Nyquist theorem thereby violated? Why not?

2.7 A data under voice system is to be designed for operation in the spectrum available below 564 kHz on a transmission system. To avoid disturbance to the FDM channels above 564 kHz, all spectral components must be 30 dB below a standard unmodulated carrier reference level in the FDM portion of the baseband. A 1.544 Mb/s data rate is required at a bit error probability of 10^{-7}. The noise level below 564 kHz is -40 dB relative to the unmodulated carrier reference level. Select the baseband transmission technique best meeting these requirements and explain the reasons for your choice.

2.8 QPSK and 4-QAM exhibit the same signal state space diagrams. Are their p_{be} performance therefore alike? Under what circumstances? Prove or disprove using the equations of this chapter.

2.9 Explain why digital techniques at baseband appear to exhibit twice as much spectral efficiency (b/s per Hz) as techniques involving the modulation of a digital waveform on a carrier.

2.10 A transmission system requires a bit error probability not to exceed 10^{-8}. The bit rate is to be 2.048 Mb/s. Determine the signal-to-noise ratio and bandwidth ($\alpha = 0.3$) required for 16-PSK. Repeat for 64-QAM and for 49-QPR.

2.11 What is the maximum (theoretical) data rate that can be sent error free over a voice bandwidth channel with a 30 dB ratio of signal to channel noise (AWGN)?

2.12 A digital transmission engineer has a 20 kHz bandwidth channel in which to transmit a 56 kb/s stream. Can QPSK be used to meet this requirement? If not, would 8-PSK be feasible? Would 16-QAM be preferable?

2.13 Why are the higher stream rates of the digital hierarchy not integral multiples of the lower stream rates?

2.14 Explain why the tolerable channel noise level decreases as the number of modulation levels increases, assuming the bit error probability is to be held constant.

2.15 Why can a 9.6 kilobaud transmission rate not be sent on a voice bandwidth line? What is the maximum rate according to Nyquist's theorem?

2.16 Draw the eye diagram of a 1.544 Mb/s baseband BRZ signal assuming an ideal brick-wall low-pass filter (linear phase) with the following cut-off frequencies: 15.44 MHz, 1.544 MHz, 772 kHz, 386 kHz, 193 kHz. Estimate the intersymbol interference and the peak-to-peak jitter caused by the filter in each case.

2.17 A 135 Mb/s 64-QAM system has an available C/N = 30 dB in a 30 MHz receiver bandwidth. What p_{be} is expected theoretically?

2.18 Compare the S/N requirements of 49-QPR and 225-QPR with 64-QAM for $p_{be} = 10^{-8}$. If bandwidth limitations are paramount, which technique would you use? If power, rather than bandwidth, is limited, which technique would you use?

2.19 A binary source has outputs with probabilities 0.6 and 0.4. What is the entropy of the source?

2.20 Design a rate 1/2 convolutional encoder with a three-stage shift register. Select the connections such that the output with a binary 1 input is the complement of that with a binary 0 input.

2.21 Determine the frequency at which a baseband raised-cosine channel response is -20 dB assuming the Nyquist frequency is 772 kHz and $\alpha = 0.2$.

2.22 A 16-QAM signal is to be transmitted through a limiting amplifier. Sketch the effect which the limiting has on the signal state space diagram and, using this diagram, describe the effect of the limiting on the p_{be} performance.

2.23 Explain why the performance of a bandwidth limited MPSK signal becomes degraded by being transmitted through an amplitude limiting amplifier. Is the performance of unfiltered MPSK signals degraded by transmission through nonlinear memoryless amplifiers?

2.24 With respect to sinusoidal interference 16-QAM was shown in Sec. 2.6.4 to be 1.59 dB superior to 16-PSK. However, with respect to AWGN, 16-QAM is about 3.8 dB superior to 16-PSK. Explain why the difference between the two techniques increases with the peak factor of the interference. In general, why do higher noise peak factors cause increased degradation of any form of digital modulation?

2.25 The main spectral lobe of MSK has its first null at $(f - f_c)T_b = 0.75$, as shown in Fig. 2.41. Explain why MSK can achieve a 2 b/s per Hz spectral efficiency.

2.26 Explain why trellis-coded modulation is important in achieving spectral efficiency in high-level modulation systems.

2.27 Many error correcting techniques are found to be nearly useless in a mobile communications environment. Explain why. What must be done to correct errors in a channel exhibiting frequent burst errors?

2.28 Error-correcting codes provide coding gains of up to 6 dB in most practical systems. Are such codes more likely to be found on systems designed for highly stable or for highly variable propagating media? Why?

2.29 The reference frequency for the digital transmission system of a given country or of a given common carrier often is located near the geographical center of the overall area served. Propagation delay however, is not a consideration in achieving synchronous terrestrial transmission. Explain how propagation delay problems are avoided in synchronous transmission.

2.30 A message consisting of 10^6 blocks of data, each 1000 bits long, is transmitted over a channel in which $p_{be} = 10^{-7}$. The extended framing format (CRC-6) is used. What average number of blocks is likely to be received with undetected bit errors?

REFERENCES

1. D. R. Smith, *Digital Transmission Systems*, Van Nostrand Reinhold, New York, 1985.

2. H. D. Goldman and R. C. Sommer, "An Analysis of Cascaded Binary Communication Links," *IRE Trans. Comm. Systems*, CS-10, no. 3, (September, 1962), 291–99.

3. *Error Performance of an International Digital Connection Forming Part of an Integrated Services Digital Network*, COM XVIII, No. 95-E, CCITT, Geneva, (1984), 155–163.

4. CCIR XVth Plenary Assembly, Vol. IX, Part 1, *Fixed Service Using Radio-Relay Systems*, ITU, Geneva, (1982).

5. CCIR XVth Plenary Assembly, Vol. IV, Part 1, *Fixed Satellite Service*, ITU Geneva, (1982).

6. *Digital Networks-Transmission Systems and Multiplexing Equipment*, CCITT Yellow Book, Vol. III. 3, ITU, Geneva, (1981).

7. *Transmission Systems for Communications*, Bell Telephone Laboratories, Inc., published by Western Electric Co., Inc., Winston-Salen, NC, (1970).

8. Nyquist, H., "Certain Topics in Telegraph Transmission Theory," *Trans. AIEE*, 47, (April, 1928), 617–44.

9. K. Feher, *Digital Communications: Microwave Applications*, Prentice-Hall, Englewood Cliffs, NJ, (1981).

10. K. J. Leuenberger, "Digital Radio Systems Examined—Part II, Modulation and Transmission Characteristics," *Microwave Systems News and Communications Technology*, 16, no. 2, (Feb. 1986), 131–43.

11. K. Feher, *Digital Communications: Satellite/Earth Station Engineering*, Prentice-Hall, Englewood Cliffs, NJ, (1983).

12. C. E. Shannon, "A Mathematical Theory of Communications," *BSTJ*, 1948, pp. 379–423, 623–56.

13. J. P. Costas, "Synchronous Communications," *Proc. IRE,* Dec. 1956, pp. 1713–18.

14. J. C. Bellamy, *Digital Telephony*, Wiley, New York, 1982.

15. W. Stallings, "Digital Signaling Techniques," *IEEE Communications Magazine*, 22, no. 12, (Dec. 1984), 21–25.

16. V. E. Benes, "Traffic in Connecting Networks when Existing Calls are Rearranged," *BSTJ*, 49, (1970), 1471–82.

17. Technical Reference TR-TSY-000210, "Low Bit Rate Voice (LBRV) Terminals," Issue 1, September 1986, Bell Communications Research, Livingston, NJ, © 1986.

18. CCITT Yellow Book, Vol. III. 3, *Digital Networks—Transmission Systems and Multiplexing Equipment*, ITU, Geneva, (1981).

19. American Telephone and Telegraph Co., *Telecommunications Transmission Engineering*, Vol. 2-Facilities, Western Electric, Winston-Salem, NC, (1977).

20. A Lender, "Duobinary Technique for High-Speed Data Transmission," *IEEE Trans. Comm. Electr.*, May 1963, pp. 214–18.

21. E. R. Kretzmer, "Generalization of a Technique for Binary Data Communications," *IEEE Trans. Comm. Tech.*, COM-14, (Feb. 1966), 67–68.

22. D. W. Jurling and A. L. Pachynski, "Duobinary PCM System Doubles Capacity of T1 Facilities," *IEEE International Communications Conference,* 1977, Paper 32.2, pp. 297–301.

23. N-S Lin, D. A. Hodges, and D. G. Messerschmidt, "Partial Response Coding in Digital Subscriber Loops," *IEEE Globecom,* 1985, pp. 1322–28.

24. C. A. Belfiore and J. H. Parks, Jr., "Decision Feedback Equalization," *Proc. IEEE,* 67, (Aug. 1979), 1143–56.

25. A. Yongaçoğlu and K. Feher, "DCTPSK: An Efficient Modulation Technique for Differential Detection," *IEEE International Conference on Communications,* 1985, pp. 31.1.1–31.1.5.

26. J. S. Seo and K. Feher, "Performance of SQAM Systems in a Nonlinearly Amplified Multichannel Environment," *IEEE International Conference on Communications,* 1985, pp. 48.1.1–48.1.5.

27. J. W. Bayless, R. D. Pedersen, and J. C. Bellamy, "High Density Digital Data Transmission," *National Telecommunications Conference,* 1976, pp. 51.3-1–51.3-6.

28. K-T Wu, I. Sasase, and K. Feher, "Improved Efficiency 15-Level Modified Duobinary PRS Above the Nyquist Rate," *IEEE International Conference on Communications,* 1985, pp. 31.3.1–31.3.5.

29. K-T Wu and K. Feher, "Multi-level PRS/QPRS Above the Nyquist Rate," *IEEE International Conference on Communications,* 1985, pp. 31.4.1–31.4.5.

30. CCITT Yellow Book, Vol. VIII.1, *Data Communications Over the Telephone Network,* ITU, Geneva, (1981).

31. A. B. Carlson, *Communication Systems: An Introduction to Signals and Noise in Electrical Communication,* McGraw-Hill, New York, (1975).

32. J. M. Wozencroft and I. M. Jacobs, *Principles of Communication Engineering,* Wiley, New York, (1967).

33. H. Ishio, et al, "A New Multilevel Modulation and Demodulation System for Carrier Digital Transmission," *IEEE International Conference on Communications,* ICC-76, Philadelphia, PA, (June, 1976), pp. 29.7–29.12.

34. "ADX-120 Transmultiplexer," Brochure 523-0604791-102A3J, 7-1-85, Collins Transmission Systems Division, Rockwell International, Dallas, TX.

35. Specification for T1 Transmission Systems, Technical Advisory TA-34, AT&T, Bell Communications Research, Inc.

36. F. Bradley, "The Hidden Treasures of ESF," *Data Communications,* 15, no. 10, (Sept., 1986), 204–13.

37. S. C. Taylor, "ESF: Its Time Has Come," *Telephone Engineer & Management,* 91, no. 1, (Jan. 1, 1987), 98–99.

38. G. R. Ritchie, "SYNTRAN-A New Direction for Digital Transmission Terminals," *IEEE Communications Magazine,* 23, no. 11, (Nov. 1985), 20–25.

39. B. R. Saltzberg and H. M. Zydney, "Digital Data System: Network Synchronization," *Bell Sys. Tech. Jour,* 54, no. 5, (May–June, 1975), 879–92.

40. A. H. Burgi-Schmelz, W. J. Felts, and L. A. Palumbo, "Public Switched Digital Service Capability," *IEEE Globecom,* 2, (1985), 675–77.

41. C. W. Smith, "Accunet Switched 56 Service: A Dial-Up Digital Network," *IEEE Globecom,* 2, (1985), 678–80.

42. L. Lewin, *Telecommunications: An Interdisciplinary Survey,* Artech House, Inc., (1979).

43. B. Sklar, "A Structured Overview of Digital Communications—A Tutorial Overview," *IEEE Communications Magazine,* 21, no. 5, (Aug. 1983), 4–17 and 21, no. 7, (Oct., 1983), 6–21.

44. V. K. Bhargava, "Forward Error Correction Schemes for Digital Communications," *IEEE Communications Magazine,* 21, no. 1, (Jan. 1983), 11–19.

45. G. D. Forney, Jr., "Coding and Its Application in Space Communications," *IEEE Spectrum,* 7, no. 6, (June, 1970), 47–58.

46. R. J. McEliece, *The Theory of Information and Coding,* Addison-Wesley, Reading, MA, (1977).

47. G. C. Clark, Jr., and J. B. Cain, *Error Correction Coding for Digital Communication,* Plenum Press, New York, (1981).

48. A. J. Viterbi, "Convolutional Codes and Their Performance in Communication Systems," *IEEE Trans. Comm. Tech.,* COM-19, no. 5, (Oct. 1971), 751–72.

49. J. A. Heller and I. M. Jacobs, "Viterbi Decoding for Satellite and Space Communication," *IEEE Trans. Comm. Tech.,* COM-19, no. 5, (Oct. 1971), 835–48.

50. V. K. Bhargava, D. Haccoun, R. Matyas, and P. Nuspi, *Digital Communications by Satellite: Modulation, Multiple Access and Coding,* Wiley, New York, (1981).

51. G. Ungerboeck, "Channel Coding with Multilevel Phase Signals," *IEEE Trans. Information Theory,* IT-28, (Jan. 1982), 55–67.

52. "The Evolution of 64-State, 8-Dimensional Trellis Coded Modulation," *Modememos,* vol. 5, no. 2, Codex Corporation, Canton, MA, (Jan. 1986).

53. "Codex Develops High Speed Modem Technology to Transmit Data at 19.2 kb/s Over Voice Grade Lines," Codex Corporation News Release, Sept. 17, 1985.

54. J. E. McNamara, *Technical Aspects of Data Communication,* Digital Equipment Corporation, Bedford, MA, (1977).

55. J. Mazzaferro, "Program Emulation Role in Satellite Delay Compensation," *Communications News,* (March 1985), p. 61.

3

Video Encoding

Moving images are three-dimensional, the dimensions being horizontal, vertical, and time. However, the transmitted signal is simply a one-dimensional function of time. Accordingly, images for remote reproduction must be scanned both horizontally and vertically to provide for the transmission of each picture element or *pixel*. This chapter begins with a review of the standard analog techniques used for image transmission, then considers techniques for increasing picture quality. An understanding of the analog techniques has been found to be important in comprehending the digital techniques, which then form a major portion of the contents of this chapter. The chapter then continues with a discussion of the application of digital techniques in the improvement of video reception as well as their application in teleconference video at relatively low bit rates for transmission economy. Standards considerations and potential future applications then conclude the chapter.

3.1 ANALOG VIDEO STANDARDS

This section describes how an image is scanned to provide its analog video representation using the standards of the U.S. National Television Systems Committee (NTSC). Following this is a brief description of the European standards.

The image scanning sequence is performed horizontally, left to right, and vertically, top to bottom. The scanning of a black and white image is done at a rate of 60 *fields* per second, where a field consists of alternate horizontal scan lines. This field rate is numerically equal to the power line frequency to aid in minimizing the appearance of power line interference effects. A total of 525 horizontal scan lines are used and the scanning is interlaced, which means that the scanning sequence in terms of lines numbered from top to bottom is 1, 3, 5 . . . 523, 525, 2, 4, 6 . . . 524, 1, 3 . . . . This scan sequence is illustrated in Fig. 3.1 [Ref. 1]. Thus a picture is produced by 525 lines per frame, interlaced two to one. (About 7% of these lines are devoted to vertical retrace of the picture tube's beam.) The use of interlace helps to reduce flicker and to mask the line-to-line differences, and thus to make the scan lines less noticeable. Accordingly, a total of 30 pictures per second is transmitted. This rate, considering picture tube persistance as well as the image retention characteristics of the human eye, provides a picture that is relatively free of flicker. In reality, the eye is being presented a rapid sequence of still pictures, as is done in motion picture films, but the perceived effect is one of motion. The combination of 525 lines per picture and 30 pictures per second results in a scan frequency of 15 750 lines per second, corresponding to a 15 750 Hz fundamental frequency in the analog video waveform. The spectrum of the *monochrome* (black-and-white) video signal consists of concentrations of energy at 15 750 Hz and its harmonics up to about 4.2 MHz.

For color transmission, the vertical rate is modified to 59.94 fields per second, resulting in 15 734.2 lines per second, and consequent concentration of energy at a 15 734.2 Hz fundamental frequency and its harmonics. This modification avoids high-frequency multiples of 60 Hz.

The waveform of a typical scan line of a monochrome picture is shown in the upper half of Fig. 3.2, based upon NTSC standards. Note that the 63.5 μs period corresponds to the 15 750 Hz frequency, and that the higher amplitudes correspond to lower picture luminance. The standard picture has an *aspect ratio* of 4 to 3, which means that the picture is four units wide for every three units high. Corresponding to 525(1 − 0.07) = 488 lines in the vertical direction there should be the (4/3) × 488 or 650 pixels in the horizontal direction. However, transmission of this much resolution was not provided in the original standards because circuit components with adequately fast response were not available. Moreover, to keep the bandwidth within a 4.2 MHz value for spectral economy, the standards are based on a *Kell*

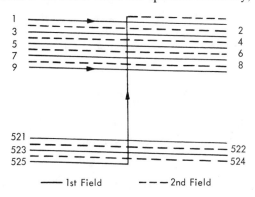

Figure 3.1 Image scan sequence. (Courtesy RCA, © 1959.)

— 1st Field   − − − 2nd Field

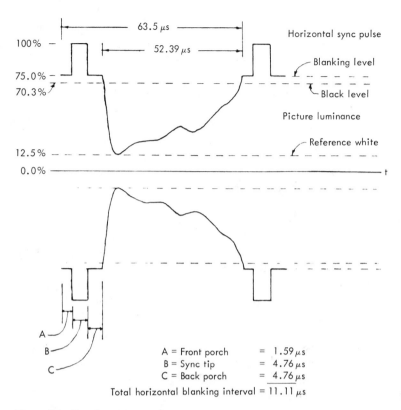

Figure 3.2 Envelope of radiated NTSC signal.

factor (ratio of vertical to horizontal size of pixel) of 0.66. Thus only $650 \times 0.66 = 429$ pixels must be produced along a horizontal line. According to Nyquist, with 52.39 μs per scan line, the required minimum bandwidth is 4.1 MHz. Many receivers actually reproduce the equivalent of only 330 pixels along a horizontal line.

Figure 3.2 actually shows the envelope of a carrier amplitude modulated with the video waveform, as is done in domestic television service. The term *negative polarity* is used to denote the fact that greater *luminance* is conveyed by lesser carrier amplitude. The amplitudes sometimes are described in *IRE units,* named after the Institute of Radio Engineers,* which was active in developing television standards. Figure 3.3 compares the modulation levels (negative half of the envelope) with the IRE units. As can be seen from Fig. 3.3, 1.6 IRE units correspond to 1.0% in terms of modulation percentage.

3.1.1 Color Transmission

Color transmission requires conveying both *hue* and *saturation* information along each scan line of the image. Hue is the color, while saturation is the extent to which the hue is mixed with white. Thus pink is low saturation red, while brilliant crimson

---

* In 1963, the IRE became a part of the Institute of Electrical and Electronics Engineers (IEEE).

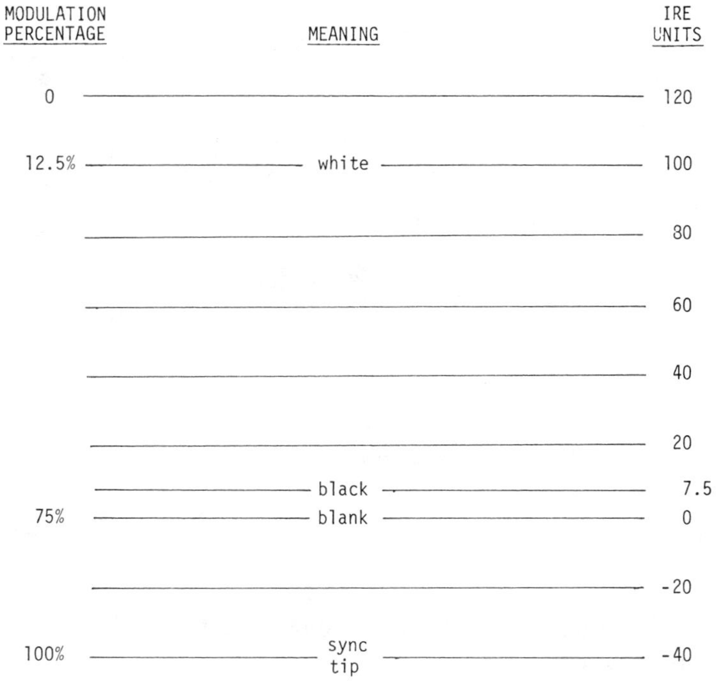

MODULATION PERCENTAGE	MEANING	IRE UNITS
0		120
12.5%	white	100
		80
		60
		40
		20
	black	7.5
75%	blank	0
		-20
100%	sync tip	-40

Figure 3.3 Comparison of video modulation levels with IRE units.

is high saturation red. To transmit color, a color subcarrier is inserted at the 455th harmonic of half the 15 734.2 Hz scan frequency, placing it at 3.579545 MHz, one of the many energy minima of the luminance spectrum. The amplitude of the color subcarrier represents the saturation information, with a large amplitude corresponding to a high saturation, or brilliant color and a low amplitude corresponding to a low saturation, or pale color. The phase of the color subcarrier represents hue. Proper phase detection by the receiver requires a phase reference, and this reference is sent at the beginning of every scan line by means of a color *burst,* consisting of at least 8 cycles of the color reference frequency sent during the back porch interval shown in Fig. 3.2. The peak-to-peak amplitude of the color burst equals 40 IRE units, i.e., the height of the sync tip over the blanking level.

In color television the three primary colors are red, green, and blue, and they are reproduced on the receiver screen by three corresponding beams. The proper combination of these three colors then can approximate any desired color. Thus, red and green can be combined to produce yellow, red plus blue yields purple, and green plus blue gives cyan. All three primary colors together produce white. Conversely, any image can be broken down into the three colors by using a system of dichroic mirrors which shunt the red and blue light to red and blue pickup tubes and allow the green to pass through to the green pickup tube, as shown in Fig. 3.4, [Ref. 1].

The use of a color television standard compatible with monochrome involves the production of a *composite* color signal based on four techniques: matrixing,

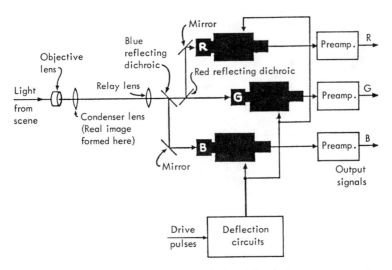

Figure 3.4 Simplified block diagram of optical and electrical components producing RGB signals. (Courtesy RCA, © 1959.)

bandshaping, quadrature amplitude modulation, and frequency interlace. These techniques are required because compatibility implies that (1) color transmissions can be received on monochrome receivers, (2) monochrome transmissions can be received on color receivers, (3) color or monochrome transmission can be accommodated within the same bandwidth.

Matrixing is a process for repackaging the information contained in the red, blue, and green signals for efficient use of the transmission channel. The matrix output signals are the Y (luminance) and the I and Q (chrominance) signals. The Y signal corresponds closely to the output of a monochrome camera, and thus provides good service to monochrome receivers. It is obtained by using a resistive combining network to produce a signal consisting of 30% red, 59% green, and 11% blue. The I and Q chrominance signals convey information which describes how the colors differ from monochrome. The I (in-phase) signal consists of 60% red, -28% green, and -32% blue, with the negative values being achieved using phase inversion. The Q (quadrature) signal is 21% red, -52% green, and 31% blue. The matrix then is as follows:

$$Y = 0.30R + 0.59G + 0.11B$$

$$I = 0.60R - 0.28G - 0.32B \qquad (3.1)$$

$$Q = 0.21R - 0.52G + 0.31B$$

Note that when red, green, and blue are equal, both I and Q go to zero, i.e., the result is a monochrome signal described by the Y component. This is required because "white" light, as perceived by the eye, actually results from a uniform spectrum often described as consisting of "all colors" of visible wavelengths.

Because the eye has less acuity in detecting variations in color than it has for resolving brightness differences, the I and Q signals do not require as much bandwidth as the Y signal, which uses a 4.2 MHz bandwidth to convey fine details. For color differences extending from orange to blue-green, which are handled by the I signal, a bandwidth of 1.5 MHz has been found to be adequate, whereas for color differences ranging from green to purple, which are handled by the Q signal, a 0.5 MHz bandwidth has been found sufficient.

As noted previously, a color subcarrier is inserted at an odd harmonic of half the line frequency. Since it is modulated at the 15 734.2 Hz line rate, the result is energy clusters at the color subcarrier frequency of 3.579545 MHz $\pm n$ 0.0157342 MHz, where n is any integer, including zero. These energy clusters fall between the clusters of the luminance signal in the spectrum and thus do not produce objectionable interference with it. The phase of the color subcarrier, moreover, reverses on successive scans of the same area of the picture. Thus interference from the color subcarrier tends to be self-canceling, especially since the eye responds to the average result of two or more scans.

The color subcarrier is quadrature amplitude modulated with the I and Q signals of Eq. (3.1). Figure 3.5 shows that the I signal lags the reference burst by an arbitrary 57° (chosen to simplify receiver design), and the Q signal lags I by 90°. Also shown is the phase and amplitude produced by pure red, i.e., blue and green are zero. The result is a 0.63 amplitude at a 346.5° phase. Figure 3.6, [Ref. 1], shows the subcarrier phase and amplitude values for the three primary colors and their one-to-one mixtures. This figure illustrates the direct relationship between the hue and the phase of the color subcarrier. The relationship between color saturation and amplitude is an indirect one. If the phase of the color subcarrier and the level of the monochrome signal remain constant, an increase in the amplitude of the subcarrier indicates an increase in color saturation, and vice versa.

Note that the Q component sidebands fall within the 4.2 MHz monochrome bandwidth whereas the I component upper sideband must be limited to about 0.6 MHz to conform to standard channel limitations. However, the full lower sideband of the I component is transmitted and used at the receiver.

The result, as described thus far, is called composite NTSC video. The color transmission is called *dot sequential,* which means that the red, green, and blue information is sent on a time division multiplexed basis, as illustrated in Fig. 3.7. As illustrated there, the R, G, and B signals can be viewed as modulating three sinusoidal carriers that differ from one another by 120° (refer to Fig. 3.6). Each

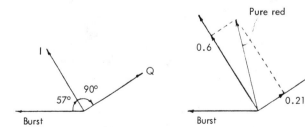

Figure 3.5 Phase relationships in modulation of color subcarrier for pure red.

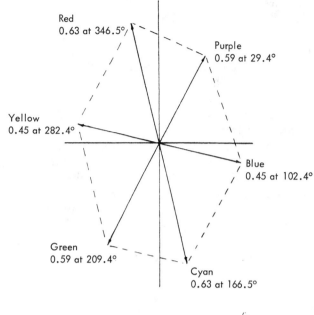

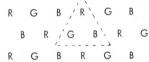

Figure 3.6 Composite vector diagram showing subcarrier phase and amplitude for each of six colors.

Figure 3.7 Dot sequential transmission of color.

picture element or *pixel* is represented by a triad. Interlace on alternate lines corresponds to frequency interleaving of the color and luminance components.

3.1.2 Modulation for Transmission

Section 3.1.1 showed that a composite video signal can be produced within a 4.2 MHz bandwidth. Standard television channels within the U.S. have a 6 MHz width. To accommodate both the composite video signal and a FM audio signal within a 6 MHz wide channel, the video amplitude modulates a picture carrier which is 1.25 MHz from the lower edge of the channel, and the lower sideband is heavily attenuated below 0.75 MHz from the picture carrier. Figure 3.8 shows the corresponding relationships, both in terms of frequencies within the channel and baseband frequencies relative to the picture carrier. The result is called *vestigial sideband* (VSB) transmission because only a vestige of the lower sideband is transmitted. The sound carrier level is 10% to 20% of the peak visual transmitter power. If the video is transmitted through a satellite or via a microwave radio system, FM video is used within a channel wide enough to accommodate all significant sidebands.

The spectrum shown in Fig. 3.8 is that which is transmitted. For the receiver to produce an undistorted baseband spectrum out of the detector, the receiver frequency response must attenuate the picture carrier frequency to 50% and must attenuate lower frequencies by a correspondingly greater amount.

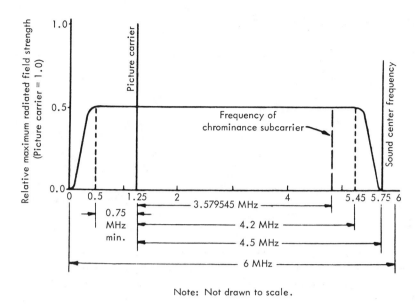

Note: Not drawn to scale.

Figure 3.8 Idealized picture transmission amplitude characteristic (transmitter output).

3.1.3 International Standards

The NTSC standards described for the U.S. are used also in Canada, Japan, Korea, Mexico, Panama, Peru, and the Netherlands Antilles. A 625-line, 50 fields/second system with a 4:3 aspect ratio is used in most other countries of the world. This system produces 15 625 lines/second and a video bandwidth of 5 MHz, although 5.5 MHz is used in the United Kingdom and Ireland, and 6 MHz is used in France, in eastern Europe, and in the USSR. A 7 to 8 MHz RF bandwidth is required for these systems. A special 819-line, 50 fields/second system with a 4:3 aspect ratio is used by some transmitters in France and Monaco. This system produces 20 475 lines/ second and operates with a 10 MHz video bandwidth and requires a 14 MHz RF bandwidth. The use of 50 fields/second in the above systems is geared to the 50 Hz power supply used in the corresponding countries. The resulting 25 pictures per second exhibits a slight degree of flicker, especially noticeable to those who are not accustomed to watching the pictures on a regular basis.

Systems of countries using the 625-line, 50 fields/second standard are compatible with one another on a monochrome basis, but use two different (incompatible) methods for color transmission. Both of these methods are similar in that they separate luminance and chrominance information, and transmit the chrominance in the form of two color difference signals which modulate a color subcarrier. The lack of compatibility results from the ways in which the chrominance information is processed. In one system, called *phase alternation line* (PAL), the phase of the subcarrier (4.43361875 MHz) is changed from line to line. This requires that a line switching signal be sent in addition to a color burst. The other system, *sequential*

TABLE 3.1 SPECIAL USES OF THE VERTICAL INTERVAL

Lines	Use
1, 2, 3	Equalizing pulse interval
4, 5, 6	Vertical sync pulse interval
7, 8, 9	Equalizing pulse interval
10, 11, 12	Unused (may be used for text services)
13, 14, 15, 16	Teletext or Videotex
17, 18	Vertical interval test signals (VITS)
19	Vertical interval reference (VIR)
20	Station identification (Field 1)
21	Captioning: Field 1—data
	Field 2—½ line framing code
22, 23, 24	Coded patterns for electronic identification of TV broadcast programs and spot announcements less than one second in duration

with memory (SECAM) has a color subcarrier that is frequency modulated alternately by the color difference signals. This switching is done by an electronic line-to-line switch. The switching information is transmitted as a line-switching signal.

3.1.4 Uses of the Vertical Interval

The vertical sync pulse has a length which is 0.07 to 0.08 of the overall vertical sweep. This means it consists of 19 to 21 or more lines per field. During the vertical retrace interval, the picture tube beam is blanked so it does not mar the picture. Table 3.1 lists special uses of the lines following the vertical sync pulse. The vertical interval test signals (VITS) consist of reference modulation levels for light intensity, transmission system test signals, and cue and control signals related to TV station operation. The vertical interval reference (VIR) provides chrominance, luminance, and black reference signals to the TV receiver to allow it to adjust itself automatically.

Text services such as Teletext and Videotex are discussed in Chap. 7.

3.2 TECHNIQUES FOR INCREASING PICTURE QUALITY

Advances in circuit technology during the 40 plus year period since the establishment of the existing analog television standards allow appreciable increases in picture quality. However, the standards are geared to circuit capabilities of a much earlier era. Standards cannot be changed significantly without obsoleting the billions of dollars (and other currencies) that the public has invested in television receivers. Thus efforts to increase picture quality are focused heavily on compatibility with existing standards.

3.2.1 Transmission Format Categories

Transmission formats can be categorized into the existing ones, enhanced formats, and high definition formats.

3.2.1.1 Existing Formats. The existing formats, NTSC, PAL, and SECAM, were described in Secs. 3.1.1 and 3.1.3. In attempting to improve quality within the framework of the existing formats, changes are required at the transmitter or the receiver or both. Section 3.2.2 describes a number of improvement techniques. As noted there, digital techniques are being applied before transmission and after detection. The use of such techniques results in some significant quality improvements.

3.2.1.2 Enhanced Quality. The concept of enhanced quality entails extended definition television (EDTV) in which a change in format is implemented, but the existing number of lines and aspect ratio are retained. Display can be done on existing receivers through the use of a format converter. An example is the provision of RGB inputs to receivers. Other examples are discussed in Sec. 3.2.2.

3.2.1.3 High Definition Television (HDTV). A high-definition format involves increased horizontal resolution, usually more than 1000 lines of vertical resolution, a wide aspect ratio (such as 2 : 1) and stereo sound. Systems using special HDTV formats are discussed in Sec. 3.2.3.

3.2.2 Improvement Techniques

Numerous techniques have been developed for the improvement of picture quality within the framework of the existing standards [Ref. 2]. Some, understandably, require the use of a format converter with the receiver.

3.2.2.1 Comb Filters. Sec. 3.1.1 described the interleaving of the luminance and chrominance components in the NTSC signal. This interleaving is done as a spectrum economy measure, allowing color to be transmitted entirely within the luminance bandwidth. However, some crosscoupling does exist between the luminance and chrominance components. This crosscoupling causes such picture artifacts as crawling color dots on the edges of alphanumerics as well as flashing colors on gray herringbone fabrics. Often receiver designers have chosen to reduce such problems by using a low-pass filter on the luminance signal. However, the result is degraded horizontal resolution. The comb filter for luminance, as the name implies, provides a separate passband for each multiple of 15 734.2 kHz above about 2.1 MHz and a stop band for each of the interleaved chrominance components. (The comb filter actually is implemented on a transversal, i.e., delay line, basis.) Significant picture improvements have been demonstrated through the use of comb filters [Ref. 2].

3.2.2.2 Digital Techniques. Digital techniques include pulse-code modulation (PCM) in handling the signal prior to transmission (see Sec. 3.3.5.1) and the use of digital processing within the television receiver (see Sec. 3.4). Digital techniques reduce the degradation resulting from cascades of encoders and decoders in the television plant. From an all-digital studio, the only NTSC encoding is just prior to the last over-the-air link to the receiver.

3.2.2.3 Apparent Resolution. The apparent resolution of a display can be improved in two ways. One is through the elimination of the line structure artifacts that are inherent in the interlace scanning of displays. These artifacts include (1) vertical aliasing, in which nearly horizontal lines exhibit jumps (from one scan line to the next), and (2) flicker at the 30 Hz rate of the aliasing components, which may result in the appearance of horizontal motion along nearly horizontal lines. Such line structure artifacts can be eliminated by using two-field addition electronically, based upon storing the previous field on a chip.

A second way of improving the apparent resolution of a display starts with an HDTV camera providing 1049 lines, 2 : 1 interlaced. Double-rate scanning then is done using interpolation from a frame store, [Ref. 2]. On rapidly moving objects, double images could result, so a technique called motion adaptation (see Sec. 3.3.6.3) is used in substituting the previous field line for intrafield interpolation.

3.2.2.4 Time-Multiplexed Analog Components (TMAC). The foregoing discussion has demonstrated some of the problems that result from the use of a color subcarrier. Not only does the resulting spectral interleaving of luminance and chrominance components result in cross-coupling between them, but in FM transmission the color subcarrier is in the part of the baseband which is adversely affected by the FM noise spectrum. The pre-emphasis and de-emphasis used in FM transmission only partially correct this problem.

In TMAC each luminance line is time compressed from 53.3 μs to 40.0 μs, i.e., by 1.33 : 1. One chrominance signal, e.g., I, then is time compressed from 53.3 μs to 13.3 μs, i.e., by 4 : 1. The remaining 10.3 μs is used for line sync, sound, and auxiliary data. After the next luminance line, the other chrominance signal, e.g., Q, is sent.

As a result of the foregoing changes, the vertical chrominance resolution is reduced by about 2 : 1, thus becoming comparable to the resolution of the horizontal chrominance. The luminance bandwidth is increased to $1.33 \times 4.2 = 5.6$ MHz. For a fixed FM deviation and transmission system bandwidth, the luminance noise increases, but the chrominance noise is lower. Overall, this provides a subjective improvement. Compared with the FM transmission of composite video, TMAC results in a softer FM threshold (see Chap. 4), better color fidelity on receivers with RGB inputs, and better balance between chrominance and luminance noise. TMAC applications are discussed in Sec. 3.6.

3.2.2.5 Extended Aspect Ratio. The objective of extended aspect ratio television is motion picture distribution by direct broadcast satellite (DBS) or by cable television. Typical NTSC receivers overscan by about 5 μs horizontally and about 10 lines vertically. Overall, about 28% of the frame time is used for the horizontal and vertical retrace functions. An aspect ratio of 5 : 3 could be reached either by nonlinear horizontal compression of the image in the overscan region (beyond the displayed edges), or by encroachment into the blanking region [Ref. 2]. An aspect ratio of 1.85 : 1, a wide-screen motion picture standard, could be reached by an additional compression factor of about 5% in the visible portion of the image.

3.2.2.6 Compatible High-Definition Television. The approach to achieving an HDTV signal that is compatible with existing standards is to use two standard channels, one of which carries a standard signal, while the other channel carries the high definition components and the outer panels of the wide scene.

3.2.3 Systems Using High-Definition Formats

The motivations for high-definition television (HDTV) include display improvement for large-screen, e.g., projection, receivers, as well as added realism in video conferencing services. The quality objective in HDTV is achievement of the quality of 35 mm color film. The proposed systems range from 1023 to 2125 lines/frame, corresponding to 16 MHz to 50 MHz luminance bandwidths, with some smaller bandwidths in the case of video compression. Proposed aspect ratios range from 4:3 to 8:3. The standard recommended by the U.S. Advanced Television Systems Committee (ATSC),* HDTV Technology Group to the U.S. State Department for CCIR implementation worldwide has 1125 lines/frame, a 5.33:3 aspect ratio, 60 fields/second, and 2:1 interlace. The 1125 lines/frame will be noted to be a compromise between twice the North American 525 line and twice the European 625 line standards.

A system whose parameters are very close to the one recommended by the ASTC is that of the Japanese Broadcasting Corporation (NHK) which provides a 5:3 aspect ratio and can be transcoded to 525 or 625 lines for compatibility with existing standards. The NHK system has a luminance bandwidth of 20 MHz and chrominance bandwidths of 7.0 MHz (*I*) and 5.5 MHz (*Q*). The chrominance information may be contained *partially or totally* within the luminance bandwidth. Delivery to the home would be via DBS, CATV, or 11 GHz broadcast.

NHK also has developed a 250 Mb/s digital HDTV system requiring a 150 MHz bandwidth using QPSK. The p_{be} should be $\leq 10^{-5}$, which can be achieved if $C/N \geq 18.8$ dB. The system uses both intraframe and interframe coding, which are discussed in Sec. 3.3.

A "semi-compatible" U.S. HDTV system using 1051 lines/frame and providing a 4.7:3 aspect ratio with 2:1 interlace has a 15.1 MHz luminance bandwidth and a 0.55 Kell factor. Stereo audio is provided. The chrominance is sent using QAM, as in NTSC, with chrominance/luminance frequency interleaving, using a color subcarrier frequency of $(18/5) \times 3.579$ MHz = 12.88 MHz. The chrominance bandwidths are 4.8 MHz (*I*) and 2.3 MHz (*Q*). Delivery to the home would be via satellite or CATV.

A system called Multiple Sub-Nyquist Sampling Encoding (MUSE) has been developed by NHK for home delivery using UHF television. The total bandwidth required is less than 9 MHz, allowing the transmission to be achieved in 1 1/2

---

* The ATSC is a group established jointly by the Electronics Industries Association (EIA), the Institute of Electrical and Electronics Engineers (IEEE), the National Association of Broadcasters (NAB), The National Cable Television Association (NCTA), and the Society of Motion Picture and Television Engineers (SMPTE).

standard 6 MHz channel widths [Ref. 3]. The principles of motion detection and compensation used in this system are described in Sec. 3.3.6.3. MUSE is a 1125 lines/frame, 60 fields/second, 2:1 interlace system with a 16:9 aspect ratio. The occupied bandwidth (-6 dB) is 8.1 MHz. Effective bandwidths are as follows:

For stationary portions of the picture

> 20–22 MHz for luminance
> 7 MHz for chrominance

For moving portions of the picture

> 12.5 MHz for luminance
> 3.1 MHz for chrominance

Several of the digital techniques discussed in Sec. 3.3 are used in achieving these effective bandwidths. Sub-Nyquist sampling, i.e., sampling at a rate less than twice the video bandwidth, normally would cause aliasing distortion. However, the energy in the video signals is concentrated at multiples of the line frequency. The sub-Nyquist rate is chosen so that the aliasing components are interleaved between the video spectral lines (luminance and chrominance). Sinusoidal jitter must be kept to a minimum if sub-Nyquist sampling is to be used successfully.

3.3 DIGITAL VIDEO CODING

The advantages of digital transmission delineated in Chap. 2 are especially pertinent in video transmission where the need exists to reproduce a high-quality color image at a distance. Also important, however, is the channel capacity required for the transmission. To this end, an understanding of the characteristics of both the source and the receiver is important, together with the statistical properties of both video signals and the human visual system. This section includes a discussion of the two major categories of digital video coding: intraframe and interframe, as well as hybrid coding.

3.3.1 Source and Receiver Statistics

In achieving coding efficiency, i.e., a minimum number of bits/pixel, redundancies in the source image can be exploited. For example, an image that contains large runs of the same brightness level can be encoded with a set of bits that represents that brightness level plus an indication as to the location (start and end) of the run (see Sec. 3.3.5.5).

Receiver statistics also affect the number of bits/pixel required in image coding. For example, if the receiver is a human viewer, the coding can be based upon what is called the *differential sensitivity* of the eye [Ref. 4]. This includes (1) picture-independent sensitivity variations and (2) picture-dependent sensitivity variations. In the first category, the noise-detection threshold increases with increasing noise frequency, i.e., finer grained noise is not as noticeable as coarser grained noise at a given luminosity. In the second category, the noise-detection threshold increases with increasing picture detail and also increases with increasing luminance. Because of such properties of the human visual system, certain levels of detail can be omitted from a picture without the viewer noticing the omission. However, this is not true if the receiver is a computer. In that event the coding preferably is of the information-preserving or reversible type.

Other factors in video encoding are the permissible level of complexity of the coder as well as channel requirements. Most telecommunications channels are the constant rate type, which call for a constant rate coder or the buffering of the data for transmission at a constant rate.

3.3.2 Video Signal Characteristics

A video signal can be characterized by its power spectrum, autocorrelation function and probability density functions.

3.3.2.1 Power Spectrum. Figure 3.9, [Ref. 4], shows the power spectrum of a typical video signal. Note that at 4 MHz the relative power is about −50 dB relative to the level at the lowest frequencies, and that the envelope is nearly flat out to about twice the line rate (about 31 kHz for NTSC video), beyond which the spectrum drops at about 6 dB per octave. The low frequencies provide the large area brightness levels while the high frequencies provide the picture edges. This is why the high frequencies, in spite of their low level, are very important. Picture edges must be reproduced sharply and accurately, but constitute only a negligible portion of the area of a picture. For this reason their relative power level is low.

3.3.2.2. Autocorrelation Function. A typical horizontal autocorrelation function of a picture is shown in Fig. 3.10, [Ref. 4]. The vertical autocorrelation function is similar to it. The autocorrelation function is related to the power spectral density by the Fourier transform. Correlation indicates the amount of redundant information present in a signal. Redundancies can be removed by the use of linear prediction or preemphasis filters, which thus allow a reduction in the required

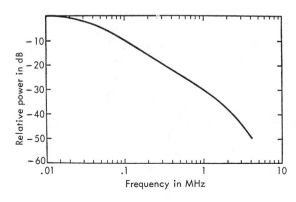

Figure 3.9 Typical spectrum of a video signal. (From D. J. Connor, R. C. Brainard, and J. O. Limb, "Interframe Coding for Picture Transmission," *Proc. IEEE,* July 1972, © 1972, IEEE. Reprinted by permission.)

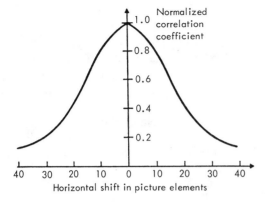

Figure 3.10 Typical autocorrelation function of a video signal, horizontal direction. (From D. J. Connor, R. C. Brainard, and J. O. Limb, "Intraframe Coding for Picture Transmission," *Proc. IEEE*, July 1972, © 1972, IEEE. Reprinted by permission.)

average number of bits per pixel. The inverse filter then is used at the receiver. Substantial average power reduction is possible using correlation with just the previous element. Often little further reduction is found possible using more of the adjacent elements on the same or preceding lines.

In general, the correlation between pixels decays exponentially with distance in any direction. The greatest part of the linear redundancy can be removed by using either the horizontally adjacent or the vertically adjacent element.

3.3.2.3 Probability Density Functions. The amplitude density or luminance density is nonuniform for single pictures but uniform for ensembles of pictures [Ref. 5]. The horizontal element difference density is highly peaked at zero, a fact useful in estimating the redundancy in a video signal.

As an example of the use of horizontal element difference density, [Ref. 5], a 5-bit original picture was found to have an average entropy (information content) of 2.6 bits/pixel, meaning that 2.4 bits/pixel of redundancy can be removed via linear prediction using only the previous picture element. Correspondingly, 6-bit originals have been found [Ref. 6] to have an average of 1.85 bit/pixel for simple scenes to 3.36 bits/pixel for complex scenes.

3.3.3 Characteristics of the Human Visual System

The differential sensitivity of the eye was noted in Sec. 3.3.1. Since the noise detection threshold increases with increasing noise frequency except at very low frequencies, high-frequency noise tends to mask quantization noise. In addition, the fact that the noise detection threshold increases with increasing luminance can be exploited by logarithmic compression/decompression.

Figure 3.11 [Ref. 7] illustrates the sine-wave response of the human visual system based upon a 1 MHz (262-line) image viewed at a 1 meter distance. The eye tends to act like a low-pass filter and to obscure irregularities of a fine-grained nature. Figure 3.12 [Ref. 8] shows the normalized impulse response of the human visual system, also based upon a 1 MHz (262-line) image viewed at a 1 meter distance. This impulse response is called the point spread function of the eye in psychophysical literature [Ref. 9].

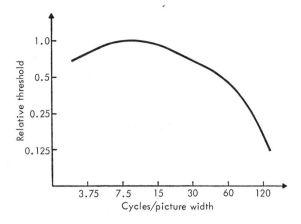

Figure 3.11 Sine-wave response of the human visual system. (Reprinted with permission from the *AT&T Technical Journal,* © 1967, AT&T.)

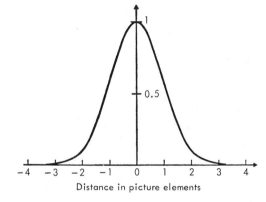

Figure 3.12 Normalized impulse response of the human visual system. (Reprinted with permission from the *AT&T Technical Journal,* © 1969, AT&T.)

3.3.4 Picture Coding Approaches

Numerous approaches have been developed for picture coding, as outlined in Fig. 3.13. Space permits a discussion of only the more commonly applied ones here. Underlying many of the approaches is the concept of allowing for distortions that are least objectionable to the human eye, and removing redundancies. A knowledge of the image source as well as the characteristics of human vision thus are important in determining what image information is required and what types of distortion are acceptable.

The concept of reversibility in coding often arises. A *reversible* process is one in which the original signal can be reconstructed. An example is the generation and transmission of a difference signal. The original can be restored by integration at the receiver. In an *irreversible* process information is lost irretrievably. However, in proper design, that which is irretrievable has been deemed to be insignificant. An example is quantization, in which the signals lying between decision levels all are assigned to a given level. In general, bit reduction on a reversible basis can be done if the symbols from the quantizer have a nonuniform probability distribution (variable word length coding), or if the symbols from the quantizer are statistically

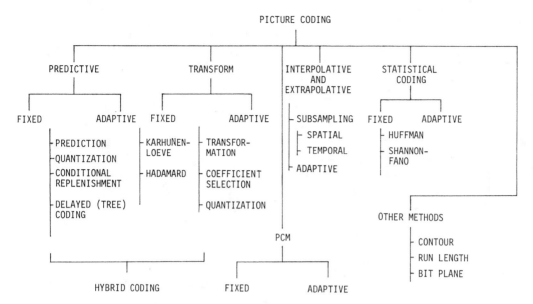

Figure 3.13 Approaches for picture coding.

dependent, i.e., redundant, in which case linear prediction techniques (see Sec. 3.3.5) can be used.

The digital coding of video signals, irrespective of the method used, allows picture quality to be determined largely by terminal equipment rather than by the transmission medium. In fact, error control techniques, as described in Sec. 2.11, can improve the tolerance of a digital video system to channel bit errors. Moreover, digital video can be encrypted to protect privacy. Digital transmission at reduced bit rates also is advantageous in terms of reducing the required power for transmission. Figure 3.14 [Ref. 10] illustrates the fact that as the radio channel bandwidth is decreased for an analog FM system, increased transmitter power is required because the FM improvement factor (see Chap. 4) decreases. For digital transmission, however, the lower bit rates, achieved by careful video coding, require less bandwidth, and because the noise power in the channel is correspondingly lower, the transmitter power can be decreased.

3.3.5 Intraframe Coding

Numerous intraframe video coding techniques have been developed. This section begins with PCM and then describes differential PCM (DPCM) and other techniques useful in reducing the number of bits/pixel. Note that in discussing intraframe coding, the issue of motion is not present. Accordingly, the measure used is bits/pixel since the coding is done based on the pixels of a given picture, and not on the basis of picture changes from frame to frame.

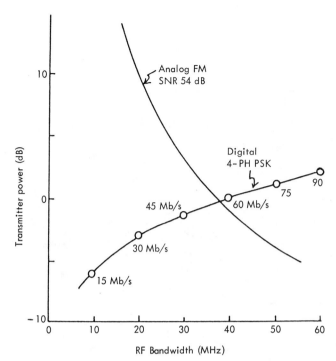

Figure 3.14 Relative transmitter power levels required for analog and digital video as functions of RF bandwidth. (From H. Kaneko and T. Ishiguro, "Digital Television Transmission Using Bandwidth Compression Techniques," *IEEE Communications Magazine*, July 1980, © 1980, IEEE. Reprinted by permission.)

3.3.5.1 Pulse Code Modulation (PCM). Pulse code modulation (PCM) is a commonly used technique for converting an analog waveform to a sequence of bits. Several steps are required. First, the waveform is band limited to a specific maximum frequency. In the case of NTSC video, this maximum is 4.2 MHz. This band limiting process then allows the application of the Nyquist sampling theorem, which states that a waveform of bandwidth W can be reconstructed completely if it is sampled at regular intervals at a rate of at least $2W$. The samples are pulses each of whose amplitudes equals the amplitude of the original waveform at the sampling instant. The sampling process can be described as follows. Let $f(t)$ be a bandlimited signal that has no spectral components above W Hz. Multiply $f(t)$ by a uniform train of impulse functions $\delta_T(t)$. The product function $f(t)\delta_T(t)$ is a sequence of impulses located at regular intervals of T seconds and having amplitudes equal to the values of $f(t)$ at the corresponding instants. Figure 3.15 provides a parallel illustration of what is happening in the time domain (left side of figure) and the frequency domain (right side of figure). The sampling function $\delta_T(t)$ has a spectrum consisting of a fundamental at $\omega_o = 2\pi/T$ and its harmonics. The sampled function, $f_s(t)$, is the pulse amplitude modulated sequence. Its frequency domain representation, $F_s(\omega)$, consists of a set of spectral functions which are nonoverlapping if the sampling rate is at least $2W$. The filtered response to these pulses, Fig. 3.17(g), represents the reconstructed waveform at the receiver.

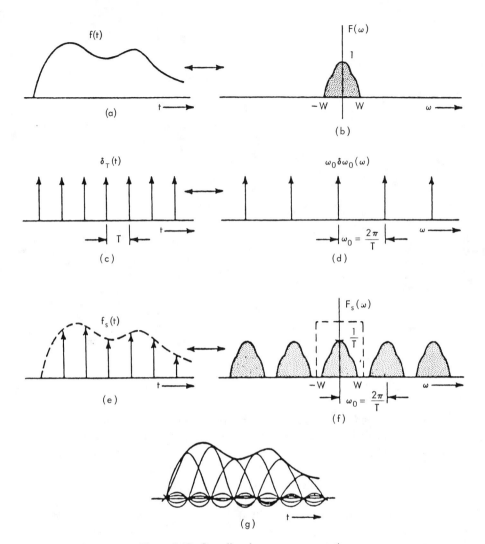

Figure 3.15 Sampling theorem representation.

In analytical terms, letting $f_s(t)$ be the sampled function,

$$f_s(t) = f(t)\delta_T(t) = \sum_{n=-\infty}^{\infty} f(nT)\delta(t - nT) \tag{3.2}$$

Let $F(\omega)$ be the frequency spectrum of $f(t)$. The Fourier transform of $f(t)\delta_T(t)$, according to the frequency convolution theorem, is given by

$$2\pi f_s(t) \leftrightarrow F(\omega) * \omega_o \delta_{\omega_o}(\omega) \tag{3.3}$$

Let $\omega_o = 2\pi/T$,

$$f_s(t) \leftrightarrow (1/T)F(\omega) * \delta_{\omega_o}(\omega) \tag{3.4}$$

The convolution of $F(\omega)$ and $\delta_{\omega_o}(\omega)$ is shown in Fig. 3.15(f). As seen there, this function reproduces every ω_o radians. If $\omega_o > 2\pi W$, the spectral representations of $F(\omega)$ do not overlap, i.e., $2\pi/T \geq 2(2nW)$, or $T \leq 1/2W$. Thus, if $f(t)$ is sampled at regular intervals less than $1/2W$ seconds apart, the sampled spectral density function $F_s(\omega)$ will be a periodic replica of the true $F(\omega)$. Accordingly, $F_s(\omega)$ contains all of the information of $f(t)$. $F(\omega)$ can be recovered from $F_s(\omega)$ by low-pass filtering the sampled signal to allow only frequency components below W Hz to pass.

From the foregoing, one can see that if $2\pi/T < 2(2\pi W)$, or $T > 1/2W$, the spectral repetitions of $F(\omega)$ will overlap, with a result known as *aliasing*, a form of distortion in which higher frequency components are folded over half the sampling frequency and appear superimposed on the desired signal.

The steps required to produce PCM are shown in Fig. 3.16. Sampling is accomplished by the pulse train generator input to the amplitude modulator, whose output is a pulse-amplitude modulated (PAM) sequence. The quantizer assigns a binary number to each sample. This binary number is the one that most closely describes the amplitude of the input at the sampling instant, as illustrated in Fig. 3.17. The vertical lines designate the sampling instants while the horizontal lines designate the quantized levels.

A total of 2^m gray levels can be implemented by describing each sampled value by a sequence of m bits. If an insufficient number of bits is used, one or both of two types of distortion may become evident. The first is called *contouring,* and is illustrated in Fig. 3.18 for a picture of medium complexity and in Fig. 3.19 for a highly detailed picture. In both figures, (a) is the original picture, and (b) is the picture quantized at 4 bits. Note the obvious contouring at 4 bits, and the fact that this contouring is noticeable especially in large areas of slowly varying brightness.

The second type of distortion resulting from an insufficient number of quantization bits is *quantizing noise*. As will be noted from Fig. 3.17, the process of quantization entails the production of small luminance errors which generally are random and appear as noise in the picture.

The use of 8 bits per sample has become established as the number required to digitize an image satisfactorily, [Ref. 11, 12], based upon viewer tests, although much of the work on video coding has been based upon tricking the eye into accepting a much smaller number, at least on the basis of an average number of bits/pixel.

The quantizing levels normally are spaced evenly, but nonlinear quantization has proven helpful in reducing the number of bits/pixel, based upon the nonlinear properties of the eye.

The last step in producing PCM is *coding*. The word coding here refers to the assignment of a particular set of binary digits to a particular luminance level, as illustrated in Fig. 3.17 for the case of 3-bit coding.

The satisfactory reception of PCM video generally requires a $p_{be} \leq 10^{-4}$. In addition to bit errors, jitter and slips also can affect video performance adversely.

3.3.5.1.1 Composite Video Coding.   The discussion thus far has not specified how color is handled in PCM coding. In composite signal coding, the composite waveform (NTSC, PAL, or SECAM) is coded as such, with the color subcarrier and sync pulses being a part of the waveform. Sampling often is done at three times the

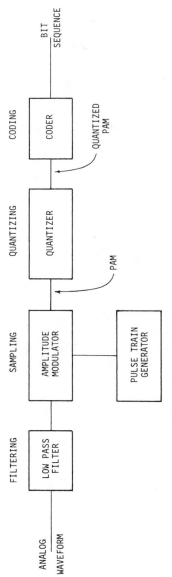

Figure 3.16 Steps in producing PCM.

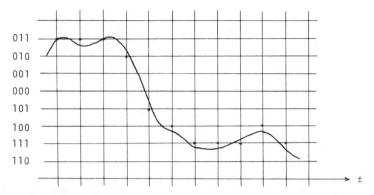

Figure 3.17 Quantization of analog waveform.

Figure 3.18 Contouring in a scene of medium complexity. (Courtesy Dr. Edward J. Delp, Laboratory for Information and Signal Processing, Purdue University, West Lafayette, IN.)

color subcarrier frequency, or at 10.74 MHz in the case of NTSC. This sampling rate is about 2.5 times the 4.2 MHz bandwidth. A multiple of the subcarrier frequency is convenient since this frequency is readily available and precisely controlled. At 8 bits/pixel (sample), the resulting bit rate for NTSC is 85.92 Mb/s, which can be transmitted readily, at twice the DS3 rate of about 90 Mb/s.

Broadcasters often use composite video coding because it can be interfaced easily with studio analog equipment. Thus decoding and reencoding of the analog signal is not needed. However, composite video coding is not the best for digital signal processing tasks such as special effects and expanded pictures. It retains the quality compromises inherent in the composite analog systems such as limited chrominance bandwidth, cross-coupling between luminance and chrominance, and edge effects. It is subject to subcarrier phase problems as well as problems in video tape program editing.

Figure 3.19 Contouring in a scene of high complexity. (Courtesy Dr. Edward J. Delp, Laboratory for Information and Signal Processing, Purdue University, West Lafayette, IN.)

3.3.5.1.2 Component Video Coding. Component video coding refers to the coding of the individual RGB components, and is used often in digital image distribution between units having digital input and output interfaces. A matrix is used which converts the RGB camera outputs into a luminance (Y) signal and two color difference signals, R-Y and B-Y. The three components then are digitized individually by separate PCM converters.

The three components may be combined with sync and then time-division multiplexed into a serial bit stream, or may be distributed in serial-parallel form. With component coding, the luminance and chrominance bandwidths are not constrained by the composite standards. As a result, special effects and expanded pictures can be handled without degradation. A component coded signal still can be transmitted at a 90 Mb/s rate, if required. One arrangement for doing this uses a grid of 512 horizontal by 480 vertical pixels that are 8-bit coded and sampled at 30 pictures/second. The resultant luminance signal requires 59 Mb/s. Color is added by sampling each component, with a result of 59 Mb/s $\times$ 3 = 177 Mb/s. Reduction of the sampling rate to 15 pictures/second allows transmission at nearly 90 Mb/s, but requires special sample sequencing to avoid the appearance of flicker.

A further advantage of component coding is that it allows the international adoption of CCIR Recommendation 601 as a set of basic digital television parameters, as discussed in Sec. 3.6.

Component coding arrangements can be described by an *extensible* family of digital codes, [Ref. 13], which use a simple ratio to relate the sampling frequencies of the luminance and the color difference signals. Three digits, $a : b : c$, are used, in which a is a symbol for the Y signal sampling frequency, b represents the R-Y frequency, and c represents the B-Y frequency. In most codes considered thus far, $b = c$. In this family of codes the luminance and color difference frequencies are related in the ratio $4 : 2 : 2$, with the actual frequencies being multiples of 2.25 MHz, the lowest common multiple of the line frequencies in 525/60 and 625/50 systems.

The recommended luminance signal sampling frequency is 13.5 MHz, and the sampling frequency for each color difference signal is 6.75 MHz, with tolerances corresponding to the tolerance for the line frequency of the relevant color television standard, [Ref. 13, Table 1]. The 4 : 2 : 2 member is applicable to studio distribution and exchange. For top quality production, 4 : 4 : 4 might be used. In this member all sampling frequencies are 13.5 MHz. For documentaries, the 4 : 1 : 1 or 2 : 1 : 1 member might be used. The CCIR luminance sampling frequency, 13.5 MHz, is designated as "4" in the ratios. Thus, this ratio arrangement provides a family of codes related in a binary manner, with each member being associated with a program quality level.

For the 4 : 2 : 2 member of the family, the use of 8 bits per sample results in 108 Mb/s for luminance and a total of 108 Mb/s for the two-color difference signals, for a total bit rate of 216 Mb/s. However, note that bits must be added for timing information, general housekeeping, and audio, but some of the horizontal and vertical blanking intervals of the picture will not be digitized. Adjustments in signal parameters will be needed for transmission purposes if a level of the digital hierarchy (see Chap. 2) is used, depending on the national standards being followed. Often these adjustments are achieved using the intraframe or interframe coding techniques described in the remainder of this chapter.

3.3.5.2 Differential PCM (DPCM).

Differential PCM (DPCM) is used in many telecommunications applications in which an analog signal must be coded at rates lower than can be achieved by the brute-force PCM approach. The DPCM principle can be applied on either an intraframe or an interframe basis, but here is discussed as an intraframe technique. It can be applied on either a component or composite basis. DPCM is based on sending differences rather than total input values. The difference that is sent is obtained by subtracting from the input a predicted value of the input, based upon the past history of the encoded signal. The term *predictive coding* often is used to describe those techniques which work on a differential basis. Note that the difference is not taken between the present and the previous input value because this approach could allow an accumulation of quantizing errors at the receiver and consequent gross streaking in the received image.

Error bursts in the channel may produce a "streaking" effect in DPCM video transmission as a result of the feedback action. These streaks cease, however, at the end of the scan line in which the error burst ended.

Figure 3.20 illustrates the intraframe DPCM principle of operation using the approach known as analog differencing and integration. The *integrator* obtains a weighted sum of all of the past differences and uses this as its prediction of the decoded sample value. The decoder and integrator units in the transmitter and the receiver are identical. The coder and decoder need handle only the dynamic range of the difference signal in using analog differencing and integration.

As implied by Figure 3.20(a), the difference between the input and the prediction is quantized into one of 2^m levels and a code m bits long is transmitted indicating which of the levels has occurred. If $m = 2$, the result is called *delta coding*. A tapered scale may be used to assure that large differences are quantized more

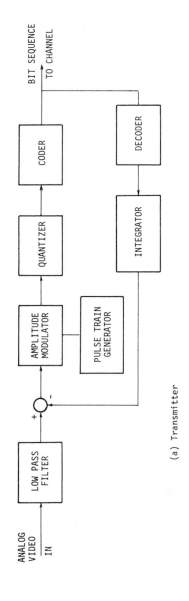

(a) Transmitter

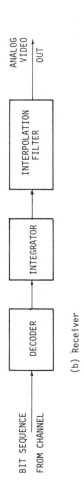

(b) Receiver

Figure 3.20 Intraframe DPCM principle of operation.

coarsely than small ones. Figure 3.21, [Ref. 4, Fig. 5], illustrates a tapered quantization scale.

The advantages of DPCM for intraframe coding are that it can exploit source (image) properties by using appropriate linear or nonlinear prediction algorithms. It can exploit receiver (human eye) properties by an appropriate selection of the quantizing scale. However, DPCM is subject to several impairments. *Slope overload* is an impairment in which a sudden change in luminosity along a scan line cannot be represented by the differentials as the sudden change that it is. Figure 3.22 illustrates this problem. A related problem, *granular noise,* also shown in Fig.

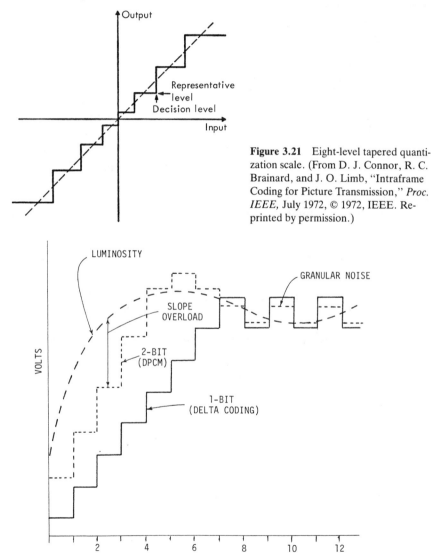

Figure 3.21 Eight-level tapered quantization scale. (From D. J. Connor, R. C. Brainard, and J. O. Limb, "Intraframe Coding for Picture Transmission," *Proc. IEEE,* July 1972, © 1972, IEEE. Reprinted by permission.)

Figure 3.22 Slope overload distortion.

3.22, results from the finite size limits of the quantizer steps. This problem becomes especially severe in the 1-bit case of DPCM known as delta coding. Slope overload can be reduced by the use of larger steps, but larger steps increase the granular noise. Techniques for reducing the magnitudes of these problems are discussed later in this section.

3.3.5.3 Noise-Feedback Coding.

The principle of using feedback to reduce the errors generated within a system is well established [Ref. 14]. This principle is used in the noise-feedback coder as a means of reducing quantization noise, which is detected by subtracting the input to the quantizer from the output. It can be applied to DPCM video on either a component or composite basis. The noise then is filtered to emphasize its high-frequency components and then is subtracted from the input signal, as shown in Fig. 3.23, [Ref. 4, Fig. 6]. In operation, the noise causes the quantizer to oscillate between levels, thus obscuring the quantization contours which otherwise would be apparent in the picture. The average output is maintained equal to the input.

An alternative method for reducing granular noise is the addition of dither prior to quantization [Ref. 15]. The probability density function of the dither signal (noise) should be rectangular and should have an amplitude equal to the step size of the quantizer. Figure 3-24(a), [Ref. 4, Fig. 7], shows the quantizer output and the perceived luminance without dither, while Figure 3-24(b), [Ref. 4, Fig. 7], shows the output and perceived luminance with dither. As can be seen, the addition of dither makes the perceived luminance follow the actual input more closely. With dither, the perceived waveform lies closer to the input waveform because visual filtering attenuates the error, which now is at higher spatial frequencies. The retinal size of the pixel determines the effectiveness of this technique since the size of the pixel (visibility of high-frequency error) decreases as the square of the viewing distance. If the dither is made pseudorandom, it can be reproduced at the receiving end, (see Sec. 2.11), and subtracted there. As a result, the rms noise level is cut in half.

The addition of high-frequency noise to the signal before quantization has been done in two ways: (1) a closed-loop technique using noise feedback and (2) an

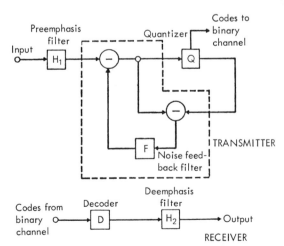

Figure 3.23 Noise-feedback coder. (From D. J. Connor, R. C. Brainard, and J. O. Limb, "Inraframe Coding for Picture Transmission," *Proc. IEEE,* July 1972, © 1972, IEEE. Reprinted by permission.)

open-loop approach using an additive dither signal [Ref. 4]. The closed loop direct feedback coder is shown in Fig. 3.25 [Ref. 16]. The integrating amplifier is functionally equivalent to the loop inside the dashed lines in the block diagram of the noise-feedback coder. Filters H and H^{-1} have characteristics that are based upon the assumption that the quantizer adds uncorrelated noise to the signal. These characteristics are determined by the signal spectrum, the frequency weighting function for the visibility of uncorrelated noise, and the transfer function of the amplifier A, which consists of a simple integration with a long time constant.

The open-loop approach with dither is based upon using a 3- or 4-bit PCM encoder operating on a signal to which noise has been added. The advantage is simplicity. The dither may be both temporal, e.g., with a two-frame period, and spatial, e.g., pseudorandom, to disperse the flickering contours. The noise visibility is greatest when the original signal coincides with a quantizer decision level, and decreases rapidly as the correlation changes from $+1$ to -1.

3.3.5.4 Special Time Domain Coding Techniques.
Time domain encoding is done assuming that the video image, either component or composite, consists of a large array of separate pixels, which are obtained by sampling the video wave-

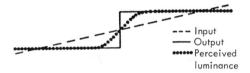

--- Input
— Output
•••••• Perceived luminance

(a) Quantizer output and perceived luminance without dither

Figure 3.24 Alternative noise-feedback coder performance. (From D. J. Connor, R. C. Brainard, and J. O. Limb, "Intraframe Coding for Picture Transmission," *Proc. IEEE,* July 1972, © 1972, IEEE. Reprinted by permission.)

(b) Quantizer output and perceived luminance with dither

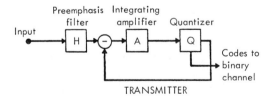

Preemphasis filter   Integrating amplifier   Quantizer

Input → H → ⊖ → A → Q → Codes to binary channel

TRANSMITTER

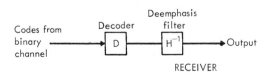

Codes from binary channel → Decoder D → Deemphasis filter H^{-1} → Output

RECEIVER

Figure 3.25 Closed loop direct feedback coder. (From R. C. Brainard and J. C. Candy, "Direct Feedback Coders: Design and Performance with Television Signals," *Proc. IEEE,* May 1969, © 1969, IEEE. Reprinted by permission.)

form at or above the Nyquist rate [Ref. 4]. In flat regions (areas without detail), the amplitude should be encoded accurately, whereas at edges, some amplitude distortion is permitted provided the edge position is reproduced accurately. A basic example is the DPCM encoder with a companded quantizing scale. Time-domain video encoders may be fixed format, edge adaptive, or area adaptive.

3.3.5.4.1 Fixed Format Encoders. Fixed format encoders use linear prediction to take advantage of statistical redundancies in the source, and use nonuniform quantization of the prediction error to exploit the changing sensitivity of vision. Accumulators at the transmitter and receiver are reset at the end of each line to limit the effect of transmission errors.

3.3.5.4.2 Edge Adaptive Encoders. Edge adaptive encoders adapt on an "instantaneous" (every sample) basis to improve the subjective rendition of rapidly changing signals at the edge of an image. This principle has been applied most successfully in improving the response of delta coders. Delta coding is a one-bit version of DPCM in which the coder output at each sampling time is a bit that represents either a positive or a negative step. Compared with multibit differential (DPCM) encoders, delta coders require a higher sampling rate to increase the correlation between successive samples. Their advantage lies in circuit simplicity. The step size is made dependent on the slope of the video waveform. Figure 3.26(a) shows the input and output code from a linear delta coder, [Ref. 4, Fig. 11]. The step size has been chosen so that the level of quantization noise in the flat areas has been balanced against slope overload noise on the sharp vertical edges. Since the output code can be used to detect the presence of an edge (series of 1s in the figure), the step size can be made dependent on the previous history of ones and zeros. This is known as high information delta modulation (HIDM), and is shown in Figure 3.26(b) [Ref. 4, Fig. 12]. In one implementation, [Ref. 17], if three successive pulses have the same polarity, the step size associated with the third pulse is double the step size of the second pulse. On the other hand, if two successive pulses differ in polarity, the step size for the second pulse is half that for the first. Figure 3.26(b) compares HIDM response with that of a simple delta coder at an edge.

The problem of selecting the rules by which the slope is increased or decreased has been treated by Jayant [Ref. 18]. A technique called "delayed encoding" has been applied by Cutler, [Ref. 19], to a video delta coder. This technique uses double integration in the predictor and an adaptive step size algorithm to obtain a rapid change in step size at an edge. The use of delayed encoding allows otherwise unstable conditions to be anticipated and thus avoided.

Another approach, the variable rate edge adaptive encoder, is based on the fact that since edges usually occur rarely, they can be transmitted efficiently using a large number of quantizer levels and a variable length code. For transmission via a constant rate channel, a buffer is needed to smooth the data flow.

The fixed rate edge adaptive encoder is simpler and less expensive than the variable rate edge adaptive coder. For an element-to-element difference greater than 6% of the peak signal amplitude, a 4-bit sample is sent. For an element-to-element difference less than 6% of the peak signal amplitude, a 7-bit sample is sent every alternate sample period. The resulting signal can be sent using 4 bits/pixel

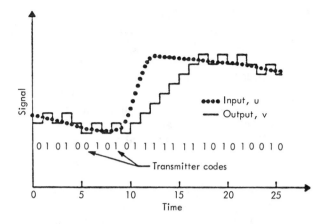

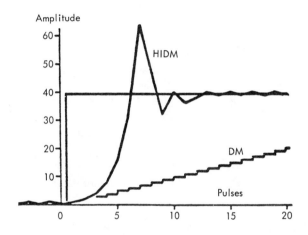

(a) Input and output from linear delta coder

(b) Output of high-information delta modulator (HIDM)

Figure 3.26 Delta coder performance at an edge. (From D. J. Connor, R. C. Brainard, and J. O. Limb, "Intraframe Coding for Picture Transmission," *Proc. IEEE,* July 1972, © 1972, IEEE. Reprinted by permission.)

although certain PCM values must be deleted to allow for the code change information [Ref. 4].

A coarse-fine edge adaptive encoder, [Ref. 20], in rapidly changing areas, sends only the three most significant bits of a 6-bit PCM signal. The occurrence of two pixels with the same PCM value causes the coder to transmit the three least significant bits instead (fine information). Mode change information is entered by inhibiting the transmission of fine data just after transition to the fine mode. The result is only a small reduction in picture quality relative to 6-bit PCM.

3.3.5.4.3 Area Adaptive Encoders. Area adaptive encoders adapt on the basis of taking an average of the luminance value of a line of pixels. This is the video equivalent of the syllabic companding used by some speech coders. The principle is one of selecting the coding operation best suited to the local characteristics of the image. One approach, due to Limb, [Ref. 4], examines eight adjacent pixels in the same line based on how the quantizing levels are used in a differential quantizer. On this basis, the picture is divided into high and low detail areas. High detail is sent at an average of about 2.2 bits/pixel, whereas low detail is sent at an average of about 1.0 to 1.5 bit/pixel. The coding process consists of an irreversible stage followed by a reversible stage. In the irreversible stage low-detailed and high-detailed segments are coded differently. For the low-detailed segments sharp edges are reproduced with full spatial accuracy and small amplitude changes are reproduced with reduced spatial resolution. For the high-detailed segments, the quantization accuracy is reduced.

3.3.5.5 Run Length Encoding. If a horizontal line or an area within an image consists merely of a constant luminance level, the value of that level can be transmitted along with the addresses of the start and end of the "run." This technique has the potential for a considerable amount of reduction in the average number of bits/pixel that must be transmitted for a picture. However, the result is a nonuniform coder output rate which may require a considerable amount of buffering if a constant rate channel is to be used.

3.3.5.6 Transform Picture Encoders. Transform picture encoding is a special intraframe technique in which blocks of pixels, often in a square configuration, are mapped by using an index number which represents the average luminance or a characteristic pattern of the pixels in that block [Ref. 21]. Uniform areas without special features can be coded with a single "index" number. Often the square configuration will be a block of 16×16 adjacent pixels. Within such a block size, most pictures contain significant correlations.

Transform coding works based on picture *structure*, where structure is defined as a departure from randomness. The coding approach, then, is to determine the structure of the data and then to develop encoding algorithms that are efficient for data having that structure. The more structure a block has, the greater is the efficiency achievable by matching the encoder to the data structure. An encoder designed for one structure will exhibit degraded performance if it is used on a different structure. Thus transform coders may be *nonadaptive*, which means they are matched to an average data structure, or *adaptive*, which means they are matched to the local structure. Accordingly, an adaptive transform coder must determine the local structure and then process that local data with an algorithm efficient for that structure. Examples of picture structure include areas of nearly constant brightness, for which a determination must be made as to the number of such areas, their brightness value, and their sizes. Another example is the boundaries between areas of nearly constant brightness, which usually are smooth lines. Other examples include line and bar patterns.

Transform coders perform a sequence of two operations: statistical coding and psychovisual coding [Ref. 22]. Statistical coding is done to provide a match to data statistics that are gross measures of picture structure, such as means, covariances, and first order probability densities. Psychovisual coding is based on the sensitivity of the human visual system to errors in the reconstructed picture. This sensitivity depends on the frequency spectrum of the error, the gray level, and detail in the picture in the vicinity of the error. Therefore, coder efficiency can be increased by allowing distortions that do not degrade subjective quality.

An error in the transmission of a transform coefficient leads to errors in all of the pixels reconstructed from it. Generally these errors will be confined to the subpicture in which the error occurred. A p_{be} of 10^{-3} results in only minor picture flaws; $p_{be} = 10^{-2}$ results in numerous flaws, but the basic picture is still discernable. Table 3.2, [Ref. 22], compares several coding methods in terms of the number of bits per pixel required to achieve approximately the same quality as 7-bit PCM for pictures of moderate detail.

From Table 3.2 the conclusion can be reached that nonadaptive transform coding (one- or two-dimensional) has no general utility because adaptive two-dimensional DPCM provides essentially the same performance and is simpler to implement. Adaptive transform coding appears to be the only technique of those listed that is capable of operation near one bit/pixel.

Table 3.2 applies to pictures containing a moderate amount of detail. For pictures of relatively low detail, i.e., head and shoulders portraits such as Figure 3.18, the same subjective quality can be achieved with 0.5 bit/pixel less. Highly detailed pictures, i.e., aerial photographs, require about 0.5 bit/pixel more for the same quality. Composite color requires about 0.75 bit/pixel more than indicated in Table 3.2.

In comparing transform coding with DPCM, transform coding usually achieves superior coding performance at fewer bits/pixel because it distributes the coding degradation in a manner less objectionable to the human viewer, shows less sensitivity to data statistics (picture-to-picture variation), and is less vulnerable to channel noise. DPCM systems that take advantage of spatial correlations of the data achieve better coding performance at 3 or more bits/pixel, require minimal equipment complexity and delay, can be designed easily, and are readily capable of high-speed operation.

3.3.5.7 Vector Quantization. Vector quantization (VQ) is a pattern-matching process in which each "vector," usually in the form of a block, is encoded by comparison with a set of stored reference patterns (vectors) known as a code book. At the sending end, the pattern most closely resembling the input block of the

TABLE 3.2 COMPARISON OF CODING METHODS

Method	Bits/Pixel
PCM	7.0
DPCM	3.0
DPCM, two-dimensional, adaptive	2.3
Transform, one-dimensional	2.3
Transform, two-dimensional	2.0
Transform, two-dimensional, adaptive	1.0

Source: From P. A. Wintz, "Transform Picture Coding," *Proc. IEEE,* July 1972, © 1972, IEEE. Reprinted by permission.

picture is selected, and the bit sequence corresponding to this pattern is sent to the receiver. The code book must be selected carefully to provide a relatively low number of bits/pixel, and an efficient search algorithm must be used.

Both VQ and transform coding are effective in redundancy removal on a block basis. VQ provides more compression than transform coding because it does a better match to the input picture by adapting the patterns in its code book as a function of time. However, VQ generally requires more computing power than transform coding.

3.3.5.8 Summary. In conclusion, the main gain achievable from adaptive processing comes from the different types of irreversible processing that are possible due to the different perceptions by the eye in the high-detailed and low-detailed portions of an image.

Reversible intraframe coding processes are those in which the original signal can be reconstructed, such as the generation of a difference signal. Irreversible processes delete information judged to be insignificant, such as happens in quantization, in which signals lying between decision levels are assigned to a given level. Bit reduction on a reversible basis can be done if the symbols from a quantizer have a nonuniform probability distribution (variable word length coding), or if the symbols from the quantizer are statistically dependent, i.e., redundant, in which case linear prediction can be applied.

For good quality picture reproduction, assuming a good predictive algorithm is being used, a companded quantizer with eight to sixteen levels is needed to quantize the difference between the actual luminance and the prediction. For transmission of the quantizer output, the requirements, [Ref. 4], are 3 to 4 bits/pixel for a fixed-length code, 2 to 3 bits/pixel for a variable length code, 1.2 to 2.2 bits/pixel using adaptive techniques, and from 1 to 2 bits/pixel using transform techniques.

3.3.6 Interframe Coding

The foregoing intraframe techniques have dealt with coding on a one-dimensional (line) and two-dimensional (line and column, or pixel) basis. The subject of interframe coding deals with three dimensions: line, column, and picture-to-picture.

Interframe coding encompasses redundancy reduction techniques which use the similarity between successive frames of a video signal as well as the differing resolution requirements in the display of stationary and moving objects [Ref. 23]. The relationship between signals in successive frames depends upon the number of frames scanned per second, which in turn is governed by flicker requirements. For displaying motion, 30 pictures/second (one-half the power line frequency) is adequate. Thus for most of the picture the need does not exist to transmit fresh information for every picture displayed. Flicker can be eliminated by storing pictures at the receiver and displaying them more than once, as is done in motion picture projection.

Note that in intraframe coding efforts are made to reduce the number of bits/pixel by removing redundancies within a given frame. No mention was made of a transmission rate as such. Using standard rates of 25 or 30 pictures/second, however, the 90 Mb/s (8 bits/pixel) rate required for PCM can be reduced to as low as 30 Mb/s ($\approx$2.5 bits/pixel). The motivation for using interframe coding is that, by exploiting picture to picture redundancies, the bit rate can be reduced further by a substantial amount, as will be seen in the descriptions that follow.

Interframe coding requires picture storage at the transmitter to allow for a comparison of each new picture with the previous one to determine which areas of the picture have changed. Only the changed areas need be transmitted. In addition, the coder generally is designed to take advantage of the differing resolution requirements that users have for changing and stationary images. High resolution is required for stationary images whereas low resolution is tolerable for changing images.

3.3.6.1 Frame Repeating Techniques. Frame repeating is useful for scenes containing little or no rapid motion. A common example of frame repeating is line interlace, as is used in both NTSC and European television standards. Every other line of the frame (picture) is sent in a 1/60 second (NTSC) or a 1/50 second (European) interval. This method relies on the image retention properties of the eye.

Dot interlace, or *selective replenishment,* carries the interlace principle a step further. Figure 3.27, [Ref. 23, Fig. 1], illustrates four-to-one dot-interlaced transmission. Using this approach only one-fourth of the frame elements are sent every 1/60 second. At the receiver, each element is displayed for 1/15 second. A digital delay line is used for storage. The elements are sent in the sequence indicated. At the display (receiver) the untransmitted elements of each frame are obtained from the previous frame, which has been placed into storage. Thus a delay of one frame is required. Dot interlace provides good picture quality during times of little or no movement. During rapid motion, the edges of moving images tend to be degraded, i.e., the sampling pattern becomes visible.

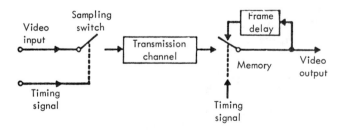

Sampling pattern

```
1 4 1 4 1 - - - -
3 2 3 2 - - - - -
1 4 1 4 - - - - -
3 2 3 - - - - - -
1 4 - - - - - - -
- -
- -
-
```

Figure 3.27 Four-to-one dot-interlaced transmission. (From B. G. Haskell, F. W. Mounts, and J. C. Candy, "Interframe Coding of Videotelephone Pictures," *Proc. IEEE,* July 1972, © 1972, IEEE. Reprinted by permission.)

In frame filtered dot interlace, a weighted average of the brightness values for each picture element in successive frames is formed. During each frame period, a subset of these average values is selected for transmission. Frame-to-frame interpolation between the received values is used to reduce the distortion. This procedure is equivalent to band-limiting, then sampling, then filtering at the receiver to reconstruct the original waveform. Stationary images are unaffected; moving images are blurred by an amount depending on the speed of movement and the number of times the picture is repeated. The sampling pattern does not become visible as it does in dot interlace.

3.3.6.2 Frame Differential Encoding.

The DPCM principle is useful not only in intraframe coding, but also in encoding frame differences. Its purpose as used in interframe coding is resolution control. In examining frame-to-frame changes, the coder must distinguish true changes from noise. In a typical implementation, [Ref. 23], picture elements that have changed by less than 1.5% of the maximum signal amplitude can be regarded as unchanged without impairing picture quality. However, frame-to-frame differences greater than 3% for signal-to-noise ratios better than 40 dB are almost certainly caused by movement. Figure 3.28 [Ref. 23, Fig. 2] is a conceptual block diagram illustrating an interframe DPCM coder. This device provides nearly perfect reproduction with 64-level (6-bit) quantization. At 16 levels (4 bits), good reproduction is provided except when an object containing large and abrupt brightness transitions moves rapidly across the screen. Moving edges of this type appear as a sequence of brightness contours, each differing from the next by an amount equal to the largest quantizer level. This effect is analogous to the slope overload problem in intraframe DPCM, but since the effect is motion dependent, it is called *temporal overload*.

In interframe DPCM the quantizer levels are companded so that small changes are reproduced more accurately than large ones. Frame differences that exceed 3% of the maximum amplitude are quantized coarsely since viewers tolerate some loss of amplitude resolution in the more rapidly changing areas of a picture. As soon as a moving object becomes stationary, it is quickly reproduced with full resolution.

Transmission errors will cause permanent faults in the picture from a coder built using only the principles illustrated in Fig. 3.28. For fault removal one can

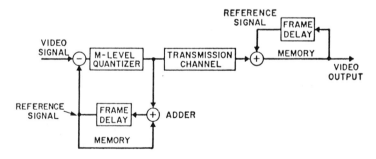

Figure 3.28 Frame-to-frame differential PCM coder. (From B. G. Haskell, F. W. Mounts, and J. C. Candy. "Interframe Coding of Videotelephone Pictures," *Proc. IEEE,* July 1972, © 1972, IEEE. Reprinted by permission.)

systematically transmit element brightness values instead of frame differences for a small part of every frame, [Ref. 24], and in this way the fault soon disappears.

3.3.6.3 Motion Compensation.
Motion compensation is based upon the premise that any motion in a given frame will continue on into the next frame. By doing successive computations of the position of an object, its velocity (speed and direction of movement) can be determined. Thus a prediction is formed in the direction of motion, and the coder sends the difference between the actual motion and that which was predicted. Ideally, the decoder will make the same prediction and reconstruct the image accurately. The success of motion compensation depends upon the amount of translational motion of the objects in the scenes and the ability of the algorithm to estimate the translation with the accuracy needed for good prediction.

In the implementation of motion detection, the best method would be a full matching method using the cross-correlation between two successive frames. However, such a method requires an excessive number of computations. A *matching method using representative points* (MMRP), [Ref. 3], establishes representative points by a coarse fixed sampling of a picture. The method uses the correlation between a given frame and representative points of the previous frame.

Figure 3.29 compares motion compensation with frame difference prediction in terms of the number of bits required per pixel in the moving area for a typical scene containing fairly active head and shoulders movement. As can be seen, motion compensation reduces the entropy by about 1.5 bits/pixel as an average.

Because motion detection is based on the assumption that each pixel within a block moves in the same way, distortion may appear in the background of a moving object, [Ref. 21]. Technique improvements may allow this distortion to be reduced.

3.3.6.4 Subsampling in Moving Areas.
The spatial resolution of an image can be reduced in its moving areas because observers cannot easily focus their eyes

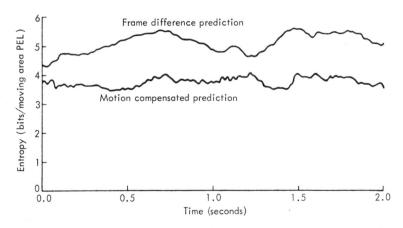

Figure 3.29 Comparison of motion compensation with frame difference prediction. (From A. N. Netravali and J. O. Limb, "Picture Coding: A Review," *Proc. IEEE,* March 1980, © 1980, IEEE. Reprinted by permission.)

on the fine detail of moving objects except when the movement is regular and predictable. In fact, rapidly moving objects tend to be blurred because television cameras integrate the light falling on the target over one frame time. Viewers have become accustomed to this blurring. Subsampling is the simplest and most direct way of reducing the spatial resolution in an area in which changes are occurring. Subsampling involves transmitting information for only a fraction of the picture elements in the changing areas. The value of the remaining elements then is set to an average of the transmitted values. Horizontal subsampling on a $2:1$ basis, i.e., sending only every other element, and setting the value of the others equal to the average of their neighbors, produces excellent picture quality [Ref. 25]. Vertical subsampling already exists in the form of interlace.

Figure 3.30, [Ref. 23, Fig. 3], illustrates interlaced scan. Each frame consists of two interlaced fields which are $1/60$ second apart. For horizontal subsampling, A and C are transmitted, while $B = (A + C)/2$. For vertical subsampling, $J = (A + D + A' + D')/4$. The form of picture degradation noticeable in using this technique is that horizontal edges that move rapidly in the vertical direction are noticeably distorted.

Filtering should be used to limit the spatial bandwidth in the changing areas of the picture prior to using a spatial subsampling algorithm such as $2:1$ horizontal subsampling. *Temporal filtering* (averaging corresponding values in adjacent frames) should be done prior to using a temporal subsampling technique such as field interpolation. The advantage of prefiltering is that the blurring which results is less objectionable than the aliasing that would be visible otherwise. Blurring also masks the high-frequency noise which may be present in the camera output signals.

Frame repeating and subsampling can be combined to provide low-bit rate stationary scenes using frame repeating and low-bit rate moving scenes using subsampling. Figure 3.31, [Ref. 23, Fig. 4], illustrates the use of temporal resolution

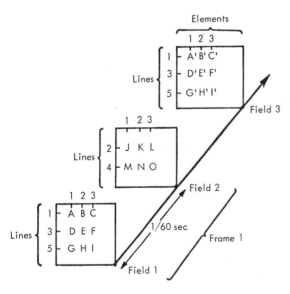

Figure 3.30 Illustration of interlaced scan. (From B. G. Haskell, F. W. Mounts, and J. C. Candy, "Interframe Coding of Videotelephone Pictures," *Proc. IEEE,* July 1972, © 1972, IEEE. Reprinted by permission.)

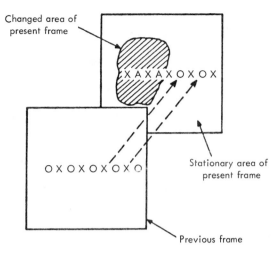

Changed area of
present frame

X A X A X O X O X

O X O X O X O X O

Stationary area of
present frame

Previous frame

X – Transmitted element value
O – Previous frame value
A – Average value of two adjacent
elements in the present frame

Figure 3.31 Use of temporal resolution
reduction in stationary parts of a picture
and horizontal spatial resolution reduction in changing areas. (From B. G.
Haskell, F. W. Mounts, and J. C. Candy,
"Interframe Coding of Videotelephone
Pictures," *Proc. IEEE,* July 1972, ©
1972, IEEE. Reprinted by permission.)

reduction in the stationary parts of the picture and horizontal spatial resolution
reduction in the changing areas. The result is a relatively constant data rate.

3.3.6.5 Conditional Replenishment. *Conditional replenishment* is a technique in which information is transmitted only when the difference between
corresponding pixels in successive frames exceeds a predetermined threshold. As
such, it is a simple form of DPCM. Thus, transmission capacity is used only to
replenish those areas of a picture that have changed significantly since the previous
frame. Figure 3.32, [Ref. 23, Fig. 7], illustrates the principle. Elements that change
significantly are fed along with their addresses to a buffer to await transmission over
a constant-rate channel. A motion detector measures differences between the incoming picture and the reference (previous) picture, noting when the difference
magnitude is more than 1.5% of the maximum signal level. At the receiver, the
transmitted information enters the delay line memory in time to update the stored
data before displaying it. Elastic stores or buffers are used to smooth the data flow
because the data rate fluctuates with movement in the scene.

The bit rate produced by a conditional-replenishment coder is a function of
the amount of movement in the picture. Figure 3.33, [Ref. 23, Fig. 8], provides
statistics that describe the amount of movement in a videotelephone scene. The
probability that the amount of changed area in a frame exceeds $x\%$ of the total area
is plotted versus x. The data were obtained from 75 minutes of imitated videotelephone conversations. An interlaced 30 Hz frame rate was used. On the average,
only 9% of the visible picture area changes from frame to frame. The changed area
constitutes less than 25% of the total visible picture area more than 90% of the
time. Tests have shown that the peak data rate is on the order of ten times the

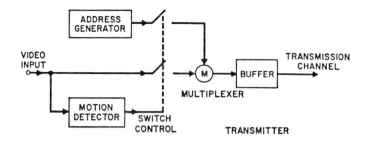

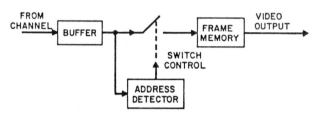

Figure 3.32 Implementation of conditional replenishment. (From B. G. Haskell, F. W. Mounts, and J. C. Candy, "Interframe Coding of Videotelephone Pictures," *Proc. IEEE,* July 1972, © 1972, IEEE. Reprinted by permission.)

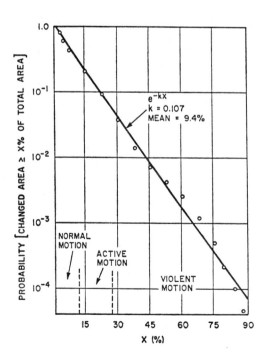

Figure 3.33 Statistics describing the amount of movement in a videotelephone scene. (From B. G. Haskell, F. W. Mounts, and J. C. Candy, "Interframe Coding of Videotelephone Pictures," *Proc. IEEE,* July 1972, © 1972, IEEE. Reprinted by permission.)

average data rate. The required channel capacity depends on the size of the buffer available for smoothing the peaks in the data. The larger the buffer, the closer the channel rate can be made to the average data generated.

Since peaks of high activity may last for several seconds, smoothing such peaks requires either buffers with a one megabit storage capacity or delays in excess of ⅓ second between talker and viewer. Such delays are distracting in teleconference situations. The solution is to transmit the changing areas with reduced amplitude and spatial resolution during active periods. One measure of activity is the storage level in the buffer. When the buffer has filled, the resolution is reduced. Other measures of activity are the number of changed elements per field and the number of bits used by the conditional replenishment coder to code a field.

During very active scenes, the resulting high degree of changes between frames requires that the threshold be increased. The image blocks are not coded uniformly because the portions of the image that contain large movements are coded while the portions containing smaller movement are not. This nonuniformity may result in picture break-up, [Ref. 21].

3.3.6.6 Picture Segmenting.   Changes in a picture tend to occur in runs. Advantage can be taken of this fact by sending the address only for the beginning and end of each run of changes. The problem that may result from the use of this approach, however, is that noise may appear as a change. If two runs are close together on a line, they should be formed into a single run for efficient addressing. Noise can be rejected by ignoring changes that are immediately preceded and followed by two unchanged elements.

3.3.6.7 Effect of Transmission Errors.   The increased redundancy removal in interframe coding means an increased vulnerability to transmission errors. Address and synchronization information require the greatest amount of protection. This protection can be achieved by adding redundancy on a controlled basis. (See Sec. 2.11, Error Control.)

3.3.7 Hybrid Coding

Hybrid coding attempts to combine the attractive features of both transform coding and DPCM on both an intraframe and interframe basis. Hybrid coding exploits the correlation of data in the horizontal direction by taking a one-dimensional transform of each line of the picture and then operating on each column of the transformed data using a one-element predictor DPCM system. In implementation, the pictorial data is scanned to form n lines. Each line is sampled at the Nyquist rate. The sampled image then is divided into arrays of picture elements. Such a system uses a cascade of transform and DPCM encoders and typically operates in the range of 2, 1, or 0.5 bits/pixel.

Motion compensation has been combined successfully with hybrid coding [Ref. 26]. In implementing such a combination, the use of adaptive techniques has been shown to be especially important. Overall transmission rates as low as 384 kb/s, averaging 0.05 bit/pixel, were achieved.

3.4 DIGITAL PROCESSING WITHIN TELEVISION RECEIVERS

The term *digital television* is being used to describe the use of a variety of digital signal processing techniques in achieving improved image quality [Ref. 27], as well as in implementing a variety of added features. Improved image quality includes the partial removal of ghosts through echo cancellation, improved sync lock for the suppression of interference from airplane flutter or electrical appliances, and flicker suppression through frame refreshing, especially important where a 50 Hz standard is used.

Added features include the simultaneous viewing of two stations, one as an inset of the other, zoom-in capability on any part of a picture, and teletext processing. An image storage capability allows slow motion for video recording. Another capability is the availability of noise-reduction chips to reduce snow in weak signal areas.

Using digital television, a pseudohigh resolution can be achieved, (see Sec. 3.2.2.3), through image storage. In operation a linear interpolation is obtained between the scan lines of the picture, resulting in a second set of scan lines being produced between those of the original set. However, inaccurate interpolation on moving objects can result in blurring due to reversion to standard resolution. A motion detection circuit can be added to alter the interpolation for moving objects.

Digital television techniques also, of course, allow the direct processing of digital video and audio signals. This eliminates the need to convert digital satellite and fiber optic transmissions to analog, and also simplifies the construction of multistandard (NTSC/PAL/SECAM) receivers, as are found frequently in certain areas of Europe.

Receiver resolution requirements for digital television are:

Luminosity	8 bits
Color	6 bits
Deflection	13 bits (for linearity)
Sound	14 bits (for high fidelity)

Digital television receivers have been implemented using very large scale integration (VLSI), in which eight chips perform all digital processing functions within the receiver. These receivers have been designed, and are being produced by ITT and by Mitsubishi.

3.5 VIDEO BANDWIDTH REDUCTION

Video bandwidth (bit rate) reduction uses several approaches: reducing spatial resolution, reducing allowable temporal variations, and reducing gray-scale resolution [Ref. 28]. Spatial resolution can be reduced during periods of motion, allowing transmission capacity to be traded between motion and resolution. Temporal variations can be limited in teleconference applications, in which the need does not exist for rapid motion. In this case, rapid movements may result in momentary blurring or jerky motion.

The reduction of gray-scale resolution below 6 bits/pixel (PCM) requires the introduction of special techniques. False contouring becomes clearly evident in PCM at 4 bits/pixel. The effects of false contouring can be reduced by adding pseudorandom noise (dither) at the transmitter and by deleting it at the receiver on a digital basis (see Sec. 3.3.5.3). In DPCM the degradation caused by slope overload can be overcome by using an integrator in the feedback path and tapered (weighted) quantization. False contouring also can be corrected using a technique known as *bit-plane encoding*, which is based on run-length encoding combined with line-to-line encoding and gray coding.

Video bit rate also can be reduced by redundancy removal from the picture. This is based upon the fact that many television pictures have highly detailed backgrounds of little interest to the viewer. The important details are faces, action scenes, and edge contours. In fact, in 80% of the transmissions, the area of detailed interest is only about 5% of the picture. One useful redundancy reduction technique (interframe) is frame-to-frame correlation (see Sec. 3.3.6.2) in which only the pixels that change from frame to frame are transmitted. A memory (buffer) stores a given frame as a reference picture for comparison, pixel by pixel, with the next frame, etc. The receiver must reinsert the horizontal and vertical blanking intervals within the reconstructed video. Fast motion may cause buffer overflow and picture breakup. However, a combination of this technique with dot interlace partially overcomes the breakup problem.

Parallel-serial scan and readout is a technique in which a solid-state camera using charge-coupled devices (CCDs) in a focal plane array provides a parallel readout of multiple, e.g., 13, scan lines simultaneously. Transmission on a multi-channel basis then requires a correspondingly lower bit rate per channel. The corresponding receiver would use an electroluminescent flat-plate display. Use of the intraframe and interframe techniques of Sec. 3.3.5 and 3.3.6 readily allows operation at 0.66 bit/pixel for a 13-channel system and a 0.25 bit/pixel for a 25-channel system.

Table 3.3, [Ref. 28], provides a list of numerous digital video techniques, describing the basebandwidth required, as well as the ability of each technique to handle objects in motion effectively. A few of the techniques listed are proprietary. The others are described elsewhere in this text or in its references. *Dither* refers to the random low-level altering of the thresholds which determine how the input will be quantized, as described in Sec. 3.3.5.3.

3.5.1 Teleconference Video Systems

A variety of systems have been devised for teleconference video transmission. One is the GEC McMichael Codec Mark II, which converts video to/from the 1.544 Mb/s or the 2.048 Mb/s rates, [Ref. 29], and is shown in conceptual block diagram form in Figure 3.34. This codec can operate in either a real-time or a high-resolution mode. The real-time mode uses conditional replenishment coding consisting of interframe

TABLE 3.3 COLOR DIGITAL VIDEO PERFORMANCE COMPARISON

Method Used	Required Bits/Pixel	Transmission Bandwidth (MHz)	Handling of Objects in Motion	Available Now
Robert's Dither System	3	32.1	Excellent	Yes
Thompson's Dither System	3	32.1	Excellent	Yes
Non-Random Dither System	3	32.1	Excellent	Yes
DPCM	5	53.5	Excellent	Yes
DPCM + Dither	3	32.1	Excellent	Yes
Delta Modulation	3	32.1	Excellent	Yes
Synthetic Highs and Lows	2	21.4	Poor	No
Bit-Plane Encoding	2	21.4	Excellent	Yes
Contour Interpolation	3	32.1	Fair	No
Significant Bit Selection with Dither	3	32.1	Good	Yes
Frame-to-frame Correlation plus Conditional Replenishment	1.5	16.0	Poor	No
Frame-to-frame Correlation plus Dot Interlace	2.5	26.8	Poor	No
Frame-to-frame Differential Encoder	2.5	26.8	Fair	No
Frame-to-frame Differential Encoder with Dot Interlace	2.5	26.8	Fair	No
Frame Repeating + DPCM	2.5	26.8	Fair	No
FFT with Run-Length Encoding	2	21.4	Good	Yes
Haar Transform	2	21.4	Good	Yes
Slant Transform	2.5	26.8	Excellent	Yes
Cosine Transform with Pipelining and FFT	2	21.4	Excellent	Yes
Sine Transform	2	21.4	Excellent	Yes
FFT with DPCM	2.5	26.8	Excellent	Yes
Hadamard Transform + DPCM	2	21.4	Excellent	Yes
Pulse Position Modulation with Dither	2	21.4	Excellent	Yes
Reed-Solomon + PPM + Dither	2	21.4	Excellent	Yes
PPM with Dither (13 Channel Parallel-Serial Mode)	0.66	7.1	Excellent	No
PPM with Dither (25 Channel Parallel-Serial Mode)	0.25	2.7	Excellent	No

Source: Reprinted with permission of *Satellite Communications Magazine,* 6300 S. Syracuse Way, Suite 650, Englewood, CO 80111.

and intraframe DPCM. The resolution is equivalent to what can be obtained with an effective bandwidth of 2.5 MHz. The high-resolution mode (for graphics) uses systematic replenishment coding with a dot-interlace pattern having a 1.5 second update period. Its resolution is equivalent to what can be obtained with an effective bandwidth greater than 6 MHz. Audio (300 to 400 Hz) is provided, either digitally coded into the video waveform (sound in sync) or as 64 kb/s digital sound encoded per CCITT Standard G.711.

The Compression Labs, Inc., Rembrandt system [Ref. 30] also has international capabilities. It uses adaptive transform coding with interframe DPCM and provides a user selectable range of transmission rates from 384 kb/s to 3.136 Mb/s.

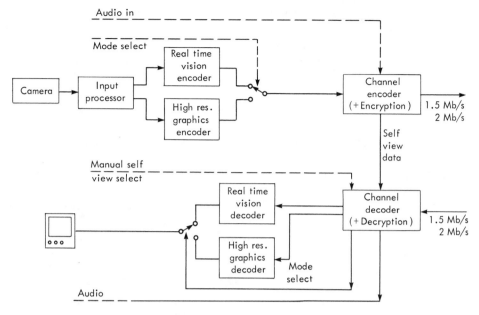

Figure 3.34 Codec for teleconference video. (© 1983. Reprinted by permission of Horizon House-Microwave, Inc., and GEC Video Systems.)

Video also can be transmitted simultaneously with still-frame graphics, alphanumeric data, and audio.

Teleconference service is provided via AT&T's Accunet Reserved T1.5 service in which customer premises equipment (CPE) supports fully interactive (full duplex) audio and video connections, including microphones, color cameras, monitors, and a *room controller,* which samples the audio from each microphone to determine which camera signal to transmit. The picture processor uses a conditional replenishment algorithm to provide transmission at 3.152 Mb/s or at 1.544 Mb/s. It also decodes the incoming signals to supply audio and video to monitors and speakers. The transmission facilities used are digital radio systems, satellites, and fiber optic systems.

3.5.2 Full Motion Video at 56 kb/s

Codecs have been built providing full motion video at 56 kb/s. Essentially every available means is used to send the best possible picture, given the 56 kb/s limit. The input is analog color video that first is digitized at 88 Mb/s. Next, spatial averaging and filtering are used to reduce the stream rate to 22 Mb/s. At this point the image resolution has become equivalent to 262 lines. Next, temporal averaging reduces the stream rate to 2.2 Mb/s. In this process, six consecutive images are stored and their pixel values are averaged. Conditional replenishment then reduces the stream rate to a value in the range 220 kb/s to 450 kb/s. This process involves dividing the entire picture into 8×8 pixel blocks. The codec compares each block with the previous one in its memory. Only the changed blocks are transmitted. The final reduction to 56 kb/s is achieved by Huffman encoding, in which 8-bit pixel values are reduced to as little as one bit, depending on the frequency with which the value appears. Thus the conditional replenishment and Huffman coding complement one another.

For minimal motion in the picture ($\leq 10\%$) the quality is good [Ref. 31]. As the motion increases, however, the moving area decomposes into small squares of varying color and light intensity. Thus a head and shoulders closeup of a person speaking involves only about 5% motion, which is reproduced well. However, a person walking across the screen entails about 20% motion. Such motion first tends to appear jerky and then goes into picture breakup. The quality rendition returns when the motion stops. Delays occur in the picture while the codec is adjusting to motion. Such delays are on the order of 0.1 to 0.2 second. To keep the sound synchronized with the speaker's lip movements, a corresponding delay must be introduced into the sound channel. Generally the voice is transmitted separately from the video, but 2.4 kb/s or 4.8 kb/s voice can be time-division multiplexed with the video within an overall 64 kb/s (DS0) stream.

Viewers have evaluated 56 kb/s video as superior to 56 kb/s freeze frame transmission (one new still picture every 13 seconds), but inferior to 1.544 Mb/s video [Ref. 31]. The initial development work on 56 kb/s video was sponsored by the Defense Advanced Research Projects Agency (DARPA). The first manufacturer was Widergren Communications, Inc., San Jose, CA. Video codecs at 56 kb/s also are produced by Picturetel, Inc., Peabody, MA.

3.6 CONFORMANCE OF VIDEO CODING TO INTERNATIONAL STANDARDS

For broadcasting purposes the CCIR has adopted its Recommendation 601 as a basis for digital coding standards for television studios internationally, [Ref. 13]. These standards are based on PCM coding (see Sec. 3.3.5.1). Component coding is emphasized, using the Y, R-Y, and B-Y components. The recommendation calls for an "extensible family" of compatible digital coding standards based on $4:2:2$ coding as the main studio system. Sampling is to be done using "a static orthogonal sampling pattern," i.e., the picture elements are in fixed positions. Each pair of color-difference samples should be "spatially cosited" rather than arranged in the dot sequential manner of Fig. 3.7. The purpose of this arrangement is to facilitate signal processing. To foster "worldwide acceptance and application in operation," 720 luminance samples and 360 color-difference samples per active line are recommended for both 525-line and 625-line systems. This includes a 1.3 μs margin to allow for variations in the timing of the horizontal blanking intervals among the various analog television standards [Ref. 32]. Encoding parameter values for the $4:2:2$ member of the family are shown in Table 3.4, [Ref. 13, Table I]. These values define the "standard digital interface between main digital studio equipment and [the] international programme exchange." The 13.5 MHz sampling frequency can

TABLE 3.4 CCIR 601 ENCODING PARAMETER VALUES FOR STANDARD DIGITAL INTERFACE BETWEEN MAIN DIGITAL STUDIO EQUIPMENT AND INTERNATIONAL PROGRAM EXCHANGE

Parameters	525-line, 60 field/s[1] systems	625-line, 50 field/s[1] systems
1. Coded signals: Y_G, C_R, C_B	These signals are obtained from gamma pre-corrected signals, namely: E'_Y, $E'_R - E'_Y$, $E'_R - E'_Y$ (Annex II, § 2 refers)	
2. Number of samples per total line: —luminance signal (Y) —each colour-difference signal (C_R, C_B)	858 429	864 432
3. Sampling structure	Orthogonal, line, field and frame repetitive, C_R and C_B samples co-sited with odd (1st, 3rd, 5th, etc.) Y samples in each line	
4. Sampling frequency: —luminance signal —each colour-difference signal	13.5 MHz[2] 6.75 MHz[2] The tolerance for the sampling frequencies should coincide with the tolerance for the line frequency of the relevant colour television standard	
5. Form of coding	Uniformly quantized PCM, 8 bits per sample, for the luminance signal and each colour-difference signal	
6. Number of samples per digital active line: —luminance signal —each colour-difference signal	720 360	
7. Analogue-to-digital horizontal timing relationship: —from end of digital active line to 0_H	16 luminance clock periods	12 luminance clock periods
8. Correspondence between video signal levels and quantization levels: —scale —luminance signal —each colour-difference signal	0 to 255 220 quantization levels with the black level corresponding to level 16 and the peak white level corresponding to level 235. The signal level may occasionally excurse beyond level 235 225 quantization levels in the centre part of the quantization scale with zero signal corresponding to level 128	
9. Code-word usage	Code-words corresponding to quantization levels 0 and 255 are used exclusively for synchronization. Levels 1 to 254 are available for video	

Source: From the CCIR Green Book, Vol. XI.1, 1986, "Broadcasting Service (Television)." Reprinted with permission.

(1) See Report 624, Table 1.

(2) The sampling frequencies of 13.5 MHz (luminance) and 6.75 MHz (colour-difference) are integer multiples of 2.25 MHz, the lowest common multiple of the line frequencies in 525/60 and 625/50 systems, resulting in a static orthogonal sampling pattern for both.

be divided by 858 to achieve the NTSC line scanning frequency, 15.7342 kHz or by 864 to achieve the 15.625 kHz PAL scanning frequency.

Section 3.2.2.4 discussed the TMAC format for component video. A version of this format has become standardized for DBS transmission in Europe. The European Broadcasting Union (EBU) has adopted the "C-MAC/packet system" for direct broadcast satellite (DBS) applications. The "C" prefix indicates a particular digital sound-and-data modulation system and "packet system" refers to the organization of the digital data stream [Ref. 33]. A modification of C-MAC known as D2-MAC modulates the digital sound-and-data in a different manner [Ref. 34]. This modification was developed for DBS services in France and Germany.

3.7 FUTURE USES OF VIDEO CODING

The incentive to pursue low-bit-rate video coding is reduction in transmission rate, and thus cost. However, reducing the bit rate of the video coder results in increased coder cost. This means that inexpensive coders, e.g., PCM, are most cost effective for local transmission links, whereas the high costs of low-bit-rate coders, e.g., 56 kb/s to 1.544 Mb/s, can be justified only for long-distance transmission requirements. Continued improvements in low-bit-rate coder quality are expected for long-distance transmission. Moreover, reduced costs for such coders in the future will make their use economically feasible over shorter distance circuits for video conferencing as well as for surveillance television applications.

For the network transmission of broadcast television signals, digital encoding must not degrade the quality of the studio signal. Accordingly, broadcasters generally demand 90 Mb/s to 135 Mb/s rates. Highly efficient coders ($\leq$30 Mb/s) produce noticeable degradation on some of the extreme types of material occasionally encountered, and thus are unsatisfactory to broadcasters. Moreover, digital transmission facilities, e.g., DS3, are of limited availability.

High resolution (>1000 line) television compatible with existing standards is receiving major attention from several manufacturers as well as regulatory bodies, and is expected to become a reality in the future.

PROBLEMS

3.1 The upper sideband of the I-chrominance signal must be attenuated before transmission. What corresponding treatment should be provided at the receiver to prevent distortion of the received spectrum? Sketch the baseband response for which the I-chrominance detector should be designed.

3.2 For a given resolution, explain why occupied luminance bandwidth is proportional to the area of a picture.

3.3 Why are intraframe coders described in terms of bits/pixel whereas interframe coders are described in terms of bits/second?

3.4 The MUSE system uses sub-Nyquist sampling. Chapter 2 explained that sampling at less than the Nyquist rate results in aliasing. Explain the kind of effect that can be expected from a small amount of aliasing in video transmission. How does MUSE minimize this effect?

3.5 A television test pattern consists of seven vertical color bars of constant luminance progressively increasing in color saturation from left to right. Sketch the time domain envelope as it would appear on an oscilloscope.

3.6 Quadrature amplitude modulation, the technique used to modulate hue and saturation information on the NTSC color subcarrier, is said to be a suppressed carrier form of modulation. Explain why.

3.7 The color subcarrier is transmitted continuously along the length of each scan line. Explain why it doe not produce noticeable line effects in a high-quality monochrome receiver.

3.8 Both reversible and irreversible coding techniques are used to reduce the number of bits/pixel that must be transmitted. On what basis can a complete restoration of the original pixels be achieved in reversible coding after the number of bits/pixel has been reduced substantially?

3.9 The transmission of an image under multipath conditions results in ghosting. Explain why the ghost usually appears to the right of the main image, occasionally to the left, but never above or below.

3.10 In what sense does digitization already exist in the present analog video standards?

REFERENCES

1. *Color Television Theory, Equipment, Operation,* Manual for Television Technical Training, Broadcast, and Television Equipment, Radio Corporation of America, Camden, NJ, 1959.

2. K. H. Powers, "Techniques for Increasing the Picture Quality of NTSC Transmissions in Direct Satellite Broadcasting," *IEEE Journal on Selected Areas in Communication,* SAC-3, (Jan. 1985), 57–64.

3. Y. Ninomiya, et al, "A Motion Video Detector for MUSE Encoder," *IEEE International Conference on Communications,* ICC-86, pp. 41.1.1–41.1.5.

4. D. J. Connor, R. C. Brainard, and J. O. Limb, "Intraframe Coding for Picture Transmission," *Proc. IEEE,* 60, (July, 1972), 779–91.

5. E. R. Kretzmer, "Statistics of Television Signals," *Bell System Technical Journal,* 31, (July, 1952), 751–63.

6. W. F. Schreiber, "The Measurement of Third Order Probability Distributions of Television Signals," *IRE Trans. Information Theory,* IT-2, (Sept. 1956), 94–105.

7. R. C. Brainard, "Low Resolution TV: Subjective Effects of Noise Added to a Signal," *Bell System Technical Journal,* 46, (Jan. 1967), 233–60.

8. J. O. Limb, "Design of Dither Waveforms for Quantized Visual Signals," *Bell System Technical Journal,* 48, (Sept. 1969), 2555–82.

9. H. R. Blackwell, "Neural Theories of Simple Visual Discriminations," *Jour. Optical Society of America,* 53, (Jan. 1963), 129–60.

10. H. Kaneko and T. Ishiguro, "Digital Television Transmission Using Bandwidth Compression Techniques," *IEEE Communications Magazine,* 18, no. 4, (July, 1980), 14-22.

11. V. G. Devereux, "Pulse Code Modulation of Video Signals: Subjective Study of Coding Parameters," BBC Research Dept., Report No. 1971/40.

12. A. A. Goldberg, "PCM Encoded NTSC Color Television Subjective Tests," *SMPTE Journal,* 82, (Aug. 1973), 649–54.

13. "Encoding Parameters of Digital Television for Studios," CCIR Rec. 601–1, Recom-

mendations and Reports of the CCIR, 1986, vol. XI, Part 1, Int. Telecommunications Union, Geneva, Switzerland.

14. H. W. Bode, *Network Analysis and Feedback Amplifier Design,* D. VanNostrand Co., Inc., New York, NY, 1945.

15. L. G. Roberts, "Picture Coding Using Pseudo-random Noise," *IRE Trans. Information Theory,* IT-8, (Feb. 1962), 145–54.

16. R. C. Brainard and J. C. Candy, "Direct-feedback Coders: Design and Performance with Television Signals," *Proc. IEEE,* 57, (May, 1969), 776–86.

17. M. R. Winkler, "High Information Delta Modulation," *IEEE Int. Conv. Record,* Part 8, (1963), 260–65.

18. N. S. Jayant, "Adaptive Delta Modulation with One-bit Memory," *Bell System Tech. Journal,* 49, (Mar. 1970), 321–42.

19. C. C. Cutler, "Delayed Encoding, Stabilizer for Adaptive Coders," *IEEE Trans. Comm. Tech.,* COM-19, (Dec. 1971), 898–907.

20. W. T. Bisignani, G. P. Richards, and J. W. Whelan, "The Improved Gray Scale and the Coarse-Fine PCM Systems, Two New Digital Bandwidth Reduction Techniques," *Proc. IEEE,* 54, (Mar. 1966), 376–90.

21. K. S. Kim and P. Li, "Video Telephone: Gone Today, Here Tomorrow?," *Data Communications,* 15, no. 12, (Nov. 1986), 124–36.

22. P. A. Wintz, "Transform Picture Coding," *Proc. IEEE,* 60, (July 1972), 809–20.

23. B. G. Haskell, F. W. Mounts, and J. C. Candy, "Interframe Coding of Videotelephone Pictures," *Proc. IEEE,* 60, (July 1972), 792–800.

24. J. C. Candy, M. A. Franke, B. G. Haskell, and F. W. Mounts, "Transmitting Television as Clusters of Frame-to-Frame Differences," *Bell System Tech. Journal,* 50, (July–Aug. 1971), 1889–1917.

25. R. F. W. Pease and J. O. Limb, "Exchange of Spatial and Temporal Resolution in Television Coding," *Bell System Tech. Journal,* 50, (Jan. 1971), 191–200.

26. A. Furukawa, T. Koga, and K. Niwa, "Coding Efficiency Analysis for Motion-Compensated Interframe DPCM with Transform Coding," *IEEE Globecom '85,* pp. 22.5.1 to 22.5.5.

27. H. C. Andrews, *Digital Image Processing,* IEEE Computer Society, IEEE Catalog no. EHO 133-9 (1978).

28. R. H. Stafford, "Digitizing Video," *Satellite Communications,* 7, no. 3, (March 1983), 28–34.

29. "Video Teleconference Codec," *Telecommunications,* Jan. 1983, p. 51–1.

30. C. Fuller, "DSC™, A Technical Backgrounder," Compression Labs, Inc., San Jose, CA.

31. E. E. Mier, "Pictures for Pennies," *Data Communications,* 12, no. 8, (Aug. 1983), 42–43.

32. L. Stenger, "Digital Coding of TV Signals for ISDN-B Applications," *IEEE Journal on Selected Areas in Communications,* SAC-4, no. 4, (July 1986), 514–28.

33. "Television Standards for the Broadcasting Satellite Service-Specification of the C-MAC/Packet System," EBU Spec. SPB 284, Dec. 1984.

34. "Methods of Conveying C-MAC/Packet Signals in Small and Large Community Antenna and Cable Networks Installations, Chapter B: Specification of the D2-MAC/Packet System," EBU Spec. SPB 352, Dec. 1984.

4

Microwave Radio Systems

Microwave radio systems provide the transmission facility for a significant portion of the broadband communications in use today. Applications include not only large multiplexed groupings of voice channels, but also broadband data and video.

Individual circuit lengths range from a few kilometers, in the case of small private systems, to cross-country distances over 6000 km. The route cross-sectional capacity (equivalent number of voice channels carried) ranges from less than 24 to more than 22 000 channels.

While many new point-to-point facilities are being built using optical fibers (see Chap. 6), microwave systems have the advantage of being able to provide transmission without requiring the acquisition of a continuous right of way. This feature is especially useful in bringing facilities along new routes into heavily populated areas.

Microwave systems are designated *short-haul* if their end-to-end length is 400 km or less. Such systems often are used for intrastate service, e.g., by a wireline common carrier serving a metropolitan area and its surroundings. A short-haul system also may serve as a feeder into a *long-haul* system, which designates a system whose length exceeds 400 km, and which may be used for interstate service, or as a backbone route. Backbone routes generally interconnect major metropolitan centers and provide for transmission at multiples of the DS3 rate (see Chap. 2), i.e., numerous mastergroups* in analog terminology.

* A mastergroup is often defined as 600 voice channels. The DS3 rate can handle 672 voice channels at 64 kb/s each.

Sec. 4.1   Microwave Propagation   **177**

Microwave radio systems use both analog and digital modulation techniques. The analog techniques, amplitude, and frequency modulation, are described in this chapter. The digital modulation techniques are based on the same principles as were described in Chap. 2 for voice-band modems, i.e., combinations of amplitude and phase shift keying, as well as the use of correlative coding. Some applications of these techniques in microwave radio are described later in this chapter.

Microwave radio systems, irrespective of the modulation techniques used, suffer from the four basic categories of impairments described in Chap. 1. These are noise level and co-channel interference, intermodulation, intersymbol interference, and adjacent channel interference. All four contribute to the bit error probability in a digital system. In the case of an analog system, intermodulation and intersymbol interference contribute to signal distortion and, in some cases, are related to echo. In a microwave system the noise level generally results from noise produced by the amplifying stages themselves, with the noise of the first stages being the most significant because such noise is amplified by the gain of all the following stages. Intermodulation in amplitude modulated systems results from nonlinearities in the amplifying stages of the system, primarily in the repeaters. In frequency modulated systems, transmission gain and delay deviations can cause intermodulation distortion, in an amount that increases with the extent of the frequency deviation. Intersymbol interference can be produced either by inadequate bandwidths in the system stages, or by echoes, which usually result from impedance mismatches. Adjacent channel interference, as the name implies, results when receiver selectivity is inadequate to prevent some of the modulation sidebands of an adjacent signal from being detected within the desired channel.

4.1 MICROWAVE PROPAGATION

The design of a microwave radio system requires an understanding of the mechanisms by which radio wave propagation takes place at microwave frequencies. This section describes the basic propagation modes.

4.1.1 Radiation from a Point Source

A basic term used in describing microwave propagation is free space path loss. This "loss" results from the spreading of the wave front as it propagates outward from its source.

To understand the concept of free space path loss, consider an isotropic (omnidirectional) source of electromagnetic energy. Let p_t denote the power in watts radiated by this source. This power spreads out uniformly in all directions as indicated in Fig. 4.1a. Consider the power flux density at a distance d meters from this source. Since the power spreads out uniformly in all directions, we ask what is the locus of all points a distance d from the origin of a coordinate system centered at this isotropic source? The answer is a sphere with radius d, and thus area $4\pi d^2$. Accordingly, the power spreads out over the area $4\pi d^2$, whence the power flux density at distance d is $p_t/4\pi d^2$ watts/m^2.

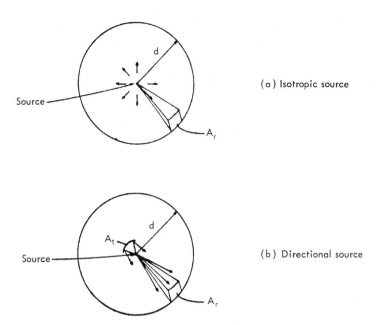

(a) Isotropic source

(b) Directional source

Figure 4.1 Geometrical relationships resulting in free space path loss.

Next assume that a parabolic reflector is placed with its focal point at the isotropic source, as shown in Fig. 4.1b. In this case, the antenna on-axis gain g_t can be shown [Ref. 1, p. 416] to be

$$g_t = \frac{4\pi A_t}{\lambda^2} \qquad (4.1)$$

where

$$A = \text{effective area of transmitting antenna, m}^2$$

$$\lambda = \text{wavelength, m}$$

The actual physical area of the reflector will be greater than A_t because the antenna's efficiency is not 100%. Typical parabolic reflector antennas have efficiencies on the order of 55% to 70%.

The gain g_t has been achieved by limiting the directions of radiation from the antenna. Previously, the power p_t was spread over an area $4\pi d^2$. Now, a higher effective power $g_t p_t$ has been produced, but the area covered at distance d will have been reduced from the 4π steradians (solid radians) of the isotropic source to $4\pi/g_t$ steradians. Thus the new beam angle, designated Ω, is

$$\Omega = \frac{4\pi}{g_t} = \frac{\lambda^2}{A_t} \qquad (4.2)$$

The solid angle Ω is proportional to the product of an azimuthal beamwidth θ_a and an elevation beamwidth θ_c. As can be seen from the first equality of (4.2), the gain of an antenna equals $4\pi/\Omega$. Thus gain is uniquely related to beamwidth.

The received power p_r at distance d equals the power flux density, $g_t p_t / 4\pi d^2$ multiplied by the effective area of the receiving antenna, A_r. Thus

$$p_r = \frac{g_t p_t A_r}{4\pi d^2} = p_t \left(\frac{4\pi A_t}{\lambda^2}\right)\left(\frac{A_r}{4\pi d^2}\right)$$

$$= p_t \left(\frac{4\pi A_t}{\lambda^2}\right)\left(\frac{4\pi A_r}{\lambda^2}\right)\left(\frac{\lambda}{4\pi d}\right)^2$$

$$= p_t g_t g_r \left(\frac{\lambda}{4\pi d}\right)^2 \tag{4.3}$$

The reciprocal of the term $(\lambda/4\pi d)$ constitutes the spreading loss, or free space loss. Expressed in decibels, this loss is

$$L = 20 \log_{10}\left(\frac{4\pi d}{\lambda}\right) \text{ dB} \tag{4.4a}$$

If d is expressed in kilometers instead of meters, and if λ is replaced by the corresponding frequency in MHz,

$$L = 32.44 + 20 \log_{10}(d_{\text{km}}) + 20 \log_{10}(f_{\text{MHz}}) \text{ dB} \tag{4.4b}$$

Note that from the first equality of (4.3), for a given radiated power, $g_t p_t$, the received power using a given size of receiving aperture A_r, depends only on d, not on λ. Thus the dependence of L on λ in (4.4a) and of L on f_{MHz} in (4.4b) is somewhat fictitious because it results from the fact that antenna gains have been referenced to isotropic antennas whose physical dimensions are proportional to wavelength.

The *polarization* of an electromagnetic wave is defined as the direction of the electric field vector. Figure 4.2 illustrates the fact that a propagating wave consists of an electric field $\vec{E}$ measured in volts/meter, and a magnetic field $\vec{H}$, measured in amperes/meter. These two field components always accompany one another in a

DIRECTION OF ELECTRIC
VECTOR IS DEFINED AS
DIRECTION OF POLARIZATION

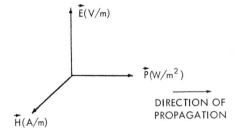

$\vec{E} \times \vec{H} = \vec{P}$

Figure 4.2 Vector relationships for wave propagation.

propagating electromagnetic wave. Their vector cross product, $\vec{E} \times \vec{H} = \vec{P}$, is the power flow or Poynting vector. Its units are watts/meter^2.

Circular polarization is achieved by causing $\vec{E}$ and $\vec{H}$ to rotate about the $\vec{P}$ axis 2π radians for each cycle of the carrier frequency. Thus a 4 GHz circularly polarized wave consists of $\vec{E}$ and $\vec{H}$ vectors that are rotating 4×10^9 revolutions per second. This rotation is achieved by using crossed dipole excitation in the antenna, with the dipoles being driven by voltages that differ in phase by $\pi/2$ radians. Either right-hand circular (RHC) or left-hand circular (LHC) polarization can be produced depending on which dipole's excitation leads that of the other.

Polarization is useful in minimizing adjacent channel interference along a given microwave path. In addition, the alternation of polarization along a path from one repeater to another can aid in minimizing interference caused by propagation ducting (See Sec. 4.1.4), also known as *overreach,* and the cause of co-channel interface.

Although precipitation tends to convert linear polarization into elliptical, especially at frequencies above 10 GHz, the undesired, or cross-polarized, signal generally is 25 to 30 dB below the desired signal, making polarization alternation a very useful technique in microwave radio systems. In fact, separate digital channels can be sent on the two polarizations under conditions such that cross-polarization is sufficiently low.

4.1.2 Line-of-Sight Propagation

The term line-of-sight (LOS) often is used to refer to the propagation path of a microwave radio system. In LOS propagation no obstacles are present in the transmission path. The signal will undergo a free-space loss as described in Sec. 4.1.1. The free-space path loss is the most significant loss between the microwave transmitter and receiver of a link. However, it is a fixed loss that is known in advance and can be accounted for in design.

Such factors as diffraction around obstacles and tropospheric propagation are assumed to be absent in LOS propagation. However, refraction in the lower atmosphere, discussed in Sec. 4.1.4 and diffraction around the earth, discussed in Sec. 4.1.5, are assumed to be present. Absorption in the atmosphere also will be present, and must be added to L to obtain the total path loss. Figure 4.3 [Ref. 2, p. 52] shows that atmospheric absorption is a function of the moisture and oxygen contents of the atmosphere. It becomes greater as wavelength decreases since the moisture particle, e.g. raindrop, sizes become significant relative to the wavelength λ.

As noted previously, line-of-sight propagation is said to take place when no obstacles are present in the propagation path. To make this statement, however, we must define what is meant by "in the propagation path." Figure 4.4 [Ref. 2, pp. 48–51] is helpful in this connection. Path clearance over obstacles is described in terms of Fresnel zones. The boundary of the nth Fresnel zone consists of all points from which the reflected wave is delayed $n/2$ wavelengths. By geometry, then, the distance from the line-of-sight path to the boundary of the nth Fresnel zone, H_n, is

$$H_n = \sqrt{\frac{n\lambda d_1(d - d_1)}{}} \text{ meters} \tag{4.5}$$

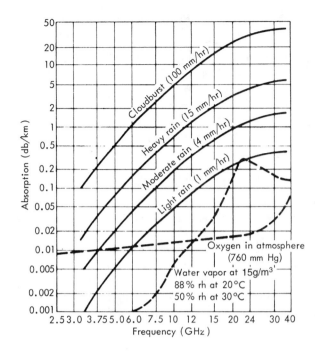

Figure 4.3 Absorption in the atmosphere. (Copyright 1972, American Telephone and Telegraph Company. Reprinted with permission.)

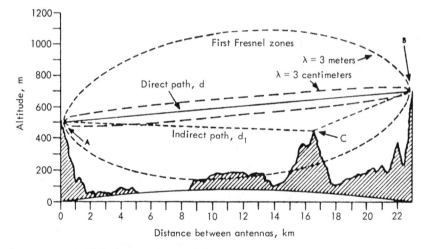

Figure 4.4 Path clearance in line-of-sight propagation. (Copyright 1977, American Telephone and Telegraph Company. Reprinted with permission.)

where

d_1 = path length from reflecting point to receiving antenna, m

d = distance between antennas, m

For free space transmission, the clearance should be at least 0.6 of the first Fresnel zone. Much greater clearances usually are provided, however, because of refraction, which is discussed in Sec. 4.1.4.

Microwave LOS propagation occurs via what is known as a *space wave,* which is part of the class of propagation modes known as *ground wave.* The ground wave includes those forms of radio wave propagation other than ionospheric and tropospheric, which are designated *sky wave,* and thus not included in a discussion of LOS. The ground wave consists of a surface and a space wave. Since the surface wave is not of significance at microwave frequencies over distances on the order of kilometers [Ref. 1, p. 633], our discussion deals only with the space wave.

The four components of the space wave are the direct wave, which suffers a spreading loss L given by Eq. (4.4), a ground reflected wave (Sec. 4.1.3), a refracted wave (Sec. 4.1.4), a diffracted wave (Sec. 4.1.4).

4.1.3 Ground Reflection

Reflection at the surface of a finitely conducting plane with conductivity σ Siemens/meter (S/m) and dielectric constant ϵ_r is based upon solutions to Maxwell's equations for the geometry of Fig. 4.5. In applying these solutions, a partially conducting dielectric such as the earth is treated as a dielectric that has a complex dielectric constant $\epsilon' = \epsilon(1 + \sigma/j\omega\epsilon)$.

Typical earth conductivities range from 10^{-2} S/m or more to 10^{-3} S/m or less. Values of ϵ_r range from 5 to 10 for poorly conducting earth ($\leqslant 10^{-3}$ S/m) to about 30 for earth with good conductivity ($\geqslant 10^{-2}$ S/m).

The reflection factor ρ is defined as the ratio of the reflected electric field, E_r, to the incident electric field, E_i. The reflection factor depends upon the polarization

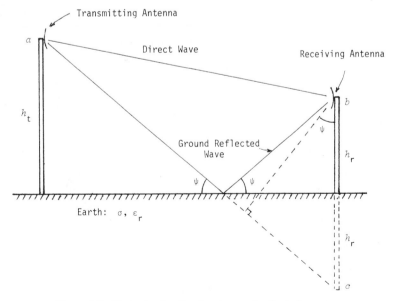

Figure 4.5 Geometry for direct and ground-reflected waves.

of the incident wave. For horizontal polarization, the reflection factor is [Ref. 1, p. 611]

$$\rho_h = \frac{\sin \psi - \sqrt{(\epsilon_r - jX) - \cos^2\psi}}{\sin \psi + \sqrt{(\epsilon_r - jX) - \cos^2\psi}} \qquad (4.6)$$

where

$$X = \frac{\sigma}{\omega\epsilon_o}$$

$$\epsilon_o = \text{permittivity of free space} = \frac{1}{36\pi \times 10^9} \text{ Farad/meter}$$

For vertical polarization, the reflection factor is

$$\rho_v = \frac{(\epsilon_r - jX) \sin \psi - \sqrt{(\epsilon_r - jX) - \cos^2\psi}}{(\epsilon_r - jX) \sin \psi + \sqrt{(\epsilon_r - jX) - \cos^2\psi}} \qquad (4.7)$$

Reflection is most significant for smooth surfaces, such as calm water. By contrast, rough terrain scatters the incident waves diffusely. Figure 4.6 shows the values of reflection coefficients [Ref. 3, Chap. 5] for sea water for grazing angles up to 10°.

At the lowest angles of incidence, as encountered in propagation beyond 20 km, the earth's curvature tends to reduce the effective value of the reflection coefficient. At any angle of incidence, the phase is 180° for horizontal polarization over a smooth surface. For vertical polarization over sea water the phase ϕ_v behaves as shown in Figure 4.7.

The effect of reflection on the received signal level can be determined through use of the geometry of Fig. 4.4. The difference in length between the direct and the reflected path is $2h \sin \psi$, where h is the smaller of the two heights in Fig. 4.4. As drawn, this is h_r. For long transmission paths, ψ is very small, so $\sin \psi \simeq (h_t + h_r)/d$. In relatively flat terrain, $h_t \simeq h_r$, so $\sin \psi \simeq 2h_r/d$. Then the path length difference is $2h_r \times 2h_r/d = 4h_r^2/d$. The corresponding phase difference ϕ_d is

$$\phi_d = \frac{2\pi}{\lambda} \left(\frac{4h_r^2}{d} \right) \text{ radians} \qquad (4.8)$$

To this must be added the phase shift ϕ_r which results from the reflection of the wave. This will be $\simeq \pi$ radians for horizontal polarization, or the radian equivalent of the value shown in Fig. 4.7 for vertical polarization.

The roughness of the surface of the earth is of prime importance in determining the nature and effects of the reflected wave. The reflection coefficient (vertical or horizontal) for average terrain is on the order of 0.2 to 0.5 at frequencies above 1.6 GHz except at low angles of incidence. Accordingly, ground-reflected waves are of most concern along paths involving water or flat terrain covered with ice.

4.1.4 Refraction

Refraction is the altering of the direction of propagation of a radio wave. In the lower atmosphere, refraction occurs because of changes in the relative permittivity, or dielectric constant, of the atmosphere through which the wave is propagating.

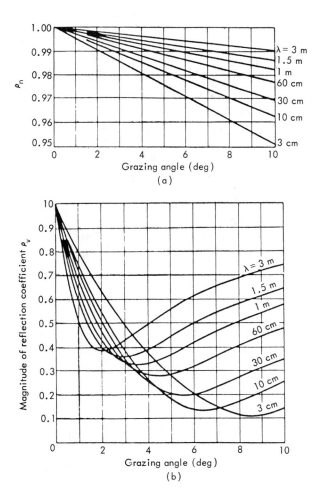

Figure 4.6 Reflection coefficients (magnitude) for sea water.

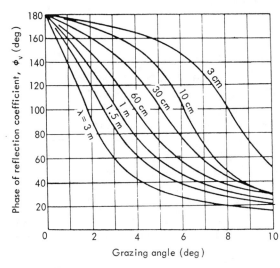

Figure 4.7 Reflection coefficient phase (vertical polarization) for sea water.

The dielectric constant, and thus the refractive index of the atmosphere, varies with height above the surface of the earth. Dry air has a dielectric constant only slightly greater than that of free space. Moisture in the air causes further increases in the dielectric constant. This causes the dielectric constant (usually) to be greater at the surface of the earth, and to decrease with altitude, especially with decreasing air density. Along with this, the temperature decreases with altitude at a nominal 6.5°C/km. The variation in dielectric constant is treated in computations as if the earth had a radius of curvature K times its actual radius of curvature. Frequently $K \simeq 1.33$, but at times K may reach very large values corresponding to the existence of propagation ducts within the atmosphere. These ducts occur when the temperature in the atmosphere increases with height, rather than decreasing as usual. An increase in temperature with height is called a *temperature inversion*. Under ducting conditions, propagation may occur over several times the normal LOS distance. This causes *overreach* to occur in a microwave system, resulting in co-channel interference if the signals from a given repeater reach repeaters beyond the next one.

The refractive index is essentially independent of frequency for all frequencies presently used for microwave radio. At optical wavelengths, $K \simeq 1.2$ rather than 1.33.

Some weather conditions may cause what is called *substandard* propagation, in which the effective value of K may drop to 1.00 or even as low as 0.66. Often a repeater chain will use spacings close enough to tolerate the $K \simeq 0.66$ condition as a means of providing high transmission reliability.

The distance d_1 from a point on the surface of the earth to the radio horizon can be shown by geometry to be

$$d_1 = 3.55 \sqrt{Kh} \text{ km} \qquad (4.6a)$$

where h = height of antenna in meters.

The LOS distance between two elevated antennas thus is

$$d_2 = 3.55 \sqrt{K} \left(\sqrt{h_1} + \sqrt{h_2} \right) \qquad (4.6b)$$

4.1.5 Diffraction

An electromagnetic wave incident upon a surface discontinuity produces diffracted waves, as illustrated in Fig. 4.8 for the case of a knife edge. Diffraction thus is a significant factor in wave propagation. As Fig. 4.8 shows, diffraction occurs in all directions from the knife edge. However, it is the forward and downward region that is of most interest and concern in microwave propagation. The theory of diffraction is described in such texts as Schelkunoff, Chap. 9 [Ref. 4]. At a given angle θ with respect to the direction of arrival of the wave, the attenuation increases as wavelength decreases. At a given wavelength λ, the field strength decreases as one moves downward into the obstruction zone. Figure 4.9 [Ref. 5, Fig. 14] shows this effect. There the parameter R describes the nature of the discontinuity, with $R = 0$ corresponding to the knife edge, $R = -1$ corresponding to diffraction over a smooth sphere, and $R = -0.3$ representing the common experience on many paths.

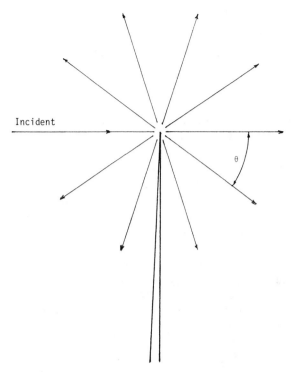

Incident

θ

Figure 4.8 Diffracted wave directions.

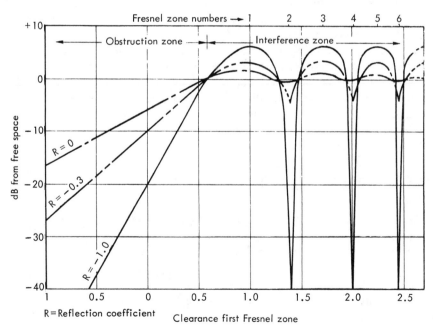

Fresnel zone numbers → 1 2 3 4 5 6

Obstruction zone

Interference zone

dB from free space

+10

0

−10

−20

−30

−40

$R = 0$

$R = -0.3$

$R = -1.0$

1 0.5 0 0.5 1.0 1.5 2.0 2.5

R = Reflection coefficient

Clearance first Fresnel zone

Figure 4.9 Attenuation versus path clearance. (Reprinted from *Engineering Considerations for Microwave Communication Systems* with permission of Siemens Transmission Systems, Inc.)

Distance into the obstruction zone is described in terms of Fresnel zones (see Eq. 4.5).

Analytical methods for computing diffracted fields are provided in Rice, et al. [Ref. 6].

4.1.6 Tropospheric Scatter

Tropospheric propagation is based upon the forward scattering of electromagnetic waves within the troposphere, which is the region of the earth's atmosphere immediately adjacent to the earth and extending up to about 10 kilometers. The frequencies may be in the VHF, UHF, or SHF frequency range. Distances of 500 km and greater have been achieved using this mode of propagation.

Prior to the advent of satellite transmission systems, numerous long haul troposcatter systems were built, largely for governmental communication purposes. High-power transmitters, e.g., 2 to 10 kW, are usually required, along with large billboard-shaped antennas.

Fast fading found on tropospheric paths exhibits a Rayleigh distribution and is caused by multipath transmission. Space and frequency diversity are useful in reducing the effects of such fading. Antenna spacings of 60λ often are used for this purpose. Slow fading, having periods of hours to days, results from changes in the refractive index gradient. Diversity cannot combat this type of fading. Increased power must be used.

Because the received power comes from a volume in the troposphere, high antenna gains are not fully effective. The larger the gain, the smaller the beamwidth and thus the smaller the illuminated volume. The antennas are said to suffer an antenna-to-medium coupling loss.

Multipath causes limits to the bandwidth that can be used on a given modulated carrier, although narrow beam antennas and diversity help in reducing multipath effects. The propagation thus is characterized by a spread in transmission delay times. The standard deviation of the delay power spectrum is called σ. The rms delay spread thus is 2σ. For digital transmission, the symbol duration τ also is important, and the ratio $2\sigma/\tau$ is used as a criterion in predicting the feasibility of achieving a given bit error rate on a digital troposcatter link.

Figures 4.10 and 4.11 [Ref. 7], respectively, show estimated values of delay spread and the resulting symbol error probabilities that can be expected.

Example

Given a median value of $E_b/N_o = 20$ dB, a 4.7 GHz carrier frequency, a 4.6 m antenna diameter, a 200 km transmission path, and a 0° takeoff angle, what is the symbol error probability using QPSK and quad diversity at a 1.544 Mb/s rate?

Solution Using QPSK, the symbol rate is $1544 \times 10^3/2 = 772 \times 10^3$ baud, corresponding to a symbol interval of 1.295 μs. From Figure 4.10, the estimated rms delay spread is $2\sigma = 94$ ns. Then $2\sigma/\tau = 0.072$. Using Figure 4.11, the symbol error probability is about 0.5×10^{-6}.

The foregoing example illustrates the feasibility of DS1 rate transmission via troposcatter. However, an attempt to double the bit rate results in a doubling of $2\sigma/\tau$, and a bit error probability well over 10^{-4}.

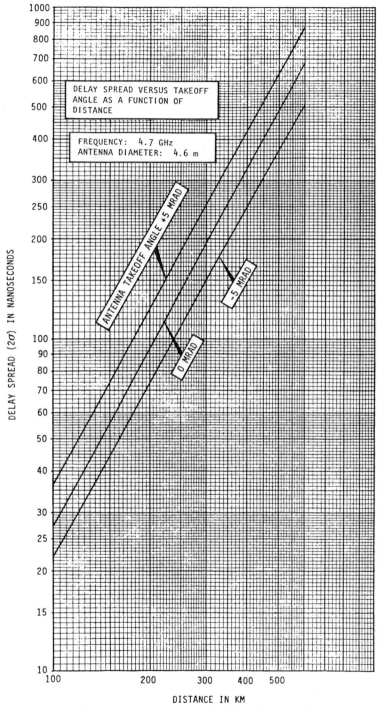

Figure 4.10 Estimated delay spread at 4.7 GHz. (Courtesy REL Incorporated. Reprinted with permission.)

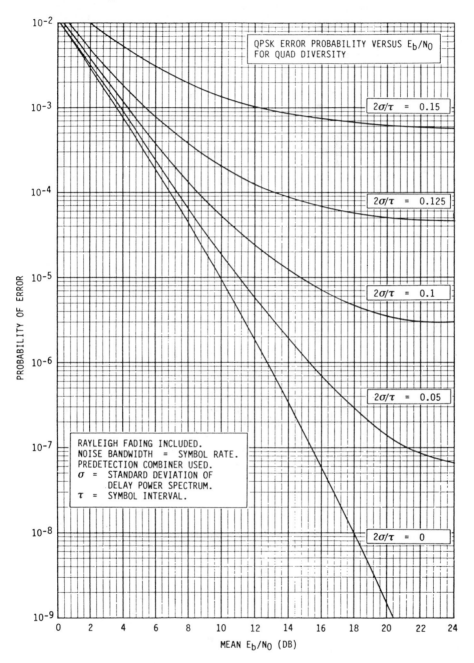

Figure 4.11 Effect of delay spread on symbol error rate versus carrier-to-noise ratio. (Courtesy REL Incorporated. Reprinted with permission.)

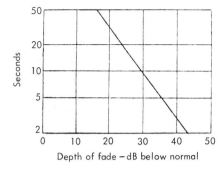

Figure 4.12 Median duration of fast fading on 50 km paths. (Copyright 1970, Bell Telephone Laboratories, Inc. Reprinted by permission.)

Delay spread, as well as the large power and antenna requirements, have discouraged further extensive development of troposcatter systems. Their use has continued, however, in the far north where geosynchronous satellite communication involves significant propagation losses because of the low elevation angles of the satellites above the horizon.

4.1.7 Fading

Fading on a microwave path is the result of changes in atmospheric refraction as well as ray interference (variations in reflection from the surface of the earth), and thus multipath propagation. Atmospheric refraction and its variations were discussed in Sec. 4.1.4.

Ray interference results when a ray reaches its destination by more than one path, i.e., the direct path and a ground reflected path. Ray interference also can result from an irregular variation in dielectric constant with height. Unlike atmospheric refraction, ray interference tends to be fast and frequency selective. Figure 4.12 illustrates the statistics of ray interference at 4 GHz. Deep fades, fortunately, are only of brief duration.

In the design of microwave radio systems (see Sec. 4.6) the probability of fades below a given level must be ascertained and a fade margin must be incorporated into the power budget corresponding to the percent availability for which the system is being designed. Space diversity is helpful in combatting fading.

As can be understood from the foregoing sections, multipath fading on LOS paths results from horizontally stratified atmospheric layers that produce multiple propagation paths in the vertical plane. The corresponding rays arrive with different elevation angles at the receiver. The use of vertically separated receiving antennas thus is effective in decreasing the outage durations caused by multipath.

4.2 MICROWAVE ANTENNAS

4.2.1. Introduction

The purpose of the antenna is to radiate electromagnetic energy produced by the transmitter, directing this energy as desired, and to minimize radiation in unwanted directions. The antenna's receiving characteristics will be the same as its transmitting characteristics at a given frequency, and nearly the same at a nearby frequency.

An *omnidirectional* antenna is defined as one that radiates uniformly in all directions and is also called an *isotropic* radiator. All radio antennas actually exhibit some directivity, but the concept of the isotropic radiator provides a useful reference for gain comparison purposes.

The radiation pattern of an antenna shows its gain versus angle. Usually a plot of gain versus azimuthal angle is of most interest, but a complete description of an antenna's pattern also will include gain versus elevation angle.

4.2.2 Antenna Gain

Equation (4.1) related the gain g_t of an antenna to its effective area A_t. The accompanying discussion noted that antenna efficiencies are not 100%. Correspondingly, a complete expression for antenna gain must include an efficiency factor η. Then if A_t is the physical area of the antenna's reflector,

$$g_t = \frac{4\pi\eta A_t}{\lambda^2} \tag{4.7}$$

Typical values for η are 0.5 to 0.7. Factors contributing to loss of efficiency are discussed in Sec. 4.2.4.

Example

What is the gain of a microwave antenna with a 3.0 m diameter aperture and a 60% efficiency at a frequency of 4.0 GHz?

Solution

$$\lambda = \frac{c}{f} = 3 \times \frac{10^8}{4} \times 10^{-9} = 0.075 \text{ m}$$

$$A_t = \left(\frac{\pi}{4}\right) D^2 \text{ where } D = \text{diameter of aperture}$$

$$A_t = \left(\frac{\pi}{4}\right) (3)^2 = 7.068 \text{ m}^2$$

Then

$$g_t = 4\pi \times 0.6 \times \frac{7.068}{(0.075)^2} = 9474, \text{ or } 39.77 \text{ dBi}$$

Note that the designation *dBi* is used to indicate that the gain is expressed in decibels relative to an isotropic source; note also that the numerical gain is a power gain, as will be apparent from the discussion accompanying Eq. (4.1). Thus the conversion to dBi was on the basis of $10 \log_{10}$ (ratio).

4.2.3 Antenna Patterns

Equation (4.7) described the gain of an antenna in the direction normal to its aperture. Since the aperture usually is a reflector, often parabolic in shape, the direction will be a unique one. In all other directions the gain of the antenna will be less. A plot of antenna gain versus angle off the normal is called an antenna *pattern*. Often this is a polar plot showing gain versus azimuth. Gain versus elevation angle may be of interest for the range from about $-5°$ to $+5°$ for a microwave radio antenna to ascertain its performance over specific terrain types.

Figure 4.13, [Ref. 2, Fig. 2.19], shows how antenna gain and beamwidth vary as functions of aperture area. The abscissa is the actual antenna area. The ordinate is the value at the -3 dB down level, which is the edge of the "beamwidth."

Important pattern characteristics are the *front-to-back ratio* and *sidelobe levels*. The front-to-back ratio is defined as the ratio g_t/g_π where g_π is the gain of the antenna in the direction opposite the center of the beam. Sidelobe levels usually are expressed as being a certain number of dB down from the main lobe (g_t) level. Figure 4.14 illustrates the terms that are important in an antenna pattern description.

Antenna patterns are *far field* descriptions of antenna characteristics. The far field of a high-gain antenna is the field that exists at a distance $\geq 4D^2/\lambda$. This is a sufficiently great distance from the antenna that both the amplitude and the phase of the wavefront are constant, i.e., the wave is a *plane wave*. This distance is required only in the direction of the main beam. For sidelobes and backlobes, far field relationships are present much closer to the antenna.

If two antennas are operated in close proximity to one another, i.e., on the same tower, they may exhibit appreciable side-to-side or back-to-back coupling. Such forms of close coupling must be taken into account in system design because of the interference coupling that may result. Often close coupling is best evaluated by measurement. Antenna patterns alone cannot be used because patterns represent far-field behavior.

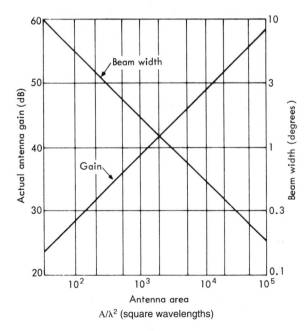

Figure 4.13 Antenna gain and beamwidth versus aperture area. (Copyright 1970, Bell Telephone Laboratories, Inc. Reprinted by permission.)

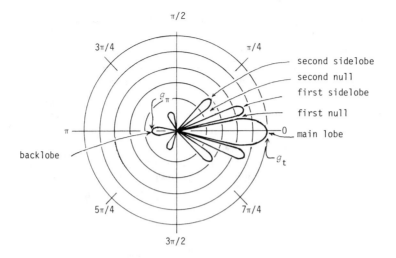

Note: Terminology is the same on both sides of the main
      lobe. Only one side has been labeled in this figure.

Figure 4.14 Antenna pattern terms.

4.2.4 Antenna Types

The two most commonly used antenna types for microwave radio transmission are the focal-fed parabolic reflector and the horn parabola. The focal-fed parabola is a simple antenna of comparatively low cost suitable for short-haul systems and for long-haul routes that are geographically separate from other microwave routes. This limited suitability results from the fact that the feed partially blocks the radiation from the reflector. The blockage not only has an adverse effect on antenna efficiency, but also results in increased side and back lobes. Figure 4.15 illustrates these problems. Ray A is blocked by the feed. Ray B is properly reflected by the parabola. Ray C is diffracted at the edge of the parabola and results in side and back lobe radiation. Ray C can be reduced by using a feed with a smaller beamwidth.

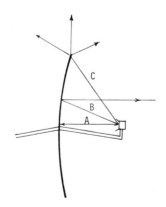

Figure 4.15 Reflection and diffraction
paths for focal-fed parabola.

However, this means (1) a larger feed and consequently more blockage, and (2) a smaller illuminated area on the parabola, with a resulting broader overall radiated main lobe.

The blockage problem can be eliminated through the use of an offset feed. This is the approach used in the horn parabola antenna, shown in diagram form in Figure 4.16. The lower side and back lobe structure of the horn parabola make it useful in well populated areas in which microwave routes run in closer proximity to one another than would be possible with the focal-fed parabola. Table 4.1 provides a comparison of the three antenna types based on published radiation pattern envelope data from one of the manufacturers [Ref. 8]. These antennas have 3-meter apertures and are designed for single-band operation. The values shown are specification limits and thus represent worst case values for the given antenna type. Cross-polarization is specified at the values shown on all three bands.

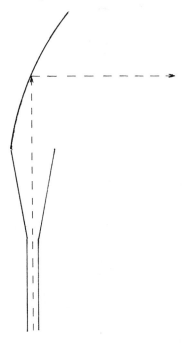

Figure 4.16 Horn parabola antenna.

TABLE 4.1 COMPARISON OF FOCAL-FED PARABOLA WITH HORN PARABOLA (ALL VALUES ARE IN DECIBELS)

	Standard Parabola	High-Performance Parabola	Horn Parabola
Cross-polarization			
Boresight Null	−30	−33	−20
Minimum	−30	−33	−30
Back Lobe			
4 GHz	−47	−67	−80
6 GHz	−51	−79	−90
11 GHz	−54	< −80	−90

4.3 MODULATION OF AN RF CARRIER

Modulation is the process in which the amplitude or angle of a wave is varied in accordance with the information to be transmitted. Both amplitude and angle modulation are used in microwave radio systems. Angle modulation in the form of frequency modulation (FM) has been used most commonly. Some new systems use amplitude modulation in the form of single sideband (SSB). The digital modulation techniques are the same as were described in Chap. 2. Digital modulation often involves combinations of amplitude and phase shift keying.

In discussions of modulation it is useful to describe a current wave of amplitude A, carrier frequency $\omega = 2\pi f$ and phase ϕ as

$$i(t) = A(t) \sin [\omega(t)t + \phi(t)] \tag{4.8}$$

Any one of the variables A, ω, and ϕ may be changed at a rate slow compared with that of the carrier frequency ω. Significant factors in any discussion of modulation are the sideband structure, as it affects the occupied bandwidth, and the ability to remove the modulation from the carrier at the receiving system, in the presence of noise. These factors are discussed next for both amplitude and frequency modulation.

Because digital modulation techniques were covered in Chap. 2, the discussions that follow are oriented toward analog modulation systems.

4.3.1 Amplitude Modulation (AM)

With reference to Eq. (4.8), AM is defined by letting $A(t) = A_0[1 + m_a S(t)]$, where $S(t)$ is the modulating signal, and m_a is the modulation index, such that $0 \leq |m_a S(t)| \leq 1$. The sideband structure in amplitude modulation can be described readily by considering the transmission of a modulating sine wave of frequency ω_s. Thus let $S(t) = \sin \omega_s t$. Then $A(t) = A_0(1 + m_a \sin \omega_s t)$. Substitution of the assumed variation of $A(t)$ into Eq. (4.8), with $\phi = 0$, yields

$$i = A_0(1 + m_a \sin \omega_s t) \sin \omega_c t$$

$$= A_0[\sin \omega_c t + m_a \sin \omega_s t \sin \omega_c t] \tag{4.9}$$

$$= A_0[\sin \omega_c t + \left(\frac{m_a}{2}\right) \cos (\omega_c - \omega_s)t - \left(\frac{m_a}{2}\right) \cos (\omega_c + \omega_s)t]$$

As can be seen from an examination of Eq. (4.9), three frequencies now are present, $\omega_c - \omega_s$, ω_c, and $\omega_c + \omega_s$. The frequencies $\omega_c - \omega_s$ and $\omega_c + \omega_s$ are the sidebands. A fully modulated ($m = 1$) carrier wave will be accompanied by sidebands, each of whose amplitude is half that of the carrier. Since power is proportional to the square of the current i, each sideband has a power level of 0.25 that of the carrier. Thus the continuous power output at 100% modulation is 1.5 times the output at zero modulation. The peak power output at modulation peaks, however, will be 4.0 times the output at zero modulation. This results from the doubling of the instantaneous value of $i(t)$ at modulation peaks.

Because both sidebands convey the same information, one of them can be eliminated. For example, this has been done for many years in frequency division multiplexed (FDM) wireline telephony. The result is called single sideband (SSB). In commercial television, most of the lower sideband is eliminated (see Chap. 3), but the carrier is transmitted. The result is called vestigial sideband (VSB).

Since the carrier conveys no information, it can be eliminated as well, provided that the proper carrier frequency and phase, if needed, can be reinserted at the receiver. Elimination of the carrier and one sideband allows full use of the power handling capabilities of the transmission circuits for information bearing signals, in addition to doubling the utilization of the spectrum. Correct carrier reinsertion at the receiver is accomplished by the transmission of pilot frequencies between certain of the mastergroups in SSB microwave radio systems.

In an AM system, input noise, as well as desired signal, produces a detector output. In other words, no discrimination against noise is provided, so the output signal-to-noise ratio, at best, equals the input signal-to-noise ratio.

Two factors are important, however, in the numerical evaluation of the performance of an AM analog system and are applicable also to angle modulated systems. These are the companding advantage (if companding is used), and an improvement due to C-message weighting. Because both companding and C-message weighting relate primarily to voice-band transmission, they will be treated only briefly here. The reader interested in further details should consult one of the references (Ref. 9, pp. 6–20 to 6–22 and 10–28 to 10–29; Ref. 10, pp. 35–31 to 35–32).

Companding involves *com*pressing the dynamic range of the transmitted signal, e.g., from 60 dB to 30 dB, transmitting the compressed signal, and then ex*panding* the dynamic range of the received signal to the original range. Table 4.2 illustrates the level modifications produced by a compandor.

Compandors provide gain for low-level speech sounds, thus preventing channel noise from masking them. High-level sounds are transmitted at or near their original level. Thus compandors can provide significant subjective improvement in the noise performance of a speech channel. Low levels of crosstalk, correspondingly, can be reduced through the use of compandors. Improvements on the order of 20 to 22 dB are common [Ref. 10, p. 35–32], although for computations a more conservative value of 17 dB often is used. Companding applied on a digital basis can provide on the order of 26 to 32 dB improvement. [Ref. 11, p. 579].

TABLE 4.2 COMPANDOR-LEVEL MODIFICATIONS

Compressor Input	Compressor Output = Expandor Input	Expandor Output
+10 dBm	+7.5 dBm	+10 dBm
+5 dBm	+5.0 dBm	+5 dBm
+0 dBm	+2.5 dBm	+0 dBm
−10 dBm	−2.5 dBm	−10 dBm
−20 dBm	−7.5 dBm	−20 dBm
−30 dBm	−12.5 dBm	−30 dBm
−40 dBm	−17.5 dBm	−40 dBm
−50 dBm	−22.5 dBm	−50 dBm

A C-message weighting curve is a specific audio frequency response curve that is obtained by combining the frequency response of a Type 500 Western Electric telephone set with the hearing characteristics of the average subscriber. It indicates the disturbance value of various tone frequencies in the audio spectrum relative to that of a tone of 1000 Hz. For example, the response at 500 Hz is -8 dB, which means that a 500 Hz tone of given power is 8 dB less disturbing than a 1000 Hz tone of the same power. Because the human ear and the end instrument do not fully respond to the noise in the entire 300 to 3400 Hz passband, an "improvement" factor of 1.4 dB is included in calculations based upon flat noise in the audio band.

4.3.2 Angle Modulation

Angle modulation is a general term used to describe frequency and phase modulation. With reference to Eq. (4.8), frequency modulation (FM) is defined by letting $\omega(t) = [\omega_0 + m_f S(t)]$, where m_f is the modulation index in rad/s/volt of $S(t)$. Phase modulation (PM) is defined by letting $\phi(t) = [\phi_0 + m_p S(t)]$, where m_p is the modulation index in rad/volt of $S(t)$. Frequency and phase modulation are related in that $\omega = d\phi/dt$. The difference lies in the fact that in FM, the instantaneous frequency deviation from the carrier is proportional to the amplitude of the modulating signal, whereas in PM, the instantaneous phase deviation is proportional to the amplitude of the modulating signal. As a consequence, noise accompanying a phase modulated signal produces a detected output that is independent of the noise frequency. However, noise accompanying a frequency modulated signal produces a detected output that is directly proportional to the frequency difference between the noise and the carrier. Thus the noise spectrum for PM is flat with frequency in the baseband, whereas the noise spectrum for FM increases with frequency in the baseband.

The discussions which follow are in terms of FM signals, but comparable results exist for PM signals because of the close relationship between these two forms of angle modulation.

To examine the FM sideband structure as it affects the occupied bandwidth, let

$$S(t) = S_0 \sin \omega_s t. \text{ Then } \omega(t) = (\omega_0 + m_f S_0 \sin \omega_s t) \text{ and}$$

$$i(t) = A(t)\sin\left[(\omega_0 + m_f S_0 \sin \omega_s t)t + \phi(t)\right] \tag{4.10}$$

By definition of FM,

$$A(t) = \text{constant. Letting } A(t) = A_0 \text{ and } \phi(t) = 0,$$

$$i(t) = A_0 \sin\left[\omega_0 t + m_f S_0 \sin \omega_s t\right] \tag{4.11}$$

The deviation ratio β is defined as

$$\beta = \text{peak frequency deviation/baseband rate at which peak occurs}$$

$$\beta = m_f S_0 / (\omega_s)_{\text{max}} \tag{4.12}$$

In more general terms, $(\omega_s)_{max}$ is the maximum significant frequency in the spectrum of $S(t)$.

Equation (4.11) can be expressed in terms of its Fourier components. The coefficients are Bessel functions. They satisfy Bessel's equation,

$$\frac{d^2y}{dx^2} + \frac{1}{x}\frac{dy}{dx} + 1 - \frac{n^2}{x^2}\,y = 0 \tag{4.13}$$

which results from attempts to solve the wave equation in cylindrical coordinates. The Bessel functions are as follows:

$$J_0(x) = 1 - \frac{1}{2^2}x^2 + \frac{1}{2^2 \cdot 4^2}x^4 - \frac{1}{2^2 \cdot 4^2 \cdot 6^2}x^6 + \cdots + (-1)^k \frac{1}{2^{2k}(k!)^2}x^{2k} + \cdots \tag{4.13a}$$

$$J_n(x) = \frac{x^n}{2^n n!}\left[1 - \frac{1}{2(2n+2)}x^2 + \frac{1}{2 \cdot 4(2n+2)(2n+4)}x^4 + \cdots \right.$$

$$\left. + (-1)^k \frac{n!}{2^{2k}k!(k+n)!}x^{2k} + \cdots \right] \tag{4.13b}$$

As a result, the current $i(t)$ of Eq. (4.11) can be expressed in terms of its Fourier spectral components as

$$i(t) = A_0\{J_0(\beta)\sin\omega_0 t + J_1(\beta)[\sin(\omega_0 + \omega_s)t - \sin(\omega_0 - \omega_s)t]$$

$$+ J_2(\beta)[\sin(\omega_0 + 2\omega_s)t + \sin(\omega_0 - 2\omega_s)t]$$

$$+ J_3(\beta)[\sin(\omega_0 + 3\omega_s)t - \sin(\omega_0 - 3\omega_s)t]$$

$$+ J_4(\beta)[\sin(\omega_0 + 4\omega_s)t + \sin(\omega_0 - 4\omega_s)t]$$

$$+ \cdots$$

$$+ J_n(\beta)[\sin(\omega_0 + n\omega_s)t + (-1)^n\sin(\omega_0 - n\omega_s)t]\} \tag{4.14}$$

Note that Eq. (4.14) shows that $i(t)$ consists of numerous sideband components, $\sin(\omega_0 \pm n\omega_s)$, whose magnitudes are those of the Bessel function $J_n(\beta)$. The upper sideband components, $\sin(\omega_0 + n\omega_s)$ are of like sign, but the lower sideband components, $\sin(\omega_0 - n\omega_s)$ alternate in sign. Because of this lack of symmetry, both sidebands are required for correct demodulation of the signal.

Note that since the magnitude of an FM wave remains constant, the appearance of sidebands means that the carrier magnitude must decrease as the argument (β) increases. This decrease indeed occurs, as one can see from the behavior of the $J_0(\beta)$ function in Fig. 4.17. As the modulation index m_f or input magnitude S_0 increase further $J_0(\beta)$ exhibits an oscillatory behavior, but at successively decreasing maximum values, as higher order sidebands become predominant.

The foregoing discussion leads to the question, "What bandwidth is required to transmit an FM signal?" Equation (4.14) implies an infinite number of sidebands and, theoretically, energy spread over the entire radio spectrum. Actually, the magnitudes of arbitrarily high-order sidebands are very low, and thus these high-order sidebands can be removed by filtering without significant degradation to FM transmission.

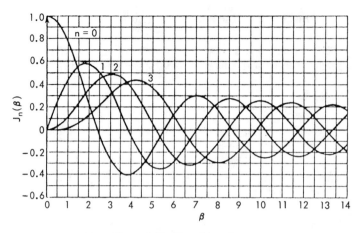

Figure 4.17 Bessel functions.

4.3.2.1 Carson's Rule. A study of the power levels contained within the FM spectrum shows that 99% of the power is within a bandwidth B, where

$$B = 2\left[\Delta f + \frac{(\omega_s)_{max}}{2\pi}\right] \qquad (4.15)$$

where

$$\Delta f = \text{maximum frequency excursion from carrier}$$

This is thus a −20 dB bandwidth. Equation (4.15) is known as Carson's Rule. It is used widely in determining the bandwidth needed for wide-deviation FM transmission or, conversely, given an available RF bandwidth and baseband width, in determining the maximum deviation frequency. It is equally applicable to PM systems, requiring only that Δf be known.

A more familiar form of Carson's Rule is obtained by defining $(\omega_s)_{max}/2\pi = f_m$ and noting that the maximum frequency excursion $\Delta f = m_f S_0/2\pi$. Then from Eq. (4.12), $\beta = \Delta f/f_m$ and

$$B = 2f_m(\beta + 1) \qquad (4.16)$$

For $\beta \ll 1$, $B = 2f_m$. Higher order sidebands, corresponding to the $J_2(\beta)$ and higher terms, are eliminated by filtering.

Example

A microwave radio system is designed for minimum spectrum occupancy while still using nonlinear (limiting) power output amplifiers. Therefore FM with a very low deviation index is selected. If the baseband consists of three frequency-division multiplexed mastergroups with a maximum baseband frequency of 8.284 MHz, what is the occupied RF bandwidth to the −20 dB level? Assume all channels are equally deviated.

Solution: $B = 2f_m = 2 \times 8.284 \times 10^6 = 16.57 \times 10^6 = 16.57 \text{ MHz}$

4.3.2.2 Preemphasis. Section 4.3.2. noted the fact that in FM transmission the detected noise spectrum increases with baseband frequency, unlike PM, in which the detected noise is uniform with frequency. Thus if a number of voice channels are frequency-division multiplexed together and the result then frequency modulates a carrier, those channels occupying the higher frequency slots in the baseband will be received with a degraded signal-to-noise ratio. Video transmission similarly will suffer because of the degraded signal-to-noise ratio about the color subcarrier frequency, 3.579 MHz. To overcome such problems, the upper baseband frequencies are transmitted at a higher than normal level, i.e., they are preemphasized, while at the receiver, the upper baseband frequencies, along with channel noise, are attenuated to achieve an overall flat spectrum.

The idle noise power density at the baseband level in the output of an FM radio system is assumed to be of the form:

$$n = n_0 \left[1 + \left(\frac{f}{f_0} \right)^2 \right] \tag{4.17}$$

where n_0 is the flat noise spectrum, such as may result from shot noise, and f_0 is the frequency at which the flat noise spectrum and the FM triangular noise spectrum cross. For uniformity among transmitters and receivers, certain standards have been established for f_0. For example, in U.S. broadcast FM systems, $f_0 = 2122$ Hz, corresponding to a 75 μs time constant for the determining network. Thus at the transmitter, a 3 dB emphasis is applied to the signal at f_0, with increased emphasis, in accordance with Eq. (4.17), at increased frequencies. Thus if s_0 is the unpreemphasized message signal power density spectrum in watts/Hz,

$$s = s_0 \left[1 + \left(\frac{f}{f_0} \right)^2 \right] \quad f_B \leqslant f \leqslant f_T \tag{4.18}$$

where s_0 is the unpreemphasized message signal power density spectrum in watts/Hz at the same baseband point, and f_B and f_T are the bottom and top frequencies of the spectrum, respectively.

Figure 4.18 illustrates the noise, original signal, and preemphasized signal spectra. For $f_B \approx 0$, the shaping of the signal spectrum effectively increases the total signal power by the ratio

$$\frac{1}{f_T} \int_0^{f_T} \left[1 + \left(\frac{f}{f_0} \right)^2 \right] df = 1 + \left(\frac{1}{3} \right) \left(\frac{f_T}{f_0} \right)^2 \tag{4.19}$$

Accordingly, for a given rms signal deviation, the overall signal power must be reduced by the amount indicated in Eq. (4.19). The result is the final preemphasis shape. Thus the preemphasized signal spectrum is

$$s = 10 \, s_0 \log_{10} \left\{ \frac{\left[1 + \left(\frac{f}{f_0} \right)^2 \right]}{\left[1 + \left(\frac{1}{3} \right) \left(\frac{f_T}{f_0} \right)^2 \right]} \right\} \text{ dB} \tag{4.20}$$

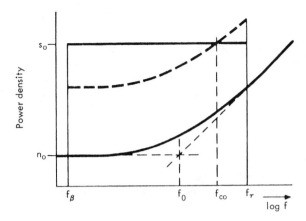

Figure 4.18 Baseband signal and noise spectra with preemphasis. (Copyright 1970, Bell Telephone Laboratories, Inc. Reprinted by permission.)

Note the frequency f_{co} at which the s curve crosses the s_0 level. At this frequency preemphasis causes no change in the transmission level point of the baseband signal, and thus has no effect on system idle noise. For example, the use of CCIR emphasis in an FDM/FM microwave radio system results in a crossover point of $0.608 f_T$. Channels at the lowest baseband frequencies have deviations about 4 dB lower than this reference deviation, whereas channels near the top of the baseband have deviations 4 dB higher than the reference amount. A reference deviation of 200 kHz rms (282.8 kHz peak) is used for systems of 960 or fewer voice channels whereas a reference deviation of 140 kHz rms (200 kHz peak) is used for systems of 1200 or more channels.

Preemphasis applied to a video signal is known as television predistortion. The result is an improvement in color transmission because of (1) the enhancement of the color subcarrier (3.579 MHz for an NTSC signal) as well as, (2) the reduction of the lower frequency spectral components, thereby reducing the magnitude of the intermodulation products that fall near the color subcarrier.

4.3.2.3 FM Threshold. Consider the combination of a desired carrier of peak amplitude A_0 and frequency ω_0 and an unwanted carrier of peak amplitude A_n and frequency $\omega_0 + \omega_n$. The two are assumed to be at slightly differing frequencies. Figure 4.19 shows that the sum of two signals that differ in frequency can be

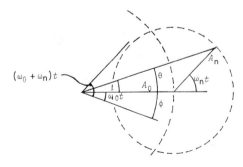

$|A_n| << |A_0|$

Figure 4.19 Amplitude-phase diagram of desired carrier A_0 and unwanted carrier A_n.

regarded as a single signal that is modulated in amplitude and frequency. The desired signal is assumed to be the stronger of the two.

As noted at the beginning of Sec. 4.3.2, $\omega = \dfrac{d\phi}{dt}$. From Figure 4.19,

$$\phi = \omega_0 t + \theta = \omega_0 t + \tan^{-1} \frac{A_n \sin \omega_n t}{A_0 + A_n \cos \omega_n t} \tag{4.21}$$

Since $|A_n| \ll |A_0|$,

$$\phi \simeq \omega_0 t + \left(\frac{A_n}{A_0}\right) \sin \omega_n t \tag{4.22}$$

and

$$\omega \simeq \omega_0 + \left(\frac{A_n}{A_0}\right) \omega_n \cos \omega_n t \tag{4.23}$$

Thus the frequency varies by $(A_n/A_0)\omega_n$ *about the carrier* ω_0, and the deviation caused by the interference is directly proportional to the frequency difference ω_n.

If a noise peak causes $|A_n| > |A_0|$, then the variation no longer is about ω_0, but instead, is about ω_n. Because of the high-peak factor of random noise, the effects of noise peaks become significant for noise power on the order of 9 dB below carrier power. Thus the FM threshold occurs at a carrier-to-noise ratio of 9 dB, with the noise being measured in the receiver's IF bandwidth.

The threshold extension demodulator uses a frequency tracking loop, allowing a threshold decrease from 9 dB to values on the order of 6 dB. In satellite communication systems, whose signal margins are generally on the order of 10 dB or less, the threshold extension demodulator provides a significant contribution to overall link performance. However, on microwave circuits with fade margins on the order of 30 dB or more, as discussed later in this chapter, a simpler form of demodulator providing the standard 9 dB threshold is adequate.

An expression for the threshold can be developed as follows. Electrons in a conductor are continuously in random motion in thermal equilibrium with the molecules, and exhibit a mean square velocity proportional to the temperature. Such noise was originally observed by J. B. Johnson in 1927 [Ref. 12] at Bell Telephone Laboratories, and is called Johnson or *thermal noise*. The available noise power P_n (watts) at temperature T (Kelvin) in a bandwidth B (Hertz) is given by the equation

$$P_n = kTB \qquad \text{watts} \tag{4.24}$$

where

$$k = \text{Boltzmann's constant} = 1.38 \times 10^{-23} \ \frac{\text{J}}{\text{K}}$$

The bandwidth is the noise bandwidth defined by taking the circuit's frequency response, $H(f)$, and integrating the square of this response over all frequencies, because noise is being measured in power, whereas $H(f)$ generally is in units of voltage or current. Then

$$B = \frac{1}{|H_0|^2} \int_0^\infty |H(f)|^2 \, df \qquad \text{Hz} \tag{4.25}$$

where

$$H_0 = \text{maximum value of } H(f).$$

The actual noise level of a circuit may differ from the value shown in Eq. (4.24). Such a difference can be described through the use of an equivalent noise temperature, which may be less than the ambient for a low-noise amplifier. Sometimes the term *noise figure,* defined in Section 4.4, is used, rather than effective temperature, to define the noise characteristics of an amplifier.

Example

A microwave radio relay system has a receiving system whose effective noise temperature is 70 K. The system bandwidth is 20 MHz. What is the FM threshold?

Solution The FM threshold is 9 dB above the receiver noise level, which is $kTB = (1.38 \times 10^{-23})(70)(20 \times 10^6) = 1.93 \times 10^{-14}$ watt. Thus the FM threshold is 1.53×10^{-13} watt, or -128.1 dBW, which is -98.1 dBm.

4.3.2.4 Improvement Factors. For a received carrier level above the threshold, the signal power in the entire signal bandwidth contributes to the output signal power, but only noise power within twice the baseband width (upper and lower sidebands) contributes to the output noise power. The result is an output signal-to-noise ratio, $(S/N)_o$, that may be significantly larger than the input carrier-to-noise ratio $(C/N)_i$. Figure 4.20 [Ref. 13, Fig. 14.2] shows the relationship between $(S/N)_o$ and $(C/N)_i$.

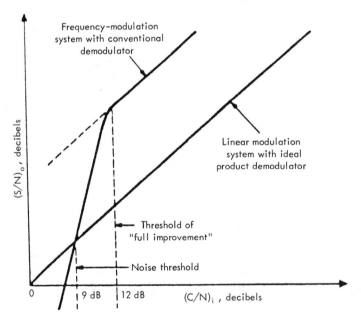

Figure 4.20 Noise performance of FM receiver. (From P. F. Panter, *Modulation, Noise and Spectral Analysis,* © 1965, McGraw-Hill, NJ.)

For a frequency discriminator, the improvement is

$$\frac{(S/N)_0}{(C/N)_i} = \frac{3\beta^2 B}{2f_m}$$

(4.26)

For a phase detector, the improvement is

$$\frac{(S/N)_0}{(C/N)_i} = (\Delta\Phi)^2$$

(4.27)

where

$$\Delta\Phi = \text{peak phase deviation.}$$

Note that the improvement factor is negative for very small deviations.

4.4 SYSTEM IMPAIRMENTS

Chapter 1 noted the four categories of system impairments that may be found in a communications system. These are background noise and co-channel interference, intermodulation, intersymbol interference, and adjacent channel interference.

4.4.1 Background Noise and Co-Channel Interference

4.4.1.1 Noise Types. Background noise found in microwave radio systems includes thermal, shot, and impulse noise. Thermal noise was introduced in Sec. 4.3.2.3 where it was noted that thermal noise power is directly proportional to the bandwidth as well as to temperature, as can be seen from Eq. (4.24). Since thermal noise results from the Brownian motion of electrons in a conductor, its amplitude fluctuations are described mathematically by the Gaussian distribution. This distribution is the limiting form for the distribution function of the sum of a large number of independent quantities that may have different distributions individually. The result is known in statistics as the central limit theorem. Thermal noise thus satisfies the conditions for a Gaussian distribution. In terms of the instantaneous voltage V of the fluctuation, assuming zero mean, the probability density function is

$$p(V) = \frac{1}{\sigma_n \sqrt{2\pi}} \exp\left(\frac{-V^2}{2\sigma_n^2}\right)$$

(4.28)

The cumulative distribution is given by the integral of $p(V)$,

$$P(V) = \frac{1}{\sigma_n \sqrt{2\pi}} \int_{-\infty}^{v} \exp\left(\frac{-x^2}{2\sigma_n^2}\right) dx$$

(4.29)

The statistically expected value of V^2, or the mean square voltage, is equal to the variance, σ_n^2. Accordingly, the rms voltage of a noise having a Gaussian distribution is σ_n, the standard deviation. A knowledge of the Gaussian distribution is significant in determining the bit error rate in digital transmission at a given ratio of carrier-to-noise power.

Noise may have a Gaussian distribution without being "white" or broadband. In fact, filtered noise still retains its probability distribution regardless of the amount of filtering applied. Conversely, a very broadband noise does not necessarily have a Gaussian distribution. An example is a single impulse which is not Gaussian, but whose frequency spectrum is very wide in bandwidth.

Shot noise is caused by the discrete nature of electron flow. It is found in most active electronic devices. Shot noise results from a large number of independent contributions and thus exhibits a Gaussian distribution. It differs from thermal noise in that it does not depend on temperature, but rather on signal amplitude, being proportional to the square root of the current through the device.

Impulse noise consists of brief spikes of energy with essentially a flat spectrum over the frequency range of interest. Impulse noise results from switching transients in communication systems as well as from corona discharges along transmission lines. The effects of impulse noise include bit errors in data transmission as well as flaws in both voice and video transmission.

If pulses occur at random times on an independent basis, the number that are found in any fixed interval follows a Poisson process [Ref. 14]. The probability that n pulses occur in time T, if v is the average number of pulses occurring in unit time, is

$$P(n) = \frac{(vT)^n e^{-vT}}{n!} \tag{4.30}$$

The actual noise found in telecommunication circuits exhibits a number of arrivals per unit time that is approximately log normal, i.e., the decibel equivalent follows a Gaussian curve.

Impulse noise differs from steady noise since the impulses exhibit a very low duty cycle, i.e., they are short relative to the time between them. The peak voltages of the impulses vary directly with bandwidth, whereas thermal noise voltage peaks vary as the square root of bandwidth. This behavior is a result of the fact that the impulse noise peaks represent the addition of nearly equal in-phase components that are uniformly distributed in frequency. Bandwidth reduction deletes a proportional number of equal contributors. The rms value is proportional to the square root of the average power which is directly proportional to the bandwidth. Accordingly, the peak factor of impulse noise can be changed by filtering. Broadband peak clipping circuits can reduce the effects of impulse noise appreciably, and are most effective if applied before band limiting, and consequent pulse smoothing, occurs.

4.4.1.2 Noise Temperature. Equation (4.24) provides a means whereby the noise level in a circuit can be expressed as a temperature, and whereby noise levels can be combined analytically, since noise power is directly proportional to noise temperature. For a thermal noise source, the noise temperature is the actual physical temperature. Other noise sources can have their levels expressed in terms of an equivalent noise temperature. Thus a low noise amplifier has an effective noise temperature that may be on the order of only 50 K to 100 K, well below the physical ambient.

In general, if a noise source produces P watts over a bandwidth B, its effective noise temperature is P/kB, in accordance with Eq. (4.24). The temperature of a noise source may vary with frequency. In this case, the noise power should be measured in very small bandwidths and the result then expressed versus frequency.

The term *antenna noise temperature* expresses the noise at the output terminals of an antenna. Such noise results from radiation intercepted by the antenna from objects on the earth as well as in outer space.

4.4.1.3 Receiving System Noise.

All stages of a receiver produce noise, but the noise generated by the first stage is amplified more extensively than that generated by the following stages. Given the cascade of stages shown in Fig. 4.21 with gains $G_1, G_2 \ldots G_n$ and noise temperatures $T_1, T_2 \ldots T_n$, what is the equivalent noise temperature of the cascade? Assume the bandwidth B is made arbitrarily small, so that noise variation with frequency is not an issue. Then:

Output of second amplifier due to T_0 is $G_1G_2kT_0B$
Output of second amplifier due to T_1 is $G_1G_2kT_1B$
Output of second amplifier due to T_2 is G_2kT_2B

The total noise out of the second amplifier is $G_2k B(G_1T_0 + G_1T_1 + T_2')$
The total noise out of the second amplifier due to internal sources is

$$G_2k B(G_1T_1 + T_2)$$

The effective input temperature of a two-stage amplifier is

$$\frac{G_2k B(G_1T_1 + T_2)}{G_1G_2k B} = T_1 + \frac{T_2}{G_1}$$

In general, for n stages in cascade, the effective input noise temperature is

$$T_e = T_1 + \frac{T_2}{G_1} + \ldots + \frac{T_n}{G_1G_2\ldots G_{n-1}} \tag{4.31}$$

Note that Eq. (4.31) has been developed on a completely general basis. It is applicable to transmission functions whose gain is less than 1.0. However, in the case of passive components such as transmission lines, what noise temperature is to be used? The noise power at the input to the line is $kT_0 B$. At the output of the line, the noise power is $kT_0 B/L$ where L = line loss, expressed as a numeric. Thus the amount of power absorbed by the line is $kT_0 B(1 - \frac{1}{L})$, and is equal to the power radiated by the line in the form of heat. The effective noise temperature of the line T_e corresponds to an output noise power $kT_e B$. Thus,

$$\frac{kT_e B}{L} = kT_0 B \left(1 - \frac{1}{L}\right) \tag{4.32}$$

Therefore, $T_e = T_0(L - 1)$

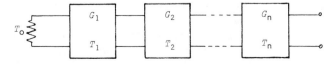

Figure 4.21 Cascade of stages in receiving system.

Example

A section of coaxial transmission line has a 2.0 dB loss between a receiving antenna and the input terminals of the receiver. If the ambient is 290 K, what is the effective noise temperature at the line input?

Solution   The 2.0 dB loss corresponds to a power ratio of $10^{0.2} = 1.585$.

$$T_e = 290 \, (1.585 - 1) \, \text{K} = 169.6 \, \text{K}$$

Although this noise is attenuated by the line, so is the desired signal level. Accordingly, an ideal receiver ($T = 0$ K) would still exhibit a 169.6 K *receiving system* noise if fed by the above transmission line.

A frequently used figure of merit of a receiving system is the ratio of receiving antenna gain G to effective noise temperature T. The G/T ratio, expressed in "dB/K," but actually having dimensions of K^{-1}, is commonly used in transmission link bridgets. The G/T ratio provides a single number which characterizes the sensitivity of a given receiving installation.

The noise figure F is directly related to the effective temperature T by the equation

$$F = 1 + \left(\frac{T}{290}\right) \tag{4.33}$$

This commonly used expression can be derived, [Ref. 14, pp. 86–87], from the basic definition of noise factor, which is

$$F = \frac{P_i/N_i}{P_o/N_o} \tag{4.34}$$

where

$$P_i = \text{available input signal power}$$

$$P_o = \text{available output signal power}$$

$$N_i = \text{available input noise power}$$

$$N_o = \text{available output noise power}$$

Thus noise figure is a measure of the extent to which the signal-to-noise ratio is degraded as a result of passing through an amplifier. The noise figure often is expressed in decibels.

$$\text{Noise figure} = 10 \log_{10} F \tag{4.35}$$

Note that a circuit or component whose noise corresponds to the ambient temperature of 290 K has a noise figure of 3.0 dB.

4.4.1.4 Co-Channel Interference.   Co-channel interference results when attempts to receive a desired channel are disturbed by the presence of an unwanted signal on that channel. The unwanted signal usually is present because of an unexpected propagation condition. Co-channel interference results in an increased bit error probability as well as in crosstalk or picture disturbances in analog transmission. Co-channel interference must be reduced by path changes or increased antenna pattern discrimination. Orthogonal polarization also can help to provide needed isolation.

4.4.2 Intermodulation

Intermodulation noise is produced whenever the strength of a signal is sufficient that operation occurs on a nonlinear portion of the characteristics of the transmission equipment. Intermodulation is the cause of numerous system impairments, including bit error probability increase in digital systems, as well as distortion and background disturbances in analog systems.

A major cause of intermodulation is gain compression, which results from the nonlinear characteristics of amplifiers. This problem is found in both vacuum tube and solid state amplifiers. Figure 4.22 [Ref. 15, p. 82] shows that saturation produces gain compression near the power limits of the device. This figure also illustrates the meaning of the 1 dB and the 3 dB compression points as those points at which the power has dropped 1 dB and 3 dB, respectively, below the output level that would exist if the devices were perfectly linear.

A characteristic of the type shown in Fig. 4.22 can be expressed on a voltage basis as well, since a decibel change in power is equivalent to a decibel change in voltage. The Taylor series expansion can be used to describe a nonlinear voltage transfer characteristic as follows:

$$e_0 = a_1 e_1 + a_2 e_i^2 + a_3 e_i^3 + \cdots + a_n e_i^n \tag{4.36}$$

The generation of harmonic frequencies by a nonlinearity can be illustrated by letting $e_i = A \cos \omega t$ and, to keep the illustration simple, by letting $a_n = 0$ for $n > 3$.

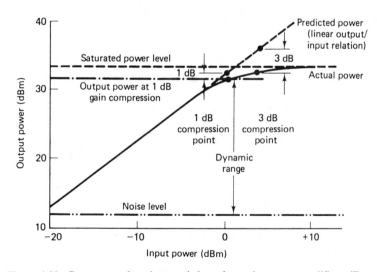

Figure 4.22 Power transfer characteristics of a microwave amplifier. (From Kamilo Feher, *Digital Communications: Microwave Applications*, © 1981, p. 82. Reprinted by permission of Prentice-Hall, Inc., Englewood Cliffs, NJ.)

Then

$$e_0 = a_1A \cos \omega t + a_2A^2 \cos^2 \omega t + a_3A^3 \cos^3 \omega t$$

$$= 0.5 \, a_2A^2 + [a_1A + 0.75 \, a_3A^3] \cos \omega t$$

$$+ 0.5 \, a_2A^2 \cos 2\omega t + 0.25 \, a_3A^3 \cos 3\omega t$$

As an exercise, the student can use the same principles to show that the simultaneous application of two frequencies ω_1 and ω_2 will result in an output that contains, *inter alia*, sum and difference frequencies, i.e., $\omega_1 + \omega_2$ and $\omega_1 - \omega_2$. In general, higher order values of a_n will be present and the output will contain frequencies consisting of $\pm m\omega_1 \pm n\omega_2$, where m and n are positive integers. The sum $m + n$ is known as the *order* of the intermodulation product.

Example

A microwave radio amplifier is designed to pass all frequencies from 3 940 to 3 960 MHz. Carrier frequencies of 3 949 and 3 951 MHz are transmitted through the amplifier. What will be the frequencies of the intermodulation products within the passband?

Solution   The intermodulation frequencies are at $\pm m\omega_1 \pm n\omega_2$ or, in frequency terms, $\pm mf_1 \pm nf_2$. Those within the passband are:

$$2 \times 3\,951 - 3\,949 = 3\,953$$

$$3 \times 3\,951 - 2 \times 3\,949 = 3\,955$$

$$4 \times 3\,951 - 3 \times 3\,949 = 3\,957$$

$$5 \times 3\,951 - 4 \times 3\,949 = 3\,959$$

$$2 \times 3\,949 - 3\,951 = 3\,947$$

$$3 \times 3\,949 - 2 \times 3\,951 = 3\,945$$

$$4 \times 3\,949 - 3 \times 3\,951 = 3\,943$$

$$5 \times 3\,949 - 4 \times 3\,951 = 3\,941$$

The amount of intermodulation distortion present in a system can be defined by using the *third-order intercept point*. Figure 4.23, [Ref. 15, p. 83], illustrates the concept. Note that for an input below --25 dBm the amplitude of the third-order product is negligible, but for greater inputs it increases rapidly. In fact, for each dB increase of the fundamental, the third-order level increases 3 dB (just as the second-order level increases 2 dB). The third-order intercept point is the intersection of the asymptotes of the output signal and the third-order product level. Hoefer [Ref. 15, p. 83], provides a means of calculating the amplitude of the intermodulation products from the third-order intercept point and the desired signal output levels as follows:

$$P_{im3} = 2P_1 + P_2 - 2P_{3i} \text{ dBm} \quad (\text{for } 2f_1 \pm f_2) \qquad (4.37A)$$

$$P_{im3} = 2P_2 + P_1 - 2P_{3i} \text{ dBm} \quad (\text{for } 2f_2 \pm f_1) \qquad (4.37B)$$

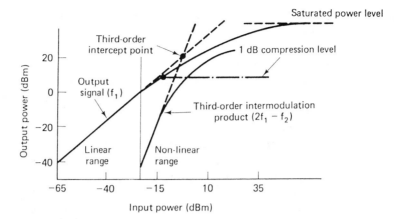

Figure 4.23 Illustration of third-order intercept point. (From Kamilo Feher, *Digital Communications: Microwave Applications,* © 1981, p. 83. Reprinted by permission of Prentice-Hall, Inc., Englewood Cliffs, NJ.)

where

P_{im3} = output power of third-order intermodulation product (dBm)

P_1 = output power at frequency f_1 (dBm)

P_2 = output power at frequency f_2 (dBm)

P_{3i} = third-order intercept level (dBm)

In systems using angle modulation a significant cause of intermodulation is differential gain and phase, also known as low-order transmission deviation. Such deviation is a time invariant characteristic, and thus produces no new frequencies as such. However, the amplitude and phase information of the sidebands relative to the carrier is changed, and these changes are interpreted by the demodulator as modulation. As a result, distortion appears in the recovered signal. [Ref. 11, pp. 272, 492].

Differential gain is the difference in gain encountered by a low-level, high-frequency sinusoid at two stated instantaneous amplitudes of a superimposed low-frequency signal, usually zero and the maximum handled by the system.

Differential phase is the difference in phase shift encountered by a low-level, high-frequency sinusoid at two stated instantaneous amplitudes of a low-frequency signal, usually zero and maximum.

As can be seen from the definitions, a video baseband signal, as described in Chap. 3, is a primary example of the type of signal that is degraded by differential gain and phase.

One cause of differential gain is a situation in which the high-level low-frequency component suffers gain compression at its peaks. The result will be less gain at all frequencies at times corresponding to these peaks. As a consequence, the high-frequency component will exhibit amplitude modulation at the low-frequency rate.

Another cause of differential gain and phase is simple lack of uniformity of the transmission characteristics of a system due to spurious reactive components, or imperfect equalization.

A cause of intermodulation that is significant in both digital and analog transmission is AM to PM conversion. Such conversion is defined by the phase shift of an amplifier that results from a 1 dB change in input power. Usually the conversion factor shows a significant variation with respect to input power level.

An alternative definition expresses AM to PM conversion in dB as $20 \log_{10}(k_p/m)$ where k_p is the peak phase deviation in radians and m is the modulation index of the applied amplitude modulated waveform. Values of AM to PM conversion may range from as low as -34 dB for a well-designed limiter to as high as -6 dB. In a highly linear circuit, AM to PM conversion usually can be ignored. A good microwave repeater may exhibit an AM to PM conversion of less than $2°$ per dB. For video transmission, the differential gain and phase should not exceed 2 dB and $5°$, respectively. Values appreciably greater result in picture streaking, smearing, and overshoot (outlines to the right of objects).

The two methods of describing AM to PM conversion can be related by converting radians to degrees and fractional changes to dB as follows:

$$\text{degrees/dB} \approx 6.6 \text{ antilog} \left[\frac{20 \log \left(\frac{k_p}{m} \right)}{20} \right] \approx 6.6 \frac{k_p}{m} \qquad (4.38)$$

Another significant source of intermodulation disturbance is echoes. Echoes frequently result from impedance mismatches, but also may occur due to mode conversion within waveguides or via "sneak" transmission paths (inadvertently designed into the equipment) at harmonic or product frequencies. Echoes occur when a primary transmission path is paralleled by an unwanted secondary path over which a portion of the original signal arrives at the receiver delayed relative to the signal via the primary path. Echoes due to impedance mismatch often result from reflections occurring where an antenna is connected to its transmission line, and where the transmission line is connected to the transmitter or receiver.

In general, given the signal $e_1(t) = A_c \sin [\omega_c t + \phi]$, to which is added an echo of relative amplitude r and delay τ, after limiting, the resulting phase modulation can be shown, [Ref. 11, p. 519], to be $\phi(t) + \phi_D(t)$, where

$$\phi_D(t) = r \sin [-\omega_c \tau + \phi(t - \tau) - \phi(\tau)] \qquad (4.39)$$

4.4.3 Intersymbol Interference

Intersymbol interference (ISI) was discussed in Chap. 2 in connection with correlative level encoding. In general, ISI is the condition in which a given transmitted symbol produces signals beyond its allocated time slot, and thus interferes with following symbols. Thus echoes can be classified as one form of ISI. Usually, however, ISI is caused by the use of circuits whose bandwidth is insufficient to pass pulses at the desired rate. Narrowband circuits store some of the energy of a symbol during its designated time slot, and release this energy during subsequent time slots.

Since ISI is governed by factors that relate to the time domain, it is unaffected by pure system gain changes. Thus if a transmission's bit error probability is degraded by ISI, an increase in signal power will not improve matters, because the ISI will increase along with the signal. For example, the delay spread (ISI) characteristic of troposcatter transmission, as portrayed in Fig. 4.11, shows a situation in which the bit error probability reaches a lower limit dependent on the amount of delay spread, $2\sigma/\tau$, rather than upon the signal-to-noise ratio, E_b/N_0.

Eye diagrams often are used to display ISI, the open eye showing the absence of ISI, while partially closed eyes indicate increasing levels of ISI.

The seriousness of ISI is a function not only of its magnitude, but also its time spread. For example, in the case of echo degradation to NTSC video, Fig. 4.24, [Ref. 11, p. 699], shows that echoes spaced less than 4µs from the desired signal are less serious than those having greater spacings. The reason is that echo in a video signal is displayed as a ghost to the right of the desired image. An echo spacing of 0.5 µs has a −10 dB rating because a 0.5 µs displacement corresponds to 0.5/52.4 = 0.00954, or less than 1% of the horizontal width of a picture. Such an echo appears more like a double contour than a ghost, i.e., it begins to blend into the picture itself, thus becoming less objectionable.

In data transmission, ISI whose duration is small relative to a symbol period similarly may contribute little or nothing to the bit error probability, and thus will be of much less concern than if its delay time were on the order of a symbol period or more.

4.4.4 Adjacent Channel Interference

Adjacent channel interference (ACI) results when the sidebands from one channel extend into the other. Such interference leads to increases in bit error probability as well as to disturbances in analog transmission. Filters are needed to remove the disturbing higher order sidebands from the adjacent channel, but in so doing, the filters cause some distortion to the desired signal in the form of ISI. Adequate channel spacing along and near a given route thus becomes important. Orthogonal polarization in adjacent channels also can help to provide isolation.

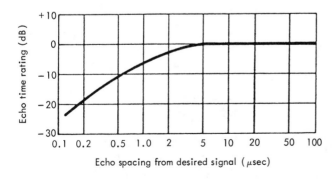

Figure 4.24 Echo time weighting. (Copyright 1970, Bell Telephone Laboratories, Inc. Reprinted by permission.)

4.5 REGULATORY LIMITS

The design of a microwave radio system must be done in accordance with the standards accepted by the governing body of the land. Internationally, the basis for microwave radio system standardization is the set of recommendations promulgated by International Radio Consultative Committee (CCIR) of the International Tele-communications Union (ITU). Within the United States, the regulation of radio transmission is governed by the Federal Communications Commission (FCC) for all but Federal government usage. Federal government usage is under the control of the Interdepartment Radio Advisory Committee (IRAC), a part of the National Telecommunications and Information Administration (NTIA). The FCC and the IRAC work together closely, especially regarding situations in which interference may occur between Federal and non-Federal frequency allocations. Table 4.3 shows the major frequency bands allocated to the "fixed" service within the United States [Ref. 16]. The details of international allocations can be obtained from the reference, which specifies the allocation in terms of regions as follows:

Region 1   Europe, Africa, the Arabian peninsula, and the USSR portion of Asia
Region 2   North and South America, including Greenland and Hawaii
Region 3   Australia, the South Pacific islands and Asia outside the USSR

TABLE 4.3 MAJOR FREQUENCY BANDS
ALLOCATED TO THE FIXED SERVICE
WITHIN THE UNITED STATES

Government (Federal) (MHz)	Nongovernment (MHz)
1 700–1 850	
	1 850–2 200
2 200–2 300	
	2 450–2 500
	3 700–4 200
4 400–4 900	
	5 925–6 425
	6 525–7 125
7 125–8 500	
	10 550–10 680
	10 700–11 700
	12 200–13 250
14 500–14 714.5	
15 136.5–15 350	
	17 700–19 700
21 200–23 600	21 200–23 600
25 250–27 500	
	27 500–29 500
	31 000–31 300
36 000–39 500	36 000–40 000

The United States allocations are within the general framework of those of Region 2.

Table 4.4 lists the radio channel width and the minimum allowable number of voice channels per radio channel in the most commonly used nongovernment bands.

Emission limits beyond the allocated radio channel widths have been defined to help reduce the amount of ACI present. Meeting these limits requires the use of carefully designed filters, generally operating at intermediate frequency (IF). The emission limits are especially important since failure to meet them may result in serious degradation to the use of analog transmission in radio channels adjacent to those carrying digital transmission. Other combinations, i.e., digital to adjacent digital and analog to adjacent digital, also may suffer degradation, but of a less serious nature.

Microwave radio systems using analog modulation must provide for the attenuation of their sidebands in accordance with the regulations [Ref. 17, Part 21] shown in Table 4.5, where

f = frequency of a given sideband, MHz

f_0 = carrier frequency, MHz

B = bandwidth, MHz

$b = 100|f - f_0|/B$

P = mean output power, watts

TABLE 4.4   RADIO CHANNEL WIDTH AND MINIMUM
NUMBER OF VOICE CHANNELS

Band (GHz)	Radio Channel Width (MHz)	Min. Voice Channels
2.11 – 2.13	3.5	96
2.16 – 2.18	3.5	96
3.70 – 4.20	20	1152
5.925– 6.425	30	1152
10.70 –11.70	40	1152

TABLE 4.5   SIDEBAND LIMITS, ANGLE MODULATED
SYSTEMS

b	Attenuation below P
$0 \leq b < 50$	0
$50 \leq b < 100$	≥ 25 dB
$100 < b < 150$	≥ 35 dB
$b > 150$	$\geq 43 + 10 \log_{10} P$ or 80 dB, whichever is less

For a microwave radio system using digital modulation in a band below 15 GHz, the emission limits are expressed in terms of the attenuation $A(f)$ below the mean wideband power output in a 4 kHz band as follows:

$$A(f) = \begin{cases} 0 & \text{dB} & \text{for } 0 < b < 50 \\ 35 + 0.8\,(b - 50) + 10\log_{10} B & \text{dB} & \text{for } 50 < b < 250 \\ \text{(at least 50 dB but no more than 80 dB)} \end{cases} \quad (4.40)$$

Figure 4.25 is a plot of the expressions of Eq. (4.40). Note that the power is expressed in a 4 kHz band. Based on a uniform spread of energy over, e.g., a 30 MHz radio channel, the power spectral density is $10\log_{10}(4 \times 10^3/30 \times 10^6) = -38.75$ dB relative to the unmodulated carrier power.

For systems operating at carrier frequencies above 15 GHz, the emission limits are expressed in terms of the attenuation $A_m(f)$ below the mean wideband power output in a 1 MHz band as follows:

$$A_m(f) = \begin{cases} 0 & \text{dB} & \text{for } 0 < b < 50 \\ 11 + 0.4\,(b - 50) + 10\log_{10} B & \text{dB} & \text{for } 50 < b < 250 \\ \text{(at least 11 dB but no more than 56 dB)} \end{cases} \quad (4.41)$$

For $b \geq 250$, $A(f) = A_m(f) = 43 + 10\log_{10} P$ or 80 dB, whichever is less.

Reference to Table 4.4 shows that for PCM digital voice transmission, the minimum number of voice channels per radio channel in the 2 GHz bands corresponds to a DS2 stream rate of 6.312 Mb/s. In the 4, 6, and 11 GHz bands, however, the minimum requirement of 1 152 voice channels does not correspond to a number found in the digital hierarchy (see Chap. 2). Designers have chosen to go to the next

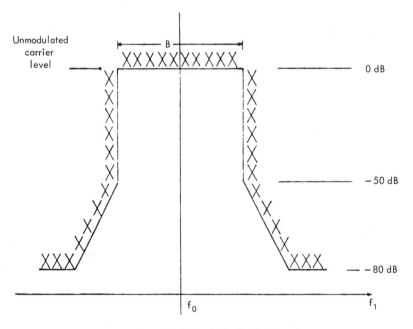

Figure 4.25 Emission limits for digital radio.

higher standard number of channels, 1 344, which corresponds to two DS3 stream rates, or 90 Mb/s, as the minimum to be implemented in these bands. The use of multilevel modulation techniques and, in some cases, orthogonal polarization, is needed to achieve the corresponding transmission efficiencies. For example, transmitting 90 Mb/s in a 20 MHz bandwidth requires 4.5 b/s/Hz efficiency.

The regulatory agencies not only demand good spectral efficiency in microwave radio, but also have specifications concerning the minimum permissible path distance. For the U.S. [Ref. 17], in the 6 GHz band, this distance is 17 km, while in the 11 GHz band, it is 5 km. In addition, discrete spectral lines must not be produced. Accordingly, digital stream scramblers are used.

4.6 SYSTEM DESIGN

The design of a successfully operating microwave radio system demands careful attention to a number of preliminary steps. These steps are outlined in this section.

4.6.1 Coordination

Once a decision has been made to build a microwave system from one point to another, a preliminary path layout will be drawn showing the tentative locations of the various repeater sites, the operating bands, modulation type (digital, FM or SSB), antenna types, and expected transmitter power levels. The services of an organization possessing a data bank describing the existing frequency assignments then are obtained to determine the availability of radio channels along the desired path and in the desired operating band. Coordination is the process of determining *a priori* (1) whether a new microwave system will interfere with existing users of the bands, and (2) whether existing users of the bands will interfere with the new system. By "existing users" is meant not only other microwave radio systems, but also satellite communication links that may occupy the same bands. Coordination thus is vital in assuring system operation free of interference.

The use of large scale maps, such as aeronautical charts, as well as aerial surveys of the proposed path, are useful in identifying possible problems, such as path obstructions, in advance. Attempts should be made to locate possible sources of interference such as radars whose harmonic outputs may fall in or near the planned operating bands.

During the coordination process, parallel or intersecting microwave paths will be identified and the potential interference levels to and from them will be computed. A field survey may be undertaken to provide path profile details that are not otherwise available, especially possible obstructions that may have been newly constructed.

Actual path tests involve transmitting over the path and measuring the field strength at the planned receiving site. Path tests allow the location of reflection points to be identified, and the values of reflection coefficients to be determined. The observed path loss will correspond to the value of K (see Sec. 4.1.4) at the time of measurement. Antenna height can be varied to determine the heights at which free space loss is obtained, as well as the best heights to minimize fading caused by ground reflections, as might result from the presence of a highway or airport near a ground reflection point. Because of the cost of path tests, however, such tests usually are justified only for heavy route planning, or where terrain details are such that advantageous obstructions exist which are not taken into account in the usual coordination computations. Often the computations are based simply on a smooth earth assumption.

4.6.2 System Layout

Microwave repeaters must be placed so that they are within radio line of sight of one another. Secs. 4.1.2 through 4.1.5 discussed the basics of line of sight propagation, ground reflection, refraction and diffraction. Repeater spacing depends not only upon LOS path clearance, but also upon fading, including rain attenuation. Other factors affecting repeater spacing are tower costs, interference to and from other systems, and system requirements in terms of the points to be served along the route. Tower costs can be traded versus repeater spacing, with taller (costlier) towers allowing fewer repeaters overall. Parallel paths should be avoided because of their interference potential. Where routes must cross one another, the crossing should be done at right angles if possible.

The design of a microwave path involves several considerations. These are related to (1) path clearance over obstacles, (2) the avoidance of specular reflection along the path, and (3) minimization of the effects of "overreach" conditions.

Path clearance over obstacles is achieved by recognizing that the refraction of microwaves usually occurs based upon an effective earth radius that is 4/3 of the true earth radius. Good design practice dictates that the first Fresnel zone surrounding the microwave beam clear the surface of the earth based upon the 4/3 radius criterion. In addition, since refraction corresponding to as little as 2/3 of the true earth radius may occur at times, an additional criterion calls for 0.3 Fresnel zone clearance at K = 2/3.

The path profile and antenna heights over local terrain at the end points of a given path will determine whether or not the Fresnel zone clearance criteria are met for a given path. In addition, however, at the point of closest approach of the path to the surface of the earth, there must be no mirror-like or specular reflection. Thus rivers and lakes at such a location must be avoided. Changes in the refractive index over the path may even cause changes in the location of the specular point.

The best method of controlling the specular point along a given path is by adjustment of the antenna heights. Fig. 4.26 illustrates this concept. In Fig. 4.26a, severe fades may result from reflections from the smooth water surface. In Fig. 4.26b, the specular point has been shifted to land existing near the lower antenna. Usually mirror-like reflection does not occur from a land surface.

Occasional refraction conditions may occur in which K assumes very large values, corresponding to atmospheric ducting along a given path. The output of a given repeater then may be received not only at the intended repeater, but also at other repeaters further down the chain. By dog-legging the chain, i.e., avoiding a straight-line design, the antenna pattern characteristics can be used to help decrease

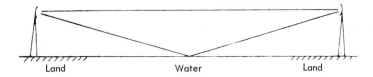

(a) Equal antenna heights; specular point at path midpoint (water surface)

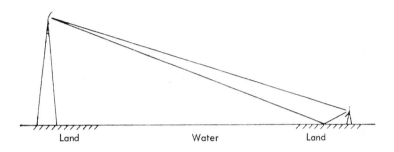

(b) Unequal antenna heights; specular point near low antenna (land surface)

Figure 4.26 Control of specular point by adjustment of antenna height.

overreach problems. Such problems may be especially severe in coastal areas or in regions of considerable land-water interface. Other means of minimizing the results of overreach include the use of alternate frequencies from one hop to another, and the use of orthogonal polarizations. The latter is especially helpful where adjacent channels are used by two nearby systems.

Diversity is a means of combatting the problems of fading caused by changes in the refractive index. Diversity can be implemented on either a frequency or a space basis. Frequency diversity requires two separate frequencies and thus does not make efficient use of the radio spectrum. Accordingly, tight regulations exist regarding frequency diversity, and industrial users in the U.S. and elsewhere are not allowed to use it.

Vertical space diversity is especially effective against ground- or water-reflective fading, as well as against atmospheric multipath fading. Although space diversity is more expensive than frequency diversity because of the additional antennas and waveguides it requires, it generally can provide better protection than frequency diversity, especially where the latter is limited to small frequency spacing intervals. Suitable spacings have been found to be 20 m at 2 GHz, 15 m at 4 GHz, 10 m at 6 GHz, and 5–8 m at 11 GHz.

Horizontal space diversity has been found useful in digital radio systems through the use of antennas having differing beamwidths or beam cross sections [Ref. 18]. Spacings are comparable to those used for vertical space diversity. The success of horizontal space diversity in digital radio systems is attributed to the fact that digital radio is affected more strongly by multipath dispersion than by total power fade depth, as is the case in analog radio.

Where numerous microwave routes converge on a metropolitan area, interference problems among the converging routes may demand that many of the links be brought in at higher frequencies than those used by the major portions of these routes. Thus an intercity route may use the 4 or 6 GHz band along most of its length, but may be brought into its terminating cities or large intermediate cities in the 11 GHz band.

4.6.3 Link Budget

A link budget is an essential element of any radio system design. The purpose of the budget is to assure the reception of adequate signal strength through the use of suitable transmitter power and antenna sizes, while not using excessive power and thereby creating interference problems. The use of decibel expressions is convenient in structuring link budgets because the decibel values can be simply added to or subtracted from one another.

The basic link budget equation for a line-of-sight microwave radio system is

$$(p_r)_{\text{dBm}} = (p_t)_{\text{dBm}} + (g_t)_{\text{dB}} - (L_a)_{\text{dB}} + (g_r)_{\text{dB}} \tag{4.42}$$

where L_a is the link path loss, which consists of (1) spreading loss, L, determined by Eq. (4.4), (2) absorption, described in Fig. (4.3), (3) fading (see Sec. 4.1.7), and (4) polarization loss. Means of determining a suitable fade margin are outlined later in this section. Polarization loss, assuming correct antenna alignment, results from atmospheric moisture, which causes linear polarization to become elliptical; this problem is most significant above 10 GHz but usually results in only one dB or less loss. It is discussed in detail in Chap. 5 because its effects are most serious in satellite transmission.

Based upon the received power p_r and the receiver noise level, the carrier-to-noise ratio, C/N, at the receiver input can be determined. Very often the limiting factor in the link budget is not C/N, but C/I, the ratio of carrier level to interference. The criterion usually is $C/I = 25$ dB, with turn down values being 18 dB for analog video and 15 dB for digital data. Turn down is required only in the event of unusual propagation conditions (raising the interference level or decreasing the desired signal) or degradation in the transmitter output level.

The term *section loss* is defined as the dB loss between the radio transmitter output and the following radio receiver input. Thus it is link path loss plus waveguide and combining network losses, as decreased by the gains of the transmitting and receiving antennas. Accordingly,

$$\text{Section loss} = (L_a)_{\text{dB}} + (L_{wg})_{\text{dB}} + (L_n)_{\text{dB}} - (g_t)_{\text{dB}} - (g_r)_{\text{dB}} \tag{4.43}$$

where L_{wg} and L_n are the waveguide and network losses, respectively.

The term *hop* is used to denote the distance between successive repeaters.

Example

Determine the receiver input power for a 4 GHz radio hop given the following conditions:

Transmitter output power = 5 watts	37.0 dBm
Gain of each antenna (3 m diameter)	39.6 dB
Waveguide loss, each end	2.1 dB
Network losses, each end	1.9 dB
Path length	46 km

Solution   The free space loss is computed using Eq. (4.4b). The result is 137.5 dB. The received power then is found by adding the antenna gains and subtracting the losses. Thus

$$\text{Receiver input power} = 37.0 - 1.9 - 2.1 + 39.6 - 137.5 + 39.6$$
$$- 2.1 - 1.9 = -29.3 \text{ dBm}$$

In addition to the received carrier level, the receiver's noise level must be determined. Assuming a 20 MHz radio channel bandwidth as is standard for the 4-GHz band, the receiver noise level can be determined if the receiver's noise figure or noise temperature is known. The noise figure is defined by Eq. (4.33). The effective temperature T represents noise contributions of both the receiver and noise entering the antenna from external noise sources. Since the antenna is looking along the horizon of a noisy earth, the noise temperature associated with the antenna, T_a, easily may be several hundred Kelvin. The noise temperature associated with the receiver, T_e, will depend largely upon the type of preamplifier used in the receiver.

4.6.3.1 Noise Figure.   Following the definition presented in Eq. (4.33), the overall noise figure F_r of a receiving system is defined as

$$F_r = 10 \log_{10} \left\{ \left(\frac{T_a + T_e}{290} \right) + 1 \right\} \tag{4.44}$$

Noise figure is discussed further in Sec. 4.6.4. The overall system noise temperature is $T = T_a + T_e$. The corresponding noise level then can be computed from Eq. (4.24) as kTB with $k = 228.6$ dBW/HzK.

Example

In the foregoing problem, if $T_a = T_e = 290$ K, then $T = 580$ K = 27.6 dBK, which, from Eq. (4.44), is $F_r = 4.77$ dB. In a 20 MHz bandwidth, the noise level N will be $kTB = -228.6 + 27.6 + 73.0$ dBHz $= -128$ dBW $= -98$ dBm.

4.6.3.2 Multiple Hops.   For n hops, assuming identical repeaters and identical received power levels at each receiver, the noise adds as $10 \log_{10} n$ dB. Thus for nine hops, $N = -98.0 + 9.5 = -88.5$ dBm in the above example. This obviously is well below the -29.3 dBm signal level. However, numerous factors must be taken into account between these two levels, as will be seen in the next section.

4.6.3.3 Fade Margin.   Microwave systems are subjected to propagation fades caused by multipath transmission and by rain attenuation. Thus if a common carrier wants to keep propagation outages as low as equipment outages, a two-way annual fading allocation of 0.01% over a 400 km route (53 minutes per year) may be specified, [Ref. 15]. This is equivalent to 7 minutes per year over a 50 km hop. The achievement of such a reliability may require a fade margin on the order of 40 dB, thus leaving a 19.2 dB carrier-to-noise-plus-interference ratio in the preceding example in order to assure an adequately low bit error probability with the modulation technique used, including a margin for modem losses and other forms of circuit degradation.

How much fade margin is required to provide a given level of path availability? The answer to this question has been developed in the Barnett-Vigants equation for fade margin [Ref. 20,21]. This equation, based on experimental data, is

$$M_f = 30 \log_{10} d + \log_{10} (6ABf_{GHz}) - 10 \log_{10} (1-R) - 70 \text{ dB} \qquad (4.45)$$

where

d = path length, km

R = availability objective (one way) for a 400 km route

A = roughness factor

B = conversion factor, worst month to annual probability

f_{GHz} = carrier frequency, GHz

Values of A are as follows:

4 for very smooth terrain, including over water

1 for average terrain

0.25 for mountainous, very rough terrain

Values of B are as follows:

0.5 for lake areas, especially if hot or humid

0.25 for average inland areas

0.125 for mountainous or very dry areas

To obtain the fade margin for the worst month, set $B = 1$. Thus if the required $R = 0.9999$,

$$M_f = 30 \log_{10} d + 10 \log_{10} (6Af) - 30 \qquad \text{dB}. \qquad (4.46)$$

For any two-way path length d,

$$1 - R = \frac{0.0001 \, d}{400} \qquad (4.47)$$

to achieve $R = 0.9999$ over a 400 km path.

4.6.3.4 Special Propagation Techniques. The need for large antenna heights to overcome Fresnel clearance and specular reflection problems may make the use of periscope antennas seem attractive. However, such techniques have been found effective only at frequencies of 6 GHz and higher, and are not recommended at lower frequencies. Thus at 4 GHz and below, use can be made of the fact that waveguide and coaxial line losses are lower. Alternatively, if line loss is a problem, the RF components of the repeater can be mounted at or near the antenna feed and powered from below.

The use of passive repeaters (back-to-back dishes connected by coaxial cable or waveguide) and passive reflectors (billboards) may appear attractive in certain terrain types. However, these techniques usually are practical only at 6 GHz and higher frequencies, and then only relatively close, e.g., within a few km, to an active repeater. Below 6 GHz, antenna beamwidths generally are too large to permit the use of passive repeaters.

4.6.4 Repeaters

Repeaters are of two basic types, baseband and heterodyne (IF or RF). A baseband repeater is one in which the modulating information is transferred at baseband frequencies, as shown in Fig. 4.27. Circuits can be added or dropped readily at any of the baseband repeaters in a chain. Baseband repeaters thus often are used in short-haul service, and are commonly found in the 6 and 11 GHz bands.

Heterodyne repeaters avoid the conversion to and from baseband, as is done in baseband repeaters. Instead, as shown in Fig. 4.28, the radio-frequency input is converted to an intermediate frequency, amplified, and then converted back to radio frequency. Alternatively, the input frequencies may be simply translated (converted) to the output frequencies, as is done in the RF repeater. These approaches avoid the added noise associated with the demodulation and remodulation processes. In addition, the modulation is unchanged through the repeater, so adjust-

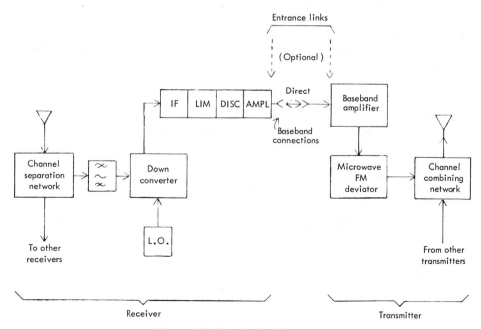

Figure 4.27   Baseband radio repeater.

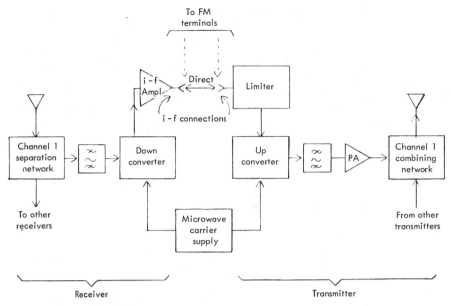

Figure 4.28 Intermediate frequency radio repeater.

ment problems are fewer. Channels still can be added and dropped at IF repeater sites, on an off-line basis, i.e., by separately converting between IF and baseband.

4.6.4.1 Small-Signal Amplifiers. Small-signal amplifiers in microwave radio repeaters often use gallium arsenide field-effect transistors (GaAsFETs). Such devices typically exhibit noise figures on the order of 1 dB (75K noise temperature). Linear operation is very important in a small signal amplifier if intermodulation problems are to be minimized. In areas where strong signals are present on nearby frequencies, preselection may be required ahead of the preamplifier to prevent its overload.

GaAsFETs are capable of covering entire microwave bands with noise figures of 3 dB and lower. Gain values of 25 dB, output levels of 10 dBm and third-order intercept points as high as 20 dBm are readily available.

4.6.4.2 Power Amplifiers. Power amplifiers for use in microwave radio systems may be either traveling wave tube amplifiers (TWTAs) or solid-state power amplifiers (SSPAs) and generally provide 2 to 20 watts output. New systems at frequencies below 10 GHz now generally incorporate SSPAs, while systems at higher frequencies still make extensive use of TWTAs, but with further technological development of SSPAs, the latter are expected to become popular in the higher frequency systems also.

Specifications for microwave power amplifiers describe their gain or output power versus frequency and also indicate the effect of temperature on gain. Temperature has a significant effect on the gain of SSPAs. The efficiency of a power amplifier is defined as its output less its input relative to the supplied dc power.

An amplifier's power transfer characteristic describes the output power as a function of input power. An example of a power transfer characteristics was shown in Fig. 4.22. Nonlinearities of the power transfer characteristic manifest themselves in the generation of intermodulation products, as well as in errors in the amplified input amplitude. In addition, a phase shift is produced that depends on the input power level. These two factors cause distortion of SSB signals and alter the digital signal-state diagram (see Chap. 2) in terms of both amplitude and phase. Accordingly, compensation for these nonlinearities must be achieved for the transmission of SSB as well as such multiamplitude digital modulation forms as 16-QAM, 64-QAM, and 256-QAM.

Operation in the most linear portion of a power amplifier's characteristic also is important in minimizing ACI since unwanted spectral sidelobes, which are inherent in the digital modulation process, may have been filtered out in low-level transmitter stages, but then restored in the power amplifier because of its nonlinearity.

The advent of SSB and multiamplitude digital modulation systems has created the need for the predistortion linearization of microwave amplifiers. The predistortion approach calls for cancelling distortion generated by the power amplifier by preinserting distortion components into the input of the power amplifier [Ref. 22, 23]. The predistortion approach is recognized as the most effective and practical linearization technique for SSB transmission by both microwave radio and satellite systems, and is being found useful for QAM systems as well. The technique has been applied to both TWTAs and SSPAs. Figure 4.29 illustrates the principles of predistortion. The distortion generator also is referred to as a "cuber" since it produces third-order distortion. The gain of the distortion amplifier must be limited to minimize the thermal noise it adds back into the main path. The delay line in the main path is added to compensate for the delay of the cuber path. The delay is adjustable to account for manufacturing tolerances. By proper adjustment of the gain and phase shift through the cuber path the third-order distortion products can be minimized.

Predistortion improvements of 35 to 40 dB have been achieved on 30 MHz bandwidth TWTA circuits [Ref. 22], as well as on SSPA circuits. In addition, SSPA

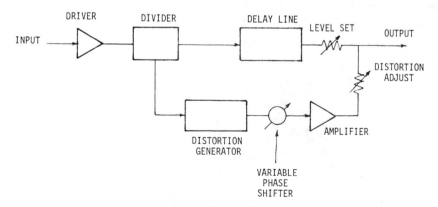

Figure 4.29 Predistorter block diagram.

improvements ranging from 6 to 8 dB over a 500 MHz bandwidth have been achieved, [Ref. 23].

4.6.4.3 Antennas*.

Antennas used for microwave radio relay purposes usually are either the parabolic or the horn reflector type. Parabolic apertures normally range from 0.6 to 4.6 meters in diameter, and can be used for multiband operation with a separate feed for each band of operation. The gain G of such an antenna at a wavelength λ meters ($\lambda = c/f$, where $c \approx 3 \times 10^8$ m/s and $f =$ frequency in Hz) is given by Eq. (4.7) as $G = 4\pi A\, \eta / \lambda^2$, where A is the reflector area and η is the efficiency of the antenna, typically 55–70%. The beamwidth of the parabolic antenna to the -3 dB points is approximately

$$\theta \approx \frac{70\lambda}{D} \qquad \text{degrees} \qquad (4.48)$$

where D is the diameter of the reflector in meters. Such antennas have patterns with front-to-back response ratios of 40 to 80 dB, although the sidelobes may be only 13 to 20 dB down from the main lobe. The polarization is that of the feed, and is usually either horizontal or vertical. Alternate radio channels often are transmitted using alternate polarization to help reduce adjacent channel interference. A standard parabolic antenna is pictured in Fig. 4.30.

Even though parabolic reflector antennas can be built with quite good characteristics, situations arise in which even lower sidelobe levels must be achieved than

Figure 4.30 Parabolic antenna, PXL-series standard microwave antenna. (Courtesy Andrew Corp., © 1982. Reprinted with permission.)

*The material in this section also appears in Ref. 23, pp. 178-79. Both are taken from B. E. Keiser, "Wideband Communications Systems," Course Notes, © 1981 and 1985.

the parabola can provide. Such situations call for the use of a horn-reflector antenna which uses a vertically mounted horn under a section of a parabolic surface. Figure 4.31 shows several of these antennas on a repeater tower. Such antennas not only have front-to-back ratios of 80 to 90 dB, but also can be built to have a beam pattern that continues to drop in amplitude off boresight rather than exhibiting the prominent sidelobes characteristic of the parabola.

Figure 4.32 shows the radiation pattern envelope of a horn-parabolic antenna, Andrew Type Number SHX10B, which has a 3-meter aperture and provides a 42.7 dBi gain in the 6 GHz band [Ref. 25]. The envelope shown is for a horizontally polarized antenna. The actual antenna pattern, except at 0°, is equal to, or lower than, the levels described by this envelope. Minor variations may occur in the pattern itself as a result of reflections from nearby objects. The manufacturer includes a full set of digital data for each pattern in order to save time and maintain accuracy when interpreting from the analog pattern envelopes. One reason for the excellent characteristics of the horn reflector is the fact that the feed does not block the main path of radiation from the reflector, but rather is offset from this direct path. The gain and −3 dB beamwidths of the horn reflector depend on its aperture area, as do those of the parabola, so Eq. (4.7) and (4.48) are applicable to it. Horn reflectors are suited to locations where frequency usage is heavy. Usually they allow

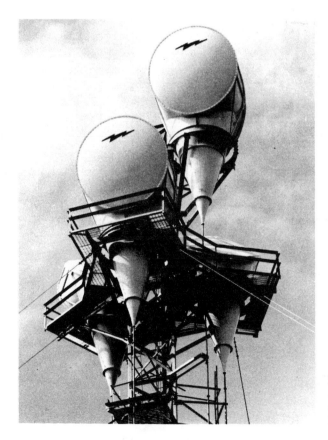

Figure 4.31 Horn-reflector antennas, SHX™ super high-performance antennas. (Courtesy Andrew Corp., © 1982. Reprinted with permission.)

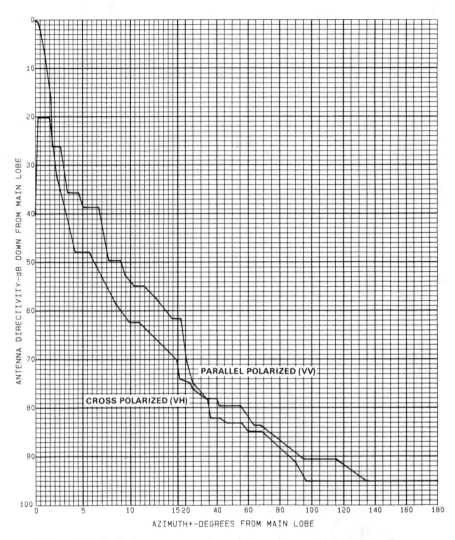

Figure 4.32 Radiation pattern envelope of a 3 m horn-parabola antenna Type SHX10B at 6.175 GHz. (Courtesy Andrew Corp., © 1984. Reprinted with permission.)

the use of identical radio channels in the repeating and branching directions of a repeater site.

4.6.5 System Design Tradeoffs

The needs for spectrum conservation are becoming increasingly significant in microwave radio system planning. Now that three basic types of system, FM, SSB, and digital, are available, which one should be chosen for new system implementation, what channelization arrangement should be chosen, and how well can band sharing be done among systems of different types? This section addressed these issues.

4.6.5.1 Channel Loading and Bit Rate. Until the mid 1970s only FDM/FM microwave radio systems were available. Then some 8-PSK digital systems operating at 90 Mb/s in the 6 GHz band made their appearance. However, the early digital systems were not felt to provide a high degree of spectrum economy because, at 64 kb/s per voice channel, 90 Mb/s is equivalent to only 1 344 voice channels, whereas the FDM/FM systems could provide as many as 2 700 voice channels in the same 30 MHz radio channel bandwidth. Since that time, however, several new developments have entered the scene. One, the advent of SSB microwave radio, allows 6 000 voice channels in a 30 MHz bandwidth. The development of SSB microwave radio, however, required the development of the predistortion linearization of amplifiers, which now is permitting the use of high-level digital modulation techniques such as 64-QAM and the development of 256-QAM. Simultaneously, a digital voice standard at 32 kb/s has been announced by the CCITT. The 64-QAM systems provide 135 Mb/s in a 30 MHz bandwidth; at 32 kb/s per voice channel, this is the equivalent of 4 200 voice channels. Moreover, a 256-QAM system is capable of 5 600 voice channels in a 30 MHz bandwidth. With the implementation of 256-QAM, no longer can it be said that digital transmission wastes bandwidth!

Thus far, the discussion has been in terms of equivalent voice channels. If the criterion is analog video, similar arguments apply if the video requirement is taken to be a given bandwith, e.g., 4.0 MHz, which can be expressed as an equivalent number of voice channels (1 000 for a 4.0 MHz bandwidth). If the criterion is digital, the important factors are bit rate and bit error probability. [Ref 26] However, the bit rate deliverable to the user equals or approximates that on the transmission facility only if the user has a digital subscriber line to his premises. If only analog service is available to the user, the deliverable digital rate will be restricted by the need to convert to analog at the user's premises. For example, if the user attempts to transmit a maximum of 19.2 kb/s and can tolerate a 10^{-5} bit error probability, he can obtain a modem using trellis coding that will place the 19.2 kb/s on a voice bandwidth analog line. Long-haul transmission of the analog bandwidth then may be done at a 64 kb/s rate. Lower rates will not provide suitable characteristics for the transmission. This examples illustrates the importance of digital end-to-end connectivity if spectrum conservation is to be obtained for digital transmission.

In conclusion, end-to-end digital transmission has the best long term potential for spectrum conservation, whether the end-to-end requirement is analog or digital. Until the widespread implementation of 256-QAM, however, SSB microwave radio will be a strong competitor to digital transmission. No doubt FM/FDM will continue in use as well, because it is well established as the most extensively used type of microwave radio system.

4.6.5.2 Multiplexing and Modulation Tradeoffs. Given the requirement to transmit a number of voice or other small bandwidth channels, should each such channel be transmitted on its own carrier or should all be frequency- or time-division multiplexed together first and transmitted on one carrier?

From a strictly theoretical viewpoint, the same information transmission efficiency should be possible irrespective of whether the multiplexing is done on a frequency-division or a time-division basis. However, frequency channelized systems, whether frequency-division multiplexed (FDM) or channelized time-division multiplexed (TDM), require guard bands because of filter roll-off characteristics as well as the time delay distortions that occur at the band edges, both of which result in intermodulation interference. If a system is not frequency channelized, then the entire transmission bandwidth is made available to each burst, a burst conveying the information to be transmitted from a given source during a specific period of time. Transmissions from the individual sources then are separated from one another by time-gating. A time interval, often on the order of 1% of the burst interval, is used to separate the transmissions of the individual sources from one another.

In a system using the FDM hierarchy (groups, supergroups, etc.), the individual channels are separated from one another in the frequency domain by means of channel filter guard bands which may occupy as much as 20% of the available bandwidth. Thus in a standard channel group, the channel slots are each 4 kHz wide, but the actual passband typically is from 200 Hz to 3 200 Hz, meaning that only 3 kHz out of a possible 4 kHz are used. Thus 25% of the spectrum is lost in guard bands. Nevertheless, considerable expense would be entailed, and serious performance degradation would result, if attempts were made to reduce this 25% to the 1% value possible with the time-division multiplexing of digital transmissions. (A sharp cutoff filter will introduce either phase distortion or ripples in the amplitude characteristics or both.)

Use of the full 500 MHz bandwidth in the 4 GHz and 6 GHz common carrier bands as a single large channel is not done because of the problems of dynamic range that would result with available circuit components. Briefly, these problems are (1) the thermal noise over these extensive bandwidths, (2) the saturation level of available amplifiers with an adequately low-noise figure, and (3) amplifier linearity. Factors (2) and (3) may cause serious intermodulation problems. For these reasons, as well as regulatory ones, channelization is done in the 4, 6, and 11 GHz common carrier bands. However, the greatest transmission efficiency results from using time-division multiplexing in the largest possible channel width because guard time slot percentages can be kept lower than guard band percentages.

4.6.5.3 Band Sharing Between Analog and Digital Transmission. Certain radio channels in an overall common carrier band may be used for digital transmission while others are used for analog transmission. This means that digital and analog modulation may be used, respectively, in adjacent radio channels. While the established FCC emission limits ensure that out-of-band levels from a digital radio are low enough not to interfere directly with adjacent analog radios of 960 channels or less, the limits are not sufficient to allow adjacent FM/FDM systems of 1 200 channels or more to meet long-haul noise objectives. Accordingly, the interference produced by the one modulation type may be detrimental to the other, especially with respect to adjacent channel effects, and also with respect to possible effects in other than adjacent channels. In some cases, both analog and digital modulation may share the same channel as is done with the data under voice (DUV) and data above voice (DAV) systems (see Chap. 2).

Compatibility between digital and analog systems is a measure of the ability of the two system types to co-exist successfully within a given common carrier band, especially on an adjacent channel basis, and may be expressed in terms of a signal-to-interference ratio, with the interference being that produced by a system of the other type in an adjacent channel. The most prominent compatibility problem is the interference produced by a digital system in an analog system. Analog detectors must be able to reproduce small amplitude changes accurately, whereas digital detectors need be sensitive only to the relatively abrupt changes produced by digital modulation.

Figure 4.33 [Ref. 27] shows several adjacent radio channels in a microwave band. Channel 2 is the desired FM/FDM channel. Channel 1 is an adjacent FM/FDM channel transmitted using the orthogonal polarization. For this reason, it is about 30 dB lower in strength than Channel 2. Channel 3 is an adjacent 90 Mb/s digital channel using 16-QAM. A noise sensing slot is used so that if the desired signal (Channel 2) fades or is interrupted, an RF squelch is initiated. This prevents receiver noise from being amplified and transmitted needlessly along the repeater chain. The noise level is sensed using a bandpass filter centered 15 to 16 MHz above the IF center frequency with a 3 dB bandwidth of about 2 MHz. This is a good band for noise sensing because it is generally above the second-order sidebands for 1 800 channel message loading, but below the adjacent channel sidebands. The transmit power of the noisy channel thereby is reduced by about 30 dB.

Field tests as well as analyses [Ref. 27, 28] have shown that analog radio channels adjacent to digital ones may suffer serious degradation based upon the use of existing FCC mask limits. For example, next to an 8-PSK channel in the 6 GHz band, an FDM/FM system has its capacity limited to 1 200 channels, rather than the 2 700 channels that could be transmitted otherwise. An SSB/AM system will have all of its channels in one direction degraded by varying amounts, depending on their location within the RF channel.

Digital channels adjacent to analog channels suffer degradation if the analog

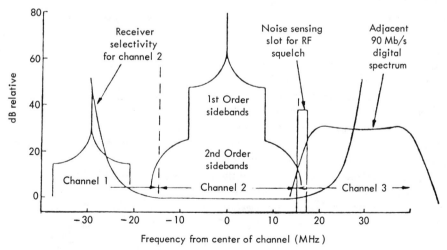

Figure 4.33 Adjacent channels in a microwave band. (Reprinted with permission from *Bell System Technical Journal,* © 1971, Bell Telephone Laboratories, Inc.)

channels are malfunctioning, i.e., transmitting noise only or transmitting sinusoidal carriers only.

Band sharing based upon hybrid (analog combined with digital) transmission has been developed in the forms of DUV, DIV, DAV, and DAVID (see Chap. 2). These systems have demonstrated successful operation based upon designs which limit the E_b/N_0 degradation to 2 to 3 dB, while allowing analog operation to continue with imperceptible degradation.

Looking at an entire RF band, however, hybrid systems must be regarded as having a role primarily in overbuild situations. If it is known in advance that a given RF band is to be devoted partly to digital and partly to analog transmission, then the channels should be assigned in the following sequence for minimum interference between digital and analog transmissions:

> High-capacity digital (e.g., 16-QAM or 64-QAM)
> Medium-capacity digital (e.g., QPSK or 8-PSK)
> Hybrid (e.g., DUV, DAV, DAVID, etc.)
> Low-capacity analog (e.g., 960 channel FDM/FM)
> Medium-capacity analog (e.g., 1 200 or 1 800 channel FDM/FM)

or

> High-capacity analog (e.g., 6 000 channel SSB/AM)

This sequence is based upon the sideband components produced by each of the modulation techniques, as well as the sensitivity of typical receiving systems to ACI.

4.6.6 Reliability and Availability*

The terms *reliability* and *availability* sometimes are used interchangeably. Reliability, however, often denotes the percentage of time during which the equipment performs its intended function, whereas the actual system availability is less because of propagation outages. Thus, if equipment failures disrupt service 0.01% of the time and if propagation outages also disrupt services 0.01% of the time, then the overall system availability is 99.98%.

Availability objectives for U.S. common carrier short-haul systems (<400 km) specify that two-way service failure be less than 0.01% per year. This is equivalent to 53 minutes per year. Industrial microwave systems, especially electric, oil, and gas utilities, allow no more than 0.01% outage during the worst month, because of the potentially serious effects of outages on their operations.

The major factors related to equipment down time are hardware reliability, redundancy, spares availability, and power source reliability. Hardware reliability has increased appreciably with the move to all solid-state components. Redundancy

---

* The material in this section also appears in Ref. 24, p. 176. Both are taken from B. E. Keiser, "Wideband Communications Systems," Course Notes, © 1981 and 1985.

can be applied both to the radio equipment, in the form of duplication, and to the power source in the form of a diesel back-up generator.

Propagation outages can be minimized through the use of an adequate fade margin as well as space diversity. The Barnett-Vigants equation (4.45) allows the computation of fade margin for various propagation path conditions and propagation availability requirements.

4.7 SYSTEM EXAMPLES

This section describes examples of microwave radio systems used by common carriers in the 2, 4, 6, and 11 GHz bands, as well as specialized systems used at 2 GHz, 10 GHz and higher frequencies.

4.7.1 Common Carrier Systems

4.7.1.1 FM Systems. Figure 4.34 shows the basic functions of an FM system for FDM transmission. Voice supergroups and master groups are multiplexed together to form the overall baseband. Alternatively, the baseband may be analog video. The *predistorter* performs the preemphasis function. The frequency deviator in a typical microwave system provides several megahertz deviation upon application of a baseband consisting of two or three mastergroups.

The peak deviation ΔF is split among all the subchannels [Ref. 9, p. 16-14]. For a small number n of sinusoidal tones

$$\text{Peak deviation per tone} = \frac{\Delta F}{n} \qquad (4.49)$$

$$\text{RMS deviation per tone} = \frac{\Delta F}{\sqrt{2}n} \qquad (4.50)$$

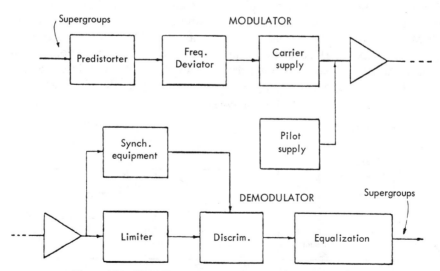

Figure 4.34 FDM/FM modulation-demodulation block diagram.

For a large number, e.g., $n > 100$, of voice channels, the peak values of the waveforms combine statistically. From the central-limit theorem the composite signal's characteristics approach those of white Gaussian noise. Based upon the Gaussian distribution, the peak-to-rms ratio often is taken to be 3.52, which corresponds to an overload expectation of 4×10^{-4}, or 0.04%. Thus the rms modulation level of n channels is

$$\Delta F_n = \frac{\Delta F}{3.52} \tag{4.51}$$

and if all subchannels carry equal average power, the rms deviation of one channel is

$$\Delta F_1 = \frac{\Delta F}{3.52n}, \qquad n > 100 \tag{4.52}$$

FM/FDM systems are built to handle 1 200, 1 800, 2 100, 2 400, or 2 700 channels. Systems handling 600 or 960 channels are authorized commercially only if they use dual polarization so they meet the requirements shown in Table 4.4.

4.7.1.2 Single-Sideband Systems. Figure 4.35 is a block diagram of a single-sideband (SSB) AM system. As shown there, 5 mastergroups, or 3 000 voice channels, are transmitted in each direction, for a total of 6 000 channels on the system. Figure 4.36 shows the spectrum of an SSB-AM radio channel [Ref. 29].

Table 4.6 shows a typical SSB/AM power budget. The required postdetection signal-to-noise ratio of 40 dB is achieved by providing a basic 21.6 dB and noting that the use of companding and the C-message weighting characteristic provide an additional 17.0 and 1.4 dB, respectively (see Sec. 4.3.1). The link budget shows the achievement of a 40.0 dB signal-to-noise ratio without space diversity; 50.0 dB with space diversity. Note that the transmitter power and antenna sizes can be increased readily to provide added margin for multihop service.

An increasing number of situations are arising in which digital transmission must be achieved over an SSB microwave radio system. In the case of PCM or ADPCM voice or voice-band data, a transmultiplexer (TDM to FDM converter) can be used for the interface, and transmission can be done on an analog basis. If a portion of the transmission is digital data, however, a transmultiplexer cannot be used. A clear channel modem is required instead. One type [Ref. 30] places a DS1

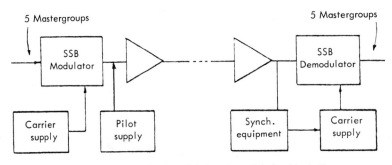

Figure 4.35 SSB/AM modulation-demodulation block diagram.

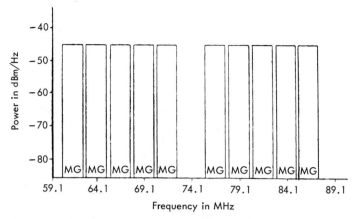

Figure 4.36 Intermediate frequency spectrum of SSB/AM radio channel. (Reprinted with permission from the *AT&T Technical Journal,* copyright 1983, AT&T.)

TABLE 4.6 SSB/AM POWER BUDGET

System parameters	
Message circuit channel capacity	6000 channels
Frequency band	5925 to 6425 MHz
Transmitter power	24.6 dBm
Nominal RF channel bandwidth	29.65 MHz
Receiver noise figure (typical)	3.0 dB
Performance requirement assumptions	
Fade margin, space diversity	46 dB
Fade margin without space diversity	36 dB
Distance	41 km
Design assumptions	
Antenna diameters	2.6 m
S/N in any channel	21.6 dB
Companding advantage	17.0 dB
C-message weighting	1.4 dB
Required Received S/N	40.0 dB
Link budget	
Transmitter power	24.6 dBm
Fixed losses (waveguide, connectors, radome)	−2.0 dB
Antenna gain, transmitting	41.5 dB
Path loss	−140.7 dB
Antenna gain, receiving	41.5 dB
Fixed losses (waveguide, connectors, radome)	−2.0 dB
Fade margin	−36.0 dB
Received signal	−73.1 dBm
Receiver noise level	−94.7 dBm
Received S/N	21.6 dB

signal in an FDM supergroup using 256-QAM. For extensive amount of digital/ analog connectivity, a modem, the Rockwell ADM-1045, using 64-QAM has been designed to place a single DS3 on a SSB baseband. The baseband signal is treated like a normal FDM baseband and the system is operated without the use of regenerative repeaters. Space diversity is important in meeting long-haul outage objectives. This modem allows analog SSB systems to convert to clear channel digital service on an as-needed basis.

4.7.1.3 Digital Radio Systems*.

A digital microwave radio system is one whose instantaneous RF carrier assumes one of a discrete set of amplitude, frequency and phase levels as a result of the modulating signal. Because of the sudden transitions from one level to another, the bandwidth of the transmitted signal is very broad. Filters thus must be used to control the bandwidth to the assigned radio channel while still allowing transmission with a minimum amount of ISI.

The term *digital radio* may be used to describe a radio system that transmits a signal whose informational content is at least partly digital. Thus the baseband may include both analog and digital signals. The FCC states [Ref. 31] that "Digital modulation techniques are considered as being employed when digital modulation contributes 50% or more to the total peak frequency deviation of a transmitted RF carrier." Thus the term digital radio may refer to any microwave radio that transmits PCM, data, or other digital carrier signals, regardless of how or at what point the signals are inserted into the radio equipment.

A digital channel bank interfaces the voice channels to the digital radio. It is followed by channel encoders, which serve to encode one or more bits of the digital input signal into a symbol signal. The bit content of the symbol signal determines the modulating effect it is to have on the amplitude, frequency and phase of the carrier. Each combination of bit values that may be encoded into a symbol signal corresponds to a logic level within the encoder. The logic level the encoder assigns to a particular bit combination defines a discrete amplitude, frequency and phase of the carrier at the moment of modulation.

Figures 4.37 and 4.38 show, respectively, the transmit and receive block diagrams [Ref. 32] of a 135 Mb/s system for operation at 6 GHz using 64-QAM and achieving 4.5 b/s/Hz. This system is the Rockwell DST-2300. The input consists of three DS3 lines, each at 44.7 Mb/s. Input conditioners and elastic buffers are used to obtain uniform pulse quality and to allow stream synchronization. A total of 329 kb/s is added for service channel functions. Scrambling is performed to allow the data stream transitions needed for receiver clock recovery. An interface with protection channel lines is provided.

In Fig. 4.38 the system monitoring and violation monitor and removal (VMR) function is performed in the output conditioner [Ref. 33]. In this unit, DS3 framing is recovered and DS3 parity is compared with parity calculated from the DS3 data. The detection of errors above a preset threshold causes switching to be initiated. The receiving equipment also contains the system DADE module, which equalizes the absolute delay between the various RF channels on a DS3 sectional basis. This helps to minimize error bursts during switching. A data alignment capability is included to align the protection channel data prior to the completion of switching. The result is found to be 10 or fewer DS3 errors per switch operation provided framing is maintained on the regular channel.

---

* Portions of the material in this section also appear in Ref. 24, pp. 181-85. Both are taken from B.E. Keiser, "Wideband Communications Systems," Course Notes, © 1981 and 1985.

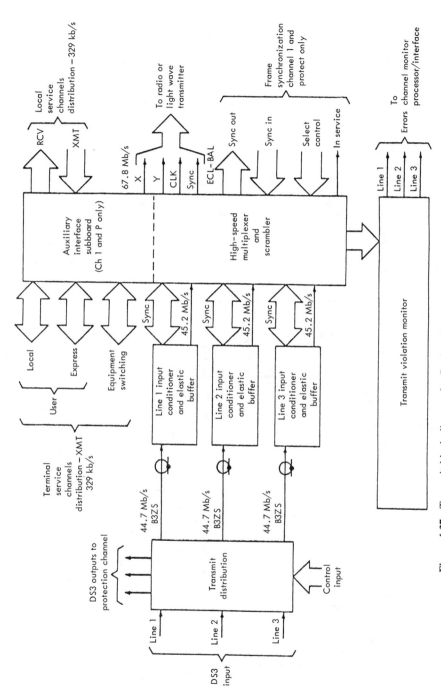

Figure 4.37 Transmit block diagram for Rockwell DST-2300. (From P. R. Hartmann and J. R. Crossett, "135 Mb/s-6 GHz Transmission System Using 64-QAM Modulation," *IEEE ICC '83*, © 1983, IEEE. Reprinted by permission.)

237

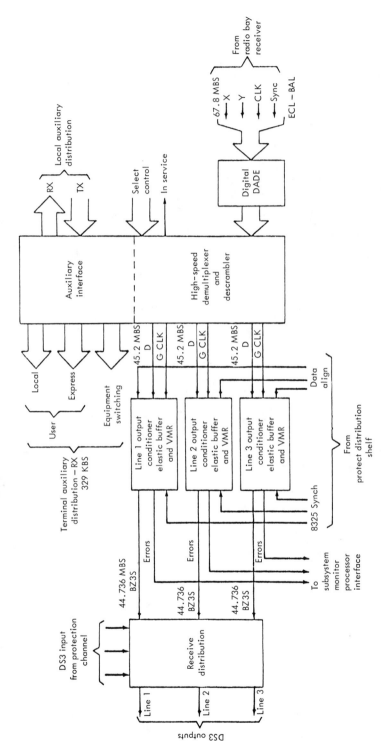

Figure 4.38 Receive block diagram for Rockwell DST-2300. (From P. R. Hartmann and J. R. Crossett, "135 Mb/s-6 GHz Transmission System Using 64-QAM Modulation," *IEEE ICC '83*, © 1983, IEEE. Reprinted by permission.)

Special techniques used in this radio system to minimize performance degradation include (1) intermediate frequency (IF) predistortion to achieve overall linearity, (2) highly accurate timing recovery, and (3) an adaptive transversal equalizer for slope and delay equalization. The timing recovery includes both control of peak jitter in carrier recovery and accurate symbol timing recovery.

Quadrature partial response signaling (QPRS) may be applied to QAM to confine the spectrum of a digital radio system to within regulatory limits by halving the required bandwidth. For example, a 49-QPRS system provides 4 b/s/Hz on a null-to-null basis. The 49-QPRS system results from the PRS encoding of 16-QAM, which provides 4 b/s/Bd. The PRS encoding to 49-QPRS effectively provides 8 b/s/Bd, or close to 8 b/s/Hz in the usually defined Nyquist bandwidth. On a null-to-null basis, this is 4 b/s/Hz.

A 256-QAM system has been developed by Fujitsu Laboratories, Ltd. It transmits 120 Mb/s at 15 MBd using 50% Nyquist roll-off filtering [Ref. 31]. Special techniques used to maintain transmission quality include a predistorter in the modulator for accurate adjustment of the symbol points in the constellation and also carrier injection to provide a predetection $S/N \geq 46$ dB. At a p_{be} of 10^{-6}, a 3 dB impairment is caused by any one of the following:

0.5 dB quadratic amplitude distortion
1.1 dB linear amplitude distortion
6% quadratic delay distortion
2° carrier phase error
1.6% filter bandwidth error
0.6° timing jitter
0.7° rms carrier phase jitter

To maintain performance during normal path and equipment variations, forward error correction using a (255, 247) BCH code has been implemented [Ref. 35] in the 256-QAM system, together with a 5-tap transversal equalizer to reduce impairments such as linear amplitude distortion and carrier phase jitter.

What is the next step beyond 256-QAM in the achievement of spectrum conservation? Increasing the number of levels in a QAM system makes it increasingly vulnerable to nonlinear distortion, fading distortion, and intersystem interference, especially in urban and suburban areas. Two techniques, co-channel dual polarization combined with one-frequency repeating, can provide an overall four-fold improvement in spectrum utilization [Ref. 36]. Techniques for achieving high degrees of polarization purity are discussed in Chap. 5, since co-channel dual polariation has been in extensive use in satellite transmission for many years, although with modulation techniques that are more robust with respect to interference than high-level QAM.

One-frequency repeating is shown conceptually in Fig. 4.39. Its achievement involves the use of an adaptive receiver capable of canceling transmitter to receiver interference. In addition, separate transmit and receive antennas are used in each direction of transmission, for a total of four antennas at each repeater site. Tests by Nippon Electric Corporation (NEC) [Ref. 36] have shown that reflective materials

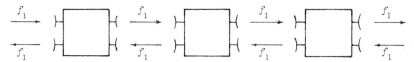

Figure 4.39 One-frequency repeating concept. (From J. Namiki, "One Frequency Repeating for Digital Microwave Radio," *IEEE Globecom '85*, © 1985, IEEE. Reprinted by permission.)

as far away as 1 to 3 km from a microwave transmitter can cause some of the transmitted beam to be reflected back into the receiving antenna, thereby causing unwanted coupling. In such cases, an increase in antenna size to produce sharper transmit and receive beams has been found helpful. Interference cancellation is achieved in the NEC tests by the use of six adaptive transversal filters.

4.7.2 Special Systems

4.7.2.1 Metropolitan Area Systems*.

Several categories of digital radio systems have been developed for the transmission of various stream rates over relatively short distance, high traffic density routes within metropolitan areas. They include digital termination systems (DTS), private systems, and common carrier systems.

Digital termination systems (DTS) are provided by competing common carriers using radio local loops. Each user has a small rooftop antenna, typically a 0.6 m dish, directed toward the service provider's location. Data rates are from 2 400 b/s to 1.544 Mb/s at distances as great as 10 km through moderate rain. The frequency band from 10.55 to 10.68 GHz is allocated for this service both to common carriers and to private users. Additional common carrier bands are: 18.36 to 18.46 GHz and 18.94 to 19.04 GHz. A 10^{-9} to 10^{-11} bit error probability is achieved using 500 mW transmitters and 4-level FSK for distances less than 10 km. The reason for the very low bit error rate is that these are *termination* systems whose performance should not significantly degrade the overall end-to-end system performance.

The two available classes of service are called "extended" and "limited." Extended service carriers serve 30 or more cities and have seven 5 MHz channel pairs in each city. Limited service carriers serve fewer than 30 cities and have six 2.5 MHz channel pairs in each city. The applications include a digital electronic message service (DEMS), high speed facsimile (to 1.544 Mb/s) and teleconferencing using motion-compensated video at 1.544 Mb/s. Satellites may link the various cities.

In operation, a central control station transmits digital traffic to the remote users sites, with the data for the various users being time-division multiplexed. Each remote site monitors the signal and processes only the data addressed to it, and then responds to the central station by sending bursts of preassembled packets of data for a predetermined or controlled time interval on another allocated frequency [Ref. 37].

---

* Much of the material in this section also appears in Ref. 24, pp. 187-88. Both are taken from B. E. Keiser, "Wideband Communications Systems," Course Notes, © 1981 and 1985.

Digital radio systems available for private (industrial or commercial) use within metropolitan areas provide DS1 or DS2 service, often using FSK in the 18.36 to 19.04 GHz band. Output powers are on the order of 100 mW, with bit error probabilities of 10^{-6} being available over distances of 5 to 16 km, depending on the local climate. Antenna diameters range from 60 to 150 cm. These are not "termination" systems, but are designed as end-to-end facilities.

A Motorola system provides DS1 or DS2 service using 2-level AM (*p-i-n* diode modulator) in the 21.2 to 23.6 GHz band. The transmitter output is 20 mW. A 10^{-7} bit error probability is achievable 99.5% of the time over a 4 km distance in an average U.S. midlatitude climate. The antenna is 38 cm $\times$ 38 cm $\times$ 23 cm deep.

The M/A-Com MA-23 DR is capable not only of DS1 and DS2 service but also CEPT-1 (2.048 Mb/s) and CEPT-2 (8.448 Mb/s). The system handles the standard AMI and zero substitution line codes, and provides wavefrom regeneration at the receiver [Ref. 38]. The modulation is FSK with a $\pm$ 4MHz deviation. The transmitter uses a Gunn diode and has a 66 m W ouput. The antenna diameter is 0.6 m or 1.2 m. The receiver noise figure is 12 dB. At a 1.544 Mb/s rate, a $p_{be} = 10^{-9}$ is available 99.99% of the time at distances from 4 to 13 km within the U.S., depending upon climate.

Digital radio facilities have been designed for DS3 transmission in metropolitan areas [Ref. 2, pp. 619–38]. The Western Electric 3A-RDS uses QPSK in the 40 MHz radio channels between 10.7 and 11.7 GHz. Eleven two-way streams are obtained within eleven radio channels using dual linear polarization. Regenerative repeaters are used and the spacing is 16 to 20 km in average climates and 26 to 32 km in dry climates. The 3.2 W transmitter output power provides better than a 17.2 *C/N* at the receivers for a 10^{-8} bit error probability. Many 3A-RDS systems transmit to distances well beyond metropolitan areas.

4.7.2.2 Community Antenna Relay Service (CARS).

Special wideband systems for analog service have been designed for operation in the 12.7 to 13.2 GHz band for several purposes: (1) video signal transmission between CATV headends, from studio to headend, and from headends to distribution points, (2) for television auxiliary broadcast, (3) for the interconnection of CATV systems, and (4) for data transmission within CATV systems. The CARS systems use transmitter powers up to 5 watts. The modulation may be FM, in which case the bandwidth may be up to 25 MHz, or VSB, in which case the bandwidth is a standard 6 MHz channel width.

PROBLEMS

4.1 Two parabolic dishes 1 km apart and each 3 m in diameter are placed so they face one another. Assuming co-polarized feeds suitably designed for each frequency used, calculate the received power if the transmitter power output is 100 mW (neglect feed losses) and if the frequency is, successively, 1 GHz, 3 GHz, 10 GHz, and 30 GHz. Explain your results in the light of Eq. (4.1) and (4.4a).

4.2 A digital radio operates in the 5.925 to 6.425 GHz band using 1.0 W. transmitter powers. The antenna diameters are 3 m and the path length is 50 km. The modulation technique requires $C/N = 20$ dB to maintain an adequately low bit error probability. The receiver noise figure is 5.0 dB. Allow 3.0 dB at each end for waveguide and network losses. Assume a 55% antenna efficiency at each end. What is the fade margin?

4.3 How does the fade margin computed in Prob. 4.2 compare with the level allowable during the worst month, assuming average inland terrain and a 0.9999 reliability requirement?

4.4 During cloudburst conditions over a 5 km section of the path length of Prob. 4.2, what additional path attenuation is encountered?

4.5 A one-hop microwave link is to operate at 10.5 GHz using 1 m diameter antennas. The required reliability is 99.99% Assume average terrain with some roughness. If the section loss is not to exceed 105 dB and diversity is not used, what is the maximum allowable distance between terminals?

4.6 An FDM/FM radio system is designed to transmit three mastergroups in the 6 GHz band. The lowest FDM frequency is to be 564 kHz. Considering the FCC emission limits, what FM deviation can be used? What is the per channel deviation?

4.7 A preamplifier designed for use in the 3.7 to 4.2 GHz band has a noise figure of 1.0 dB and a gain of 10 dB. It is followed by a stage whose noise figure is 6.0 dB. What is the effective noise figure of the receiving systems?

4.8 Draw the FCC mask for a radio channel in the 10.7 to 11.7 GHz band. A Nyquist filter with $\alpha = 0.2$ is used. What is the maximum bit rate that can be transmitted if 8-PSK is used? 64-QAM? 256-QAM?

4.9 An amplifier has a gain of 18 dB. The third-order intercept point occurs at $+25.0$ dBm. Find the third-order intermodulation products in the amplifier's output if the following two signals are present simultaneously in the input:
1. $f_1 = 3\,900$ MHz $P_{i1} = -18$ dBm
2. $f_2 = 3\,920$ MHz $P_{i2} = -20$ dBm

4.10 A system designer must transmit a maximum number of 1.544 Mb/s motion-compensated teleconference video channels within a radio channel in the 2.16 to 2.18 GHz band. He has a choice of a 64-QAM system with a guaranteed $p_{be} \leqslant 10^{-7}$ or a 256-QAM system with a guaranteed $p_{be} \leqslant 10^{-6}$. Which system should he choose and why? How many simultaneous teleconference channels can be transmitted if the channel filtering approximates $\alpha = 0.3$?

4.11 An SSB/AM system is to be designed to cover a 400 km distance along a smooth coastal path. Five mastergroups (full duplex) are to be handled by this system. A 99.99% path availability is to be provided. Select the repeater placement, spacing, antenna sizes, transmitter powers, receiver noise factors, and frequency band of operation. State the reasons for your selections.

4.12 A microwave repeater is located on a 400 m high mountain top in Colorado with an unobstructed view of the flat plains to its east. The next repeater to the east is to be 90 km away. The mountain repeater is on a 5 m high platform. What height is required for the repeater antenna in the plains if a $K = 1.0$ condition is to be met?

4.13 A flat 20 km path is being checked for obstacles that may be within 50 Fresnel zones of a 11 GHz beam. The antennas at the ends of the path are each 120 m high. How high an obstacle can be tolerated at the midpoint of the path? Assume $K = 1.0$.

4.14 A troposcatter system is built to cover a 250 km path (single hop). The median value of E_b/N_0 is 17 dB. The antennas are 4.6 m diameter with $0°$ takeoff angle and the frequency is 4.7 GHz. If QPSK and quad diversity are used, what is the maximum bit rate at which a 10^{-6} bit error probability can be achieved?

4.15 Co-channel cross-polarization is to be used as a spectrum conservation measure along a given microwave path designed to handle analog video initially, with a plan to convert later to digital transmission. You have a choice among standard parabola, high performance parabola and horn parabola antennas. The route is not a dense one in terms of other systems, but could become so in the future. Which antenna type would you select and why?

4.16 Amplitude modulated systems often use only a single sideband for transmission whereas angle modulated systems use both sidebands. Explain why, using Eq. (4.14).

4.17 Equation (4.11) shows that the amplitude, and thus the power, of an FM signal remains constant during modulation. Sidebands appear, however, during modulation. Explain how the power can remain constant irrespective of the presence or absence of modulation sidebands.

4.18 The allowable outage time for a government transmission system is a maximum of 50 minutes per year per hop. What is the section loss if the transmission is in the 7 900 to 8 400 MHz band, the transmit and receive antennas have 3 m diameters, and the hop lengths are 35 km?

REFERENCES

1. E. C. Jordan, *Electromagnetic Waves and Radiating Systems,* Prentice-Hall, NY, 1950.

2. *Telecommunications Transmission Engineering,* volume 2, *Facilities.* Bell System Center for Technical Education, Western Electric Company, Inc., Winston-Salem, NC, 1977.

3. D. E. Kerr, *Propagation of Short Radio Waves,* McGraw Hill, NY, 1951.

4. S. A. Schelkunoff, *Electromagnetic Waves,* Van Nostrand, NY, 1943.

5. R. F. White, *Engineering Consideration for Microwave Communications Systems,* GTE Lenkurt, Inc., San Carlos, CA, 1972.

6. P. L. Rice, A. G. Longley, K. A. Norton, and A. P. Barsis, *Transmission Loss Predictions for Tropospheric Communication Circuits,* National Bureau of Standards Technical Note 101, vols. I and II, revised January 1, 1967.

7. P. Gruber, "Application of Digital Tropo for Command and Control," REL, Inc., Boynton Beach, FL, May 22, 1981.

8. "Radiation Pattern Envelopes for Common Carrier Microwave Antennas," Bulletin 1055, Andrew Corporation, Orland Park, IL, 1982.

9. D. H. Hamsher, *Communication System Engineering Handbook,* McGraw-Hill, NY, 1967.

10. *Reference Data for Radio Engineers,* Howard W. Sams & Co., Inc., Indianapolis, IN, sixth ed., 1975.

11. *Transmission Systems for Communications,* Bell Telephone Laboratories, Inc., revised fourth ed., 1971.

12. J. B. Johnson, "Thermal Agitation of Electricity in Conductors," Phys. Rev., vol. 32 (1928), pp. 97–109.

13. P. F. Panter, *Modulation, Noise and Spectral Analysis,* McGraw-Hill, NY, 1965.

14. W. B. Davenport, Jr., and W. L. Root, *An Introduction to the Theory of Random Signals and Noise,* McGraw-Hill, NY, 1958.

15. K. Feher, *Digital Communications, Microwave Applications,* Prentice-Hall, NJ, 1981.

16. *Manual of Regulations and Procedures for Federal Frequency Management,* National Telecommunications and Information Administration, Washington, DC, Jan. 1984 Ed.

17. *Rules and Regulations,* Federal Communications Commission, Washington, DC, Jan. 1987. Ed.

18. M.F. Gardina and S. H. Lin, "Measured Performance of Horizontal Space Diversity on a Microwave Radio Path," *IEEE Globecom '85 Conference Record,* pp. 1104–7.

19. W. T. Bennet, "Occurrence of Selective Fading as a Functions of Path Length, Frequency and Geography," *ICC '70 Conference Record,* IEEE.

20. W. T. Barnett, "Microwave Line of Sight Propagation With and Without Frequency Diversity," *Bell System Technical Journal,* Vol. 49. pp 1827–1871 (Oct. 1970).

21. A. Vigants, "Numbers and Duration of Fades at 6 and 4 GHz," *"Bell System Technical Journal,* Vol. 50, 815–841 (March, 1971).

22. R. P. Hecken, R. C. Heidt, and D. E. Sanford, "Predistortion for the Traveling-Wave-Tube Amplifier," *Bell System Technical Journal,* 62, (Dec. 1983), 3447–64.

23. T. Nojima, T. Murase, and N. Imai, "The Design of a Predistortion Linearization Circuit for High-Level Modulation Radio Systems," *IEEE Globecom '85 Conference Record,* pp. 1466–71.

24. B. E. Keiser and E. Strange, *Digital Telephony and Network Integration,* Van Nostrand, NY, 1985.

25. "Radiation Pattern Envelopes for Horn Reflector Antenna," Bulletin 1285, Andrew Corporation, 10500 W. 153rd Street, Orland Park, IL. 1984.

26. J. J Spilker, Jr., *Digital Communications by Satellite,* Prentice-Hall, NJ, 1977.

27. "Digital to Analog Radio Interference in the 6 GHz Common Carrier Band," Rockwell International Microwave Products Marketing Bulletin, Dallas, TX, March 31, 1980.

28. M. Ramadan, et al., "Interference Effects of Digital Radios into Adjacent Analog Radios," *IEEE ICC '80 Conference Record,* pp. 34.3.1 to 34.3.5.

29. J. Gammie, et al., "System Design and Performance," *Bell System Technical Journal,* 62, (Dec. 1983), 3255-3312.

30. W. R. McClellan and W. A. Conner, "A DS3 Implementation on SSB Radio Systems," *IEEE Globecom '85,* pp. 1083-88.

31. "Establishment of Policies and Procedures for the Use of Digital Modulation Techniques in Microwave Radio and Proposed Amendments to Parts 2 and 21," Federal Communications Commission, FCC 74-985, Docket 19311, Washington, DC, Sept. 1974.

32. P.R. Hartmann and J. R. Crossett, "135 Mb/s—6 GHz Transmission System Using 64-QAM Modulation," *IEEE ICC '83 Conference Record,* pp.F2.6.1 to F2.6.7.

33. "MDR-2000 Series Digital Radio Systems," Product Description, Collins Transmission Systems Division, Rockwell International, P.O. Box 10462, Dallas, TX.

34. Y. Daido, et al., "256-QAM Modem for High Capacity Digital Radio Systems," *IEEE Globecom '84,* pp. 16.8.1. to 16.8.5.

35. Y. Takeda, et al., "Performance of 256 QAM Modem for Digital Radio System," *IEEE Globecom '85,* pp. 1455–59.

36. J. Namiki, "One Frequency Repeating for Digital Microwave Radio," *IEEE Globecom '85,* pp. 1477–81.

37. D. S. Williams, "Local Distribution in a Digital Communications Network," *IEEE ICC '81 Conference Record,* pp. 66.3.1 to 66.3.5.

38. "Video Microwave Systems," Bulletin 9236A, MA-23CC, M/A-Com MVS, Inc., 63 Third Avenue, Burlington, MA.

5

Satellite Transmission[*]

Communications satellites as we know them today had their beginning with *Syncom*, the first synchronous satellite, in 1963. Soon *Syncom* was followed by *Intelsat I (Early Bird)*, the first commercial satellite, in 1965. Numerous military satellite systems parallel the development of the commercial systems. The first domestic commercial satellite was Telesat's *Anik* (Canadian), followed by Western Union's *Westar* (U.S.). Because of the predominance of analog voice communication during those years, however, satellite earth stations throughout the world were built based upon the analog frequency-division multiplex (FDM) hierarchy. Only with the advent of Satellite Business Systems (SBS) has an all digital satellite system developed. Most satellites and their earth stations provide both analog and digital transmission.

Satellite transmission is unique in that it makes large bandwidths, e.g., hundreds of megahertz, available for intercontinental communication. Moreover, with the use of polarization and spot beaming techniques, a considerable amount of frequency reuse is feasible, which is a significant fact in view of the increasingly crowded radio frequency spectrum.

Satellite transmission is capable of providing global communication, including

---

[*] The initial sections of this chapter also appear in Ref. 1, pages 191–6. Both are taken from B. E. Keiser, "Wideband Communication Systems," Course Notes, © 1981 and 1985.

transmission to and from moving terminals such as ships, and considerable system development effort has been devoted to extending such capabilities to land and aeronautical vehicles [Refs. 2, 3]. Only the polar regions beyond about 81° latitude remain beyond line of sight of the geosynchronous satellites. Since satellites that are not geosynchronous require tracking earth station antennas, coverage of the polar regions is more practical by microwave or other transmission techniques.

The satellite may be regarded as a microwave repeater at a high enough elevation that most circuits require only that one repeater. Where a second such repeater is needed, the overall time delay may produce undesirable effects in attempts to carry on interactive communication.

Satellite transmission developed initially on an analog (frequency-division multiple access) basis. New developments in analog transmission via satellite center on the use of compandored single-sideband modulation, primarily for voice transmission. Broadband developments emphasize digital transmission using multilevel modulation techniques. The implementation of such techniques using time division multiple access (TDMA) avoids many of the intermodulation problems in satellite transponders that have plagued the analog techniques.

5.1 FREQUENCY ALLOCATIONS

Table 5.1 lists the major frequency bands allocated to satellite communications and designates the type of usage in each case [Ref. 4]. In some of the these bands the regulatory authorities have specified maximum power flux densities to minimize interference to existing terrestrial services, since such bands are not used exclusively for satellite service, but are shared with terrestrial users.

The term *allocation* means that the frequencies listed in Table 5.1 are available for the usage indicated, but not all are in actual use at the time of writing. The bands above 17.8 GHz are being used mainly on an experimental basis in the western hemisphere.

5.2 SATELLITE PROPAGATION

The propagation medium for geostationary satellite transmission is a highly stable one because most of the path is through free space. The only atmospheric effects occur near the earth stations and these generally are limited by the fact that propagation usually is upward at a relatively significant angle relative to the horizon. Only at the higher latitudes, or for satellites at a considerably different longitude than the earth station, is a low angle path required.

5.2.1 Orbits

For a satellite to remain in a fixed position in the sky relative to the earth stations it is serving, two conditions must be met. First, the satellite must be over the equator. Second, the satellite must be at an altitude of 35 784 km to 35 804 km, the exact

TABLE 5.1 MAJOR SATELLITE FREQUENCY ALLOCATIONS

Band (MHz)	Usage
225.0– 400.0	government
1530.0– 1544.0 1626.5– 1645.5	downlink ⎫ uplink ⎬ maritime
1545.0– 1559.0 1646.5– 1660.5	downlink ⎫ uplink ⎬ aeronautical
3400 – 4200 5850 – 7075	downlink ⎫ uplink ⎬ commercial
7250 – 7750 7900 – 8400	downlink ⎫ uplink ⎬ government
10700 –11700 11700 –12200	downlink, international ⎫ downlink, U.S. ⎬ commercial
14000 –14500	uplink
12200 –12700 17300 –17800	downlink ⎫ uplink ⎬ direct broadcast
17700 –20200 27500 –30000	downlink ⎫ uplink ⎬ commercial
20200 –21200 30000 –31000	downlink ⎫ uplink ⎬ government

value depending upon the longitude, because of the eccentricity of the earth. The satellite's altitude requirement results from the fact that the period of an orbiting satellite is given by the equation

$$T = 2\pi \sqrt{\frac{A^3}{\gamma}} \qquad \text{second} \qquad (5.1)$$

where

A = semimajor axis of ellipse (earth's radius, $\simeq 6\,378$ km, plus altitude, for a circular orbit)

γ = gravitational constant = 3.99×10^5 km^3/s^2

For a circular orbit to have a period identical with that of the earth's rotation, the period must equal 1 day, which is 23 h, 56 min, 4.09 s.* From a geosynchronous altitude of 35 784 km, three satellites can cover most of the earth's surface.

Actually, the satellite's orbital inclination relative to the equatorial plane will cause it to move north and south relative to the equator with a period of 1 sidereal day. The satellite's orbital eccentricity can cause an altitude variation which, in accordance with Eq. (5.1), translates into east-west motion. The combined motion causes the satellite's position to vary in an oval or figure-8 pattern about its nominal position. All of this pattern must be within the antenna beam position of the using

---

* The referenced period is known as a *sidereal day*, which is the time required for the earth to rotate back to a given constellation.

earth stations. Likewise, the pattern must be kept small enough that the satellite maintains its footprint coverage on the earth within specified limits.

Example

A satellite earth station antenna located on the equator has a 30 m diameter and transmits a pencil beam (circular cross-section) to a satellite directly overhead at 6 425 MHz. If the link degradation due to satellite motion is to be limited to 1.0 dB, how far can the satellite be allowed to move from its nominal position?

Solution   From Equation (4-2), $\Omega = \lambda^2/A_t$. At 6 425 MHz, $\lambda = 3 \times 10^8/6.425 \times 10^9$ m $= 0.0467$ m. $A_t = (\pi/4)(30)^2 = 706.8$ m^2. Then $\Omega = 3.085 \times 10^{-6}$ rad^2. Thus the beamwidth is 0.001756 radians $= 0.1°$. This is to the -3.0 dB level. The beamwidth at -1.0 dB is ≈ 0.55 this amount (see Sec. 5.3.3) or 0.0009658 radians. At geosynchronous altitude, this corresponds to $0.0009658 \times (6\ 378 + 35\ 804)$ km $= 40.7$ km.

The example describes a worst case situation in that for a typical U.S. domestic or European earth station, the slant range from the earth station to the satellite will be on the order of 40 000 km or more. In addition, the beam cross-section will be elliptical in the plane of motion of the satellite. Thus larger excursions than 40 km will be tolerable to a 30 m dish.

Other satellite motions also can occur, however. For example, the satellite may drift slowly in the East-West direction during a period of many sidereal days. Table 5.2 summarizes the satellite position changes which may occur [Ref. 5, pp. 392–3] based upon typical eccentricities and inclinations. As can be seen from the table, eccentricity does not present a serious problem, but orbital inclination can produce enough position change that either a correction will have to be implemented (see Sec. 5.5) or a large dish earth station will require a tracking capability.

Motion of the satellite not only may carry it to or near the edge of the earth station's beam, or produce footprint changes on the ground, but propagation delay may vary also, as is discussed in Sec. 5.2.2.

The geostationary orbit just discussed is the most commonly used orbit for telecommunications satellites. However, other orbits sometimes are used. The polar orbit, often at altitudes of about 730 km such that the period is on the order of 1.7 h, can be used for communication to and from the polar regions, but requires tracking antennas at the earth terminals. An elliptical orbit (12 h period) is used by the Soviet Union for their *Molniya* satellites. This orbit provides good coverage of the far north and avoids the payload handicaps of launching from a northerly latitude, since any orbit inclination less than the latitude of the launch site requires a turn, and thus loss of total satellite momentum.

TABLE 5.2   SATELLITE POSITION CHANGES BASED ON
TYPICAL ECCENTRICITIES AND INCLINATIONS
OF THE ORBIT

Cause	Change
Orbital eccentricities, $\varepsilon = 5 \times 10^{-4}$	84 km, peak-peak, E-W
	42 km, peak-peak, altitude
Orbital inclination, $\pm 0.5°$	728 km, peak-peak, N-S
Long term E-W drift	146 km

5.2.2 Time Delay

Although electromagnetic waves travel at the speed of light, $\approx 2.99 \times 10^8$ m/s, the distance to a geosynchronous satellite may range from 35 784 km for an earth station at the subsatellite point (on the equator) to 41 677 km for an earth station at the horizon relative to the satellite. Accordingly, the one way propagation time, neglecting electronic circuit delay, from one earth station to another may range from a minimum of 0.239 s to a maximum of 0.278 s. The total round trip delay time then ranges from 0.478 s to 0.556 s. As was noted in Chap. 2, such delays can have an adverse effect on systems which use ARQ protocols demanding frequent ACKs for the continuation of transmission.

In the event double hop satellite transmission is required, as might be the case if a domestic satellite is used in tandem with an international satellite, the total round trip delay time is longer than one second. International transmission is being implemented increasingly on a one-way basis only, with the return path being terrestrial, i.e., submarine cable. This allows a domestic satellite to be placed in tandem with an international satellite for an overall delay of less than 0.6 s in one direction, with the delay on the return path being kept to less than 0.1 s. The combination round trip delay, on the order of 0.6 to 0.7 s, is tolerable in most cases.

As noted in Sec. 5.2.1, satellite motion causes a variation in propagation delay time. The position of the earth station on the earth, as well as the orientation of the satellite's actual orbit, both will affect the amount of time delay variation experienced at the earth station. Based upon the orbital parameter variations [Ref. 5, p. 393] listed in Table 5.2, the maximum variation in propagation time is 550 μs peak to peak one way during a sidereal day. A reduction in the inclination of the satellite's orbital plane to 0.1° cuts the variation in propagation time to 250 μs.

The corresponding two-way Doppler shift then is

$$2 \, d/dt[275 \times 10^{-6} \sin(2\pi t/86\,400)] = 4 \times 10^{-8} \text{ s/s}$$

for the 550 μs peak to peak variation. These variations thus may be important in their production of TDMA frame rate differences (see Sec. 5.7.2), and the need for Doppler tracking in such circuits.

5.2.3 Atmospheric Attenuation

The attenuation caused by atmospheric constituents was shown in Fig. 4.3 for paths entirely within the atmosphere. The path between an earth station and a satellite, however, includes only a short section within the atmosphere. The length of this section depends, of course, on the elevation angle as measured at the earth station. Figure 5.1 [Ref. 6] shows the values of this attenuation for standard atmospheric conditions. The attenuation is the result of oxygen and water vapor in the air. Rainfall causes significant increases in the attenuation, as can be appreciated from Fig. 4.3.

Major fading mechanisms in satellite transmission include troposphere refraction, molecular absorption caused by oxygen and water vapor, and rain-induced absorption. Effects present to a small degree in the 6 GHz and lower bands are

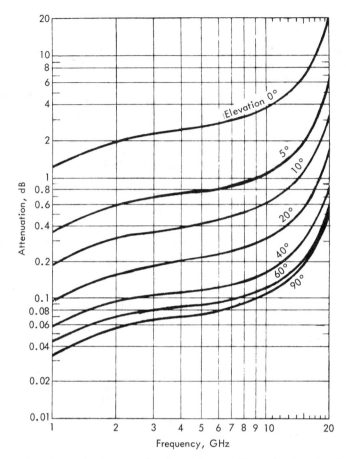

Figure 5.1 Atmospheric attenuation for earth to satellite paths. (Reprinted with permission of *Microwave Journal,* from the November 1968, issue, © 1968, Horizon House—Microwave, Inc.)

ionospheric refraction and Faraday rotation. The latter is a rotation of the polarization vector. Faraday rotation and other polarization effects are of concern mainly in satellite systems using dual polarization.

At the low elevation angles, i.e., ≤10°, tropospheric refraction is found to cause changes in the effective angle at which the signals reach the receiving antenna. In addition, rapid amplitude and phase variations known as scintillation are characteristic of tropospheric refraction.

Studies of propagation problems at low elevation angles [Ref. 7] in the 4 GHz band indicate the need for a fade margin of 2.5 dB for 99.99% annual availability if the satellite elevation angle is 5°, with greater margins for lower elevation angles. A rain attenuation allowance of 1.0 dB should be provided at 5° elevation angle if 99.99% path availability is to be achieved, whereas only 0.7 dB is needed at 10° elevation angle. Fluctuations due to ionospheric scintillation exceed 1 to 2 dB only 0.1% of the time. Figure 5.2 shows the fade margin requirements in the 6 GHz band

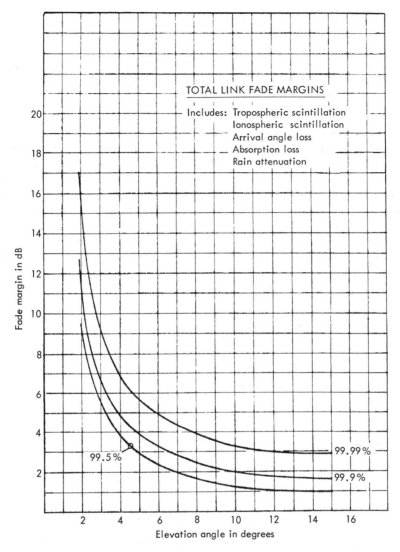

Figure 5.2 Uplink or downlink fade margin requirements for various availabilities as a function of elevation angle.

for various availabilities due to tropospheric and ionospheric scintillation, arrival angle change, absorption loss and rain attenuation.

5.2.4 Rain Depolarization

Raindrops carry small amounts of atmospheric contaminants and thus exhibit a degree of electrical conductivity. Their dielectric constant also is greater than that of air. Accordingly, they act as dipoles. At the frequencies used for satellite transmission the wavelength is short enough that rain drop dimensions begin to be a significant fraction of a half wavelength. Thus, the passing wave induces currents into them and reradiation then occurs with a polarization corresponding to the direction (cant angle) of the rain drops. Rain-caused depolarization is the result. Such depolarization increases (cross-polarization isolation decreases) with frequency, as shown in Fig. 5.3, because at the higher frequencies rain drops of a given size are a larger fraction of a wavelength, and thus better reradiators.

Cross polarization isolation is important in the dual polarized transmission systems now used on most satellites to achieve frequency reuse. The successful use of dual polarization generally requires that the unwanted (cross-polarized) signal be at least 20 dB below the desired carrier. In fact, design criteria require that the ratio of carrier to interference (C/I) be adequate for the planned bit error probability or the planned analog usage. Typically, this calls for $C/I \geq 25$ dB.

The presence of the cross-polarized signal results not only from rain depolarization but also from the characteristics of the hardware, mainly the antennas and feedline components, as described in Sec. 5.10.1.

Figure 5.3 illustrates the effect of rain on cross-polarization isolation for 5 km path lengths, which are typical of the length of atmosphere through which the radio waves pass between an earth station and a satellite. The curves are shown for both differential attenuation and differential phase over 36 MHz transponder band·

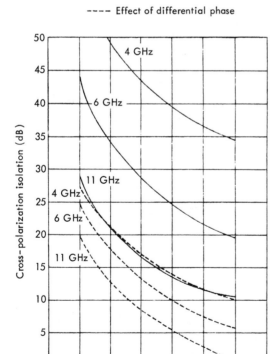

Figure 5.3 Cross-polarization isolation versus rain rate for 5 km paths lengths.

widths for 4, 6, and 11 GHz. Differential attenuation is the difference in attenuation between the horizontal and vertical polarizations, whereas differential phase is the difference in phase shift between the horizontal and vertical polarizations [Ref. 8]. As can be seen from Fig. 5.3, differential attenuation and phase are key parameters in the production of cross-polarization by precipitation.

5.3 SPACE SEGMENT

A spacecraft for telecommunications purposes consists not only of the transponders, but also of a control subsystem, solar array, batteries, monitoring systems, and a small propulsion system for repositioning as well as temperature control devices. The following sections describe those spacecraft subsystems of primary interest and concern to the telecommunications engineer, namely, the transponders, power sources, and antennas.

5.3.1 Transponders*

Each satellite contains a number of transponders whose function is to receive, amplify, and retransmit the signals reaching it within a given frequency band. The retransmitted signal must be at a different frequency from the received signal to prevent the oscillation which would occur if the transmitter output were fed back to the receiver input. Because of satellite power limitations, the downlink is more critical than the uplink, i.e., the achievement of an adequate received signal-to-noise ratio is more difficult. For this reason, the downlink band usually is lower in frequency than the uplink band. The higher frequencies suffer greater atmospheric attenuation and hardware adjustments are more critical, but these difficulties can be handled more readily at the transmitting (uplink) earth station with its greater power output capability. A single satellite antenna with multiple isolated feeds, however, may be used for both receiving and transmitting simultaneously.

A large number of signals from various earth stations usually arrives at a given satellite. They may be of various frequencies and polarizations, and may occur in different time slots. The antenna feed arrangement is used to separate the signals into two orthogonal polarizations, often linear for domestic satellites and circular for international satellites. Following this, the different frequency bands are separated by the use of channel filters so that each transponder receives the frequency band for which it is designed. Separation of the signals in the time domain, if done, occurs in a processing transponder (see Sec. 5.3.1.1). Dual polarization hardware can be built such that interference from the cross-polarized signal is about 40 dB below that of the desired signal over relatively small bandwidths, e.g., 2%, and beam widths, e.g., 2°. Over broader bandwidths and beamwidths, however, the oppositely polarized (unwanted) signal reaches higher levels. One *Intelsat* design achieved −27 dB over the entire 3 700–6 425 MHz band within a spot beam.

---

* The material of this section also appears in Ref. 1, pages 208-12. Both are taken from B. E. Keiser, "Wideband Communications Systems," Course Notes, © 1981 and 1985.

Propagation factors degrade polarization isolation by converting linear or circular polarization to elliptical. Thus both the antennas and the propagation effects must be included in a determination of interference at a receiver from an unwanted transmitted polarization.

In general, access to a given transponder from the ground is based on the polarization and frequency of the uplink signal. Selection of a given transponder in this manner may be used to control the downlink frequency and possibly the covered area on the ground since different transponders may be connected to different spot beams. In addition, transponders may serve different classes of users, with some transponders being dedicated to low-level mobile users while others handle large earth stations with mastergroup levels of traffic or television transmissions.

A transponder frequency plan is shown in Fig. 5.4, using staggered frequencies to aid in isolating the two polarizations. Staggered plans are useful for transponders having small numbers of carriers, i.e., for television or mastergroup applications. For a single voice or data channel per carrier, however, staggering is only of limited value.

A single conversion transponder is shown in block diagram form in Fig. 5.5. The preamplifier provides gain at the received radio frequency, but usually has an equivalent noise temperature on the order of 1 000 K. Lower noise temperatures are not needed because appreciable noise enters from the earth itself. Moreover, amplifiers with low-noise figures tend to be less reliable than the noisier type typically used.

The total bandwidth of a given transponder may be as little as 36 MHz or less, as in many domestic and international satellites, or as large as 72 to 241 MHz or more, as in some of the international satellites.

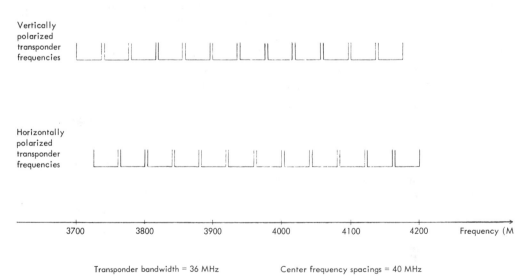

Figure 5.4 Downlink satellite transponder frequency plan.

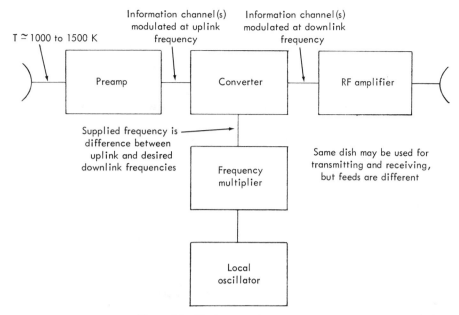

Figure 5.5 Single conversion transponder.

Most transponders provide preamplification of the uplink signal, conversion by a fixed amount to a lower frequency, and then amplification at the lower frequency, which then is transmitted down to the ground. In the 4- and 6-GHz commercial bands, 2 225 MHz usually is subtracted from the uplink frequency to produce the downlink frequency, whereas in the 7- and 8-GHz government bands, 725 MHz or 200 MHz is subtracted. These uplink- downlink frequency differences are the maximum ones available within the given frequency allocations [Ref. 9] except for the 200 MHz difference. This relatively small difference results from the fact that the 7 900–7 950 MHz link is received on board the satellite through an earth coverage horn and is adjacent in the uplink spectrum to the other channels received on the earth coverage horn. However, signals received in the 7 900–7 950 MHz transponder are cross-strapped to a 7 700–7 750 MHz downlink which is used with a narrow coverage downlink (transmit) antenna. The frequency assignment was established to place the downlink-frequency band adjacent to the other downlink narrow coverage frequency bands.

Automatic gain control amplification and limiting are used to maintain uniform signal levels, but transponder gain often is commandable from the ground as well.

The downlink beam produces a coverage area on the ground known as the *footprint*. An example of a footprint is shown in Figure 5.6 [Ref. 10].

Most transponders are built on a highly redundant basis to achieve high reliability. The block diagrams in this chapter are intended to illustrate the basic concepts and thus do not display these redundancies.

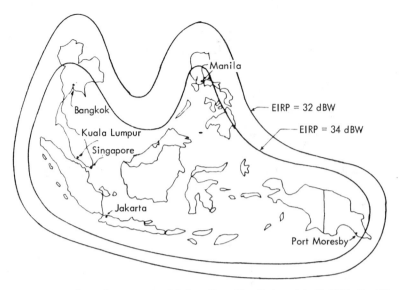

Figure 5.6 Footprint coverage of *Palapa B* satellite (Indonesia). (© 1981, Cardiff Publishing Co.; reprinted by permission.)

5.3.1.1 On-Board Processing. The transponders described thus far involved a single conversion of the uplink frequency directly to the downlink frequency, along with the needed amplification. However, various applications exist in which conversion to baseband on board the satellite is advantageous. Figure 5.7 is a conceptual block diagram of a processing transponder. As shown there, the entire transponder input is converted to baseband at which such functions as switching or signal processing can be performed. Then the processed baseband signals are remodulated and converted to the downlink frequency band.

On-board processing of weather photograph information and earth resources data from multispectral scanners has proven feasible. Such processing allows

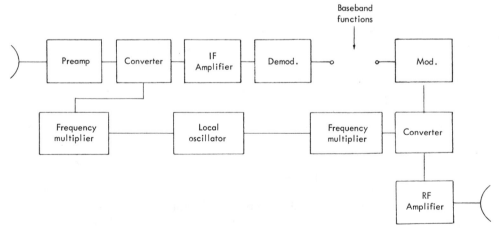

Figure 5.7 Processing transponder.

significant bit rate reductions to be achieved. Concepts for commercial applications of on-board switching and processing include on-board demand access, also known as the "switchboard in the sky" concept, and TDMA packet transmission via spot beams. On-board demand access allows the transponder input channels to be switched by command from the ground to the correct downlink channel. TDMA packet transmission, or satellite-switched TDMA, uses a preprogrammed switching sequence in which the packet addresses are used on board the satellite to switch each packet to its proper destination via the corresponding spot beam. A packet typically is 1 024 bits long, including address information.

In addition to on-board switching, signal processing can be done to regenerate uplink digital signals for downlink transmission (see Chap. 2 for a discussion of waveform regeneration). Such processing is useful both in commercial and military applications. The use of on-board regeneration with DQPSK has been shown [Ref. 5, p. 417] to provide bit error probabilities of 10^{-6} and better with 2.5 to 3.0 dB less E_b/N_o than is required otherwise.

Military uses of on-board processing include the removal of interference accompanying the uplink signals. In this manner, the repeating of interference can be minimized, and the tendency of strong signals to "capture" the transponder AGC because of nonlinearities can be reduced [Ref. 11].

Other concepts for using processing transponders include the use of uplink single sideband to conserve bandwidth, and signal conversion on board the satellite to PCM/FM for the downlink to minimize the power required from the satellite. On-board processing also can be used to minimize the signal degradation from satellite amplifier nonlinearities.

Signal processing transponders may be built to perform specific types of signal conversions. The result is a lack of flexibility with respect to changes that may be desired after the satellite has been launched. However, processing can be accomplished on a reprogrammable basis, thus overcoming this limitation. The advantages of processing transponders are such that their use in the future probably will increase significantly, especially with the problems of an increasingly crowded spectrum.

5.3.1.2 RF Amplifiers.

The RF amplifier used in each satellite transponder may be either a solid-state power amplifier (SSPA) or a traveling-wave tube amplifier (TWTA). Power outputs range from 4 watts, common in many domestic satellite systems, to over 200 watts for a direct broadcast satellite amplifier. The SSPAs are commonly used at the lower frequencies (<10 GHz), especially at the power levels typical of domestic common-carrier service.

Figure 5.8 [Ref. 12] shows the amplitude and phase characteristics typical of TWTAs used both in satellite and earth station service. The discussion which follows thus applies to earth station amplifiers as well as those used on board the satellites. Note that an input backoff of 4 dB from saturation results in an output backoff of only 1 dB. Thus the gain of the amplifier is compressed at high input levels. The characteristics of SSPAs exhibit somewhat better linearity than do TWTAs, but this is only a matter of degree. The same design approaches thus must be used with both amplifier types.

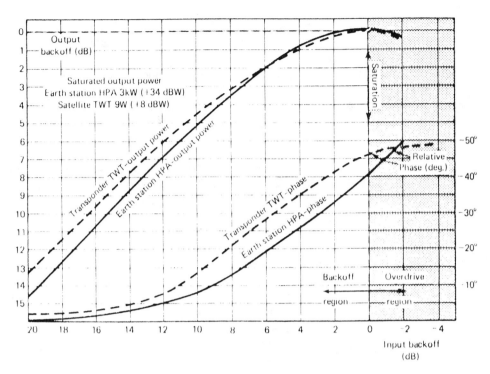

Figure 5.8 Typical TWTA and HPA amplitude and phase characteristics. (Reprinted courtesy of the International Telecommunications Satellite Organization [INTELSAT].)

Measurements made on traveling-wave tube amplifiers [Ref. 13] have shown that input backoffs on the order of 10 dB or more are needed, as indicated in Fig. 5.9, in order to achieve acceptably low values of intermodulation distortion in FDM/FM systems. As a result, such systems need precise uplink power control, which limits the flexibility of a network of earth stations to accommodate changing user requirements. Note that the input power to a transponder is the summation of the signals from all of its using earth stations. In an FDM/FM system, input power to a transponder may arrive on a different carrier(s) from each earth station. The transmitted levels from each of these earth stations thus must be suitably limited to prevent serious intermodulation problems.

Digital systems, especially those using QPSK or 8-PSK, have less stringent C/I requirements (see Chap. 2) than do FM systems. Moreover, many digital systems use time-division multiple access (TDMA), which means that only one carrier passes through the transponder at a time. In such a case, the backoff requirements can be relaxed considerably.

Amplifier nonlinearities cause both signal suppression and distortion, as well as disproportionate sharing of satellite power. Intermodulation results from the presence of multiple inputs through a limiting amplifier. As will be shown later in the next section of this chapter, intermodulation can be reduced by preplanned frequency selection within the transponder's passband. Amplifiers also exhibit

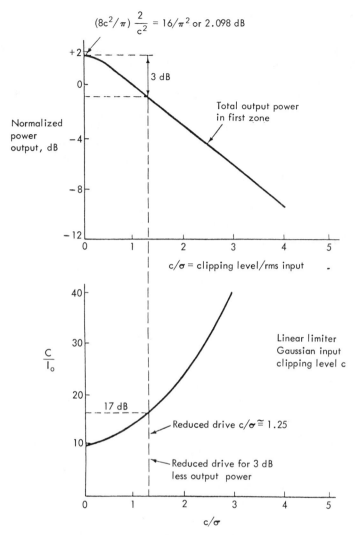

$(8c^2/\pi)\dfrac{2}{c^2} = 16/\pi^2$ or 2.098 dB

Normalized power output, dB

3 dB

Total output power in first zone

c/σ = clipping level/rms input

$\dfrac{C}{I_0}$

Linear limiter Gaussian input clipping level c

17 dB

Reduced drive $c/\sigma \cong 1.25$

Reduced drive for 3 dB less output power

c/σ

Figure 5.9 Effect of input backoff on carrier-to-intermodulation (C/I_0) ratio. (From James J. Spilker, Jr., *Digital Communications by Satellite,* © 1977, p. 240. Reprinted by permission of Prentice-Hall, Inc., Englewood Cliffs, NJ.)

AM/PM conversion, as well as combined AM/PM and AM/AM effects. These amplifier imperfections are discussed next.

Under conditions in which one of two sinusoidal inputs reach saturation, hard limiting is said to occur. Figure 5.10 illustrates a hard limiter characteristic. Under hard limiting, the smaller signal of the two can be shown [Ref. 14, pp. 226–7] to be suppressed 6 dB relative to the larger one. The same suppression occurs if the smaller "signal" actually is the sum of a large number of low-amplitude sine waves.

If strong Gaussian interference, e.g., a band of thermal noise, is present in the hard limiting amplifier, then the weak signal will be suppressed by 1.05 dB [Ref.

15]. Table 5.3, from the same reference, summarizes the output intermodulation and signal components for a hard limiter with a Gaussian input signal and rectangular input spectrum. The total power in the vicinity of the fundamental is designated P. The bandwidth of the limiter is B, and is assumed to be rectangular. The edge of the channel refers to the limits of the bandwidth B.

As can be appreciated from Table 5.3., total hard limiting produces intolerable levels of C/I because of severe signal suppression. Actual amplifiers are more closely represented by the piecewise linear limiter, or clipping amplifier, whose characteristic is shown in Fig. 5.11. The signal-to-distortion ratio within the signal passband is a function of the input power to the amplifier. Accordingly, the desired signal-to-distortion ratio is produced by reducing the drive level sufficiently.

A piecewise linear limiter is assumed to be followed by a bandpass filter which eliminates all harmonics produced by the amplifier, leaving only the signal fundamental and distortion components within a baseband width of the carrier. A typical plot of a TWT transfer function is shown in Fig. 5.12 [Ref. 14, p. 233]. Such a

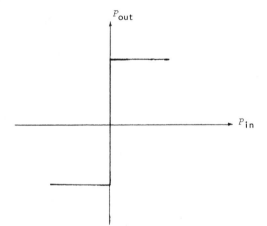

Figure 5.10 Hard limiter transfer characteristic.

TABLE 5.3 HARD LIMITER OUTPUT COMPONENTS FOR GAUSSIAN INPUT WITH RECTANGULAR SPECTRUM

Component	Watts	Decibels
Total fundamental zone output	P	0
Total signal power output	$0.785\,P$	-1.06
Signal power density output	$0.785\,P/B$	
Total intermodulation (I_0) power	$0.215\,P$	-6.7
Total signal/total I_0		5.64
Total I_0 power in tails	$0.1\,P$	-10
Total I_0 power in input band B	$0.115\,P$	-9.4
Center channel I_0 power density	$0.128\,P/B$	
Edge channel I_0 power density	$0.0912\,P/B$	
Total signal-to-inband I_0 power ratio		8.34
Center-channel-signal-to-center I_0 power ratio		7.8
Edge-channel-signal-to-edge I_0 power ratio		9.35

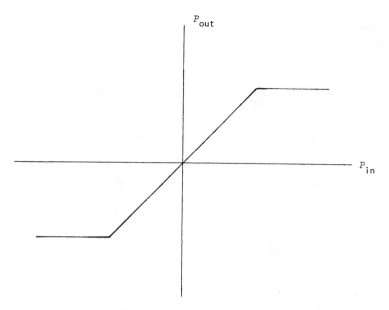

Figure 5.11 Piecewise linear limiter transfer characteristic.

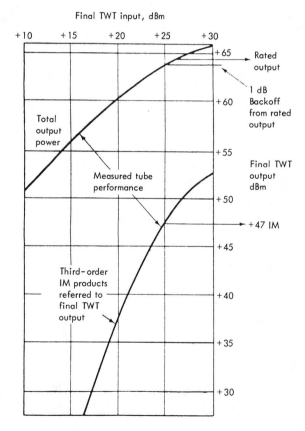

Final TWT input, dBm

Total output power

Measured tube performance

Third–order IM products referred to final TWT output

Rated output

1 dB Backoff from rated output

Final TWT output dBm

+47 IM

Figure 5.12 Typical TWT output power and intermodulation products. (From James J. Spilker, Jr., *Digital Communications by Satellite,* © 1977, p. 233. Reprinted by permission of Prentice-Hall., Englewood Cliffs, NJ.)

characteristic often is referred to as being soft limiting. The figure shows the intermodulation (I_o) level produced by two equal amplitude sine waves at 1 dB backoff from rated output.

The actual signals through a transponder will be modulated by voice, data, or video, so a large FDM baseband of these modulated signals can be considered to have characteristics similar to those of a Gaussian function. Figure 5.13 [Ref. 14, p. 233] illustrates an input spectrum that corresponds to a set of adjacent channels, one of which is turned off. Intermodulation components from amplifier nonlinearities, however, will appear within the notch in the amplifier's output. The I_o level in the notch compared with the signal power that would be present if the particular channel were turned on is called the *noise-power-ratio* (NPR). It is the inverse of the signal-to-noise ratio that would exist in the presence of signal.

The normalized power output and signal-to-intermodulation spectral density ratio have been derived by Spilker [Ref. 14, pp. 239–40] and are plotted in Fig. 5.9 in terms of the ratio c/σ, defined as clipping level/rms input. For hard limiting, $c/\sigma \to 0$. Note that under hard limiting conditions the C/I_0 power ratio drops to 9 dB

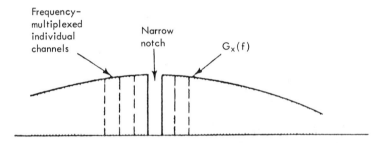

Figure 5.13 Input spectrum of frequency division multiplexed channels. (From James J. Spilker, Jr., *Digital Communications by Satellite,* © 1977, p. 233. Reprinted by permission of Prentice-Hall, Inc., Englewood Cliffs, NJ.)

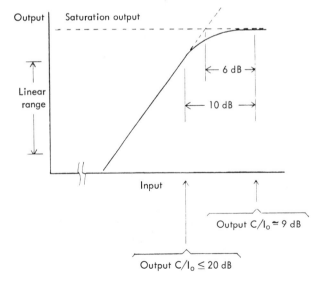

Figure 5.14 Normalized output power and C/I_0 for a linear limiter with Gaussian input.

as shown in Fig. 5.9. Note also the relationships among Figs. 5.8, 5.9, and 5.14. Figure 5.8 shows the relationship of output backoff to input backoff; Fig. 5.9 provides examples of typical C/I_o relative to input backoff; Fig. 5.14 provides theoretical results relating C/I_o to output backoff. Most of the distortion is third and fifth order I_o. Note that a 3 dB output power backoff allows C/I_o to increase to 17 dB.

In addition to nonlinear distortion, the solid state and TWT amplifiers used in transponders and earth stations also produce AM/PM conversion. A change in the amplitude of a multicarrier input results in a change in the output phase of each signal component. The effects of AM/PM conversion are present even at low input levels at which nonlinear amplitude distortion is negligible. For such low input levels, the phase modulation produced by amplitude changes is approximately proportional to the amplitude squared, i.e.,

$$\theta(A) \simeq k\left(\frac{A^2}{2}\right) \tag{5.2}$$

where A is the amplitude of the input envelope. Thus $\theta(A)$ is proportional to the input power. Many amplifiers exhibit such conversion, but with various values of k, which may be expressed in degrees/dB. Spilker [Ref. 14, pp. 256–7] shows that the AM/PM distortion products occur at the same frequencies as the third-order products from an amplitude nonlinearity, but have a different amplitude and are shifted in phase by 90°. Thus, at input levels well-below saturation, AM/PM distortion predominates whereas, at input levels driving the amplifier into limiting, amplitude distortion predominates.

The application of an FDM baseband to a frequency-modulated carrier will result in unintelligible or noise-like distortion out of a nonlinear amplifier. However, the use of a filter ahead of the AM/PM-producing stage may generate intelligible cross-talk, i.e., the FM on one channel is added to another. This results from (1) FM conversion to AM by the filter, and then (2) AM conversion to PM by the amplifier.

Figure 5.15 [Ref. 14, p. 263] is a presentation of the combined effects of AM/PM and amplitude nonlinearities. This model is used in the development of predistortion networks. The input waveform is assumed to be

$$x(t) = A(t)\cos(\omega_0 t + \phi) \tag{5.3}$$

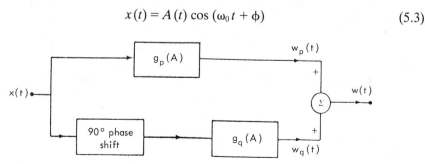

Figure 5.15 In-phase/quadrature representation of a bandpass nonlinearity. (From James J. Spilker, Jr., *Digital Communications by Satellite*, © 1977, p. 263. Reprinted by permission of Prentice-Hall, Inc., Englewood Cliffs, NJ.)

The in-phase and quadrature terms [Ref. 16] are produced by quadrature envelope nonlinearities that are related to the AM/PM and amplitude nonlinearities, $\theta(A)$ and $g(A)$ by

$$g_p(A) = g(A) \cos \theta(A) \tag{5.4}$$

and

$$g_q(A) = g(A) \sin \theta(A) \tag{5.5}$$

The resulting output components then are

$$w_p(t) = g_p[A(t)] \cos(\omega_0 t + \phi) \tag{5.6}$$

and

$$w_q(t) = g_q[A(t)] \sin(\omega_0 t + \phi) \tag{5.7}$$

Accordingly, the output is

$$w(t) = g[A(t)] \cos\{\omega_0 t + \theta[A(t)]\phi\} \tag{5.8}$$

5.3.1.3 Frequency Selection to Reduce Intermodulation (I_o) Effects.

Section 4.4.2 showed that two frequencies, f_1 and f_2, passing through a nonlinear amplifier produced a set of frequencies $\pm mf_1 \pm nf_2$. In particular, as illustrated by an example in that section, the spacing of the I_o products will be uniform as shown in Fig. 5.16. Because of this uniformity of I_o spacing, the assignment of carrier frequencies for transmission through a transponder should be made nonuniform if I_o effects are to be reduced. The worst I_o problems will result from a uniform carrier spacing. Unfortunately, uniform spacing is desired for efficient utilization of the transponder's spectrum, but, under hard limiting conditions, results in the I_o levels listed in Table 5.3 for Gaussian inputs.

Figure 5.17 [Ref. 14, page 248] illustrates an I_o spectrum for N clusters of K carriers each. Each cluster has a bandwidth W such that $B \geq 3W$. The I_o power density at the center of the cluster is $(P/NK)[(0.128)/(0.215)](0.128) = 0.076\,P/NK$, based upon the results displayed in Table 5.3. If the relative channel spacing, B/W, were to decrease to 1.0, however, the I_o power density at the center of the cluster would rise to $0.128\,P/NK$. The total power in each cluster of I_o products is weighted in the same proportion as if each cluster were treated as a line component.

Assume a transponder has been channelized into channels each of bandwidth B. Assume, however, that only W Hz of each channel is used, and that the center frequency of each transmission is selected randomly within the bandwidth B. Only W/B of the I_o power passes through the receiver's W bandwidth filter. As a result,

Figure 5.16 Spacing of intermodulation (I_o) products.

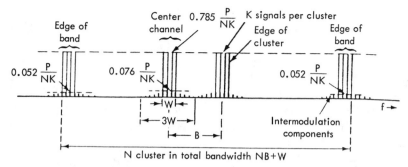

Figure 5.17 Intermodulation (I_0) spectrum for N clusters of K carriers each. (From James J. Spilker, Jr., *Digital Communications by Satellite,* © 1977, p. 248. Reprinted by permission of Prentice-Hall, Inc., Englewood Cliffs, NJ.)

the center-channel-signal-to-I_0 power ratio increases by B/W from the 7.8 dB of Table 5.3 to

$$C/I_0 = 7.8 + 10 \log_{10}(B/W) \qquad \text{dB} \qquad (5.9)$$

Thus if $B/W = 10$, then $C/I_0 = 17.8$ dB.

The complete avoidance of third- and even fifth-order products is possible using a plan devised by Babcock [Ref. 17]. However, a high price must be paid. For example, for 10 channels to be free of third-order I_0, a total of 62 channels must be allocated for a transponder utilization of only 16%. Table 5.4 [Ref. 14, p. 252] shows frequency plans that avoid third-order I_0 products with and without product spreading of $3B$ [Ref. 18]. The bandpass nature of the channel must be taken into account in computing the I_0 products.

Because the third-order I_0 product has 57.4% of the total I_0 power at mid-channel, and because the third- and fifth-order products together constitute 74.6% of the total, the use of frequency selection to eliminate these products increases the worst case C/I_0 for a large number of signals N by 3.7 and 5.9 dB, respectively.

TABLE 5.4 FREQUENCY PLANS TO AVOID THIRD-ORDER I_0 PRODUCTS

	Signals, P	Channels, N	Frequencies, f_i
Without products spreading	3	4	1,2,4
	4	7	1,2,5,7
	5	12	1,2,5,10,12
	6	18	1,2,5,11,13,18
	7	26	1,2,5,11,19,24,26
	8	35	1,2,5,10,16,23,33,35
	9	46	1,2,5,14,25,31,39,41,46
	10	62	1,2,8,12,27,46,48,57,60,62
With product spreading	3	7	1,3,7
	4	15	1,3,7,15

Source: From James J. Spilker, Jr., *Digital Communications by Satellite,* © 1977, p. 252. Reprinted by permission of Prentice-Hall, Inc., Englewood Cliffs, NJ.

For large N, a more suitable channel spacing approach is the use of random spacing, in which signals of bandwidth W Hz are spaced on the average by H Hz for $H \gg W$, each being randomly centered within its allocation H. Figure 5.18 illustrates such random spacing. From Eq. (5.9), the performance improvement for random spacing is $10 \log_{10} (H/W)$ dB. Thus for $H/W = 5$, a 7 dB improvement is obtained. While none of the I_o products are eliminated, the I_o power is well distributed across the frequency band because of the random frequency placement, and only a small portion, W/H, of the I_o power appears within the individual receive passbands.

With reference to Fig. 5.9, the output C/I_o at saturation becomes

$$C/I_0 = 9 + 10 \log_{10} (\text{BW Available/BW Occupied}) \text{ dB} \qquad (5.10)$$

This result is based on average power density results from a large number of carriers, so a check of the actual I_o product spectrum should be made for a specific frequency plan with a limited number of carriers.

Example

A transponder's 36 MHz passband is divided into 12 randomly spaced channels, each 2 MHz wide. As many of these channels as possible are to be used for BPSK service with a required $p_{be} \leq 10^{-8}$. Allow 1.5 dB degradation from theoretical E_b/N_o requirements for hardware limitations other than intermodulation. How many of the channels can be used if the transponder is operated to saturation?

Solution Reference to Chap. 2 shows that BPSK at a $p_{be} = 10^{-8}$ requires $E_b/N_o = 12.0$ dB. Hardware limitations raise this requirement to 13.5 dB. Application of Eq. (5.10), using BW Available = 36 MHz, shows that the allowable BW Occupied is 12.77 MHz. Since the channels are each 2 MHz wide, six of them can be used.

Note: the foregoing example illustrates the disadvantages of operating a transponder to saturation, especially if this operation is on a frequency division multiplex basis, even if digital traffic is being carried.

5.3.1.4 Noise Allocations. The preceding sections have addressed amplifiers and their nonlinear effects. As was seen there, intermodulation and other transmission impairments produced in the amplifiers can be treated as noise.

Satellite system noise allocations are established by the CCIR, with the noise

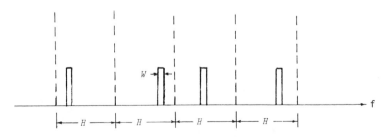

Figure 5.18 Frequency plan for random spacing of large number N of carriers of bandwidth W.

TABLE 5.5 TYPICAL NOISE ALLOCATIONS FOR SATELLITE SYSTEMS
(NOTE: ALL VALUES ARE pWp0)

Sources	Satellite	Earth Station	Subtotals	Totals
Thermal noise, TOTALS	900	1590	2490	2490
Intermodulation	1100	500	1600	
Delay distortion ripple	135	225	360	
Gain slope across message channel	40		40	
Distortion noise, TOTAL				2000
Multipath coupling		100	100	
Adjacent channel interference		150	150	
Adjacent satellite interference	700	300	1000	
Interfering terrestrial systems		1000	1000	
Other sources, TOTAL				2250
End links		1200	1200	
Miscellaneous		500	500	
SUBTOTAL				1700
TOTAL				8440

Source: Copyright 1977, American Telephone and Telegraph Company. Reprinted with permission.

being expressed in pWp0 (picowatts, psophometrically weighted,* at 0 TLP). The most significant component of distortion is that which is allocated to I_o [Ref. 19]. This level is 1 100 pWp0 for the transponder and 500 pWp0 for the earth station for a total of 1 600 pWp0 [Ref. 20]. Table 5.5 summarizes these noise allocations, based upon typical values for domestic satellites [Ref. 19, pp. 499–501].

Thermal noise depends largely on the noise generated in receiver front ends, but its effective value in terms of system performance depends, as well, on the received signal strength. Thus while the satellite receiver may have a 2 000 K noise temperature, the uplink signal strength makes this noise less significant than the 60 K noise temperature of the earth station receiver (see Sec. 4.4.1.3).

The "multipath coupling" of Table 5.5 includes internal coupling through adjacent satellite filters. The "miscellaneous" category includes FM modulators and demodulators, multiplex equipment, and echo suppressors.

The 1 000 pWp0 total for adjacent satellite interference is to occur no more than 20% of any month, and is based upon the use of earth stations which have large enough antennas to discriminate against adjacent satellites such that the interference does not exceed this total. Section 5.4.1.1 discusses required sizes of earth station antennas with respect to satellite spacing in the orbital arc.

The total of 8 440 pWp0 corresponds to 39.3 dBp or to 39.8 dBrnc0. This is comparable to noise objectives often used in microwave radio systems, in which the noise objective is expressed in terms of the noisiest message channel during the busy hour.

At certain times of the year the sun may appear behind the satellite as viewed

---

*CCITT recommendations call for the measurement of (voice) message circuit noise by a *psophometer*. It has a frequency weighting network similar to the C-message weighting used in the U.S. Psophometric weighting of a 3 kHz band of white noise decreases the average power by about 2.5 dB, compared with a 2.0 dB decrease for C-message weighting.

at a given earth station for a period on the order of a half hour. During such times the thermal noise output of the sun within the band being received can increase circuit noise significantly. Maintenance of circuit continuity then requires the use of an alternate satellite (at a different longitude) to which the circuits can be switched. A second antenna directed at the alternate satellite also is required to prevent outage time while switch-over is being accomplished.

5.3.1.5 Power Flux Density Limits.

The uplink power to a satellite must be limited, in the case of multiple carriers within a transponder, so that intermodulation is kept within suitable limits, as was discussed in Sec. 5.3.1.2. Limits also are needed to prevent interference to terrestrial microwave systems via radiation from antenna sidelobes. Specifically, CCIR requirements state that from a satellite earth station to a microwave system the interference into any 4 kHz voice channel shall not exceed 500 pWp0 for more than 20% of any month and 50 000 pWp0 for more than 0.005% of any month. No more than two sources of such interference are assumed. From a microwave system to a satellite earth station receiver, the interference in any voice channel shall not exceed 250 pWp0 for more than 20% of any month and 50 000 pWp0 for more than 0.01% of any month. No more than four sources are assumed to contribute to the 20% value. These four sources acting together will produce the 1 000 pWp0 listed for "Interfering terrestrial systems" in Table 5.5. No more than three sources are assumed to contribute to the 0.01% value of 50 000 pWp0.

The downlink power flux density produced by a satellite on the surface of the earth must be limited to prevent interference to terrestrial microwave radio systems using the same bands. The remainder of this section deals with these downlink limits.

The gain of the terrestrial system antenna is defined in terms of its elevation angle θ and its azimuth angle ζ such that

$$\Delta = \cos^{-1}(\cos \theta \cos \zeta) \qquad (5.11)$$

Then the antenna's gain pattern is assumed to be the same in any direction from boresight and to be within the following limits [Ref. 21] at 4 GHz:

$$G(\Delta) = \begin{cases} 40 \text{ dB} & 0 \leq |\Delta| \leq 0.575° \\ 34 - 25 \log_{10} \Delta \text{ dB} & 0.575° \leq |\Delta| \leq 57.5° \\ -10 \text{ dB} & |\Delta| > 57.5° \end{cases} \qquad (5.12)$$

and within the following limits [Ref. 22] at 11 GHz:

$$G(\Delta) = \begin{cases} 48 \text{ dB} & 0 \leq |\Delta| \leq 0.31° \\ 33 - 29.5 \log_{10} \Delta \text{ dB} & 0.31° \leq |\Delta| \leq 31° \\ -11 \text{ dB} & |\Delta| > 31° \end{cases} \qquad (5.13)$$

Radiation from the satellites is assumed to depend upon the elevation angle of the satellite above the local horizontal plane, and relative to 1 W/m^2 in a 4 kHz band, to be within the following limits on the maximum power flux density F(θ) at 4 GHz:

$$F(\theta) = \begin{cases} -152 & 0° \leqslant \theta \leqslant 5° \\ -152 + 0.5\,(\theta - 5) & 5° \leqslant \theta \leqslant 25° \\ -142 & \theta > 25° \end{cases} \tag{5.14}$$

and within the following limits at 11 GHz:

$$F(\theta) = \begin{cases} -150 & 0° \leqslant \theta \leqslant 5° \\ -150 + (\theta - 5)/2 & 5° \leqslant \theta \leqslant 25° \\ -140 & \theta > 25° \end{cases} \tag{5.15}$$

The above power flux density limits are those of the CCIR. These limits restrict the output *EIRP* from a satellite operating on the 4 and 11 GHz downlink bands, but do not apply to other satellite transmissions, e.g., direct broadcast satellites, which are allocated different frequencies.

5.3.2 Satellite Power Sources

Geosynchronous satellites use silicon solar cells as their source of power. These cells are responsive to a broad frequency spectrum of power from the sun. The overall solar flux is about 2 000 W/m². Present solar cell efficiency is about 15%, thus resulting in a solar cell array output of 300 W/m². The size of the solar array thus limits the power available on board the satellite. New cell developments may allow a future efficiency on the order of 50%. Over a 10 year lifetime, cell output decreases about 15%. Some of this decrease results from micrometeorite bombardment, to which the cells are continually subjected while in space.

Solar cells produce an output power directly proportional to the amount of solar flux normally incident upon them. The cells may be placed in a planar array which is continually oriented for maximum normal solar flux. To avoid the need for mechanical orientation, however, many designs configure the spacecraft so that it has multiple sides. This arrangement allows sunlight to strike more than one planar array at a time so that adequate power is obtained without the need for mechanical orientation.

Solar cell arrays are used to charge batteries on board the spacecraft so that peak power loads can be supplied. Such peak loads may occur when temperature control subsystems are actuated. In addition, for 1 or 2 weeks at the time of equinox (latter half of March and latter half of September), the satellite may be in *eclipse* (darkness) for up to 70 minutes per day. Eclipse occurs at local midnight, whereas the minimum satellite communications load often occurs between 2 and 4 AM. Consequently, there is an advantage to locating a satellite about three time zones to the west of the area where its active users are located.

Batteries for satellite power may be of either the nickel-cadmium or nickel-hydrogen type. The nickel-cadmium battery has a long and good space performance record. To maintain long lifetime and reliability, however, these batteries are discharged only 50% and then recharged again. They also are discharged and recharged ("exercised") periodically. The nickel-hydrogen battery has been used only recently (1980s) on board spacecraft, but is almost free of failure modes. It is operated until nearly fully discharged and then is recharged again. It is replacing the nickel-cadmium battery in use on board spacecraft.

While solar cells continue to be the power source of choice for geosynchronous satellites, they are less desirable for polar orbiting satellites, as may be used for special military and scientific applications. Satellites operating in polar and other nongeosynchronous orbits are in the sunlight an average of only 12 hours per day. Other power sources thus are important. The use of selenium thermoelectric materials has been a significant factor in such satellite power generating systems. Much experimentation and development work has been done toward achieving safe nuclear heat sources for the selenium cells. However, the crashes of three Soviet nuclear powered satellites have led to a search for safer thermal sources.

5.3.3 Satellite Antennas

This section presumes a basic background in microwave antennas, as presented in Sec. 4.2. The subsections which follow deal with specific issues relevant to satellite on-board antennas.

5.3.3.1 Beam Shape. Many satellite antennas provide what might be called a "conventional" beam shape in that no special effort has been made to shape the beam for uniform field strength over the field of view (FOV), or "footprint" on the surface of the earth.

The electric field pattern of a uniformly illuminated rectangular aperture [Ref. 23, pp. 567–8] is sin x/x, where $x = \pi wy/\lambda$, in which y = off-axis angle in either plane, and w = antenna dimension in that plane. The half-power beamwidth is $\theta = 0.885\ \lambda/w$. The relative gain function then can be expressed in terms of the off-axis angle y normalized to the beamwidth θ:

$$f(y) = \frac{\sin\left(\dfrac{2.783y}{\theta}\right)}{\dfrac{2.783\ y}{\theta}} \tag{5.16}$$

Figures 5.19 and 5.20 [Ref. 23, p. 568] show how this function varies with x. Note that Fig. 5.19 displays the relative amplitude and power whereas Fig. 5.20 displays the corresponding relative gain in dB.

For the commonly used circular aperture of diameter D, the gain function is

$$f(y) = \frac{2J_1\left(\dfrac{\pi Dy}{\lambda}\right)}{\dfrac{\pi Dy}{\lambda}} = \frac{2J_1(U)}{U} \tag{5.17}$$

where $U = \pi Dy/\lambda$ and J_1 is the Bessel function of the first kind, of order one. The

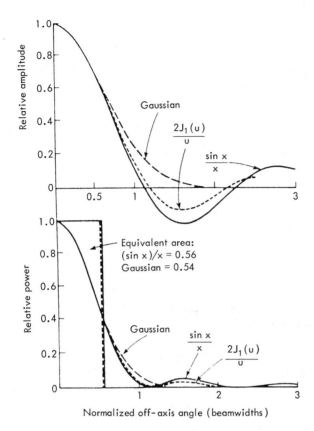

Figure 5.19 Patterns of beam field strength (amplitude) and flux density (power). (From Barton D. K., *Radar System Analysis,* Artech House, Dedham, MA, 1978. Reprinted by permission.)

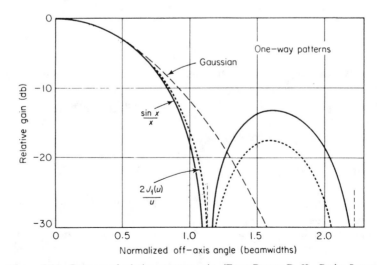

Figure 5.20 Patterns of relative antenna gain. (From Barton D. K., *Radar System Analysis,* Artech House, Dedham, MA, 1978. Reprinted by permission.)

half-power beamwidth is $\theta = 1.03\lambda/D$, so the relative gain function is

$$f(y) = \frac{2J_1\left(\frac{3.24y}{\theta}\right)}{\frac{3.24y}{\theta}} \tag{5.18}$$

As can be seen from Figs. 5.19 and 5.20, the patterns of the rectangular and circular aperture antennas are nearly the same up to $x = 1$. Figure 5.20 shows that the -1 dB beamwidth is 0.56 as great as the -3 dB beamwidth. Beamwidth equations such as 4.2 provide the -3 dB beamwidth.

The Gaussian function often is used to represent the beam pattern near the axis as a matter of mathematical convenience. This function is

$$f(y) = \exp\left[-1.385\left(\frac{y}{\theta}\right)^2\right] \tag{5.19}$$

Curves for this function also are plotted in Figs. 5.19 and 5.20. As can be seen, it is a reasonable approximation to the actual pattern functions up to $x \simeq 0.7$. However, it is not generated by any real antenna, since such an antenna would require an infinitely large reflector. Note that the Gaussian function displays no sidelobes. Sidelobe levels from an antenna can be reduced by tapering the illumination of the aperture [Ref. 24].

The actual footprint on the surface of the earth will differ from the beam cross-section because the beam will be obliquely incident on the surface of the earth at any nonzero latitude. When a beam intersects the surface of the earth at an elevation angle ε, the area A_b within the effective beam angle θ_b is

$$A_b = \frac{d_s^2 \theta_b}{\sin \varepsilon} \qquad \text{km}^2 \tag{5.20a}$$

where

$$d_s = \text{slant range in km.}$$

If the beam has an elliptical cross-section with angles θ_e and θ_a, the solid angle within the beam will be proportional to $\theta_e\theta_a$. However, the effect of the sin x/x beam pattern results in an effective solid angle only about half as great [Ref. 25]. Accordingly, the effective beamwidths are approximately $\theta_e/\sqrt{2}$ and $\theta_a/\sqrt{2}$, and the area of the footprint on the surface of the earth is

$$A_b = \left(\frac{\pi}{8}\right)\frac{\theta_e\theta_a d_s^2}{\sin \varepsilon} \qquad \text{km}^2 \tag{5.20b}$$

As can be seen from Fig. 5.19 and 5.20, conventional beam shapes do not provide uniform signal strength over the footprint. Moreover, the largest output power is required at the edge of the coverage area not only because of the antenna pattern but also because of added path loss and atmospheric attenuation. Usually the maximum (antenna boresight) gain is adjusted for adequate edge-of-coverage field strength. However, a multibeam antenna can achieve higher gain at the edge of coverage than can be done with a single horn [Ref. 26]. Special aperture distributions [Refs. 27 and 28] can produce shaped beams that compensate for the added losses along paths to different points on the surface of the earth. These special distributions use a large central feed horn surrounded by a ring of smaller horns fed 180° out of phase with the central horn. An alternative to the multihorn approach is the use of an array in which each of a number of subarrays is fed by a lower power (solid state) amplifier [Ref. 29]. Advantages include a beam forming network of modest size, and thus low loss due to such a network, and improved reliability, since amplifier failure results in graceful degradation.

An example of the type of beam shaping that can be done is illustrated in Fig. 5.21 [Ref. 29, p. 48], which shows the actual gain versus beam angle, relative to the required *EIRP*. The number of amplifiers used corresponds to the number of subarrays into which the overall array was divided.

5.3.3.2 Reflector Deployment.

Satellite reflectors having adequate sizes often cannot be launched in their fully deployed configuration. A major reason is the increasing use of spot beams which, because of their small widths, require reflectors having diameters on the order of 10 m and larger. While shuttle launches allow larger antenna apertures than ever before, spacecraft attitude stabilization capability now is better than 0.1°, thus allowing some very small spot beams to be used effectively.

The deployment of satellite reflectors has been done for many years since preshuttle era satellites also often had reflectors larger than could be launched in their fully deployed configurations. In many cases the larger reflector sizes, e.g., 10 m and larger, were required not only to produce small footprints, but also to provide adequate RF power levels in view of the limited prime power available on board the satellite (see Sec. 5.3.2).

Satellite antennas to be stowed and then deployed usually are made of a fine metallically coated mesh which can be folded in a variety of ways similar to the ways

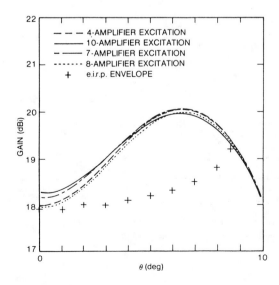

Figure 5.21 Beam shaping by use of solid-state array. (From S. Siddiqi, A. I. Zaghloul, S. M. Chou and R. E. Eaves, "An L-Band Active Array System for Global Coverage," *Comsat Technical Review,* vol. 15, no. 1, p. 48.)

in which umbrellas are folded. Toroidal stowing and deployment also are used. A mechanical deployment method using pushrods was developed by Harris; Lockheed developed a wrap-rib (toroidal) technique, and General Dynamics developed its parabolic erectable truss antenna. A recent technique consists of inflating specially prepared balloons and having them chemically rigidized in space [Ref. 30].

The satellite antennas that have been stowed, launched, and then deployed generally are the larger antennas, as has been noted above. Any large microwave parabolic dish must be made with careful attention to maintaining close to a true parabolic shape. Achieving the parabolic curvature is especially difficult if the parabolic shape is maintained by stretching a metallic fabric across ribs, as must be done with the deployable antennas. What happens if the curvature departs from true parabolic? This question is answered by Fig. 5.22 [Ref. 31], which shows that the efficiency and gain of a parabolic antenna become degraded as rms surface error increases. The gain reduction occurs as $\exp[-(4\pi\delta/\lambda)^2]$, where δ is the rms surface variation in the same units as λ. Thus surface tolerance limits the upper usable frequency of an antenna since a given error, measured in cm rms, becomes an increasing percentage of wavelength as frequency increases.

A further effect of the surface tolerance problem is that various sun angles on the geosynchronous spacecraft over the 24-hour period may produce gain variations at operational frequencies. Generally it is undesirable for such variations to exceed ± 1.0 dB. This then results in an upper limit for operational frequencies.

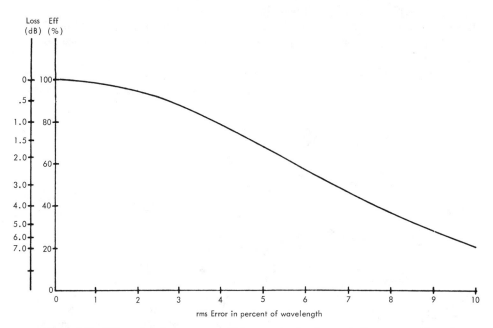

Figure 5.22 Effect of surface error on efficiency and gain of a parabolic antenna. (From J. Ruze, "Antenna Tolerance Theory, A Review," *Proc. IEEE,* April 1966, © 1966, IEEE. Reprinted by permission.)

5.4 GROUND SEGMENT*

Figure 5.23 is a simplified block diagram of a satellite earth terminal for analog transmission. The modulation most commonly used is FM, although digital modulation as well as SSB is being used also, especially on some uplinks. Figure 5.24 is a block diagram of a digital earth terminal. Many actual earth stations are hybrids in that they provide for analog service via some satellite transponders and digital service via others.

In analog service, on the order of 2 400 to 2 700 voice channels can be sent through a transponder using FM, whereas 6 000 channels can be uplinked using SSB; the downlinks then may be sent using SSB, FM, or PCM/MPSK.

Digital streams at the DS1 rate, each conveying 24 voice channels or the equivalent, are multiplexed to form a stream at the DS3 rate or higher. A single DS3 stream can be handled using QPSK in a 36 MHz transponder. Alternatively, two DS3 streams can be transmitted using 8-PSK, and correspondingly higher rates can be sent using 16-QAM. Higher rates, of course, also can be sent using larger transponder bandwidths than 36 MHz.

The frequency standard generally is of the cesium type. The tunable frequency synthesizers used in the up and down converters are phase locked to the frequency standard. (For a discussion of the handling of Doppler shift, see Sect. 5.4.2.3.) The required local oscillator frequencies then are obtained by the use of phase-locked multipliers. Although Fig. 5.24 shows only a single up-conversion step, two actually may be used, with one IF being centered at 70 MHz and another perhaps at 700 MHz. Smaller earth terminals may use only a fixed frequency local oscillator rather than a frequency synthesizer. Earth terminals operating with satellite transponders having appreciably larger bandwidths than 36 MHz use higher IF frequencies than 70 MHz.

The portions of the block diagrams of Figs. 5.23 and 5.24 described thus far are repeated for each satellite transponder through which the earth station works. A power combiner then adds the outputs of the various up converters, each of which is in a separate band of frequencies. If dual polarization is used, there will be two power combiners, one for the transponders using vertical or right-hand circular (RHC) polarization and another for the transponders using horizontal or left-hand circular (LHC) polarization.

Following the power combiner is a broadband intermediate power amplifier (IPA)** and a broadband high power amplifier (HPA). Earth station power output may be on the order of 500 W to 2 kW or more, depending on the number of channels being handled. Usually the IPA and HPA are dual redundant because of the larger number of channels they carry. Section 5.4.3 discusses earth station amplifiers further.

A diplexer is used for each of the two polarizations handled by the earth

---

* Portions of the introductory material of this section also appear in Ref. 1, pages 213–6. Both are taken from B. E. Keiser, "Wideband Communication Systems," Course Notes, © 1981 and 1985.

** Not shown in Fig. 5.23.

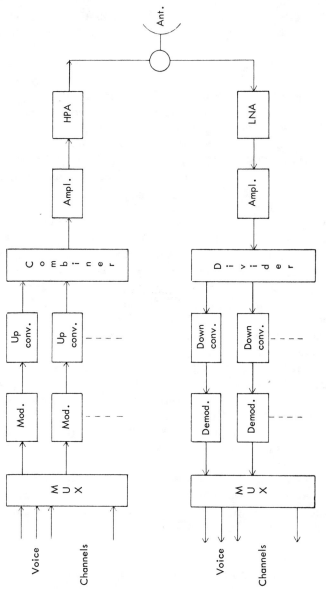

Figure 5.23   Satellite earth station for analog transmission.

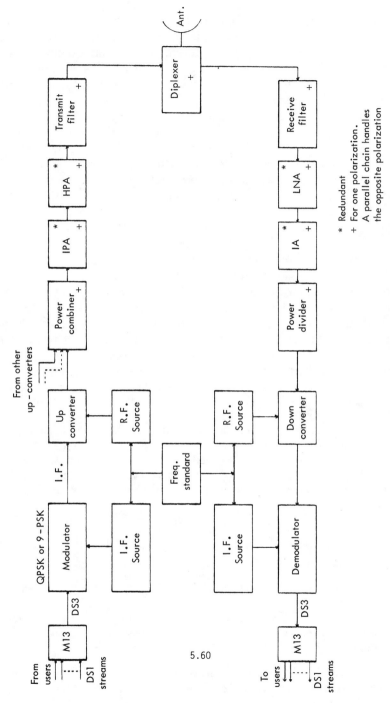

Figure 5.24 Satellite earth terminal for digital transmission.

* Redundant
+ For one polarization.
  A parallel chain handles
  the opposite polarization

5.60

277

station, as well as for each frequency band pair, i.e., 4–6 GHz, 7–8 GHz, 11–14 GHz, etc. However, dual polarization operation generally is confined to the frequency bands below 10 GHz because of the extensive depolarization caused by precipitation above 10 GHz. The diplexers and the transmit and receive filters must provide the high degree of isolation needed to prevent the transmitter output power from feeding back into the receiver input and thus producing desensitization.

An important characteristic of the earth station is the ratio G/T defined and described in Sec. 4.4.1.3. Large values of G/T allow relatively low-power satellites to be used, but these large G/T values require more expenditure for the earth station because of the cost of large antennas and low-noise temperature amplifiers (LNAs). Thus, as will be seen in Sec. 5.9, direct broadcast satellites are designed to use 200 W on-board amplifiers to allow receiving systems to be built for less than \$500 ($G/T = -8$ dB/K) whereas satellites for common carrier service often use 4 watt on-board amplifiers because the earth stations used with them often have relatively high G/T values, on the order of 22 to 41 dB/K.

A separate set of LNAs and intermediate amplifiers (IAs) is used for each received polarization and each frequency band, e.g., 4, 7, 11 GHz. In addition, the IAs and LNAs are redundant for reliability. The power divider separates the channels within the frequency domain based on the satellites's transponder frequency bands. The downconversion, demodulation, and demultiplexing steps then are the reverse of those described for the transmitting direction.

All transmitted sidebands must be attenuated sufficiently to prevent them from disturbing the receiving system. Isolation must be on the order of 140 to 180 dB depending on transmitted power level, bandwidth, and receiver noise level. This requires filters with good skirt selectively but yet with well-controlled delay distortion at the band edges to keep intersymbol interference low.

Earth stations used as part of the *Intelsat* system are classified as follows:

The standard A earth station operates in the 4 GHz downlink and 6 GHz uplink bands with $G/T \geqslant 35.0$ dB/K. This can be achieved using a 13 m dish and a 45 K LNA. The Standard B earth station differs from the Standard A only in that $G/T \geqslant 31.7$ dB/K. The Standard B requires an 11 to 13 m dish. The Standard C earth station operates in the 11 GHz downlink and 14 GHz uplink bands with the following G/T values:

$$\text{Clear sky } \frac{G}{T} \geqslant 37.0 + L_1 + \log_{10}\left(\frac{f}{11.2}\right) \frac{dB}{K} \tag{5.21}$$

where L_1 is the additional attenuation over clear sky all but 10% of the time and f is the carrier frequency in GHz.

$$\text{Degraded sky } \frac{G}{T} \geqslant 37.0 + L_2 + \log_{10}\left(\frac{f}{11.2}\right) \frac{dB}{K} \tag{5.22}$$

where L_2 is the additional attenuation over clear sky all but 0.017% of the time (1.5 hours per year). These equations are intended to keep the basic telephone channel noise power to less than 8 000 pWp0 for 90% of the time (see Table 5.5).

Equations (5.21) and (5.22) are applied next to illustrate the receiving antenna gain required in a particular case. The example chosen applies to the *Intelsat* receiving system at Etam, WV [Ref. 32]. Weather statistics and propagation studies showed that clear sky attenuation, caused by mist, fog, high strato-cumulus clouds, i.e., factors not measurable by a rain gauge, is 0.4 dB. Rain conditions for all but the worst 10% of the year contribute an additional 0.55 dB attenuation. Thus $L_1 = 0.40 + 0.55 = 0.95$ dB. Rain conditions for all but the worst 1.5 hours of the year contribute an additional 9.5 dB attenuation. Thus $L_2 = 0.40 + 9.5 = 9.9$ dB. Corresponding contributors to the temperature T are 17 K for the 18° elevation angle at Etam for all but 10% of the time and 419 K for all but 0.017% of the time.

The meeting of the Standard C earth station requirements necessitates a 16.7 to 18.9 m dish, and in rainy areas, a space diversity pair of sites may be needed. For example, the use of a second receiving site at Lenox, WV, 35 km to the northeast of Etam, operated on a diversity basis with Etam, resulted in a reduction in L_2 to $0.4 + 2.5 = 2.9$ dB and a reduction of the noise temperature all but 0.017% of the time from 419 K to 307 K. Because an unacceptably high transmit power (22 kW) would have been required at Etam without diversity, the use of the diversity pair was implemented.

Other *Intelsat* earth station classifications are summarized in Table 5.6. The Standard Z earth station must produce less than 400 pWp on an adjacent satellite carrier ($\geqslant 3°$ away), in accordance with CCIR Recommendation 465-1. A non-standard earth station requires approval on a case-by-case basis.

The sidelobes produced by the antennas of the above earth stations all must meet the criterion $G_s = 32 - 25 \log_{10} \theta$, where θ is the antenna's half-power beam-width in degrees. Many newer earth stations must meet more stringent sidelobe criteria, such as $29 - 25 \log_{10} \theta$ or $26 - 25 \log_{10} \theta$.

5.4.1 Earth Station Antennas

The gain of an antenna with aperture A_t was given by Eq. (4.7) as $4\pi\eta A_t/\lambda^2$. Section 4.1.1 showed that the gain of an antenna also equals $4\pi/\Omega$, where Ω is the solid beam angle. Based upon this expression an antenna with a half-power beamwidth θ and having a 65% efficiency will exhibit a gain g of

$$g = \frac{27\,000}{\theta^2}, \qquad \theta < 20° \qquad (5.23)$$

TABLE 5.6 *INTELSAT* EARTH STATION CLASSES

Class	Band (GHz)	G/T (dB/k)	$EIRP$ (dBW)	Ant. Dia (m)	Notes
A	4/6	$\geqslant$35.0	63.0 to 69.8	13	*EIRP* is for SCPC
B	4/6	$\geqslant$31.7	63.0 to 69.8	12	*EIRp* is for SCPC
C	11/14	See Note	—	18	G/T is defined by Eqs. (5.21), (5.22)
D1	4/6	22.7	56.6 per ch	4.5	SCPC
D2	4/6	31.7	52.7 per ch	13	SCPC
E	11/14	25 to 34	—	3.5 to 9.0	Intl. Business Svc.
F	4/6	>22.7 to 29.0	—	5 to 9	Intl. Business Svc.
Z	—	—	20.0/4 kHz carrier	—	Station accessing leased facilities

Source: Reprinted courtesy of the International Telecommunications Satellite Organization (INTELSAT).

If d_t denotes the reflector diameter, then

$$\theta \simeq \frac{70\lambda}{d_t} \text{ degrees} \tag{5.24}$$

For $d_t > 50 \lambda$, a condition which applies to most antennas used for satellite communications except those for spread spectrum applications (see Sec. 5.7.3), the gain at the peaks of the sidelobes must be restricted (FCC Docket 81–704) as follows for a transmitting antenna:

$29 - 25 \log_{10} \theta$ dBi	$1° \leqslant \theta \leqslant 7°$
8 dBi	$7° < \theta \leqslant 9.2°$
$32 - 25 \log_{10} \theta$ dBi	$9.2° < \theta \leqslant 48°$
-10 dBi	$48° < \theta \leqslant 180°$

The peak gain of a sidelobe may not exceed the envelope by more than 3 dB for $1° \leqslant \theta \leqslant 7°$, or by 10% for $\theta > 7°$. The off-axis cross-polarization isolation of any antenna shall be $\geqslant 10$ dB for off-axis angles $1° \leqslant \theta \leqslant 10°$.

Several feed types are used with parabolic reflector antennas, as illustrated in Fig. 5.25. The focal feed [feed mounted at focal point of parabola, as in Fig. 5.25(a)] is simple and economical. It is found in use on small (3–7 m) and very small (<3 m) earth stations such as those used in U.S., Japanese, and Indian domestic systems, as well as in maritime systems. In addition, some military systems such as those of NATO, as well as *Fleetsatcom* and the *Defense Satellite Communication System* (*DSCS*) use such antennas.

Medium (7–16 m) and large (>16 m) earth station antennas generally use the Cassegrain feed arrangement, which allows the primary feed to be located firmly at the center of the reflector. A subreflector and the main secondary aperture (the "dish") are arranged so they have a common focal point, as illustrated in Fig. 5.25(b). The Gregorian feed shown in Fig. 5.25(c) is used at some medium and large earth stations. In some cases its primary feed is offset to produce a narrow beam with low sidelobes. A dielectric shield may be added at the antenna's circumference to absorb off-axis energy, thus reducing the sidelobes.

The foregoing antenna types are quite satisfactory for communication through a single satellite, and thus serve well in common carrier applications for both transmitting and receiving. A cable television operator, however, has a different set of antenna requirements. He does not need to transmit, but he needs to receive signals from three or more satellites simultaneously. Multiple satellite receiving antennas have been devised for this purpose. The problem facing the designer of such an antenna is that the parabolic reflector produces a beam whose boresight is straight out from the reflector. A spherical reflector could be used for multiple beam directions, but the spherical reflector does not have the well-defined focal point of the parabola. A compromise between the two thus must be implemented. Three arrangements for this purpose are:

1. The torus, offset fed. This antenna is parabolic in the vertical plane but circular in the horizontal plane.
2. The offset spherical, which is an extremely long focal length parabola.
3. The quasi-parabolic in both planes, symmetrically fed.

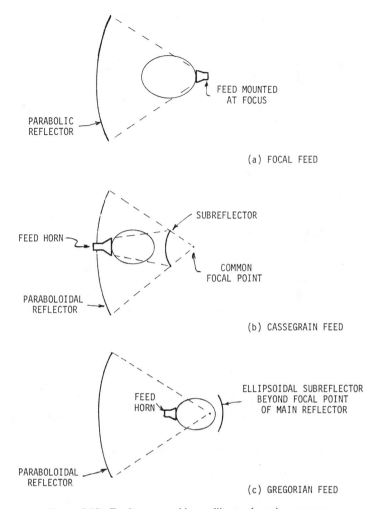

FEED MOUNTED
AT FOCUS

PARABOLIC
REFLECTOR

(a) FOCAL FEED

SUBREFLECTOR

FEED HORN

COMMON
FOCAL POINT

PARABOLOIDAL
REFLECTOR

(b) CASSEGRAIN FEED

ELLIPSOIDAL SUBREFLECTOR
BEYOND FOCAL POINT
OF MAIN REFLECTOR

FEED
HORN

PARABOLOIDAL
REFLECTOR

(c) GREGORIAN FEED

Figure 5.25 Feed types used in satellite earth station antennas.

Typical performance for a multiple satellite antenna, the "Simulsat 5" by Antenna Technology Corp., is listed in Table 5.7.

5.4.1.1 Antenna Size Requirements.
The size of a satellite earth station antenna is significant with respect to both antenna gain and beamwidth. The link budgets (see Sec. 5.6) for many satellite circuits are such that adequate gain often can be achieved with a dish diameter of only a few meters. However, much larger dishes often are required to achieve adequately narrow beams, and special attention to antenna sidelobes also may be required to keep interference levels acceptably low. The interference problems to be addressed are (1) to and from adjacent satellites, and (2) to and from other terrestrial users of the same parts of the microwave spectrum. Table 5.8 describes the effect of co-channel interference on FM video transmission. Some digital transmission can tolerate $C/I = 15$ dB.

TABLE 5.7 PERFORMANCE OF "SIMULSAT 5" MULTIPLE C-BAND SATELLITE ANTENNA

Aperture	5×8.5 m
Frequency	$3.4 - 4.2$ GHz
Gain	44 dBi
Beamwidth	1°
Polarization isolation	>25 dB
Adjacent satellite isolation	>25 dB
Arc reception	72°

Source: Courtesy Antenna Technology Corp.

TABLE 5.8 EFFECT OF CO-CHANNEL INTERFERENCE ON FM VIDEO TRANSMISSION

C/I (dB)	Effect
18	Just perceptible
20	Generally accepted commercial quality
25	Coordination limits (microwave interference to satellite earth station)
26	Internal interferences (adjacent channels in satellite system)

Equation (5.24) presents some highly significant information regarding earth station antenna diameters. It states that the beamwidth of an antenna operated at a given wavelength λ is inversely proportional to the antenna's diameter d_t. This places a lower limit on antenna diameter since the smaller the diameter, the broader the beamwidth. The result then is interference to/from adjacent satellites. U.S. domestic satellites in the 4/6 GHz bands are being spaced every 2.5°, and European spacing is 1.5°. Domestic satellites for the 11/14 GHz band are being spaced every 2°, but the smaller wavelength allows relatively small dish sizes in this band.

Studies done on the effect of antenna size on C/I for FM video reception show, for example, that the minimum size antenna for 4/6 GHz operation for a given polarization plan is a 5 m low sidelobe antenna. Adjacent domestic satellites therefore use different polarization plans to allow their reception by smaller dishes. Figure 5.26, [Ref. 33], illustrates the C/I versus satellite spacing for both standard and low sidelobe designs. The assumptions used for Fig. 5.26 are: 9.2 m transmit antennas, 35 dBW (saturated) downlink *EIRP,* 80 dBW uplink *EIRP,* terrestrial $C/I = 25$ dB and internal $C/I = 26$ dB. References in Fig. 5.26 are to the FCC *Rules and Regulations,* Part 25.209, and to FCC Docket 81.704.

Antenna design techniques required to meet the Docket 81.704 sidelobe levels include the use of a low cross-polarization prime-focus feed with a very low illumination taper (center to edge of dish) of about 8 dB, and a surface tolerance on the order of 0.075 cm. Low cross-polarization in a feed can be achieved by using a corrugated horn. Offset fed antennas also are good performers with respect to low side lobes because the feed does not block the aperture.

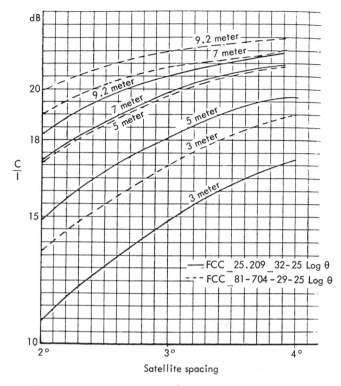

Figure 5.26 *C/I* versus satellite spacing. (© 1983, *Communications News Magazine.* Reprinted by permission.)

5.4.1.2 Earth Station Siting*. Satellite earth stations may be found in a variety of places, including building roof tops, but they are best located in valleys or other low terrain, such that their surroundings provide some shielding from interference that may reach them from terrestrial microwave relays. Before attempting to establish a new satellite earth station, a careful examination must be made of the surrounding electromagnetic environment to determine what main beam or sidelobe interference may exist between the new earth station and microwave repeaters.

An important consideration in earth station siting is the beam direction to the satellite. This can be determined using the chart of Fig. 5.27 [Ref. 34]. Knowledge of the earth station's latitude and of the relative longitude of the satellite allow the determination of the azimuth and elevation angles of the satellite using this chart.

Knowledge of the earth station's main beam direction is important in avoiding obstructions in that direction, as well as in determining the direction of the sidelobes. Sidelobes may cause interference to adjacent satellites or to other satellite earth stations or nearby microwave systems.

---

* The material of this section also appears in Ref. 1, pp. 198–9. Both are taken from B. E. Keiser, "Wideband Communications Systems," Course Notes, © 1981 and 1985.

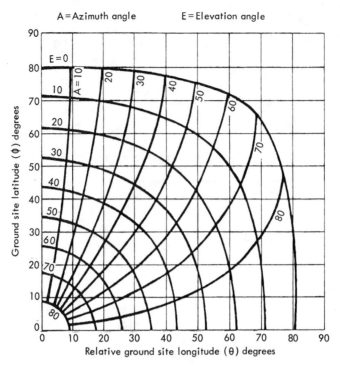

A = Azimuth angle   E = Elevation angle

Figure 5.27 Nomogram of determining look angles to the direction of a geostationary satellite. (From F. L. Smith III, "A Nomogram for Look Angles to Geostationary Satellites," *IEEE Trans. Aerospace and Electronic Systems,* May 1972, © 1972, IEEE. Reprinted by permission.)

5.4.1.3 Protective Walls. A satellite earth station cannot always be built in a valley or other area naturally shielded from terrestrial microwave systems. Artificial barriers thus may have to be erected. Such barriers serve to shield the satellite earth station from its RF environment. While the discussion which follows is written in terms of an outside source of interference, reciprocity applies, and the loss produced by the protective wall also applies to an outside system that is the recipient of interference from the subject earth station.

The *shielding effectiveness* of a solid wall of infinite extent, i.e., large enough that diffraction around the edges is not a factor, is given by the equation [Ref. 35]

$$\text{S.E.} = A + R + B \qquad \text{dB} \qquad (5.25)$$

where

A = attenuation through wall, dB

R = reflection loss on side on which wave impinges, dB

B = multiple reflection correction term, dB

The attenuation, $A = \alpha d$, where α = attenuation rate in nepers/meter (Np/m) and d = wall thickness, meters. The value of α is

$$\alpha = \sqrt{\frac{\omega\mu\sigma}{2}} \qquad \frac{\text{Np}}{\text{m}} \qquad (5.26)$$

where

μ = permeability, Henry/meter (H/m)

$\quad = \mu_0 \, \mu_r$

μ_0 = permeability of free space = $4\pi \times 10^{-7}$ H/m

μ_r = relative permeability of wall material at frequency ω

σ = conductivity of wall material, Siemens/meter (S/m)

1 Np = 8.686 dB

The value of R is based upon the impedance discontinuity that the wall presents to the wave. Thus, the reflection loss depends not only upon the surface impedance of the wall, which is given by

$$\eta_s = \sqrt{\frac{j\omega\mu}{\sigma}} \qquad \text{ohms} \qquad (5.27)$$

but also upon the wave impedance η_0, which is 377 ohms under the far-field conditions pertinent to distant sources, as well as under the off-axis conditions pertinent to antennas within the wall, since the beam axes are directed over the top of the wall, such that the wall itself is away from the beam axis. Accordingly [Ref. 36],

$$R = -20 \log_{10} \left[\left(\frac{2\eta_s}{\eta_0 + \eta_s} \right) \left(\frac{2\eta_0}{\eta_0 + \eta_s} \right) \right] \text{ dB} \qquad (5.28)$$

The value of B is

$$B = 20 \log_{10} \left| 1 - 10^{-A/10} \left(\cos 0.23A + j \sin 0.23A \right) \right| \qquad (5.29)$$

For a material for which $\sigma \gg \omega\epsilon$, the reflection loss R is given by the approximation

$$R \simeq 168 - 10 \log_{10} \left(\frac{f\mu_r}{\sigma_r} \right) \qquad \text{dB} \qquad (5.30)$$

where

σ_r = conductivity relative to that of copper, which is 5.8×10^7 S/m.

Even thin metal foils provide more than enough shielding effectiveness at microwave frequencies. The height of the wall must be limited so that it does not obstruct the earth station's beam aimed upward at the satellite. However, wave diffraction does occur over the top of the wall. The amount of diffraction loss will depend upon the height of the wall relative to the dish, as well as the radius of curvature of the wall top. In analyzing wave diffraction over wall tops, the incident wave from an external (terrestrial microwave) source is assumed to be coming from the horizon. The diffracted wave field strength then is integrated over the antenna's aperture.

The theory and computational techniques for diffraction over a knife edge [Ref. 37] can be expressed in terms of the geometry of Fig. 5.28 for the case in which the disturbance at point R is coming from (or going to) a distant point T along the horizon.

A useful mathematical tool for predicting the behavior of partially blocked electromagnetic waves [Ref. 38] is the set of Fresnel integrals,

$$y = \int_0^v \sin\left(\frac{\pi x^2}{2}\right) dx \tag{5.31a}$$

$$x = \int_0^v \cos\left(\frac{\pi x^2}{2}\right) dx \tag{5.31b}$$

The parameter v can take on all values from $-\infty$ to $+\infty$. As $v \to -\infty$, $x \to -0.5$, and $y \to -0.5$. As $v \to \infty$, $x \to 0.5$, and $y \to 0.5$. The vector from $(-0.5, -0.5)$ to $(0.5, 0.5)$ represents free space propagation. The plot of (x, y) is known as the Cornu spiral. Figure 5.29 [Ref. 37, Fig. III.10] shows the Cornu spiral.

Assuming a distant interference source propagating waves parallel to the surface of the earth, let

$r =$ horizontal distance from antenna radiation center to wall

$s =$ wall height above antenna radiation center

$\varepsilon = \tan^{-1}(s/r)$

Then

$$v = \sqrt{\frac{2r}{\lambda}} \tan \varepsilon = s\sqrt{\frac{2}{r\lambda}} \tag{5.32}$$

The radiation center of the antenna is the point from which the radiation appears to come if the antenna is used to transmit. Often it is taken to be located at the physical center of the feed, as an approximation. Thus for a given wall height and distance, at a given wavelength λ, a value of v can be defined. With reference to the Cornu spiral, the vector from the value of v corresponding to the wall height to $v \to \infty$ represents propagation over the wall to the receiving antenna location.

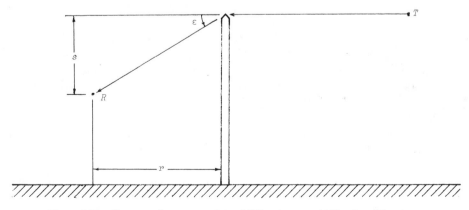

Figure 5.28 Geometry for computation of diffraction over knife edge. (Courtesy Fanwall Corporation, Arlington, VA, and Artech House, Inc., Norwood, MA.)

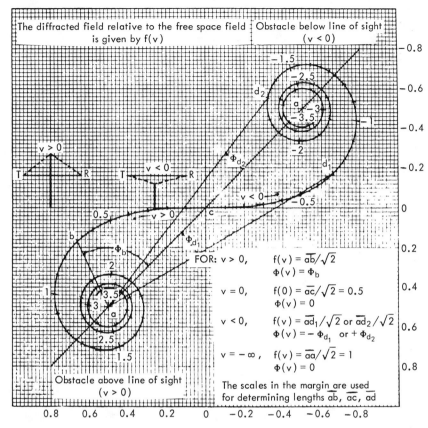

Figure 5.29 Cornu spiral. (Courtesy Fanwall Corporation, Arlington, VA, and Artech House, Inc., Norwood, MA.)

Diffraction loss over the top of a wall can be determined through the use of Figure 5.30 [Ref. 39]. Use of this figure simply requires a knowledge of r, λ, and ε.

Example

A metallic protective wall is to be used to attenuate the field from a microwave radio relay system operating in several radio channels in the 3 700 to 4 200 MHz band. What minimum attenuation is produced at a distance 30 m from the wall and 3 m below its top?

Solution The least diffraction loss occurs at the lowest frequencies. Since only a band of frequencies is given, the computation is done for the lowest frequency, 3 700 MHz. $\lambda = c/f = 3 \times 10^8/3\ 700 \times 10^6 = 0.081$ m. Since $s = 3$ m and $r = 30$ m, $\varepsilon = \tan^{-1} (3/30) = 0.10$. In addition, $r\lambda = 30/0.081 = 370$. Use of Fig. 5.30 then shows the loss to be 22 dB.

Some very high levels of attenuation can be produced through the use of a diffraction strip above the top of a wall, as illustrated in Figure 5.31, which represents a cross-section of the wall, with a strip parallel to, and just above, the top

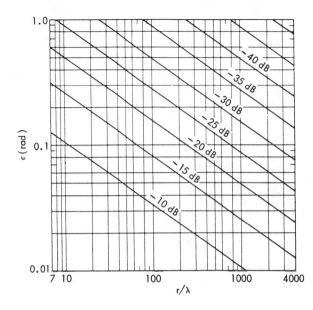

Figure 5.30 Diffraction loss. (From J. J. G. McCue, "Remarks on anti-RFI fences," *IEEE Trans. Electromagnetic Compatibility,* Feb. 1981, © 1981, IEEE. Reprinted by permission.)

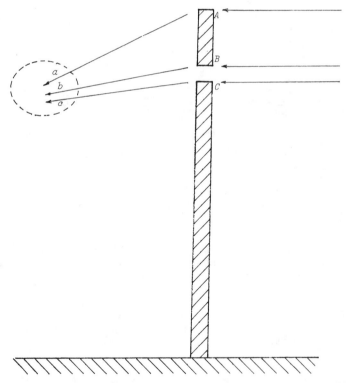

Figure 5.31 Use of strip above wall top to produce null in diffracted field. (Courtesy Fanwall Corporation, Arlington, VA, and Artech House, Inc., Norwood, MA.)

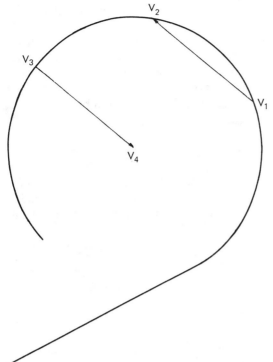

Figure 5.32 Cornu spiral representation of propagation with top strip. (Courtesy Fanwall Corporation, Arlington, VA, and Artech House, Inc., Norwood, MA.)

edge.[*] A wave is assumed to impinge on the wall from the right-hand side at points A, B, and C. Diffracted rays a, b, and c cancel, or nearly cancel, one another in the dash-encircled region. In Fig. 5.32, v_1 corresponds to the top of the wall (C), v_2 to the bottom of the strip (B), and v_3 to the top of the strip (A). Thus propagation through the gap, represented by the vector $v_1 v_2$ in Fig. 5.32, is cancelled by propagation of equal magnitude and opposite phase from the space above the strip, represented by vector $v_3 v_4$, where $v_4 \rightarrow \infty$.

A graphical procedure allows the optimum values of v_1, v_2, and v_3 to be obtained approximately, following which a computer optimization can be done. The graphical procedure is as follows:

1. From point v_1, draw a radius vector equal in magnitude to $v_1 v_4$, such that it intersects the spiral at the next larger value of v. Call the intersection v_2.
2. Draw a parallel vector to $v_1 v_2$, ending in v_4 in the direction opposite to $v_1 v_2$. This vector starts at v_3 and is approximately equal in magnitude to $v_1 v_2$.

This procedure is an approximation because the spiral radius continues to decrease as v increases. However, the graphical procedure allows the computation time to be decreased appreciably.

[*] The author acknowledges the sponsorship of this work by the Fanwall Corporation, Arlington, VA. The technique described here is the subject of U.S. patent 4 668 958.

The top strip technique provides significant increases in protection for localized regions in specific frequency bands. Thus it allows high degrees of protection without wall height increases and without large wall-to-antenna distances, which may require extra real estate. The top strip technique, as described, cannot provide simultaneous protection in different bands, but the most severe problems usually are in the 4 GHz band. Protection levels of 36 dB and more are feasible over the entire frequency range from 3.7 to 4.2 GHz. The principle can be extended, if necessary, through the use of multiple strips above the wall.

5.4.2 Interface Subsystems

Numerous interfaces are required in the transmission of signals via satellite systems. Differing international standards contribute to the interface problem. Figure 5.33 shows some of the interfacing needed, and also shows the satellite's control sub-

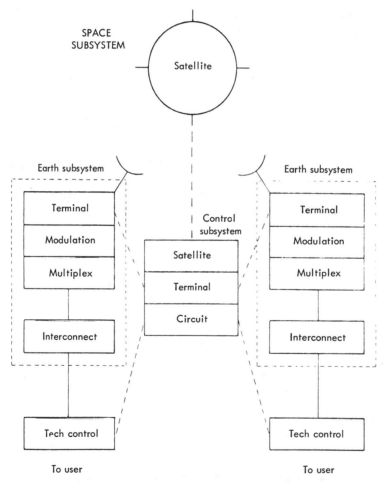

Figure 5.33 Satellite system block diagram.

system, which is the subject of Sec. 5.5. The box labelled "Interconnect" designates the point at which terrestrial circuits are interconnected with the satellite system. The boxes labelled "satellite terminal circuit" constitute the tracking, telemetry, and command subsystem (see Sec. 5.5). The "Tech Control" function maintains proper limits on the number and power level of the uplinks to prevent circuit degradation from intermodulation. The earth stations at their respective locations will interface on an analog or digital basis, depending upon the type of service to be provided. This section describes the techniques used to provide satellite system interfaces.

5.4.2.1 Transmultiplexers. The digital hierarchy was introduced in Chap. 2, where it was compared with the analog hierarchy. The purpose of a transmultiplexer is to provide two-way conversion between analog FDM and digital TDM signals based upon the standard hierarchies. Several common transmultiplexer arrangements are the following:

1. Two FDM groups (24 voice channels) to one DS1 stream. This is a conversion between two 48-kHz analog basebands and one 1.544 Mb/s stream.
2. One FDM supergroup (60 voice channels) to two CEPT-1 streams. This is a conversion between one 240 kHz analog baseband and two 2.048 Mb/s streams.
3. Two FDM supergroups (120 voice channels) to five DS1 streams or four CEPT-1 streams. This is a conversion between two 240 kHz analog basebands and five 1.544 Mb/s or four 2.048 Mb/s streams.

Other combinations, of course, also are possible.

Transmultiplexers are used at switching centers, where conversions between TDM and FDM must be done because of the differing types of facilities which must be interconnected. Either analog or digital means can be used in building transmultiplexers. As an example, a block diagram of a 60-channel transmultiplexer is shown in Fig. 5.34 [Ref. 40]. The designations S/P and P/S refer, respectively, to serial-to-parallel and parallel-to-serial. The letters R and S refer, respectively, to receiver and sender. The EX and COMP abbreviations, respectively, are for expander and compressor. The abbreviation FI is for filter, for smoothing. Since Fig. 5.34 shows the use of the European digital multiplex standards, the compressor and expander will operate based upon the A-law for speech compression and expansion [Ref. 1, pp. 28–29].

5.4.2.2 Digital Noninterpolated Interface (DNI). A digital noninterpolated interface (DNI) provides for the transmission of individual primary multiplex channels in permanently assigned satellite channels within a TDMA burst. DNI interfaces can carry selected individual multiplex channels or complete primary multiplex groups of channels. The name DNI is used to distinguish the interface from one known as digital speech interpolation (DSI), used to take advantage of the normal pauses in human speech and to use these pauses to provide additional channels for voice transmission.

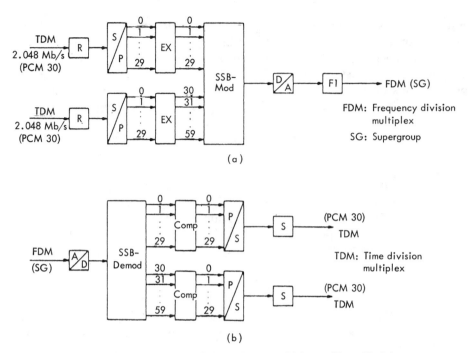

Figure 5.34 Block diagram of 60-channel transmultiplexer. (From H. Scheuermann and H. Göckler, "A Comprehensive Survey of Digital Multiplexing Methods," *Proc. IEEE,* Nov. 1981, © 1981, IEEE. Reprinted by permission.)

DNI circuits are arranged so digital rate differences between the terrestrial and the satellite circuits do not cause an excessive number of slips of the multiplexed data frames. Such slips may be caused by the plesiochronous operation of the reference clocks (see Chap. 2), or by Doppler shifts caused by motion of the satellite.

Satellite links used in international operation may interface between different national networks each of whose timing is controlled by cesium beam oscillators having accuracies on the order of $\pm 1 : 10^{-11}$. At a 2.048 MHz clock rate at each end, however, a timing difference of 1 bit can accrue in 7 hours. This is too often for high-speed data communication. However, the clocks can be reset based on the use of frame slips [Ref. 5, p. 73]. Since there are 256 bits/frame at the 2.048 Mb/s rate, a frame slip occurs on the average of only once per 72 days. This is an adequately low rate.

Satellites do not remain at an exact orbital position, but tend to deviate, over a 24 hour period, in both latitude and longitude. The deviation may be allowed to reach 0.1° or more, depending on the system and the sizes of earth stations (and therefore beam sizes) used. The path length may vary by up to 1.1 ms or more, with the rate of change of path length reaching 40 ns/s. Doppler buffering, as well as plesiochronous time difference alignment, can be provided by elastic buffers [Ref. 41] located at the interfaces to the satellite system, and capable of absorbing the path length change, corresponding to one up- and one down-path.

5.4.2.3 Doppler Buffers. The Doppler buffer is designed as a variable extension of the satellite propagation path [Ref. 5, p. 395], thus maintaining a constant propagation delay between earth stations in communication via the satellite. It functions by storing a number of message bits corresponding to the compensating delay time ΔT [Ref. 5, pp. 394–5]. The capacity of a Doppler buffer must be at least $2\Delta T$ so it can be started at the center of its range and compensate to the extent $+\Delta T$ or $-\Delta T$, as needed. As an example, if $\Delta T = 1.0$ ms and the link rate is 2.048 Mb/s, the required buffer size is 2×2.048 Mb/s $\times 1.0$ ms $= 4\,096$ bits.

Separate Doppler buffers must be used on the transmit and receive sides of all terminals in a network if Doppler shift effects are to be eliminated totally. This is vital if the individual channels within a given TDMA frame are to remain properly aligned within the frame.

The TDMA system frame reference period is established by relating it to a suitable multiple of the 125-μs frame period used in both the North American and the European standards. A selected earth station serves as the reference station and establishes the timing for the entire network.

5.4.3 Earth Station Amplifier Techniques

Section 5.3.1.2 discussed RF amplifiers for use on board the satellite. The problem of amplifier nonlinearity was analyzed, especially with respect to the need to back off the operating level from saturation—a particularly important requirement if multiple carriers are being amplified. All of the points made about satellite amplifiers apply to earth station amplifiers as well. The main differences are that the earth station amplifier usually operates at a higher power level than the satellite amplifier, the earth station amplifier can be serviced or replaced as needed, and adjustments to precompensate for nonlinearities can be made readily at an earth station.

A low-loss multiplexer has been developed for satellite earth terminals to eliminate the need for a broadband high-power transmitter [Ref. 42] with its reliability and efficiency limitations. Each 36 MHz channel in the 5 925 to 6 425 MHz uplink band (in the case of a domestic commercial satellite) is amplified by an individual solid-state power amplifier. Modular units allow the addition of channels as needed. Waveguide equalizers provide for amplitude and time delay compensation. Such modular units are well suited to small, unmanned earth terminals.

5.4.4 Echo Suppression and Cancellation

Echos arise from impedance mismatches in terminating equipment. Echos contribute to intersymbol interference in data transmission and thus to bit errors. In video transmission on an analog basis, echos result in the appearance of "ghosts" in the picture. In digital video transmission, echos cause various forms of degradation depending on the type of coding algorithm used.

Generally the adverse effects of echos increase with both echo delay and echo level. Echo problems have been controlled through the judicious use of circuit loss as well as by the use of the echo suppressor, which opens the transmission path from the listener to the talker [Ref. 43]. The basis for using circuit loss is that the echo

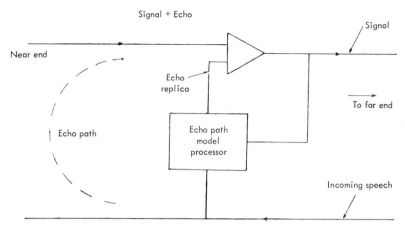

Signal + Echo

Signal

Near end

Echo
replica

To far end

Echo path

Echo path
model
processor

Incoming speech

Figure 5.35 Principle of echo cancellation. (From H. G. Suyderhoud, M. Onufry and S. J. Campanella, "Echo Control in Telephone Communications," *IEEE National Telecommunications Conference, 1976,* © 1976. Reprinted by permission.)

path is a round-trip path, and thus the echo suffers twice the attenuation encountered by the desired signal. For terrestrial circuit lengths in excess of 3 000 km, the use of loss (known as "via net loss") results in unacceptably low received levels [Ref. 44]. While echo suppressors often are used on one-way single-hop satellite circuits, their performance has been found to be unacceptable [Ref. 45] on two-way ("full hop") satellite circuits, where the echo delay is a full 540 ms or more.

Echo problems are solved most effectively through the use of the echo canceler. Echo cancellation was proposed in the early 1960s, but could not be implemented on a widespread basis at the time because of its complexity and thus high cost. However, the use of very-large-scale integration (VLSI) has allowed an entire echo canceler to be placed on a single chip [Ref. 46, 47], thus rendering the concept practical economically.

Figure 5.35 [Ref. 43] illustrates the basis on which echo cancelers are implemented. An adaptive model of the echo signal is built using a tapped delay-line filter. Adaptive feedback processing is used to obtain this model of the echo path response. The model then is stored in memory. Following this, the incoming signal is processed by convolution with the stored impulse response, thus providing a close replica of the actual echo signal. This replica then is subtracted from the actual echo signal on the sending side. As a result, the echo is removed, leaving the speech unaffected. Accordingly, the failings of the echo suppressor technique do not arise.

Usually an echo canceler is used at each end of a satellite circuit. This is called *split echo control.*

5.5 SATELLITE CONTROL

Figure 5.33 showed the basic elements of a satellite system, including the control subsystem. The control subsystem uses a special earth station, often called the tracking, telemetry, and command (TT&C) station. This station performs a cooperative (beacon aided) track on the satellite so that any deviation from desired on-orbit position is sensed quickly. In addition the TT&C station monitors space-craft telemetry, which includes such data as solar array output, the state of charge of the batteries, the amount of propulsion fuel remaining, on-board temperatures, and the operating level and load of each transponder, including the automatic gain control (AGC) level. The command function of the TT&C station is used to send corrective orbital commands, which fire gas jets on board the spacecraft, and may also be used to change transponder power levels and operating modes as well as antenna beams, or to override automatic functions, such as temperature control, which may not be performing as desired.

5.6 LINK BUDGETS*

A link budget provides a complete description of a radio transmission path from the transmitter power output to the detected signal, and often includes an expression of reception quality in terms of bit error probability for digital systems, or signal-to-noise ratio for analog systems. For a satellite system both an uplink and a downlink budget must be calculated. However, the uplink budget usually is the less critical of the two, since plentiful amounts of power normally are available to the earth-based transmitter. Uplink stations also may have significant amounts of antenna gain. Generally the satellite receiver will have a rather high-noise temperature, e.g., over 1 000 K, because the earth itself is noisy and no value would be gained with a low-noise receiver. Quite to the contrary, low-noise receivers cannot be made to operate as reliably as the high-noise (less sensitive) ones that are actually used on spacecraft.

Example

A 10 Mb/s digital signal is to be transmitted through the *Satcom F2* satellite at 119° W using QPSK modulation. Establish the uplink parameters for transmission from Los Angeles, CA to Anchorage, AK based upon the contours in Fig. 5.36 and 5.37 [Ref. 48], which show *EIRP* and *SFD* respectively, at the satellite. The satellite receiving system has a $G/T = -5.0$ dB/K.

Solution Figure 5.36 shows that the satellite provides an *EIRP* of 37 dBW in the direction of Anchorage, AK. An uplink signal from Los Angeles must be -83 dBW/m² to saturate the transponder. For an input backed off 10 dB from saturation, the following are the key link budget parameters:

SFD	-83.0 dBW/m²
Input back-off	-10.0 dB
Boltzmann's constant, k	$+228.6$ dBW/HzK
G/T	-5.0 dB/K
$10 \log_{10} (\lambda^2/4\pi)$	-37.3 dBm²
C/kT	93.3 dB Hz

*Portions of this section also appear in Ref. 1, pp. 197–8. Both are taken from B. E. Keiser, "Wideband Communication Systems," Course Notes, © 1981 and 1985.

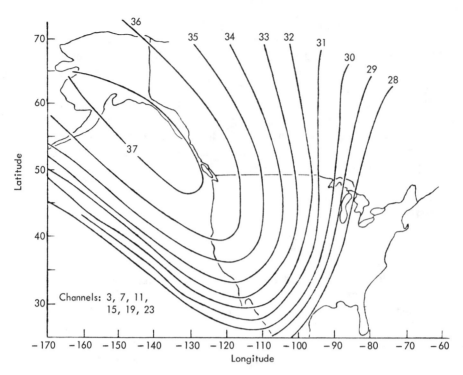

Figure 5.36 *Satcom F2* (119° W) EIRP contours (dBW).

The factor $10 \log_{10} (\lambda^2/4\pi)$ is used to convert from the uplink flux density in W/m^2 to the received power level in W. The value of C/kT is the uplink carrier-to-noise ratio in a Hz bandwidth. The actual carrier-to-noise ratio is found by subtracting the bandwidth in dBHz. Thus if the 10 Mb/s stream is transmitted using QPSK and occupies a 6 MHz bandwidth, then, since 6 MHz = 67.8 dBHz, $C/N = (93.3 - 67.8)$ dB = 25.5 dB.

The criticality of the downlink budget results from several factors. The satellite is power-limited by the amount of power available from the solar array and the number of transponders and pieces of control equipment among which this power must be divided. In addition, the physical size of the spacecraft antenna, and thus its gain, also generally is smaller than those on the ground. Another limit may be the available channel bandwidth, as well as the way in which a given transponder's bandwidth and power are allocated. A further limit is that in the 3 700–4 200 MHz band, international regulations state that the power flux density shall not exceed 12 dBW *EIRP* in any 4 kHz band.

In a purely digital time-division-multiplexed system, each user has the entire transponder for the duration of his time slot. However, many systems allocate only a portion of the transponder to digital transmission; alternatively, they may use the transponder on an FDM digital basis in which case intermodulation will exist among the carriers. For example, a single channel per carrier (SCPC) system may transmit a single PCM channel using a 45 kHz wide portion of an overall 36 MHz wide

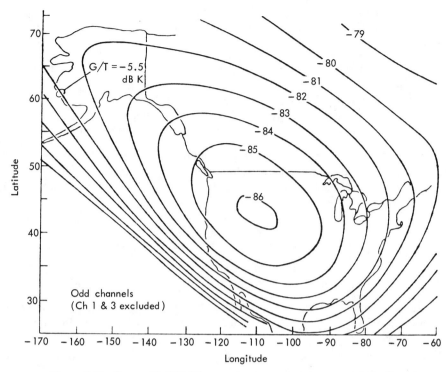

Figure 5.37 *Satcom F2* (119° W) saturation flux density contours (dBW/m²).

transponder. As many as 800 of these SCPC channels may use the same transponder.

The basic downlink power budget may be expressed in terms of the carrier-to-noise power normalized to a 1 Hz bandwidth, $(C/kT)_A$, available from a transponder or a portion thereof, as follows:

$$\left(\frac{C}{kT}\right)_A = 10 \log_{10} \left[(EIRP)_{\max} - (EIRP)_0 \right] \tag{5.33}$$

$$-(TD)_d - (TPL)_d k + \left(\frac{G}{T}\right)_{\text{eff}} \quad \text{dBHz}$$

where

$(EIRP)_{\max}$ = maximum center beam transponder effective isotropically radiated power in watts at its normal operating point, chosen to be backed off from saturation by a specified amount.

$(EIRP)_0$ = power in watts devoted to other carriers in the transponder than the carrier of interest.

$(TD)_d$ = tilt differential for the downlink in dB, the degradation from the maximum *EIRP* resulting from the position of the earth terminal relative to the boresight of the satellite antenna.

$(TPL)_d$ = total path loss in dB for the downlink.

= free space loss (*FSL*) + miscellaneous loss (*m*).

The expression for *FSL* was derived in Chap. 4 where it appears as Eq. (4.4b), which states that $FSL = 32.44 + 20 \log_{10} (d_{km}) + 20 \log_{10} (f_{MHz})$ dB. The remaining terms in Eq. (5.33) are

m = loss caused by pointing error, radome loss, atmospheric attenuation and polarization loss.
$k = -228.6$ dBW/HzK (Boltzmann's constant)
$(G/T)_{eff}$ = effective earth terminal figure of merit in dB/K, including the effect of thermal noise radiated from the satellite to the earth terminal.

System designers may use linear approximations to curves such as those of Fig. 5.12 in order to estimate the intermodulation noise level, which also must be taken into account in a link design. For example, *Telesat* [Ref. 48] uses the following linear approximation:

$$C/I_0 = 98.7 - IPBO \qquad (5.34)$$

where

C/I_o = carrier to intermodulation noise spectral density ratio.
$IPBO$ = input back-off level of the individual carrier in the transponder.

The satellite system operator is responsible for the achievement of suitably low intermodulation levels, and must instruct earth station users regarding limits on their transmit levels.

The available uplink C/kT can be expressed in terms of the saturation flux density (SFD) and the $IPBO$ as

$$\left(\frac{C}{kT}\right)_{up} = SFD - IPBO - k + \frac{G}{T} + 10 \log_{10}\left(\frac{\lambda^2}{4\pi}\right) \text{ dB} \qquad (5.35)$$

The total carrier-to-noise spectral density ratio then is

$$\left(\frac{C}{kT}\right)_{total}^{-1} = \left(\frac{C}{kT}\right)_{up}^{-1} + \left(\frac{C}{kT}\right)_{down}^{-1} + \left(\frac{C}{I_0}\right)^{-1} \qquad (5.36)$$

Intermodulation noise thus is treated statistically, as is thermal noise. Other forms of degradation usually are handled through the use of allowances in the link margins.

Equation (5.36) allows a determination to be made of the available (C/kT) at the receiving earth station. The next question is "what (C/kT) is required?" Let this value be designated $(C/kT)_R$. It is expressed as follows:

$$\left(\frac{C}{kT}\right)_R = R + \left(\frac{E_b}{N_0}\right) + L + M \qquad \text{dBHz} \qquad (5.37)$$

where

$R = 10 \log_{10}$ (bit rate, b/s)
E_b/N_o = ratio of energy per bit to noise power spectral density to achieve required bit error rate.
L = losses resulting from use of channel filters (about 1 to 2 dB).
M = satellite link margin.

Link margin values M typically are in the following ranges:

Digital modem implementation loss	1 to 2 dB
Antenna pointing error	up to 0.5 dB
Interference	
Adjacent channel	0.5 dB
Adjacent satellite	0.5 dB
Terrestrial radio	0.5 dB
Fade margin (for 99.99% availability at a 10° elevation angle)	
3.70 to 4.20 GHz	4.0 dB
7.25 to 7.75 GHz	6.0 dB
10.95 to 12.20 GHz	8.0 dB

The total margin thus is about 7 dB to 11 dB, depending upon the frequency band used.

The earth station power amplifier rating per carrier must accommodate the following factors:

1. Variations in saturation flux density and satellite *EIRP* over the earth area to be covered (typically 1 to 3 dB).
2. Variations in *SFD* and satellite *EIRP* during the life of the satellite (typically 1 to 2 dB).
3. Losses between power amplifier and antenna (typically 1 dB).

If the earth station transmits multiple carriers, e.g., if SCPC operation is included (see Sec. 5.7.2), the amplifier must be backed off to minimize odd order intermodulation noise between the carriers. The power amplifier rating thus must be 4 to 10 dB beyond the overall required transmitter output. In turn, the required transmitter output is the *EIRP* less the transmit antenna gain. Thus

$$EIRP = SFD - IPBO - FSL + 10 \log_{10} \left(\frac{\lambda^2}{4\pi} \right) \qquad \text{dBW} \qquad (5.38)$$

Example

Determine the satellite system operating parameters for the system of the foregoing example. Assume that the receiving system uses a 4.7 m dish, and that a 10^{-6} bit error probability is to be achieved.

Solution For a 10 Mb/s digital signal using QPSK, the keying rate is 5 MBd. Using a 0.2 filter roll-off factor (see Chap. 2), the maximum double-sideband transmission rate is $1/(1 + \alpha) = 1/1.2 = 0.8333$ Bd/Hz. Thus the required bandwidth within the transponder is $5.00/0.8333 = 6.00$ MHz. This is 0.166 of the total transponder bandwidth of 36 MHz, so the power through the transponder will be 0.166 of the total, or -7.8 dB relative to the total.

Figure 5.37 shows that the *Satcom F2 SFD* is -83.0 dBW/m² from Los Angeles. Thus the uplink earth station transmitting the 10 Mb/s digital signal should produce $-83.0 - 7.8$, or -90.8 dBW/m². Assume *IPBO* = 10 dB, and assume a transponder frequency (uplink) of 6 175 MHz.

To determine the uplink free-space loss (FSL), the distance to the satellite is based on a longitude difference relative to the satellite of 3.24° and a latitude of 34°N for Los Angeles. Then the satellite appears [Ref. 49] at 46.4° elevation and 7.70° west of south. The slant range to the satellite is 37 214 km, obtained by use of spherical trigonometry, and the Law of Cosines. Then, using Eq. (4.4b).

$$FSL = 32.5 + 20 \log_{10}(6\ 175) + 20 \log_{10}(37\ 214) = 199.7 \text{ dB}$$

Since $\lambda = c/f = 3 \times 10^8/6\ 175 \times 10^6 = 0.0486$ m,

$$10 \log_{10}(\lambda^2/4\pi) = -37.3 \text{ dBm}^2$$

Then using Eq. (5.37),

$$EIRP = -90.8 - 10.0 + 199.7 - 37.3 = 61.6 \text{ dBW}$$

Since the receiving system uses a 4.7 m dish, its gain can be determined using Eq. (4.7),

$$G_r = \frac{4\pi A_r \eta}{\lambda^2} = 4\pi\left(\frac{\pi}{4}\right)(4.7)^2 \frac{(0.6)}{(0.0486)^2} = 55\ 384 = 47.4 \text{ dB}$$

where the antenna efficiency η has been assumed to be 60%.

The required uplink transmitter power rating then will be $61.6 - 47.4 + 4.0$ dB $= 18.2$ dBW $= 66$ watts. If other carriers are to be handled within the 6.0 MHz subject bandwidth by this transmitter, an additional 6.0 dB back-off is required, bringing the required transmitter rating to 264 watts.

For the downlink the elevation angle of the satellite is 16.4° and the slant range is 39 383 km. Using Eq. (4.4b),

$$FSL = 32.5 + 20 \log_{10}(3\ 750) + 20 \log_{10}(39\ 383) = 195.9 \text{ dB}$$

Based on Fig. 5.36, the downlink $(EIRP)_{max} = 37.0$ dBW toward Anchorage. A total fraction of 0.166 of that power is devoted to the subject carrier, which places it at a level of 29.2 dBW. With reference to Eq. (5.33), the use of actual satellite contours eliminates the need to use the $(TD)_d$ term, and the uplink carrier is of sufficient strength that $(G/T)_{eff} \cong (G/T)_{et}$, where subscript "eff" denotes *effective,* and "et" denotes *earth terminal.*

To compute $(C/kT)_{down}$, the receiving earth station's G/T must be determined. Its low noise amplifier is assumed to have a 75 K noise temperature. At the 16.4° elevation angle at Anchorage the sky temperature is estimated [Ref. 50] to be 20 K. Feed losses are estimated to contribute another 5 K noise. Thus the receiving system has an effective 100 K noise temperature. Since $G = 47.4$ dB, $G/T = 27.4$ dB/K. Then

$$(C/kT)_{down} = 37.0 \text{ dBW} - 195.9 \text{ dB} - 4.0 \text{ dB}$$

$$+ 228.6 \text{ dBW/HzK} + 27.4 \text{ dB/K} = 93.1 \text{ dBHz},$$

where the miscellaneous loss m has been assumed to be 4.0 dB. Note that $EIRP_{max}$ is used since $(C/kT)_{down}$ is measured in W/Hz.

From Eq. (5.34), $C/I_o = 108.7$ dBHz. The value of $(C/kT)_{up}$ is obtained using Eq. (5.35) as $(C/kT)_{up} = -83.0 - 10.0 + 228.6 - 5.5 - 37.3 = 92.8$ dBHz. Again, the full value of -83.0 is used for SFD since $(C/kT)_{up}$ is in W/Hz.

Using Eq. (5.36),

$$\left(\frac{C}{kT}\right)^{-1}_{\text{total}} = [10^{9.28}]^{-1} + [10^{9.31}]^{-1} + [10^{10.87}]^{-1}$$

Thus

$$\left(\frac{C}{kT}\right)_{\text{total}} = 89.9 \text{ dB Hz} = \left(\frac{C}{kT}\right)_{\text{A}}.$$

The required C/kT is determined from Eq. (5.37). First, based upon the use of QPSK and a 10^{-6} bit error probability requirement, Chap. 2 shows that $E_b/N_o = 10.6$ dB. Then

$$\left(\frac{C}{kT}\right)_{\text{R}} = 10 \log_{10} (10 \times 10^6) + 10.6 + 1.5 + 7.0 = 89.1 \text{ dB Hz}$$

Since $(C/kT)_\text{A} > (C/kT)_\text{R}$ with all needed margins included, the system will perform as desired, with an excess margin of 0.8 dB.

Note that the small margins with which a satellite link can operate make forward error correction (see Chap. 2) especially useful; thus a coding gain of only a few dB is significant. For analog FM systems, a device known as a *threshold extension demodulator* (TED) in the receiving end of a circuit consists of a frequency tracking filter allowing the use of an instantaneous receive bandwidth theoretically as low as the information bandwidth. The filter follows the excursions of the FM carrier, thus allowing a smaller noise bandwidth than otherwise attainable. Typically a lowering of the FM threshold of 3 to 4 dB is achievable, based upon the deviation index β actually used. The theoretical maximum threshold reduction is $10 \log_{10} \beta$.

5.7 TRANSPONDER UTILIZATION

An individual transponder provides for the handling of a given amount of power over a specified bandwidth. Its utility can be measured by the parameters power, bandwidth, and time. Accordingly, its use as a resource can be shared in the frequency, time, or power domains, as illustrated in Fig. 5.38. In frequency division multiple access (FDMA), each user has some of the bandwidth and some of the power all of the time. If the carriers are of equal power and all modulated at the same modulation index, the total power out of the transponder will increase directly with the number of such modulated carriers transmitted. In time division multiple access (TDMA), each user has all of the power and all of the bandwidth part of the time. A third way of dividing the transponder resource is called code division multiple access (CDMA). Here each user has all of the bandwidth all of the time, but only part of the power. Another term often used for this approach is spread-spectrum multiple access (SSMA).

Note that multiple access (MA) is not the same as multiplexing. For example, 24 voice channels, each coded using PCM, can be time division multiplexed (TDM)

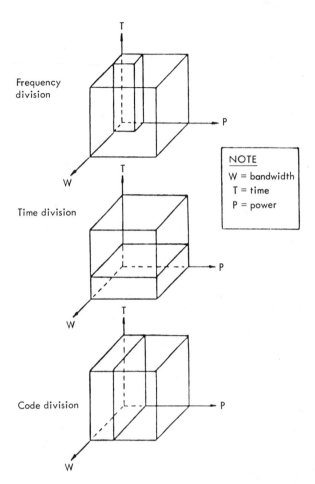

Frequency division

Time division

Code division

NOTE
W = bandwidth
T = time
P = power

Figure 5.38 Multiple access domains.

together to form a DS1 stream. This stream then can be used to QPSK modulate a carrier which is burst through a satellite during allocated time slots (TDMA). This arrangement would be designated PCM/TDM/QPSK/TDMA. Alternatively a single channel per carrier (SCPC) system, as described in Sec. 5.7.2, can be designated PCM/QPSK/FDMA. Although FDM generally is used with FDMA and TDM with TDMA, hybrid systems also exist [Ref. 11]. One is the FDM-Master Group Codec for use in the Telesat TDMA system [Ref. 51].

Many earth terminals use large numbers of dedicated channels devoted to continuous or nearly continuous traffic. However, many channels are not needed on a full-period basis. Demand assignment (DA) can achieve economies by keeping circuits connected only for the duration of a call or message burst.

The DA concept is a very old and well-established one in telephony. A user demands the assignment of a circuit by taking the telephone instrument off the hook. Receipt of dial tone then allows him to access the public switched network by dialing the desired number. A fully variable DA network pools all channels (trunks). A given channel then may be used by any station based upon the instantaneous traffic load.

In satellite systems two basic DA configurations are used, depending on whether the transponder carries an SCPC/FDMA or a multichannel TDMA system [Ref. 52, page 134]. In the case of SCPC/FDMA (see Section 5.7.2) the earth station interface in on a channel-by-channel basis. Network signaling also must be handled at the earth stations since the satellite DA system forms part of an overall switched network and includes the switching function.

In a multichannel TDMA system, however, channel capacity may be distributed dynamically among the earth stations based upon the burst length allocated at a given time to any one earth station. The switching center maintains control of the individual circuit signaling and governs burst lengths allocated to the various earth stations. Accordingly, an interface is required only between a traffic volume measuring device at the switching center and a TDMA capacity allocating processor at the earth station. Thus the satellite system simply provides transmission.

In comparing DA with fixed assignment (FA), DA is most advantageous for destinations having light traffic loads [Ref. 1, pp. 205–6]. Thus DA not only uses the space segment more efficiently than FA, but also allows for more efficient use of the terrestrial interconnect facilities. As a result, direct connections can be made more often, and thus the quality of service is better than if additional tandem connections were required.

A semivariable DA system is one in which blocks of channels are reserved for origination and/or destination stations, but still used only on demand.

A DA system is designated demand assigned multiple access (DAMA) when carriers (in FDMA systems) or bursts (in TDMA systems) are assigned on demand. Alternatively, when channels on existing carriers (FDMA) or time slots in existing bursts (TDMA) are assigned on demand, the system is said to be baseband demand assigned (BDA). The BDA concept is best suited to networks with many users but only a few large earth stations, whereas fully variable DAMA is best suited to a network with many earth stations, each of which has only low traffic needs. Mixed approaches also are useful, depending on the requirements to be met by a system.

Systems using DAMA provide for access on an individual user basis. The SPADE system, using FDMA as described in Sec. 5.7.1, is an example of a DAMA system. Other DAMA approaches are single-channel-per-burst (SCPB) TDMA and CDMA. These systems do not transmit a carrier (FDMA or CDMA) or burst (TDMA) until it is required. The carrier or burst is established only for the duration of a message connection. For control, a common TDM signaling channel allows all stations to call each other and to be aware of the available channels. An available channel can be seized on a first-come-first-served basis.

5.7.1 Frequency Division Multiple Access (FDMA)*

In FDMA the available spectrum within a satellite transponder is divided among carriers, each of which carries one or more information channels. Thus each signal is sent within an individual nonoverlapping frequency segment. The resulting power

---

* Portions of the material of this and the following section also appear in Ref. 1, pages 201–5. Both are taken from B. E. Keiser, "Wideband Communications Systems," Course Notes, © 1981 and 1985.

amplifier intermodulation products are minimized through carrier placement and input back-off (see Sec. 5.3.1.2). Frequency sources of high stability and automatic frequency control are used to keep the carriers within proper frequency tolerances. Digital transmissions result in spectra having a $\sin (f - f_o)/(f - f_o)$ characteristic, where f_o is a given carrier frequency. Filters can be used to eliminate the "spectral sidelobes" beyond the first null without significant signal degradation, but such unwanted sidebands may be restored as the signal passes through a nonlinearity [Ref. 53] and the envelope fluctuations produced by the filtering are reduced.

Guard bands between adjacent channels must allow for drifts in the frequency sources and for Doppler shifts caused by satellite motion. Satellite beacons or pilot signals can be used to help reduce frequency drifts if the beacon frequency is coherently related to the translation frequency through the satellite [Ref. 14, p. 217].

A commonly used FDMA arrangement, especially for small remote earth terminals, is single channel per carrier (SCPC). Such channels can be assigned only when actually needed, and also can be speech activated, so each one contributes to the transponder power output only when it is actually required. This helps to minimize intermodulation interference. A detailed analysis of intermodulation in FDMA satellite transponders is provided by Spilker [Ref. 14, Chap. 9].

Many SCPC systems use DAMA [Ref. 54]. Each carrier is modulated by a bit stream that comes from the voice channel of an individual user. Table 5.9 [Ref. 55] lists a number of SCPC systems and their parameters.

Intermodulation effects in SCPC systems can be reduced significantly if the carriers are not uniformly spaced. This can be achieved in several ways, one of which is uniformly spaced channels that are speech activated, thus resulting in more than 50% of them, on a random basis, being unused at any one time. Another arrangement involves placing the carriers in clusters, as was discussed in Sec. 5.3.1.3. For clusters of bandwidth W, the spacing is made to exceed $3W$.

5.7.2 Time Division Multiple Access (TDMA)

Since user traffic is generated in a continuous stream, TDMA requires that the data be stored and then read out of storage at the proper time in short bursts at a higher bit rate than that of the original stream to achieve the required frame format. Storage of the bits is done in memories, or buffers. The storage and subsequent read-out of the bits in bursts is called *compression,* since the time scale of the incoming data stream is compressed into a shorter time base than the original one. At the receiver, the inverse process occurs. The bursts enter a memory and are read out in a continuous stream. This process is called *expansion.*

Section 5.7.1 noted the need for transponder back-off in FDMA operations. Typical output back-off values are on the order of 3 dB or more, and result in a significant decrease in the power that otherwise would be available from the transponder. By comparison, TDMA operates with only one modulated carrier in the transponder at a time. The result is that the efficiency in terms of power utilization can be increased appreciably over that of FDMA since the power amplifier can be operated in saturation. Moreover, frequency guard bands are not needed in TDMA operation, and guard time slots can be kept to a very small percentage of the total

TABLE 5.9 SCPC SYSTEM CHARACTERISTICS

System	Intelsat			Inmarsat	Domsat			
					Australian RTSS		30/20	Japanese CS-2
Frequency (Ghz)	6/4			1.6/1.5	14/12		30/20	
Earth Station Type	STD-A	STD-B	STD-D	STD-A	Master	Remote	Master	Remote or Mobile
Antenna mφ	30	11 ~ 13	D1 D2 4.5/13	1.2	6.4	3.0 ~ 6.4	5	2
G/T dB/K	40.7	31.7	22.7/31.7	4	31	25 ~ 31	31	24
EIRP dBW/CH	63.0/69.8	63.0/69.8	56.6/52.7	36	45 ~ 51	44 ~ 50	52 ~ 60	52 ~ 60
Channel Operation Mode ch. Spacing (kHz) Modulation Voice Data	45 QPSK PCM A-law 48, 50, 56 kbps with FEC		45 FM 2 : 1 Syllabic —	25 FM 2 : 1 Syllabic Telex data 4.8 kbps	22.5 FM 2 : 1 Syllabic 2048 Mbps with FEC		45 FM/QPSK 2 : 1 Syllabic/ADPCM 16 kbps ~ 1.2 Mbps with FEC	
System Control Mode	DAMA (SPADE) & PAMA	PAMA	PAMA	DAMA	DAMA TPC		DAMA/PAMA TPC	
Type of Service	International Telephony & High Speed Data.		International Telephony	Maritime Telephony & Telex	Remote Area Telephony & High Speed Data		Emergency Telephony & New Services such as TV-conferencing.	

DAMA: Demand Assignment Multiple Access.
PAMA: Pre-Assign Multiple Access.
TPC: Transmit Power Control

Source: From *Signal,* © 1985, Armed Forces Communications and Electronics Association. Reprinted by permission.

on-time. Thus while frequency guard bands may occupy 10 to 15% of the frequency band, typical time guard slots often are on the order of only 1 to 2% of the total on-time. Moreover, the entirety of an FDMA channel passband often is not usable because of group delay variations near the band edge, thus resulting in a further disadvantage of FDMA relative to TDMA.

In TDMA each earth terminal transmits to the satellite in its own time slot, based on its determination of propagation time to the satellite. Guard time is used to allow for the decay of pulses so that intersymbol interference is not caused, as well as to allow for timing inaccuracies. Pulse decay is a function of the transient responses of the filters used in both the earth stations and the satellite. These filters must have good phase linearity, i.e., low group delay distortion.

Slight motions of the satellite (see Sec. 5.2.1) will cause corresponding changes in propagation time. However, satellite motion is periodic and predictable. Accordingly, elastic buffers, rather than pulse-stuffing buffers, can be used to compensate for satellite path delay variations. This presumes that highly stable clocks are used at all terminals and that the frame rate is held constant at the satellite. Actually the frame rate must be different on the up- and downlinks to the satellite by twice the satellite Doppler experienced on either link separately [Ref. 5, p. 393]. This results from the fact that the TDMA frame reference is actually on the satellite. Thus if a Doppler shift Δf occurs on the downlink, the frame rate transmitted from a given terminal must be shifted by $-\Delta f$ so that the signal reaches the satellite at the correct frequency.

The sizes of the elastic buffers must be adequate to prevent overflow or underflow. The buffers can be sized based upon the anticipated orbital characteristics of the satellite, plus a safety factor. In addition, the buffers must be reset regularly because of clock drifts at the earth terminals.

Digital transmission using TDMA is accomplished by the use of modulation during the carrier bursts. The needed phase reference must be derived during each burst since no means exists to synchronize the transmitted phases as received at the satellite. The phase reference can be obtained [Ref. 14, Chap. 10] either by (1) using a phase-locked loop or narrowband filter that can acquire each carrier rapidly in sequence, or (2) using multiple time-gated carrier recovery loops or a single time-multiplexed phase-locked loop with phase memory from frame to frame. The latter approach allows the use of narrow-band carrier recovery loops or a single time-multiplexed phase-locked loop with phase memory from frame to frame. The latter approach allows the use of narrow-band carrier recovery loops operating on each time-gated carrier.

With the development of large array antennas for use on communication satellites as well as improved attitude stabilization, narrow spot beams covering only a metropolitan area and its vicinity will become operational. The receiving and transmitting spot beams can be made independent of one another. Such antennas, together with switching on board the satellite, can allow the transmission of data packets to and from specific ground locations, thus achieving not only high transponder power utilization, but also spectrum economy through frequency reuse in various spot beam areas. Time slot coordination can be achieved by having one earth station serve as a central timing source and sending time through the satellite to all the other earth stations [Ref. 56].

Satellite-switched transmission can be accomplished using FDMA also, by using frequency bands within the transponder rather than time slots. However, the transponders then must be operated with their power levels backed off from saturation.

Terrestrial interfaces to the TDMA compression and expansion buffers may function on either a synchronous or an asynchronous basis. In synchronous operation, the clock rate of the terrestrial stream must be an integer multiple of the TDMA frame frequency. Synchronous operation can be achieved either with or without the terrestrial clock locked to the TDMA frame rate [Ref. 5, pp. 394–5]. Locking to the TDMA frame rate is the simpler of the two. The clock is derived as a multiple of the TDMA frame rate on both the transmit and the receive sides of the terminal. This method can be applied when the terrestrial digital streams terminate directly into the analog-to-digital or digital-to-analog converters, which can easily absorb the rate variations caused by satellite motion.

If the terrestrial clock is not locked to the TDMA frame rate, a buffer is placed at each interface to absorb the Doppler variation. The buffer must be able to store as many bits as occur in a time duration equal to the peak-to-peak propagation time variation on the satellite path. Separate Doppler buffers must be used on the transmit and receive sides of all terminals in the network.

If the symbol rate of the signal entering a compression buffer is not a precise multiple of the TDMA frame frequency, the interface is asynchronous. In this case, the buffer must add a symbol to, or delete a symbol from, the transmitted burst to maintain continuity of information flow. Figure 5.39 [Ref. 5] illustrates asynchronous operation at a TDMA direct digital interface.

5.7.3 Code Division Multiple Access (CDMA)

In code division multiple access (CDMA) all channels overlap in spectra, but use different codes so they can be distinguished from one another at the receiver [Ref. 57]. The codes often are based on pseudorandom sequences (see Chap. 2). By using different codes derived from such sequences, a low cross-correlation can be maintained among them, and minimum interference will occur between users. The receivers are programmed so that each one is responsive only to its own code. This allows more than one signal to be sent at a given frequency at the same time. Thus the coded modulation format allows code-division multiplexing and selective addressing.

Relative power levels must be controlled carefully in a CDMA system, and self-interference constitutes a limit on the number of users that can access a system simultaneously. (Time and/or frequency slots are assigned to users on a hopping basis to avoid self-interference.) Often the spectrum is spread by frequency hopping or by time hopping within a given band. Both transmitter and receiver derive their hopping commands from pseudorandom generators that are built alike, started in the same state at the same time, and clocked together. Clocking together can be achieved by having the receiver derive its timing from the received stream.

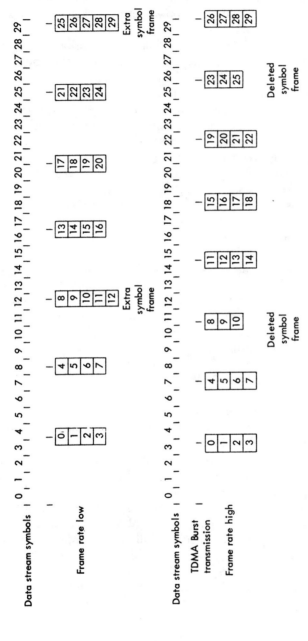

Figure 5.39 Asynchronous operation at a TDMA direct digital interface. (From Campanella/Schaefer, "Time-Division Multiple-Access Systems (TDMA)" in *Digital Communications: Satellite/Earth Station Engineering*, K. Feher, ed., © 1983, p. 395. Reprinted by permission of Prentice-Hall, Inc., Englewood Cliffs, NJ.)

Instead of devising symbols, each of which represents a specific series of bits, as introduced in Chap. 2, a CDMA system uses many symbols, called *chips,* from a pseudorandom generator to send each bit. Since the receiver has a replica of the pseudorandom code, it can perform the detection function properly.

Because of the spectrum spreading that occurs from the hopping process, the energy density of a spread spectrum signal in W/Hz is kept below the regulatory requirements for adjacent satellite interference.

A chief merit of CDMA is that it is interference resistant. Military applications therefore include antijam systems. However, the interference resistant characteristics of CDMA are equally useful in a friendly interference environment. This allows the transmit and receive antenna beams to be much broader than the width that would be required because of adjacent satellite interference. Accordingly, the criteria presented in Sec. 5.4.1.1 do not apply to CDMA systems. As a result, the antennas used in 4/6 GHz CDMA systems can be as small as 0.6 to 1.5 m in diameter. Such an earth terminal is one type of very small aperture terminal (VSAT) now in use. Because the antenna gain is relatively low compared with 3 m and larger dishes, the problem of sun outage (see Sec. 5.3.1.4) does not occur. Noise levels increase only 1 to 3 dB when the sun appears behind the satellite as viewed from the earth station.

Data transmission using CDMA allows large data networks, e.g., those of Equatorial Communications, Inc., to provide one-way transmission to hundreds of nodes at rates from 45 to 19 200 b/s; two-way transmission also is achieved on a point-to-point basis.

5.7.4 Summary

Figure 5.40 summarizes the features of the three multiple-access techniques with their advantages and disadvantages.

5.8 OPERATING SYSTEMS

Most currently operational satellite systems are strongly oriented toward analog transmission at the present time, although digital transmission capabilities are increasing steadily. The reason is that many systems had their origin in the mid-1970s, and built a sizeable number of analog earth station facilities. One exception is Satellite Business Systems (SBS), owned by MCI. SBS started later than the others, and has built an all digital system.

Transponder bandwidths typically are 36 MHz for many U.S. domestic satellites. International satellites also use 36 MHz bandwidths as well as 72 MHz, 241 MHz, and other values. Some military and maritime satellites use substantially smaller bandwidths, on the order of 4 to 30 MHz.

The *EIRP* from a satellite ranges from 17 to 21 dBW for maritime satellites, and 33 to 48 dBW for domestic and international satellites, to 56 to 68 dBW for direct broadcast satellites. Polarization generally is dual linear except for international satellites, which often use circular polarization. Power provided by solar

Technique	Characteristics	Advantages	Disadvantages
FDMA	Constant envelope signals Signals confined to nonoverlapping frequency bands MA Demultiplexing by filtering Message information by angle modulation	Uses existing hardware No network timing	Intermodulation in repeater Requires uplink power control
TDMA	Signals from different links never present simultaneously in transponder MA Demultiplexing by time gating Message information by angle modulation within carrier burst	High-efficiency in using satellite power Does not require uplink power control Peak power transmitter Bandwidth efficiency	Network timing required Analog to digital conversion required
CDMA SSMA	Constant envelope carriers Transmitted spectrum is spread over transponder bandwidth MA Demultiplexing by correlation with local replica of code Message information by angle modulation	No network timing required Can use fixed-address assignments Interference resistant	Link synchroniaztion required Uplink power control required Bandwidth inefficiency

Figure 5.40 Summary of multiple-access techniques.

arrays ranges from 850 to 2500 watts, with the smaller values pertaining to the maritime and some of the domestic satellites, midrange values to large domestic and international satellites, and the highest values being for the direct broadcast satellites.

Projected satellite lifetimes range from 7 to 10 years. Satellite repair in low earth orbit using the shuttle is expected to extend many satellite lifetimes in the future.

5.9 DIRECT BROADCAST SATELLITES (DBS)

The purpose of a direct broadcast satellite (DBS) service is to provide multichannel television programming to users beyond the coverage areas of cable television systems and local television stations. Because DBS systems are designed for direct reception by the public, they are characterized by very high transmitting powers, thus allowing relatively simple and inexpensive receiving systems [Ref. 58].

Standards for DBS systems in the Western Hemisphere were developed in the Regional Administrative Radio Conference of 1983 (RARC'83) and can be summarized as follows [Ref. 59]:

The frequency bands to be used are 17.3 to 17.8 GHz for the uplink (feeder) and 12.1 to 12.7 GHz for the downlink. Circular polarization is to be used. The modulation will be FM for video plus two sound channels. Satellite *EIRP*s will range from 56 to 68 dBW with a median of 61 dBW. This will require solar array power outputs typically on the order of 2 000 watts at beginning of life (BOL) and 1 700 watts at end of life (EOL) providing, respectively, on the order of 215 watts down to 185 watts output per transponder. The minimum elevation angle usually will be no less than 15°, and the satellites will be positioned so eclipse will occur after local midnight.

The RARC'83 plan calls for a total of 112 coverage areas encompassing all of North and South America including Greenland, Alaska, the Caribbean Islands, Hawaii, and other Pacific islands. A total of 49 orbital positions spaced 1° to 9° between 31° W and 175° W will be used with a 9° minimum spacing between satellites serving adjacent or overlapping areas.

There will be 32 equally spaced channels, each of 24 MHz bandwidth. The channels will overlap, with eight channel families each consisting of four frequencies spaced at four-channel intervals, e.g., 1-5-9-13, 2-6-10-14, etc. Assignments to countries are in terms of channel families. The U.S. has 32 channels at each of eight orbital positions. Upper and lower guard bands will be 12 MHz wide, with a channel spacing of 14.58 MHz under this staggered channel plan. Satellites providing odd numbered channels will be placed 0.2° W of their nominal positions, whereas satellites providing even numbered channels will be placed 0.2° E of their nominal positions.

Tables 5.10 and 5.11 show, respectively, typical downlink and uplink power budgets for DBS systems.

TABLE 5.10 TYPICAL DBS DOWNLINK POWER BUDGET (SATELLITE TO HOME)

Satellite *EIRP*	63.0 dBW	(median, U.S.)
Free space loss	206.1 dB	(12.5 GHz, 30° el.)
Atmospheric attenuation	7.0 dB	(rain; 9.0 dB max)
Received *EIRP*	−150.1 dBW	
$\lambda^2/4\pi$	−43.4 dBm^2	
Received power flux density	−106.7 dBW/m^2	(−107 dBW/m^2 min.)
Receiver *G/T*	10.0 dB/K	(1 m dish)
C/kT [−150.1 + 10.0 − (−228.6)]	88.5 dB Hz	
C/N	14.7 dB	(in 24 MHz bandwidth)

TABLE 5.11 TYPICAL DBS UPLINK POWER BUDGET (FEEDER LINK)

Earth station *EIRP*, max	87.4 dBW/ch	(5 m dish, 65% eff., 1 kW/ch)
Free space loss	208.9 dB	(17.6 GHz, 48° el.)
Rain attenuation, max.	13.0 dB	(to be exceeded only a few minutes/year)
Carrier, *C*	−134.5 dBW	
Boltzmann's Constant	−228.6 dBW/HzK	
Satellite *G/T*	7.7 dB/K	
kT	−236.3 dBW/Hz	
C/kT	101.8 dBHz	
C/N	28.0 dB	(in 24 MHz bandwidth)

5.10 SPECTRUM UTILIZATION*

The frequency allocations listed in Table 5.1 might seem to be perfectly adequate for satellite communications purposes in view of the large bandwidths available. However, a serious shortage of spectrum exists for several reasons. First, only one commercial frequency pair, the 3 700 to 4 200 MHz downlink and the 5 925 to 6 425 MHz uplink, is suitable for use under all possible weather conditions. The 11 and 14 GHz bands are suitable under most conditions, however, and rapidly increasing use is being made of these bands. The bands above 17.7 GHz are more severely limited by precipitation. Their extensive use may depend upon the development of some of the special techniques discussed in Sec. 5.12.

Considerable use is being made of the existing allocations below 14.5 GHz both domestically and internationally for video and multichannel telephony, as well as data transmission. Frequency reuse techniques include polarization diversity, usable primarily in the 4- and 6-GHz bands, and spot beaming, usable in all bands. Other spectrum conservation techniques include the use of multilevel modulation, as discussed in Chap. 2, companded single sideband, and the possibility of bi-directional links.

---

* Portions of the material of this section also appear in Ref. 1, pp. 200–201. Both are taken from B. E. Keiser, "Wideband Communications Systems," Course Notes, © 1981 and 1985.

5.10.1 Polarization Diversity

With polarization diversity the number of transponders occupying an overall band can be doubled, since the isolation between dual polarized beams can be as great as 30 dB, compared with the C/I requirement of 25 dB noted in Table 5.8. Table 5.12 shows four ways in which the 3 700 to 4 200 MHz band is used. Schemes A and B are dual polarization for a doubling of the number of channels that could be transmitted with single polarization.

The term *orthogonal* is used to describe two polarizations which, ideally, do not interfere with one another. Thus for linear polarization, *vertical* and *horizontal* are orthogonal to one another, whereas for circular polarization, *right-hand circular* (RHC) is orthogonal to *left-hand circular* (LHC). The term *cross-polarization* refers to the extent to which a transmitted polarization can be received on an orthogonally polarized receiving antenna. The ideal cross-polarization level is $-\infty$ dB, but in practice, values on the order of -25 dB to -35 dB often exist. In satellite communication, off-axis cross-polarization as well as sidelobes must be kept low to avoid carrier degradation via interference from other systems. Cross-polarization is caused by two factors: hardware (antenna and feed) limitations and propagation (weather) conditions.

TABLE 5.12 TRANSPONDER POLARIZATION SCHEMES FOR THE 3 700–4 200 MHz DOWNLINK BAND

Frequency	Transponder/polarization scheme			
	A	B	C	D
3720	1 V	1 H	1 H	
3740	2 H	2 V		1 V
3760	3 V	3 H	2 H	
3780	4 H	4 V		2 V
3800	5 V	5 H	3 H	
3820	6 H	6 V		3 V
3840	7 V	7 H	4 H	
3860	8 H	8 V		4 V
3880	9 V	9 H	5 H	
3900	10 H	10 V		5 V
3920	11 V	11 H	6 H	
3940	12 H	12 V		6 V
3960	13 V	13 H	7 H	
3980	14 H	14 V		7 V
4000	15 V	15 H	8 H	
4020	16 H	16 V		8 V
4040	17 V	17 H	9 H	
4060	18 H	18 V		9 V
4080	19 V	19 H	10 H	
4100	20 H	20 V		10 V
4120	21 V	21 H	11 H	
4140	22 H	22 V		11 V
4160	23 V	23 H	12 H	
4180	24 H	24 V		12 V

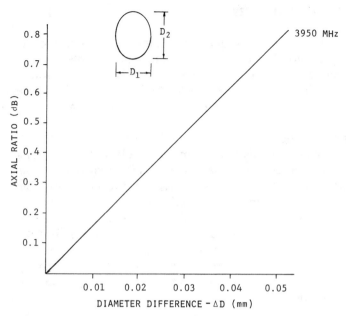

Figure 5.41 Axial ratio produced by one meter length of 5.4 cm diameter out-of-round waveguide.

5.10.1.1 Hardware Limitations*. Antennas using cross-polarization must preserve the proper polarizations over their field of view (FOV). An antenna can be adjusted for a very high degree of polarization orthogonality, e.g., cross-polarized component < -50 dB, along its axis and at a single frequency. Maintaining orthogonality (isolation) as off-axis angle increases and as frequency departs from design values, however, becomes increasingly difficult. Over a beamwidth at a single frequency, -45 to -40 dB usually is attainable. Over the entire FOV and full bandwidth, the orthogonality may be more like -35 to -32 dB. While separate transmit and receive antennas make the polarization design simpler because the covered frequency range is decreased, satellite and earth station design generally calls for only a single dish at each end.

Factors that affect polarization purity include the feed horn and its compatibility with the reflector system (rotational symmetry), the polarization diplexing arrangement, the coupling between the feed horns in a dual-feed system, and the presence of any water droplets on the feed and subreflector (a radome can prevent moisture accumulation). Depolarization can result from differential phase delay caused by polarizer phase error, waveguide dimensional distortions, e.g., out of round conditions, asymmetry in the feed horn matching device, nonsymmetrical feed patterns, and asymmetrical blockage effects. Figure 5.41 shows the axial ratio that results from a one meter length of 5.4 cm out-of-round waveguide.

Generally a satellite antenna should have a well-defined radiation center (the

---

* Much of the material in this and the following section was developed by Comsat Laboratories, Clarksburg, MD, for *Intelsat*.

point from which the radiation appears to come). In addition, circularly polarized antennas should have a small axial ratio, e.g., <0.5 dB, where axial ratio is defined, as illustrated in Fig. 5.42, as the ratio of the electric field strengths along the major and minor axes of the polarization ellipse. The relationship between axial ratio and polarization isolation is shown in Fig. 5.43. A small axial ratio and a well-defined radiation center can be achieved by using a corrugated horn feed and an offset-fed reflector.

Good impedance matches within the antenna system are vital to good polarization performance. For example, a VSWR of 1.3 : 1 on each side of a quarter-wave polarizer limits the polarization isolation to 35 dB.

A cross-polarization level of −35 dB has been achieved over a single 500 MHz band, with lower levels over subtended angles of 1° or less. One *Intelsat* antenna operating over the entire 3.7 to 4.2 and 5.925 to 6.425 GHz bands has achieved a cross-polarization level of −27 dB among a set of six simultaneous dual-polarized beams over the FOV on the earth. The antenna uses a 1.5 m diameter lens aperture. Sidelobes (into other beams) are at −27 dB.

Isolations on the order of −40 dB are realizable from horn feeds. The feed must generate currents on the reflector that radiate fields into the aperture plane of the reflector that are spatially parallel. The cross-polarization produced by the reflector depends on the ratio of focal length F to the aperture diameter D, i.e., the F/D ratio. The larger the F/D, the more nearly parallel the currents are on the reflector. The effect of F/D on cross-polarization, however, is reduced in the case of a cassegrain antenna (see Sec. 5.4.1) with a dual feed and a high subreflector gain.

Ways of simplifying the reflector design include the use of a spatial polarization filter, which can provide 50 dB isolation, or the use of wire grids or conducting strips, in the case of reflectors for a single linear polarization.

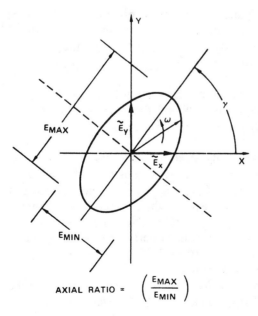

$$\text{AXIAL RATIO} = \left(\frac{E_{MAX}}{E_{MIN}} \right)$$

Figure 5.42 Polarization ellipse parameters.

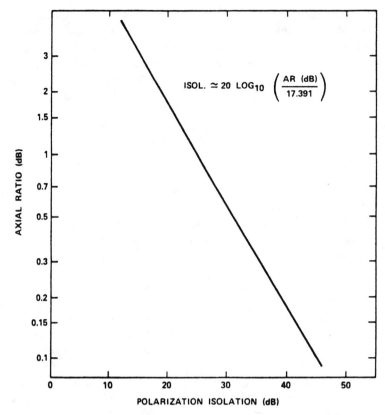

Figure 5.43 Polarization isolation versus axial ratio.

Good system design calls for earth stations to provide -40 dB receive isolation. For a circularly polarized system, Fig. 5.44 shows the effect of the axial ratio of the satellite antenna on the isolation for one path as a function of earth station isolation. As can be seen from this figure, even 0.15 dB axial ratio will reduce the link isolation to -33 dB.

Several techniques have been devised to correct for polarization errors. Since such errors result largely from propagation problems, the techniques are presented after the following discussion of propagation depolarization.

5.10.1.2 Propagation Effects on Polarization.

Transmissions between the earth and satellite orbits involve passage of the waves through both the atmosphere and the ionosphere. At frequencies below 2 GHz only the ionosphere affects propagation. Frequencies above 40 or 50 MHz almost always propagate through the ionosphere with little or no attenuation, but generally suffer a phase shift known as Faraday rotation. For this reason satellite systems operating at such frequencies, e.g., government systems operating in the 225 to 400 MHz band, usually use circular polarization for both the uplink and the downlink.

Between 2 and 3 GHz neither the ionosphere nor the atmosphere has a significant effect on propagation. However, above 3 GHz, water particles in the

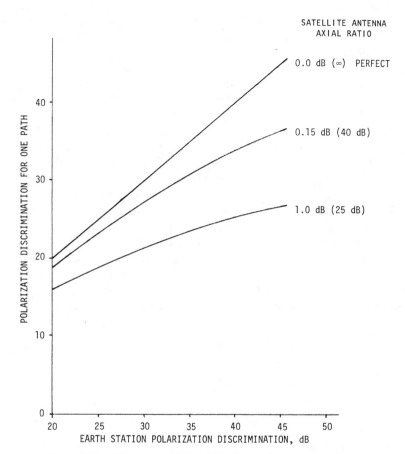

Figure 5.44 Effect of downlink polarization performance on system.

atmosphere produce both attenuation and phase shift. In fact, some weather radars operate in the 3 GHz band because rain cells reflect radio waves at such frequencies.

Figure 5.3 shows the effects of rain rate on cross-polarization isolation over 5 km path lengths, typical of propagation through atmospheric rain cells. As can be seen, the degradation caused by differential phase is significantly more serious than that caused by differential attenuation, since lower isolation values result.

The reason why rain affects propagation at the shorter wavelengths is that raindrops (also known as *hydrometeors*), especially those near the surface of the earth, carry a certain amount of atmospheric contaminants, which render them conductive. In addition, the dielectric constant of water is greater than 1, so raindrops both reflect and absorb electromagnetic radiation. A raindrop acts as a partially conducting dipole whose length begins to be a significant, e.g., 5%, fraction of a half wavelength as frequency increases in the microwave region. Accordingly, a passing electromagnetic wave induces a current in the raindrop and that current results in radiation with the electric vector directed along the length of the drop. This is the direction of polarization of the wave reradiated from the raindrop. Generally it will be different from the direction of polarization of the incident wave.

5.10.1.3 Correction of Depolarization.
The correction of rain depolarization involves the use of mechanical rotation of the feeds for alignment with the satellite's polarization to within a few minutes of arc. This generally requires independent rotation of the transmit and receive feeds because propagation at 4- and 6-GHz, for example, is affected to differing extents by precipitation. Because of the variableness of precipitation, adaptive polarization control is necessary to prevent interference between orthogonally polarized channels.

Linear polarization errors, including ellipticity, can be corrected through the use of pilot signals transmitted from the spacecraft, one for each polarization, assigned within the operational frequency bands and detected at the earth station by amplitude-phase-lock receivers. A variable rotatable differential phase shifter and a variable rotatable differential attentuator then produce the desired orthogonal output. The polarizers can be installed in circular waveguide with axial ratios less than 0.17 dB, corresponding to isolation better than 40 dB over a 500 MHz bandwidth. Polarizer loss is less than 0.03 dB, so the polarizer can be placed in the receive waveguide feed without significant degradation to its noise temperature. The polarizers also can handle typical earth station transmitter power outputs, so they can be used in the transmit portions of the antenna feed as well.

Figure 5.45 shows the use of two independently rotatable polarizers. Their

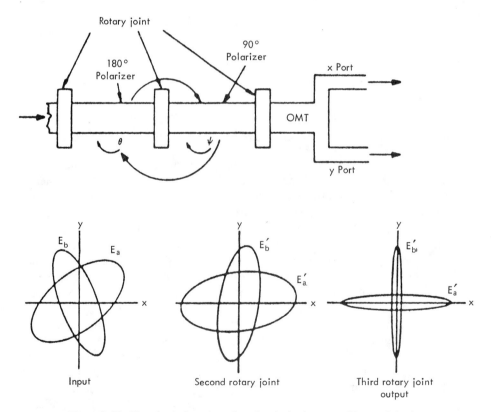

Figure 5.45 Use of polarizers to reduce depolarization caused by precipitation.

angular positions are adjusted to convert the dual elliptically polarized fields of the input to dual linearly polarized fields at the output orthomode transducer. A microprocessor controls the polarizer angular positions so that the polarizer error levels (voltages squared) are continuously minimized. Figure 5.46 [Ref. 60] shows an adaptive correction circuit. An electronic control unit, as shown in Fig. 5.47, causes digital stepping motors to drive the polarizers in 0.18° steps at up to 100 steps/ second. This is more than an adequate rate since the rate of change of rain depolarization has a 0.2 Hz cut-off with a 20 dB fall-off to about 100 Hz. Thus a correction system using mechanical polarizers has an adequate response time.

5.10.1.4 Linear Versus Circular Polarization. Both linear and circular polarization are used in satellite transmission. The advantages of linear polarization are the facts that the antenna is simpler to construct (a phase splitting network is not required) and its performance is better than that of circular polarization during

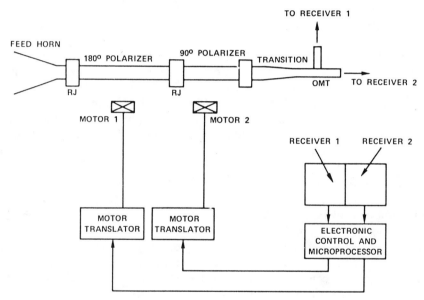

Figure 5.46 Adaptive polarization correction circuit. (From D. F. DiFonzo, W. S. Trachtman and A. E. Williams, "Adaptive Polarization Control for Satellite Frequency Reuse Systems," *Comsat Technical Review,* vol. 6, no. 2, p. 272.)

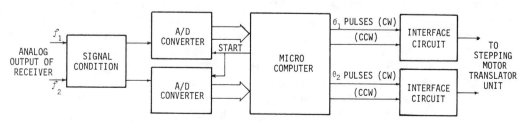

Figure 5.47 Electronic control unit for adaptive correction unit.

precipitation conditions. The worst case of linear cross-polarization occurs for a raindrop oriented at 45° to the linear vector, while the same circular cross-polarization occurs for a raindrop oriented at *any* angle. Circular polarization requires adaptive control during precipitation to reduce its cross-polarization to the level achievable with linear polarization. Linear polarization is used extensively by domestic satellite operators. The staggered channel arrangement (see Table 5.12) provides further isolation for multichannel basebands or video modulated carriers.

In favor of circular polarization is the fact that it is unaffected by Faraday rotation, and thus is the preferred technique for those satellite systems operating below 2 GHz. Circular polarization is used extensively in the 4 and 6 GHz bands by *Intelsat* since the ground station receivers can reject circularly polarized radiation emitted from their own transmitters and back-scattered from reflecting layers in the atmosphere (rain, fog, clouds) more effectively than if the radiation is linearly polarized. In addition, with circular polarization, there is no need for polarization alignment control between a transmitter and the corresponding receiver.

5.10.2 Spot Beams

Spot beams can be designed to provide specific footprint shapes by using clusters of small spots, or by feed arrangements to produce noncircular footprints. Thus an antenna can be designed to cover only a portion of a country, or a region the size of the U.S. or western Europe. Similarly, beams can be devised to cover only hemispherical regions. In all cases, the beamwidth of the satellite antenna is significantly smaller than the 17.3° width that would cover the entire surface of the earth that is within view of the satellite.

5.10.3 Bidirectional Links

Consideration has been given to the possibility of providing satellite uplinks in the 4 GHz band and downlinks in the 6 GHz band. However, this arrangement would complicate the coordination procedures required with existing 4 GHz terrestrial transmitters as well as 6 GHz terrestrial receivers. In fact, the widespread use of 6 GHz microwave radio could result in a considerable number of interference cases if 6 GHz downlinks were attempted.

5.10.4 Companded Single Sideband

Companded single sideband AM (CSSB-AM) has been implemented on an increasing number of microwave circuits as noted in Sec. 4.7.1.2. In satellite service it is capable of providing 6 000 half circuits (earth to satellite and return), or the equivalent of 3 000 full duplex circuits within a single 36 MHz transponder. By comparison, an FDM/FM system can provide, at most, 2 700 half circuits. A digital system using 32 kb/s ADPCM and 16-QAM (see Chap. 2) can provide about 3 200 half circuits. Both the CSSB-AM and FDM/FM systems are at or close to the limits of their spectrum efficiency, whereas digital design is likely to provide 16 kb/s voice and 64-QAM modulation systems via satellite, which will allow digital to transmit

TABLE 5.13 LINK BUDGET PARAMETERS FOR CSSB-AM VIA SATELLITE

SNR from link budget	>17.5 dB unweighted
Talker level	−21.0 dBm0
Compressor increase	+7.0 dB
Talker level, compressor output	−14.0 dBm0
Psophometric weighting	2.5 dB
Compandor advantage	16.0 dB
Subjective *SNR*, talker	36.0 dB (toll quality)
Test tone level	0.0 dBm0
Subjective *SNR*, test tone	50.0 dB (toll quality)
Satellite *IPBO*	−8.0 dB
Satellite SSPA outputs	8.5 W
Satellite *EIRP*	34.0 dBW
Earth station *G/T*	32.0 dB/K
SNR, satellite input	18.3 dB
S/I_o, system	≥24.0 dB
Phase jitter from $1/f$ noise	≈8.0°

the greatest number of voice channels. However, CSSB-AM provides the greatest spectrum efficiency of operational systems at the time of writing.

The implementation of satellite CSSB-AM systems involves the use of pilot tones to keep the frequency error to less than 1.0 Hz and to maintain level control. This stability also meets the requirements of CCITT Rec. G. 135, which calls for a frequency error less than 2.0 Hz for data. Table 5.13 lists the link budget parameters for a typical CSSB-AM system. Psophometric weighting is similar to C-message weighting (see Sec. 4.3.1), but uses a frequency response characteristic defined by the CCITT and a reference frequency of 800 Hz. The reference to $1/f$ noise is to that which is generated in the up and down converters.

For data modems, the data tone/noise ratio is raised to 24 dB to achieve a $p_{be} = 10^{-6}$ at 4 800 b/s.

5.11 FUTURE SATELLITE APPLICATIONS

While many of the future uses for satellites are in the voice and voiceband data areas, such applications can be extended naturally to broadband data and graphic transmission. The applications all are related to the "wireless" advantage of satellite radio. These include land mobile radio beyond the existing metropolitan areas, fixed service to remote locations which cannot be served economically via cable, aeronautical service, position location and communications for air traffic control, remote monitoring and tracking, and data communication using packet techniques.

5.11.1 Land Mobile Radio

Present land mobile radio systems are limited to the vicinity of the metropolitan areas in which they are based or, in some cases, to interstate highway corridors along which service is provided. While the most heavily traveled routes are covered, no service is provided to remote areas. The implementation of a satellite service, however, presents numerous system compatibility issues. A primary one is that of the frequencies to be used. Existing allocations are inadequate in that they are based on frequency reuse among many cells (800 MHz) or among many metropolitan area repeaters (VHF and 450 MHz). A signal transmitted to and from a satellite will cover a very wide area; correspondingly, the satellite receives over a very wide area. Such coverage is essential for remote areas but raises serious interference issues with respect to metropolitan areas within a given satellite footprint. On the other hand, if separate frequency bands, e.g., 1.5 to 1.6 GHz, are used for satellite service to solve the interference problem, users with existing equipment will be unable to receive remote area service. A second major compatibility issue is that of the mobile antenna. Existing mobile antennas are designed for omnidirectional coverage along the horizon, whereas antennas for use with satellites must provide transmission to/from elevation angles that generally are between 10° and 60°.

The satellite system for land mobile communication probably will function in the following way [Ref. 61]. The frequency band used between the mobile and the satellite will be either the 800 MHz or 1.56 GHz band. Between the satellite and base stations, gateways and control stations, the 4/6 GHz or 12/14 GHz bands will be used. System control will use DAMA, with an operations center automatically making channel assignments, performing billing functions and controlling the network. A common signalling channel will function as follows: the station initiating the call will request service and specify the number being called via the common channel. The operations center then will assign a channel (frequency pair) and notify the requesting and called stations to use that channel. Call completion causes the operations center to be notified.

The antenna on board the satellite will produce multiple spot beams covering the U.S. Circular polarization will be used because of Faraday rotation. Frequency reuse will be accomplished by using both RHC and LHC polarization.

The antenna for the mobile unit presents several requirements. The gain must be 4 to 8 dBi or more. Ground reflections must be suppressed, i.e., be in or near an antenna null. The axial ratio must be kept low. An elevation coverage of 5° to 60° must be available, with an azimuth coverage of 360°. Antenna types meeting such requirements probably will be nonsteered for economy reasons. Possibilities include the drooping dipole, with a 4 dBi gain, the quadrifilar helix, consisting of four helices wound on a cylinder, or a vertical arrangement of circularly polarized elements. While economy strongly favors the nonsteered antenna, some mechanically or electronically steered antennas may be required to provide adequate rejection of satellite interferences or to meet possible gain requirements in excess of 8 dBi in certain fringe areas by tracking the satellite being used.

Three modulation techniques are being given serious consideration for land mobile radio use: AM (CSSB), FM, and digital. The advantages of CSSB are its spectrum efficiency (4 kHz/voice channel), its modest use of limited satellite power, and the fact that satellite link budgets can be structured with adequate S/N. However, frequency stability is critical and automatic Doppler correction is required.

The use of FM with syllabic companding requires 30 kHz/voice channel and an S/N of 6.7 dB. Its feasibility for satellite mobile applications is being studied.

Digital techniques considered include adaptive delta coding at 12 kb/s per voice channel and linear predictive coding at 2.4 kb/s per voice channel. Modulation using PSK and rate 1/2 coding would result in a 35 kHz/voice channel spectrum requirement for adaptive delta coding and an E_b/N_o of 5.2 dB. Voice quality has been found to be adequate with this set of parameters.

5.11.2 Aeronautical Communication

The purposes of providing aeronautical communication via satellite are improved air traffic control by virtue of continuous communication and commercial data services, initially at rates on the order of 200 to 400 b/s. The satellite under consideration for such service is *Inmarsat* [Ref. 62]. However, increased satellite output powers are required for aeronautical service because the on-board antenna will have significantly lower gain than the dish that can be used on board a ship. The major technical problem in aeronautical communication is multipath from the surface of the earth. The best solution to this problem is the use of properly designed antenna patterns having low response in the direction of the earth. In addition, protection against multipath fading can be obtained by using DBPSK with rate 1/2 convolutional coding using symbol interleaving and soft-decision Viterbi, all of which have been described in Chap. 2. System design objectives include aircraft antennas made of microstrip patches for low drag. Such antennas having a gain on the order of 0 dBi and being circularly polarized can cover over 90% of the azimuth for elevations above 10%. Other design objectives include provisions for low data rate transmission per channel to minimize satellite power requirements as well as aircraft terminal costs.

Frequency allocations for the aircraft to satellite path are in the 1 636.5 to 1 660.5 MHz band, with the satellite to aircraft link being in the 1 545 to 1 559 MHz band. Tables 5.14 and 5.15 provide the major typical ground to aircraft and aircraft to ground link parameters, respectively, that can be expected for aeronautical communication via satellite.

5.11.3 Geostar Satellite Data Network

A satellite data network is being implemented to allow 300 b/s full duplex data transmission anywhere in North America using hand-held transceivers. Its priority service is that of airliner position and altitude determination to a 16 m accuracy for air traffic control, but this function requires only 2% of the planned system capacity. The system is known as *Geostar* [Ref. 63].

The system, using three satellites, will be able to handle 100 million users, interrogating all locations 100 times per second. The satellites will produce 15 spot beams, each providing a 500 × 800 km oval area. Each spot beam will be able to send 15 000 messages per second. The individual transceivers will send 256-bit bursts of 20 µs duration, corresponding to 12.8 Mb/s TDMA. Each transceiver will be powered by two AA batteries that will produce 375 W peak power for the

TABLE 5.14 GROUND-TO-AIRCRAFT LINK BUDGET
PARAMETERS

Ground to Satellite (6.4 GHz)	
$EIRP$, ground	61.4 dBW
G/T, satellite	−15.0 dBi/K
C/N_0, uplink	73.2 dBHz
Satellite to Aircraft (1.54 GHz)	
$EIRP$, satellite	20.8 dBW
Noise, aircraft	26.2 dBK (412 K)
C/N_0, downlink	34.1 dBHz
Combined Link	
C/N_0	34.1 dBHz
Symbol rate	400 Bd (200 b/s, $R = 1/2$)
E_s/N_0, combined	8.1 dB
C/I_0	15.0 dB
$C/multipath$	10.0 dB
E_s/N_0, available	7.3 dB
E_s/N_0, required	6.3 dB (for $p_{be} = 10^{-5}$)
Margin	1.0 dB

TABLE 5.15 TYPICAL AIRCRAFT-TO-GROUND LINK BUDGET
PARAMETERS

Aircraft to Satellite (1.64 GHz)	
Transmitter power	11.5 dBW
G/T, satellite	−15.0 dBi/K
C/N_0, uplink	34.0 dBHz
Satellite to Ground (4.2 GHz)	
Satellite gain	138.5 dBm^2
$EIRP$, satellite	−19.6 dBW
G/T, earth station	32.2 dBi/K
C/N_0, downlink	42.7 dBHz
Combined Link	
C/N_0	33.5 dBHz
Symbol rate	400 Bd (200 b/s, $R = 1/2$)
E_s/N_0, combined	7.5 dB
C/I_0	20.0 dB
$C/multipath$	10.0 dB
E_s/N_0, available	7.3 dB
E_s/N_0, required	6.3 dB (for b.e.r. $= 10^{-5}$)
Margin	1.0 dB

intermittent usage planned. The antenna length will be 5 cm. The uplink will be at
1.618 GHz (16.5 MHz bandwidth) and the downlink will be at 2.492 GHz.

5.11.4 Personal Radio

A Japanese advanced communications technology satellite experiment is planned
for the early 1990s for both fixed and mobile applications. The transmission rate will
be 64 kb/s using FSK modulation and noncoherent detection. Access to the satellite
will be FDMA/SCPC. The bit error probability is to be 10^{-4} or better.

The earth unit will have a 30 cm antenna diameter and a 0.3 W transmitter at 50 GHz. The receiver will have a 4.2 dB noise figure at 40 GHz. The satellite will transmit using 0.05 watt at 40 GHz and receive with a 4.7 dB noise figure at 50 GHz. Antenna efficiencies are estimated at 60%. The *FSL* for 38 000 km is 218.0 dB at 50 GHz and 216.1 dB at 40 GHz. With an atmosphere absorption of 2.1 dB at 50 GHz and 0.5 dB at 40 GHz, the link availability is estimated at 99%.

5.12 FUTURE TRENDS IN SATELLITE COMMUNICATION SYSTEMS

In spite of the rapid development of communication satellite systems since the mid-1970s, and the increasing implementation of digital transmission via satellite since the early 1980s, many more developments are on the horizon. The use of on-board processing was described in Sec. 5.3.1.1. It is expected to allow the implementation of on-board controlled TDMA switching possibly combined with scanning spot beams [Ref. 64]. The addresses carried by individual packets can be used for beam and time slot control.

Intersatellite links involving an up, over, and down mode of transmission have already been shown to be feasible through work done by the U.S. Air Force with its *Lincoln Experimental Satellites 8* and *9* (*LES-8* and *LES-9*), which used a 36 to 38 GHz cross link. Such intersatellite links, when implemented commercially, may help to further global telecommunications as well as to provide more widespread service to land, mobile, maritime, and aeronautical terminals.

Early satellite designs attempted to maximize satellite lifetime by keeping the satellite as simple, and therefore reliable, as possible, while allowing the earth stations to be relatively complex. The trend now, however, is toward more complex satellites but simpler earth stations. This trend is being aided by two major factors. One is the widespread use of large-scale integrated circuits, with their inherently high reliability. The other is the accumulation of many years of experience on the part of spacecraft designers. The complex satellite and the relatively inexpensive earth station make good economic sense, just as do the present complex telephone central office and the relatively inexpensive end instrument. Many earth stations may use a single satellite. By putting more of the complexity into the satellite, the savings in earth station hardware are multiplied many times.

Relatively complex satellites may provide not only higher *EIRP* (in the bands above 14 GHz where such *EIRP* is allowed) but also more satellite beams for improved orbit-spectrum utilization. More on-board processing is another feature of the more complex satellite. Such on-board processing, in addition to the applications discussed in Sec. 5.3.1.1, can allow transmission to and from cities experiencing good weather in the 20 to 30 GHz bands, while using the 4 to 6 GHz bands to and from those cities experiencing precipitation conditions. The smaller earth station sizes will be advantageous primarily from an economic viewpoint.

5.12.1 Large Space Platforms (LSP)

The large space platform (LSP) concept envisions a few giant space stations in geostationary orbit replacing many communications and sensor satellites. The motivation for building an LSP is that it would alleviate interference caused by crowding of the orbit, thus permitting relatively small earth stations. In addition, many satellite circuits can be interconnected or cross-strapped. The LSP provides economies of scale by making common support functions available to multiple payloads. A very important feature of the LSP concept is that it permits mounting very large and complex antennas and feed systems. An LSP can be designed for multiband operation. For example, 20/30 GHz transponders can be used to/from earth stations in locations experiencing good weather, and circuits going to/from earth stations surrounded by bad weather can be sent using lower frequency bands.

NASA plans a Baseline Experimental Geostationary Platform for approximately the year 1991 using the space transportation system (shuttle) to build, maintain, and repair the system.

5.12.2 Trends

Several requirements are driving satellite communication technology [Ref. 65]. One is increased bandwidth, involving greater reuse of existing bands as well as new (higher frequency) bands. Another is that of system configurations. At present international satellites over the world's oceans provide high interconnectivity while domestic/regional satellites over land provide limited coverage and connectivity. In the future the LSP is expected to serve many users, and dedicated missions will be performed by a large number of satellites. A further requirement driving the technology is the desire for services directly from customer premises. These services include video conferencing as well as worldwide data services. Other requirements include the need for integrated mobile services (land, sea, and air) as well as search and rescue. Finally, the need for increased system flexibility calls for such capabilities as dynamic antenna footprints, traffic rerouting capabilities, intercommunication between networks, and the sharing of in-orbit spare satellites.

The requirements of the preceding paragraph are resulting in technology development in the areas of spacecraft bus characteristics, connectivity in orbit, digital transmission, spacecraft life and reliability, and orbit utilization.

Spacecraft size now can be designed to occupy a full shuttle bay. Orbital transfer vehicles can be developed which allow full spacecraft deployment in low earth orbit (LEO), with transfer to geostationary earth orbit (GEO). The development of long life spacecraft will allow a modular build-up of orbital resources, including transponders and footprints adaptable to a variety of needs, as well as intersatellite traffic transfer capability.

Increased connectivity in orbit is another technology development area. This involves intersatellite links, both RF and optical. Such links can provide global business communication networks and extended coverage areas, with crosslinks extending from as little as 40 km to as much as 40 000 km. Intersatellite links eliminate double-hop transmission and thus eliminate the passage of traffic through an additional earth station. The use of intersatellite links also permits a modular build-up of orbital capacity, the direct interconnection of otherwise separate networks, and improved communication to/from high latitudes.

The area of digital transmission development includes satellite-switched TDMA (SS-TDMA), signal processing improvements, and advances in on-board processing well beyond SS-TDMA. Signal processing development areas include the widespread use of speech coding at 32 kb/s and 16 kb/s using a trunk sharing arrangement called digital speech interpolation, in which trunks are used by a given talker only when he is actually talking and not during pauses. Data transmission at 32 kb/s and 16 kb/s rates is a natural adjunct to speech transmission at these rates. In the area of video processing, standards are needed for coding and bit rates to permit the ready interconnection of video conference user networks. Under development is TDMA/DA for video. On-board processing well-beyond SS-TDMA involves improvements in TDMA flexibility at rates of 60 to 120 Mb/s and beyond for small users, as well as the use of on-board signal regeneration to combat uplink noise and interference. New interconnection modes will require integrated antenna beam and transponder switching, as well as on-board baseband switching.

Developmental areas for improved spacecraft life and reliability include improved traveling-wave tube (TWT) reliability at frequencies above 6 GHz, higher power TWTs for greater EIRP and coverage, higher power and improved efficiency for SSPAs at 11 GHz and above, and monolithic receivers at 6 GHz for mass/volume and reliability/cost improvements. In the payload support area are improved solar cells and arrays using thinner silicon cells with better radiation hardness, as well as gallium arsenide cells. Improvements are needed in the radiation hardness of high density microelectronic devices as well as in power storage. Nickel hydrogen cells with improved ampere-hour capacity as well as efficient battery management systems are under development. Electric propulsion systems are being developed for improved orbital adjustment accuracy.

Orbit utilization improvement calls for antenna technology advances. In the space segment area this means reconfigurable beam technology, wider bandwidths, large deployable antennas for narrow beams, dual reflector antennas, active phased arrays, and improved beam pointing accuracy (to $\pm 0.03°$ with RF tracking). With respect to the ground segment, technology development areas include increased antenna bandwidth for the expanded WARC allocations, dynamic depolarization compensation (improvements over the techniques of Sec. 5.10.1.3), and improved cost effectiveness of dual polarized feeds as well as improved sidelobe performance.

5.13 GLOSSARY OF TERMS [Ref. 66]

Apogee The highest point in the satellite's orbit (km).

Apogee kick motor (AKM) A rocket stage used to convert the elliptical transfer orbit into a circular geosynchronous orbit.

Ariane A European launch vehicle.

Atlas A U.S. rocket stage.

Attitude control Maintenance of the satellite's orientation with respect to the Earth and Sun.

Bandwidth The useful frequency range of a device such as a transponder. (MHz)

Beamwidth The angular coverage of an antenna beam. Earth station beams are usually specified at the half-power (or −3 dB) point. Satellite beams are based on the area to be covered.

Body stabilized A satellite attitude control system using the gyroscopic stiffness of one (or more) spinning wheels.

BOL Beginning of life.

BSS Broadcasting satellite systems, intended for transmission to small home or community receivers.

Cargo bay The part of the Shuttle used to carry satellites.

CATV Cable television.

Channel (1) A half-circuit. (2) A radio frequency assignment (which is dependent upon the frequency band and the geographic location).

Circuit (1) A complete (two-way) telecommunications loop. (2) Two half circuits.

Colocated Multiple satellites sharing (approximately) the same location.

CPU Central processing unit.

dB A logarithmic representation of a ratio.

dBi The ratio of the gain of an actual antenna to an isotropic radiator using decibels.

DBS Direct broadcasting satellite service.

dBW The ratio of the power to one watt expressed in decibels.

Delta (1) The amount of change in a quantity. (2) A U.S. launch vehicle family.

Downlink The space-to-earth path.

e.i.r.p. Equivalent isotropically radiated power, the amount of power that would need to be fed into an isotropic antenna to match the flux level from an actual antenna. (dBW)

EOL End of life.

FDMA Frequency domain (or division) multiple access.

FEC Forward error control, adding unique codes to the digital signal at the source so errors can be detected and corrected at the receiver.

FM-TV Frequency modulated TV.

FSS Fixed satellite service. The earth stations are nonmobile. This service generally provides telephony and TV distribution.

GEO Geosynchronous or geostationary.

Geostationary A geosynchronous satellite that has a zero inclination angle. This satellite appears to hover over one spot on the earth's equator.

Geosynchronous An orbit whose period exactly matches the Earth's rotation rate (about 24 hours).

GHz Gigahertz (1000 MHz).

HDTV Higher (than normal) definition TV.

HS-333 & HS-376 Families of Hughes satellites.

Hydrazine A commonly used liquid propellant for stationkeeping.

IM Intermodulation distortion, which occurs when two (or more) signals are passed through a nonlinear device (such as an amplifier).

Inclination The angle between the Earth's equatorial plane and the orbit plane of the satellite. (deg.)

Isotropic antenna A theoretical antenna that radiates (or receives) the same amount of signal in all directions.

IUS Inertial upper stage, a rocket motor system.

kg Kilograms (1 kg = 2.2 lbm).

lbf Pounds force.

lbm Pounds mass.

Location The satellites assigned longitudinal position over the equator. (East or West longitude.)

Mb/s Megabits per second.

Motor A rocket stage.

Nutation An imbalance in a spinning object.

Orbit altitude Height above the earth's surface (km).

Orbit period The time for the satellite to make one full revolution in its orbit. (min.)

Orbit spacing The angular separation (measured in degrees of longitude) between satellites using the same frequency and covering overlapping areas. (deg.)

Orthogonal At opposite (or right) angles to another form of intelligence.

PAM Perigee assist module, a rocket stage.

Perigee The lowest point in a satellite's orbit. (km)

Platform A structure in space containing multiple missions.

RARC Regional Administrative Radio Conference.

SCPC Single channel per carrier.

SCPT Single carrier per transponder.

Scramble Deliberate distortions of information to permit only authorized reception.

Solar array A power generation method using solar cells.

Spin stabilization Attitude control by spinning most (or all) of the satellite's exterior.

SSMA Spread spectrum multiple access.

SSPA Solid state power amplifier.

Station The assigned satellite location (East or West longitude).

Stationkeeping Maintaining the assigned location (deg.).

TDMA Time domain (or division) multiple access.

Thruster A small rocket motor.

Transfer orbit An intermediate orbit used to reach the geosynchronous orbit.

Transponder A combination of one or more receivers, filters, frequency converters, and transmitters to form a signal repeater.

TT&C Tracking, telemetry and control.

TWT Traveling wave tube.

TWTA An amplifier using a TWT and power supply.

Uplink Earth-to-space path.

WARC World Administrative Radio Conference.

PROBLEMS

5.1 Dual polarization is used commonly in the 4-6 GHz satellite bands, but not in the 11-14 GHz bands. Why?

5.2 Why is a satellite system's downlink budget more critical than its uplink budget?

5.3 A satellite transponder centered at 3 950 MHz is used totally for TDMA digital transmission and has a 5 W power output. For earth stations that are at the beam edge (-3 dB) and that have a 45° latitude (satellite and earth stations at the same longitude), what is the received level in a 50 dB gain dish if the satellite antenna has a 1.5 m diameter? (Neglect circuit and waveguide losses.) Assume a 55% antenna efficiency.

5.4 In the system of Prob. 5.3 the effective earth terminal figure of merit is 20.0 dB/K. What is the available C/kT?

5.5 In the system of Probs. 5.3 and 5.4, what symbol rate can be transmitted if the required $E_s/N_o = 18$ dB, assuming losses and link margin total 6.0 dB?

5.6 You have a choice between placing a satellite earth terminal dish on a building roof top or near a parking lot on the ground. The path to the satellite is unobstructed in both cases. Which location would you choose and why?

5.7 Discuss the advantages and disadvantages of uniform carrier frequency spacing in a satellite transponder being used on an FDMA basis.

5.8 Explain how the operating level of a satellite transponder is actually determined on the ground.

5.9 A satellite beam is directed at an area centered at 40° N latitude and at the longitude of the satellite. The antenna produces a conventional beam shape, with a 1.0° beamwidth to the −3 dB points. Sketch the power flux density contours for −1 dB, −2 dB, −3 dB, −4 dB, −5 dB and −6 dB.

5.10 Figure 5.8 shows the characteristic applicable to a 3 kW earth station amplifier. The need for an 8 dB input back-off has been established. The amplifier has a 36 MHz bandwidth. Three frequency-modulated carriers are to be transmitted. The first must be received at the satellite with S/N = 20 dB and occupies an 8 MHz bandwidth. The other two must be received at the satellite with S/N = 26 dB and occupy 12 MHz each. What earth station transmitter power is associated with each carrier?

5.11 A satellite in a circular low-earth orbit encircles the earth once every 90 minutes. What is its altitude?

5.12 A satellite transponder is being operated to saturation. If a requirement exists for $C/I_o = 18$ dB through the transponder, what portion of the available bandwidth can be occupied?

5.13 What footprint area on the surface of the earth is covered from a satellite at 105° W if the beam center is aimed at 90° W, 40° N and the effective beam angle is 1°?

5.14 An on-board satellite parabolic reflector is to function to frequencies as high as 12.7 GHz for DBS service. No more than 0.5 dB degradation can be allowed due to reflector surface deviation from true parabolic. What deviation in cm rms is allowable?

5.15 A spread spectrum system is designed to use portions of a transponder also allocated to other services. Explain the basis on which it can operate without interfering with the other users.

5.16 A satellite receive-only earth station uses a 6.0 m dish at a 30° elevation angle to view a geosynchronous satellite that is due south of it over the equator. Terrestrial microwave interference from the due south direction, however, has degraded the C/N to 10 dB, whereas 25 dB is required. The desired signal and the interference both are at 3.9 GHz, and of the same polarization. Determine the location and height of a protective wall that will allow C/N to 25 dB in the presence of the terrestrial interference.

5.17 Let the available $E_b/N_o = 14$ dB for both an uplink and a downlink circuit individually, and assume the power amplifiers on each circuit operate with 6 dB output back-off for linear performance. A 45 Mb/s rate is to be sent using QPSK. Calculate, on an end-to-end basis:
a. The b.e.r. if the satellite is nonregenerative.
b. The b.e.r. if the satellite is regenerative.

5.18 A transponder's 54 MHz passband is divided into 16 randomly spaced channels each 2.1 MHz wide. As many of these channels as possible are to be used for QPSK service with a required $p_{be} \leq 10^{-7}$. Allow 1.6 dB degradation from theoretical E_b/N_o requirements for hardware limitations other than intermodulation. How many of the channels can be used if the transponder is operated to saturation?

REFERENCES

1. B. E. Keiser and E. Strange, *Digital Telephony and Network Integration,* Van Nostrand Reinhold Co., New York, 1985.

2. F. S. Carr, "Aerosat—Current Status and Test and Evaluation Program," *1975 Eascon Record,* p. 13.

3. R. E. Anderson, "The Mobilesat System," *Satellite Communications,* 8, no. 3, (March, 1984), 16–18.

4. *Manual of Regulations and Procedures for Federal Radio Frequency Management,* Tables of Frequency Allocations, National Telecommunications and Information Administration, Washington, DC, Jan. 1984 Ed.

5. K. Feher, *Digital Communications: Satellite/Earth Station Engineering,* Prentice-Hall, Englewood Cliffs, NJ, 1983.

6. A. Benoit, "Signal Attenuation Due to Neutral Oxygen and Water Vapour, Rain and Clouds," *Microwave Journal,* (Nov. 1968), pp. 73–80.

7. M. Zuliani, A. R. Smalley, and H. J. Underhill, "Unattended Radar Communications System Design," Telesat Canada, Final Technical Report RADC-TR-79-300, Rome Air Development Center, Griffiss Air Force Base, NY, Nov. 1979.

8. D. Fang, "Attenuation and Phase Shift of Microwaves Due to Canted Raindrops," *Comsat Technical Review,* 5, no. 1, (Spring, 1975), 135–56.

9. R. Y. Huang and P. Hooten, "Communication Satellite Processing Repeaters," *Proceedings of the IEEE,* 57, (Feb. 1971), 238–51.

10. W. L. Morgan, "Palapa," *Satellite Communications,* 5, no. 10, (Oct. 1981), 46.

11. W. L. Pritchard, "Satellite Communication—An Overview of the Problems and Programs," *Proceedings of the IEEE,* 65, no. 3, (March, 1977), 294–307.

12. "Intelsat TDMA/DSI System Specification (TDMA/DSI Traffic Terminals)," BG 42-65 E B/6/80, Intelsat, Washington, DC, June 26, 1980.

13. A. L. Berman and E. I. Podraczky, "Experimental Determinations of Intermodulation Distortion Produced in a Wideband Communications Repeater," *IEEE 1967 International Convention Record,* Part II, pp. 69–88.

14. J. J. Spilker, Jr., *Digital Communications by Satellite,* Prentice-Hall, Inc., Englewood Cliffs, NJ, 1977.

15. F. E. Bond and H. F. Meyer, "Intermodulation Effects in Limiter Amplifier Repeaters," *IEEE Trans. Comm. Tech.,* (Apr. 1970), pp. 127–35.

16. A. R. Kay, D. A. George, and M. J. Eric, "Analysis and Compensation of Bandpass Nonlinearities for Communication," *IEEE Trans. Comm. Tech.,* Oct. 1972.

17. W. C. Babcock, "Intermodulation Interference in Radio Systems," *Bell Sys. Tech. Jour.,* (Jan. 1953), pp. 63–73.

18. J. L. Sevy, "The Effect of Multiple CW and FM Signals Passed Through a Hard Limiter or TWT," *IEEE Trans. Comm. Tech.,* (Oct. 1966), pp. 568–78.

19. American Telephone and Telegraph Company, *Telecommunications Transmission Engineering,* Vol. 2, Second Edition (Winston-Salem, NC: Western Electric Company, Inc., 1977), pp. 500–501.

20. E. D. Sunde, "Intermodulation Distortion in Multicarrier FM Systems," *1965 IEEE International Convention Record,* 13, Part 2, New York, NY, 130–46.

21. M. J. Pagones and V. K. Prabhu, "Effect of Interference from Geostationary Satellites on the Terrestrial Radio Network," *IEEE Globecom '85 Conference Record,* pp. 1482–86.

22. P. Cheilik, "Interference into Digital Radio Systems from Communications Satellites (Part I, Theory and Model Description)," *IEEE International Conference on Communications, 1985,* pp. 15.1.1 to 15.1.5.

23. D. K. Barton, *Radar System Analysis,* Prentice-Hall, Inc., Englewood Cliffs, NJ, 1964.

24. S. Silver, *Microwave Antenna Theory and Design,* McGraw-Hill Book Company, New York, 1949.

25. L. J. Battan, *Radar Meteorology,* University of Chicago Press, Chicago, IL, 1959.

26. J. S. Ajioka and H. E. Harry, "Shaped Beam Antenna for Earth Coverage from a Stabilized Satellite," *IEEE Trans. Antennas and Propagation,* AP-18, (May, 1970), 323–27.

27. E. Carpenter, "An Optimized Dual Polarization Global Beam Antenna," AIAA 9th Communications Satellite Systems Conference, San Diego, CA, March 7–11, 1982, *A Collection of Technical Papers,* pp. 736–40.

28. J. Aasted and R. Roederer, "A Multibeam Array for Communication with Mobiles," AIAA 7th Communications Satellite Systems Conference, San Diego, CA, April 24, 27, 1978, AIAA Paper 587, *A Collection of Technical Papers,* pp. 400–406.

29. S. Siddiqi et al., "An L-Band Active Array System for Global Coverage," *Comsat Technical Review,* 15, no. 1, (Spring, 1985), 39–69.

30. M. C. Bernasconi, E. Pagana, and G. Reibaldi, "Inflatable, Space-Rigidized Reflectors for Mobile Missions," *IEEE Globecom '85 Conference Record,* pp. 407–11.

31. J. Ruze, "Antenna Tolerance Theory, A Review," *Proc. IEEE,* 54, (April, 1966), 633–40.

32. L. F. Gray and M. P. Brown, Jr., "Transmission Planning for the First U.S. Standard C (14/11 GHz) Intelsat Earth Station," *Comsat Technical Review,* 9, no. 1, (Spring, 1979), 61–89.

33. M. Shoemake, "What Proposed Two-Degree Spacing Means for Satellite Antenna Users," *Communications News,* 20, no. 3, (March, 1983), 64–65.

34. F. L. Smith, III, "A Nomogram for Look Angles to Geostationary Satellites," *IEEE Trans. Aerospace and Electronic Systems,* AES-8, no. 3, (May, 1972), 394.

35. B. E. Keiser, *Principles of Electromagnetic Compatibility,* Artech House, 1987.

36. E. C. Jordan, *Electromagnetic Waves and Radiating Systems,* Prentice-Hall, Inc., New York, 1950.

37. P. L. Rice, et al., "Transmission Loss Predictions for Tropospheric Communication Circuits," National Bureau of Standards Technical Note 101, revised Jan. 1, 1967.

38. S. A. Schelknnoff, *Electromagnetic Waves,* D. Van Nostrand Co., Inc., Princeton, NJ, 1943.

39. J. J. G. McCue, "Remarks on Anti-RFI Fences," *IEEE Trans. Electromagnetic Compatibility,* EMC-23, no. 1, (Feb. 1981), 28–32.

40. H. Scheuermann and H. Göckler, "A Comprehensive Survey of Digital Trans-multiplexing Methods," *Proc. IEEE,* 69, no. 11, (Nov. 1981), 1419–50.

41. "Digital Interface Characteristics between Satellite and Terrestrial Networks," CCIR Report no. 707, vol. 4, International Telecommunications Union, Geneva, Switzerland, 1978.

42. R. W. Gruner and E. A. Williams, "A Low-Loss Multiplexer for Satellite Earth Terminals," *Comsat Technical Review,* 5, no. 1, (Spring, 1975), 157–77.

43. H. G. Suyderhoud, M. Onufry, and S. J. Campanella, "Echo Control in Telephone Communications," *1976 National Telecommunications Conference Record,* pp. 8.1-1 to 8.1-5.

44. R. W. Hatch and A. E. Ruppel, "New Rules for Echo Suppressors in the DDD Network," *Bell Laboratories Record,* 52, (Dec. 1974), 351–57.

References   **333**

45. P. S. Henry and B. S. Glance, "A New Approach to High Capacity Digital Mobile Radio," *Bell Sys. Tech. Jour.*, 60, no. 8, (Oct. 1981), 1891–1904.

46. D. L. Duttweiler and Y. S. Chen, "A Single-Chip VLSI Echo Canceler," *Bell Sys. Tech. Jour.*, 59, no. 2, (Feb. 1980), 149–60.

47. D. G. Messerschmitt, "Echo Cancellation in Speech and Data Transmission," *IEEE Journal on Selected Areas in Communications*, SAC-2, no. 2, (Mar. 1984), 283–97.

48. M. Zuliani, A. R. Smalley, and H. J. Underhill, "Unattended Radar Communications System Design," Telesat Canada, Final Technical Report. RADC-TR-79-300, Rome Air Development Center, Griffiss Air Force Base, NY, Nov. 1979.

49. N. C. Ostrander, "The Rand Sync-Sat Calculator," Report RM-5278-NASA, The Rand Corporation, Santa Monica, CA, Sept. 1967.

50. M. I. Skolnik, *Radar Handbook,* McGraw-Hill, New York, 1970, Chap. 39.

51. H. Kaneko, Y. Katagiri, and T. Okada, "The Design of a PCM Master-Group Codec for the Telesat TDMA System," *ICC'75 Conference Proceedings,* 3, (June, 1975), 44.6 to 44.10.

52. R. G. Gould and Y. F. Lum, *Communication Satellite Systems: An Overview of the Technology,* IEEE Press, New York, 1976.

53. G. Robinson, et al., "PSK Signal Power Spectrum Spread Produced by Memoryless Nonlinear TWTs," *Comsat Technical Review,* 3, no. 2, (Fall 1973), 227–56.

54. J. G. Puente, W. G. Schmidt, and A. M. Werth, "Multiple Access Techniques for Commercial Satellites," *Proc. IEEE,* 58, no. 2, (Feb. 1972), 218–29.

55. H. Shimayama, et al., "State-of-the-Art SCPC Satellite Communications Systems," *Signal,* 39, no. 6, (Feb. 1985), 64–71.

56. F. Assal, R. Gupta, J. Apple, and A. Lopatin, "A Satellite Switching Center for SS-TDMA Communications," *Comsat Technical Review,* 12, no. 1, (Spring, 1982), 29–68.

57. R. C. Dixon, *Spread Spectrum Systems,* John Wiley & Sons, New York, 1976.

58. R. G. Gould and E. E. Reinhart, Guest Editorial, *IEEE Journal on Selected Areas in Communications,* SAC-3, no. 1, (Jan. 1985), 4–7.

59. E. E. Reinhart, "An Introduction to the RARC'83 Plan for DBS Systems in the Western Hemisphere," *IEEE Journal on Selected Areas in Communications,* SAC-3, no. 1, (Jan. 1985), 13–19.

60. D. F. DiFonzo, W. S. Trachtman, and A. E. Williams, "Adaptive Polarization Control for Satellite Frequency Reuse Systems," *Comsat Technical Review,* 6, no. 2, (Fall, 1976), 253–83.

61. W. A. Sandrin, "Land-Mobile Satellite Start-up Systems," *Comsat Technical Review,* 14, no. 1, (Spring, 1984), 137–64.

62. W. Sandrin et al., "Aeronautical Satellite Data Link Study," *Comsat Technical Review,* 15, no. 1, (Spring, 1985), 1–38.

63. E. E. Mier, "Celling a Satellite Data Network," *Data Communications,* 12, no. 12, (Dec. 1983), 46–60.

64. D. O. Reudink and Y. S. Yeh, "A Scanning Spot-Beam Satellite System," *Bell Sys. Tech. Jour.,* 56, no. 8, (Oct. 1977), 1549–60.

65. D. K. Sachdev, "Satellite Communication Technology—Are We Getting Ready for the 90's?," *IEEE ICC'83 Conference Record,* (June, 1983), pp. 328–32.

66. W. L. Morgan, "Satellite Notebook #19," *Satellite Communications,* vol. 8, no. 13, 1984.

6

Optical Transmission[*]

The concept of using light for telecommunications is not new. Both guided and atmospheric optical experiments were performed in the nineteenth century, and included demonstrations by John Tyndall in 1870 that light could be guided by a stream of water, as well as A. G. Bell's demonstration of the photophone in 1880 using a beam of light. Of more direct applicability was the demonstration of the first operating laser in 1960 and the work of Corning Glass leading to fiber transmissions over one km in 1970.

While the term *optics* is used in describing telecommunications applications, the wavelengths generally are longer than the 400 to 700 nm range of visible light, and thus fall into the *infrared* range.

This chapter begins with a description of the advantages of optical fibers for telecommunications and continues with a description of the fiber materials as well as wave propagation through them, including the effects of delay distortion. Following this, both sources and detectors are described, leading to complete transmission systems and their components. The subjects of coherent optical transmission and wavelength division multiplexing then are covered. The topics of atmospheric and free-space optical transmission also are part of this chapter because of their use of

[*] Several sections of this chapter also appear in Ref. 1, pp. 221–45. Both are taken from B. E. Keiser, "Wideband Communication Systems," Course Notes, © 1981 and 1985.

sources and detectors similar to those of the fiber systems. The chapter also includes a brief summary of optical fiber system standards.

6.1 ADVANTAGES OF OPTICAL FIBERS FOR COMMUNICATIONS

A major reason frequently cited for the rapid growth of fiber optic applications is fiber's low loss (0.2 to 1.0 dB/km), allowing repeater separations up to 50 km or more. Figure 6.1, [Ref. 2], compares fiber loss with that of other guiding media. Note that the width of the fiber optic curve below 1 dB/km is on the order of 100 THz. Thus, another advantage is fiber's broad bandwidth capability, allowing data rates up to 4 Gb/s or more over intercity distances. Fiber's numerous additional advantages include a significant reduction in the weight and bulk of cable plant compared with coaxial cable, and thus the ability to replace coaxial cable with fiber in crowded underground duct banks, thereby vastly increasing transmission capacity.

Fiber ends problems with cable crosstalk, electromagnetic interference (EMI), short circuits, and grounding. The levels of crosstalk that do exist are much lower than in metallic cables and thus are generally negligible. EMI does not disturb fiber transmission because the frequencies used are vastly different; EMI, of course, can disturb electronic terminal equipment operating at baseband. There is no such thing as a short-circuited fiber, although open circuits (fiber breaks) can and do occur. Grounding is not a problem in optical fibers, except at terminals or repeaters, because the fiber is an optical waveguide. Being a cabled-type of medium, fiber operates well under all weather conditions.

Fiber transmission provides significant cost savings over metallic cable in some applications, with comparable costs in others. Cost trade-offs show fiber economies, relative to other transmission media, generally increasing with distance and with the number of channels. However, definitive answers to the question, "which

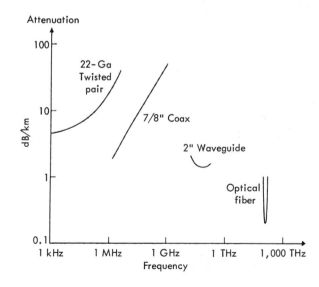

Figure 6.1 Attenuation of various guiding media. (From P. S. Henry, "Introduction to Lightwave Transmission," *IEEE Communications Magazine*, May 1985, © 1985, IEEE. Reprinted by permission.)

transmission medium is most cost effective?" require a detailed study of both installation and operating costs, and thus depend on cost factors applicable when the study is made, and for a specified topology and geographical conditions.

A further advantage of fiber transmission is security. The relatively low loss of the medium makes it difficult to tap without the operator becoming aware of the tap as a result of reflection level changes. In fact, an *optical time-domain reflectometer (OTDR)* can be used to monitor the line for such purposes. A triaxial fiber can be used with a noninformation region outside the core to monitor the reflections of pulses from the reflectometer. While taps can be built based upon directional coupler principles, and can operate without noticeable reflections, the installation of such taps requires that the fiber be broken or disconnected momentarily. At such a time the OTDR can record the location of the break for investigation by maintenance personnel.

6.2 BASIC ELEMENTS OF AN OPTICAL FIBER COMMUNICATIONS SYSTEM

Figure 6.2 shows the basic elements used in transmitting information via a fiber. The transmitter (source) is a *light-emitting diode (LED)*. Alternatively, a *laser diode (LD)*, may be used. The source operates at a wavelength in the infrared range of 0.8 to 1.55 μm. The guide is a fused silica or glass composition fiber consisting of a *core* surrounded by a *cladding*. The cladding has a lower refractive index than the core, thus directing light back along the core. The refractive index *n* is the ratio of the speed of light in free space to its speed in the propagating medium. For fibers, typical values of *n* range from less than 1.5 to as high as 1.9. For some fibers used in telecommunications applications, the difference in refractive indices between core and cladding is on the order of 0.4%. The detector is a silicon *positive-intrinsic-negative (PIN)* diode or an avalanche photodiode.

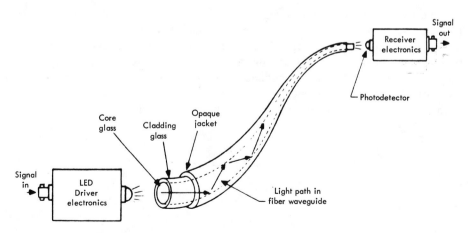

Figure 6.2 Basic fiber optics communications link. (Courtesy Dr. Leonard Bergstein.)

6.3 OPTICAL FIBER MATERIALS

Optical fiber materials may be plastic, glass, or plastic-clad silica, as described next.

6.3.1 Plastic Fibers

Plastic fibers are useful only for short distances because of their relatively high attenuation, often measured in dB/m rather than in dB/km. Their advantage is that they are rugged and thus useful in such environments as are found in automotive and aircraft applications. Plastic fibers typically have large diameters, e.g., 600 μm or more, making them well suited to use with inexpensive emitters, such as LEDs.

6.3.2 Glass Fibers

Glass fibers are used in telecommunications applications and generally have a diameter less than 200 μm. The step-index fibers have a cladding whose index of refraction is distinctly different from that of the core, while the graded index fibers have an index which varies smoothly from the core to the cladding region.

6.3.3 Plastic-Clad Silica

Plastic-clad silica fibers have a behavior like that of glass, but the core can be made larger because of the plastic cladding. These fibers are step index, and have a diameter less than 600 μm. They are easy to use with inexpensive emitters such as LEDs. Their use generally is limited to short-distance (local) applications.

6.4 WAVE PROPAGATION THROUGH FIBERS

6.4.1 Path Geometry

The basic concepts of wave propagation outlined in Chaps. 4 and 5 apply to wave propagation through fibers. These concepts include those of wave impedance as well as polarization. For example, the difference in values of n that the propagating wave encounters at the core-cladding interface results in a wave reflection at this interface because of the wave impedance discontinuity encountered there. Since the index of refraction n is the ratio of the velocity of light in vacuum ($c \simeq 3 \times 10^8$ m/s) to the velocity of light in the medium it can be expressed as

$$n = \frac{\sqrt{\frac{1}{\mu_0 \varepsilon_0}}}{\sqrt{\frac{1}{\mu \varepsilon}}} \qquad (6.1)$$

For a glass fiber, $\mu = \mu_0$, so

$$n = \sqrt{\frac{\varepsilon}{\varepsilon_0}} = \sqrt{\varepsilon_r} \qquad (6.2)$$

where ε_r, the relative permittivity, also is known as the dielectric constant. For a smooth variation in the refractive index, the wave is bent smoothly. In the case of reflection, the Law of Reflection states that the angle of incidence θ_i equals the angle of reflection θ_r. Light transmitted into a medium from the outside is governed by the Law of Refraction (Snell's Law), which is expressed by Eq. (6.3).

$$n_t \sin \theta_t = n_i \sin \theta_i \qquad (6.3)$$

in which the subscripts t designate the wave *transmitted* into the medium, i the wave incident on the medium, and the angles θ are measured normal to the surface that the wave strikes. Figure 6.3 illustrates the relationships among the directions of the incident, reflected, and transmitted waves for the case $n_i < n_t$. Light entering a medium of higher n is bent toward the normal, while light entering a medium of lower n is bent away from the normal.

For light traveling from a medium of higher to one of lower refractive index, three possibilities exist, as illustrated in Fig. 6.4. Light entering a medium of lower index of refraction is bent away from the normal. Light traveling along path 1 is incident at a large enough angle that total internal reflection occurs. Attempts to apply Snell's Law result in $\sin \theta_t > 1$, which is an impossibility. Thus a transmitted wave does not exist. Light traveling along path 2 is incident at an angle that results in a refracted angle of 90°. The incident angle is called the *critical angle*, and can be found by inserting $\theta_t = 90°$ in Eq. (6.3), whereupon $n_t = n_i \sin \theta_{crit}$, and

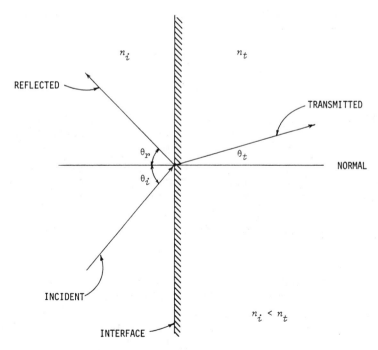

Figure 6.3 Geometrical relation among directions of incident, reflected and transmitted waves.

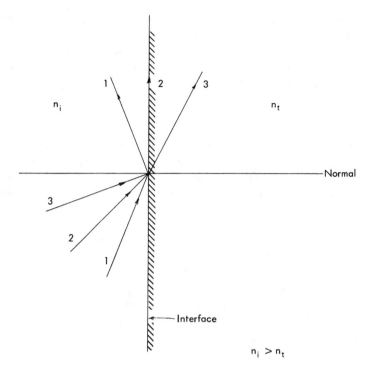

Figure 6.4 Geometrical relations among waves striking interface from medium of higher index of refraction.

$$\theta_{crit} = \sin^{-1}\left(\frac{n_t}{n_i}\right) \tag{6.4}$$

Light traveling along path 3 is refracted at the interface according to Eq. (6.3).

In the case of total internal reflection (path 1), a weak field actually exists in the medium of lower n, but it experiences a rapid exponential decrease in strength with distance from the interface. This field is said to be evanescent, and exists in the cladding of the fiber. Placement of another core glass within one to two wavelengths of the core-cladding interface allows some of the field to be coupled into the second core. This process is called *frustrated internal reflection,* and forms the basis for the operation of bidirectional couplers. Use of the cladding around the core prevents the loss of light that otherwise would occur where the core might touch a physical support, or where it may be bent sharply. Moreover, the use of n_t and n_i values that are nearly equal results in large values of θ_{crit}, which are important in causing the wave to propagate down the fiber as nearly parallel to the axis as possible. This, in turn, is important in minimizing time-domain dispersion of the transmitted pulses.

Figure 6.5 illustrates the foregoing relationships as they apply to a step-index fiber, the core having $n = n_1$ and the cladding having $n = n_2$. The index of refraction profile also is shown in Fig. 6.5. The cladding is surrounded by a protective jacket, often of plastic. The acceptance cone for the fiber is defined by the angle θ_c. An

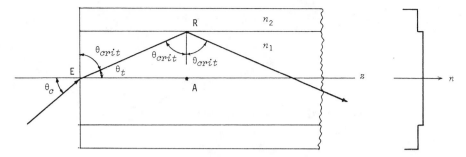

Figure 6.5 Path of transmitted signal in step-index fiber.

important parameter associated with the performance of an optical fiber is the *fractional refractive index difference*, Δ. By definition,

$$\Delta = \frac{(n_1 - n_2)}{n_1} \tag{6.5}$$

Its effects on fiber characteristics and performance will be described subsequently.

Knowing θ_{crit} from Eq. (6.4), one can determine the value of θ_c for a fiber having a given Δ. Using Snell's Law, Eq. (6.1),

$$n_i \sin \theta_c = n_1 \sin \theta_t = n_1 \sin (90° - \theta_{crit}) = n_1 \cos \theta_{crit}$$
$$= n_1 \sqrt{1 - \sin^2 \theta_{crit}} \tag{6.6}$$

Substituting Eq. (6.4) as it applies to the core-cladding interface with $n_t = n_2$ and $n_i = n_1$.

$$n_i \sin \theta_c = n_1 \sqrt{1 - \left(\frac{n_2^2}{n_1^2}\right)} = \sqrt{n_1^2 - n_2^2} \tag{6.7}$$

Let the maximum value of θ_c be called $(\theta_c)_{max}$. Then the *numerical aperture (NA)* of the fiber is defined as

$$NA = n_i \sin (\theta_c)_{max} \tag{6.8}$$

The light incident from the air, $n_i = 1$, and

$$NA = \sqrt{n_1^2 - n_2^2} \tag{6.9}$$

Since $\Delta \ll 1$ for fibers used in telecommunications,

$$NA = \sqrt{(n_1 - n_2)(n_1 + n_2)} \approx \sqrt{2n_1 (n_1 - n_2)}$$
$$= \sqrt{2n_1\Delta n_1} = n_1 \sqrt{2\Delta} \tag{6.10}$$

The time domain dispersion of the light in the fiber can be evaluated as follows. Figure 6.5 shows light entering the fiber at point E from the cone defined by angle θ_c. Light traveling along the axis (*axial ray*) follows path EA. Light entering at the critical angle (*marginal ray*) follows path ER. Note that $(EA/ER) = \sin \theta_{crit} = n_2/n_1$. If L = total fiber length, then the additional distance traveled by a marginal ray is

$$\delta L = L \left[\frac{(ER - EA)}{EA} \right] = L \left[\left(\frac{n_1}{n_2} \right) - 1 \right] = L \left[\frac{(n_1 - n_2)}{n_2} \right] \tag{6.11}$$

Since $n_1 \simeq n_2$

$$\delta L \simeq L \left[\frac{(n_1 - n_2)}{n_1} \right] = L \Delta \tag{6.12}$$

The additional time required to travel along the marginal ray thus is

$$\delta t = \frac{\delta L}{v} = \frac{L \Delta n_1}{c} \tag{6.13}$$

where δt is the time domain dispersion of the light in the fiber.

Fibers often are rated in terms of a *data rate × distance product,* e.g., a number of Gb/s − km. For a step-index fiber, this product thus is proportional to $L/\delta t = c/\Delta n_1$.

6.4.2 Modes in Fibers

The propagation of light in fibers is governed by Maxwell's equations. Incorporation of the refractive indices of the core and cladding, as well as the geometrical boundary conditions for the cylindrical core and cladding results in a wave equation that can be solved for the field distributions in the fiber. These distributions are called *modes*. The modes that can propagate along a fiber are determined by the *normalized wavenumber, V,* which is defined as

$$V = \beta_0 \, aNA \tag{6.14}$$

where β_0 is the free-space phase constant or wavenumber, and equals $2\pi/\lambda_0$ where λ_0 is the wavelength in free space. The parameter a is the radius of the core, which is assumed here to have a circular cross-section. The core diameter also is known as the *mode-field diameter.* Figure 6.6 [Ref. 3] shows the propagation constant β as a function of V, and the modes that can propagate in a fiber of given NA and radius a.

As in Figure 6.5, the z-axis is the direction of propagation. The transverse magnetic (TM) modes have $H_z = 0$ and the transverse electric (TE) modes have $E_z = 0$. Thus the TE and TM modes are radially symmetric. The designation HE or EH is given based upon whether H_z or E_z makes the larger contribution to the transverse field. These modes are called *hybrid modes*. The first subscript (Figure 6.6 modes) $\nu = 0$ for the radially symmetric modes (TE and TM) and is a positive integer for the hybrid modes. The second subscript m designates one of the roots for a given ν value. For the HE_{11} mode there is no cutoff. This is the basis for the single-mode light guide. For fibers with $V < 2.405$, only the HE_{11} mode propagates, and the fiber is said to be *single mode (monomode).* Note that for a given λ_0, the single-mode condition is achieved by making the aNA product sufficiently small. Also note that for a given aNA product, the single-mode condition becomes easier to achieve as λ_0 is increased.

Monomode fibers typically have core diameters on the order of 5 to 10 μm, while typical multimode fibers have core diameters on the order of 70 to 100 μm.

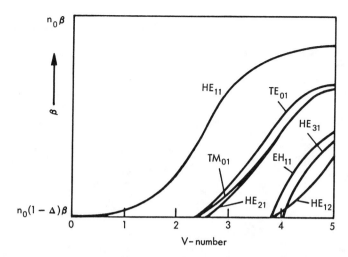

Figure 6.6 Low-order modes of an optical fiber. (M. K. Barnoski, *Fundamentals of Optical Fiber Communications*, © 1981, Academic Press, Inc. Reprinted by permission.)

Example

What is the maximum diameter a 0.15 *NA* fiber can have for single-mode operation at 1300 nm?

Solution At 1300 nm, $\beta_0 = 2\pi/1300 \times 10^{-9} = 4.833 \times 10^6$. The maximum diameter will be $2a = 2 \times 2.405/4.833 \times 10^6 \times 0.15 = 6.63 \times 10^{-6}$ m = 6.63 μm

6.4.3 Attenuation Characteristics

Light transmitted along a fiber is attenuated for several reasons. What is called *Rayleigh scattering* is caused by irregularities in the refractive index of the glass that are less than 0.1 λ in diameter. These irregularities result from thermal fluctuations while the fiber still is in a molten state. Rayleigh scattering is proportional to λ^{-4}.

At wavelengths greater than 1.6 μm an *infrared absorption tail* becomes evident. This absorption is caused by infrared resonances in silica and other fiber constituents.

A third loss is hydroxyl ion (OH⁻) absorption, which may produce loss bands in the vicinity of 0.95, 1.25, and 1.38 μm. This loss results from the presence of the OH⁻ ion, which can be reduced to values as low as 10 parts per billion, thus nearly eliminating impurities as a problem.

Other loss contributors include *microbending,* which results from stress plains (minute internal longitudinal cracks) that appear in a fiber that has been bent sharply. Nuclear (ionizing) radiation can cause yet another form of loss, a darkening of the fiber where it has been subject to such radiation. Figure 6.7, [Ref. 2], illustrates the variation of silica fiber attenuation versus wavelength, including the effects of Rayleigh scattering, the infrared absorption tail, and OH⁻ absorption at 1.35 μm.

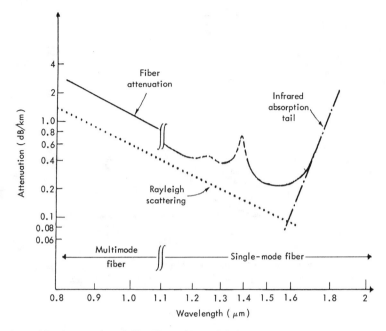

Figure 6.7 Attenuation of silica fibers. (From P. S. Henry, "Introduction to Lightwave Transmission," *IEEE Communications Magazine,* May 1985, © 1985, IEEE. Reprinted by permission.)

The response of an optical fiber to a pulse of ionizing radiation consists of three phenomena: (1) luminescence consisting of a temporary generation of blue Cerenkov radiation for several milliseconds, (2) transient absorption, a temporary increase in attenuation, and (3) permanent absorption, a permanent increase in attenuation consisting of the generation of defect centers which darken the core. Figure 6.8 illustrates the ranges of losses which occur in fibers containing phosphorous doping in the core as the result of exposure to 1 hour of gamma radiation at 10^5 rads (a *rad* is the radiation absorbed dose, consisting of 0.01 J of ionizing energy absorbed in 1 kilogram).

6.4.4 Angular Division Multiplexing

Angular division multiplexing is a special technique for multichannel transmission over short distances, e.g., on the order of a kilometer. It is accomplished by differentially exciting and detecting groups of modes, each of which is characterized by a set of plane waves propagating at a specific angle in the fiber. The propagation angle is $\theta m = \lambda m / 4an_1$, where m is the compound mode number.

The advantage of angular division multiplexing is that each channel has fewer modes and thus less pulse dispersion than if all modes were propagated and detected as a single channel. Thus more effective bandwidth per channel can be provided. The number of channels can be increased further by sending multiple wavelengths via each group of modes. This is a technique called *wavelength division*

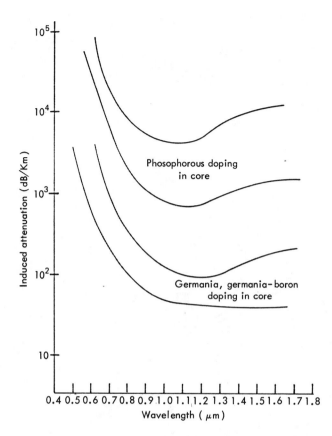

Figure 6.8 Fiber losses after 1 hour exposure to 10^5 rads. (From D. H. Rice and G. E. Keiser, "Application of Fiber Optics to Tactical Communication Systems," *IEEE Communications Magazine*, May 1985, © 1985, IEEE. Reprinted by permission.)

In the figure: Induced attenuation (dB/Km) vs Wavelength (μm). Curves labeled "Phosophorous doping in core" and "Germania, germania-boron doping in core."

multiplexing, and is the subject of Sec. 6.9.3. Crosstalk between the groups of modes is on the order of -32 dB.

6.5 FIBER TYPES AND THEIR CHARACTERISTICS

Glass fibers are manufactured having a step index or a graded index, as will be described in this section. Fiber production methods include the *outside vapor deposition* (OVD) method, which has produced the lowest loss fiber (0.16 dB/km at $\lambda = 1.55$ μm), the *modified chemical vapor deposition* (MCVD) method, which allows fundamental studies on film structures, materials and properties, and is widely accepted for the mass production of commercial fibers, the *vapor-phase axial deposition* (VAD) method, which holds the record for the highest bandwidth multimode fiber (9.7 Gb/s − km at $\lambda = 1.31$ μm), the *plasma chemical vapor deposition (PCVD)* method, which provides the highest deposition efficiency and reproducibility, and the RF plasma enhanced MCVD method, which can deposit at a rate in excess of 6 g/minute. The *double crucible method* is for fibers of high NA ($\simeq$ 0.4) and loss (up to 10 dB/km).

Figure 6.9 illustrates five types of fibers and their associated index profiles.

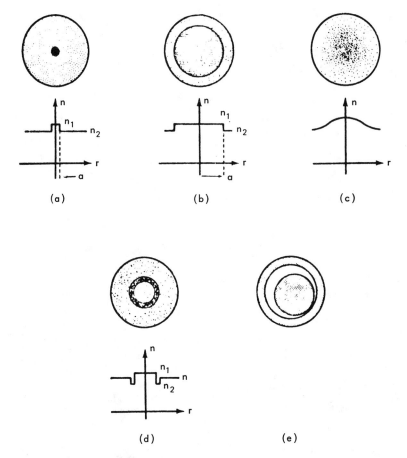

Figure 6.9 Cross sectional illustration of different fiber types and their associated index profiles. (Courtesy Dr. Leonard Bergstein.)

The single mode (a), multimode (b), and graded index (c) fibers are discussed subsequently in this section. The multiple-clad fiber (d) is discussed in Sec. 6.9.3. The plastic-clad fiber (e) was discussed in Sec. 6.3.3.

6.5.1 Single Mode Step-Index Fibers

As noted in Sec. 6.4, a step-index fiber with a core diameter $a < 2.405/\beta_0 NA$ propagates only a single mode. Such a diameter generally is less than about 10 wavelengths. The single-mode (monomode) fiber typically has a core diameter of 4 to 10 μm and a very low dispersion δt. Because of its low NA, a highly coherent high radiance source such as a laser or a laser diode is needed to drive it. Monomode fibers are more difficult to splice than types with larger core diameters, but splicing techniques for use in the field have been developed. A monomode fiber has been made to operate at 2 Gb/s over an unrepeatered fiber 130 km long at $p_{be} < 10^{-9}$.

6.5.2 Multimode Step-Index Fibers

A step-index fiber with a core diameter $a > 2.405/\beta_0 NA$ propagates multiple modes. Core diameters often are 100 μm or more. Multimode fibers generally are used for lower data rates than monomode fibers, e.g., 200 Mb/s, and for relatively short distances, e.g., 1 to 10 km or less.

6.5.3 Graded Index Fibers

As noted in Chap. 4, variations in the refractive index of a medium cause a change in the direction of propagation of a wave. In the graded index fiber, the index of refraction decreases smoothly from a maximum along the fiber axis to a minimum at the edge of the core. The result is that the waves travel faster near the edge. The core profile, $n(r)$, where r = radial distance from the axis, can be adjusted so that the travel time for the various modes is approximately the same. The corresponding light path is (ideally) sinusoidal. The graded-index fiber is a multimode fiber, but one in which the travel times of the various modes ideally are equal.

The index of refraction of a graded-index fiber usually is made to fit the following power law profile.

$$n^2(r) = n_0^2 \left[1 - 2\Delta \left(\frac{r}{a} \right)^{\rho} \right] \tag{6.15}$$

where n_0 is the index of refraction along the fiber axis and where,

$$\Delta = \frac{(n_0 - n_2)}{n_0} \tag{6.16}$$

The parameter ρ determines the profile shape. If $\rho \rightarrow \infty$, the profile is step-index, whereas if $\rho = 2$ the profile is parabolic. Figure 6.10, [Ref. 3], shows how the diverging light paths are bent back toward the fiber axis.

The analysis of graded-index fibers usually assumes an ideal parabolic profile. Actually, the refractive index may consist of a series of many very small steps, depending on how the fiber has been manufactured. Accordingly, some performance degradation usually exists, i.e., the time-domain dispersion δt between the axial and marginal rays is not eliminated.

For a graded index fiber the amount of light that can be coupled from a source is only half the amount that can be input to a step-index fiber having the same Δ. For light traveling down the axis, the travel time is $t = Lv = n_0 L/c$. For light traveling away from the axis and then back again (sinusoidal path) the travel time will be $t = n(r)L_s/c$, where L_s is the length of the sinusoidal path. The *optical path length* is defined as the geometrical path length times the index of refraction, i.e., $n(r)l$. If this product is the same for all paths, $\delta t = 0$. This condition is reached for $\rho = 2$, i.e., the parabolic profile. The data rate × distance product for a graded-index fiber ($\rho = 2$) is proportional to Δ^{-2}.

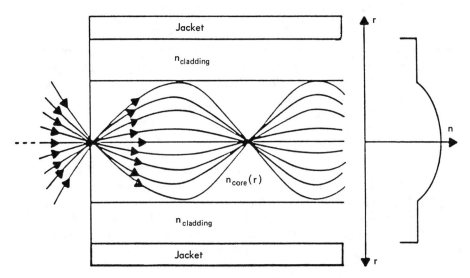

Figure 6.10 Graded-index fiber and refractive index profile. (Courtesy Newport Corporation, © 1986. Reprinted by permission.)

6.6 GROUP DELAY DISTORTION

Group delay distortion results from three types of dispersion which are discussed next. These are intermodal, material, and waveguide dispersion.

6.6.1 Intermodal Dispersion

Section 6.4.1 discussed the time domain dispersion δt of light in a fiber, which is described by Eq. (6.13). This group delay spread resulting from a variation in group delay between different propagating modes is called *intermodal dispersion*. Section 6.5.3 indicated that for the ideal graded-index fiber, as for the monomode fiber, the intermodal dispersion is zero. Figure 6.11 summarizes these conclusions by illustrating the intermodal dispersion for the three fiber types, along with the fact that (ideally) only the step-index multimode fiber exhibits intermodal dispersion.

6.6.2 Material Dispersion

Material dispersion or *chromatic dispersion* is the group delay resulting from the nonlinear dependence of the fiber's refractive index on wavelength. Accordingly, material dispersion produces a pulse spreading that is proportional to the spectral width of the optical source. Figure 6.12, [Ref. 4], shows the material dispersion for a silica core fiber. The amount of dispersion in ps per nm of source width is shown for a 1 km length of fiber. Thus for a light-emitting diode (LED) source, for which the wavelength width $\Delta\lambda = 35$ nm, the dispersion at $\lambda = 800$ nm is 110×35 ps = 3850 ps. For an injection laser for which $\Delta\lambda = 1.5$ nm, the dispersion at 1000 nm is 40×1.5 = 60 ps. For a distributed Bragg reflector laser for which $\Delta\lambda = 0.1$ nm, the dispersion at 1200 nm is $10 \simeq 0.1 = 1$ nm.

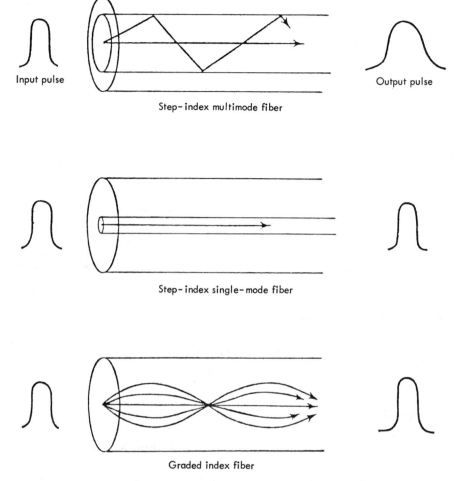

Input pulse

Output pulse

Step-index multimode fiber

Step-index single-mode fiber

Graded index fiber

Figure 6.11 Light paths in single-mode and multimode fibers illustrating inter-modal dispersion. (Courtesy Dr. Leonard Bergstein.)

Because single-mode fiber dispersion has a known wavelength dependence, measured data can be modeled. The model is known as the Sellmeier delay fit, [Ref. 5], and is given by the expression

$$D(\lambda) = \left(\frac{S_{0_{max}}}{4}\right)\left(\lambda - \frac{\lambda_0^4}{\lambda^3}\right) \qquad (6.17)$$

where

$D(\lambda)$ = total chromatic dispersion, ps/nm − km
$S_{0_{max}}$ = slope of $D(\lambda)$ at λ_0, ps/(nm)²km
λ_0 = wavelength at which dispersion is zero, nm

Chromatic dispersion can be minimized over a wide wavelength range using the multiple-clad fiber, which is discussed in Sec. 6.9.3.

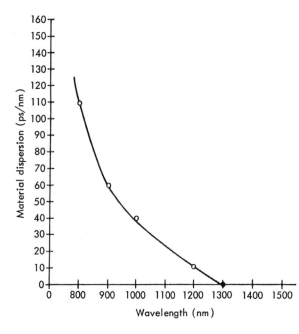

Figure 6.12 Material dispersion of a 1-kilometer length of silica core fiber. (From D. H. Rice and G. E. Keiser, "Application of Fiber Optics to Tactical Communication Systems," *IEEE Communications Magazine,* May 1985, © 1985, IEEE. Reprinted by permission.)

6.6.3 Waveguide Dispersion

Waveguide dispersion is the group delay that results from the differing dispersions for each propagating mode. This is a small effect.

6.7 OPTICAL SOURCES

Optical sources used for telecommunications applications include light-emitting diodes and laser diodes. Their actual emission wavelengths range from 800 nm to 1600 nm, placing them in the near infrared rather than optical wavelengths.

The spectral line width in nm often is expressed by the term *full width half maximum (FWHM),* which is equivalent to the −3 dB bandwidth. The term FWHM also is used to express the optical beamwidth between the −3 dB angles. The emission wavelength depends on the materials used. For the 800 to 900 nm region alloys of gallium arsenide and aluminum arsenide are used. For the 1300 nm region alloys of indium, gallium, arsenic and phosphorus are used.

6.7.1 Light Emitting Diodes

Light emitting diodes, (LEDs), are made of semiconductors with small amounts of atomic impurities to increase their conductivity. In n-type material the electrons are the majority carriers of current, whereas in p-type material, the majority carriers are *holes.* A hole is the absence of an electron. The LED consists of n-type and p-type material joined together, with the interface plane between them being called the junction. Application of a suitable forward-biased voltage across the junction results in current conduction along with light radiation from the junction resulting from the recombination of holes and electrons, and known as *recombination radiation.* The light output is directly proportional to the diode current, which in turn is proportional to the number of electron-hole pairs recombining. Accordingly, the output curve is a straight line, as illustrated in Fig. 6.13, [Ref. 6], for the light launched into a 50 μm 0.2 *NA* multimode fiber. The conversion efficiency is on the order of 0.01%.

The wavelength of the optical radiation depends on energy differences between the electrons in the *n*-type material and the holes in the *p*-type material. The light polarization is random. The high-radiance Burrus diode has been developed for efficient coupling into single fiber systems. The Burrus diode is a surface emitter. Medium radiance large-area diodes are used to couple into fiber bundles with more than one fiber per data channel. Modulation rates up to 200 MHz are possible, depending on material doping levels, which affect carrier recombination lifetimes. The spectral bandwidth is on the order of 35 to 50 nm.

6.7.2 Laser Diodes

In the *current injection laser diode (ILD)* the voltage applied across the diode causes current flow, but at a greater density than in the LED. Instead of producing a spontaneous recombination of electron-hole pairs, the current flow stimulates the pairs to emit light coherently, producing a higher output power as illustrated in Fig. 6.14, [Ref. 6], for the light launched into a 50 μm 0.2 *NA* multimode fiber. Outputs up to 100 mW have been achieved. The process is called *stimulated emission,* a characteristic of all lasers. As illustrated in Fig. 6.14, the current must reach a threshold value, e.g., about 100 mA, before lasing action begins. Beyond the

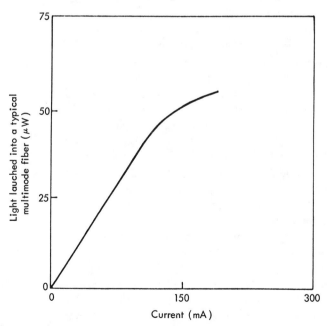

Figure 6.13 Light emitting diode characteristic. (From S. D. Personick, "Review of Fundamentals of Optical Fiber Systems," *IEEE Journal on Selected Areas in Communications,* April 1983, © 1983, IEEE. Reprinted by permission.)

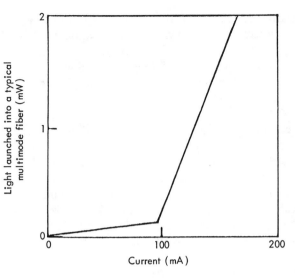

Figure 6.14 Laser diode characteristic. (From S. D. Personick, "Review of Fundamentals of Optical Fiber Systems," *IEEE Journal on Selected Areas in Communications,* April 1983, © 1983, IEEE. Reprinted by permission.)

threshold, light emission increases sharply. The surfaces of the semiconductor crystal act as partially reflecting mirrors to redirect part of the light output back into the junction. Correspondingly, the output becomes partially collimated, although diffraction by the edges of the junction region results in the production of a fan beam with a width of 15° to 30° perpendicular to the plane of the junction. The polarization is parallel to the plane of the junction. Efficiencies (light output power/dc input power) of 30% to 40% have been reached.

Conventional laser diodes emit a spectrum of lines or "modes" spread over a width of several nm. Because of the chromatic dispersion of the fibers, except at 1.3 µm, these *multifrequency* lasers are not suitable for high-rate long distance transmission, [Ref. 7]. In addition, the power of each line (or frequency) fluctuates, especially during intensity modulation, even though the total power is constant from pulse to pulse. The power fluctuation among the spectral lines (modes) is converted via chromatic dispersion into pulse shape variations at the receiver. These variations are called *mode partition noise.* Because mode partition noise impairs system performance, sources for high data rate systems must be *single frequency* lasers.

Single frequency operation is achieved by using a *distributed feedback (DFB)* or a *cleaved-coupled-cavity (C³)* laser. The DFB laser uses a grating to obtain distributed, but frequency-selective, feedback that confines the output to a "single frequency" (actually a spectral width on the order of 50 MHz, rather than the 10 to 20 GHz width that may be produced otherwise). The C³ laser has two cavity sections which are coupled optically but isolated electrically. The drive current through each section is adjusted to achieve "single frequency" operation.

During intensity modulation, drive current variations produce changes in the instantaneous frequency of the laser, resulting in pulse spreading at the receiver because the refractive index of the laser is a function of carrier density. The result is known as *chirp* since the frequency shifts during the output pulse duration.

The improved spatial coherence of the laser output, compared with the LED, allows the laser to achieve a better coupling efficiency to a fiber, as will be seen in

Sec. 6.9.1.1. The fact that the spectral width is less than that of an LED results in less chromatic dispersion, as was illustrated in Sec. 6.6.2.

6.7.3 Comparison Between Light Emitting Diodes and Lasers

The LED generally is useful for distances encountered in local and metropolitan applications. Some LEDs emit milliwatts of power at modulation rates up to 200 MHz. The LED with its wide angle output couples efficiently into the relatively large diameter multimode fibers.

The laser diode is used for intercity and long-haul applications, especially those involving modulation rates in excess of 200 MHz. The relatively narrow beam and narrow spectral width output of the laser diode suit it well to coupling into single mode fibers. Systems using laser diodes are more costly than those using LEDs because of the additional device sophistication as well as the need for a stabilization network.

Both the LED and the laser have made significant progress in terms of reliability since their initial introduction, with measured lifetimes exceeding 10^5 hours, and projected lifetimes on the order of 7×10^5 hours for lasers and 10^8 hours for LEDs, [Ref. 8]. Table 6.1 compares typical LED and laser diode characteristics for operation at 800 to 850 nm wavelengths. The reliability of LEDs is somewhat better than that of lasers, their cost is lower, and they are less sensitive to temperature changes than lasers.

Because the chromatic dispersion of fibers reaches a minimum at 1.3 μm, LEDs can be used readily at this wavelength for systems having moderate rate and distance requirements.

6.7.4 Light Source Modulation

Numerous methods exist for modulating light sources. The techniques discussed in this section relate to the noncoherent operation of light sources. Techniques for coherent optical systems are discussed in Sec. 6.10.

A light source can be intensity modulated by varying its drive current; alternatively, a laser diode can be operated at constant output and an electro-optic crystal such as lithium niobate ($LiNbO_3$) or lithium tantalate ($LiTaO_3$) can be used to modulate the polarization of the output light externally. The bits 0 and 1 then can be

TABLE 6.1 COMPARISON OF LED AND LASER DIODE

Parameter	Laser	LED
Power	5–100 mW	1–10 mW
Modulation	$\simeq$4 GHz	$\leq$200 MHz
Threshold	40 mA	None
Lifetime (measured)	>100 000 h	>100 000 h
Coupling loss to NA = 0.14 fiber	−2 to −3 dB	−10 to −17 dB
Line width, $\Delta\lambda$	1–20 Å	200–400 Å

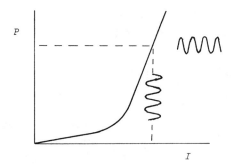

Figure 6.15 Intensity modulation of a laser. (Courtesy Dr. Leonard Bergstein.)

represented by the two orthogonal linear polarizations or by the opposite-sense circular polarizations.

The remainder of this section discusses sinusoidal and pulse intensity modulation of optical sources.

6.7.4.1 Sinusoidal modulation.

Optical source intensity can be modulated by a sine wave which, in turn, is either amplitude or frequency modulated. Figure 6.15 illustrates the basic principle of intensity modulation using a response curve characteristic of a laser. Note that the laser is operated beyond its threshold at all times. This allows the production of subnanosecond pulses and thus operation at rates of several Gb/s, with a limit set only by fiber chromatic dispersion. By contrast, if attempts were made to operate between zero input current and a value beyond the curve, the laser would be turned on and off but a delay of several ns would occur for each pulse. Such a problem does not exist for the LED, but LEDs cannot be modulated at GHz rates.

6.7.4.1.1 Amplitude Modulation.

A baseband signal can be used to amplitude modulate a light source above and below a given operating point such that the output always remains above a minimum value, such as the laser threshold. Alternatively, one or several sinusoidal carriers, each at a different frequency, and each modulated independently, can be applied to the light source drive current. In this way, as many as four to eight television signals, each using vestigial sideband (VSB), as described in Sec. 3.1, can be applied to the light source. This technique allows analog transmission having the bandwidth of the corresponding TV channels, but entails amplitude modulation of the light source with its inherent nonlinearities.

The *depth of modulation* of a laser is defined [Ref. 8] by the equation

$$P(t) = P_b [1 + ms(t)] \tag{6.18}$$

where

$$P(t) = \text{output power of laser}$$
$$m = \text{modulation depth}$$
$$P_b = \text{average laser optical power}$$
$$s(t) = \text{modulating signal}$$

To keep distortion satisfactorily low, *m* usually is limited to 0.25 to 0.50. Typical values of distortion for single-mode lasers operating at $m = 0.5$ are:

2nd order: -30 dB to -45 dB
3rd order: -45 dB to -60 dB

The spread in values results from the fact that lasers do not have consistently good linearity. Accordingly, VSB/AM systems require careful spectrum planning. Moreover, the dynamic range requirements of AM transmission limit the allowable loss, and thus the distance between repeaters in overall system design. As many as 30 VSB/AM channels per fiber can be accommodated with careful laser selection and the development of linearization circuits for the optical transmitter [Ref. 9]. Broadband linearization techniques are discussed further in Chap. 7.

6.7.4.1.2 Frequency Modulation. The sinusoidal carrier or carriers referenced above can be frequency modulated, thus alleviating the distortion and dynamic range problems characteristic of AM, but requiring more bandwidth occupancy instead, typically 32 to 36 MHz for each video channel using NTSC standards. Because of the multiple carriers, intermodulation from laser nonlinearities is present, so the carrier frequencies must be selected to minimize this intermodulation. The analysis of Sec. 5.3.1.3 describes the method used for carrier frequency selection.

The occupied bandwidth is based on Carson's Rule (see Sec. 4.3.2.1). For video, the sync tip to peak white (STPW) deviation should be at least 8 MHz, [Ref. 10], yielding an occupied bandwidth of 24.4 MHz. The guard band between adjacent channels is on the order of 30% resulting in a 32 MHz minimum center-to-center spacing.

6.7.4.2 Pulse modulation. Pulse modulation of the intensity of a light source can be done using either PCM or pulse position modulation (PPM). Pulse frequency modulation (PFM) also has been used. PPM can be used with either an analog or digital input, but the input generally is multilevel digital. As noted in Sec. 6.7.4.1, the laser must be operated beyond its threshold at all times for maximum modulation rate. The term *high-low keying* refers to pulse modulation in which high and low light output levels represent the two binary states.

The majority of digital optical fiber communication systems use binary intensity modulation (IM) of the laser or the LED, [Ref. 11]. To maintain timing at repeaters and receivers a *complementary bit* (to the previous one) is added after each m information bits to prevent long runs of the same bit. The result is called an *mB1C* code. This code allows error detection by checking the C bit, [Ref. 12].

If PCM source coding has been used, the result is referred to as PCM/IM. An attractive alternative to PCM/IM is digital PPM/IM. In M-ary PPM, the time slots are each divided into M equal intervals, and a pulse is sent during one of these intervals for each time slot. Each interval corresponds to a symbol, each of which corresponds to $\log_2 M$ bits. In each time slot, the receiver counts the number of photons in each of the intervals and takes the interval with the largest count to represent the transmitted symbol.

A detailed discussion of modulation techniques for optical sources can be found in Ref. 11.

6.8 PHOTODETECTORS

Photodetectors suitable for telecommunications use must meet several basic requirements. They must provide a high response to incident optical energy, they should add the least possible internal noise to the detected signal, they should exhibit the lowest possible susceptibility to changes in environmental conditions, especially temperature, and provide an adequate instantaneous bandwidth to respond to the information bandwidth on the optical carrier. Photodetectors are used both as receivers, and in the monitoring of source output to control source level through feedback.

6.8.1 Detector Types

Photodetectors used in telecommunications applications are silicon semiconductor devices, basically reversely biased diodes. Usually they are either the positive-intrinsic-negative (PIN) photodiode or the avalanche photodiode (APD). The APD provides internal amplification of the generated signal (by 10 to 100 times) and thus can detect lower signal levels than the PIN photodiode. For both types, the minimum detectable signal is determined by the level of internally generated noise. In the case of the PIN diodes the noise is primarily *shot noise,* resulting from random thermally generated currents. The main source of noise in APDs is the probabilistic avalanche process, in which pairs of photogenerated carriers undergo multiplication. Signal amplification results from this process [Ref. 8]. Figure 6.16 [Ref. 8]

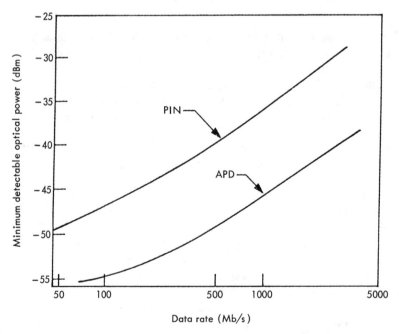

Figure 6.16 Minimum detectable optical power for $P_{be} = 10^{-9}$. (Reprinted with permission from the *AT&T Technical Journal,* copyright 1987, AT&T.)

compares the minimum detectable PIN and APD optical power levels (time-average) as a function of data rate, with minimum power being defined as the value needed to obtain $p_{be} = 10^{-9}$. The minimum power increases with data rate because binary coding is assumed, and the noise level increases with bandwidth.

A fundamental factor establishing the minimum detectable optical power is the quantum noise limit. At optical and infrared wavelengths the thermal noise limit kT, based upon the quantum mechanics principles, must be replaced by the expression.

$$P_n(f) = \frac{hf}{\left[\exp\left(\frac{hf}{kT}\right) - 1 \right]} \quad \frac{W}{Hz} \tag{6.19}$$

This means that at sufficiently high frequencies the thermal noise spectrum drops to zero, but the quantum noise term,

$$P_n(f) = hf \tag{6.20}$$

takes its place. Figure 6.17 [Ref. 13] shows how thermal noise at various temperatures compares with quantum noise up to 10 THz. Most optical sources operate at wavelengths up to 1.55 μm, corresponding to frequencies no lower than about 130

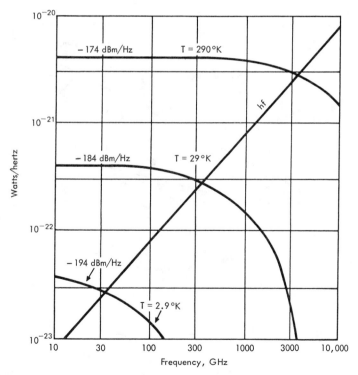

Figure 6.17 Comparison of thermal and quantum noise levels. (Copyright 1971, American Telephone and Telegraph Co. Reprinted with permission.)

THz. Thus, at and below normal room temperature, the noise limit clearly is quantum rather than thermal noise.

Silicon APDs are the choice for most telecommunications applications which need highly sensitive receivers in the vicinity of 0.8 μm. For operation at λ > 1 μm, PIN diodes are used extensively and some are capable of Gb/s operation. High sensitivity APDs are useful for long distances between repeaters, as well as at transmission rates in excess of 1.5 Gb/s.

The PIN diodes do not have the internal gain needed for high data rate long distance transmission. In addition, high *dark current* noise caused by tunneling and degraded frequency response caused by charge accumulation at heterojunction interfaces have led to the development of the *separate absorption, grading, multiplication, (SAGM) APD*. The SAGM-APD has several layers of indium-gallium arsenide-phosphide (InGaAsP) in varying compositions. It uses a narrow bandgap InGaAs layer to absorb input light and a wide bandgap indium-phosphide (InP) layer to provide carrier multiplication to solve the dark current problem. A grading layer in InGaAsP is added at the heterojunction to reduce the charge accumulation. The SAGM-APD performs well in high data rate applications, especially at 1.5 μm.

Figure 6.18, [Ref. 7], compares PIN diodes with APDs designed for 1.3 to 1.5 μm wavelengths. The PIN diodes use GaAs field-effect transistor (FET) preamplifiers with a 50 mA/V transconductance, a capacitance of 1 or 2 pF, and no

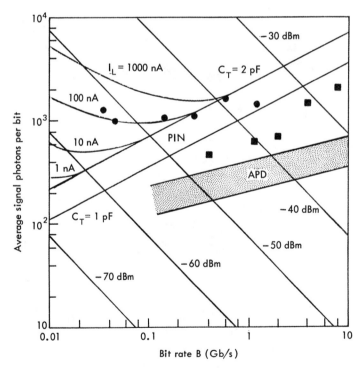

Figure 6.18   Receiver sensitivities for optical repeaters for $p_{be} = 10^{-9}$. (Reprinted with permission from the *AT&T Technical Journal*, copyright 1987, AT&T.)

leakage currents except for the values indicated on the curves sloping upward to the left. The diagonal lines sloping downward convert the energy per bit into power in dBm assuming $\lambda = 1.5$ μm. The ultimate sensitivity limit is 10 photons/bit. System noise (see Sec. 6.9) causes degradations from this limit.

The disadvantage in using APDs lies in their greater circuit complexity and bias voltage requirements. However, above 100 Mb/s, the APD has an advantage in required detector power which often justifies its use.

6.8.2 Methods of Detection

The two basic methods of detection used in optical transmission are direct detection and *heterodyne* or *homodyne* detection. Figure 6.19 illustrates the fundamental differences between these techniques. *Heterodyne* detection involves the use of a local oscillator at a frequency which differs from the signal by an intermediate frequency, whereas *homodyne* detection uses a local oscillator whose frequency is identical to that of the incoming signal. Both heterodyne and homodyne detection are discussed further in Sec. 6.10, Coherent Optical Systems.

Direct detection is used commonly in optical fiber systems to recover the information that has been transmitted over the optical waveguide channel. The varying optical intensity falling on the photodetector thus produces an electrical output proportional to the original modulating signal, whether analog or digital.

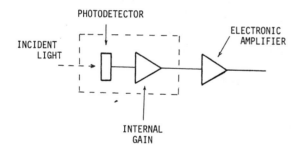

(a) Direct detection

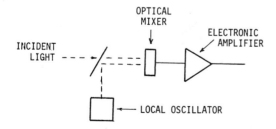

(b) Heterodyne or homodyne detection

Figure 6.19 Methods of detection. (Courtesy Dr. Leonard Bergstein.)

6.9 OPTICAL FIBER TRANSMISSION SYSTEMS

Optical fiber transmission systems exhibit two fundamental types of limits: loss and dispersion. Fiber loss is discussed in Sec. 6.4.3, and dispersion in Sec. 6.6. The loss problem must be viewed in connection with system noise level. Section 6.8 treated the noise types found in photodetectors, together with the basic quantum and thermal noise limits. Other noise types include shot noise generated in the preamplifier and speckle or modal noise resulting from source polarization fluctuations; modal noise is negligible for a single-mode fiber if no polarization dependent components are in the line.

In a *loss limited system,* the loss of the fiber, connectors, and splices equals the difference between the transmitter output and the effective receiver sensitivity, which depends upon system noise. In a *delay distortion limited system,* pulse spreading causes unrecoverable interference between pulses such that the loss limit is not reached.

Figure 6.20, [Ref. 7], illustrates the system limits reached at laboratories in the U.S., Japan, and England. The solid lines show loss and dispersion limits based upon the assumptions listed on the figure. The distance is the amount allowable between regenerative repeaters. The highest attenuation limit is achievable at 1.56 μm, and is on the order of 0.2 dB/km, with a somewhat shorter distance limit being achievable at 1.3 μm, where the dispersion limit is most favorable. However, comparison of a multiwavelength source at 1.3 μm with a single-wavelength source at 1.56 μm, [Ref. 8], shows superior performance (twice the data rate capability) at 1.56 μm with chirp being the most significant factor in setting the limit.

Most long-haul optical fiber systems in the U.S. operate at a multiple of the DS3 rate and interface with other facilities at the DSX-3 cross-connect. European

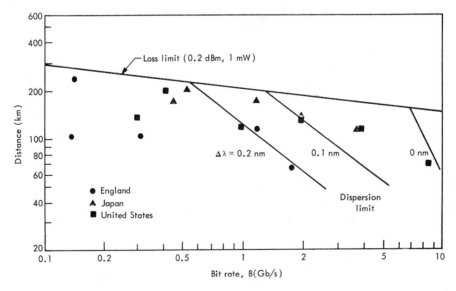

Figure 6.20 System limits. (Reprinted with permission from the *AT&T Technical Journal,* copyright 1987, AT&T.)

systems generally interface at the European fourth level (139.264 Mb/s), and Japanese systems at the Japanese fifth level (397.20 Mb/s). Generally the North American DSX-4 cross-connect has not been used for optical fiber systems [Ref. 14].

6.9.1 System Components

The major components of an optical fiber transmission system are the sources (Sec. 6.7), the fiber (Sec. 6.5), and the detectors (Sec. 6.8). Additional major system components, couplers, and repeaters, are discussed next.

6.9.1.1 Couplers. Couplers are needed to match light sources to fibers, as well as in channeling light from one fiber to another, as may be needed for a line tap or for mixing or for multiterminal applications.

In launching light into a multimode fiber, the angular divergence of the rays from the source may be greater than can be accepted by the fiber, especially if the NA of the fiber is smaller than the NA of the input rays. In addition, the radius of the input beam may exceed the core radius of the fiber. Under such conditions, the fiber is considered to be *overfilled,* i.e., the fiber cannot accept all of the light being directed into it, so a coupling loss occurs. Figure 6.21(a), [Ref. 3], illustrates the

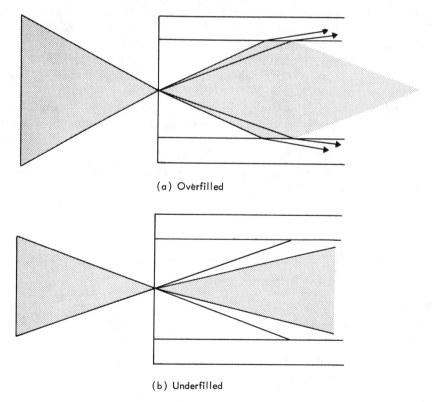

(a) Overfilled

(b) Underfilled

Figure 6.21 Light launching conditions in a multimode optical fiber. (Courtesy Newport Corporation, © 1986. Reprinted with permission.)

overfilled condition. On the other hand, for an input beam NA less than the fiber NA and an input beam radius less than the fiber's core radius, the fiber is *underfilled*, as illustrated in Fig. 6.21(b). In this case, only low-order modes will be excited in the fiber. The coupling loss for the underfilled case is much less than for the overfilled case.

In developing efficient couplers, an understanding of the directionality of the radiation from the source is important. An *isotropic* source is one that radiates uniformly in all directions, whereas a *collimated* source radiates in only one direction. In general, the angular distribution of a source is

$$W(\theta) = W_0(\cos \theta)^m \qquad \theta < (\theta_c)_{max} \tag{6.21}$$

where $(\theta_c)_{max}$ is the maximum angle at which light is admitted into the fiber as determined by Eq. (6.8). If $m = 1$ the source is called a *Lambertian* source. Large values of m correspond to a nearly collimated source. For sources from which the light is highly divergent, such as an LED, a short focal length lens may be used to focus the light on the end of the fiber. In this case the lens will be overfilled. A surface-emitting LED closely approximates a Lambertian source.

From the foregoing discussion, there are four parameters that determine the efficiency of the source-to-fiber coupling. These are the NAs of the source, the fiber, the dimensions of the source, and the fiber core. The source diameter times the NA of the source is a constant independent of the focal length of the imaging lens. If the diameter × NA product of the source is greater than the diameter × NA product of the fiber, reducing the source NA to fit the fiber NA will not increase the coupling because the result will be an enlargement of the diameter of the source image on the end of the fiber.

Coupling light to a multimode fiber is easier than coupling to a single-mode fiber. Not only must the single-mode fiber be aligned precisely to the incoming beam, but the incident electromagnetic field distribution must be matched to that of the mode to be propagated by the fiber. The profile of the HE_{11} mode in a step-index single-mode fiber can be approximated by a Gaussian distribution with an e^{-2} spatial half width, [Ref. 15], given by

$$W = a(0.65 + 1.619 \, V^{-3/2} + 2.879 \, V^{-6}) \tag{6.22}$$

where

W = width parameter of the Gaussian field
a = fiber core radius

Example

To what spot size should the incident light be focused at the fiber end face if $a = 3$ μm and $V = 2.1$?

Solution $W = 3 \times 10^{-6}[0.65 + 1.619(2.1)^{-1.5} + 2.879(2.1)^{-6}]$

$= 3.64 \times 10^{-6}$, or 3.64 μm

Thus, the incident light should be focused to a spot size which is about 1.21 times the fiber core diameter at the fiber end face.

Optical Transmission   Chap. 6

Equation (6.22) shows that, for a given fiber core size, as V becomes smaller, i.e., as λ becomes longer, the spot size must increase. Thus, the field of the mode is less well-confined within the core. Accordingly, single-mode fibers usually are selected so that the cut-off wavelength is on the order of 80% to 90% of the planned operating wavelength.

A fiber can be *butt-coupled* to its source by placing the fiber end directly on the source and using epoxy to secure the attachment. For butt coupling, the coupling efficiency η (power accepted by fiber/power emitted by source) is, [Ref. 16],

$$\eta = 0.5\,(m+1)\left[\frac{\rho}{(\rho+2)}\right] NA^2 \qquad (6.23)$$

Note that since $\rho = 2$ for a parabolic graded index profile, but $\rho \to \infty$ for the step-index profile, the parabolic graded index fiber accepts only half as much light as the step index, i.e., it exhibits an added 3 dB coupling loss. In general, the coupling loss is $10 \log_{10}(P_s/P_f)$, where P_s is the power from the source and P_f is the power launched into the fiber. Figure 6.22 [Ref. 3] shows how coupling loss varies with NA and m for $\rho \to \infty$.

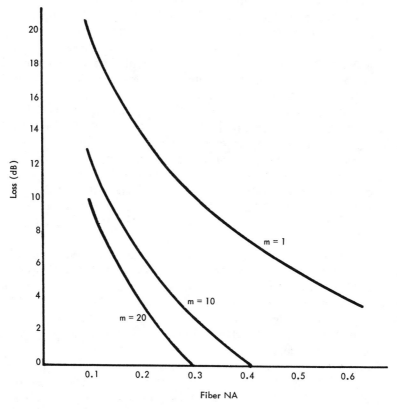

Figure 6.22 Fiber coupling loss versus *NA* and *m* for step-index fibers. (Courtesy Newport Corporation, © 1986. Reprinted with permission.)

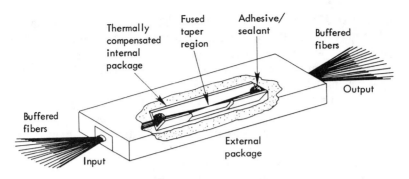

Figure 6.23 Fused biconical taper star coupler. (From D. R. Porter, P. R. Couch and J. W. Schelin, "A High-Speed Fiber Optic Data Bus for Local Data Communications," *IEEE Journal on Selected Areas in Communications,* April 1983, © 1983, IEEE. Reprinted by permission.)

Simple T and star couplers are used in a variety of data and video distribution applications. The T-coupler usually is designed with a given tap ratio, e.g., −10 dB, such that only a small portion of the optical power is intercepted at a single tap, thereby allowing an adequate amount to flow to other taps on the line. The star coupler can be designed to distribute the optical power equally among a number of lines, each feeding a terminal or other load at a distance. For the star coupler, the division loss is $10 \log_{10} n$, where n is the number of terminals to be served by the star.

Data bus applications also may require the combining of a large number of fiber lines into a single one, or the distribution of information (broadcast) to a large number of terminals simultaneously. Figure 6.23 [Ref. 17] shows a fused biconical taper (FBT) star coupler which combines a 16×16 array of fibers at rates up to 100 Mb/s. It is constructed by removing the buffer material of the individual fibers to expose their outer surfaces. The fibers then are twisted together, maintaining uniform tension, and the twisted portion is heated to form a taper region. In operation, light in the tapered fiber is coupled progressively from the fiber core as the diameter diminishes. Light then is distributed to the other fibers fused together in the taper region. As the diameter increases to the nominal value, the light is recaptured by the fiber cores. The excess loss of this coupler 2.6 dB ± 1.2 dB.

6.9.1.2 Repeaters. Regenerative repeaters are required on optical fiber lines for the same reasons as on copper cables: noise and pulse distortion. Figure 6.24 illustrates the basic features of an optical fiber regenerative repeater. Note that conversion to baseband is done to perform pulse regeneration, following which the signals are reconverted to an optical carrier for further transmission.

The basic functions performed by a regenerative repeater are pulse reshaping, retiming, regeneration, and error monitoring. A reshaping circuit amplifies the signal, compares it with a preset threshold for a decision, and reshapes the waveform. This function generally is aided by a feedback loop which serves to provide gain control. The retiming function includes timing extraction, filtering, and a limiting amplifier. Regeneration is completed through a decision circuit that discriminates between spaces and marks in the reshaped waveform and resets the

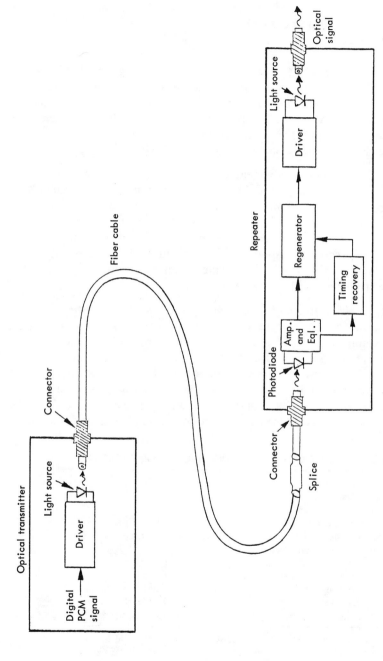

Figure 6.24 Regenerative repeater for use in fiber optic transmission. (Courtesy Dr. Leonard Bergstein.)

timing of the data using the clock signal from the retiming circuit. Error monitoring is achieved using the C bit of an *mB1C* code such as 10B1C. An alarm circuit is used to detect loss of input signal, decrease in optical output, or increase in laser diode bias current. Loss of input signal is detected by loss of timing signal.

A detailed description of the techniques used in building a 1.6 Gb/s repeater can be found in Ref. 18.

6.9.1.3 Fiber Cables. Typical specifications for a single mode fiber as used in intrastate and interstate networks, [Ref. 19], are listed in Table 6.2. Graded index fibers have cores on the order of 50 μm and greater dispersion and attenuation, but in some cases are useful for intrastate applications as well. Multimode fibers in new systems are used primarily for applications up to 10 km, although early interstate systems used such fibers in long haul applications.

6.9.1.3.1 Cable Types. Fiber cables must be built to survive inadvertent damage caused by construction work. To this end, the cables are built using Kevlar strength members, or steel or aluminum jackets, as illustrated in Figs. 6.25, 6.26, and 6.27. The cable of Fig. 6.25 is an all dielectric light weight cable with excellent crush resistance. The cable of Fig. 6.26 has an external construction that follows traditional telephone cable principles. It is a heavy duty cable that can be installed by regular crews. The cable of Fig. 6.27 achieves superior optical performance by minimizing the stress on the fiber in cable manufacture.

6.9.1.3.2. Cable Splices and Connectors. Splices and connectors both join fibers together, but splices generally are permanent joints whereas connectors are used where disconnection may be required. The major concern in the use of splices and connectors is the loss that results from such factors as fiber alignment, the end conditions of the fibers, and fiber-core parameters, such as core diameter, as well as peak index difference in multimode fibers and mode-field diameter in single-mode fibers [Ref. 20]. Figure 6.28 illustrates these and other loss causes, classifying them as *intrinsic* (mismatches) and *extrinsic* (separation, misalignment, and offset).

TABLE 6.2 TYPICAL SPECIFICATIONS FOR SINGLE-MODE FIBER

Core diameter	8.7 ± 1.3 μm
Surface diameter	125 ± 3 μm
Surface noncircularity	$\leqslant 2\%$
Coating diameter	250 ± 15 μm
Core/cladding offset	$\leqslant 1.0$ μm
Refractive index difference, Δ	$0.003 \pm 0.5\%$
Zero dispersion wavelength	1310 nm nominal
Maximum dispersion at 1310 nm ± 20 nm	3.5 ps/nm − km
Dispersion at 1550 nm	17.0 ± 2.0 ps/nm − km
Attenuation at 1310 nm	0.5 dB/km max
Attenution at 1550 nm	0.4 dB/km max

Source: From C. M. Siperko, "LaserNet—A Fiber Optic Intrastate Network (Planning and Engineering Considerations," *IEEE Communications Magazine,* May 1985, © 1985, IEEE. Reprinted by permission.

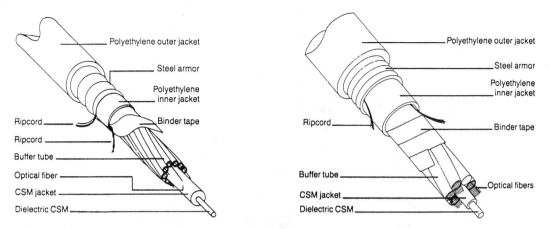

Figure 6.25 Alcatel fiber optic cables. (Courtesy Alcatel Cable Systems.)

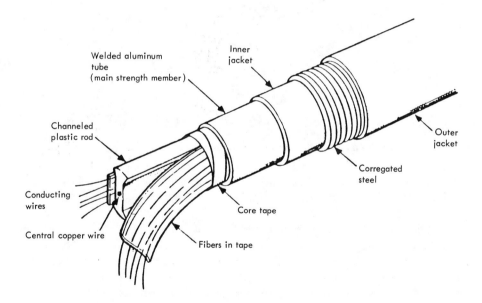

Figure 6.26 General Cable fiber optic cable. (Courtesy General Cable Co.)

Except for such short distance applications as residential distribution, local area networks (LANs) and computer/terminal connections, new fiber installations are largely single mode, with core diameters on the order of 5 to 10 μm. Splice losses are related directly to alignment acccuracy, as illustrated in Fig. 6.29, [Ref. 21], with respect to lateral offset, the largest contributor to splice loss. The larger core of the multimode fiber, on the order of 50 μm or more, makes alignment accuracy much less critical than for the single-mode fiber. Accuracy requirements

Sec. 6.9   Optical Fiber Transmission Systems   **367**

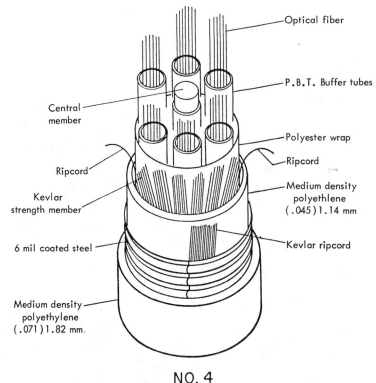

Optical fiber

P.B.T. Buffer tubes

Central member

Polyester wrap

Ripcord

Ripcord

Kevlar strength member

Medium density polyethlene (.045) 1.14 mm

6 mil coated steel

Kevlar ripcord

Medium density polyethylene (.071) 1.82 mm.

NO. 4
POLYETHYLENE STEEL POLYETHYLENE (G.P. Armor)

Figure 6.27 Siecor fiber optic cable. (Courtesy Siecor Corporation.)

are related directly to the cost of a splice or a connector. Low loss, e.g., 1 dB or less, splices are of most importance for long-haul applications to allow maximum distance between regenerative repeaters.

Splicing is done both by fusion welding and mechanical joining. For both methods the basic steps are fiber end preparation, fiber alignment, and retention of the aligned fibers as the splice is achieved. Figure 6.30 illustrates fusion welding. For single-mode fibers, alignment is done with micropositioners driven by a feedback signal to peak the signal through the splice. In spite of automatic alignment using feedback, however, resplicing often is needed to eliminate lossy splices.

Several mechanical splicing techniques are shown in Figs. 6.31, 6.32, and 6.33. In the snug-fitting tube technique of Fig. 6.31, a hole is provided for the insertion of an index-matching fluid. The collapsed-tube splice of Fig. 6.32 begins with an empty sleeve (a). The sleeve is collapsed over one fiber (b), and then the second fiber is inserted and epoxied in place (c). In the bent-fiber V-groove technique of Fig. 6.33, a platelet is brought up, bending the fibers to the groove bottom (a), then epoxy is applied and one fiber is moved (to the left) to close the gap (b). The completed splice is shown in (c). Fibers are being spliced increasingly in arrays, and connectors for arrays also are being used, allowing a multiplicity of fibers, e.g., a 12-fiber array,

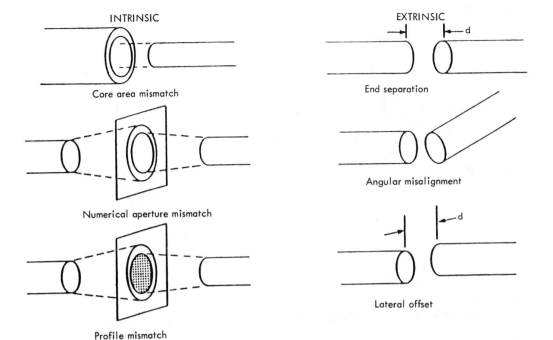

Figure 6.28 Conditions causing losses in splices and connectors. (Courtesy Mr. Robert Hoss and ITT E/O Products Divn.)

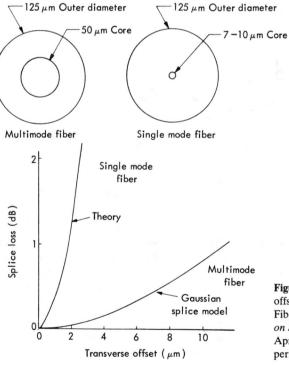

Figure 6.29 Splice loss due to lateral offset. (From C. M. Miller, "Optical Fiber Cables and Splices," *IEEE Journal on Selected Areas in Communications*, April 1983, © 1983, IEEE. Reprinted by permission.)

Sec. 6.9   Optical Fiber Transmission Systems

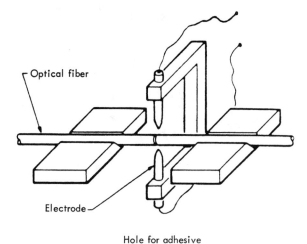

Optical fiber

Electrode

Figure 6.30 Fusion welding. (Courtesy Mr. Robert Hoss.)

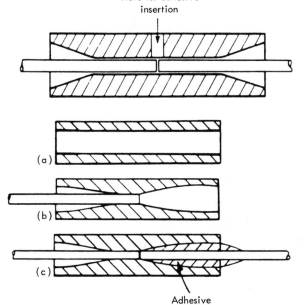

Hole for adhesive insertion

Figure 6.31 Splice using snug-fitting tube. (Courtesy Mr. Robert Hoss.)

(a)

(b)

(c)

Adhesive

Figure 6.32 Collapsed tube splice. (Courtesy Mr. Robert Hoss.)

to be joined simultaneously. Array splicing is done on both multimode and single-mode fibers. Arrays can be placed on the cable at the factory [Ref. 20]. In the field, specially formed silicon chips are used to complete the splice between two mating arrays. These chips mate with the grooves on the outside of the arrays. Mechanical springs are used to maintain alignment, and a matching gel between the arrays is used to keep the loss low over a wide range of temperature and humidity conditions. The grooved chip approach can be used in a sandwich array termination as illustrated in Fig. 6.34.

Field techniques have been developed that allow 12-fiber ribbons to be spliced in as little as 20 to 30 minutes. Short splice times are especially important in achieving rapid service restoration. For individual fiber splices, a rotary alignment

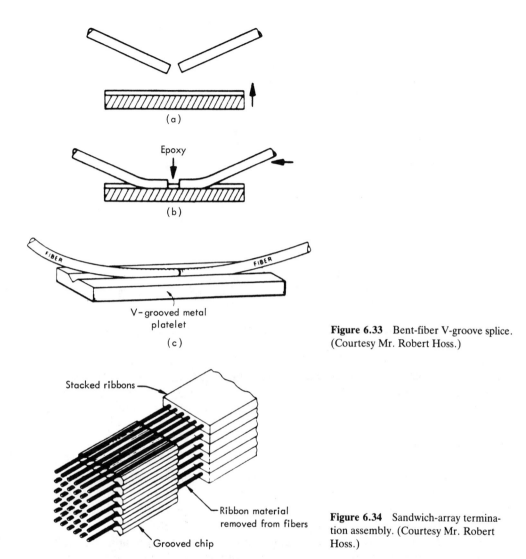

(a)

Epoxy

(b)

V-grooved metal
platelet

(c)

Figure 6.33 Bent-fiber V-groove splice. (Courtesy Mr. Robert Hoss.)

Stacked ribbons

Ribbon material
removed from fibers

Grooved chip

Figure 6.34 Sandwich-array termination assembly. (Courtesy Mr. Robert Hoss.)

technique has been developed that reduces the loss to 0.05 dB and requires only 10 minutes per splice, including testing.

Fiber connectors usually are precision-aligned butt joints with ground and polished ends. The fibers are positioned and held in supporting ferrules as the ends are ground and polished. The ferrules, usually cylindrical or conical, then are aligned in sleeve couplings. Figure 6.35, [Ref. 20] shows three types of fiber connectors, the cylindrical ferrule, the conical ferrule, and the expanded beam lens. Connectors usually have higher losses than splices because the fiber alignment cannot be optimized and matching gels normally are not used. With contacting end faces, connector losses are on the order of 0.3 to 0.5 dB or more. Loss also may result from eccentricity, e.g., 1 μm, between the bore and alignment-surface axes, diametral clearance, e.g., 2 μm, between the largest bore and the smallest fiber,

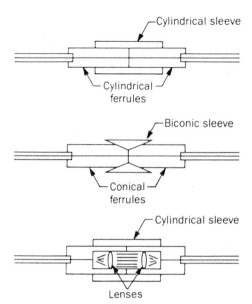

Figure 6.35 Fiber connectors. (Reprinted with permission from the *AT&T Technical Journal*. Copyright 1987, AT&T.)

and angular misalignment, e.g., 0.5°, between the bore and the alignment-surface axes.

Automated micromachining techniques yield single-mode connector losses that typically are less than 0.5 dB, with a maximum of 1.0 dB. Single-mode biconic connectors exposed to thermal cycling between −20°C and +60°C typically show loss variations of less than 0.1 dB, with a maximum of 0.3 dB, [Ref. 20].

6.9.2 Link Budgets

The link budget in a fiber optic system is calculated in a manner very similar to the link budget for a microwave radio (Chap. 4) or a satellite system, (Chap. 5). The transmitter output power is attenuated along the transmission path. The received level then is compared with the level required for a given performance criterion, usually p_{be}. The "link" under consideration in a fiber optic transmission system is the fiber connecting the laser in one regenerative repeater to the photodiode in the next regenerative repeater. Loss limits and delay distortion limits on fiber optic systems were illustrated in Fig. 6.20, which showed the loss limit to be most significant in terms of the allowable distance between regenerative repeaters, whereas delay distortion (dispersion) plays a major role in limiting transmission rate, plus a secondary role in limiting distance, especially at the highest data rates.

The factors that enter a link budget and that determine actual link margin are illustrated in Table 6.3, which consists of two examples, a 5 km T1 system and a 70 km 2 T3 system. The T1 system might be used for local area network (LAN) applications, whereas the 2 T3 system might be used for broadcast video or for a multiplexed combination of lower data rate applications. The T1 system is assumed to use an LED, whereas the 2 T3 system is assumed to use an ILD. The transmitter

TABLE 6.3 LINK BUDGET EXAMPLES

		5 km T1 System (LED)		70 km 2 T3 System (ILD)
Average transmitter output power		3.0 dBm		5.0 dBm
Transmitter performance margin		−3.0 dB		−2.0 dB
Coupling loss		−15.0 dB		−4.0 dB
Connector loss, transmitter		−1.0 dB		−1.0 dB
Fiber loss	(multimode)		(single mode)	
Loss/km	3.0 dB/km		0.4 dB/km	
Length	5 km		70 km	
Fiber loss	15.0 dB		28.0 dB	
Performance margin	2.0 dB		2.0 dB	
Loss/splice	0.2 dB		0.2 dB	
No. of splices	5		7	
Splice loss	1.0 dB		14.0 dB	
Total loss along fiber		−18.0 dB		−44.0 dB
Connector loss, receiver		−1.0 dB		−1.0 dB
Received power		−35.0 dBm		−47.0 dBm
Required power for $p_{be} = 10^{-8}$		−44.0 dBm		−53.0 dBm
System margin		9.0 dB		6.0 dB

performance margin allows for a decrease in transmitter output power with age, as well as with changes in temperature. The T1 system is assumed to use a multimode graded-index fiber, whereas the 2 T3 system is assumed to use a single-mode fiber. Note that all loss factors are entered as negative dB since they constitute subtractions from the transmitter power.

The receivers are assumed to have a *quantum efficiency* (fraction of incident photons which produce election-hole pairs) of 63%, corresponding to a 2.0 dB loss. However, this loss is incorporated into the required receive power level for $p_{be} = 10^{-8}$, so does not appear as a separate line item in the example. For the T1 system, the photodiode is assumed to be a PIN diode, whereas for the 2 T3 system the receiver is assumed to be an APD.

The link budget may be used to determine if an adequate system margin exists. Alternatively, it may be used to determine what design parameters a system must have to meet given performance requirements.

Digital fiber optic systems generally use two-level coding and an NRZ line code. As noted in Sec. 2.5.5.1, the NRZ code has its first null at $1/T_s$, which is equivalent here to $1/T_b$. Consequently, the bandwidth numerically equals the bit rate. Multilevel digital transmission generally is associated with coherent optical systems, which are described in Sec. 6.10.

Dispersion limited fiber optic systems often are described in terms of a data rate x distance product, which is a function of the operating wavelength, the source spectral width, and the profile parameter ρ. Manufacturers may refer to length dependent factor γ such that the distance × data rate product actually equals (distance)$^{\gamma}$ × data rate, where $0.7 \leqslant \gamma \leqslant 1.0$.

The *system rise time* is defined as the time required for the output voltage to rise from 10% to 90% of its final value. For NRZ pulses the system rise time should not exceed 0.7 T_b. The overall system rise time is the root sum square of the transmitter rise time, receiver rise time, and the time delay spreads due to material dispersion and to multimode dispersion. A 10% increase in this root sum square value normally is added, [Ref. 22, Eq. 8.44; Ref. 3, Eq. 8.1].

6.9.3 Wavelength Division Multiplexing

Wavelength division multiplexing (WDM) functions using the same principle as does frequency-division multiplexing. Each optical carrier uses a unique wavelength (frequency). This permits the simultaneous transmission of different types of signals, as well as bidirectional transmission, on a single fiber. Figure 6.36 illustrates the WDM concept. The WDM multiplex coupler consists of wavelength-selective components such as gratings, prisms, or thin-film filters for combining the signals from the input fibers onto the single transmission fiber. The wavelength demultiplex coupler uses similar components. Wavelengths as closely spaced as 1.5 nm have been distinguished from one another in laboratory tests [Ref. 23].

The performance of WDM multiplexers and demultiplexers is evaluated in terms of their insertion loss and crosstalk. The insertion loss is defined as the output power divided by the sum of the input powers. Insertion loss usually can be kept as low as 1 to 2 dB for laser sources. Crosstalk measurements at the demultiplexer output show that crosstalk levels usually are on the order of −25 dB or less.

A fiber development of special significance in WDM is the quadruply clad fiber [Ref. 24]. This technique provides depressions (wells) in the index of refraction that allow shifts in the wavelength of minimum dispersion. Thus the material dispersion can be minimized at two wavelengths for a wide spectral range of operation. Fig. 6.37 illustrates the measured material dispersion of an experimental quadruply clad fiber. Such a fiber alleviates mode-partition noise problems associated with the use of multilongitudinal mode lasers, allowing many high bit rate channels to be wavelength division multiplexed together.

Applications of WDM are widespread. Systems using WDM are operational in Japan, Europe, and the U.S. with one major U.S. system, Lightnet, using WDM

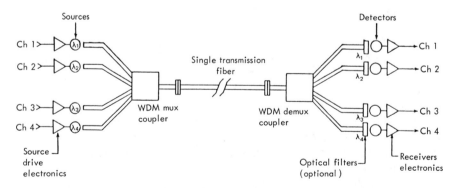

Figure 6.36 Wavelength division multiplexing. (Courtesy Alcatel Cable Systems.)

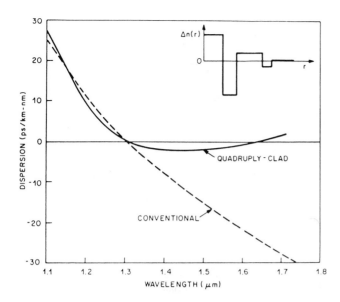

Figure 6.37 Dispersion of quadruply clad fiber. (From T. Li, "Advances in Optical Fiber Communications: An Historical Perspective," *IEEE Journal on Selected Areas in Communications,* April 1983, © 1983, IEEE. Reprinted by permission.)

extensively. The applications include not only intercity networks, but also wideband multiservice networks, CATV and multiservice subscriber systems.

6.9.4 Optical Fiber Applications

As shown in the subsequent portions of this section, fiber optic transmission is applicable to a wide variety of systems for telephony (switched systems). Applications to broadband cable systems and data bus configurations are discussed in Chap. 7. Systems being installed operate at transmission rates of 400 to 800 Mb/s for long-haul applications, as well as for some short distance purposes and achieve values of $p_{be} \leqslant 10^{-9}$ using regenerative repeater spacings of 40 km and greater. The fibers used typically are single mode at 1.3 μm and achieve attenuations well-under 1 dB/km. Analog systems often use FM of one or several RF carriers, while digital systems commonly use PCM for voice and video. Fiber optic transmission technology has been applied extensively to systems for telephony and related applications. Described next are operational systems for long-haul applications followed by those for shorter distance and then local loop applications.

6.9.4.1 Operational Long-Haul Systems. Long haul fiber optic systems have been installed across all of the developed countries of the world, and also span the Atlantic and Pacific Oceans. The rapid advances that have been achieved mean that a system may be out of date by an order of magnitude in performance within a few years of its first deployment [Ref. 25]. Thus lightwave systems must be designed for easy upgrading to higher line rates. One way of achieving upgrading is through the use of WDM. Table 6.4, [Ref. 19] illustrates some of the possibilities.

TABLE 6.4 GROWTH CAPACITY OF FIBER OPTIC SYSTEMS

Voice Channel Coding	64 KBPS PCM	64 KBPS w/DSI (2:1)	32 KBPS ADPCM	32 KBPS w/DSI (2:1)
Optical Channel Transmission Speed	Number of Available Voice Channels			
405 Mbps	6048	12096	12096	23192
1.3 Gbps	18144	36288	36288	72576
1.8 Gbps	24192	48384	48384	96768

Wave Division Multiplexing

Development of single longitudinal mode (SLM) or single frequency lasers will provide reduced spectral width and improved spectrum stability permitting multiplexing of many lightwave channels on a single fiber.

For example, if 3, 5, and 10 optical channels are multiplexed on a single fiber, the number of available voice channels (32 Kbps ADPCM with DSI) are:

Number of Optical Channels	Number of Available Voice Channels
3	290304
5	483840
10	967680

Source: From C. M. Spierko, "LaserNet—A Fiber Optic Intrastate Network (Planning and Engineering Considerations)," *IEEE Communications Magazine*, May 1985, © 1985, IEEE. Reprinted by permission.

The major electronics components of a lightwave system are (1) terminal multiplex equipment, which combines incoming digital streams into the line rate, (2) terminal regenerators, which convert between the electrical line rate and pulses of light on the fiber, (3) line regenerators to reconstruct the original optical pulses, when needed, and (4) a maintenance subsystem that monitors error performance, provides for automatic protection switching, and alerts maintenance personnel to system problems, including the diagnosing of terminal failures as well as fault location.

The link budget parameters for the AT&T FT Series G 417 Mb/s and 1.7 Gb/s systems, [Ref. 26], are shown in Table 6.5. Because the system is designed for upgrading from the 417 Mb/s to the 1.7 Gb/s capability, the link budgets are the same, allowing for reliable operation at regenerative repeater spacings up to 40 km for either system. The architectures of the two systems are similar, except for the multiplexing schemes. The increase from 417 Mb/s to 1.7 Gb/s is achieved at a single wavelength, 1.31 μm, through the use of higher speed multiplexing and electro-optic conversion on the same circuit pack to minimize connection length. In addition, a new laser using the *metal-organic chemical vapor deposition (MOCVD)* process was developed having an improved frequency response. Moreover, high-speed multiplexing circuits use submicron silicon *n-type metal-oxide semiconductors (NMOS)* to achieve the overall 1.7 Gb/s rate while maintaining modest power

TABLE 6.5 LINK BUDGET PARAMETERS FOR AT&T
FT SERIES G SYSTEMS

Transmitter output power	−2.0 dBm
Receiver sensitivity ($p_{be} = 3 \times 10^{-11}$)	−32.3 dBm
System gain	30.3 dB
System allowance	6.0 dB
Facility loss	24.3 dB
Connector loss	1.3 dB
Available for outside plant, office jumper cables, and additional connectors	23.0 dB

Source: Reprinted with permission from the *AT&T Technical Journal.* Copyright 1987, AT&T.

consumption and dissipation. Achieving the 1.7 Gb/s rate in the FT Series G 1.7 Gb/s system without using WDM results in a cost saving in that the electronics did not have to be replicated for each wavelength used. Thus costs of electronic multiplexing are significantly less than those of WDM.

The achievement of modulation rates beyond 2 Gb/s probably will require the replacement of high-speed silicon technology with gallium arsenide (GaAs) technology [Ref. 26]. Coherent optical systems (see Sec. 6.10) using external modulators made of lithium niobate may achieve modulation rates as high as 8 Gb/s or more.

New submarine cable systems such as the transatlantic TAT-8 and TAT-9 use fiber optic transmission, as does the transpacific HAW-4/TPC-3. A transatlantic fiber link for video transmission is being built by Submarine Lightwave Cable. Reliability of utmost importance in a submarine cable system [Ref. 27]. Any deepwater failure would entail not only very high repair costs but also a huge loss of revenue. The reliability target for TAT-8 is fewer than three system repairs in 25 years of system life. This requirement translates into minimal parts counts and single mode fiber to maximize repeater spacing. Redundancy of critical components further enhances system reliability. Fiber strength and cable design as well as repeater design must protect the system during cable laying as well as during operation in the deep-sea environment. Back-up satellite circuits on *Intelsat* will be implemented should a circuit failure occur.

6.9.4.2 Subscriber Carrier Systems. Laser diodes or edge-emitting diodes and single-mode fibers form the basis for many new feeder cable systems designed for subscriber carrier system service between central offices and clusters of remote subscribers. By using a lightwave multiplexer a large number of voice channels can be accomodated on a single fiber. Moreover, the capacity of such an arrangement allows local telephone operating companies to upgrade the bit rate provided to subscribers by upgrading the electronics. Examples of subscriber carrier systems are the AT&T DDM-1000 lightwave multiplexer and the SLC® Series 5 carrier system for loop applications, [Ref. 28]. The DDM-1000 contains two DS3 muldems which can be connected through a DSX-3 cross-connect, or connected internally to a 90 Mb/s lightwave transmitter/receiver. The SLC® Series 5 carrier system is microprocessor based and is capable of BRZ or B8ZS line coding, selectable with dip switches. The Series 5 interfaces with the DDM-1000 at the DS1 rate.

6.9.4.3 Subscriber Loop Applications.

Subscriber loops generally connect business and residential subscribers to local telephone exchanges using twisted-pair copper wire. (The term local loop includes both the feeder system of Sec. 6.9.4.1.2 and the final connection to the subscriber's instrument.) The use of twisted-pair copper to the subscriber limits the total bit rate or bandwidth that can be provided. Replacement of the entire subscriber loop with fiber thus would remove the existing bandwidth limitation. Such replacement largely is a matter of economics. In order for economics to favor the large scale usage of fiber all the way to the end instrument, a low cost, e.g., less than $100, optical transceiver combining the light source and detection functions into a single unit must be achieved. The use of LEDs with single-mode fiber may allow such a transceiver to be built, allowing a 140 Mb/s upstream rate. The downstream rate from the telephone exchange could be on the order of 565 Mb/s, readily achievable by using laser diodes at the exchange end [Ref. 29].

6.9.5 Photonic Switching

The use of fiber for the transmission of optical signals motivates the implementation of switching in the optical domain as well, to avoid the need for conversion of signals from the optical to the electrical form. The term *photonic switching* implies an optically controlled switching process. Such processes have been developed, but the term also is being applied more generally to the switching of optical signals [Ref. 30]. A major portion of the research activity actually lies in the electronic switching of optical signals.

By definition an optical switch receives an optical signal at an input port and directs that signal to one of two or more output ports in response to a control signal. A *relational* optical switch is one whose switching behavior is independent of the bits traversing it whereas a *logical* optical switch is controlled by the input signals in such a way that some Boolean function is performed on the inputs [Ref. 31]. Note that *switching* as used in this section refers to the changing of the current state of a device to an alternate state, as opposed to the "switching" that is analogous to an interconnection network configuration.

Electro-mechanical switching uses mechanically activated optical switch crosspoints. Switching times are on the order of milliseconds, but loss is low and the switch is not sensitive to wavelength or polarization.

Acousto-optic switching is achieved by deflecting the input light by means of an acoustical wave propagating in a Bragg cell. Switching is somewhat faster than for the electro-mechanical approach, but is wavelength dependent.

Fiber switching can be done using an all-fiber Mach-Zehnder interferometer with fiber directional couplers. The light sent into either of the two output ports depends on the path imbalance of the interferometer. Changes are produced by the piezo-electric effect or thermally, so switching speeds are slow and the result is wavelength dependent.

Electro-optic switching uses an optical directional coupler controlled electrically using lithium niobate or a III-V semiconductor material. An electrode structure is positioned so it changes the relative refractive indices in two optical waveguides. The device actually has two input ports A and B and two output ports C and D with data beng transferred from A to C and B to D (bypass mode) or from A to D and B to C (exchange mode). Application of the electrical control signal causes the device to switch between the bypass and the exchange modes. Electro-optic switching is attracting the most research activity, with major interest being focused on devices formed using titanium diffused guides in lithium niobate. Electro-optic switches can achieve subnanosecond switching times, but are several millimeters in size, making large switching matrices bulky. Crosstalk may be a problem. The devices are wavelength dependent and have limited optical bandwidths.

Optically activated switching can be achieved using several approaches consisting either of nonlinear optical techniques or optical plus electronic techniques. Interest in optically activated switching has been stimulated by the possibility of using two dimensional arrays of devices along with free-space optical systems. The free-space systems allow the parallel switching of many beams, and thus increased speed through parallel transmission. One approach to optically activated switching is based on angular deflection produced by a dynamic holographic grating recorded in a photorefractive crystal or on a thermoplastic film [Ref. 30]. The angle of deflection is changed by changing the wavelength of the light. Switching times are on the order of milliseconds. Another approach uses optically bistable devices constructed using a Fabry-Perot etalon structure containing a nonlinear material. The transmission of the device depends on the intensity of the incident light. The transfer characteristic shows a threshold optical switching intensity and bistability. Switching speeds vary from milliseconds to picoseconds. However, the power requirements for large switch arrays using this principle thus far have been excessive. A third approach to optically controlled switching is the application of hybrid technology using opto-electronic switching elements that consist of photodetectors and modulators linked with electronic logic elements. Systems of 64×64 ports operating at 1 Gb/s and higher appear to be feasible using this approach [Ref. 30].

The power required to switch equals the switching energy divided by the switching time. Switching energy is determined by normal operating region of a device and usually is fixed. Thus as switching time is decreased, the required power increases.

Example:

A photonic device has an area of 80 μm^2 and a switching energy of 1 fJ/μm^2 to change states. How much power is required to change states in 1 ps? In 1 ns?

Solution The power required to change states in 1 ps is 80 fJ/1 ps or 80 mW. The power required to change states in 1 ns is 80 fJ/1 ns or 80 μW.

The use of photonic switching together with the other techniques discussed earlier in this section leads to the optical telecommunications network of Fig. 6.38.

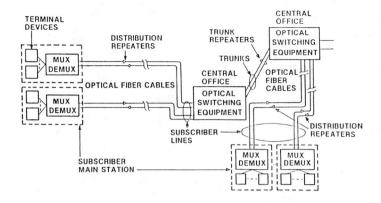

Figure 6.38 Optical telecommunications network. (Courtesy Mr. Robert Hoss and ITT E/O Products Divn.)

6.10 COHERENT OPTICAL SYSTEMS

6.10.1 Description

While lasers often are referred to loosely as "monochromatic" sources, the discussions of Sec. 6.6.2 and 6.7.3 indicated that lasers actually emit light within a band of wavelengths $\Delta\lambda$ or, alternatively, a spectral bandwidth Δf, which may actually exceed the information bandwith W.

The spectral bandwidth Δf can be expressed in terms of the free-space wavelength width $\Delta\lambda$ as

$$\Delta f = \frac{\Delta\lambda c}{\lambda^2} \tag{6.24}$$

where λ is the free-space wavelength emitted by the source.

A *coherent optical communication system* is one in which light is treated as a carrier that can be modulated in amplitude, frequency or phase. Fig. 6.39 [Ref. 32] shows the basic configuration of a coherent optical system. Note the use of a laser control function at the transmitter as well as a local oscillator control function at the receiver. Modulation of the laser may be internal rather than the external type shown in Fig. 6.39. In some cases a post-amplifier is added to the transmitter output to compensate for modulator power loss as well as to provide the maximum input power for the fiber being used.

The receiver may operate on the *heterodyne* principle, in which case $\lambda_1 \neq \lambda_2$, or on the *homodyne* principle, for which $\lambda_1 = \lambda_2$. Homodyne detection obtains the demodulated baseband signal directly via optical mixing. Heterodyne detection uses a square-law detector since a difference frequency, or intermediate frequency (IF), must be formed. The baseband then is recovered from the IF using envelope, differential, or synchronous detection.

Coherent optical detectors are sensitive to the polarization of both the received signal and that of the local oscillator. Accordingly, the optical fiber must maintain the polarization of the transmitted light or the receiver must have a means of correcting the received polarization. Single-mode fibers are used with coherent optical systems so that the optical phase front does not become distorted. Optical

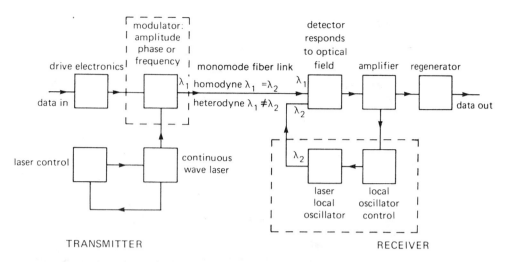

Figure 6.39 Coherent optical communication system. (From I. W. Stanley, "A Tutorial Review of Techniques for Coherent Optical Fiber Transmission Systems," *IEEE Communications Magazine,* Aug. 1985, © 1985, IEEE. Reprinted by permission.)

amplifiers or injection locked laser oscillators may be installed along the fiber to compensate for fiber loss.

6.10.2 Advantages

Coherent optical systems exhibit numerous advantages. Direct detection APD receivers at 1.3 to 1.55 μm require about 700 photons/bit for binary NRZ signals to achieve $p_{be} = 10^{-9}$. By comparison, coherent detection requirements are shown in Table 6.6 [Ref. 33]. While this table shows that ideal direct detection receivers require only 10 photons/bit, the best receivers are 17 to 20 dB worse than that ideal, and probably will remain at 10 dB from the ideal even with expected noise level reductions in the photodetector and electronic amplifier following it. By contrast, the best coherent receivers are only about 3 dB from the ideal. Such reductions in receiver noise leave the main remaining noise source as quantum noise of the transmitted light signal.

Coherent systems allow an improvement of the power handling level in single-mode fibers using angle modulation, [Ref. 34]. While industrial multimode fibers are capable of continuous wave power densities of $10^3 W/mm^2$ and total levels of 2 kW or more, the limits are quite different for single-mode fibers in view of the nonlinear interaction that occurs in their core in the form of *stimulated Brillouin scattering (SBS)* or *stimulated Raman scattering (SRS)*. SBS limits the power handling capability of noncoherent intensity modulated direct detection systems to 2 to 3 mW at $\lambda = 1.55$ μm. (The limit is not evident in noncoherent systems because of the significant amount of frequency chirping produced.) Angle modulation of a coherent system (constant amplitude) not only alleviates SBS, but also suppresses self-phase modulation, which limits the input power to a fiber to several hundred

TABLE 6.6 SENSITIVITY LIMITS FOR OPTICAL
DETECTION TECHNIQUES

Detection Technique	Sensitivity Limit, Photons/bit
Direct detection	10
Coherent heterodyne	
ASK	36
FSK	36
PSK	18
Coherent homodyne	
ASK	18
PSK	9

Source: From R. A. Linke and P. S. Henry, "Coherent Optical Detection: A thousand Calls on One Circuit," *IEEE Spectrum,* Feb.
1987, © 1987, IEEE. Reprinted by permission.

milliwatts. This leaves SBS as the remaining limiting factor, at a level of several watts, [Ref. 34].

Another advantage of coherent optical systems is the removal of the chromatic dispersion limit exhibited by single mode fibers with noncoherent sources. The WDM of large numbers of carriers also becomes feasible. Improvements of up to 20 dB in receiver sensitivity and on the order of 30 dB in transmitted level (see Sec. 6.10.3) allow appreciable increases in the length of an unrepeatered span. At a 1 Gb/s data rate (two-level coding) a coherent system can tolerate a transmission loss up to 90 dB, corresponding to a fiber length on the order of 400 km [Ref. 34]. This has very significant implications for undersea cable systems, in which the number of repeaters must be minimized for reliability reasons.

A further advantage lies in the use of heterodyne or homodyne detection followed by an electronic filter for removing unwanted noise outside the baseband. Such noise may arise from the spontaneous emission produced by optical ampli-fiers.

6.10.3 Amplifiers

A variety of optical amplifiers are available for either linear or saturated power output. Linear amplifiers such as the resonant-type Fabry-Perot and traveling-wave type amplifiers are capable of 0 to 10 dBm output levels at 1.55 μm. Injection locked lasers can be used to amplify angle modulated signals and achieve outputs of 10 to 20 dBm. Phase-locked array oscillators can achieve several watts of output on a saturated basis for amplifying angle modulated signals. Their levels thus are on the order of 30 dB higher than the Fabry-Perot or traveling-wave type amplifiers.

6.10.4 Modulation and Detection

Angle modulation is the preferred approach for coherent optical systems because higher level amplifiers can be used than for amplitude modulation and because of the good receiver sensitivities possible. Fig. 6.40 [Ref. 34] illustrates five transmitter

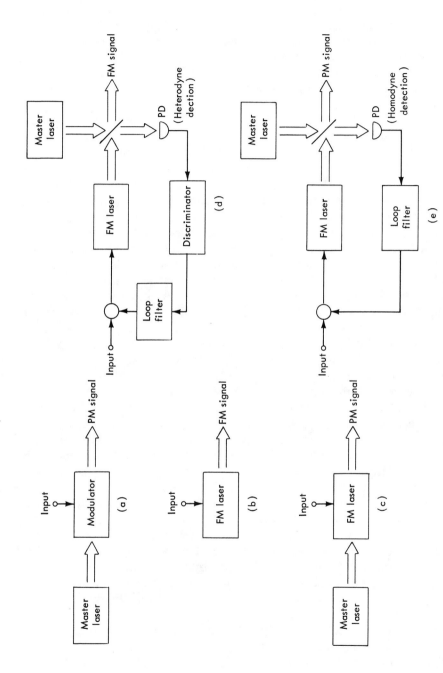

Figure 6.40 Transmitter configurations for angle modulation. (From T. Kimura, "Coherent Optical Fiber Transmission," *Journal of Lightwave Technology*, April 1987, © 1987, IEEE. Reprinted by permission.)

configurations for angle modulation. In Fig. 6.40(a), PSK (digital PM) is produced using a guided-wave electrooptic phase modulator after a frequency stabilized CW laser. Direct FSK (digital FM) is illustrated in Fig. 6.40(b). An optical FSK signal is obtained by modulating the injection current of a single-longitudinal mode semiconductor laser. A frequency shift of 100 MHz to 1 GHz can be obtained without serious intensity modulation. An external cavity can be used to narrow the overall spectral output of the laser with only modest degradation of the FM. In addition, the modulation input current can be electrically equalized to precompensate for nonuniform FM characteristics.

Direct PSK is illustrated in Fig. 6.40(c). This is achieved by direct current modulation of a semiconductor laser into which coherent laser light is injected. Phase modulation is produced by detuning the injected laser frequency away from the input light frequency to the locking bandwidth limit. The cutoff modulation frequency is controlled by the injecton locking bandwidth. Even if the injection locked laser has a broad inherent spectral linewidth, the width is reduced to the level of the injected signal linewidth.

Frequency modulation using optical FM feedback (FMFB) is illustrated in Fig. 6.40(d). Here a fraction of the output signal from an FM semiconductor laser is demodulated by a heterodyne detector followed by a frequency discriminator. The "master laser" has a very stable frequency and a narrow linewidth. The demodulated signal is phase reversed (to produce negative feedback) and fed back to the input. This FMFB approach suppresses both the FM noise and the nonuniform FM response of a semiconductor laser.

Fig. 6.40(e) illustrates a phase-locked loop (PLL) using homodyne detection for producing PSK. Here the loop bandwidth of the PLL determines the modulation cutoff frequency. Loop delay time limits the effective modulation bandwidth so it must be minimized through careful circuit integration.

Amplitude-shift keying (ASK) is of interest primarily for local distribution applications because of its simplicity and its less stringent requirements regarding source linewidth. The performance of an ASK system becomes degraded substantially only when the laser linewidth becomes broad enough that the IF bandwidth must be increased to pass all the signal energy. The result then is greater noise bandwidth and poorer performance [Ref. 35].

Coherent detection systems require a narrow linewidth if they are to produce low bit error probability. For $p_{be} = 10^{-9}$, the curves of Fig. 6.41, [Ref. 34], apply. Generally the spectral linewidth of the optical carrier as well as that of the local oscillator must be no more than 10^{-3} to 10^{-4} times the transmission data rate. Fig. 6.42 [Ref. 32] shows typical linewidths of several optical sources. For the external cavity, the linewidth is determined by mechanical vibrations of the cavity. An AFC loop reduces the linewidth further. A tuning range of 55 nm has been achieved for the external cavity.

Because optical PLLs (for homodyne detection) present construction difficulties, most coherent systems have used heterodyne detection. However, heterodyne detection is not as sensitive as homodyne detection, as can be seen from Table 6.6. In the heterodyne systems the carrier and local oscillator continually slip in and out

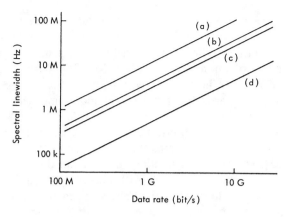

(a) FSK heterodyne detection with frequency shift equal to symbol rate

(b) PSK heterodyne differential detection

(c) FSK heterodyne detection with frequency shift of 0.5 × symbol rate

(d) PSK heterodyne synchronous detection and PSK homodyne detection (PLL bandwidth = 0.01 × symbol rate)

Figure 6.41 Spectral linewidth required for coherent detection systems. (From T. Kimura. "Coherent Optical Fiber Transmission," *Journal of Lightwave Technology,* April 1987, © 1987, IEEE. Reprinted by permission.)

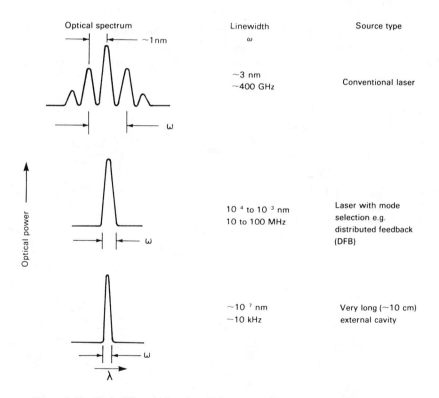

Figure 6.42 Typical linewidths of optical sources. (From I. W. Stanley, "A Tutorial Review of Techniques for Coherent Optical Fiber Transmission Systems," *IEEE Communications Magazine,* Aug. 1985, © 1985, IEEE. Reprinted by permission.)

of phase with one another. The receiver's sensitivity is best at the in-phase condition, but approaches zero as the 90° condition is approached. The IF signal constitutes an average of these conditions, resulting in the sensitivity of a heterodyne receiver being 3 dB poorer than that of a homodyne receiver [Ref. 33]. With OOK, heterodyne detection is 6 dB porrer than homodyne, with $p_{be} = 10^{-9}$ requiring 36 photons/bit. Fig. 6.43 [Ref. 32] compares the heterodyne and homodyne approaches versus direct detection.

For wavelength division multiplex applications, the minimum channel spacing when using heterodyne detection is two to five times the bandwidth of the modulated optical spectrum, [Ref. 35], whereas with homodyne detection the channel spacing need only equal the bandwidth. Binary ASK with prefiltering requires a bandwidth of 2 *W*. For wide-deviation binary FSK the bandwidth may be 5 *W* to 10 *W*. For MSK, the bandwidth may be approximately *W*, but with increased demodulator complexity. Binary PSK requires a bandwidth of 2 *W*. The choice of line code also enters into the bandwidth determination, as was outlined in Chap. 2.

6.10.5 Application Areas

The potential applications of coherent optical systems in long-haul telecommunications are very significant, as has been noted in Sec. 6.10.2. For such applications, PSK with homodyne detection appears to offer the best long term potential. Coher-

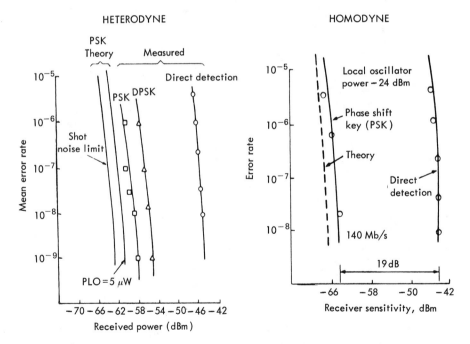

Figure 6.43 Coherent optical system performance comparisons with direct detection. (From I. W. Stanely, "A Tutorial Review of Techniques for Coherent Optical Fiber Transmission Systems," *IEEE Communications Magazine,* Aug. 1985, © 1985, IEEE. Reprinted by permission.)

ent systems also are applicable to shorter distance usage such as for local networks. For such networks, coherent system advantages lie in the provision of very large bandwidths, e.g., 50 THz, with the topological flexibility of locating such components as multiplexers, power splitters, and photonic switches where most convenient. One may ask the purpose of such bandwidths as 50 THz. No one source or destination on a network would require anything close to such bandwidth, but each source on such a network may produce its own wideband information, just as each destination will access only a small portion of the bandwidth at a time. The key is the network flexibility afforded by the bandwidth capability. Switching functions then may be located at the exchange, at customers' terminals, or at intermediate points. Such a network need not be dependent on a particular modulation format or information rate [Ref. 35]. Switching could be done on a space, wavelength, or time basis. Detection could be on either a coherent or a direct basis. The use of single-mode fiber also is under consideration for the local loop plant, thus reducing the likelihood of premature obsolescence of the installed fiber plant. Such fiber plant can serve direct modulation and detection systems initially and coherent systems in the future providing interconnection with 50THz local networks. In fact, standards committees meeting to define broadband ISDN interface rates have been discussing feeder loop bit rates in the range of several Gb/s [Ref. 29]. A special long-term advantage of coherent optics for the local loop, where many terminals may receive signals simultaneously, is that the large gain available with coherent optics can compensate for the bridging loss that predominates in passive distribution systems [Ref. 34].

6.10.6 Implementation Requirements

The rapid increases that have been achieved in fiber bandwidth-distance product may reach 1000 Tb/s-km using coherent detection, MFSK, WDM, and SiO_2 fiber [Ref. 29]. For coherent optical transmission to be implemented commercially, demultiplexing techniques for closely spaced WDM carriers will be useful. Tunable low-cost heterodyne receivers and single-mode optical star couplers also must be made available commercially.

For subscriber loop applications, large scale integration (LSI) of the regenerator, multiplexer and switches of the terminal electronics must be achieved. Optoelectronic integrated circuits (OEICs) are being developed to provide such terminal control functions as modulation, switching, and tunable filtering. *Titanium-diffused lithium niobate (Ti:LiNbO$_3$)* waveguide modulators have become available commercially for use in loop applications [Ref. 29].

6.11 OPTICAL FIBER SYSTEM STANDARDS

In any telecommunications system, standardization is important so that fiber interfaces between different owners or operators, known as *midfiber meets,* can be specified without lengthy negotiations. Work toward standardization has been done in the areas of optical, signal, and physical parameters.

Optical parameter standardization is being addressed [Ref. 36] in the areas of wavelength, spectrum line width, fiber attenuation and dispersion, and waveshape, as well as sources and detectors. Such parameters, especially attenuation and dispersion, are difficult to standardize because of the rapid technological advances being made. Standards must serve present-day situations without hampering future creativity, especially as increased capabilities become available. Areas for optical parameter standardization include definitions and measurement techniques, methodologies for regenerative section design, and values of parameters for transmission systems [Ref. 36].

Signal parameter standardization includes the establishment of standard rates and formats. Many present optical systems are being built to operate at a multiple of DS3 (44.736 Mb/s) or DS4E (139.268 Mb/s), and these levels often are used for interconnection. Physical parameter standardization includes fiber core size, splicing and coupling techniques as well as connectors.

Standards developed for local area networks include the ANSI X3T9.5 *Fiber Distributed Data Interface (FDDI)*, the AT&T Information Systems *Premises Distribution System (PDS)*, and the IBM Cabling System, Type 5 Fiber. All three call for the use of multimode fiber, use LED sources, and provide transmission distances to 2 km.

An alternative to the ANSI Fiber Distributed Data Interface (FDDI) is FDDI-II which is circuit switched and allocates the 100 Mb/s rate in increments of 6.144 Mb/s isochronous channels [Ref. 37]. Each of the 16 isochronous channels provides a full duplex capability that may be reallocated into three 2.048 Mb/s or four 1.536 Mb/s streams. A token channel at a 1 Mb/s rate also is available. FDDI-II allows a total of 1000 physical connections (500 stations) over a total path of 200 km (100 km of cable). FDDI connections between stations are made with a dual fiber cable using a duplex connector. FDDI-II is fully interoperable with basic FDDI prior to the assignment of isochronous channels. The presence of non-FDDI-II capable stations in a ring, however, prevents the assignment of isochronous channels. FDDI is being developed consistent with the *Open Systems Interconnection (OSI)* model of the International Organization for Standardization (ISO). The OSI model is outlined in Chapter 7.

Data encoding for FDDI has 4 information bits for every 5 transmitted bits and is called 4B/5B. Of the 32 member symbol set, 16 are data symbols, 3 symbols are used for line-state signaling, 2 are control indicators, and 3 are used for starting and ending delimiters. The remaining 8 symbols are not used since they violate code run length and DC balance requirements. Information is transmitted in frames around a ring with a token being used (see Chap. 7) to designate the terminal being allowed to transmit.

The FDDI-II standard is being developed to meet a variety of requirements, including both packet and circuit switching of voice, video and data, for such applications as the distributed processing environment. The dual-ring topology approach of FDDI is especially useful since fiber transmission is best suited to point-to-point applications. Point-to-point topology leads to active hub-star and ring connections [Ref. 38]. (Passive stars may lead to too much loss because of signal strength division.) The active star may be subject to a single point failure that can disable an entire local area network. Single ring networks also may fail at any node. The dual-ring approach of FDDI alleviates this problem.

Fiber standards for long-haul applications include the *Synchronous, Optical Network (SONET), Metrobus,* and the EIA Class 4A Fiber, Nondispersion-shifted. SONET is sponsored by Bell Communications Research (BELLCORE) and the Exchange Carriers Standards Association (ECSA) and is known as T1 × 1.2/.4. Metrobus is sponsored by AT&T Network Systems. The EIA standard is designated F06.6. All three call for monomode fiber with laser sources. Distances between repeaters range from 30 to 52 km.

6.12 ATMOSPHERIC OPTICAL AND INFARED TRANSMISSION

The techniques used to transmit data through fibers also are used, in modified forms, for transmission through the atmosphere. One such application is to local area networks. The purpose is to provide broadband, e.g., 30 MHz, access to larger communication systems such as fiber optic, microwave, or satellite, where such access is hindered by local obstructions such as roads or buildings [Ref. 39]. One such system, by General Optronics, Edison, NJ, has the following characteristics:

Transmitter: 2 mW GaAℓAs injection laser diode
Transmit antenna: 7.5 cm exit aperture (Galilean telescope)
                  1.6 mr beam divergence
Receive antenna: 20 cm aperture (f/5 Schmidt-Cassegrain receiver)
                  0.8 mr FOV
APD gain: 100 (RCA C30817)
Wavelength: 820 nm
Optical filter bandwidth: 10 nm
System bandwidth: 300 MHz
Receiver bandwidth: 20 MHz
System loss margin: 40 dB

Atmospheric attenuation at 820 nm is 0.31 dB/km during 25 km visibility (sunny, clear weather) and 1.36 dB/km during 5 km visibility (hazy weather with weak turbulence). Accordingly, an AGC compensates for atmospheric turbulence intensity fluctuatons along the link.

Infared (IR) transmission also is applicable indoors to allow the interconnection and the remote control of devices without the use of wires. Such a capability is especially useful in avoiding extensive wiring as well as in providing flexibility in locating terminals [Ref. 40]. Advantages of IR over RF techniques are that it does not interfere with existing RF systems and generally IR signals cannot be detected outside the office in which they are being used.

Studies of wireless indoor data links using diffusely scattered radiation at 950 nm and distances up to 50 m have shown that time dispersion (multipath) limits the transmission rate to 260 Mb/s-m, [Ref. 41], but background noise from ambient daylight limits the actual rate to less than 1 Mb/s. Other sources of ambient noise are fluorescent and incandescent lights. In general, sunlight exhibits a broad peak in the 400 to 600 nm range, fluorescent lights have a rather narrow peak around 650 nm, and incandescent lights produce a very broad peak from 800 to 1600 nm. Transmission may be limited further by the rise and fall time characteristics of the diodes used.

Modulation techniques for indoor IR links generally are analog, pulse, or digital [Ref. 40]. Analog FM of a carrier which, in turn, intensity modulates the source is a means of shifting the signal spectrum from that of the ambient lights, and also allows FDM for multiple user requirements. The carrier frequency may range from 90 kHz to 500 kHz or higher. Such pulse modulation techniques as *pulse position modulation (PPM),* or *pulse duration modulation (PDM)* are suitable for analog inputs such as voice. Digital modulation may be accomplished using PCM coding from which a Manchester coded NRZ stream is produced that intensity (2-level) modulates the IR. Ambient light interference is below most of the baseband of the digital stream and good timing extraction can be achieved at the receiver. Binary data can be used to modulate the IR carrier using MPSK or MFSK.

6.13 FREE-SPACE OPTICAL TRANSMISSION

Free-space optical transmission is applicable to intersatellite links (ISLs) that are of interest both commercially and for military purposes. The link advantages of coherent optical transmission point toward its use for ISLs. Acquisition and tracking is required relative to the frequency of the optical signal, the direction (azimuth and elevation) of the other end of the link, polarization, and also symbol and bit timing [Ref. 42]. Based upon a 10 mW transmitter power and a 1 mr pointing uncertainty, acquisition time may be on the order of 1 to 10 seconds. Tracking must be designed to accommodate spacecraft attitude disturbances. Frequency tracking will be required to handle doppler shift as well as laser frequency jitter. Polarization changes will result largely from satellite movement and should be negligible relative to the tracking loop response time constants.

Lasers are expected to be single-frequency types for both the transmitter and the receiver local oscillator (LO). Single-frequency GaAs lasers can be tuned well beyond the requirements of Doppler shift. The receiver LO must be capable of frequency or phase locking to the incoming signal depending on the type of modulation being used. Receiver sensitivities within 1 dB of the quantum limit have been shown to be feasible through demonstration [Ref. 42].

System link parameters for ISLs under consideration, [Ref. 38], are the following:

Transmitter: 30 mW GaAlAs laser at 0.83 μm
Antenna: 20 cm diameter
Data rate: 100 Mb/s, BFSK
System implementation loss: 12 dB

Link margin: 7 dB

Performance: $p_{be} = 10^{-10}$ at 80 photons/bit

A significant advantage of the coherent optical link over the noncoherent link is its 20 dB or greater improvement in link margin, which results from a smaller effective receiver bandwidth, and which reduces interference from the sun in the field of view of the receiver.

6.14 GLOSSARY OF TERMS

Absorption loss The loss of optical flux or energy caused by impurities in the transmission medium as well as intrinsic material absorption. Expressed in dB/km.

Acceptance angle The solid angle within which all incident light rays will enter the core of an optical fiber. Expressed in degrees.

Acceptance cone A cone with an included angle twice that of the acceptance angle.

Bundle A collection of glass or plastic fibers that transmit data in the form of optical energy.

Cladding The outer portion of an optical fiber having an index of refraction lower than that of core.

Core The center portion of an optical fiber. It is the light transmitting medium.

Coupling loss Attenution of the optical signal due to coupling inefficiencies between the flux source and the optical fiber, or between fibers, or between the fiber and the detector in a receiver. Expressed in dB.

Dispersion The undesirable effect of the broadening of optical pulses caused by lengthening of rise and fall times as the pulse travels along the fiber. Sometimes referred to as "pulse spreading," it results from either modal or material effects in the fiber that reduce bandwidth. Expressed in ns/km.

Fiber A clear glass or plastic optical "cable," consisting of a core and cladding, designed to propagate optical energy. The diameter of a fiber can vary from about 10 to 1000 μm, depending on type.

Flux The rate of energy flow passing to, from, or through a surface or other geometric entity. Radiant flux is expressed in watts. Luminous flux is expressed in lumens. Flux is sometimes erroneously referred to as optical power.

Graded-index fiber An optical fiber made with a refractive index that gets progressively lower as the diameter increases. See *Step-index fiber*.

Index of refraction The physical property of a material that describes the behavior of optical energy passing through it. It is defined as the ratio of the velocity of light in a vacuum to the velocity of light in the material.

IRED A diode that emits photons in the infared spectrum when forward biased.

Mode Each different path that a light ray can take to travel down an optical fiber.

Multimode fiber An optical fiber that propagates optical energy in more than one mode.

Numerical aperture A measure of the light-gathering capability of a fiber. Mathematically, it is expressed as the sine of the acceptance angle.

Optical port An opening through which optical energy can pass.

Refraction The deflection from a straight path undergone by a light ray passing from one medium into another having a different index of refraction.

Responsivity A measure of how much output current can be obtained from a photodetector for a given optical energy input. Expressed in A/W.

Single mode fiber An optical fiber that allows propagation of optical energy in only one mode.

Step index fiber An optical fiber made with an abrupt change in refractive index at the core-to-cladding interface. *See* Graded-index fiber.

PROBLEMS

6.1 A 10 μm diameter fiber has an $NA = 0.10$. How long must the optical wavelength be for single mode operation?

6.2 A fiber has a core whose index of refraction is 1.505 and a cladding whose index of refraction is 1.500. What is the fiber's NA?

6.3 What is the time-domain dispersion for a 50 km length of the fiber of Prob. 2?

6.4 A multimode telecommunications fiber has $\Delta = 0.01$ and $n_1 = 1.48$. What is the NA? How large is the acceptance cone?

6.5 Explain why the cladding of an optical fiber always has a smaller index of refraction than the core.

6.6 An optical fiber with a 0.5 dB/km attenuation is to be used with a 40 km repeater spacing. The fiber is capable of 5.4 Gb/s−km. If digital video at 135 Mb/s per channel is to be transmitted, how many video channels can this system accommodate? If the repeaters were placed 20 km apart instead, what number could be handled?

6.7 A single-mode fiber has a chromatic dispersion given by the equation

$$D(\lambda) = 0.025 \left(\lambda - \left[\frac{2.85 \times 10^{12}}{\lambda^3}\right]\right) \frac{ps}{nm - km}$$

This fiber is to be used with an injection laser for which $\Delta\lambda = 2.0$ nm. What is the material dispersion at 1320 nm in a 40 km length of the fiber?

6.8 A laser is to be used to transmit ten analog video signals (NTSC standards) on a fiber. Describe the modulation technique you would use, including appropriate numerical parameters, for maximum distance between repeaters. Include laser and fiber parameters within readily available ranges of values.

6.9 What is the dispersion in a 3 km length of fiber for which $\Delta = 0.004$ and $n = 1.5$?

6.10 A fiber has a core diameter of 8 μm, an $NA = 0.1$, and is to be operated at $\lambda_0 = 1.2$ μm. To what spot size should the incident light be focused for coupling into this fiber?

6.11 Two graded-index fibers ($\rho = 2$) are to be butt-coupled together. Their $NA = 0.25$ and $m = 5$. What is the coupling loss?

6.12 A fiber optic system is to be designed to transmit 12 television signals per fiber, each at 135 Mb/s, over the 18 km distance from a cable television headend to a major system distribution point. Develop the link budget parameters for the system assuming that $p_{be} \leq 10^{-5}$.

6.13 Explain why the spectral linewidth of a source to be coherently modulated must be less than the information bandwidth to be impressed upon that source.

REFERENCES

1. B. E. Keiser and E. Strange, *Digital Telephony and Network Integration,* VanNostrand Reinhold Co., New York, 1985.

2. P. S. Henry, "Introduction to Lightwave Transmission," *IEEE Communications Magazine,* 23, no. 5, (May 1985), 12–16.

3. *Projects in Fiber Optics: Applications Handbook,* Newport Corporation, Fountain Valley, CA, 1986.

4. D. H. Rice and G. E. Keiser, "Application of Fiber Optics to Tactical Communication Systems," *IEEE Communications Magazine,* 23, no. 5, (May 1985), 46–57.

5. "On the Way—a New Dispersion Specification Format," *Guidelines,* Corning Telecommunications Products Division, Corning Glass Works, Corning NY.

6. S. D. Personick, "Review of Fundamentals of Optical Fiber Systems," *IEEE Journal on Selected Areas in Communications,* SAC-1, no. 3, (April 1983), 373–80.

7. T. Li, "Advances in Lightwave System Research," *AT&T Technical Journal,* 66, Issue 1, (Jan.–Feb. 1987), 5–18.

8. R. W. Dixon and N. K. Ditta, "Lightwave Device Technology," *AT&T Technical Journal,* 66, Issue 1, (Jan.–Feb. 1987), 73–83.

9. J. Koscinski, "Feasibility of Multi-channel VSB/AM Transmission on Fiber Optic Links," *1987 NCTA Technical Papers,* National Cable Television Association, Washington, DC, pp 17–25.

10. H. Gysel, "Properties and Systems Calculation of Optical Supertrunks for Multichannel TV Transmission, Using Analog Intensity Modulation, Single Mode Fibers and High Deviation FM," *1987 NCTA Technical Papers,* National Cable Television Association, Washington, DC, pp. 12–16.

11. J. M. Senior, *Optical Fiber Communications: Principles and Practice,* Prentice-Hall, Inc., Englewood Cliffs, NJ, 1985.

12. N. Yoshikai, K.-I. Katagiri, and T. Ito, *"mB1C* Code and Its Performance in an Optical Communication System," *IEEE Transactions on Communications,* COM-32, no 2, (Feb. 1984), 163–68.

13. *Transmission Systems for Communications,* Bell Telephone Laboratories, Inc., revised fourth ed., 1971.

14. I. Jacobs, "Design Considerations for Long-Haul Lightwave Systems," *IEEE Journal on Selected Areas in Communications,* SAC-4, no. 9, (Dec. 1986), 1389–95.

15. D. Marcuse, "Loss Analysis of Single Mode Fiber Splices," *Bell System Technical Journal,* 56, (May–June, 1977), 703–18.

16. M. K. Barnoski, *Fundamentals of Optical Fiber Communications,* Academic Press, Inc., New York, 1976.

17. D. R. Porter, P. R. Conch, and J. W. Schelin, "A High-Speed Fiber Optic Data Bus for Local Data Communications," *IEEE Journal on Selected Areas in Communications,* SAC-1, no. 3, (April 1983), 479–88.

18. H. Nishmoto, et al. "Fully Integrated 1.6 Gb/s Optical Repeater," *IEEE Globecom '86,* pp. 49.1.1 to 49.1.5.

19. C. M. Siperko, "LaserNet-A Fiber Optic Intrastate Network (Planning and Engineering Considerations)," *IEEE Communications Magazine,* 23, no. 5, (May 1985), 31–45.

20. J. M. Anderson, D. R. Frey, and C. M. Miller, "Lightwave Splicing and Connector Technology," *AT&T Technical Journal,* 66, Issue 1, (Jan.–Feb. 1987), 45–64.

21. C. M. Miller, "Optical Fiber Cables and Splices," *IEEE Journal on Selected Areas in Communications,* SAC-1, no. (April 1983), 533–40.

22. D. R. Smith, *Digital Transmission Systems,* VanNostrand Reinhold, New York, 1985.

23. "Fiber Technology: Brilliant Advances Seen as Likely," *Data Communications,* 15, no. 12, (Nov. 1986), 60.

24. T. Li, "Advances in Optical Fiber Communications: An Historical Perspective," *IEEE Journal on Selected Areas in Communications,* SAC-1, no. 3, (April 1983), 356–72.

25. R. J. Sanferrare, "Terrestrial Lightwave Systems," *AT&T Technical Journal* 66, Issue 1 (Jan.–Feb. 1987), 95–107.

26. J. E. Rogalski, "Evolution of Gigabit Lightwave Transmission Systems," *AT&T Technical Journal,* 66, Issue 3, (May–June 1987), 32–40.

27. P. K. Runge and P. R. Trischitta, "Undersea Lightwave Communications," *IEEE Journal on Selected Areas in Communications,* SAC-2, no. 6, (Nov. 1984), 782–83.

28. T. D. Nantz and W. J. Shenk, "Lightguide Applications in the Loop," *AT&T Technical Journal,* 66, Issue 1, (Jan.–Feb. 1987), 108–18.

29. M. Gawdun, "Lightwave Systems in the Subscriber Loop," *Telecommunications,* 21, no. 5, (May 1987), 65–85.

30. G. Parry and J. E. Midwinter, "Principles of Photonic Switching," *IEEE ICC'87 Conference Proceedings,* (June 1987), pp. 1556–58.

31. H. S. Hinton, "Applications of the Photonic Switching Technology for Telecommunications Switching," *IEEE ICC'87 Conference Proceedings,* (June 1987), pp. 1559–64.

32. I. W. Stanley, "A Tutorial Review of Techniques for Coherent Optical Fiber Transmission Systems," *IEEE Communications Magazine,* 23, no. 8 (Aug. 1985), 37–53.

33. R. A. Linke and P. S. Henry, "Coherent Optical Detection: A Thousand Calls on One Circuit," *IEEE Spectrum,* 24, no. 2, (Feb. 1987), 52–57.

34. T. Kimura, "Coherent Optical Fiber Transmission," *Journal of Lightwave Technology,* LT-5, no. 4, (April 1987), 414–28.

35. I. W. Stanley, G. R. Hill, and D. W. Smith, "Application of Coherent Optical Techniques to Wide-Band Networks," *Journal of Lightwave Technology,* LT-5 no. 4, (April 1987), 439–51.

36. R. J. Boehm, et al. "Standardized Fiber Optic Transmission Systems—A Synchronous Optical Network View," *IEEE Journal on Selected Areas in Communications,* SAC-4, no. 9 (Dec. 1986), 1424–31.

37. F. E. Ross, "FDDI-A Tutorial," *IEEE Communications Magazine,* 24, no. 5, (May 1986), 10–17.

38. J. F. McCool, "The Emerging FDDI Standard," *Telecommunications,* 21, no. 5, (May 1987), 54–62.

39. J. D. Fridman and J. Svacek, "Atmospheric Optical Communications Link for a Local Area Network," *Laser Focus,* 19, no. 3, (March 1983), 95–97.

40. K. Pahlavan, "Wireless Data Communication Techniques for Indoor Applications," *IEEE International Conference on Communications,* ICC'85, Paper 13.1, pp. 372–78.

41. F. R. Gfeller and U. Bapst, "Wireless In-House Data Communication via Diffuse Infrared Radiation," *Proceedings of the IEEE,* 67, no. 11, (Nov. 1979), 1474–86.

42. V. Chan, "Space Coherent Optical Communication Systems," *Journal of Lightwave Technology,* LT-5, no. 4, (April 1987), 633–37.

7

Broadband Cable Systems

Broadband cable systems have their origin in cable television systems devised to bring entertainment television to subscribers located in remote areas without over-the-air service. Since the introduction of cable television in the late 1940s, systems have grown substantially both in sophistication and in number of channels carried. The technology also is being applied to broadband local area networks for inter-active data exchange, as well as to such applications as multichannel surveillance television. Users of broadband cable systems for nonentertainment purposes in-clude business, industry, and government. Advanced systems for entertainment purposes now bring a wide variety of programs to areas that already have multi-channel over-the-air television services. In the newest systems, optical fibers are beginning to replace the coaxial cable for the main trunk run, and as noted in Chap. 6, work is in progress toward bringing fiber all the way to the subscriber.

Cable systems possess one inherent difference from switched telephone sys-tems. Cable systems generally are built on a nonswitched basis, which means that everyone receives the same set of channels or bandwidth unless specific restrictions are implemented within the system. Privacy thus requires passwords and encryption.

7.1 PERFORMANCE STANDARDS AND QUALITY

Broadband cable system standards generally are geared to analog signal delivery. This implies a signal-to-noise ratio on the order of 54 dB for all subscribers, and also means that transmission reflections must be kept to a minimum. While some of the smaller older systems may provide only a 42 dB signal-to-noise ratio at the worst point in the system, the standards still are well beyond the demands of digital transmission. Figure 7.1 relates the video signal-to-noise ratio to viewer evaluations of picture quality as determined in a study by the Television Allocations Study Organization (TASO) [Ref. 1].

Broadband cable systems can be designed for a full duplex capability either by using separate cables for each direction of transmission, or by using one part of the overall cable spectrum for one direction and another part for the opposite direction.

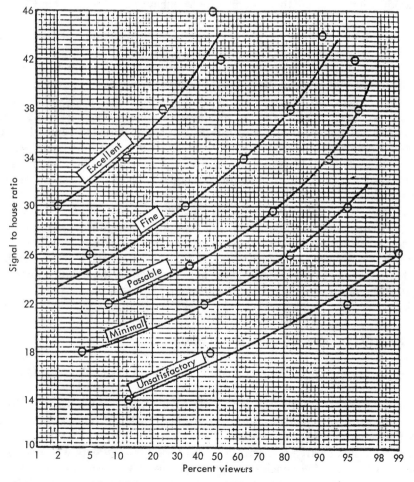

Figure 7.1 Viewer evaluations of picture quality as a function of video signal-to-noise ratio.

Transparent service can be achieved readily since cable systems simply use amplifiers (linear repeaters) to compensate for cable loss. Synchronous transmission of digital signals is readily possible. Compared with switched telephony circuits, the lowest economical digital rate on a cable system for a user may be anywhere from 1200 b/s to 19 200 b/s depending on telephone company tariffs as well as cable system charges, assuming that the cable system and the telephone system both serve the end points to be connected.

The use of cable systems for data transmission may entail certain problems, however, as follows. First, some cable systems transmit jamming signals at 2.25 and 4.50 MHz above certain video carriers to prevent unauthorized reception of the corresponding channels. Some system use sweep generators periodically as a means of system test. Either jammers or sweep generators can produce bursts of bit errors if used. In a heavily loaded system (signals on all or nearly all channels), intermodulation may be produced by slight amplifier nonlinearities. The effects of intermodulation in raising the system noise level have been discussed in Chap. 5. A related problem is the incidental phase modulation that may be caused by modulators and frequency converters in the system. Such incidental phase modulation can have an adverse effect on PSK or APK systems.

Another class of problems includes power ingress, in which 60 Hz levels accompany the channels. Because of its numerical proximity to the video field rate, power ingress generally is not noticed in a video signal if its level is sufficiently low. External signal ingress may ocur as FM broadcast signals or strong local TV signals leak into the cable, a problem which is especially significant in systems whose cable sheath is a braided, rather than a solid, conductor. Ingress into a cable system, as well as unwanted reflections, may occur from the presence of unterminated ports. This makes the proper use of directional couplers important in the prevention of such problems.

Finally, some cable systems suffer a lack of proper maintenance. Loose, broken, or corroded connectors can result in ingress, reflection, or intermodulation problems (the corrosion causes diode, or mixing, action), as can broken or cracked cable sheaths, leakage through the braid, and loose cover plates or broken housings. However, all of the problems noted in this section can be handled by the cable operator who desires to carry data on a system.

7.2 SPECTRUM UTILIZATION ON CABLE SYSTEMS

Cable systems generally transmit signals to the subscriber on 6 MHz wide channels in the "LO-VHF" (54–88 MHz), "MID-BAND" (120–174 MHz), "HI-VHF" (174–216 MHz), "Super-Band" (216–300 MHz), and "Ultra Band" (300–450 MHz). FM voice may be transmitted in the 88–108 MHz FM band. Return signals from the subscriber may occupy the "SUB-VHF" (5.75–47.75 MHz) band, although the usable upstream spectrum on the subscriber network generally ends at about 30 MHz. The frequencies are significant both in terms of cable loss versus frequency characteristics, and in terms of over-the-air use of the respective frequencies in the event of cable leakage, leading to problems of outside signal ingress and

TABLE 7.1 CABLE CHANNEL DESIGNATIONS AND FREQUENCY RANGES

Channel	Freq. Range (MHz)	Channel	Freq. Range (MHz)
T- 7	5.75–11.75	P	252–258
T- 8	11.75–17.75	Q	258–264
T- 9	17.75–23.75	R	264–270
T-10	23.75–29.75	S	270–276
T-11	29.75–35.75	T	276–282
T-12	35.75–41.75	U	282–288
T-13	41.75–47.75	V	288–294
2	54–60	W	294–300
3	60–66	X or AA	300–306
4	66–72	Y or BB	306–312
5	76–82	Z or CC	312–318
6	82–88	M1 or DD	318–324
A	120–126	M2 or EE	324–330
B	126–132	M3 or FF	330–336
C	132–138	M4 or GG	336–342
D	138–144	M5 or HH	342–348
E	144–150	M6 or II	348–354
F	150–156	M7 or JJ	354–360
G	156–162	M8 or KK	360–366
H	162–168	M9 or LL	366–372
I	168–174	M10 or MM	372–378
7	174–180	M11 or NN	378–384
8	180–186	M12 or OO	384–390
9	186–192	M13 or PP	390–396
10	192–198	M14 or QQ	396–402
11	198–204	M15 or RR	402–408
12	204–210	M16 or SS	408–414
13	210–216	M17 or TT	414–420
J	216–222	M18 or UU	420–426
K	222–228	M19 or VV	426–432
L	228–234	M20 or WW	432–438
M	234–240	M21 or XX	438–444
N	240–246	M22 or YY	444–450
O	246–252		

cable signal egress through the cable shield. Such problems are most noticeable in the frequency ranges not otherwise used for the service provided, i.e., in the SUB-VHF, MID-BAND, Super Band, and Ultra Band frequency ranges. Table 7.1 lists the channel designations and frequency ranges of the channels. Within each channel, the picture carrier, color subcarrier, and sound carrier are arranged as shown in Fig. 3.8.

7.3 BASIC COMPONENTS OF A CATV SYSTEM

Figure 7.2 [Ref. 2] illustrates the basic components of a CATV system. In addition to the headend, main trunk, and distribution system, a studio for local origination often is included. By contrast, a master antenna television system (MATV) or

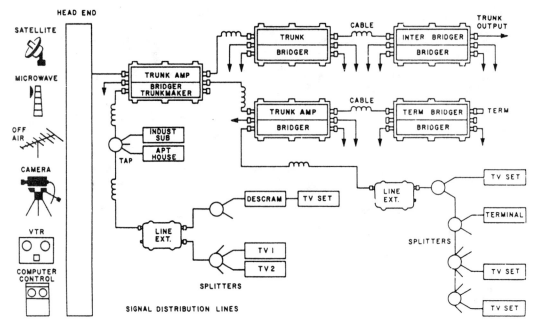

Figure 7.2 Basic components of a CATV system. (Courtesy Texscan Corp. Reprinted with permission.)

satellite MATV (SMATV) simply receives available over the air channels possibly combined with one or more channels via satellite, and usually includes only a distribution system, the size being too small to require a main trunk or to warrant a studio.

7.3.1 Headend

The headend is the source of signals for the CATV system. It receives its signals from nearby stations directly over the air, from distant stations via microwave or satellite systems, and perhaps from a local studio, which may include videotape sources. The CATV headend amplifies and signal conditions each channel individually, as distinguished from an MATV system, which simply amplifies all received signals together on a broadband basis. The headend also programs the channels to be seen on the system, and drives the main trunk cable, providing uniform channel levels. Uniformity of levels is especially important in those systems whose operation depends upon the selectivity of the subscriber's receiver, since receiver rejection typically is only −20 dB at channel edges. Uniform levels thus are essential if a separate picture is to be placed on every channel.

An additional headend function is the monitoring of system performance. Monitoring includes not only video quality checks but also transmission performance. Leakage may be tested through the use of signal generators at 108 MHz or 216 MHz. Attenuation measurements may be done by using selected TV channel carriers as pilots. System sweep generators serve to evaluate transmission versus frequency. Figure 7.3 [Ref. 3] shows the basic headend equipment.

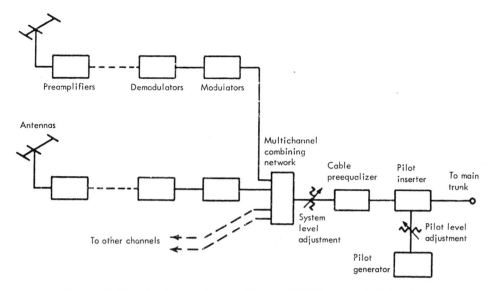

Figure 7.3 Basic headend equipment. (Courtesy TAB Books, © 1970. Reprinted by permission.)

7.3.2 Main Trunk

The main trunk may be coaxial cable with a repeater approximately every 500 to 600 m to compensate for cable loss, which is as great as 35 dB/km at 400 MHz. Alternatively optical fiber may be used. Systems providing the maximum possible number of channels per cable use the VSB techniques described in Sec. 7.5. For main trunk runs, other techniques may be used, such as FM video, as illustrated in Fig. 7.4 [Ref. 4]. This system requires 12 to 16 MHz/channel, and uses a repeater every kilometer.

An important main trunk design concept is that of the unity gain repeater section illustrated in Fig. 7.5 [Ref. 5]. Such a section, combined with a specified length of coaxial cable, ideally provides a unity gain at all channels on the system. The AGC is an automatic gain control to compensate for gain changes caused by changes in cable temperature as well as repeater temperature. The AGC control voltage may be derived from a pilot tone on the system or a selected TV visual carrier may be used. The ASC and ASGC functions are automatic slope control and automatic slope and gain control, respectively. Slope control is derived either from two separate pilot tones or two separate TV visual carriers.

Many main cable trunks are being implemented using fiber optics. An analog video approach is illustrated in Fig. 7.6 [Ref. 4]. This arrangement uses FM video signals frequency-division multiplexed with the center frequencies selected to minimize intermodulation problems that may result from laser nonlinearities. Wider FM deviation can be used than for the system of Fig. 7.4. The overall FDM spectrum then intensity modulates a laser. Several lasers, each operating at a different wavelength, can be operated simultaneously through the use of WDM. The overall system thus can be described as FM/FDM/IM/WDM. The WDM combiner entails a

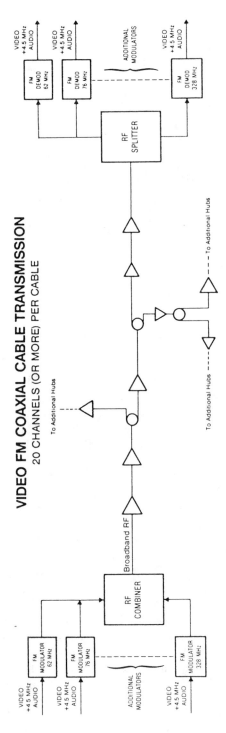

Figure 7.4 FM video on coaxial cable. (From J. A. Chiddix in *NCTA Cable '85 Technical Papers*, 1985, © NCTA, 1985. Reprinted by permission.)

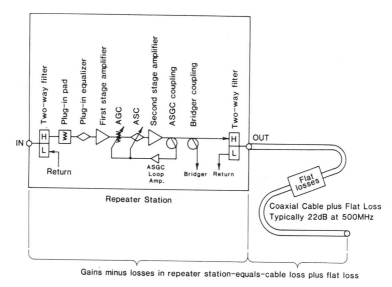

Figure 7.5 Typical unity gain repeater section. (From V. Bhaskaran and M. Davidov in *NCTA Cable '84 Technical Papers,* 1984, © NCTA, 1984. Reprinted by permission.)

loss on the order of 2 to 3 dB. The fiber system provides transmission distances of 25 to 30 km without the use of a repeater.

One FM/FDM/IM/WDM system by North American Phillips provides 10 video plus two DS1 channels and transmits for 45 km without repeaters. Each video channel has 8 MHz FM deviation. Five such video channels plus one DS1 are frequency-division multiplexed and the resulting spectrum intensity modulates a laser. The same is done to modulate a second laser, with the lasers operating at 1275 nm and at 1316 nm.

A digital video fiber system is illustrated in Fig. 7.7 [Ref. 4]. The composite video is sampled at three times the color subcarrier frequency, or 10.74 Mb/s. Coding is done either at 8 bits for a 63 dB SNR (broadcaster preference), or at 7 bits for a 57 dB SNR (adequate for CATV). The result is a digital rate of 75.2 Mb/s or 85.9 Mb/s per channel. Two such digital channels are time-division multiplexed together and used to intensity modulate a laser at 1234 nm, 1267 nm, 1300 nm, or 1333 nm, for a total of eight digital channels on a fiber. A TDM/IM system is shown in Fig. 7.8 [Ref. 4]. Here all eight video channels are time-division multiplexed and transmitted as a single digital stream by the laser. Digital video offers several advantages, the major one being that it is not subject to the common intermodulation impairments suffered by analog video transmission such as composite triple beat (CTB) and composite second order beats (resulting in the "windshield wiper effect"), as described in Sec. 7.5. Digital transmission is not adversely affected by laser nonlinearities. Detection sensitivity is better than with analog transmission and the terminal equipment has been proven to be more reliable and stable.

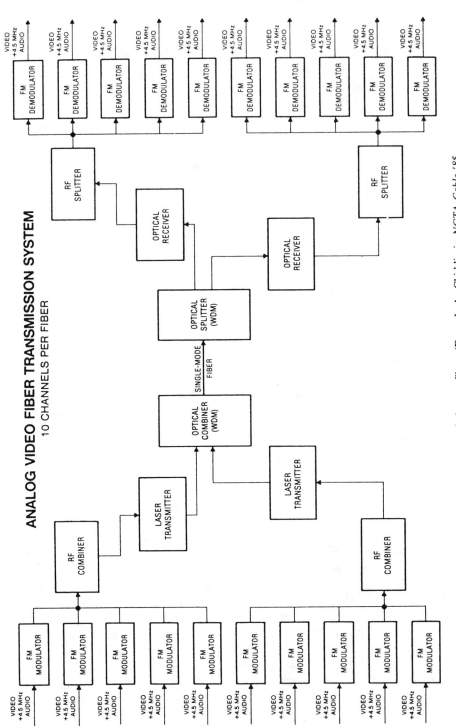

Figure 7.6 Analog video transmission on fiber. (From J. A. Chiddix in *NCTA Cable '85 Technical Papers*, 1985, © NCTA, 1985. Reprinted by permission.)

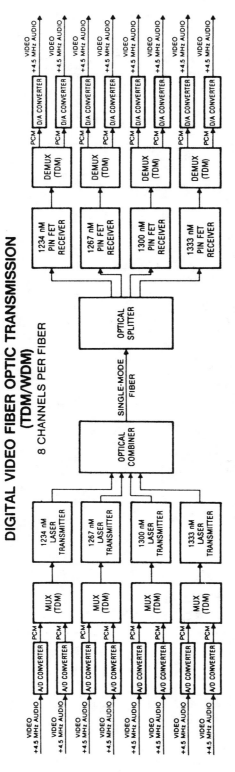

Figure 7.7 Digital video via fiber: TDM/IM/WDM. (From J. A. Chiddix in *NCTA Cable '85 Technical Papers*, 1985, © NCTA, 1985. Reprinted by permission.)

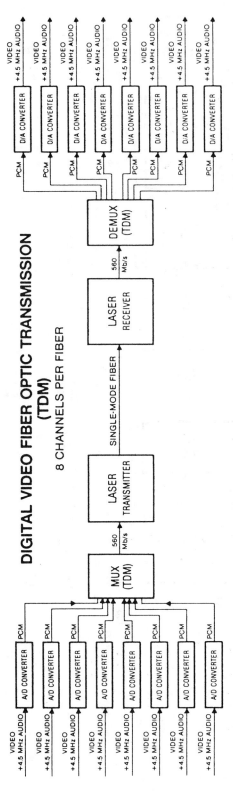

Figure 7.8 Digital video via fiber: TDM/IM. (From J. A. Chiddix in *NCTA Cable '85 Technical Papers*, 1985, © NCTA, 1985. Reprinted by permission.)

7.3.3 Distribution System

The distribution system in CATV takes the signals from a bridging amplifier on the main trunk and provides them to subscribers as indicated in Fig. 7.2. The distribution system is that portion of the overall system that takes the signals from the main trunk via a bridger and transmits them, via repeaters known as *line extenders,* to the actual delivery points. As many as four subscribers may be served from *splitters,* as shown in Fig. 7.2.

7.3.4 Studio for Local Origin

Many CATV systems provide for locally originated program material. The simplest form is a time and weather display using character generators, with the results often overlaid on another program channel. Such information as news and stock market quotations may use a full screen of alphanumeric characters. More advanced program origination utilizes remote pickup vans containing cameras, a video chain (amplifiers and signal conditioners), and a microwave relay for transmission to the headend. Video tape units are used commonly for later replay. A permanent studio may be located at the headend or at system headquarters.

7.4 TEXT DISPLAY SYSTEMS

Various text display systems have been devised to present alphanumeric information and simple graphics, usually in response to user requests. Such material is organized into "pages," each consisting of a video screen of material. The display unit usually is a color television receiver. The information to be transmitted is digitally encoded in alphanumeric form.

Text display systems are categorized by the CCITT as *videotex* (television text service), which may be *teletext* or *videotext,* and *viewdata.* Teletext is television text service which may use available lines of the vertical blanking interval (see Table 3.1) to send one-way data streams. Videotext refers to interactive systems typically using twisted pair or broadband cable technology to send two-way data streams. Viewdata is telephone interactive videotex in which a digital code is modulated onto an audio-frequency carrier that usually is transmitted over a telephone channel. Viewdata is an interactive system in which the terminal requets pages that are sent individually.

Table 7.2 [Ref. 6] is a sample list of videotext systems and their main transmission features.

Teletext originated in attempts to transmit signals within the television plant, with an intermediate goal of captioning for the deaf. Teletext pages often are used to present perishable information, with the data base being organized on a menu basis. Each of eight "magazines" may contain up to 100 pages, with a page consisting of a video screen of 24 rows of up to 40 characters each. In operation, a digital code is embedded in lines of the vertical blanking interval of the television signal and cyclically repeated. The receiving converter selects the page of interest and stores it internally for presentation. Each line of data starts after the TV line sync

TABLE 7.2 VIDEOTEXT SYSTEMS
SAMPLE LIST OF VIDEOTEX SYSTEMS AND THEIR MAIN TRANSMISSION FEATURES
(Cost information is only approximate as of end of 1983)

Videotex Systems

Design Authority	System and year of availability	Installed to Date		Downstream Design Parameters						Upstream Design Parameters						Nodes Served and upstr'm protocol	Approximate Cost	
		Head-end	Sub-scriber	Recd Freq MHz	Carrier Level dBmV	Modulation Type	Bwdth KHz	Bit Rate bps	Bps per Hertz	Trxd Freq MHz	Carrier Level dBmV	Modulation Type	Bwdth KHz	Bit Rate bps	Bps per Hertz		Per Home $	Per Headend $
Cox cable	Indax 1981	2 beta sites	300		−15 min	biphase	300	28K	0.09			biphase	300	28K	0.09	CSMA/CD	300 target	
Jerrold	Communi-com 1984	0	0		−15 min		400	128K	0.32				400	128K	0.32	16,000 homes CSMA/CD		
Packet-cable	Packet-cable 1983	0	0	Features strand-mounted Control Processor			6000	2M	0.33				6000	1M	0.167			
Videoway	The Vida-Network 1984	1 beta site	450 when cmpltd	108 to 120	−15 min	NRZ nosync	6000	4000K	0.67	any sub band		MSK	1000	500K	0.50	65M homes BTMA*/CD	225 target	

* BTMA: (Busy Tone Multiple Access)

Source: From M. B. Akgun and P. Parkinson, "The Development of Cable Data Communications Standards," *IEEE Journal on Selected Areas in Communications*, March 1985, © 1985, IEEE. Reprinted by permission.

pulse and comprises a string of shaped binary pulses representing NRZ-coded data at over 5 Mb/s. The data represent synchronizing waveforms for bit and byte recovery, addresses to identify the character row, control words, and encoded teletext characters. Hamming codes are used to correct single errors and to detect double ones. The transmission rate is approximately 1.7 pages/second per TV line. Graphics can be sent using a mosaic approach.

In the United States, the National Broadcasting Company (NBC) and Columbia Broadcasting System (CBS) television networks have been transmitting teletext based on the North American Broadcast Teletext Specification (NABTS) [Ref. 6]. In addition, television station WTBS, available nationally via satellite, transmits a version of teletext based on Keyfax, a U.S. proposed version of the British Broadcasting Corporation (BBC) Ceefax.

Full channel teletext uses 200 active lines of a video field for a capacity of 10 000 pages or more. Each line of the video field can be programmed independently for rapid access time. As an example, the TOCOM 5510A concept would use the 200 lines as shown in Table 7.3 [Ref. 7].

Applications of full channel teletext include airline guides, movie reviews, and classified advertising. Table 7.4 [Ref. 6] is a sample list of teletext systems and their main transmission features.

7.5 TECHNIQUES FOR MAXIMIZING SYSTEM BANDWIDTH

Coaxial cable systems suffer bandwidth limits because cable loss increases steadily with frequency. For a typical *gas-injected dielectric (GID)* polyethylene cable, letting α = cable loss per unit length,

$$\alpha = a\sqrt{f} + bf, \qquad b < 0.01a \text{ for } f \text{ in MHz} \tag{7.1}$$

where a and b are constants which depend upon the cable conductor dimensions and the type of dielectric used. Thus while a given cable may exhibit relatively low loss at frequencies well below 100 MHz, the loss increases steadily as frequency increases. A typical CATV cable loss at 400 MHz is 30 to 35 db/km. Repeaters, therefore, must be used so that sufficient gain is provided to transmit the entire cable spectrum satisfactorily. Moreover, the greater the bandwidth to be handled by the repeater, the more channels are likely to be present. Large bandwidth repeaters thus must

TABLE 7.3 TOCOM 5510A FULL CHANNEL TELETEXT LINE ALLOCATION

Lines	Use	Pages/Line	Average Access Time(s)
1–40	Index	1	0.5
41–100	Rapid access information	10	5
101–200	Catgeorized information	100*	50

* Each line contains 10 categories of 10 pages each.

A downsized version of this concept became the current family of TOCOM 55 PLUS addressable converters and systems.

Source: Courtesy TOCOM, Inc. Reprinted with permission.

TABLE 7.4 TELETEXT SYSTEMS
SAMPLE LIST OF TELETEXT SYSTEMS AND THEIR MAIN TRANSMISSION FEATURES
(Cost information is only approximate as of end of 1983)

TELETEXT SYSTEMS

DESIGN AUTHORITY	SYSTEM and year of Availability	INSTALLED TO DATE		Modu-lation	Rec'd Carrier		CHARACTERISTICS OF TRANSMITTED SIGNAL								APPROXIMATE COST	
		Head End Eqpt	Sub scriber Eqpt		Freq Mhz	Level dBmV	Data Levels as % Carrier	Data Lines per Field	Number of Sub Chnls	Instnt Data Rate Mbps	Band Width capital MHz	Bps per Hertz	Thru-Put Charac-ters/Sec cps	Address-able System? (Y/N)	per Home $	per Headend $
Cabledata	HTU Delivery System 1984	0	0	VSB/AM	normal TV vid	0	75.0 −31.25 =43.75	10 lines per field		3000	6 TDM	0.5	192K	Yes	25 units plus HE offered at $20K as experimental (alpha) test site	
EEG	Captioning/Text System 1980	300	70,000 approx	VSB/AM	normal TV vid	0	75.0 −37.5 =37.5	21 odd field	4	503.5	6 TDM	0.08	60 2 bytes /line	No	725	6,000 to 14,000
The Games Network	The Games Network 1983	0 Huntington Beach, et al introduction		?	?	?	N/A	N/A	?	2,000	2	1.00	240K approx	Yes	50 instaln +14 per mon	offered free of charge
Jerrold /Mattel	Playcable 1982	20	10,000 approx	FSK+/− 75Khz dev	107.5 homing ch +7 others	−15	N/A	N/A	5	14	+/− 2	0.035	12K aprx using 8 channels	No	150 cmptr 10/mon adaptor	12K cmptr (PDP-11)

Nabu	The NABU Network 1983	1 / 1,000 Ottawa Cable / 1 25 Vancouver	OQPSK	centre of any video chan.	−10	N/A	N/A	31 tiers	6,300	6	1.05	750K max per vid channel (6 poss)	Yes	400 comptr or 15/m rental	110K/150K standalone Future sat link expld
Norpak	Teletext Encoder System (TES-2) 1st models 1979	10 / 900 approx	VSB/AM	normal TV vid	0	75.0 −31.25 =43.75	1 of 10/20 or FF	4096 data ch's	5727.3	6 TDM or FF	0.9	1.68K to 441K(FF) 28b/line	No	400 Mark IV	790,000 approx
Time Inc Matsushita	Time Teletex Service	2 beta sites / 100 to 400	VSB/AM	normal TV vid	0	75.0 −31.25 =43.75	Full Field	4096 data ch's	5727.3	6 Full Field	0.95	441K(FF) 28 bytes per line	Yes	75 target (8/m)	?
Tocom	Tocom 55 Plus optional subsystem 1984	0 / 0	VSB/AM	normal TV vid	−10 min	75.0 −31.25 =43.75	17/18 or FF 200 lines	1 per TV ch	1736	6 TDM or FF	0.29	0.7K to 138K FF	Yes	375 approx	?
Videoway	Vidacom phase I (1-way) 1984	0 / 0 500 sample planned	VSB/AM no vid sync	normal TV vid	−2 min	100.0 −12.5 =87.5	FF	?	4000	6	1.00	418K max less games data etc	Yes	225 approx	?
Zenith	Z-Text 1984	0 / 900 ex	VSB/AM	normal TV vid	0	75.0 −31.25 =43.75	14-20 or FF	2	5727.3	6 TDM	0.95	1.68K to 441K(FF)	Yes	?	?

Source: From M. B. Akgun and P. Parkinson, "The Development of Cable Data Communications Standards," *IEEE Journal on Selected Areas in Communications*, March 1985, © 1985, IEEE. Reprinted by permission.

exhibit a high degree of linearity, as described in Sec. 5.3.1.2 to assure low-intermodulation levels among large numbers of channels. As noted in Sec. 7.3.2, intermodulation results in two major forms of distortion. One, called *composite triple beat (CTB)* is defined as

$$\text{CTB} = \frac{\text{average power of all beats at carrier frequency}}{\text{carrier power in all carriers unmodulated}} \tag{7.2}$$

CTB results in horizontal streaks in those channels that are affected. Another problem, *composite second-order beat (CSB)* results in a windshield wiper effect in the picture. Efforts to improve amplifier linearity often entail lower amplifier gain, but this means that more amplifiers are required for a given cable length, resulting again in aggravation of the intermodulation problem.

Cable system designers have continually improved system bandwidth in response to demands for larger numbers of channels on the part of cable operators. Systems typically transmit the spectrum from 54 MHz upward, often excluding 88 to 108 MHz because of FM intrusion, and may function as high as 400 MHz (54 channel cable), 450 MHz (60 channel cable), or 550 MHz (77 channel cable). Cable operators requiring larger numbers of channels must use a dual cable system. The spectrum below 54 MHz commonly is reserved for reply transmission from the subscriber's location, as described in Sec. 7.7.

Techniques for increasing system bandwidth thus focus on minimizing intermodulation distortion. This is done through several approaches: (1) reducing amplifier distortion, including minimizing the total number of amplifiers in cascade, (2) using a special channeling plan, and (3) using special techniques involving the sync pulses. The performance objective to be met through the use of these techniques is an overall relative distortion level $\leqslant 53$ dB, based upon subjective viewer evaluations [Ref. 8]. The individual amplifiers contributing to this distortion must be limited to significantly lower distortion levels, depending on the total number of such amplifiers in cascade. The -53 dB value is based upon disturbances from modulated carriers. Figure 7.9 [Ref. 9] shows the perceptible carrier-to-interference ratio as a function of interference frequency within the channel. As can be seen from this curve, interferences near the picture carrier and the color subcarrier produce the most noticeable effects. These interference levels, e.g., -58 dB, thus establish the criteria to be met by cable transmission systems.

7.5.1 Reduction of Amplifier Distortion

A CATV repeater may be constructed in any of the three ways illustrated in Fig. 7.10. The (a) portion of the figure represents a conventional amplifier. In the (b) portion, the input power is divided between two parallel amplifiers, allowing each a 3 dB lower input operating point. As was noted in Sec. 5.3.1.2, the distortion levels will be reduced by 4 dB for second-order products and by 9 dB for third-order products using this approach. However, an even more powerful technique is required for CATV amplifiers handling as many as 60 or more channels. This technique is called feedforward, as illustrated in Fig. 7.10(c).

Feedforward involves two cancellation loops. The first loop isolates noise and

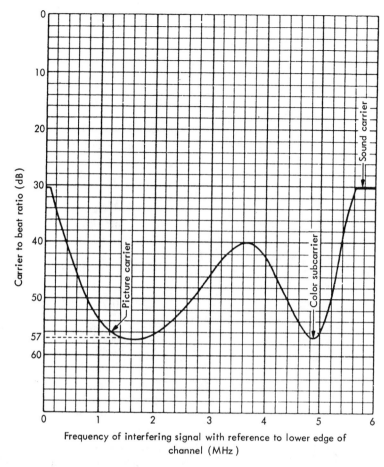

Figure 7.9 Perceptible carrier-to-interference ratio versus interference frequency in channel. (Courtesy Texscan Corp. Reprinted with permission.)

distortion produced by the main amplifier and the second loop provides distortion cancellation. Figure 7.11(a) [Ref. 10] shows the first loop cancellation process. Most of the output of the main amplifier, (signal + distortion + noise, designated $S + D + N$) passes through directional coupler DC2 to the output. However, some of the main amplifier output is applied to DC3, where it is combined out of phase with the original signal S_1 resulting in simply $D + N$. Figure 7.11(b) shows that $D + N$, via the error amplifier, is subtracted at DC4 from $S + D + N$, resulting in S only. Generally 22 to 26 dB of cancellation can be achieved, [Ref. 10], of which about 18 dB is CTB. By comparison, the parallel-hybrid approach typically provides CTB reduction of only about 5 dB [Ref. 11].

Because of the cancellation process, feedforward amplifiers tend to lack gain flatness with frequency at temperature extremes. In addition, their higher noise figures compared with conventional amplifiers reduce their dynamic range, making them less desirable as trunk station preamplifiers.

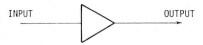

(a) Conventional

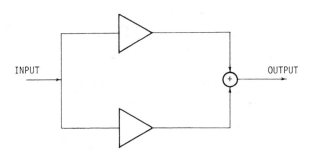

(b) Parallel-hybrid

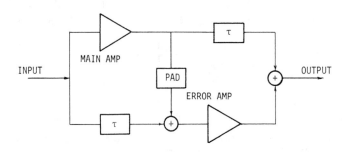

(c) Feedfordward

Figure 7.10 CATV amplifier arrangements.

The design of the basic feedforward gain block is illustrated next using the notation of Fig. 7.12 [Ref. 12]. In this figure,

G_M = gain of main amplifier
G_E = gain of error amplifier
L_{11}, L_{12}, L_{21}, L_{22}, L_{31}, L_{32}, L_{41}, and L_{42} are coupler losses
L_{d1} and L_{d2} are delay line losses

The gain of the feedforward stage, G_{FF}, is

$$G_{FF} = G_M - L_{11} - L_{21} - L_{d2} - L_{41} \tag{7.3}$$

Letting $L_{21} = L_{31}$, the gain G_{FF} also must equal the gain of the error path. Thus,

$$G_M - L_{11} - L_{21} - L_{d2} - L_{41} = G_E - L_{12} - L_{d1} - L_{31} - L_{42} \tag{7.4}$$

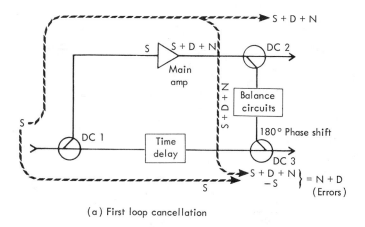

(a) First loop cancellation

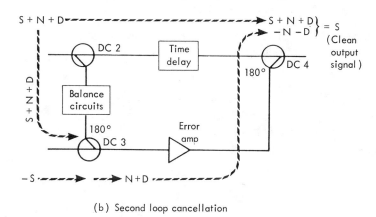

(b) Second loop cancellation

Figure 7.11 Feedforward cancellation of noise and distortion components. (From J. P. Preschutti in *NCTA Cable '84 Technical Papers*, 1984, © NCTA, 1984. Reprinted by permission.)

Four circuit configurations meeting the conditions of Eq. (7.3) and (7.4) are illustrated in Fig. 7.13 [Ref. 12]. In this figure, K_D = distortion improvement factor (distortion cancellation less circuit losses), and R_{max} = maximum reach in dB.

The factor K_D is a measure of the increase in output capability compared with that of the main amplifier. Distortion cancellation is directly proportional to the amplitude and phase balance within the loop. For 24 dB of cancellation, the amplitude balance must not vary by more than 0.25 dB peak-to-valley and the phase error must be held to within 2° [Ref. 13]. Based upon the foregoing [Ref. 12],

$$K_D = 12 - (L_{21} + L_{d2} + L_{41}) \text{ dB} \tag{7.5}$$

The noise figure of the feedforward gain stage is determined by the noise figure of the error amplifier path. Noise produced by the main amplifier is assumed

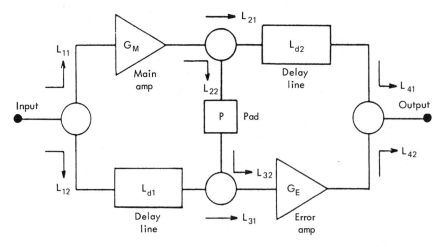

Figure 7.12 Feedforward gain block. (From J. C. Pavlic in *NCTA Cable '83 Technical Papers*, 1983, © NCTA, 1983. Reprinted by permission.)

to be cancelled by the first loop. Then if NF_{GE} = noise figure of the error amplifier, then the noise figure of the feedforward stage, NF_{FF}, is

$$NF_{FF} = NF_{GE} + L_{21} + L_{d1} + L_{12} \qquad (7.6)$$

The maximum reach is the longest cascade in dB over which the gain blocks can be cascaded, given a specific noise and distortion performance. Based upon achieving an end-to-end $C/N \geqslant 43$ dB and $CTB \geqslant 59$ dB, and letting N = number of gain blocks in cascade,

$$R_{max} = NG_{FF} \qquad (7.7)$$

$$N = 10^x \qquad (7.8)$$

where

$$X = \frac{V_{spec} - V_{opt}}{10} - \frac{59 - CCTB_{spec}}{20} \qquad (7.9)$$

$$V_{opt} = V_{spec} + \frac{43 - CNR_{spec}}{2} - \frac{59 - CCTB_{spec}}{4} \qquad (7.10)$$

where

V_{spec} = specified gain block output level
$CCTB_{spec}$ = specified gain block carrier-to-composite triple beat ratio
CNR_{spec} = specified gain block carrier-to-noise ratio

Note that of the four gain blocks in Fig. 7.13, FF1 simultaneously produces minimum noise and maximum distortion cancellation. In addition, it also provides the maximum cascade in trunk use.

Any efforts at minimizing amplifier distortion must be done bearing in mind the total number of amplifiers to be placed in cascade. As bandwidth increases the allowable number of repeaters decreases. This decrease is accompanied by the need

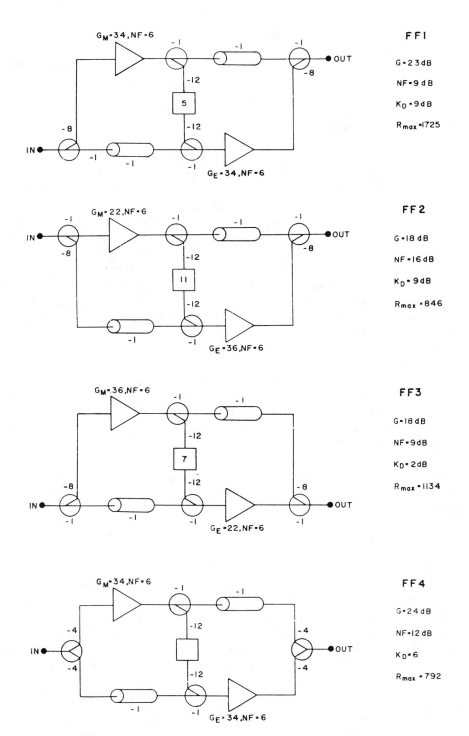

Figure 7.13 Examples of feedforward gain blocks. (From J. C. Pavlic in *NCTA Cable '83 Technical Papers,* 1983, © NCTA, 1983. Reprinted by permission.)

Sec. 7.5   Techniques for Maximizing System Bandwidth   **417**

for closer repeater spacing because of higher cable loss. Thus a system using low-loss 1.9 cm cable such a Commscope PIII with foamed plastic dielectric (34.4 dB/km) or GC Fused Disc III air dielectric (30.5 dB/km) can operate to 400 MHz using 45 repeaters for a 23 km length, or to 450 MHz using 40 repeaters for a 19 km length.

7.5.2 Special Channeling Plans

Special channeling plans are used to avoid intermodulation by moving certain of the carrier frequencies so that the intermodulation components fall directly on carrier frequencies. The result is the removal of intermodulation distortion in the demodulation process. Sideband intermodulation products, of course, remain. An overall subjective improvement of 4 to 6 dB can be achieved. One such technique, called *harmonically-related carriers (HRC)* allows each visual carrier to be phase locked to an integral multiple of a 6 MHz reference oscillator to a tolerance of several parts per million (ppm), which corresponds to several Hz per MHz. This arrangement places most of the VHF visual carrier frequencies 1.25 MHz below those of the standard channel allocations, except for Channels 5 and 6, which are placed 0.75 MHz above those of the standard allocations. The *incrementally-related carriers (IRC)* plan provides for each visual carrier to be phase locked to $(1.25 + 6n)$ MHz, where n is an integer. Again, the tolerance is several ppm.

The HRC and IRC offsets may render some channels unusable for TV purposes because of possible system leakage (radiation) at frequencies critical to safety, air navigation, or other special purposes. The FCC specifies a limit [Ref. 14] of 10 μV/m in the airspace 450 m above a CATV system in the 108 to 136 MHz and the 225 to 400 MHz bands. Even without HRC or IRC, certain channels may require *aeronautical offsets,* in which the visual carriers are offset by up to 100 kHz or reduced in power to less 10 μW. Channels that are not usable for TV because of offsets or power reduction still may be usable for data transmission at the 10 μW level or less. The aeronautical offset rules primarily affect cable channels using the 108 to 136 MHz and the 225 to 400 MHz bands.

7.5.3 Special Techniques

Special techniques involving the sync pulses include synchronizing the sync pulses on all channels to cause the worst distortion to occur outside the picture. This reduces the visible distortion effects by a subjective 2.5 dB. Another technique is called *sync suppression and active video inversion (SSAVI).* The actual purpose of SSAVI is scrambling, but it reduces CTB by 10 dB if all channels are scrambled. In operation, the sync pulses are suppressed and the video is inverted when the average level is less than 50 IRE units (100 = white, while 0 is blank). The result is a lower average RF level in the channel.

7.5.4 Special Systems

Cable transmission at frequencies up to 900 MHz is feasible, [Ref. 15], using VHF/UHF amplifier technology, general purpose hybrids, and feedforward gain

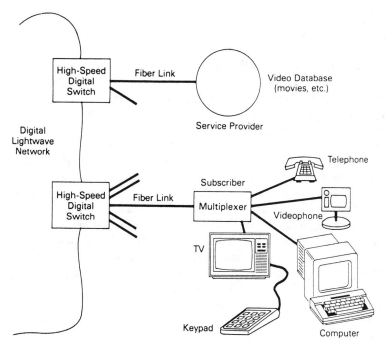

Figure 7.14 Subscriber-switched optical fiber. (From S. B. Weinstein, *Getting the Picture,* IEEE Press, © 1986. Reprinted by permission.)

blocks built from such components. Transmission up to 900 MHz provides many more channels on a single cable, especially for relatively short MATV systems, and avoids the ingress/egress problems encountered at certain non-TV frequencies, inasmuch as the 470 to 806 MHz portion of the spectrum is devoted largely to over-the-air UHF television.

Another special system concept, subscriber-switched optical fiber, is illustrated in Fig. 7.14 [Ref. 16]. Here each subscriber has an individual fiber link to a high-data rate digital switch, providing not only telephone, TV and personal computer connections, but also personal movie selection and full duplex videotelephony.

7.6 ADDRESSABLE CONTROL

Addressable control is the technique whereby the CATV channels made available to a given subscriber are controlled by means of digital signals sent from a controlling computer at the headend to a terminal at the subscriber's location. This terminal is a device that is placed between the cable and the subscriber's TV receiver. Addressable control allows the cable operator to provide the subscriber only those channels for which the subscriber is paying or wishes to receive. Control may be on a per channel basis, e.g., for subscription channels, or in terms of groupings of channels, e.g., various program levels for which the subscriber is paying. Parental access control allows parents to have certain channels eliminated if such channels are deemed undesirable for their children.

7.6.1 System Operation and Features

In operation, addressable control is achieved by having a *home channel* in which each terminal may be addressed using lines in the vertical interval. The digital rate at which addressing information is sent may be a submultiple of the color subcarrier frequency, i.e., 3.579/n MHz. A *program control word* may be sent in the vertical interval of another channel and contain such data as service class identification, program identification, channel type, and parental access control information.

Some addressable control systems provide that a terminal disconnected for longer than 10 seconds or some other specified period of time loses its *authorization* (a predetermined appropriate bit sequence) to provide channels to the subscriber. The authorization may be retained for 3 to 10 minutes or longer, however, in the event of a power loss. Upon reconnection, a new authorization must be sent from the control center. Therefore, the incentive to tamper with, steal, or relocate the terminal is minimized. A terminal that is turned off by the subscriber goes to its home channel for possible new addressing information.

7.6.2 Security

Security is important to any cable operator to prevent theft of service. Such early security techniques as traps (band-stop or band-pass filters) and converters were called *soft* techniques in that they lacked addressability and could be compromised easily by someone wishing to steal service. *Hard* security involving denial of one or all channels by the system operator is provided readily by means of addressable control. This denial is achieved by one of a variety of forms of scrambling. One of the more popular forms of scrambling involves suppression of the horizontal sync with restoration by the decoder. A decoding pulse or sine wave can be sent as part of the program material. Decoding can be delivered or denied through addressable control. Figure 7.15 [Ref. 17] illustrates the suppression of the sync pulse by a scrambling pulse or sine wave inserted at the headend and the subsequent restoration of sync at the terminal. Table 7.5 [Ref. 18] provides a summary of selected video scrambling methods.

Scrambling may be either *static,* in which fixed descrambling signal parameters are used, or *dynamic,* in which the descrambling signal parameters are variable [Ref. 19]. For descramblers to be cost-competitive, they must be designed with components commonly found in the TV set itself. Most existing scrambling methods constitute only minor deviations from NTSC standards, and thus are vulnerable to pirate designs. The most secure alternative is dynamic scrambling with an encrypted key signal.

The Video Cipher II system [Ref. 20] uses the Data Encryption Standard (DES) of the National Bureau of Standards to provide for the secure satellite distribution of TV programming. Audio and control information are sent during the horizontal sync interval, eliminating the need for an audio subcarrier. In operation,

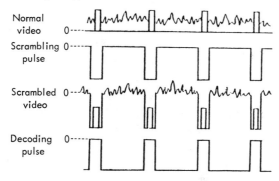

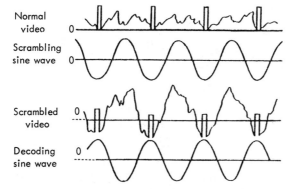

Figure 7.15 Sync suppression and restoration. (From C. O. Eissler in *NCTA Cable '81 Technical Papers,* 1981, © NCTA, 1981. Reprinted by permission.)

subscriber requests are telephoned to a control center, which has an input to the scrambler subsystem at the satellite uplink earth station. The uplink scrambler accepts a standard NTSC video input (composite video), two audio inputs, and an auxiliary data stream. A *channel control computer* transforms user authorization information into addressing and control data that is applied to the scrambler. The video output from the scrambler is confined to the standard 4.2 MHz NTSC bandwidth. At the receiving locations (users may be CATV systems or individuals), a descrambler, if specifically authorized for a given program, reverses the steps performed at the scrambler to produce both video and stereo audio. An auxiliary 88 kb/s data channel also is provided.

Video security is achieved by total elimination of the vertical and horizontal sync, by inversion of the video waveform, and by centering the color burst at a nonstandard level. Since an audio subcarrier is not used, a 2 dB improvement results relative to an unscrambled signal.

The DES algorithm is based on a 56-bit *key,* which is analogous to a password. New keys are sent periodically along with service authorizations via the control channel encrypted with each descrambler's unique key. Each program also carries its own key, which can be decrypted only by those descramblers possessing the periodic key. As many as 600 000 descramblers per hour can be addressed.

TABLE 7.5 SUMMARY OF SELECTED VIDEO SCRAMBLING METHODS

Scrambling Technique	Scrambling Depth	Video Security	Residual Effects in Descrambled Video	Descrambler Hardware Complexity	Cost
RF METHODS					
Tone jammer	Marginal. Scrambles audio also	Inadequate	Useful luminance energy lost	Low. 1 Trap per scrambled channel	Low
Video inversion	Marginal	Inadequate	Luminance and chrominance distortions due to imperfect carrier recovery	Complex	High
Sinewave sync suppression	Adequate	Adequate	Noise transfer from descrambling signal to video	Low	Low
Squarewave sync suppression	Adequate	Inadequate (sync easily restored)	Video jitter due to inaccurate timing	Low	Low
Frequency inversion	Good. Scrambles audio also	Good	Scrambled picture due to inaccurate timing	Moderate	Moderate
Nonlinear filter	Good	Good	Distortions due to filter mismatch	Low	Low

7.6.3 Interface Between Cable System and Television Receiver

The widespread advent of addressable control has brought with it the need for an interface between the cable and the TV receiver. This interface may involve programmable descrambling, addressable from the headend, as described in Sec. 7.6.2, or it may involve teletext decoding, parental control, or such specialized requirements as baseband video and audio connections for video cassette recorders (VCRs) and video projectors, or RGB connections for special monitor functions such as high-quality teletext display.

The terminal provided by the CATV operator generally duplicates the tuner of the receiver. One attempted solution has been the "cable-ready" television receiver. However, such a receiver will not be cable ready from the cable operator's viewpoint in that it has no provision for addressable control. A more useful approach is the modular TV receiver consisting of a baseband monitor and a two-channel receiver.

TABLE 7.5 SUMMARY OF SELECTED VIDEO SCRAMBLING METHODS (*cont.*)

Scrambling Technique	Scrambling Depth	Video Security	Residual Effects in Descrambled Video	Descrambler Hardware Complexity	Cost
BASEBAND METHODS					
Video inversion/ sync suppression	Adequate	Adequate	Distortion due to inaccurate DC restoration	Moderate	Moderate
Video jitter	Good	Excellent	Jittered video due to inaccurate timing	Moderate	High
Line reversals	Good	Adequate	Negligible	Low	Moderate
Line permutations	Excellent	Excellent	Negligible	High	High
Line dicing	Excellent	Excellent	Significant segment distortions in CATV links due to VSB filtering and multipath	High	High
MAC A, B, or C	Good, in conjunction with other scrambling methods	Good	Not presently applicable to 6MHz CATV links	Not Known	Not Known

Source: From V. Bhaskaran and M. Davidov in *NCTA Cable '84 Technical Papers,* 1984, © NCTA, 1984. Reprinted by permission.

A further interface problem is the accommodation of VCR features. Many VCRs are programmable in that they can be set to record six or more different channels over a two-week or longer period on an unattended basis. The channel programmability feature is lost in a cable system, where all channels are selected manually at the terminal (or a remote extension thereof) by the subscriber. One solution, implemented in the Pioneer BA-5000 terminal, is that of having programmability built into the terminal with timing being sent from the headend.

7.7 TWO-WAY CABLE SYSTEMS

Systems for entertainment television generally have reply circuits of audio bandwidth only, whereas industrial, government, and commercial systems may require full 6 MHz channels in both directions.

7.7.1 Two-Way System Techniques

A two-way cable system may have a reply circuit that is separate from the forward circuit, or the reply channels may be obtained by backfeeding over the main cable. A *subsplit* system is one in which the forward direction of transmission (also called *downstream*) uses the band above 54 MHz, whereas the reverse direction of transmission (also called *upstream*) uses frequencies typically below 30 MHz on the cable. In a *midsplit* system, the forward channels use frequencies above 159 MHz (usually up to 400 MHz), whereas the reverse channels occupy the 5 to 116 MHz spectrum. In a *high-split* system, the forward channels are from 232 to 400 MHz, whereas the reverse channels are 5 to 175 MHz.

7.7.2 Two-Way System Design

A basic repeater system for two-way CATV (subsplit) is shown in Fig. 7.16. The downstream direction functions the same as does any one-way system. Two-way operation is achieved by providing the reverse transmission direction using the 5 to 35 MHz spectrum. Some of the problems encountered in two-way design are described next.

7.7.2.1 Intrusion Problems.
The 5 to 35 MHz spectrum over the air contains numerous signals that may be of considerable strength, and which may enter (or intrude into) the cable system. These signals include short-wave radio, teletype, business radio services, and amateur and even citizens transmitters. Intrusion is a sign of a leaky cable system, so the operators of the intruding systems cannot be faulted. An additional form of intrusion that may occur, even without a two-way system, is the inadvertent response of the TV receiver to signals below 50 MHz. In addition, the drop cables to the subscribers' homes also may pick-up signals below 50 MHz, even though they are shielded. Moreover, leaky connectors can affect interference levels by as much as 20 dB, with a major leakage source being found to be the cable-connector-repeater housing interface. Intrusion problems at HF often are accompanied by VHF intrusion also. In fact, FM signals can be used as indicators of such intrusion problems.

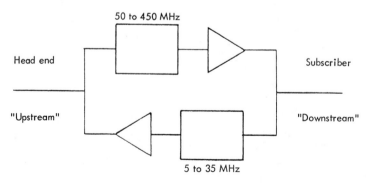

Figure 7.16 Basic repeater system for two-way CATV (subsplit).

Solutions have been devised for the various intrusion problems noted in the previous paragraph. High-pass filters at the TV receiver (50 MHz cut-off) help to prevent unwanted responses to signals below 50 MHz. Foil cable shields rather than braid are useful in reducing cable intrusion at all frequencies, especially at VHF. The leaky connector problem can be avoided by using connectors that require a torque wrench for tightening, rather than those that bottom out. Interfering signals can be isolated quickly by using code-operated switches that insert 6 dB of attenuation in a given section of a system rather than requiring experimentation with complete shutdowns of portions of the system into which intrusion is suspected. High VSWR levels on a cable system may indicate loose fittings or broken cable sheaths. In fact, at HF, the VSWR can become quite high because of the low loss of coaxial cable at HF. End-of-line test oscillator levels as observed at the headend can be useful indicators of upstream plant quality.

Note that the foregoing problems, except for intrusion into the TV receiver, are related to the use of coaxial cable, and will not occur if an optical fiber system is used for the main trunk, distribution, and house drop functions.

7.7.2.2 Upstream Signal Stability.

Good downstream signal stability does not guarantee good upstream stability. Upstream levels from home terminals may vary by several dB from unit to unit. Portable test oscillators (PTOs) and field strength meters are used to test upstream plant leakage. A PTO placed at the end of the longest feeder can inject specific frequencies such as 11 MHz or 32 MHz into the system. The field strength meter then is used to look for the corresponding frequency just outside the cable at various places along its route.

Problems causing a significant VSWR to appear can be identified by using end-of-line test oscillators (ELOs) that send pilot frequencies continuously in bands not used for subscriber channels. These oscillators typically have a 20 ± 0.5 dBmV output. A spectrum analyzer at the headend provides an immediate check on system performance. Alternatively, a computer program can provide a scan of all ELO levels. Subscriber terminals typically have a $+36$ dBmV output that must be received at the headend within ± 5 dB of a design reference level.

7.7.3 Two-Way System Operation

As an illustration of the operation of a two-way CATV system, this section describes the operation of the TOCOM system [Ref. 21]. Fig. 7.17 is the system block diagram. As can be seen there, each repeater consists of a two-way amplifier, the major direction being downstream. The system as designed is capable of 1000 *remote transmit-receive (RTR)* subscriber terminals per group and 30 groups per trunk. The number of groups is expandable to 100. N trunks can be implemented, to a total RTR capacity of 180 000. The central data terminal provides for emergency subscriber calls to police, fire, and ambulance services, and also allows power, water, and gas meter information or other data from the subscriber premises, with the consent of the subscriber, to be relayed to the appropriate recipients. In operation, the central data terminal sends interrogations to the various RTRs, the total interrogation time being 30 seconds. The RTR samples certain data and sends it

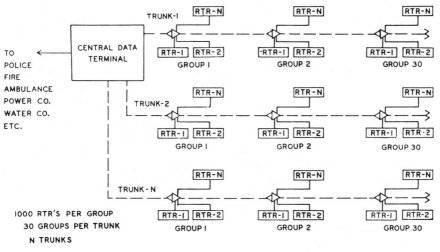

TO
POLICE
FIRE
AMBULANCE
POWER CO.
WATER CO.
ETC.

1000 RTR'S PER GROUP
30 GROUPS PER TRUNK
N TRUNKS

TOTAL RTR CAPACITY = 180,000

TOTAL INTERROGATION TIME 30 SECS.

Figure 7.17   TOCOM system block diagram. (Courtesy TOCOM, Inc. Reprinted with permission.)

back to the central data terminal. The reply can be up to seven 16-bit words, each requiring 30 ms.

Figure 7.18 shows the central data terminal. In addition to the usual headend functions, it contains a 50 MHz transmitter for RTR interrogation and system control, as well as a 6 to 30 MHz receiver decoder. A display is provided for rapid identification of any portion of the system requiring maintenance. The control data processor has access to the public telephone and teletype networks, as well as to a variety of memory devices such as disc, magnetic tape, etc.

Figure 7.19 shows the RTR. In addition to the converter for entertainment television, a 50 MHz receiver is provided to receive interrogation and commands from the central data terminal. The receiver output is acted upon only if the identification bits match those of the RTR. The word code register causes one of the seven 16-bit words to be read out to the data register. (Note that nine possible examples of 16-bit words actually are listed.) The data register then outputs the data on command to the transmitter, which operates at a frequency within the 6 to 30 MHz band. Provisions for RTR test from the central data terminal are included. The RTR has a hand-held portion which may be operated up to 8 m from the RTR itself. Each RTR has one address in a block of 1024 and one frequency of 60. Thus over 60 000 unique addresses are possible. The hard-wired controller in the central data terminal generates sequential interrogations for all terminal units during a 6-second cycle. Interrogations are sent to all RTRs in a group on a common interrogation frequency. Responses are received at the central data terminal as TDM signals within each frequency group. Detected signals are fed to the hard-wire control console logic for decoding and display or transmission of the returned data.

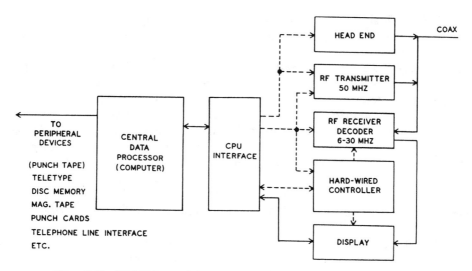

Figure 7.18 TOCOM central data terminal. (Courtesy TOCOM, Inc. Reprinted with permission.)

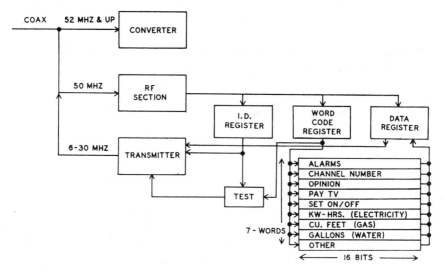

Figure 7.19 TOCOM remote transmitter receiver. (Courtesy TOCOM, Inc. Reprinted with permission.)

7.7.4 Two-Way Cable System Applications

A two-way cable system provides a transmission medium for a wide variety of applications of both a residential and business nature. In addition, a two-way system provides certain functions directly useful to the system operator.

7.7.4.1 Residential Applications. Residental applications of two-way CATV systems include home protection services as a major commodity. Such services include the ability to call the fire and police departments, as well as ambulances. In such cases, the cable system may provide transmission instead of, or as a back-up to, the telephone line. Other applications allow the subscriber to request premium (pay) television channels, or specially controlled channels, limited to a specific set of subscribers, such as special professional education courses for credit from local universities. Downstream addressable control can be used to fulfill the request using the techniques discussed in Sec. 7.6. Other applications, as described in Sec. 7.7.3, include the reading of gas, electric, and water meters, instant "subscriber response" polls and television program rating surveys, credit card payment for services, and the remote use of computers from the home. The provision of all or many special services may justify the system economically, whereas only one service may not.

Major applications for two-way systems lie in the provision of interactive text services, as described in Sec. 7.4, in the interrogation of large-data bases, and for access to transactional two-way services, such as banking or shopping from the home. Numerous telemetry systems have been devised to handle such functions as alarms and meters, as well as energy management switches in the home. Table 7.6 [Ref. 6] is a sample list of CATV telemetry systems and their main transmission features.

7.7.4.2 Applications Within the System. The operator of a two-way CATV system has the means of amplifier level monitoring readily available, as well as a means of detecting intruding signals and isolating them. By virtue of the return path, line disturbances that produce standing waves can be sensed readily at the headend by observing pilot levels from sources connected to remote parts of the system.

7.8 LOCAL AREA NETWORKS (LANs)

A *local area network (LAN)* is a privately owned network that provides a shared, high-data rate communication channel. Usually the LAN is limited in distance to within several kilometers and is interconnected by packet switches, circuit switches, bus structures, or in/out (I/O) channels [Ref. 22]. The medium is shared sequentially by the using stations each of which can get on and off quickly, thus providing fair access to all and desirably preventing any one station from limiting access by the others.

A closely associated concept is that of the *metropolitan area network (MAN),* which links separate LANs through gateways, and provides point-to-point communication between subscriber pairs, often using matched modems. A MAN can be thought of as a wide-radius LAN.

In viewing the functions of a LAN, those who are familiar with telephone switching technology may ask how a LAN differs from a *private branch exchange (PBX).* The PBX is well suited to voice, but not to the bursty traffic often handled

TABLE 7.6 TELEMETRY SYSTEMS: SAMPLE LIST OF TELEMETRY SYSTEMS AND THEIR MAIN TRANSMISSION FEATURES
(Cost information is only approximate as of end of 1983)

TELEMETRY SYSTEMS

DESIGN AUTHORITY	SYSTEM and year of availability	INSTALLED TO DATE Head-end	INSTALLED TO DATE Sub-scriber	DOWNSTREAM Recd Freq MHz	DOWNSTREAM Carrier Level dBmV	DOWNSTREAM MOD Type	DOWNSTREAM MOD Bwdth KHz	DOWNSTREAM Bit Rate bps	DOWNSTREAM Bps per Hertz	UPSTREAM Trxd Freq MHz	UPSTREAM Carrier Level dBmV	UPSTREAM MOD Type	UPSTREAM MOD Bwdth KHz	UPSTREAM Bit Rate bps	UPSTREAM Bps per Hertz	NODES SERVED and upstr'm protocl	Per Home $	Per Headend $
CableBus	Cable Alarm 1980	40	2,000 (mostly private)	73.5	−20 min	FSK +−50K async	250 spaced	1.2K to 9.6K	0.0048 to 0.0380	31.4	+41 max	CW	30 spaced	1200 to 2400	0.04 to 0.08	17,500 homes 64K pos	110	60K (Micro 1)
E-Com	Tru-Net 100	30	1,000 (mostly private)	any	−20 min	FSK	250	38.4K	0.15	any	+40 max	FSK	250	38.4K	0.15	4,000 homes	635 i/p inc	7K comp+modem
	Tru-Net 500 (upper level)	1 beta site		any		FSK	1500	307.2K	0.20	any	+40 max	FSK	1500	307.2K	0.20	250 areas	1.5K/ area	50K
	(lower level) 1984			any		FSK	250	38.4K	0.15			FSK	250	38.4K	0.15	1,000 homes	335/ home	+ area cost as shown
Jerold	Cable Security System 1982	2 beta sites	200	FM band	−15 min	FSK	400	13.9K	0.035	T9 2 chs used in parallel	+50 max	FSK	400	13.9K	0.035	16,000/ headend X8 max	100 plus sensors	10K for modem & cmptr + controller
Pioneer	VIP Home Security	1	3,000 approx	121.3	−7 min	FSK	4000	256K	0.064	24.0	+54 max	PSK	6000	256K	0.004	1,000 homes & up	280/ home	13K for 1,000 homes & up
Rogers	Rogers Interactive System	2 op +2 beta sites	7,200 mostly polling & PPVTV*	any	−20 min to COS**	FSK	60	19K	0.32	below 13.0 above 5.0	+40 max	FSK +−3K	15 X500= 7500 total	2K	0.13	500 hs/ bridger switch	25 for add on to Z-TAC	75 approx
Tele Eng	Tele-Dat II 1984	1 beta site		A-2 band	−20 min	PWM	2000	9.6K	0.0048	T-10 band	+50 max	PWM	2000	9.6K	0.0048	65,500 homes		
Tocom	Cable-guard	1 CAN 3 USA	8,000 approx	217.3 typ	−5 min	FSK +−1M	400	56K	0.14	18.2 to 26.2	+55 max	FSK +−1M	400	28K	0.07	2,000 to 64,000	120 without sensors	20K approx for 2k hhs

*—PPVTV: Pay-Per-View TV; **—Computer Operated switch

Source: From M. B. Akgun and P. Parkinson, "The Development of Cable Data Communications Standads," *IEEE Journal on Selected Areas in Communications,* March 1985, © 1985, IEEE. Reprinted by permission.

by a LAN. In data applications, the capacity of the PBX may not be well utilized because of idle periods in the data. Moreover, PBX ports usually are limited to 64 kb/s and most PBXs do not readily provide host multiplexing of several channels through a common host port. The LAN, on the other hand, provides a high-speed channel that interconnects all devices, thus providing efficient bandwidth sharing among all of them. The LAN can achieve host channel multiplexing by forming packets, each with its source and destination address. A combination PBX and ring-type LAN is useful, where both analog voice and digital data must be switched.

7.8.1 CATV System Characteristics and the Development of LANs

The technological development of LANs has built, in part, on CATV technology. In a CATV system, all signals are everywhere within the system, i.e., switching is not done. Privacy requires passwords and encryption. Full-duplex transparent operation, however, is possible, as is synchronous transmission. Section 7.1 outlined some of the problems that may be encountered in attempts to use CATV systems for data transmission. However, many of these problems result from simultaneous use of a system for entertainment television, and are not present in a system dedicated to data.

Digital modulation methods suitable for data on a cable system include ASK, FSK, and PSK. ASK may activate AGC circuits in repeaters and thus delay receiver stabilization. Delays are undesirable in that modems must respond rapidly in multi-drop and polled applications. (Polling is discussed in Sec. 7.8.2.3.) FSK usually is preferred for cable modems although coherent modulation products (from other channels on the system) may be detrimental to performance under distortion conditions. PSK usually is used only for synchronous data streams because of difficulties in phase ambiguity resolution. Multilevel phase shift keyed systems are useful where spectrum efficiency is important.

7.8.2 LAN Classification

LANs can be classified in terms of their architecture, transmission technology, or access method, as illustrated in Fig. 7.20 [Ref. 23].

7.8.2.1 Architecture. As shown in Fig. 7.20, the LAN architecture may be a bus, tree, ring, or hybrid configuration. The digital bus is a common information channel into which each subscriber can enter information that is accessible by all others. Topologically, busses may be connected in tree or ring configurations. In fact, each branch of a tree is a bus. The basis for digital bus operation usually is a time-division structure in which information is transferred in discrete blocks or packets. The bus must have a bandwidth that can handle the total data movement. In addition, interconnecting devices must have a processing speed high enough to be able to examine each data message, e.g., packet, to determine its relevance to the subscriber. The number of subscribers that can be handled depends upon the bus transmission rate as well as subscriber utilization in terms of transmission duty

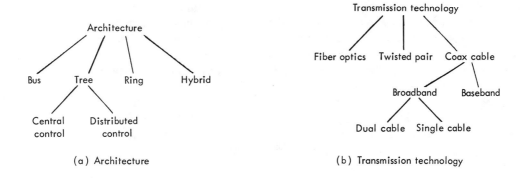

(a) Architecture

(b) Transmission technology

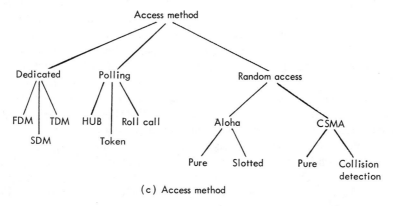

(c) Access method

Figure 7.20 Methods of classifying local area networks. (Copr. 1983. Reprinted by permission of Horizon House-Microwave, Inc., and GEC Video Systems.)

cycle and access time needs. The bus is popular in institutional networks as well as in CATV systems.

The ring architecture is simply a bus that is closed back on itself. The tree architecture is a configuration that may be built from a number of star connections and busses. The star topology is found in the local twisted-pair telephone network, as well as in PBXs and in computer branch exchanges (CBXs). As noted in Fig. 7.20(a), the tree may use either central or distributed control. A *hybrid* architecture is a combination of two of the above architecture types.

7.8.2.2 Transmission Technology. The transmission technology used for a LAN may be any guided medium, as illustrated in Fig. 7.20(b). In addition, short range radio also is used, as described in Sec. 4.7.2.1. Coaxial cable has formed the basis for much LAN development, but is expected to be replaced by fiber optics in many cases because of fiber's vastly greater bandwidth. As can be seen from Fig. 7.20(b), a coaxial cable system can be either *broadband* or *baseband*. In broadband transmission, the cable is channelized, i.e., it operates on an FDM basis. Each input is translated to a carrier within an assigned channel using an RF modem. Terminal addressing is by band-pass filtering. In a broadband system, a dual cable may be used, one coaxial for each direction of transmission, or a single cable may be used, with the upper portion of the spectrum being used for one direction of transmission and the lower portion being used for the opposite direction.

In baseband transmission, the entire available spectrum on the cable is devoted to a single high-speed data stream. The individual inputs are time-division multiplexed by a muldem. Each terminal to be individually addressed must be able to recognize its own address. In some applications, [Ref. 23], a broadband network may link all network branches through a headend and serve individual baseband subnetworks, each of which is carried on one or more channels of the backbone broadband network.

7.8.2.3 Access Protocols.

How does a terminal obtain use of the LAN to which it is connected? Certain time slots or frequency bands may be *dedicated* to the terminal, but the dedicated approach is inflexible for many data processing environments and often wasteful of network resources. Another approach is *token passing*. A token is a special block of data allowing the terminal possessing it to transmit. Thus no data collisions occur on the network. An alternative is *polling,* in which a host computer or control center addresses each terminal in sequence, asking it if it has data to send. *Contention* protocols, of which there are several, are detailed in Sec. 7.8.4. *Adaptive message division multiple access (AMDMA)* operates in both contention and dedicated modes with variable and fixed message lengths.

Space does not permit a detailed discussion of protocol development and standardization. For such a treatment, the reader is referred to Tanenbaum [Ref. 24]. Much of the development work has been done under the overall purview of the International Standards Organization (ISO) and the IEEE 802 committees. The IEEE committees and their associated LAN standards are the following:

802.1 Network Management

802.2 Logical Link Control Specifications

802.3 Carrier-Sense Multiple Access with Collision Detection (CSMA/CD)

802.4 Token-Passing Bus Access Method and Physical Layer Specifications

802.5 Token-Ring Access Method and Physical Layer Specifications

802.6 Metropolitan Area Networks

802.7 Cable Management Task Force

7.8.3 Communication Protocols and Interfaces

The ISO has defined several distinct protocol layers with the intent that different systems have as many layers in common as possible to permit a maximum degree of "openness" for internetwork communications. The purpose of each layer is to provide certain services to the higher layers. These layers and their relationships to one another constitute the basis for the ISO's model for *open system interconnection (OSI).* Its intent is the international standardization of the various protocols [Ref. 25]. Figure 7.21 illustrates the key features of the model.

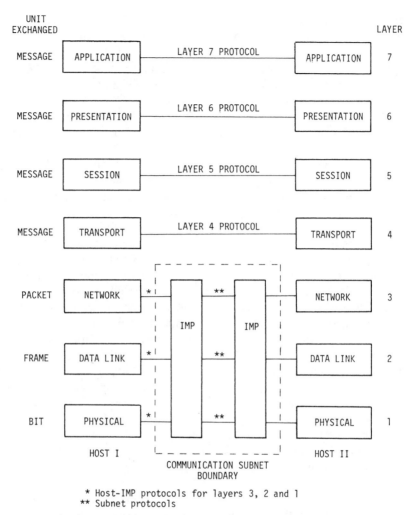

MESSAGE	APPLICATION	LAYER 7 PROTOCOL	APPLICATION	7
MESSAGE	PRESENTATION	LAYER 6 PROTOCOL	PRESENTATION	6
MESSAGE	SESSION	LAYER 5 PROTOCOL	SESSION	5
MESSAGE	TRANSPORT	LAYER 4 PROTOCOL	TRANSPORT	4
PACKET	NETWORK	IMP IMP	NETWORK	3
FRAME	DATA LINK		DATA LINK	2
BIT	PHYSICAL		PHYSICAL	1

HOST I

COMMUNICATION SUBNET
BOUNDARY

HOST II

* Host-IMP protocols for layers 3, 2 and 1
** Subnet protocols

Figure 7.21 The ISO OSI reference model.

The *physical layer* is responsible for the transmission of *bits* transparently over the channel, including such characteristics as bit amplitude and duration, as well as the establishment and termination of the connection. Included are the connector pin assignments.

The *data link layer* is responsible for the transfer of information over the physical link with the needed synchronization, error-control, and flow control functions. Thus data *frames* are transmitted and acknowledgment frames returned from the receiver are processed. Buffering for rate conversion is included.

The *network layer* is responsible for the switching and routing functions needed to route *packets* within the communications subnet, which consists of specialized computers known as *interface message processors (IMPS),* as well as transmission lines. The network layer controls the operation of the subnet, and determines the chief characteristics of the IMP-host interface. It accepts messages from the source (host), converts messages to packets, and directs packets toward their destinations. The network layer also controls traffic to avoid congestion.

The *transport layer* provides end-to-end control and information exchange. It accepts the *message* from the session layer, breaks it into smaller units, if necessary, passes the units to the network layer, and ensures that the units all arrive correctly at the other end. The transport layer isolates the session layer from changes in hardware technology. It makes multiplexing transparent to the session layer, and creates a distinct network connection for each transport connection required by the session layer.

The *session layer* supports the dialog between cooperating *application processes (APs)*. A *session* is a connection between users. Thus the session layer is the user's interface into the network, adding application-oriented functions to the transport layer. The session layer is absent in networks whose users only want raw communication services.

The *presentation layer* furnishes the services which permit the AP to interpret the meaning of the information being transferred. Accordingly, it performs those functions that are requested sufficiently often to warrant finding a general solution for them. Examples are text compression, based on common words and phrases (Huffman coding of words), encryption, code conversion (Baudot, ASCII, EBCDIC), file format conversion, and terminal standards conversion.

The *application layer* directly serves the AP by providing access to the OSI environment. It makes distributed information services available to support the AP and manage the communications process. The content of the application layer thus depends upon the user, and may involve network transparency, problem partitioning among various machines to take maximum advantage of the network, and industry-specific protocols allowing computers from different companies to access each other's data bases.

The protocols for layers 1, 2, and 3 are known collectively as X.25. For layer 1, the protocol is X.21, which was approved by the CCITT in 1976. The X.21 interface specifies how the customer's computer (DTE) sets up and clears calls by exchanging signals with the carrier's equipment (DCE). Thus the physical, electrical, and procedural interface between the host and the IMP are specified. The signal lines used in X.21 appear on a 15-pin connector and carry the following designations.

From DTE to DCE:

    T (Transport) for data

    C (Control) for on-hook/off-hook supervision

    Ga (DTE common return)

    G (Ground)

From DCE to DTE:

    R (Receive) for data

    I (Indication) for control

    S (Signal) for bit timing

    B (Byte timing) for framing (optional)

The X.25 interface provides for addressing, flow control, delivery confirmation, and interrupts. For terminals that are not designed for X.25 the interface is a *packet assembler-disassembler (PAD)* using a protocol designated X.3, and including the X.28 protocol between terminal and PAD and the X.29 protocol between PAD and network. Using the X.25 interface, call establishment and termination between DTEs involves the set up of a *virtual circuit* in which a call request packet is sent from the DTE to its DCE. The network then delivers the call request to the destination DCE which, in turn, delivers it to its DTE. The destination DTE returns a *call accepted packet*. Upon receipt of the call accepted packet by the originating DTE, the virtual circuit is established. Both DTEs then use the full-duplex virtual circuit to exchange data packets. Termination consists of a clear request with a clear confirmation response.

X.25 is a bit-oriented protocol that allows the transmission of characters with an arbitrary number of bits per character. Thus the frame size need not be an integral multiple of any specific character size. Data transparency is achieved by bit stuffing. A *flag character* consisting of the sequence 0 1 1 1 1 1 1 0 is sent at the start and end of each frame. A "0" is stuffed after any sequence of five 1s, and the receiver destuffs using the same rule. The flag character is sent as 0 1 1 1 1 1 1 0, and thus is not subject to stuffing.

The *Systems Network Architecture (SNA)* is a network architecture devised by IBM that allows IBM customers to construct their own networks. Layer 1 is the physical layer. Layer 2 is called *synchronous data link control (SDLC)*, and corresponds to the OSI second layer. Layer 3, *path control,* is concerned with routing and congestion control within the subnet. It corresponds to the OSI third layer, plus parts of the fourth layer. Layer 4, *transmission control,* creates, manages and deletes transport connections called sessions, and provides a uniform interface to higher layers, independent of the properties of the subnet. It corresponds to portions of OSI layers 4 and 5. Layer 5, *data flow control,* keeps track of which end of a session is to transmit next, and also handles error recovery. It corresponds to portions of OSI layer 5. Layer 6 is called *network addressable unit (NAU)* services. It includes presentation services such as text compression and session services for establishing connections. Also included are network services for operation of the network as a whole.

The Digital Equipment Corporation (DEC) has a *Digital Network Architecture (DNA)* to allow any of DEC's customers to establish a private network. Many isolated DECNETs thus exist. A DECNET is a collection of nodes (machines) which may run user programs or do packet switching or both. The lowest four layers correspond closely to those of OSI. There is no session layer. The application layer is a combination of the OSI presentation and application layers. Unique aspects of DECNET are that the frames (Layer 2) contain a character count describing the length of the frame (a multiple of 8 bits), and Layer 3 routes each packet independently of its predecessors.

7.8.4 Network Utilization and Capacity Allocation

Network utilization U is defined as the throughput divided by the data rate R. The propagation delay between stations is designated τ. Thus $R\tau$ is the length of the transmission path in bits. If the length of a packet is designated L_p, then let

$$a = \text{length of path in bits/ length of packet}$$

$$a = \frac{R\tau}{L_p} \tag{7.11}$$

Typically a will be found to be on the order of 0.01 to 0.1. The parameter a determines the upper bound on U. This follows from the fact that the time required for transmission is L_p/R. Thus, the upper bound is

$$U_{max} = \frac{\dfrac{L_p}{\left(\dfrac{\tau + L_p}{R}\right)}}{R} = \frac{1}{(1 + a)} \tag{7.12}$$

This upper bound is independent of the medium access protocol. It assumes that maximum propagation time is incurred on each transmission and that only one transmission occurs at a time. Overhead causes decreases from U_{max}. Overhead includes address bits, synchronization, and administrative overhead to control protocol.

A number of access protocols are *contention-based*. This means that the network users *contend* for the use of the network. The contention arrangement has a significant effect on capacity allocation and thus on network utilization. The purpose of using a contention-based design is to accommodate the need for a high-data rate for a short period of time to or from a given terminal. The principle is that the entire channel capacity is available to all users. Individual users then contend for the channel. The problem that arises is that a collision occurs when two or more users attempt to transmit, causing message overlap, and therefore destruction of the corresponding portions of the messages. The solution to this problem is that upon detection of a collision, users reschedule their transmissions at pseudo-randomly determined times. The result of using a contention-based design is that the network's capacity can be allocated closer to the average aggregate rate of the subscribers rather than to the sum of the peak rates, as must be done in static assignment.

In the *aloha* design, users transmit speculatively. The maximum utilization is $1/2e$, or about 18%. This utilization is reached at about 0.4 attempts per packet time, and otherwise is lower. In *slotted aloha*, all transmissions start at the beginning of a time slot. The maximum utilization is $1/e$, or about 37%. This utilization is reached at about 1.0 attempts per packet time, and otherwise is lower. Aloha and slotted aloha can be used on networks without specific limits on propagation delay, and thus are used on satellite networks.

In the *listen before talk* and *listen while talk* designs, however, propagation delay is a significant parameter, so such designs are not used on satellite networks. Listen before talk also is called *carrier sense multiple access (CSMA)*. The user transmits only if the channel is free, and a collision only occurs because of finite propagation time. For long messages, the utilization approaches 90%. In nonpersistent CSMA the station senses the channel only at random intervals and sends when it finds the channel idle. For slotted channels, p-persistent CSMA is used. If the channel is idle, the station transmits with probability p. With probability $1-p$ it waits until the next slot. If the slot is idle, it transmits with probability p, etc. If $p = 1$, the station transmits whenever it finds the channel idle, thus ignoring propagation delays. The maximum utilization of 1-persistent CSMA is about 53%, and is reached near one attempt per packet time. For 0.5-persistent and 0.1-persistent CSMA, the maximum efficiencies reach 68% and 88%, respectively, and occur at more than one attempt per packet time. While the utilization becomes quite high for many attempts per packet time, the throughput becomes quite low and the delays become long.

Listen while talk is used by Ethernet. This approach minimizes the time period of a collision to a maximum of 2τ. The utilization approaches 99% for long messages. If two or more stations attempt to transmit simultaneously, a collision occurs, but each station detects the collision, stops its transmission, and restarts only after a random period of time has passed. An Ethernet terminal can be in one of three states: contention, transmission, or idle. The process of listening while transmitting actually is achieved by listening between packets. The IEEE 802.3 standard for bus contention systems is based on Ethernet and describes a passive (nonrepeatered) cable bus system operating in a 30 MHz baseband. A *local interface unit (LIU)* provides the interface between the system and a given station. The LIUs transmit and receive at 10 Mb/s. The access protocol is referred to as CSMA with collision detection (CD), or CSMA/CD. As many as 1024 stations within 2.5 km can access the system. The message protocol uses a variable frame message size with a best effort delivery.

An alternative method of capacity allocation is *reservation,* which is useful in situations in which a few users need a high-speed information interchange in a point-to-point mode for a period of time. The reservation approach provides a high-capacity information channel and a low-capacity control channel. The response time depends upon the capacity of the high-speed bus, the duration of transmissions, the number of users, and the efficiency of the control process.

The *multidrop* approach to capacity allocation is used in situations in which a group of processing elements provides data to a distributed set of subscribers. Implementation involves a high-capacity information channel and a transaction channel.

7.8.5 LAN Applications

Applications for LANs include computer terminal interconnections within universities, industrial complexes, military bases, and government establishments. Other applications include surveillance TV, intercom and paging, automotive quality control, the remote loading and monitoring of networks of process controllers, energy management and control systems in factories, health care facility applications, and closed-circuit TV for training, conferences, etc. Table 7.7 [Ref. 6] lists the main features of various local and metropolitan area networks.

TABLE 7.7 LOCAL AND METROPOLITAN AREA NETWORKS
MAIN FEATURES OF VARIOUS LOCAL AND METROPOLITAN AREA NETWORKS
(Areas of incompatibilities between systems can easily be recognized. The listed systems represent only a sample of products that were known by end of 1983.)

LOCAL & METRO AREA NETWORKS

DESIGN AUTHORITY	SYSTEM	NETWORK ARCHITECTURE Type	Max Radius Km	Modulation Type	SUPER-CHANNEL PARAMETERS Super Chnls Spaced	Downstrm Alloc-ation	Upstream Alloc-ation	Bps per Hertz	BER & CNR	Data Rate Mbps	Freq Agile LIU	LOCAL INTERFACE UNIT PARAMETERS LIU PROTOCOL Chl Access	Logic Link	Interface	Data Rate Kbps	Ports /LIU (max)	NUMBER OF SYSTEMS IN USE
Condord Data Systems	Token/Net	mid split BUS	40	AMPSK (IEEE 802)	6 MHz	P Q R S T U (six ch)	59.75 to 65.75MHz etc. to 89.75 MHz	0.83	10^{-8} at 36 dB	5	YES	TDMA/token passing (IEEE 802 ECMA)	as per IEEE 802 and ECMA	RS-232C V.24 RS-449 V.35	up to 230	32	alpha sites
Contel Information Systems	ContelNet (800 Series)	mid split TREE	8	FSK	6 MHz	156 MHz to 300 MHz	12 MHz to 156 MHz	0.33	10^{-9} at 30 dB	2	NO	CSMA/CD, token passing (IEEE 802)	as per IEEE 802	RS-232C	up to 19.2	16	?
	High Speed	mid split TREE	8	QPSK	12 MHz	156 MHz to 300 MHz	12 MHz 156 MHz	0.83	not available	10	NO	CSMA/CD, token passing (IEEE 802)	as per IEEE 802	RS-232C	up to 19.2	16	?
Gould	Modway	CATV BUS 5 active 2.5 nonamp	*	*	6 MHz	*	*	*	*	up to 1.544	NO	token passing similar to IEEE 802	extended HDLC similar to IEEE 802	RS-232C + special control interface	up to 1540	?	?
LDO M/A COM	CAPAC	mid Split TREE	no limit	DQPSK	2 MHz	180 MHz to 300 MHz	6 MHz to 120 MHz	1.05	10^{-8} at 26 dB	2.1	NO	FDM/TDM downstream FDM/TDMA upstream	similar to X.21	RS-232C RS-449	up to 2048	32	3 systems
Phasecom	Intelligent Cable Network (ICN)	dual mid 802 Sub TREE	4 to 80	VSBASK	6 MHz	50-440, 160-440, 182-300, 50-440.	50-440, 5-120, 5-108, 5.75-29.75	0.26	10^{-13}	1.544	YES	CSMA/CD	X.25	RS-232C 12 bit parallel	up to 19.2	4	beta sites

438

Company	System	Topology	Max nodes	Modulation	Channel BW	Freq (228-262 midsplit / 226-244 subsplit)	Freq (70-106 midsplit / 10-28 subsplit)	Eff.	BER	Data rate	Std	Access method	Data link protocol	Interface	Async rate	No.	Installed base
Sytek	Locainet 20	mid split or sub split TREE	50	FSK	300 KHz	228-262 midsplit 226-244 subsplit	70-106 midsplit 10-28 subsplit	0.43	10⁻⁹	0.128	YES	CSMA/CD	HDLC derivative	DEC compatible	up to 19.2	2	300 systems 10,000 units
	Locainet 40	mid/sub split TREE	10	FSK	6 MHz	216 to 246 MHz	23.75 to 53.75 MHz	0.33	10⁻¹³	2.0	YES	CSMA/CD	HDLC derivative	DEC compatible	up to 9.6	8	5 alpha sites 20 units
3 M/IS	Videodata	mid sub split TREE	no limit	FSK	800KHz	0 to S	2, 3, 4, 4A & 5	0.125	1 at 30 dB	0.1	NO	FDM or TDM auto poll	SDLC	RS-232C or 8-bit parallel	up to 100	4	300 systems in US & Europe
	Videodata LAN/1	mid split TREE	11	CPFSK	6 MHz	P+Q, R+S, T+U (3 chs)	62.75 to 86.75 MHz (3 chs)	0.417	10⁻¹³ at 26 dB	2.5	NO	token passing non IEEE 802	SDLC	RS-232C	up to 19.2	2	beta sites
	Videodata LAN/3	mid split BUS	?	AMPSK (IEEE 802)	12 MHz	156 to 300 MHz	5 to 120 MHz (3 chs)	0.83	?	10	?	TDMA/token passing (IEEE 802 ECMA)	as per IEEE 802 and ECMA	RS-232C V.24 RS-449 V.35	up to 230	?	?
Ungermann Bass	Net/One	mid split TREE	16	AM	6 MHz			0.833	10⁻⁹ at 26dB	5.0	Y/N both types made	CSMA/ED** (IEEE 802)	HDLC derivative (IEEE 802)	RS-232C V.35 RS-422 IEEE 488	up to 2000	24	13 CAN. 200 US. +100 others
Wang	Wangnet Interconnect Band	dual cable TREE	22	FM&FSK	20 KHz 187.5 KHz	10-20.6 and 49.6 to 81.6MHz	10-20.6 and 49.6 to 81.6MHz	0.48 to 0.34	?	1200 bps to 64 Kbps	Y/N both types made	FDM & TDM		RS-449 V.35 V.24 RS-366	up to 64	1	approx 20 full systems +
	Peripherals Band			?	8 MHz	97.5 to 145.5 MHz	93.5 to 149.5 MHz	0.534	?	4.27	YES	FDM & TDM		?	?	8	
	Wang Band			PSK	27 MHz	216 to 243 MHz	216 to 243 MHz	0.4 approx	?	10	NO	CSMA/CD	HDLC	Wang VS & OLS		8	
	Utility Band		no limit	—	6 MHz	channels 7 to 13, 174-216 MHz	channels 7 to 13, 174-216 MHz	—	—	—	—	—	—	Wang VS & OLS 12K		1	many individual service band installations

The 6 MHz dual-cable channels are provided for user-defined video communications applications.

User provides own modem to special control interface
ED Error Detection

Source: From M. B. Akgun and P. Parkinson, "The Development of Cable Data Communications Standards," *IEEE Journal on Selected Areas in Communications*, March 1985, © 1985, IEEE. Reprinted by permission.

439

7.9 INTEGRATED SERVICES DIGITAL NETWORK (ISDN)

The Integrated Services Digital Network (ISDN) is a unified, global digital telecommunications network providing the user a common interface to which telephones, computers, and other communications devices can be attached. Initial work on the ISDN focuses on the use of existing wire-pairs whose bandwidth is limited to the support of rates not exceeding the first level (DS1 in North American systems and CEPT-1 in European systems). The CCITT views the ISDN as evolving from the digital telephone networks of various countries. A single architecture thus will provide not only telephone service but also telex, facsimile, and data retrieval, with such capabilities as video conferencing and computer aided design being added thereafter [Ref. 26].

User interfaces have been defined as follows:

Basic Rate Digital Subscriber Line
  2 B (bearer) channels @ 64 kb/s for voice or data
  1 D (data) channel @ 16 kb/s for signaling and customer packet data at 16 kb/s
Primary Rate Digital Subscriber Line (North American)
  23 B channels @ 64 kb/s
  1 D channel @ 64 kb/s
Primary Rate Digital Subscriber Line (European)
  30 B channels @ 64 kb/s
  1 D channel @ 64 kb/s

The general purpose of the D channel is to set up calls, disconnect them, and correctly route data on the B channels through the network (common-channel signaling). The basic rate is intended for residential service. The basic rate interface between customer-premises equipment and the ISDN node is called the *U interface*. The primary rate is intended for large business customers with PBX service. Old terminals not having an ISDN interface can be connected via an adapter.

The ISDN is based upon the ISO OSI model, described in Sec. 7.8.3. In the case of a B channel used for an end-to-end circuit-switched connection, e.g., for voice, the ISDN node provides only an OSI Layer 1 interface to the terminal. All higher layers are defined by the user. However, in the case of a B channel used for packet switching to send data over multiple virtual circuits to numerous terminals on the user's premises, the ISDN node provides an interface to each terminal for the OSI Layer 2 and 3 functions also. All signaling messages on the D channel require Layers 1, 2, and 3. The Layer 2 link-access procedures for the D channel are called LAP-D (link access protocol-D) functions.

Extension of the ISDN to broadband services is related to conversion of the subscriber line to optical fiber, allowing an increase in the digital stream rate from the vicinity of 2 Mb/s to 30 Mb/s or more. Broadband applications include video telephony, video conferences, high-volume file transfers, and the delivery of radio and TV programs, including HDTV.

ISDN supports various concurrent applications via a single *user-network interface (UNI)*. This interface has a number of positioned channels carried within a frame, which is a periodically recurring set of serial time slots. Specific slots are assigned for overhead functions such as frame delimitation. The remaining slots carry the data being sent. The use of specific periodic time slots assigned to a channel is called *synchronous transfer mode (STM)*. By contrast, *asynchronous transfer mode (ATM)* does not have such slots deterministically assigned to a channel [Ref. 27]. In ATM, information is organized into blocks or packets, each having a header that includes channel identifiation. Such a channel is called a *labeled channel*. If labeled channels are multiplexed onto a stream of blocks, the stream is called a *label multiplex*. ATM thus serves as a multiplexing technique for the dynamic allocation of bit rate. Such dynamic allocation may be very useful in those forms of digital video calling for a nonconstant channel rate, with significant increases when rapid motion is occurring in the picture.

Broadband channel rates under consideration by the CCITT are on the order of 30 to 45 Mb/s for the H_2 channel, 60 to 70 Mb/s for the H_3 channel, and 120 to 140 Mb/s for the H_4 channel. The CEPT-3 or DS3 rate thus may become designated as H_2, or possibly as H_{21} and H_{22}, respectively. The H_4 rate is considered especially important because it is needed for high-quality video and high-data rate transmission between computers.

Associated with the broadband ISDN concept is that of the *broadband universal telecommunications network (BUTN)* [Ref. 28]. Its proponents view it as a step beyond the broadband ISDN. The BUTN would combine broadband circuit switched and high-speed packet switched services onto an optical fiber system at rates on the order of 560 Mb/s.

PROBLEMS

7.1 A system using GID cable is being designed for a 1200 dB reach, and is to be used in a 450 MHz CATV system. The cable has a loss of 32 dB/km at 400 MHz and a loss characteristic $a\sqrt{f} + bf$, where $b = 0.005\ a$. How many 20 dB repeaters will the system have on its longest cable run? What will be the length of that run in km?

7.2 In the examples of Fig. 7.13, explain why FF1 has a lower NF than FF4 even though both use a main amplifier with $NF = 6$.

7.3 What is the maximum network utilization for a fiber optic LAN operating at the DS1 rate if the fiber $\epsilon_r = 2.25$ and each packet is 512 bits long?

7.4 A cable system is found to be interfering with an emergency radio system that operates at 243 MHz. However, the cable system is not actually transmitting on Channel N. The interference is found to consist of a combination of Channels J and L. Explain what is causing this problem.

7.5 The transmission stability of coaxial cables appears to make them well suited to the use of multilevel modulation techniques. You are asked to design a system capable of transmitting full motion digital video (derived from NTSC composite) within a 6 MHz channel width. What modulation technique would you select, and what video bit rate would you use?

7.6 A 60 Hz ingress problem in a cable system is found to produce a broad horizontal bar that moves vertically through each color picture over a time interval of approximately 17 seconds. The system's single monochrome channel, however, is unaffected. Explain why not.

REFERENCES

1. Television Allocations Study Organization, *TASO Report to the FCC,* March 16, 1969.
2. "CATV Data Handbook," Texscan Corporation, 3102 North 29th Avenue, P.O. Box 27548, Phoenix, AZ 85061.
3. W. A. Rheinfelder, *CATV System Engineering,* TAB Books, Blue Ridge Summit, PA.
4. J. A. Chiddix, "Fiber Optic Technology for CATV Supertrunk Applications," *NCTA Cable '85 Technical Papers,* pp. 157–65.
5. A. S. Taylor, "Characterization of Cable TV Networks as the Transmission Media for Data," *IEEE Journal on Selected Areas in Communications,* SAC-3, no. 2, (March 1985), 255–65.
6. M. B. Akgun and P. Parkinson, "The Development of Cable Data Communications Standards," *IEEE Journal on Selected Areas in Communications,* SAC-3, no. 2, (March 1985), 273–85.
7. "Tocom 55 Plus General Information Manual," TOCOM, 3301 Royalty Row, Irving, TX 75062.
8. "Standards of Good Engineering Practice for Measurements on CATV Systems," National Cable Television Association, NCTA 008-0477, 1977, Washington, DC.
9. "Sylvania Pathmaker CATV Data," CATV Division, GTE Products Corporation, El Paso, TX.
10. J. P. Preschutti, "Limitations and Characteristics of Broadband Feedforward Amplifiers," *NCTA Cable '84 Technical Papers,* pp. 109–17.
11. N. J. Slater and D. J. McEwen, "Composite Second Order Distortions," *NCTA Cable '84 Technical Papers,* pp. 129–34.
12. J. C. Pavlic, "Some Considerations for Applying Several Feedforward Gain Block Models to CATV Distribution Amplifiers," *NCTA Cable '83 Technical Papers,* pp. 297–302.
13. R. G. Meyer, R. Eschenbach, and W. M. Edgerley, "A Wideband Feedforward Amplifier," *IEEE Journal on Solid State Circuits,* Dec. 1974.
14. Opinion and Order, Docket 21006, Federal Communications Commission, Washington, DC, ¶76.611(a)(2).
15. G. Luettgenau, "TV Cable Transmission Up to 900 MHz," *NCTA Cable '84 Technical Papers,* pp. 47–51.
16. S. B. Weinstein, *Getting the Picture,* IEEE Press, 1986, pp. 139–40.
17. C. O. Eissler, "Addressable Control," *NCTA Cable '81 Technical Papers,* pp. 29–33.
18. V. Bhaskaran and M. Davidov, "Video Scrambling—An Overview," *NCTA Cable '84 Technical Papers,* pp. 240–46.
19. M. T. Hayasi, "Effectiveness of Static Scrambling versus Dynamic Scrambling Systems: A Classification Method," *NCTA '83 Technical Papers,* pp. 309–13.
20. M. Madras, "M/A Com's Video-Cipher Systems Offer Security Quality, Flexibility," *Ku Band World,* 1, no. 3, (March 1986), 42–50.
21. TOCOM System Description, TOCOM, 3301 Royalty Row, Irving, TX 75062.

22. H. Frank, "Broadband versus Baseband Local Area Networks," *Telecommunications,* 17, no. 3, (March 1983), 35–38.

23. M. A. Lawrence, "The Case for Broadband LANs," *Telecommunications Products and Technology,* 5, no. 7, (July 1987), 36–40.

24. A. S. Tanenbaum, *Computer Networks,* Prentice-Hall, Inc., Englewood Cliffs, NJ, 1981.

25. M. Edwards, "Development of Standards Promises to Ensure the Multivendor Interoperability of Networks," *Communications News,* 23, no. 7, (July 1986), 58–63.

26. S. N. Pandhi, "The Universal Data Connection," *IEEE Spectrum,* 24, no. 7, (July 1987), 31–37.

27. S. E. Minzer, "Toward an International Broadband ISDN Standard," *Telecommunications,* 21, no. 10, (Oct. 1987), 94–164.

28. D. J. Harrold and R. D. Strock, "The Broadband Universal Telecommunications Network," *IEEE Communications Magazine,* 25, no. 1, (Jan. 1987), 69–79.

8

Transmission System Alternatives

This concluding chapter briefly describes two transmission technologies, coaxial carrier systems and millimeter waveguide systems, which constitute alternatives to the optical fiber for long haul transmission. The first, coaxial carrier, is in extensive use in the United States and elsewhere. The second, millimeter waveguide, has been developed and tested, but not deployed. The chapter concludes with a comparison of the various broadband transmission technologies in terms of their areas of applicability, especially in the foreseeable future.

8.1 COAXIAL CARRIER CABLE SYSTEMS

Coaxial carrier cable systems are used for significant amounts of voice, data, and video transmission. Such systems provide for the transmission of FDM signals at carrier frequencies as high as 70 MHz to distances of 6400 km. Most of the systems operate on an analog basis. Separate coaxial lines are used for each direction of transmission. Numerous coaxial lines are placed in a common sheath to form the overall cable.

The principle of operation of a coaxial carrier transmission system is similar to that of a CATV transmission system, but the maximum frequency is held to less than 70 MHz to allow a 6400 km reach. The bandwidth allows the transmission of as many as 13 200 analog voice channels per coaxial pair, or a total of 132 000 channels per cable, with a cable consisting of 22 coaxial units. (One pair out of ten is reserved for line protection.) The channels are arranged in the FDM hierarchy, listed in Table 8.1. Two mastergroups provide a 4.8 MHz bandwidth, sufficient for the transmission of an NTSC video signal.

Table 8.2 summarizes the development of coaxial carrier systems in the U.S. by the Bell System [Ref. 1]. The L1 system was placed into service in 1941 with 480 4 kHz two-way channels per pair of 0.7 cm diameter coaxial cables with a repeater every 9 km. The cable diameter then was increased to 1.0 cm for a 600 circuit capacity and a 12.9 km repeater spacing. The descriptions that follow deal with the L5 and L5E systems since their principle of operation is essentially the same as that of the earlier systems.

TABLE 8.1 FREQUENCY DIVISION MULTIPLEX HIERARCHY

Unit	Equivalence	Spectrum
Message Channel	—	200 to 3350 Hz
Group	12 Message Channels	60 to 108 kHz
Supergroup	5 Groups (60 message channels)	312 to 552 kHz
Mastergroup*	10 Supergroups (600 message channels)	60 to 2788 kHz or 564 to 3084 kHz
Jumbogroup*	6 Mastergroups (3600 message channels)	0.564 to 17.548 MHz
L5 Line*	3 Jumbogroups (10 800 message channels)	1.59 to 68.78 MHz

*Other definitions exist beyond the supergroup. For example, the CCITT *basic mastergroup* is 5 supergroups, or 300 message channels. The CCITT *supermastergroup* is 3 *basic mastergroups,* or 900 message channels.

TABLE 8.2 ANALOG COAXIAL CARRIER TRANSMISSION SYSTEMS

System	First Service	Capacity, Voice Circuits Per Coax Pair	Per Cable*	Coax Units per Sheath (typical)	Repeater Spacing (km)	Repeater Type
L1	1941	600–720	720	4	12.9	Vacuum tube
			2160	8		
			5580	8		
L3	1953	1860	9300	12	6.4	Vacuum tube
L4	1967	3600	32400	20	3.2	Discrete transistor, printed board wiring
L5	1974	10800	108000	22	1.6	Discrete transistor hybrid integrated circuit
L5E	1976	13200	132000			

* One pair reserved for protection of failed regular lines.

Source: Reprinted with permission from the *AT&T Technical Journal,* copyright 1974, AT&T.

Sec. 8.1   Coaxial Carrier Cable Systems

445

8.1.1 System Features

The L5 and L5E systems use fixed gain repeaters every 1.6 km and adaptive regulating repeaters every 11 km (maximum) to compensate for cable characteristic changes due to temperature. Adjustable gain equalizing repeaters are placed at maximum intervals of 60 km. Power feed main station repeaters are placed at 120 km maximum intervals, and line protection switching on a basis of one standby line per ten in-service lines is done at 240 km maximum intervals. Figure 8.1 [Ref. 1] illustrates the main features of the L5 switching span.

8.1.2 Frequency Allocation

The frequency allocation on the L5 cable is based on the fact that parasitic effects in transformers, inductors, and capacitors, especially losses and stray capacitance, limit one's ability to control the transmission characteristic at the highest and lowest frequencies. The ratio of upper to lower frequencies, accordingly, is limited to about 5.5 octaves. To maximize the bandwidth, the lowest frequency requiring control is raised above 1.5 MHz.

Guard-band selection is based on providing the ability to interchange an entire analog jumbogroup with a high-speed digital signal. In addition, design limits were based upon the use of economical band-stop and band-pass filters. Figure 8.2 [Ref. 1] shows, respectively, the basic jumbogroup and the L5 frequency allocation.

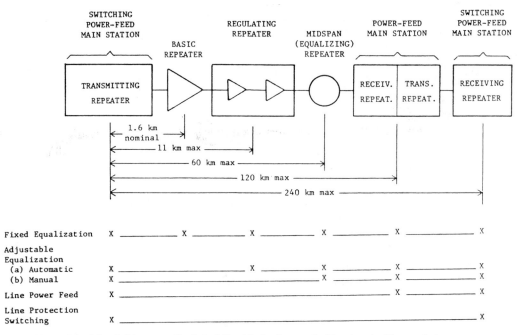

Figure 8.1 L5 switching span (basic building block of system). (Reprinted with permission from the *AT&T Technical Journal,* copyright 1974, AT&T.)

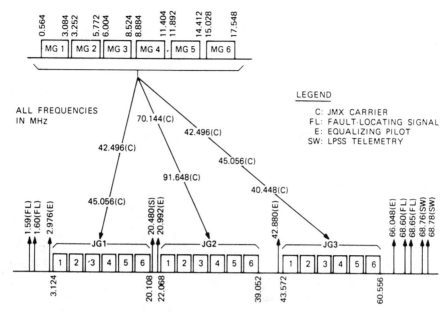

Figure 8.2 Basic jumbogroup and L5 frequency allocation. (Reprinted with permission from the *AT&T Technical Journal,* copyright 1974, AT&T.)

The basic jumbogroup is equivalent to the L4 line spectrum. The *JMX carrier (C)* frequencies shown are used to translate the basic jumbogroup to the L5 line frequencies.

8.1.3 Cable Characteristics

The *coax-22 cable* used for the L5 and L5E system consists of 22 disc-insulated coaxial cables plus 42 polyethylene-insulated conductor pairs for order wire (coordination) and fault location purposes as well as air-pressure telemetry. The loss equation is of the form of Eq. (7.1):

$$\alpha = 2.4235 \left(\frac{1 + 0.0062}{\sqrt{f}} \right) \sqrt{f} + 0.0029f + 0.0049 \left(T - T_o \right) \sqrt{f} \text{ dB/km} \quad (8.1)$$

where f is in MHz, T is the temperature in °C, and $T_o = 12.77$°C. The loss consists of a resistance loss of $2.4235(1 + 0.0062/\sqrt{f})\sqrt{f}$, which includes skin effect, a power factor term $0.0029f$ from dissipation in the disc spacers, and a factor to account for the temperature dependence of the copper resistivity, $0.0049(T - T_o)\sqrt{f}$.

The cable loss exhibits certain distortions at frequencies beyond the 70 MHz bandwidth utilized. These distortions include a structural return loss from cable stranding during manufacture, resulting in a resonance at 157 ± 2.5 MHz. In addition, seam interaction or "back twist" from cable stranding in the outer coaxials results in a resonance in the vicinity of 170 MHz.

8.1.4 Repeater Design Objectives

The L5 and L5E systems are designed for a long-haul noise objective of 40 dBrncO, with residual transmission deviations less than 0.01% of the top channel cable loss. In transmission planning, therefore, the bandwidth, repeater spacing, and signal transmission levels had to be adjusted to realize the system objectives over its expected lifetime. Repeater spacing thus is governed by the available gain, noise figure, load-carrying capacity, and linearity of the repeater, as well as the margins needed to account for cable and repeater variations because of temperature changes, manufacturing limits, and aging. Table 8.3, [Ref. 1], summarizes the design objectives for L-type repeaters.

8.1.5 System Layout

Factors affecting system layout are the power feeding techniques, the equalization strategy, the need to interface with existing systems, and system reliability.

8.1.5.1 Powering. Figure 8.3 [Ref. 1] is a simplified diagram of the L5 line power feed. The voltage is developed by dc-dc converters and applied to the line, then removed at each repeater using a power separation filter.

8.1.5.2 Equalization. Equalization is needed, as explained in Chap. 7, because cable attenuation per unit distance increases in dB as $\sqrt{f}$. To achieve a 40 dBrnc0 noise objective over a 6400 km circuit requires the equalization of 132 000 dB near 70 MHz. This calls for broadband circuits that are low in noise, highly linear, and very stable. Fixed equalizers compensate for normal cable loss, for average design error, and for deviations from nominal repeater spacing. Line build-out networks are used to simulate the loss of 0.16 km to 0.80 km lengths of line. Manual adjustments on an out of service basis can be used to compensate for constant transmission deviations. Adjustable equalizers (manual or automatic) compensate for cable temperature, repeater temperature, manufacturing deviations,

TABLE 8.3 DESIGN OBJECTIVES FOR L-TYPE REPEATERS

System Data	L3	L4	L5
Top frequency (MHz)	8.3	17.5	60.6
Repeater performance, referred to top channel:			
Noise figure (dB)	11	6.5	5.5
Load capacity (dBm)	16	21	24
Nonlinearity			
Second order (dB)	−61	−70	−70
Third order (dB)	−96	−100	−110*
Insertion gain (dB)	44	33	31
Transmission level (dB)	−11	−14.2	−13.6

* Using special phase-shaping networks providing an intentional nonlinearity of the phase frequency characteristic to reduce the correlation of third-order product addition.

Source: Reprinted with permission from the *AT&T Technical Journal,* copyright 1974, AT&T.

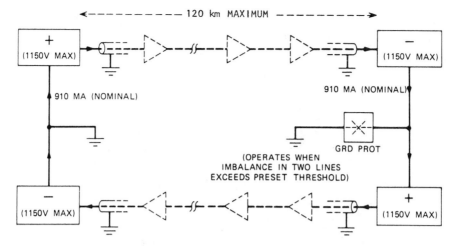

Figure 8.3 L5 line power feed arrangement. (Reprinted with permission from the *AT&T Technical Journal,* copyright 1974, AT&T.)

aging effects and the replacement of failed repeaters with spares having slightly different characteristics.

Cable characteristic changes due to temperature constitute the largest time-variant transmission deviation. This effect is compensated by regulating repeaters every 11 km, as illustrated in Fig. 8.1. The compensation is achieved in two ways. A *closed-loop postequalizer* compensates for a portion of the preceding regulating section and an *open-loop preequalizer* senses the resistance of a buried thermistor to compensate for a portion of the ensuing regulating section. Repeater characteristic changes due to temperature are compensated by a *dynamic equalizer,* which is an adaptive equalizer with memory, permitting the transmission response to remain unchanged if any of the pilots are lost. Statistical manufacturing deviations are compensated by manually adjusted equalizers.

8.1.6 Reliability

The large circuit capacity of the L5 and L5E systems dictates that the probability of failure be minimized and that outage times be kept as short as possible. Reliability considerations were paramount in establishing the length of the switching span as a maximum of 240 km, and in determining the number of lines required as standbys to achieve the availability objective. For DDS applications, this objective is 0.9996. Because of the use of L5 and L5E for DDS, this objective must be met.

8.1.7 LD-4 Digital Cable System

The LD-4 digital cable system was placed into operation in 1975 by Bell Canada between Toronto and Montreal, a 700 km length [Ref. 2]. It has a 274.176 Mb/s data rate capability and an availability objective of 0.99999 per 160 km of path length. The cable is buried at least 1.2 m at all points, with direct burial being used in rural

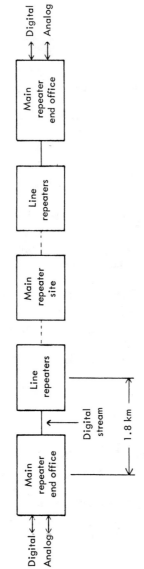

Figure 8.4 Major elements of the LD-4 system. (Reprinted from *Telesis*, Vol. 5, No. 3, p. 68, © Bell Northern Research, Ltd., 1977.)

areas and ducts being used in urban areas. Multiplex equipment at the terminals provides digital streams at the DS3, DS2, and DS1 rates plus analog conversion for voice. Figure 8.4 illustrates the major elements of the LD-4 system.

The major digital impairments in the system are bit errors and line jitter. Bit errors are caused by imperfections in repeater operation, e.g., protection switch actuation, and increase with the number of line repeaters and multiplexers in use. Line jitter is caused by 60 Hz induction, as well as variations in the line rate in the repeaters. Line jitter also increases with the number of repeaters.

8.1.8 Future of Coaxial Carrier

Coaxial carrier systems having even greater capacity than the L5 and L5E are technologically possible. However, the need for, and the economic desirability of such systems is doubtful in view of such alternatives as optical fiber systems, as well as satellite and digital microwave radio systems.

8.2 MILLIMETER WAVEGUIDE SYSTEM

A millimeter waveguide system, designated the WT4, was developed by the Bell System in the mid-1970s. It provides 59 DS4 channels in each of two directions plus 3 protection channels in each direction.

8.2.1 System Characteristics

The WT4 system is designed to use the 38.0 to 104.5 GHz spectrum with repeaters spaced 60 km maximum in gentle terrain and superhighway rights of way and 50 km maximum in rugged mountainous terrain. Figure 8.5 [Ref. 3] is a block diagram of a repeater *hop* (repeater and transmission medium to next repeater). The system is designed for $p_{be} < 10^{-9}$ over a 6400 km distance with a service availability > 0.9998. The modulation is DBPSK, providing up to 238 000 full duplex voice channels. An upgrade to DQPSK called the WT4A provides 476 000 full duplex voice channels.

As many as six repeater stations within a protection span ($\leqslant 500$ km) can be arranged to add or drop channels. The solid-state circuits are operated in a dry nitrogen environment for high reliability. Protection system signaling and an order wire channel are interleaved into the digital data streams of the designated channels. Automatic transfer to protection channels is provided in the event of a service channel failure.

8.2.2 Waveguide Structure and Characteristics

The waveguide has a 60 mm internal diameter and is installed in 140 mm outside diameter steel sheath, in which it is supported by spring rollers. The installation depth is at least 0.6 m. The structure is that of fusion-joined steel tube sections encased in a fusion-joined protective steel outer casing, which is highly resistant to damage. The waveguide can follow the horizontal bends and vertical contours of the

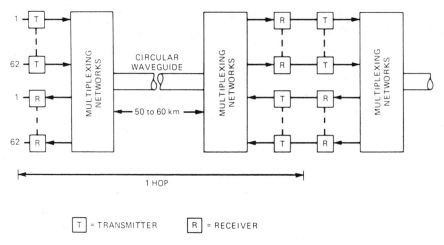

Figure 8.5 Block diagram of WT4 repeater hop. (Reprinted with permission from the *AT&T Technical Journal*, copyright 1974, AT&T.)

right-of-way without undue performance penalties. Its minimum bend radius is 75 m, based upon the yield stress of the sheath pipe and the limited elastic range of the roller support. Heavy shielding is provided by the sheath and the waveguide, allowing even high-voltage power line right of way to be utilized without interference (intermodulation due to ingress). Waveguide loss is less than 1.0 dB/km from 40 to 110 GHz, based on measurements during a field evaluation test [Ref. 3]. The various loss components add as shown in Fig. 8.6 [Ref. 3]. The projected WT4A system loss composite is shown in Fig. 8.7 [Ref. 3]. The installed waveguide is a mix of 99% dielectric lined guide and 1% helix-type mode-filter guide. The two types are illustrated in Fig. 8.8 [Ref. 3].

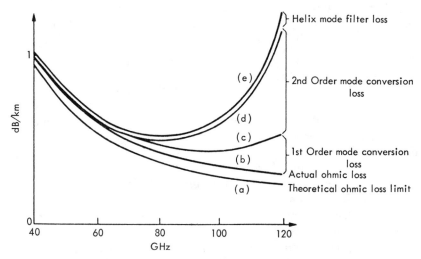

Figure 8.6 Addition of various loss components in WT4 waveguide. (Reprinted with permission from the *AT&T Technical Journal*, copyright 1974, AT&T.

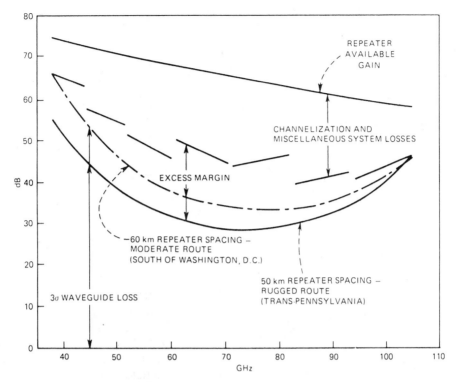

Figure 8.7 Projected WT4A system loss composite. (Reprinted with permission from the *AT&T Technical Journal*, copyright 1974, AT&T.)

8.2.3 Link Budget

The transmitters selected for the WT4 system are silicon IMPATT diode oscillators whose output is at least 70 mW at 108 GHz. The receiver noise is approximately 1000 K. Line attenuation between repeaters is a maximum of 70 dB. The noise floor in a 500 MHz bandwidth accordingly is -228.6 dBW/HzK $+ 87.0$ dBHz $+ 30.0$ dBK $= -111.6$ dBW. The link budget then is:

Transmitter output	-11.5 dBW
Line attenuation	70.0 dB
Received signal	-81.5 dBW
Noise level	-111.6 dBW
Signal-to-noise ratio at receiver	30.1 dB

8.2.4 Repeater Stations

The repeater station spacing is 60 km or less. Repeater stations include protection switching equipment and emergency standby power, but normally would be powered from commercial sources.

The multiplexing networks consist of band diplexers made of circular wave-

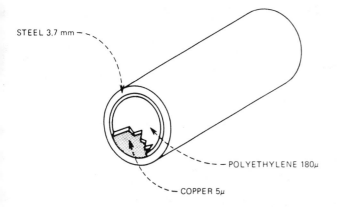

STEEL 3.7 mm

--- POLYETHYLENE 180μ

--- COPPER 5μ

(a) Dielectric-lined waveguide

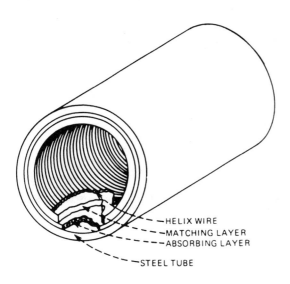

---HELIX WIRE
---MATCHING LAYER
---ABSORBING LAYER

---STEEL TUBE

(b) Helix waveguide

Figure 8.8 WT4 waveguide. (Reprinted with permission from the *AT&T Technical Journal*, copyright 1974, AT&T.)

guide operating in the TE_{110} mode to split the overall 38 to 104.5 GHz band into subbands (see Fig. 8.7). Channel diplexers consisting of resonant cavities have half-power bandwidths of 475 MHz and center frequency spacings of 500 MHz. Their purpose is to drop or add DS4 channels within each subband. Low-pass filters are included to control harmonics. One direction of transmission uses the 38.0 to 69.0 GHz frequencies, while the opposite direction uses the 73.5 to 104.5 GHz frequencies.

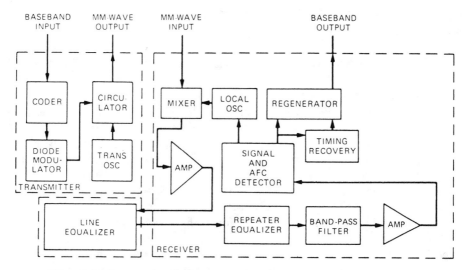

Figure 8.9 Regenerative line repeater. (Reprinted with permission from the *AT&T Technical Journal,* copyright 1974, AT&T.)

Figure 8.9 [Ref. 3] is a block diagram of a regenerative line repeater. The link budget assures a received signal level at each repeater that will result in $p_{be} < 10^{-9}$ even at temperature extremes and maximum supply voltage variations. The repeater *intermediate frequency (IF)* is kept fixed through the use of an AFC circuit. The transmitter frequency can drift ± 25 MHz without causing excessive unequalized delay in the system. The baseband stream (DS4) is scrambled using pseudorandom bit generators in the TDM multiplexers that feed the system. Thus the need to transmit a dc component is eliminated.

The technologies used in making the repeaters assure long lifetime and ease of maintainability. The millimeter wave parts all use standard rectangular waveguide, with three sizes covering the 38.0 to 104.5 GHz band. The tolerances typically are 2.5 μm. The IF and most of the baseband circuits are made of hybrid integrated circuits. Line widths in the IF networks are 75 $\pm$6 μm. Line separations must be controlled to ± 10 μm. Some IF circuits require the dielectric constant of the alumina substrate to be held within $\pm 1\%$ of a fixed value. Printed boards are used in the AFC and AGC circuits associated with the IF amplifiers and the power supply circuits.

8.2.5 System Status

A WT4 system field evaluation using a 14 km run was conducted successfully in northern New Jersey in 1975 and 1976 using the 40 to 110 GHz band. A date for commercial deployment has not been set because fiber optic transmission now appears to offer a greater degree of cost-effectiveness.

8.3 COMPARISON OF BROADBAND TRANSMISSION TECHNOLOGIES

This text has described five different transmission technologies, four of which (microwave radio, satellite radio, optical fiber, and cable) are in active use. Why so many? Will all survive? With the possible exception of copper cable, all will indeed survive because each offers unique capabilities not provided by the others. A microwave radio system can provide transmission over terrain so rugged and to locations so remote that the laying of a fiber along a right-of-way, especially in view of installation labor costs, is not feasible. Radio, of course, is essential to land mobile communication. A satellite communication system can transmit to vehicles in motion, especially those over and on the oceans. Fiber-optic systems can provide low-cost high-data rate transmission between fixed points.

Additional continuing uses for the foregoing technologies also are evident. Microwave radio is finding increasing usage for wideband local distribution, especially in urban areas. Satellite transmission is very well-suited to broadcast applications, especially to large numbers of remote receivers, and is experiencing increased usage by private networks as a result of their use of VSATs. Optical fiber is superior for point-to-point transmission not only on a long-haul basis, but for local distribution within cities as well. Increasing emphasis is being placed on the use of optical fiber in the subscriber loop, especially in future broadband ISDN and BUTN applications. Copper cable is useful in short-distance low-capacity applications, but eventually is expected to yield its place to optical fiber.

REFERENCES

1. F. C. Kelcourse and F. J. Herr, "L5 Coaxial-Carrier Transmission System: Overall Description and System Design," *Bell System Technical Journal,* 53, no. 10, (Dec. 1974), 1897–99.
2. B. Johnston and W. Johnston, "LD-4: A Digital Pioneer in Action," *Telesis,* 5, no. 3, (June 1977), 66–72.
3. D. A. Alsberg, J. C. Bankert, and P. T. Hutchison, "The WT4/WT4A Millimeter-Wave Transmission System," *Bell System Technical Journal,* 56, no. 10, (Dec. 1977), 1829–48.

Appendix A

International System of Units (SI)

Unit	*Symbol*	*Meaning*
ampere	A	Unit of electric current
ampere per meter	A/m	Unit of magnetic field strength
angstrom	Å	10^{-10} m
bel	B	
bit	b	
centimeter	cm	10^{-2} m
coulomb	C	Unit of electric charge
decibel	dB	0.1 B
degree Celsius	°C	
electronvolt	eV	
farad	F	Unit of capacitance
gigahertz	GHz	10^9 Hz
henry	H	Unit of inductance
hertz	Hz	Unit of frequency
hour	h	
joule	J	Unit of energy

Unit	Symbol	Meaning
Kelvin	K	Unit of temperature
kilogram	kg	Unit of mass
kilohertz	kHz	10^3 Hz
kilohm	kΩ	10^3 Ω
kilometer	km	10^3 m
kilovolt	kV	10^3 V
kilowatt	kW	10^3 W
megahertz	MHz	10^6 Hz
megawatt	MW	10^6 W
megohm	MΩ	10^6 Ω
meter	m	Unit of length
microampere	μA	10^{-6} A
microfarad	μF	10^{-6} F
microhenry	μH	10^{-6} H
micrometer	μm	10^{-6} m
microsecond	μs	10^{-6} s
microwatt	μW	10^{-6} W
milliampere	mA	10^{-3} A
millihenry	mH	10^{-3} H
millimeter	mm	10^{-3} m
millisecond	ms	10^{-3} s
millivolt	mV	10^{-3} V
milliwatt	mW	10^{-3} W
nanometer	nm	10^{-9} m
nanosecond	ns	10^{-9} s
neper	Np	8.686 dB
ohm	Ω	Unit of electric resistance
picofarad	pF	10^{-12} F
picosecond	ps	10^{-12} s
picotesla	pT	10^{-12} T
picowatt	pW	10^{-12} W
second	s	Unit of time
siemens	S	$1\,\Omega^{-1}$
steradian	sr	Unit of solid angle
Tesla	T	Unit of magnetic flux density = 1 Wb/m^2
volt	V	Unit of electromotive force
watt	W	Unit of power
weber	Wb	Unit of magnetic flux; 1 Wb = 1 Vs

Appendix B

Frequency Band Nomenclature

30 to 300 Hz	ELF	Extremely Low Frequency
300 to 3000 Hz	VF	Voice Frequency
3 to 30 kHz	VLF	Very Low Frequency
30 to 300 kHz	LF	Low Frequency
300 to 3000 kHz	MF	Medium Frequency
3 to 30 MHz	HF	High Frequency
30 to 300 MHz	VHF	Very High Frequency
300 to 3000 MHz	UHF	Ultra High Frequency
3 to 30 GHz	SHF	Super High Frequency
30 to 300 GHz	EHF	Extremely High Frequency

Index

Absorption:
atmospheric, 181–82, 187, 249–51
hydroxyl ion, 343–44
Absorption loss, 391
Acceptance angle, 391
Acceptance cone, 340, 391
Accunet Reserved T1.5 Service, 99, 171
Accunet Switched-56, 98
Accunet T1.5, 99
Accunet T45, 99
Acknowledgment (ACK), 100, 117, 249
negative (NAK), 100–101, 117
Adaptive ARQ, 101
Adaptive delta coding, 323
Adaptive differential PCM (ADPCM), 234, 320
Adaptive equalizer, 52
Adaptive message division multiple access (AMDMA), 432
Adaptive transform encoders, 158–59
Add-drop multiplexer, 93–94
Addressable control, 419–23
Adjacent channel interference (ACI), 178, 181, 213, 215, 225, 226, 230–32, 267

Adjacent satellite interference, 267
Advanced data communications control procedure (ADCCP), 117
Advanced Television Systems Committee (ATTSC), 139
Advantages, optical fibers, 336–37
Aeronautical communication, 323–24
Aeronautical offsets, 418
AFSATCOM, 104
Air traffic control, 323
Aliasing, 138, 147, 164
vertical, 138
Allocation, 246
frequency, 246–47, 255
Aloha, 436
Alternate mark inversion, (AMI), 39–40, 241
Altitude, geosynchronous, 247
AM to PM conversion, 212, 259, 263, 264
Amplifier:
power, solid state, 224–25
traveling wave tube, 224–25
Amplifier distortion, 412–18

Amplifiers:
  power, 224–26
  small-signal, 224
Amplitude modulation (AM), 54–56, 196–98
Amplitude-phase keying (APK), 68–72, 398
  M-ary, (MAPK), 68–71, 81, 83
Amplitude-shift keying (ASK), 54–56, 77, 80, 384–86, 430
Analog differencing and integration, 151–52
Angle, critical, 339
Angle modulation, 198–205, 381–86
Angular division multiplexing, 344–45
Anik, 245
Antenna:
  beamwidth, 193
  dual reflector, 327
  earth station, 279–83
  gain, 179, 192–93
  horn parabola, 194–95, 226–28
  microwave, 191–95, 226–28
  multiple satellite, 280–82
  noise temperature, 207
  parabolic, 194–95, 226–27
  pattern, 192–94
  periscope, 222–23
  satellite, 270–74
  size requirements, 281–83
  surface error, 274
  tracking, 246, 248
Antenna-to-medium coupling loss, 188
Antijam systems, 309
Antipodal coding, 38
Aperture, antenna, 192
Apogee, 327
Apogee kick motor (AKM), 327
Architecture, LAN, 430–31
Area, effective, 180
Area adaptive encoder, 157–58
Ariane, 327
ARQ:
  adaptive, 101
  continuous, 101
  stop and wait, 100
ASCII, 434
Aspect ratio, 129, 137, 138
Asynchronous, 84, 118
Asynchronous TDM (ATDM), 21
Asynchronous transfer mode (ATM), 441
AT&T:
  DDM-1000 lightwave multiplexer, 377–78
  FT Series G System, 376–77

Atlas, 327
Atmospheric optics, 335, 389–90
Attenuation, 3
  atmospheric, 181–82, 187, 249–51
  differential, 252–53
  guiding media, 336
Attitude control, 327
Authorization, 420
Autocorrelation function, video, 141–42
Automatic frequency control (AFC), 384, 455
Automatic gain control (AGC), 389, 401, 403, 430, 455
Automatic repeat query (ARQ), 100–101, 117, 249
Automatic slope and gain control (ASGC), 401, 403
Automatic slope control (ASC), 401, 403
Availability, 11–12, 118, 119, 232
Avalanche photodiode (APD), 356–59, 373
Axial ratio, 314–16, 322
Axial ray, 341

Back lobe, antenna, 195
Back-off, 298–300, 304
Back porch, 130
Backbone route, 177
Bands, filter guard, 9
Bandwidth, 4–5, 23–24, 327
  maximizing, 409, 412–13
Bandwidth-limited operation, 34
Bandwidth reduction, video, 168–72
Barnett-Vigants equation, 222
Baseband, 9, 431–32
Baseband demand assignment (BDA), 303
Baseband office, 118
Baseband transmission, 37–53
Basic System Reference Frequency (BSRF), AT&T, 93, 97
Batteries:
  nickel cadmium, 269–70
  nickel hydrogen, 269–70
  satellite, 269–70
Baudot, 434
Beam:
  direction to satellite, 283–84
  reconfigurable, 327
  shape, 270–73
  spot, 245, 273, 306
Beamwidth, 179, 193, 328
Beginning of life (BOL), 311, 328
Bell, A. G., 335

Bell Communications Research
    (BELLCORE), 389
Bell System, 445, 451
Bessel functions, 199–200
Bidirectional couplers, 340
Bidirectional links, 320
Billboard, 223
Binary, 7
Binary digit, 31
Binary symmetric channel, 31
Binomial error distribution, 15
Bi-phase shift keying (BPSK), 54, 78, 80,
    118
Bipolar coding, 38–40, 43
Bipolar NRZ, 118
Bipolar return-to-zero (BRZ) code,
    38–42, 85, 118, 119
Bipolar violation (BPV), 39, 41–42, 89,
    118
Bit, 31
Bit count integrity, 12, 15, 17
Bit error probability, 12, 13, 15
Bit error rate (BER), 13
Bit interleaving, 84
Bit-plane encoding, 169, 170
Bit stuffing, 91
Bit synchronization, 17, 34
Black level, 130
Blanking interval:
    horizontal, 130
    vertical, 129–30
Blanking level, 130
Block code, 102–4, 107–8, 111–12
Block error rate, 12, 15
Blocking, 20
Blurring, 164
Body stabilized, 328
Boresight null, antenna, 195
Bose-Chaudhuri-Hocquenghem (BCH)
    code, 104, 108, 239
Bragg cell, 378
Bragg reflector, distributed, 348
Brick-wall channel, 25–27, 46
British Broadcasting Corporation (BBC),
    409
Broadband modems, 76
Broadband services, 98–99
Broadband system, 431–32
Broadband universal telecommunications
    network (BUTN), 441, 456
Broadcast, 19
Broadcasting satellite service (BSS), 328
Bundle, 391
Burrus diode, 351
Burst, 230

Burst error correction, 110–11
Bus, 20, 430–31
Butt-coupling, 363
By-pass, 6
Byte, 118
Byte stuffing, 118

Cable channels, 398–99
Cable-ready receiver, 422
Cable television (CATV), 138, 139, 241,
    328, 396–441, 444
    two way, 424, 428
Cables, fiber, 366–72
Call accepted packet, 435
Captioning, 136
Cargo bay, 328
Carrier injection, 239
Carrier recovery, 35–36
Carrier sense multiple access (CSMA) (see
    Listen before talk), 436
Carrier-to-interference (C/I) ratio, 220,
    252, 258, 259, 260, 281–82, 313
Carrier-to-noise (C/N) ratio, 8, 9, 204–5,
    296–98
Carson's Rule, 24, 200, 355
Cassegrain feed, 280–81, 315
Ceefax, 409
Cells, nickel hydrogen, 327
Cerenkov radiation, 344–45
Cesium beam oscillators, 292
Channel, 118, 328
    binary symmetric, 31
Channel bank, 83, 84, 90
    D5, 90
Channel capacity, 31
Channel coding, 9
Channel control computer, 421
Channel encoders, 236
Channel service unit (CSU), 95–96, 118
Character interleaving, 84
Charge-coupled device (CCD), 169
Chip, 309
Chirp, 352, 360
Chopped spectra, 75
Chromatic dispersion (see Material
    dispersion), 348–49, 352, 353, 354,
    382
Chrominance, 132, 136, 137, 138, 139, 150
Circuit, 118, 328
Circuit switching, 20
Circuit Switched Digital Capability
    (CSDC), 98–99
Cladding, 337, 340, 391
Cleaved-coupled-cavity (C³) laser, 352

Closed-loop postequalizer, 449
C-MAC packet system, 174
C-message weighting, 197–98, 234–35, 321
Coarse-fine edge adaptive encoder, 157
Coaxial cable, 401–3, 409
Coaxial carrier cable systems, 444–51
Co-channel interference (CCI), 178, 186,
    205, 208–9
Code:
  B3ZS, 42, 93
  B6ZS, 41–42, 93
  B8ZS, 41
  bipolar return-to-zero (BRZ), 38–42,
    93, 95
  diphase, 38
  4B3T, 42
  4B/5B, 388
  high-density bipolar-3 (HDB-3), 42, 93
  Manchester, 39
  mB1C, 355, 366
  Miller, 39
  MS43, 42–43
  nonreturn-to-zero (NRZ), 38–40, 60,
    65, 73, 77, 373, 381, 390, 409
  return-to-zero (RZ), 38–40
Code conversion, 20
Code division multiple access (CDMA),
    301, 307, 309, 310
Code tree, 104–6
Codec, 169–72
Coded mark inversion (CMI), 43, 93
Coder, 10, 174
Coding, 3, 4, 38–43, 147, 173
  antipodal, 38
  bipolar, 38–40, 43
  channel, 9
  delta, 9, 151–54, 156–57
  digital video, 140–67
  error, 9
  line, 9
  noise-feedback, 154–55
  partial response, 46–52
  polar, 38, 77
  predictive, 151
  psychovisual, 158–59
  source, 9
  statistical, 158
  unipolar, 38, 43, 54, 77
Coding gain, 102
Coherent optical systems, 380–87, 390–91
Collimated source, 362
Colocated satellites, 328
Color burst, 131
Color subcarrier, 131, 138, 149
Columbia Broadcasting System (CBS), 409

Comb filter, 137
Common-channel signaling, 87, 93
Commscope PIII, 418
Community antenna relay service
    (CARS), 241
Companding, 197, 234–35
Complementary bit, 355
Component video, 150–51, 172–73
Composite color, 131, 133, 147
Composite second order beat (CSB), 403,
    412
Composite triple beat (CTB), 403, 412
Compound mode number, 344
Compression:
  (amplitude), 211
  (time), 304
Compression Labs, Inc., 170
Computer, 19
Computer branch exchange (CBX), 431
Concatenation, 108, 112, 115
Concentrator, 2
Conditional replenishment, 165–67, 169,
    171–72
Conditioner, 236
Conductivity, earth, 183–85
Conference of European Postal and
    Telegraph Agencies (CEPT), 17
Connectors, fiber, 368, 371–72
Constellation, 61–62, 113–16, 239
Constraint length, 104–5, 109
Consultative Committee International for
    Radio (CCIR), 13, 139, 150, 151,
    172–74, 202, 214, 266, 268–69, 279
Consultative Committee International for
    Telephony and Telegraphy
    (CCITT), 13, 76, 92, 113, 118, 170,
    267, 321, 434, 440
Contention protocol, 432, 436
Continuous ARQ, 101
Contouring, 147, 149, 169
Control signals, 118
Controlled transition processor, 65–67
Converging routes, 220
Convolutional code, 104–14
Coordination, 217–18
Core, 337, 340, 391
  profile, 347
Correlative level encoding, 46–52
Costas loop, 36
Coupler:
  bidirectional, 340
  Fused biconical taper (FBT) star, 364
  optical, 361–64
  star, 364
  tee, 364

Coupler (*cont.*)
  loss, 363, 391
CPU, 328
Critical angle, 339
Cross polarization, 195, 252, 253, 280,
    282, 313–19, 374
Crosstalk, 197, 208, 336, 345
Cuber, 225
Current injection laser diode (ILD),
    351–53
Customer Controlled Reconfiguration
    (CCR), 99
Customer service unit (CSU), 95–96
Cyclic code, 104
Cyclic redundancy check (CRC), 88–90,
    93–94, 103

DADE module, 236
Dark current, 358
Dark fiber, 6
Data above video (DAVID), 95, 232
Data above voice (DAV), 95, 230, 232
Data circuit terminating equipment
    (DCE), 19
Data communications equipment (DCE),
    19, 34, 119, 434
Data Encryption Standard (DES), 420–21
Data in voice (DIV), 232
Data link, 119
Data mode, 119
Data over voice (DOV), 95
Data rate × distance product, 342, 373
Data service unit (DSU), 95–96, 119
Data terminal equipment (DTE), 19, 34,
    119, 120, 121, 122, 434
Data transition jitter, 29
Data under voice (DUV), 94–95, 119,
    230, 232
Datapath, 98
Dataphone Digital Service (DDS), 95–98,
    119, 449
Dataphone Switched Digital Service
    (DSDS), 119
Day, sidereal, 247, 249
dB, 328
dBi, 328
dBW, 328
DDS loop, 119
Decision feedback equalizer, 53
DECNET, 435
Decoder, 10
Decoding techniques, 107–10
Dedicated access, 432
De-emphasis, 138

Defense Advanced Research Projects
    Agency (DARPA), 172
Defense Satellite Communication System,
    280
Delay:
  group, 3–4, 9
  response, 12
Delay compensation through program
    emulation, 118
Delay distortion, 81–82, 267, 335, 348–50
Delay spread, 188–91
Delayed encoding, 156
Delta, 328
Delta coding, 9, 151–54, 156–57, 170
  adaptive, 323
Demand assigned multiple access
    (DAMA), 303–5, 322
Demand assignment (DA), 302–5
Demodulator, 10, 65
  coherent, 65
Demultiplexer, 10, 238
Depolarization, rain, 251–53, 316–18
Depolarization correction, 318–19, 327
Depth of modulation, 354
Descrambler, 10, 44–46, 109, 238
Desensitization, 278
Detector sensitivity, optical, 381–82
Deviation, 233–34, 236
Deviation ratio, 198–99
Deviator, frequency, 233
Diameter, mode-field, 342
Dichroic mirrors, 131–32
Dielectric constant:
  earth, 183–86
  glass, 339
Differential attenuation, 252–53
Differential decoder, 64
Differential encoder, 64
Differential gain, 211
Differential MPSK (DMPSK), 78
Differential PCM (DPCM), 9, 151–54,
    156, 162–63, 167, 170
Differential phase (amplifier), 211
Differential phase (polarization), 252–53
Differential phase demodulator, 65–66
Differential QPSK (DQPSK), 64, 257
Differential sensitivity, 140–41, 142
Diffraction, 181, 186–88, 285–90
Diffuse threshold decoding, 111
Diffusing, 109
Digital Access and Cross-Connect System
    (DACS), 99
Digital channel bank, 236
Digital Cross-Connect System 3/1, 93
Digital Data System (DDS), 95–98

Digital electronic message service
(DEMS), 240
Digital FM, 76
Digital hierarchies, 85, 92–94
Digital modulation, 53–83
Digital multiplex equipment, 92–93
Digital Network Architecture (DNA), 435
Digital noninterpolated interface (DNI),
291–92
Digital private branch exchange (DPBX), 2
Digital radio, 236
Digital serving area (DSA), 119
Digital speech interpolation (DSI), 327
Digital television, 168
Digital termination service (DTS), 6,
240–41
Digital transmission, 85–95
definition, 7–11
Digroup, 85
Diplexer, 275–78
Direct broadcast satellite (DBS), 138, 139,
174, 278, 311–12, 328
Discriminator, 233
Dispersion, 342, 391
chromatic, 348–49, 352, 353, 354, 382
intemodal, 348–49
material (*see* Dispersion, chromatic)
waveguide, 348–50
Distortion:
amplifier, 412–18
cumulative, 8
group delay, 12, 335, 348–50
linear amplitude, 239
picture, 4
quadratic amplitude, 239
quadratic delay, 239
slope overload, 153
Distributed Bragg reflector, 348
Distributed feedback (DFB) laser, 352
Distribution system, CATV, 399–400, 407
Dither, 154, 169, 170
Diversity:
frequency, 188, 219
space, 188, 219–20, 234–35
Doppler buffer, 293, 307
Doppler correction, 322–23
Doppler shift, 249, 292, 304, 306, 390
Dot interlace, 161, 169, 170
Dot sequential, 133
Double crucible method, 345
Double sideband (DSB), 54
suppressed carrier (DSB-SC), 54
Downconverter, 10
Downlink, 328
Downstream, 424

Downtime, 119
Dot interlace, 161–62
Drift, 67
Drooping dipole, 322
Dual polarization, 252
Dual polarized feeds, 327
Dual-reflector antenna, 327
Ducting, propagation, 181, 186
Duobinary, modified, 51
Duobinary technique, 46–52
Duplex, 119
Duty cycle, 119
Dynamic equalizer, 449
Dynamic routing, 21
D2 MAC, 174

Early Bird, 245
Earth station:
amplifiers, modular, 293
antenna, 279–83
satellite, 275–94
siting, 283–84
Earth terminal, digital, 275–77
EBC-DIC, 434
Eccentricity, orbital, 247–48
Echo, 5, 212–13, 293–94
Echo cancellation, 168, 294
Echo checking, 100
Echo control, split, 294
Echo suppressors, 267, 293–94
Echo time weighting, 213
Eclipse, 269, 311
Edge adaptive encoder, 156–57
Effective isotropically radiated power
(EIRP), 269, 273, 297–300, 309,
311, 325, 327, 328
Effective noise temperature, 208
Efficiency, 12, 120
Efficiency:
antenna, 179, 192
code, 103
power amplifier, 224
Egress, 399, 419
EIA Class 4A Fiber,
Nondispersion-shifted, 389
EIRP contours, 296
Elastic buffer, 236, 292, 306
Elastic store, 67, 98, 165
Electric propulsion, 327
Electromagnetic interference (EMI), 336
Electron, 350
Electronic Industries Association (EIA),
119, 120, 139
Emission limits, 214–17, 230

Encoder:
  area adaptive, 157–58
  edge adaptive, 156–57
  edge adaptive, coarse-fine, 157
  edge adaptive, variable rate, 156
  fixed format, 156
  hybrid, 167
  transform, 158–59, 167
  transform, adaptive, 158–59, 170
  frame differential, 162–63
  run length, 158
Encryption, 144, 171, 396, 430, 434
End links, 267
End of life (EOL), 12, 311, 328
End office, 120
End-of-line test oscillator (ELO), 425
End terminal (ET), 19, 120
Entropy, 31
Equalization, 52–53, 239
Equalizer, 10–11, 53, 239
  adaptive, 52, 239
  decision feedback, 53
  dynamic, 449
Equatorial Communications, Inc., 309
Erasure, 110
Error allocation, 16
Error coding, 9
Error control, 12, 100–116, 121
Error detection, 100–101
Error distance, 78
Error-free blocks, 14
Error-free seconds (EFS), 14–15, 97, 120
Error parameters, 13–15
Error probability, bit, 4
Errored second (ES), 14, 91
Ethernet, 437
Euclidean distance, 61–62, 68, 113
European Broadcasting Union (EBU),
  174
Exchange Carriers Standards Association
  (ECSA), 389
Expansion, 304
Extended aspect ratio, 138
Extended definition television (EDTV), 137
Extended service carrier, 240
Extended superframe format (ESF),
  88–91
Extensible family of digital codes, 150–51,
  172–73
Extrinsic losses, 366, 369
Eye pattern, 18, 213

Fabry-Perot amplifier, 382
Fabry-Perot etalon, 379

Facility, 1
Facility data link (FDL), 89–90
Facsimile, 2, 240
Fade margin, 191, 221–22, 250–51
Fading, Rayleigh, 81, 188
Failed state, 91–92
Failed second, 14, 91–92
Failure, 12
Failure rate, 12
Faraday rotation, 250 316, 320, 322
Far field, 193
F-bit, 89–90
FCC Rules and Regulations, 280, 282
FDM hierarchy, 445
Federal Communications Commission
  (FCC), 214
Feedforward, 412–18
Feeds, dual polarized, 327
Fiber:
  glass, 338, 391
  graded index, 338, 346, 373
  multimode, 342, 346–47, 366, 370, 392
  multiple clad, 346, 349
  optical, 335–38, 401, 403–6
  plastic, 338, 391
  plastic-clad, 338, 346
  quadruply clad, 374–75
  single mode, 342, 346, 366, 370, 373,
    377, 380, 381, 392
  step index, 338, 345–47, 392
  subscriber-switched, 419
  triaxial, 337
Fiber cables, 366–72
Fiber connectors, 368, 371–72
Fiber Distributed Data Interface (FDDI),
  388–89
Fiber splices, 366–71
Field, 129
Field effect transistor (FET), 358
Field interpolation, 164
Field of view (FOV), 270, 314, 315
Field survey, 217
Filter:
  comb, 137
  matched, 56, 58, 60
  transversal, 49, 240
Filter roll off, 27–29, 230
Fixed assignment (FA), 303
Fixed format encoder, 156
Fixed path routing, 21
Fixed satellite service (FSS), 328
Fixed service frequency bands, 214
Flag character, 435
Fleetsatcom, 280
Flicker, 129, 135, 138, 155, 160, 168

Flux, 391
FM improvement factor (FMIF), 204–5
FM-TV, 328, 401
FM video, 281–82, 401–4
Focal feed, 280–81
Footprint, 255–56, 270, 272, 320
    dynamic, 326
Foreign exchange (FX), 6
Forward channel, 120
Forward error correction (FEC), 100–112,
    239, 301, 328
Four-wire circuit, 120
Fractional refractive index difference,
    341
Frame alignment, 17, 34, 88
Frame differential encoding, 162–63
Frame repeating, 161–62
Frame synchronization, 17
Framing, 86–90, 116, 236
Framing, distributed bit, 86
Framing bits, bunched, 87–88
Framing pattern sequence (FPS), 89–90
Free-space path loss (FSL), 178–81, 221,
    297–300
Frequency allocations, 246–47
Frequency convolution theorem, 146
Frequency deviation, 58
Frequency deviator, 233
Frequency division multiple access
    (FDMA), 303–4, 310, 328, 390
Frequency-division multiplexing (FDM),
    9, 53, 83–85, 197, 231–35, 245, 258,
    262, 263, 266, 291, 296, 301–4, 320,
    401–4, 432, 444
Frequency interlace, 132
Frequency modulation (FM), 57–60,
    198–205, 241, 257, 275, 322
Frequency plan, transponder, 254–55
Frequency shift keying (FSK), 57–60, 80,
    240, 241, 384–86, 430
    M-ary (MFSK), 57–60, 78
Frequency standard, cesium, 275
Fresnel integrals, 286–87
Fresnel zone, 181–83, 188
Front end processor, 19, 120
Front porch, 130
Front-to-back ratio, 193–94
Frustrated internal reflection, 340
Fujitsu Laboratories, Inc., 239
Full width half maximum, 350
Fused biconical taper (FBT) star coupler,
    364
Fusion welding, 368, 370
Future trends, satellite communication,
    325–27

Gain:
    antenna, 179, 192–93
    differential, 211
Gain slope, 267
Gallager adaptive burst-finding scheme,
    111
Gallium arsenide (GaAs) FET, 358
Gas-injected dielectric (GID), 409
Gaussian function, 271–72
GC Fused Disc III, 418
GEC McMichael, 169, 171
General Dynamics, 274
Geostar satellite data network, 323–24
Geostationary, 328
Geostationary earth orbit (GEO), 246–48,
    326, 328
Geosynchronous altitude, 247
Geosynchronous orbit, 329
Ghosts, 293
GHz, 329
Glass fibers, 338
Golay code, 104
Graded index fiber, 338, 346, 347, 366,
    373, 391
Granular noise, 153–54
Graphics, 4, 170–71
Gray coding, 44, 169
Gray levels, 147, 159, 168–69
Gregorian feed, 280–81
Ground reflection, 183–85
Ground wave, 183
Grounding, 336
Group delay distortion, 12
G/T ratio, 208, 278, 298–300
Guard bands, 230
Guard time slots, 306
Gunn diode, 241

Half duplex, 120
Half-power bandwidth, 23–24
Hamming code, 409
Hamming distance, 101, 109, 113
Hamming weight, 101
Hard decision detector, 102, 107, 109
Harmonically-related carriers (HRC), 418
Harris, 274
Headend, 399–400, 426
Heterodyne detection, 359, 380, 382, 386
HI-VHF, 398
High Capacity Terrestrial Digital Service
    (HCTDS), 99
High frequency (HF), 101
High Speed Switched Digital Service
    (HSSDS), 99

Hiearchy:
  Digital, 85, 92–94
  FDM, 83, 230, 445
High definition television (HDTV),
  137–40, 174, 329
High frequency (HF), 425
High information delta modulation
  (HIDM), 156–57
High-level data line control (HDLC), 117
High-low keying, 355
High power amplifier (HPA), 258, 275
High-split, 424
Hit, 120
Hole, 350
Home channel, 420
Homochronous, 120
Homodyne detection, 359, 380, 382, 384,
  386
Hop (microwave), 220
Hop (waveguide), 451
Hops, multiple, 221
Horn parabola antenna, 194–95
HS-333 & HS-376, 329
Hub office, 95
Hue, 130
Huffman encoding, 172, 434
Human visual system, characteristics,
  142–43
Hybrid (circuit), 418
Hybrid (network), 430–31
Hybrid coding, 167
Hybrid modes, 342
Hydrazine, 329
Hydrometeor, 317
Hypothetical reference circuit, 12

IBM Cable System, 388
Idle code, 120
Impairments:
  analog, 4
  graphic system, 4
  transmission, 3–4
  video, 4
IMPATT diode, 453
Impulse, 25
Impulse noise, 206
Inclination, orbital, 247–48, 329
Incrementally-related carries (IRC), 418
Index of refraction, (see Refractive index),
  391
Indium-gallium arsenide-phosphide
  (InGaAsP), 358
Infant mortality, 12
Information, mutual, 31

Information channel, 120
Information path, 120
Infrared, 335
Infrared absorption tail, 343–44
Infrared (IR) transmission, 389–90
Ingress, (see Intrusion), 398, 419, 452
Injection laser diode (ILD), 348, 351–53,
  372–73
Inmarsat, 323
Institute of Electrical and Electronics
  Engineers (IEEE), 139, 432
Integrated Services Digital Network
  (ISDN), 16–17, 94, 99, 440–41, 456
Integrator, 151–52
Intelsat, 253, 258, 278–79, 315, 320, 377
Intelsat I, 245
Intelsat V, 104
Intensity modulation (IM), 352, 355, 401,
  403
Interconnectivity, 326
Interdepartment Radio Advisory
  Committee (IRAC), 214
Interface, CATV to TV receiver, 422–23
Interface message processor (IMP),
  433–34
Interference:
  adjacent channel, 5
  adjacent satellite, 267
  cochannel, 4–5
  intersymbol (ISI), 5, 18, 23, 25–30,
    46–47, 51, 52, 53
Interframe coding, 139–40, 160–67, 169, 170
Interlace, 129, 138
Interleaving, 109–12
Intermediate power amplifier (IPA),
  275–77
Intermediate terminal, 121
Intermodal dispersion, 348–49
Intermodulation (IM), 5, 178, 202,
  209–12, 224–25, 230, 246, 258,
  260–63, 264–68, 291, 296, 298, 304,
  398, 401, 403, 412, 418
Intermodulation reduction, 264–66
International objectives, 16–17
International standards, video, 172–74
International Standards Organization
  (ISO), 432, 440
International Telecommunications Union
  (ITU), 76, 214
International Telephone and Telegraph
  (ITT), 168
Intersatellite link (ISL), 325, 326, 390
Intersymbol interference (ISI), 5, 18, 23,
  25–30, 46–47, 51, 52, 53, 102, 178,
  212–13, 236, 239, 278, 293

Intraframe coding, 139–60, 169, 170
Intrinsic losses, 366, 369
Intrusion (*see* Ingress), 424–25
Ionizing radiation, 343–45
IRE units, 130–31, 418
IRED, 392
Irreversible process, 143
Isochronous, 99, 121, 388
Isotropic antenna, 329
Isotropic source, 178–79, 192, 362
IUS, 329

Jamming, 398
Japanese Broadcasting Corporation
    (NHK), 139
Jitter, 12, 17, 29, 147
    carrier phase, 239
    data transition, 29
    pattern, 36
    phase, 12, 17, 35–37, 67
    timing, 37
    zero crossing, 18
Jount Tactical Information Distribution
    System (JTIDS), 104
Justification, 91

Kell factor, 129–30, 139
Kevlar, 366, 368
Key, 421
Keyfax, 409
Keying, on-off, 54, 77, 78
kg, 329
Knife edge, 186–87

Label multiplex, 441
Labeled channel, 441
Lambertian source, 362
LAN architecture, 430–31
Large space platforms (LSP), 325–26
Laser:
    injection, 348
    multifrequency, 352, 360
    single frequency, 352, 360
Laser diode (LD), 337, 346, 353, 377, 378
    current injection (ILD), 351–53
Law of Reflection, 339
Law of Refraction, 339
lbf, 329
lbm, 329
LD-4 cable system, 449–51
Left-hand circular (LHC) polarization,
    313, 322

Level, 4–5, 7
L5 cable system, 445–48
L5E cable system, 445–48
Light-emitting diode (LED), 337, 338,
    348, 350–51, 353, 354, 362, 372–73,
    377, 378
Light source modulation, 353–55
Limited service carrier, 240
Limiter, 233, 259–61
Lincoln Experimental Satellites, 325
Line, scan, 129
Line build-out network, 448
Line coders, 38–44
Line coding, 9
Line control, 116
Line decoders, 38–44
Line extender, 407
Line-of-sight propagation, 181–83, 218–20
Linear modulation, 55
Linear prediction, 141, 156, 160
Link access protocol-D (LAP-D), 440
Link budget:
    microwave, (*see* Power budget,
        microwave), 220–21, 234–35
    optical fiber, 372–74
    satellite, (*see* Power budget, satellite),
        295–301, 322
    waveguide, 453
Listen before talk, (*see* Carrier sense
    multiple access), 436
Listen while talk, 436
Lithium niobate, 353, 377, 379
    titanium diffused, 387
Lithium tantalate, 353
LO-VHF, 398
Local area network (LAN), 2, 372, 389,
    396, 428–39
Local interface unit (LIU), 437
Local loop, 1, 121, 378
Location, 329
Lockheed, 274
Logic level, 236
Logical multiplexing, 20
Long haul, 121
Long haul access multiplexing, 121, 177
Loop checking, 100
Looping, 121
Loss:
    coupling, 363
    spreading, 178–80
Losses:
    extrinsic, 366, 369
    intrinsic, 366, 369
Low earth orbit (LEO), 326
Low noise amplifier (LNA), 276–78

Luminance, picture, 130, 136, 137, 138, 139, 141, 147, 150, 154, 158, 160, 173

Mach-Zehnder interferometer, 378–79
M/A-Com, 241
Main trunk, 399–406
Manchester code, 39, 390
Marginal ray, 341
Mark, 38, 54
M-ary APK (MAPK), 68–71, 81, 83
M-ary FSK (MFSK), 57–60, 78, 387, 390
M-ary PPM, 355
M-ary PSK (MPSK), 60–65, 78–83, 258, 275, 390, 451
M-ary PSK, differential (DMPSK), 78
M-ary QAM (MQAM), 80–81, 235, 236, 275, 320
M-ary QPR (MQPR), 80–81
Mask, FCC, 214–17, 231
Master antenna television system (MATV), 399–400, 419
Mastergroup, 233, 234–35
Matched filter, 56, 58, 60
Matching method using representative points (MMRP), 163
Material dispersion, (*see* Chromatic dispersion), 348–49, 353, 374–75
Materials, optical fiber, 338
Matrixing, 131–32
Maximum likelihood decoding, 109–10, 113
Maximum reach, 416–17
Mb/s, 329
Mean time between failures (MTBF), 12
Mean time to repair (MTTR), 12
Mean time to replace (MTTR), 12
Mean time to service restoral (MTSR), 12
Message switching, 20
Metal-organic chemical vapor deposition (MOCVD) process, 376–77
Metrobus, 389
Metropolitan area network (MAN), 428, 437–39
Metropolitan area systems (Microwave), 240–41
Microbending, 343
Microwave antennas, 191–95
Microwave propagation, 178–91
MID-BAND, 393–99
Midfiber meet, 387
Midsplit, 424
Miller code, 39
Millimeter waveguide system, 451–56

Minimum shift keying (MSK), 30, 59–60, 73, 82
Mitsubishi, 168
Mobile radio, 321–23
Mode:
    alternation, 42
    hybrid, 342
    number, compound, 344
    partition noise, 352, 374
    spectral, 352
    waveguide, 342–44, 392
Mode-field diameter, 342
Modem, 1, 9, 19, 71
    broadband, 76
Modified chemical vapor deposition (MCVD), 345
Modified duobinary, 51
Modulation, 9, 53–83, 196–205
    amplitude, 54–56, 196–98
    analog, 196–205
    angle, 198–205, 381–86
    depth of, 354
    digital, 53–83
    index, 58
    intensity (IM), 352, 355
    light source, 353–55
    trellis-coded, 9, 100, 101
Modulator, 10
Molniya, 248
Monitoring, 236
Monochrome video, 129
Monomode, 342
Motion adaptation, 138, 140
Motion compensation, 163, 167, 240
Motion detector, 165
Motor, 329
Motorola, 241
Movement in videotelephone scene, 166
Multidrop, 437
Multiframe, 88–90
Multifrequency laser, 352, 360
Multimode fiber, 342, 346, 347, 366, 370, 392
Multipath, 188, 267, 323
Multiple access (MA), 301–2
Multiple Sub-Nyquist Sampling Encoding (MUSE), 139–40
Multiple satellite antennas, 280–82
Multiplex equipment, digital, 92–93
Multiplexer, 2, 10, 17, 19, 83–85, 237
    add-drop, 93–94
    T1, 86
Multiplexing:
    frequency-division (FDM), 9, 53, 83–85, 229–30, 432, 444

statistical, 21–22
time-division (TDM), 9, 83–85, 229–30, 426, 455
wavelength division (WDM), 83, 335, 344–45, 374–77, 382, 386, 387
Multipoint network, 19, 95, 99, 120, 121
Multistandard receiver, 168
Mutual information, 31
Mux, 121

National Aeronautical and Space Administration (NASA), 326
National Association of Broadcasters (NAB), 139
National Broadcasting Company (NBC), 409
National Bureau of Standards (NBS), 420
National Cable Television Association (NCTA), 139, 445
National Telecommunications and Information Administration (NTIA), 214
National Television Systems Committee (NTSC), 128, 129, 137, 147, 161, 168, 174, 202, 213, 355, 420, 421
Negative polarity, 130
Network addressable unit (NAU), 435
Network Channel Terminating Equipment (NCTE), 99
Network utilization, 435
NHK, (*see* Japanese Broadcasting Corporation), 139
Nickel hydrogen cells, 327
Nippon Electric Corporation (NEC), 239–40
Noise:
    additive white Gaussian (AWGN), 30–31, 43, 51, 68
    background, 5, 178, 205–8
    granular, 153–54
    mode partition, 352, 374
    quantum, 357–59, 381
    receiving system, 207–8, 221
    shot, 206, 356
    speckle, 360
    thermal, 4, 30–31, 203–8
Noise bandwidth, 23
Noise-feedback, 154–55
Noise figure, 208, 221, 415–17
Noise level, 3–4
Noise power ratio (NPR), 262
Noise sensing slot, 231
Noise temperature, 206–8
Normalized wavenumber, 342

North American Broadcast Teletext Specification (NABTS), 409
North American Phillips, 403
N-type metal oxide semiconductor (NMOS), 376–77
Nuclear radiation, 343–45
Numerical aperture (NA), 341, 361–63, 392
Nutation, 329
Nyquist:
    bandwidth, 24, 239
    limit, 25, 46
    sampling, 145, 156
    theorems, 25–30

Objectives, end-to-end, 13
Office channel unit (OCU), 96, 119
Offset feed, 195
Offset keying, 73
Offset QPSK (OQPSK), 73
Omnidirectional source, 178–79, 192
On-board demand access, 257
On-board processing, 256–57, 325
On-off keying (OOK), 54, 77, 78, 80, 386
One-frequency repeating, 239–40
Open circuits, 336
Open loop preequalizer, 449
Open Systems Interconnection (OSI), 388, 432–35, 440
Optical fiber materials, 338
Optical path length, 347
Optical port, 392
Optical sources, 350–55
Optical switch:
    logical, 378
    relational, 378
Optical time-domain reflectometer (OTDR), 337
Optics, 335
    atmospheric, 335
Opto-electronic integrated circuit (OEIC), 387
Orbit:
    altitude, 329
    geostationary, 246–48
    period, 329
    polar, 248
    satellite, 246–48
    spacing, 329
Orbital eccentricity, 247–48
Orbital inclination, 242–48
Orbital transfer vehicles, 326
Orthogonal, 329
    polarization, 313

Orthogonal (*cont.*)
  signal set, 78
Orthomode transducer, 318–19
Open System Interconnection (OSI),
  432–34
OSI:
  application layer, 434
  data link layer, 433
  network layer, 433–34
  physical layer, 433
  presentation layer, 434
  session layer, 434
  transport layer, 434
Outage, 121
Outside vapor deposition (OVD), 345
Overfilled fiber, 361–62
Overfiltering, 46
Overreach, 181, 186, 218–19

**Packet assembler-disassembler (PAD),
  435**
Packet switching, 20–21, 240, 257, 306,
  325, 388
Palapa B, 256
PAM, 329
Parabolic reflector antenna, 194–95
Parallel-hybrid, 413–14
Parity, 101–3, 107, 236
Partial response coding, 46–52
Partial response filtering, 46–48, 76
Partial response signaling:
  classes, 49–51
  quadrature (QPRS), 73–75
Passive reflector, 223
Passive repeater, 223
Path tests, 217–18
Pattern, antenna, 192–94
Pattern jitter, 36
Performance allocations, 13
Performance measures, 11–19
Performance objectives, 11–12
Perigee, 329
Periods, time guard, 9
Periscope antenna, 222–23
Permutation decoding, 108
Personal radio, 324–25
Phase, differential:
  (amplifier), 211
  (polarization), 252–53
Phase alternation line (PAL), 135, 137,
  147, 168, 174
Phase jitter, 12, 35–37, 67
Phase locked loop (PLL), 35–37, 121, 306,
  383–84

Phase modulation (PM), 60–67, 198
Phase reference, 64–67
Phase reversal keying (PRK), 54
Phase shift, 3
Phase shift keying (PSK), 60–67, 384–86,
  398, 430
  M-ary (MPSK), 60–65, 78–83, 231, 232
  quaternary, 29, 62, 64
Photodetectors, 356–59
Photodiode:
  avalanche (APD), 356–59, 373
  PIN, 356–58, 373
Photonic switching, 378–80
Photophone, 335
Picture coding approaches, 143–44
Picture quality, viewer evaluation, 397
Picture segmenting, 167
Picture Tel, Inc., 172
Pilot tones, 32
Pioneer BA-5000, 423
Pixel, 128, 130, 134
Plane wave, 193
Plasma chemical vapor deposition
  (PCVD), 345
Plastic-clad silica fiber, 338
Plastic fibers, 338
Platform, 329
Plesiochronous, 84, 98, 121, 292
Point-to-point segment, 95, 121
Polar coding, 38, 77
Polar orbit, 248
Polarization, 180–81, 184, 213, 219, 220,
  231, 245, 252, 253, 309, 312, 338
  circular, 181, 311
  dual, 252, 278
  left-hand circular (LHC), 313, 322
  linear vs. circular, 319–20
  orthogonal, 313
  right-hand circular (RHC), 313, 322
Polarization diversity, 313
Polarizer, 318–19
Polling, 430, 432
Polybinary, 51
Polynomial code, 104
Portable test oscillator (PTO), 425
Positive-intrinsic-negative (PIN) diode,
  337
Postal service, 5–6
Power amplifiers, 224–26
Power budget:
  microwave (*see* Link budget,
    microwave), 220–21, 234–35
  satellite (*see* Link budget, satellite),
    295–301
Power flux density, 180

Power flux density limits, satellite, 268–69, 296
Power level, saturated, 211
Power-limited operation, 34
Power sources, satellite, 269–70
Power spectrum, video, 141
Power transfer characteristic, 225
Poynting vector, 181
Preamplifier, 224, 255
Precipitation effects, 249–53
Precoding, 48–49
Predictive coding, 151
Predistorter, 233, 239
Predistortion, television, 202
Predistortion linearization, 225–26, 229, 239, 263
Pre-emphasis, 138, 141, 201–2, 233
Prefiltering, 164
Premises Distribution System (PDS), 388
Private branch exchange (PBX), 6, 428, 430, 440
Probability density functions, video, 142
Processing transponder, 256–57
Program control word, 420
Propagation, 181–86, 246–53
   fiber, 335, 338–44
   line-of-sight, 181–83
   substandard, 186
   tropospheric, 181
Propagation time, 306
Propulsion, electric, 327
Protection switching, 17
Protective walls, 284–90
Protocol:
   binary synchronous (BISYNC), 117–18
   bit oriented, 117
   bit stuffing, 117
   byte count oriented, 117
   character oriented, 117
   contention based, 436
   conversion, 20
   digital data communications message (DDCMP), 117
Protocols, transmission, 116–18, 121
Pseudorandom generator, 307–8, 455
Pseudorandom sequence, 44–46
Psophometer, 267
Psophometric weighting, 267, 321
Psychovisual coding, 158–59
Public Switched Digital Service (PSDS), 98–99
Pulse amplitude modulation (PAM), 145, 147

Pulse code modulation (PCM), 9, 121, 137, 144–51, 161, 172, 174, 234, 236, 257, 275, 355
Pulse duration modulation (PDM), 390
Pulse frequency modulation (PFM), 355
Pulse position modulation (PPM), 355, 390
Pulse stuffing, 17, 84, 91, 92
   positive, 91, 92
   positive-zero-negative, 91

Quadrature amplitude modulation
   (QAM), 54, 101, 113, 115, 122, 132, 133, 225, 232, 239
   M-ary (MQAM), 80–81, 235, 236
   superposed, 71–72
Quadrature partial response (QPR), 73–74
   signaling (QPRS), 73–75, 239
   M-ary (MQPR), 80–81
Quadrifilar helix, 322
Quadrupling loss, 36
Quadruply clad fiber, 374–75
Quality, 12
Quantization, 143, 160, 173
Quantizing noise, 147, 149, 154
Quantum efficiency, 373
Quantum noise, 357–59, 381
Quaternary, 7, 33
Quaternary phase-shift keying (QPSK), 29, 122, 139, 241, 257
   offset, (OQPSK), 73

Rad, 344
Radiation, 178–81
   recombination, 351
Radio channel widths, 215
Rain depolarization, 251–53
Raised-cosine function, 28
Rate:
   CEPT-1, 85, 241, 440
   CEPT-2, 87–88, 241
   CEPT-3, 441
   code, 103
   DS0, 43
   DS1, 43, 85–86, 241, 275, 291, 302, 403, 440, 451
   DS1C, 43
   DS2, 43, 451
   DS3, 43, 92–94, 236, 241, 275, 360, 377, 388, 441, 451
   DS4, 43, 451, 454, 455
   DS4E, 388
Ray interference, 191
Rayleigh fading, 81

Rayleigh scattering, 343–44
Reach, maximum, 416–17
Receiver, multistandard, 168
Receiving system noise, 207–8
Recombination radiation, 351
Reconfigurable beams, 327
Red-green-blue (RGB), 137, 138
Reed-Solomon (RS) code, 104, 112, 170
Reflection:
  frustrated internal, 340
  law of, 339
Reflection factor, 183–84
Reflectometer, optical time-domain
    (OTDR), 337
Reflector, passive, 223
Reflector deployment, 273–74
Refraction, 181, 184–86, 250, 392
  law of, 339
Refractive index, 186, 337, 338–39, 343,
    347, 374
Regeneration:
  on-board, 257, 327
  waveform, 8, 241
Regional Administrative Radio
    Conference (RARC), 311, 329
Regulatory limits, 214, 217, 230
Reliability, 12, 232
  equipment, 15
  propagation, 15
Remote transmit-receive (RTR) terminal,
    425–26
Repeater, 10, 223–24
  baseband, 223
  heterodyne, 223–24
  passive, 223
  regenerative, 10–11, 19, 360, 364–66,
    368
  unity gain, 401, 403
Repeating, one-frequency, 239–40
Reservation, 437
Residual error rate, 122
Resolution, 137, 138, 168, 169, 171
  apparent, 138
  high, 169
Response delay, 12
Responsivity, 392
Reuse, bands, 326
Reverse channel, 122
Reversible process, 143
RF amplifiers, satellite, 257–64
Right-hand circular (RHC) polarization,
    313, 322
Ring, 20, 430–31
Rockwell:
  ADM-1045, 235

ADX-120 transmultiplexer, 84–85
DST-2300, 236–38
Roll-off factor, 28
Room controller, 171
Rotation, Faraday, 250
Routes, converging, 220
Routing, fixed path, 21
Routing control, 21
Run length encoding, 158, 169, 170

Sampling, 145–46, 172–73
Satcom F2, 295–301
Satellite, geosynchronous, 117
Satellite antennas, 270–74
  circular aperture, 270–72
  rectangular aperture, 270–71
Satellite Business Systems (SBS), 245, 309
Satellite control, 294–95
Satellite MATV, 400
Satellite position changes, 248
Satellite systems, trends, 326–27
Saturation, 4
  color, 130, 133
Saturation flux density contours, 297
Saturation level, 3–4
Scan frequency, 129, 131
Scanning, 128–29
Scanning spot beams, 325
Scintillation, 250
SCPT, 329
Scramble, 330
Scrambler, 10, 44–46, 109, 237
Scrambling, 9, 236, 420–22
  dynamic, 420
  static, 420
Section loss, 220
Security:
  fiber system, 337
  hard, 420
  soft, 420–22
Segment, 13
Selective replenishment, 161
Selenium thermoelectric cells, 270
Sellmeier delay fit, 349
Sensitivity:
  differential, 140–41
  optical detector, 381–82
Separate absorption, grading,
    multiplication (SAGM)APD, 358
Sequence control, 116
Sequential decoding, 109, 112
Sequential with memory (SECAM),
    135–37, 147, 168
Service channel, 236

Session, 21
Severely errored second, 14, 91–92
Shannon bound, 34, 102
Shannon-Hartley Law, 33
Shannon Theorem, 30–34
Shaped beams, 272–73
Shielding effectiveness, 284–85
Short circuits, 336
Short-haul, 122, 177, 223, 232
Shot noise, 206, 356
Sideband limits:
    angle modulated systems, 215–17
    digital radio, 216
Sidelobe levels, 193–94
Sidereal day, 247, 249
Signal converter, 19, 122
Signal point classes, 113–16
Signal set, orthogonal, 78
Signal states, 61–62
Signal state space diagram, 61–62
Signal-to-interference ratio, 220, 231
Signal-to-noise ratio, 77, 204–5, 234, 239
Signaling, 90
    common-channel, 87, 93
    robbed bit, 90
Single channel per burst (SCPB), 303
Single channel per carrier (SCPC),
    296–99, 302–5, 329
Single frequency laser, 352, 360
Single mode fiber, 342, 346, 366, 370, 373,
    377, 380, 381, 392
Single sideband (SSB), 54, 197, 225, 231,
    232, 234–36, 275, 320, 322
Sky wave, 183
Skynet 1.5 service, 99
Slip, 12, 17, 122, 147
    controlled, 17
    frame, 87
    uncontrolled, 17
Slope overload distortion, 153, 169
Slotted aloha, 436
Sneak paths, 212
Snell's law, 339
Snow, 4
Society of Motion Picture and Television
    Engineers (SMPTE), 139
Soft decision detector, 102, 107, 109
Solar array, 310–11, 327, 330
Solar cells, silicon, 269–70
Solid state power amplifier (SSPA),
    224–25, 257, 263, 327, 330
Source:
    directional, 179–80
    isotropic, 178–79
    optical, 350–55

Source coding, 9
Space, 38, 54
Space wave, 183
SPADE, 303
Speckle noise, 360
Spectra, chopped, 75
Spectrum conservation, 229
Spectrum mask, 24
Spectrum utilization, 312–21
Specular point control, 218–19
Speed conversion, 20
Speed of propagation, 4
Spill, 91
Spin stabilization, 330
Splices, fiber, 366–71
Split echo control, 294
Splitter, 68, 70, 400, 403
Spot beams, 245, 257, 306, 312, 320, 325
Spread spectrum multiple access (SSMA),
    301, 307, 309, 330
Squelch, 231
Standards:
    analog video, 128–36
    optical fiber system, 387–89
Star, 20
Star coupler, 364
Starting control, 117
State, encoder, 105
Station:
    (data), 122
    (orbital), 330
Stationkeeping, 330
Statistical coding, 158
Statistical multiplexing (STAT-MUX),
    21–22
Statistics:
    source, 140–41
    receiver, 140–41
Step-index fiber, 338, 345–47, 392
Stimulated Brillouin scattering, 381
Stimulated emission, 351
Stimulated Raman scattering, 381
Stop and wait ARQ, 100
Structure, picture, 158
Studio, 399–400, 407
Stuffing, positive-zero-negative, 91
SUB-VHF, 399
Subcarrier, color, 131, 138
Subchannel, 233
Submarine cables, 377
Submarine Lightwave Cable, 377
Subsampling, area, 163–65
Subsplit, 424
Substandard propagation, 186
Super Band, 398–99

Index

Superframe, 88–90
  extended (ESF), 88–90
Supergroup, 233
Superposed QAM (SQAM), 71–72
Surface error, antenna, 274
Surface wave, 183
Surveillance television, 174
Sweep generator, 400
Switchboard in the sky, 257
Switching, 20–22
  acousto-optic, 378
  circuit, 20
  electro-mechanical, 378
  electro-optic, 379
  fiber, 378–79
  message, 20
  optically activated, 379
  packet, 20–21
  photonic, 378–80
Symbol, 10
Symbol error probability, 13–14
Symbol signal, 236
Symbol timing recovery, 29, 36–37, 58, 65
Sync pulse:
  horizontal, 130
  vertical, 136
Sync pulse synchronization, 418
Sync suppression and active video
      inversion (SSAVI), 418
Sync suppression and restoration, 420–21
Sync tip, 130
Sync tip to peak white (STPW), 355
Synchronization, 34–37, 236
  bit, 17, 34
  frame, 17
Synchronous data link control (SDLC),
      116–17, 435
Synchronous Optical Network (SONET),
      389
Synchronous signals, 122
Synchronous TDM (STDM), 21–22, 83
Synchronous transfer mode (STM), 441
Synchronous transmission, 398
Syncom, 245
Syndrome, 107
Syntran, 92–94
System:
  delay distortion limited, 360
  loss limited, 360
  T1, 85, 372–73
  T3, 372–73
System layout, microwave, 218–20
System rise time, fiber optic, 373
System segment, 122
System Network Architecture (SNA), 435

T-carrier systems, 14
TDMA:
  demand assigned (TDMA/DA), 327
  satellite switched (SS-TDMA), 257, 326,
      327
Tee coupler, 364
Teleconference video systems, 169–71,
      174, 240
Telemetry systems, 428–29
Telesat, 298, 302
Teletext, 136, 168, 407, 409–11
  full channel, 409
Television, high definition, 2
Television Allocations Study Organization
      (TASO), 397
Television predistortion, 202
Temperature inversion, 186
Temporal filtering, 164
Temporal overload, 162
Temporal resolution reduction, 164–65
Terminal configuration, 122
Ternary, 7, 33
Terrestrial interfaces, 290–93
Text display systems, 407–9
Thermal noise, 4, 30–31, 203–8, 259, 267,
      268
Third order intercept point, 210–11, 224
Threshold, 7, 8, 10, 61–62, 64, 138
Threshold decoding, 108
Threshold extension demodulation
      (TED), 203, 301
Threshold, FM, 138, 202–4
Throughput, 12
Thruster, 330
Tie trunks, 6
Tilt differential (TD), 296–97
Time compression multiplexing (TCM),
      98–99
Time delay, satellite, 246, 249
Time division multiple access (TDMA),
      246, 249, 257, 258, 291, 293, 301–7,
      310, 323, 325, 326, 327, 330
Time-division multiplexing (TDM), 9,
      83–85, 122, 133, 234, 240, 291, 296,
      403, 405–6, 426, 455
  asynchronous, 21
  synchronous, 21–22, 83
Time-multiplexed analog components
      (TMAC), 138, 174
Time slot interchange, 93
Timeout control, 116
Timing, 12, 34–37
  data-aided joint recovery, 37
Timing jitter, 37, 239
Timing recovery, symbol, 29, 239

Timing recovery loop, 17
Timing supply:
    nodal, 97
    secondary, 97
Titanium-diffused lithium mobate
    (Ti : LiNbO₃), 387
TOCOM, 409, 425-27
Token passing, 432
Tracking:
    antenna, 246, 248
    telemetry and command (TT&C),
        290-91, 294-95, 330
Transfer delay, 122
Transfer orbit, 330
Transform encoders, 158-59, 167, 170
Transmission:
    digital, 85-95
    level point (TLP), 267
    principles, 3-5
    video, 4
Transmultiplexer, 84-85, 291-92
    Rockwell ADX-120, 84-85
Transmission technologies, comparison,
    456
Transparency, 116
Transponder, 330
    processing, 256-57
    satellite, 246, 253-69
    single conversion, 254-55
Transponder utilization, 301-9
Transversal equalizer, adaptive, 239
Transversal filter, 49, 52, 137
Traveling wave tube amplifier (TWTA),
    224-25, 257-64, 327, 336
Tree, 430-31
Trellis, code, 105, 109, 113
Trellis-coded modulation (TCM), 9, 100,
    101, 112-16
Trends, satellite systems, 326-27
Tropospheric propagation, 181, 188-90
Two-way CATV, 424-28
TWT, 330
Tyndall, John, 335

U interface, 440
Ultra Band, 398-99
Underfilled fiber, 362
Unipolar coding, 38, 43, 54, 77
Unity gain repeater section, 401, 403
Upconverter, 10
Uplink, 330
Upstream, 424
User-network interface (UNI), 440-41
Utilization, network, 435

Vapor-phase axial deposition (VAD), 345
Vector quantization (VQ), 159-60
Vertical interval, uses of, 136
Vertical interval reference (VIR), 136
Vertical interval test signals (VITS), 136
Very small aperture terminal (VSAT),
    309, 456
Vestigial sideband (VSB), 54, 134, 197,
    241, 354-55, 401
Video:
    coded, 82
    digital, 403, 405
    full motion, at 56 kb/s, 171-72
Video bandwidth reduction, 168-72
Video cassette recorder (VCR), 422-23
Video Cipher II, 420
Video conference, 2, 326
Video signal characteristics, 141-42
Videotex, 2, 136, 407-8
Videotext, 407-8
Viewdata, 407
Violation monitor and removal (VMR),
    236
Virtual circuit, 21, 435
Viterbi decoding, 109-10, 112, 113
Voltage standing wave ratio (VSWR), 425

Wander, 67
Waveguide dispersion, 348-50
Wavelength, 342
Wavelength division multiplexing (WDM),
    83, 335, 344-45, 374-77, 382, 386,
    387, 401, 403-5
Wavenumber, normalized, 342
Welding, fusion, 368, 370
Westar, 245
Western Electric, 241
Western Union, 245
White, reference, 130
Widergren Communications, Inc., 172
Windshield wiper effect, 403, 412
Word interleaving, 84
World Administrative Radio Conference
    (WARC), 327, 330
WTBS, 409
WT4 system, 451-56
WT4A system, 451-53

X.3 protocol, 435
X.21 protocol, 434
X.25 protocol, 89, 117-18, 434-35
X.29 protocol, 435